Diary and Autobiography of John Adams

L. H. BUTTERFIELD, *EDITOR*

LEONARD C. FABER AND WENDELL D. GARRETT

ASSISTANT EDITORS

———————— ☆ ————————

Volume 2 · *Diary* 1771–1781

ATHENEUM

NEW YORK

1964

Published by Atheneum
Reprinted by arrangement with Harvard University Press

Copyright © 1961 by the Massachusetts Historical Society
All rights reserved
Printed in the United States of America by
The Murray Printing Company, Forge Village, Massachusetts
Bound by The Colonial Press, Inc., Clinton, Massachusetts
Published in Canada by McClelland & Stewart Ltd.

First Atheneum Edition

Funds for editing *The Adams Papers* have been provided by Time, Inc.,
on behalf of *Life*, to the Massachusetts Historical Society, under whose
supervision the editorial work is being done.

The Adams Papers

L. H. BUTTERFIELD, EDITOR IN CHIEF

SERIES I

DIARIES

Diary and Autobiography of John Adams

ORIGINALLY PUBLISHED BY
HARVARD UNIVERSITY PRESS

Contents

Illustrations

Illustrations

nicipal officials. See the Diary entries at p. 409–410. (From the original in the Adams Papers.)

8. TRADE CARD OF JOHN ADAMS' PARIS STATIONER, CABARET, AT THE SIGN OF THE GRIFFIN, 1778   291

Examples of this engraved trade card appear in two of John Adams' folio letterbooks bound in white parchment and purchased in Paris soon after his arrival on his first diplomatic mission. See his Personal Receipts and Expenditures, 1778–1779, p. 327 and note at p. 343. (From an original in the Adams Papers.)

9. "I HAVE TAKEN AN HOUSE ON THE KEYSERS GRAGT NEAR THE SPIEGEL STRAAT" (AMSTERDAM, 1781)   322

Engraving of John Adams' residence in Amsterdam from early 1781 to early 1782, from Caspar Phillips' *Het Grachtenboek*, published in Amsterdam, 1771. In contracting with the firm of Sigourney, Ingraham, & Bromfield for the house, Adams wrote, 9 April 1781: "When I return it will be necessary for me to have an House to put my Head in and Furniture, suitable for a Minister Plenipotentiary from the United States to recieve and entertain Company and not in the Style of Sir J[oseph] Y[orke] of 80,000 Guilders a Year, but however decent enough for any Character in Europe to dine in, with a Republican Citizen." On 13 April he added: "I wish you to be particularly carefull about the House, that it be in a good and pleasant Situation, that it be large, roomly and handsome, fit for the Hotel des Etats Unis de L'Amerique." According to a document by which John Adams sublet the house on 19 March 1782, because he was moving to The Hague, the owner was Abraham Jacobsz. Vorsterman. See note on Diary entry of 28 February 1781, p. 456. (Courtesy of the Gemeentelijke Archiefdienst, Amsterdam, through Dr. Simon Hart.)

10. KEIZERSGRACHT NO. 529 IN 1960   322

Recent view of the residence (with white door frame) of John Adams in Amsterdam shown in the engraving above. (Photograph by George M. Cushing Jr.)

11. JOHN ADAMS PRINTS THE DOCUMENTS LEADING TO DUTCH RECOGNITION OF THE UNITED STATES, 1782   323

Titlepage of an anonymous publication entitled *A Collection of State-Papers . . .*, The Hague, 1782, with a note by John Adams on his authorship. Between Adams' Memorial of 19 April 1781 and the final act of his accreditation as minister plenipotentiary precisely one year later, 19 April 1782, many petitions and resolves were passed by merchants, municipalities, and provincial assemblies which he gathered and printed in this pamphlet. See his Diary entries of July 1781 and April 1782 and notes, p. 457 and vol. 3:4. (Courtesy of the Massachusetts Historical Society.)

12. THE PRO-AMERICAN JOURNAL BEGUN BY JOHN ADAMS'
FRIEND CERISIER AT AMSTERDAM, 1781 323

Titlepage of the first volume of John Adams' copy of Antoine Marie
Cerisier's weekly paper, *Le politique hollandais*, begun in 1781, in
which Cerisier "inserted every thing that he thought would do honor
to America, or promote our reputation and interest." This volume
remains among Adams' books in the Boston Public Library. The
allegorical engraving shows "Congress" in classical garb and Indian
headdress holding a United States flag and sword over a vanquished
Britannia accompanied by a lion. France, wearing a robe ornamented
with fleurs-de-lis, is coming to America's assistance with a drawn
sword and beckoning to a crowned female figure, obviously representing Spain, to accompany her. In the background another female
figure representing the Dutch Republic watches the scene while
holding a copy of the Treaty of Westminster of 1674 by which
she was allied with Great Britain. In the foreground lies a map of
the American scene of conflict. On Cerisier and his journal see
Adams' Diary entry of 13 January 1781 and note, p. 453–454.
(Courtesy of the Boston Public Library.)

VOLUME 2

Diary 1771–1781

Diary of John Adams

1771. JANY. 10. THURSDAY.[1]

Dined at the Honble. John Ervings, with Gray, Pitts, Hancock, Adams, Townsend, J. Erving Jur., G. Erving, Boardman. We had over the Nominations of Nat. Hatch to be Judge of the common Pleas, and Ed. Quincy to be a Justice of the Quorum, and H. Grays Story of a Letter from a repentant Whigg to him.

H. Gray. "The general Court is a good School for such Conversation as this"—i.e. double Entendre, Affectation of Wit—Pun—Smut, or at least distant and delicate Allusions to what may bear that Name.

Gray said He could sometimes consent to a Nomination when he could not Advise to it. And says he I can illustrate it to you Mr. Hancock.—Suppose a young Gentleman should ask his Father's Consent that he should marry such a young Woman, or a young Lady should ask her father's Consent that she should marry such a young Man. The Father says I cant advise you, to have a Person of his or her Character, but if you have a Desire, I wont oppose it. You shall have my Consent. —Now Mr. Hancock I know this Simile will justify the Distinction to a young Gentleman of your Genius.

A light brush happened too between Pitts and Gray. Pitts hinted something about the strongest Side. Gray said, there were 2 or 3 of Us last May, that were Midwives, I kn[ow]. But you have been always of the strongest side, you have been so lucky.

When the Co[mpany] 1st. came in, they began to banter Blair Townsend, upon his approaching Marriage which it seems is to be this Evening, to one Mrs. Brimmer. Treasurer punned upon the Name. (N.B. Shenstone thanked God that his Name was obnoxious to no Pun). And We had frequent Allusions, Squints, and Fleers about entering in &c. among the Merchants and Widowers and Bachelors, &c.

---

[1] First entry in "Paper book No. 16" (our D/JA/16), consisting of several gatherings of leaves stitched together in a rough gray paper cover.

To fill the five-month gap preceding the present entry there are: (1) a few entries in the Suffolk Bar Book (MS, MHi), showing that JA attended meet- ings of the bar (and recorded the min- utes) on [3] Oct., 21 Nov., 1 Dec. 1770, and 2 Jan. 1771. (2) The Mass. *House Journal*, 1770–1771, which records a very large number of committee assign- ments to JA during the second session of this House, 26 Sept.–20 Nov. 1770. (3) Data in JA's own papers and the Su-

I

perior Court Minute Books on his attendance at various courts in the latter part of 1771; these show that he handled cases in Suffolk Superior Court in its August term, in Suffolk Inferior Court and Middlesex (Cambridge) and Bristol Superior Courts in their October terms, and in Essex Superior Court (Salem) in its November term.

The cases included two which are remembered to this day and are at least vaguely known to many who know nothing else whatever about JA's career as a lawyer. These were Rex v. Preston and Rex v. William Wemms et al., the British officer and the eight soldiers under his command indicted for the murder of Crispus Attucks and four others in King Street, Boston, on the night of 5 March 1770. Despite the enormous amount that has been said and written about the "Boston Massacre," no satisfactory account of the ensuing trials exists, though the published and unpublished materials available for such a purpose are abundant. As to JA's part specifically, he states in his Autobiography that he was engaged the "next Morning, I think it was," for one guinea to defend Preston and his men. To let feelings cool, the criminal proceedings against them were repeatedly postponed. At length on 7 Sept. the accused (including four civilians charged with firing at the mob from inside the Custom House) were arraigned in Suffolk Su-

perior Court, but there were eventually three separate trials: (1) Preston's trial, 24–30 Oct., in which Paine and Samuel Quincy acted for the crown, and JA, Josiah Quincy Jr., and Auchmuty defended Preston, who was acquitted. (2) The soldiers' trial, 27 Nov.–5 Dec., with the same attorneys on both sides except that Auchmuty was replaced by Sampson Salter Blowers; six of the prisoners were acquitted and two found guilty of manslaughter. (3) The trial of Edward Manwaring and the three other customs employees, 12 Dec., in which Samuel Quincy prosecuted, the defense counsel are unknown, and "The Jury acquitted all the Prisoners, without going from their Seats" (*The Trial of William Wemms ... Taken in Short-Hand by John Hodgson*, Boston, 1770, Appendix, p. 211–217; this appendix is omitted in all reprints of the *Trial*).

Since the court records and the Hodgson report are vague in respect to dates and the so-called *History of the Boston Massacre* by Frederick Kidder (Albany, 1870), though the only work of its kind, is deficient in nearly every respect, the precise chronology of the trials can best be established from the Diary of Robert Treat Paine (MS, MHi) and the Diary of the younger Benjamin Lynde, the acting chief justice of the Superior Court (*The Diaries of Benjamin Lynde and of Benjamin Lynde, Jr.*, Boston, 1880, p. 194, 198, 200–201).

FRYDAY FEBY. 7 [*i.e.* 8?]. 1771.[1]

Met a Committee of the House at the Representatives Room, to consider of a Plan for a society for encouraging Arts, Agriculture, Manufactures and Commerce, within the Province.[2]

Such a Plan may be of greater Extent and Duration than at first We may imagine. It might be usefull at any Time. There are in this Prov[ince] natural Productions eno. Hemp, Silk, and many other Commodities might be introduced here, and cultivated for Exportation. The Mulberry Tree succeeds as well in our Climate and Soil, as in any.

[1] Friday fell on 8 Feb. 1771.
[2] This committee, appointed 16 Nov. 1770, was ordered to report at the next session (Mass., *House Jour.*, 1770–1771, p. 164), but its report has not been found.

At a Time, when the Barriers against Popery, erected by our Ancestors, are suffered to be destroyed, to the hazard even of the Protestant Religion: When the system of the civil Law which has for so many Ages and Centuries, been withstood by the People of England, is permitted to become fashionable: When so many Innovations are introduced, to the Injury of our Constitution of civil Government: it is not surprizing that the great Securities of the People, should be invaded, and their fundamental Rights, drawn into Question. While the People of all the other great Kingdoms in Europe, have been insidiously deprived of their Liberties, it is not unnatural to expect that such as are interested to introduce Arbitrary Government should see with Envy, Detestation and Malice, the People of the British Empire, by their Sagacity and Valour defending theirs, to the present Times.

There is nothing to distinguish the Government of Great Britain, from that [of] France, or of Spain, but the Part which the People are by the Constitution appointed to take, in the passing and Execution of Laws. Of the Legislature, the People constitute one essential Branch—And while they hold this Power, unlimited, and exercise it frequently, as they ought, no Law can be made and continue long in Force that is inconvenient, hurtful, or disagreable to the Mass of the society. No Wonder then, that attempts are made, to deprive the Freeholders of America and of the County of Middlesex, of this troublesome Power, so dangerous to Tyrants and so disagreable to all who have Vanity enough to call themselves the better Sort.—In the Administration of Justice too, the People have an important Share. Juries are taken by Lot or by Suffrage from the Mass of the People, and no Man can be condemned of Life, or Limb, or Property or Reputation, without the Concurrence of the Voice of the People.

As the Constitution requires, that, the popular Branch of the Legislature, should have an absolute Check so as to put a peremptory Negative upon every Act of the Government, it requires that the common People should have as compleat a Controul, as decisive a Negative, in every Judgment of a Court of Judicature. No Wonder then that the same restless Ambition, of aspiring Minds, which is endeavouring to lessen or destroy the Power of the People in Legislation, should attempt to lessen or destroy it, in the Execution of Lawes. The Rights of Juries and of Elections, were never attacked singly in all the English History. The same Passions which have disliked one have detested the other, and both have always been exploded, mutilated or undermined together.

The british Empire has been much allarmed, of late Years, with Doctrines concerning Juries, their Powers and Duties, which have been said in Printed Papers and Pamphlets to have been delivered from the highest Trybunals of Justice. Whether these Accusations are just or not, it is certain that many Persons are misguided and deluded by them, to such a degree, that we often hear in Conversation Doctrines advanced for Law, which if true, would render Juries a mere Ostentation and Pagentry and the Court absolute Judges of Law and fact. It cannot therefore be an unseasonable Speculation to examine into the real Powers and Duties of Juries, both in Civil and Criminal Cases, and to discover the important Boundary between the Power of the Court and that of the Jury, both in Points of Law and of Fact.

Every intelligent Man will confess that Cases frequently occur, in which it would be very difficult for a Jury to determine the Question of Law. Long Chains of intricate Conveyances; obscure, perplext and embarrassed Clauses in Writings: Researches into remote Antiquity, for Statutes, Records, Histories, judicial Decisions, which are frequently found in foreign Languages, as Latin and French, which may be all necessary to be considered, would confound a common Jury and a decision by them would be no better than a Decision by Lott. And indeed Juries are so sensible of this and of the great Advantages the Judges have [to] determine such Questions, that, as the Law has given them the Liberty of finding the facts specially and praying the Advice of the Court in the Matter of Law, they very seldom neglect to do it when recommended to them, or when in any doubt of the Law. But it will by no Means follow from thence, that they are under any legal, or moral or divine Obligation to find a Special Verdict where they themselves are in no doubt of the Law.

The Oath of a Juror in England, is to determine Causes "according to your Evidence"—In this Province "according to Law and the Evidence given you." It will be readily agreed that the Words of the Oath at Home, imply all that is expressed by the Words of the Oath here. And whenever a general Verdict is found, it assuredly determines both the Fact and the Law.

It was never yet disputed, or doubted, that a general Verdict, given *under the Direction of the Court* in Point of Law, was a legal Determination of the Issue. Therefore the Jury have a Power of deciding an Issue upon a general Verdict. And if they have, is it not an Absurdity to suppose that the Law would oblige them to find a Verdict according to the Direction of the Court, against their own Opinion, Judgment and Conscience.

4

[It] has already been admitted to be most advisable for the Jury to find a Special Verdict where they are in doubt of the Law. But, this is not often the Case—1000 Cases occur in which the Jury would have no doubt of the Law, to one, in which they would be at a Loss. The general Rules of Law and common Regulations of Society, under which ordinary Transactions arrange themselves, are well enough known to ordinary Jurors. The great Principles of the Constitution, are intimately known, they are sensibly felt by every Briton—it is scarcely extravagant to say, they are drawn in and imbibed with the Nurses Milk and first Air.

Now should the Melancholly Case arise, that the Judges should give their Opinions to the Jury, against one of these fundamental Principles, is a Juror obliged to give his Verdict generally according to this Direction, or even to find the fact specially and submit the Law to the Court. Every Man of any feeling or Conscience will answer, no. It is not only his right but his Duty in that Case to find the Verdict according to his own best Understanding, Judgment and Conscience, tho in Direct opposition to the Direction of the Court.

A religious Case might be put of a Direction against a divine Law.

The English Law obliges no Man to decide a Cause upon Oath against his own Judgment, nor does it oblige any Man to take any Opinion upon Trust, or to pin his faith on the sleve of any mere Man.

[1] The following essay on the rights of juries, an issue being warmly debated in both England and America, has every appearance of having been written for a newspaper, but no printing has been found. Samuel M. Quincy, the editor of Josiah Quincy Jr.'s *Reports*, plausibly suggested that at least some passages in it were originally "part of [JA's] preparation for the argument" in the case of Wright and Gill *v.* Mein, which had come before the Suffolk Inferior Court, Jan. 1771, and was appealed to the next sitting of the Superior Court (Quincy, *Reports*, Appendix II, p. 566–567). JA's extensive notes and authorities for his successful argument in this case—that a jury can find against the instructions of a court—are in Adams Papers, Microfilms, Reel 185.

THURSDAY FEBY. 14. 1771.

Dined at Mr. Hancocks with the Members,[1] Warren, Church, Cooper, &c. and Mr. Harrison and spent the whole Afternoon and drank Green Tea, from Holland I hope, but dont know.—

[1] Of the "Boston seat" in the House of Representatives.

FRYDAY [15 FEBRUARY]. EVENING.

Going to Mr. Pitts's, to meet the Kennebeck Company—Bowdoin, Gardiner, Hallowell, and Pitts. There I shall hear Philosophy, and Politicks, in Perfection from H.—high flying, high Church, high state from G.—sedate, cool, Moderation from B.—and warm, honest, frank

Whiggism from P. I never spent an Evening at Pitts's. What can I learn tonight.

Came home and can now answer the Question. I learned nothing. The Company was agreable enough.—Came home in great Anxiety and distress, and had a most unhappy Night—never in more misery, in my whole Life—God grant, I may never see such another Night.

SATURDAY. FEBY. 16.

Have had a *pensive* day.[1]

[1] The next entry in the present Diary booklet (D/JA/16), curiously, is dated 21 Nov. 1772; this is followed by 18 blank leaves and then by scattered entries from [ca. 20] July 1771, through 28 [i.e. 27?] Nov. 1772.

1771. APRIL 16. TUESDAY EVENING.[1]

Last Wednesday my Furniture was all removed to Braintree.[2] Saturday, I carried up my Wife and youngest Child,[3] and spent the Sabbath there, very agreably. On the 20th. or 25th. of April 1768, I removed into Boston. In the 3 Years I have spent in that Town, have received innumerable Civilities, from many of the Inhabitants, many Expressions of their good Will both of a public and private Nature. Of these I have the most pleasing and gratefull Remembrance. I wish all the Blessings of this Life and that which is to come, to the worthy People there, who deserve from Mankind in general much better Treatment than they meet with. I wish to God it was in my Power to serve them, as much as it is in my Inclination.—But it is not.—My Wishes are impotent, my Endeavours fruitless and ineffectual, to them, and ruinous to myself. What are to be the Consequences of the Step I have taken Time only can discover. Whether they shall be prosperous or Adverse, my Design was good, and therefore I never shall repent it.

Monday Morning, I returned to Town and was at my Office before Nine, I find that I shall spend more Time in my Office than ever I did. Now my family is away, I feel no Inclination at all, no Temptation to be any where but at my Office. I am in it by 6 in the Morning—I am in it, at 9 at night—and I spend but a small Space of Time in running down to my Brothers to Breakfast, Dinner, and Tea.[4]

Yesterday, I rode to Town from Braintree before 9, attended my Office till near two, then dined and went over the ferry to Cambridge, attended the House the whole Afternoon, returned, and spent the whole Evening in my Office, alone—and I spent the Time much more profitably, as well as pleasantly, than I should have done at Clubb.

This Evening is spending the same Way. In the Evening, I can be alone at my Office, and no where else. I never could in my family.

[1] First entry in "Paper book No. 17" (our D/JA/17), a stitched gathering of leaves containing fairly regular entries from this date through 14 June 1771.

[2] The return to Braintree, as JA explains in detail in his Autobiography, was in order to improve his health and to avoid continuous overwork; but he kept his law office in Boston and after about a year and a half returned to live in town (see 22 Sept. 1772, below).

[3] "1770 May 29. Charles, Son of said John and Abigail was born, Thursday Morning at Boston, and the next Sabbath was baptized by Dr. Cooper" (entry by JA in his father's copy of Willard's *Compleat Body of Divinity*; see HA2, *John Adams's Book*, Boston, 1934, p. 5, and facsimile of family record).

[4] Doubtless William Smith Jr. (1746–1787), AA's brother, whose somewhat remarkable Boston household is briefly described in the entry of 23 July, below.

1771. FEB. [*i.e.* APRIL] 18. THURSDAY. FASTDAY.

Tuesday I staid at my Office in Town, Yesterday went up to Cambridge. Returned at Night to Boston, and to Braintree, still, calm, happy Braintree—at 9. o Clock at night. This Morning, cast my Eyes out to see what my Workmen had done in my Absence, and rode with my Wife over to Weymouth. There we are to hear young Blake—a pretty fellow.

SATURDAY [20 APRIL].

Fryday morning by 9 o Clock, arrived at my Office in Boston, and this Afternoon returned to Braintree. Arrived just at Tea time. Drank Tea with my Wife. Since this Hour a Week ago I have led a Life Active enough—have been to Boston twice, to Cambridge twice, to Weymouth once, and attended my office, and the Court too. But I shall be no more perplexed, in this Manner. I shall have no Journeys to make to Cambridge—no general Court to attend—But shall divide my Time between Boston and Braintree, between Law And Husbandry. Farewell Politicks. Every Evening I have been in Town, has been spent till after 9. at my Office. Last Evening I read thro, a Letter from Robt. Morris Barrister at Law and late Secretary to the Supporters of the Bill of Rights, to Sir Richd. Aston, a Judge of the K[ing]'s Bench. A bold, free, open, elegant Letter it is. Annihilation would be the certain Consequence of such a Letter here, where the Domination of our miniature infinitessimal Deities, far exceeds any Thing in England.

This mettlesome Barrister gives us the best Account of the Unanimity of the Kings Bench that I have ever heard or read. According to him, it is not uncommon abilities, Integrity and Temper as Mr. Burrows would perswade us, but sheer fear of Lord M[ansfiel]d, the Scottish Chief which produces this Miracle in the moral and intellectual

World—i.e. of 4 Judges, agreeing perfectly in every Rule, order and Judgment for 14 Years together. 4 Men never agreed so perfectly in Sentiment, for so long a Time, before. 4 Clocks never struck together, a thousandth Part of the Time, 4 Minds never thought, reasoned, and judged alike, before for a ten thousandth Part.

SUNDAY [21 APRIL].

Last night went up to Braintree, and this Evening down to Boston, call'd at S. Adams's and found Mr. Otis, Coll. Warren and Dr. Warren. Otis as Steady and Social, and sober as ever and more so.

MONDAY [22 APRIL].

In the Morning mounted for Worcester, with Pierpoint, Caleb and Rob. Davis, Josa. Quincy, &c. Baited the Horses at Brewers, and at Coll. Buckminsters.

THURSDAY. APRIL 25TH. 1771.

Dined last Monday at Brighams in Southborough, and lodged at Furnasses in Shrewsbury. Next day dined at Mr. Putnams in Worcester, and at the same Place, dined on Wednesday. This day dined at Mr. Paines—with much Company. At about 2 O Clock this day We finished the famous Cause of Cutler vs. Pierpont and Davis—an Action of Trespass for compelling the Plaintiff to store his Goods with the Committee at Boston and carting him &c.[1]

We had Stories about Fort George, the Duke of York, and a warm Gentleman at Cambridge, Bob. Temple.

The D. of York was in a Battle at Sea, a cannon Ball hit a Mans Head and dashed his Blood and Brains in the Dukes Face and Eyes. The Duke started, and leaped quite out of the Rank. The Officer, who commanded, said, pray your Highness dont be frightened.—The Duke replyed Oh sir, I am not frightened but I wonder *what Business that fellow had here with so much Brains in his Head.*

The warm Gentleman at Cambridge was Bob. Temple. A Number of Gentlemen at Cambridge his Friends got into a Quarrell and Squabble and somebody knowing they all had a great Esteem of Temple begged him to interpose and use his Influence to make Peace. At last he was perswaded, and went in among the Persons, and one of the first Steps he took to make Peace was to give one of the Persons a Blow in the Face with his fist.

Strong insinuated privately at the Bar, another Story. He said the Defence put him in Mind of the Answer of a Young fellow to the Father of a Girl. The Father caught the young Fellow in naked Bed

8

with his Daughter. The old Man between Grief and Rage broke out into Reproaches.—You Wretch, what do [you] mean by trying to get my Daughter with Child? The Young fellow answered him, I try to get your Daughter with Child! *I was trying not to get her with Child.*

Thus, the Defendants are to be laughed and storied out of large Damages no doubt.

However the Jury gave none. They could not Agree. 8 were for Defendants, 4 for Plaintiff.

[1] In June 1770 Ebenezer Cutler, a merchant of Oxford, tried to run two wagonloads of boycotted English goods out of Boston under cover of night. The watch at Boston Neck having observed him, a crowd of indignant citizens pursued and overtook him at Little Cambridge (Brighton), and forced him to return with his goods, which were impounded by the committee to enforce the nonimportation agreement. Cutler brought suit against Robert Pierpont, the Boston coroner, and Caleb Davis, two of the more respectable persons who had been present and who had, according to evidence adduced at the trial, actually tried to protect Cutler from the mob. Cutler asked £5,000 damages for assault, false arrest, and other "enormities" and won his case in the Worcester Inferior Court in September. JA was first involved in the case as counsel for the defendants in their appeal. The case was tried *de novo* in the current term of the Superior Court at Worcester, but despite eighteen hours of deliberation the jury could not agree, and it was continued until September, when the jury found for the defendants. JA could not take credit for this victory, but a year later, thanks to a writ of review, the case was argued again; JA's client Davis was cleared altogether, and Pierpont was found liable for £15. Cutler's final frantic effort to appeal to the King in Council seems to have come to nothing. Though "famous" in its day, as JA says, the Cutler case was soon forgotten. But since the trials took place in Worcester and the evidence was taken by deposition to avoid the cost of bringing witnesses from Boston, the record of this typical incident of the era of nonimportation is peculiarly full and graphic. Some 130 documents relating to it are on file in the Suffolk co. Court House. See Superior Court of Judicature, Minute Books 90, 97; Records, 1771, fol. 140; 1772, fol. 124–125; Early Court Files, &c., Nos. 152615, 152686; also *Boston Gazette*, 29 April, 23 Sept. 1771, 21 Sept. 1772.

MAY 1ST. 1771. WEDNESDAY.

Saturday I rode from Martins in Northborough to Boston on horse back, and from thence to Braintree in a Chaise, and when I arrived at my little Retreat, I was quite overcome with Fatigue. Next Morning felt better, and arose early and walked, up Pens Hill and then round, by the Meadow, home.

After Meeting in the Afternoon Mr. Tudor and I rambled up the western Common, and took a View of a Place which I have never seen since my Removal to Boston. I felt a Joy, I enjoyed a Pleasure, in revisiting my old Haunts, and recollecting my old Meditations among the Rocks and Trees, which was very intense indeed. The rushing Torrent, the purling Stream, the gurgling Rivulet, the dark Thickett, the rugged Ledges and Precipices, are all old Acquaintances of mine. The young Trees, Walnutts and Oaks which were pruned, and trimmed by me, are grown remarkably. Nay the Pines have grown the better for lopping.

This Evening at the Bar Meeting, I asked and obtained the unanimous Consent of the Bar to take Mr. Elisha Thayer of Braintree Son of Captn. Ebenr. Thayer Jur. as a Clerk.[1] How few Years are gone since this Gentleman was pleased to call me a *petty Lawyer* at Majr. Crosbys Court. Now [he] is soliciting me to take his Son, and complementing &c. me, with being the first Lawyer in the Province, as he did, in express Words, tho it was but a Compliment, and if sincere in him was not true, but a gross Mistake, nay what is more remarkable still complimenting me with his Seat in the House of Representatives, as he did by assuring me in Words, that if I had an Inclination to come from Braintree, he would not stand in my Way.—Such are the Mistakes we are apt to make in the Characters of Men, and in our Conjectures of their future Fortune. This however is a wretched Tryumph, a poor Victory, a small Antagonist to defeat—And I have very few of this Kind of Conquests to boast of. The Governor tells of a vast No. of these Changes in Sentiment concerning him—and will be able to tell of many more.

[1] Young Thayer stayed in JA's office less than two years, for in Feb. 1773 the members of the Suffolk bar voted that "the remaining part of Mr. Thayer's three years [with JA] be dispensed with under the peculiar circumstances of his case, but not to be drawn into precedent" and not to prejudice the bar's recommendation of Thayer to practice after another year ("Suffolk Bar Book," MHS, *Procs.*, 1st ser., 19 [1881–1882]: 151). The "peculiar circumstances" no doubt related to Thayer's health; he died early in 1774 (JA to Ebenezer Thayer, 25 April 1774, Tr in CFA's hand, Adams Papers, Microfilms, Reel No. 114).

MAY 2. 1771.

The Tryumphs, and Exultations of Ezekl. Goldthwait and his pert Pupil Price, at the Election of a Register of Deeds, are excessive.[1] They Crow like dunghill Cocks. They are rude and disgusting. Goldthwait says he would try the Chance again for 20 dollars, and he would get it by a Majority of 100 Votes even in this Town. Nay more he says, if he would be Rep[resentative] and would set up he would be chose Rep. before Adams.—Adams the Lawyer dont succeed in the Interest he makes for People, he is not successfull.—N.B. very true!

Price says to me, if you was to go and make Interest, for me to be Clerk in the Room of Cook, I should get it no doubt.

These are the Insults that I have exposed myself to, by a very small and feeble Exertion for S. Adams to be Register of Deeds. Thus are the Friends of the People after such dangerous Efforts, and such successfull ones too left in the Lurch even by the People themselves. I have acted my sentiments, with the Utmost Frankness, at Hazard of all, and the certain Loss of ten times more than it is in the Power of the People to give me, for the sake of the People, and now I reap nothing but Insult, Ridicule and Contempt for it, even from many of the People themselves. However, I have not hitherto regarded Consequences to myself. I have very chearfully sacrificed my Interest, and my Health and Ease and Pleasure in the service of the People. I have stood by their friends longer than they would stand by them. I have stood by the People much longer than they would stand by themselves. But, I have learn'd Wisdom by Experience. I shall certainly become more retired, and cautious. I shall certainly mind my own Farm, and my own Office.

[1] In April Samuel Adams competed with Goldthwait for the office of register of deeds for Suffolk co. Goldthwait, who had tory leanings, had been elected "unanimously" for several successive terms and had won the recent election by 1123 votes to 467 (MHS, *Procs.*, 2d ser., 14 [1900–1901]:47).

MAY 3D. 1771. FRYDAY.

Last Evening I went in to take a Pipe with Brother Cranch, and there I found Zeb. Adams. He told me, he heard that I had made two very powerfull Enemies in this Town, and lost two very valuable Clients, Treasurer Gray and Ezek. Goldthwait, and that he heard that Gray had been to me for my Account and paid it off, and determined to have nothing more to do with me. Oh the wretched impotent Malice! They shew their teeth, they are eager to bite, but they have not Strength! I despize their Anger, their Resentment, and their Threats. But, I can tell Mr. Treasurer, that I have it in my Power to tell the World a Tale, which will infallibly unhorse him—whether I am in the House or out. If this Province knew that the public Money had never been counted this twenty Year—and that no Bonds were given last Year, nor for several Years before, there would be so much Uneasiness about it, that Mr. Gray would loose his Election another Year.[1]

It may be said that I have made Enemies by being in the general Court. The Governor, Lieutenant Governor, Gray, Goldthwait, The Gentry at Cambridge, &c. are made my bitter Foes. But there is nothing in this. These People were all my Foes before, but they thought it for their Interest to disguise it. But Now they think themselves at Liberty to speak it out. But there is not one of them but would have done me all the Harm in his Power secretly before.

This Evening Mr. Otis came into my Office, and sat with me most of the Evening—more calm, more solid, decent and cautious than he ever was, even before his late Disorders.—I have this Week had an Opportunity of returning an Obligation, of repaying an old Debt to that Gentleman which has given me great Pleasure. Mr. Otis was one of the 3 Gentlemen, Mr. Gridley and Mr. Thatcher were the other two, who introduced me to Practice in this County. I have this Week strongly recommended 14 Clients from Wrentham and 3 or 4 in Boston, to him, and they have accordingly by my Perswasion engaged him in their Causes, and he has come out to Court And behaved very well, so that I have now introduced him to Practice. This Indulgence to my own gratefull Feelings, was equally my Duty and my Pleasure.

He is a singular Man. It will be amusing to observe his Behaviour, upon his Return to active Life in the Senate, and at the Bar, and the Influence of his Presence upon the public Councils of this Province. I was an Hour with him this Morning at his Office, and there he was off his Guard and Reserve with me. I find his Sentiments are not altered, and his Passions are not eradicated. The fervour of his Spirit is not abated, nor the Irritability of his Nerves lessened.

[1] In November and again in April JA had served on committees to protest or investigate Treasurer Harrison Gray's conduct of his office (Mass., *House Jour.,* 1770–1771, p. 155, 220).

MAY 9. 1771.

From Saturday to Wednesday Morning I staid at Braintree, and rode, walked, rambled and roamed. Enjoyed a Serenity and Satisfaction to which I have been 3 Years a Stranger.

Yet I have had upon my Mind, a puzzling perplexing affair. The Purchase of Elijah Belchers Homestead and two Pastures, has occasioned a Journey to Germantown, where I had not been for three Years, and which Mr. Palmer has made a little Paradise, to treat with Mrs. Palmer about Terms and Conditions, and many Walks about the Land, to see the Condition of the Fences &c. The Fences are in a ruinous Condition and require a large Expence for Repairs.

Wednesday, after Court I waited on Dr. Gardiner, Secretary Fluker [Flucker], Mr. Josa. Quincy Jur. and John Erving Jur. Esqr., and was very politely treated by each of those Gentlemen, each of them very readily agreeing, to take my single Note for the Money, and two of em Fluker and Quincy giving me Assignments of their Mortgages, in Exchange for my Note. A droll Adventure with Mr. Erving. He took my Note and gave me up Elijah Belchers for upwards of £56 Prin[ciple]

and Int[erest] and seemed mightily pleased. In the Evening, upon seeing Mr. Greenleaf, I discovered that Deacon Palmer had never any
Thing to do with this Debt, and that it was not in the List which I was
to discharge. So that I had given my Note, without Authority, and to
my own Prejudice. But, waiting the next Morning on Mr. Erving, and
explaining the Facts to him, he very genteelly gave up my Note and
took back that of Belcher.

This Day arrived Hall from London with News of the Committment
of the Mayor and Mr. Alderman Oliver to the Tower, by the House of
Commons. I read this Morning in the English Papers and the Political
Register for April, all the Proceedings against the Printers Thompson
and Wheble, and vs. the Mayor and Alderman Wilks, and Oliver.
What the Consequence will be, of these Movements, it is not easy to
foresee or Conjecture. A Struggle, a Battle, so serious and determined,
between two such Bodies as the House and the City, must produce
Confusion and Carnage, without the most delicate Management, on
both sides, or the most uncommon Concurrence of Accidents.

TUESDAY. MAY. 14. 1771.

Yesterday came to Town with my Wife. A fine Rain all night.
Captn. Bradford sent his Compliments, and desired me to meet the
Clubb at his House this Evening which I did—Dr. Cooper, Mr. Lathrop,
Otis, Adams, Dr. Greenleaf, Wm. Greenleaf, Dr. Warren, Thom.
Brattle, Wm. Cooper, C. Bradford. A very pleasant Evening. Otis
gave us an Account of a present from Dr. Cummings of Concord to
H[arvard] Colledge Chappell of a brass Branch of Candlesticks, such
as I. Royal Esqr. gave to the Representatives Room, and that it was
sent to N. Hurds to have an Inscription engraven on it. The Inscription is

> In Sacelli hujusce ornatum et splendorem
> phosphoron hoc Munus, benigne contulit
> Cummings Armiger, Medicus concordiensis.[1]

Danforth. The Inscription was much faulted, by the Witts at Clubb
—and as it was to be a durable Thing for the Criticisms of Strangers
and of Posterity, it was thought that it ought to be altered.

Dr. Cooper mentioned an old Proverb that an Ounce of Mother Wit,
is worth a Pound of Clergy. Mr. Otis mentioned another which he
said conveyed the same Sentiment—an Ounce of Prudence is worth a
Pound of Wit. This produced a Dispute, and the sense of the Company
was that the Word Wit in the 2d. Proverb, meant, the faculty of

suddenly raising pleasant Pictures in the Fancy, but that the Phrase Mother Wit in the first Proverb meant, natural Parts, and Clergy acquired Learning—Book Learning. Dr. Cooper quoted another Proverb, from his Negro Glasgow—a Mouse can build an House without Timble [2] —and then told us another Instance of Glasgows Intellect, of which I had before thought him entirely destitute. The Dr. was speaking to Glasgow about Adams Fall and the Introduction of natural and moral Evil into the World, and Glasgow said they had in his Country a different Account of this matter. The Tradition was that a Dog and a Toad were to run a Race, and if the Dog reached the Goal first, the World was to continue innocent and happy, but if the Toad should outstrip the Dog, the world was to become sinfull and miserable. Every Body thought there could be no danger. But in the Midst of the Career the Dog found a bone by the Way and stopped to knaw it, and while he was interrupted by his Bone, the Toad, constant in his Malevolence, hopped on, reached the Mark, and spoiled the World.

[1] John Cuming of Concord, Mass., was voted an honorary A.M. by Harvard in 1771; the present gift (lost in a fire in the 19th century) was only one of his benefactions to Harvard (Quincy, *History of Harvard Univ.*, 2:422–423; note by CFA in JA, *Works*, 2:262). The inscription as recorded by JA might be translated "For the adornment and splendor of this Chapel, the Honorable Cummings, a physician of Concord, has presented this gift, a bearer of light."

[2] Thus in MS. CFA silently corrects to "trouble," but a better guess would be "Timber."

WEDNESDAY MAY 15TH. 1771.

Argued before the Sessions the Question whether the Court had Authority by Law to make an Allowance of Wages and Expences, above the Fees established by Law to the Jurors, who tryed C[aptain] Preston and the Soldiers. The two Quincys, Otis and Adams, argued.[1] Otis is the same Man he used to be—

He spares nor Friend nor Foe, but calls to Mind
like Doomsday, all the faults of all Mankind.

He will certainly soon relapse into his former Condition. He trembles. His Nerves are irritable. He cannot bear Fatigue.—"Brother A. has argued so prodigiously like a Rep[resentative] that I cant help considering him as the Ghost of one"—&c.[2]

[1] The subject thus argued was explained and commented on by Josiah Quincy Jr. in an anonymous article in the *Boston Gazette*, 20 May 1771, which will also be found in Quincy's *Reports*, p. 382–386. The trials of Preston and the soldiers had for the first time in the history of the Massachusetts courts required keeping the jury together for more than one day, and the Superior Court therefore "Ordered, that it be recommended" to the Court of General

Sessions to make "a reasonable Allowance" of money to the jurors for their protracted service. The jurors then petitioned for this allowance, but the Court of Sessions "having a Doubt of their Power touching the Grant of the Prayer thereof, ordered the Petition to stand over for Argument at the Sessions in April." The argument took place on 15 May, as JA records, and required the whole day. The prayer was refused on the ground "that the only Power of the Sessions to *grant Monies* must be derived from *provincial Law*," and certainly not from an order or recommendation of the Superior Court. The itemized bill for lodging and subsisting the jurors in the soldiers' trial, a highly interesting document, is printed by John Noble in Col. Soc. Mass., *Pubns.*, 5 (1902): 59–60.

[2] On 7 May Otis had been elected a Boston representative to the General Court in the place of JA.

WEDNESDAY. MAY 22. 1771.

At Plymouth. Put up at Wetheralls, near the County House—lodged with Mr. Angier, where we had a Chamber wholly to ourselves—very still and retired—very serene and happy. Mrs. Howland and her Family, I hear are very much grieved, and hurt, and concerned about my passing by their House. But my Health is my Excuse of all my Removals. I am not strong enough to bear the Smoke and dirt, and Noise, of Howlands, and their late Hours at night.—Heard of the Election of Coll. Edson at Bridgwater, and Coll. Gilbert of Freetown. Which proves to me, that the System of the Province will be different, this Year, from what it was the last. The House was very near equally divided, the whole of the last Session, and these two Members will be able to make a ballance in favour of Timidity, Artifice, and Trimming. How easily the People change, and give up their Friends and their Interest.

1771. WEDNESDAY 29. MAY.

General Election. Went to Boston and to Cambridge, and returned to Boston at night.

1771. THURSDAY MAY 30.

Mounted my Horse for Connecticutt. Stopped, and chatted an Hour with Tom Crafts who is very low with Rheumatism and an Hectic, but the same honest, good humoured Man as ever. Stopped again at little Cambridge[1] at the House by the Meeting House, and gave my Horse Hay and Oats, at Mr. Jacksons. Rode alone. My Mind has been running, chiefly upon my Farm and its Inhabitants and Furniture, my Horses, Oxen, Cows, Swine, Walls, Fences &c. I have in several late Rambles very particularly traced, and pursued every Swamp and

Spring upon the North Side of Penns Hill from its Sourse to its Outlet. And I think if I owned the whole of that Side of the Hill I could make great Improvements upon it, by Means of Springs, and Descents and falls of Water.[2]

The first is the Swamp in the Pasture, by John Curtis, which my father gave me, which Swamp is fed by Springs which come from Land that was Curtis's. This Swamp discharges its Waters two Ways. The first is by a range of low, wet, rocky ground, which runs down directly to Plymouth Road, near S. Curtis's Lane, and the Bars of my new Pasture, and therefore flows down Pens hill in Wash. The other turns round and runs down into a Meadow in the lower Part of the Pasture, I purchased of Curtis, and from thence flows thro a range of low Land of S. Curtis into Bridgwater Road, and so in great freshitts, and plentifull Rains, flows down across the Road into my Pasture, and Coll. Verchilds, and mine again and Jo. Fields, into the fresh Meadow and Brook.

In the next Place there is a Spring, a living Spring never dry, which originates in my new Pasture opposite S. Curtis's lane. It arises directly beneath a great Rock, and flows in a Rivulet, down, thro S. Pennimans Land, and the narrow Lane, and Nat. Belchers and into my Meadow, which was Deacon Belchers, and then into Deacon Belchers Pond and thence thro Mrs. Vesey, Bass, Gay, Ruggles, Winslow, Peter Adams across the Road, and over Peter Adamss Meadow and into the Brook by Major Millers Bridge.

Now the Questions are, what Improvement could I make of these Courses of Water, if I owned the whole North Side of the Hill? And what Improvements can I make with what I own already.

I can clear my Swamp, and cutt a Ditch through it and extend that Ditch down to my Pasture Barrs, along the low, rocky, Spungy Valley there.

Then I can cutt another Ditch, down to the lower Part of my Pasture, and another Ditch thro the Meadow there, and if there was a Ditch to communicate with it, thro S. Curtis's Land, down to the long slough in the Road on one side of the Causey opposite to my Pasture, a Gutter might be opened directly into my Pasture, or it might be carried round by a Channell in the Road along side of the Causy, by my Pasture and Verchilds, and all turned directly into my four Acres, and Orchard— and carried all round the Walls of that and shed upon the Land as I pleas'd. And as to the other Spring and Rivulet, I might make a Dam just within my Meadow and turn half the Water, by a Channell, round by Nat. Belchers Wall and by my Wall against the Street and round by the House, and thence down into the Pond, and the other half, round the Side of the bushy Pasture Hill, so as to oose over several Acres there before it fell down into the Pond.

Rode along to Captn. Brewers in Waltham, and turned my Horse out to Pasture, about 11. O. Clock perhaps, so that I have spent the forenoon in getting about 9 Miles. I rode this forenoon from little Cambridge to Brewers, with Mr. Ruggles of Roxbury, the Butcher, and I find him my Relation.—His Mother, who is still living above 70, is Sister to my Grandmother, Aunt Fairfield, Aunt Sharp, and Aunt Ruggles of Rochester, and Parson Ruggles of Rochester, and the Butchers Father were Brothers, so that Tim and he are very near—both by fathers and Mothers side.[3] We talked about Family, Cattle fat and lean, and Farms, and Improvement of Land &c. He says that Roxbury People make no Profit, by carting Dung out of Boston, it must be done every Year, and they must put on 10 Load to an Acre, which will cost them 12 or 15£ in Boston besides the Labour of Carting, and when all this is done, they may get 30 Hundred of Hay—besides after feed. Roxbury People dont dung their Grass Land so much as they used to do—for of late Years they have got more into gardening, and 4 or 5 Acres of Garden takes all the dung they can get. Dr. Davis, he says, dungs his Close vs. Warrens, but little. The Wash helps it, and he dont feed it till quite Winter.

Dined at Brewers, and spent good Part of the Afternoon there. A vast Drove of fat Cattle went by while I was there from the River Towns. Rode from Brewers to Munns in Sudbury, where I drank Tea and put out my Horse to Pasture, and put up myself for the Night.

Spent the Evening at Munns, in Conversation with him about the Husbandry of the River Towns, Hatfield, Deerfield, Springfield, Northampton and Hadley, &c. and about Captn. Carvers Journal of his Travells in the Wilderness, among the Savages in search of the South sea.[4]

The Farmers upon Connecticutt River, fat their Cattle on the very best of English Hay, and Oats and Pees, ground to meal. They would not digest the Corn whole, so they grind their Provender. One of the great Farmers, will fatten 20 Head of Cattle in a Year, and it is the whole Business of one Man to take the care of em—to feed, Water, and curry them. They give an Ox but little Provender at first, but increase the Quantity till an Ox will eat a Peck at a Time, twice a day. The County of Hampshire is the best Place to send to for Stock—Oxen, Cows, Horses, young Cattle of all Ages, their Breed is large and excellent and store Cattle are much cheaper there than below.—Lodged at Muns.

¹ Now Brighton.

. ² For reasons only partly apparent, CFA omitted in his text of the Diary all the rest of the present entry, together with all of the entry of the following day except the last six words.

³ This passage may be elucidated as follows: JA's maternal grandmother was Ann (White) Boylston, and her sisters, the various aunts mentioned here, were of course his great-aunts, one of whom had married the late Rev. Timothy Ruggles of Rochester, father of "Tim" Ruggles, the well-known soldier, judge, and loyalist, of Hardwick. Another White sister had evidently married the father of JA's chance acquaintance, Ruggles the Roxbury butcher, who was thus a double first cousin of the younger Timothy.

⁴ Jonathan Carver's *Travels through the Interior Parts of North-America, in the Years 1766, 1767, and 1768*, was not issued until 1778, and then in London after tedious difficulties with the Board of Trade and Plantations, instead of in Boston as the author had at first hoped (*Travels*, p. xiii–xiv; *DAB*). A native of Weymouth, Carver for a time kept his friend Edmund Quincy informed of his plans after sailing to England early in 1769, where he was to remain the rest of his life. Several of his letters written to Quincy in 1769 have come to rest in the Adams Papers. In one of them, dated at London, 2 Aug. 1769, he reports:

"I have sold my Journals and Plans to the Booksellers in London For Thirty Guineas down and on the sale of every 250 Copies in N. America am to receive ten Guineas more let it amount to what number it will in the same proportion, and a reserve of Forty Books neatly Bound to dispose of among my friends, tis now making ready for the Press and with the Plans and cutts annexed tis thought it will be a prety Elegant piece of work considering the subject being the first English Journal ever printed of so extensive Travels in the interiour parts of North America. The many late discoveries and writings of Countries much more frequent of late Years then formerly which continually fill the presses here has greatly less[ened] the Prices of all Manuscripts on those subjects. I beleave such a Journal te[n] Years ago would have sold for six times the money."

It seems very likely that JA met Carver, and saw his MS journal, when Carver was in Boston upon his return from the West in 1768.

1771. MAY 31. FRYDAY.

A fair, soft, pleasant Morning.—I believe the Peasants round about the Town of Boston are as contracted, in their Views and Notions, as any People in the Province. On the North Side of Charlestown Ferry, their Lands are divided into little Strips and they spend the whole Year in providing for a few Cows and in carrying their Milk in Bottles over the ferry and Wheeling it about the Town of Boston. On the South Side of the Neck, they raise Garden Stuff and Hay, for the Market. But they have less Conversation with Travellers And Strangers, and therefore less Civility, Knowledge &c. than Countrymen at a greater Distance.—Turned out my Horse at Coll. Williams's Marlborough. Dined at Martins, Northborough, where I met with my Class Mate Wheeler of George Town the Episcopal Priest. He says the Deer in St. James's Park are as tame as Catts, they will come up to you and eat any Thing out of your Hands. There is a large Number of them in the Park, and it is a rare Thing to have one of them stolen or kill'd. It is transportation to do Either. So there is a Number of Swans upon the Thames, none of em get killed, nor any of their Eggs destroyed.— Mr. Wheeler informed me, that Coll. Lithgow of George Town, had a Son which he designed to get me to take. He is 20 Years of Age, has studied Latin with Mr. Wheeler, but has never been at Colledge, &c. He gives a pitifull Account of our Classmate, his Brother Bayley [Bailey], and his Wife, their want of Œconomy, and their wretched Living, &c.—Oated, and drank Tea at Furnaces, lodged at Mr. Putnams in Worcester.

1771. SATURDAY JUNE 1ST.

Spent the Day at Worcester in Riding about with Mr. Putnam to see his Farm. He does what he pleases with Meadows and Rivers of Water. He carries round the Streams wherever he pleases.

Took one Ride up to Baggachoag Hill, one Way, and another up the Lane by Doolittles shop, and I found that great Alterations have been made, and many Improvements, in 13 Years, for it is so long since I was in Either of those Parts of the Town of Worcester before. In the latter Road, I missed many objects of my former Acquaintance, many shady Thicketts and gloomy Grottos, where I have sat by the Hour together to ruminate and listen to the falls of Water.

This Pleasure of revisiting an old Haunt is very great. Mr. Putnam says he was lately at Danvers, and visited the very Path where he used to drive the Cows to Pasture when he was 7 Years old. It gave him a strange Feeling. It made him feel young, 7 Year old.

I visited Dr. Willard, I see little Alteration in him or his Wife in 16 Years, his Sons are grown Up. Sam, the eldest who has been to Colledge is settled at Uxbridge in the Practice of Physick, Levi is at home.

I met Coll. Gardiner Chandler. He said he heard I was in Quest of Health—if I found more than I wanted he begged a little—no poor Creature ever suffered more for Want of it. Thus he is the same Man. 16 Years, I have been a Witness to his continual Complaints of Weakness, and Want of Health.

This Day, Mr. Putnams eldest Daughter Eleanor, brought to the World her first Daughter, being married to Rufus Chandler, Son of Coll. John.

Heard Mr. Wheeler, late Minister of Harvard, at Worcester all day.

Here I saw many Faces much altered and many others not at all, since I first knew this Place which is now 16 Years. Here I saw many young Gentlemen, who were my Scholars and Pupils, when I kept School, here—Jno. Chandler Esq. of Petersham, Rufus Chandler, the Lawyer, Dr. Wm. Paine, who now studies Physick with Dr. Holyoke of Salem, Nat. Chandler, who studies Law with Mr. Putnam, and Dr. Thad. Maccarty, who is now in the Practice of Physick at Dudley. Most of these began to learn Latin with me.

Mem[orandum]. Gard. Chandler Yesterday said, that many Regulations were wanting, but the Town of Boston more than any Thing—and that after Election every Body used to be enquiring, who was chosen Councillors, very anxious and inquisitive to know. But now no Body asked any Thing about it. And Putnam said Yesterday He did not like the Town of Boston, He did not like their Manners—&c. I record these curious Speeches, because they are Characteristick of Persons, and of the Age.

Drank Tea at Mr. Putnams with Mr. Paine, Mrs. Paine, Dr. Holyokes Lady and Dr. Billy Paine. The Dr. is a very civil, agreable and sensible young Gentleman.

Went in the Evening over to G. Chandlers and chatted with him an Hour. He is very bitter vs. the Town of Boston. I hate 'em from my Soul says he.—Great Patriots—were for Non Importation, while their old Rags lasted, and as soon as they were sold at enormous Prices, they were for importing—no more to be heard about Manufactures—and now, there is a greater Flood of Goods than ever were known—and as to Tea, those who were most strenuous against it are the only Persons who have any to sell.

Jno. Chandler Esqr. of Petersham came into P.s in the Evening from Boston Yesterday, and gave us an Account of Mr. Otis's Conversion to Toryism.—Adams was going on, in the old Road, and Otis started up and said they had gone far enough in that Way, the Governor had an undoubted Right to carry the Court where he pleased, and moved for a Committee to represent the Inconveniences of sitting there, and moved for an Address to the Governor. He was a good Man—the Ministers said so—the Justices said so and it must be so—and moved to go on with Business, and the House voted every Thing he moved for.—Boston People say he is distracted, &c.[1]

[1] On the first day of the new assembly, 29 May, Otis opposed Samuel Adams' uncompromising position that the removal of the General Court to

Cambridge was a violation of the Province charter and succeeded in substituting much more conciliatory language in the usual House remonstrance to Hutchinson (who had received his commission as governor in March) on this subject. See Mass., *House Jour.*, 1771–1772, p. 6; Wells, *Samuel Adams*, 1:393–396.

1771. MONDAY JUNE 3D.

A fine Morning—a soft, sweet S.W. Wind. Oated in Spencer—turned my Horse to grass at Wolcotts in Brookfield. I ride alone, I find no Amusement, no Conversation, and have nothing to think about. But my Office and Farm frequently steal into my Mind, and seem to demand my Return. They must both suffer for Want of my Presence.

The Road to Stafford turns off, by Brookfield Meeting House, into Brimfield in the County of Hampshire.

Dined at Cheneys of Western in the County of Hampshire. An old Man came in, and after some Conversation with the old Landlady, she asked him, if he was not the Man who called here about 17 Years ago and was intrusted with a Jill of W. India Rum? He said Yes. Hant you had your Money?—No.—Well I sent it by a Brimfield Man, within a fortnight after. I'le at him about it. I'm desperate glad you mentioned it. I had the Rum. I was driving down a drove of Hogs. My two Boys were with me, I lost em both in the Year 1759, one at Crownpoint and one about 10 mile from Albany. They drinked the Rum with me. I'm glad you mentioned it—the Money is justly your due. I'le pay you now—how much is it.—2s:4d.—But says I, interposing for Curiosity, that will hardly do justice for the Interest is as much as the Principall. The whole Debt is 4s:8d.—I'm a poor Man says he. Landlady wont ask me Interest.—I was much amused with the old Womans quick and tenacious Memory, and with the old Mans Honesty. But it seems to be, that the whole Anecdote shews that these are but two Penny People.

This honest Man whose Name is Frost, hearing that I was bound to the Spring, and unacquainted with the Way, very obligingly waited for me, to shew me the Way as far as he went which was several Miles. His father came from Billerica, to Springfield. Mrs. Cheney says her Husband came from Roxbury. I found that Frost was a great Partisan of the mineral Spring. He said, He had been weakly this 30 Year, and the Spring had done him more good in a few days, than all the Drs. had done, in 30 Year—and he went on and told of a great Number of marvellous Instances of Cures wrought there by Washing and drinking while he was there.[1]

Oated at Silas Hodges's in Brimfield, near the baptist Meeting House. There I find they have not so much faith in the Spring. Lodged at

Colburns the first House in Stafford. There I found one David Orcutt, who came from Bridgwater 30 Years ago, a Relation of the Orcutts in Weymouth. He I find is also a great Advocate for the Spring. He was miserable many Years with Rheumatism &c., and by means of the Spring was now a comfortable Man. The Landlord came with [his] Father 30 Years ago from Roxbury. He has a farm of 200 Acres of Land, 100 under Improvement, keeps near 30 Head of neat Cattle, 3 Horses, 50 sheep, and yet offers to sell me his Place for £500 L.M.

[1] Contemporary opinions on the curative powers of the mineral springs at Stafford, Conn., which first attracted wide public attention in 1766, are well summarized by Carl Bridenbaugh in an article on "Baths and Watering Places of Colonial America," *WMQ*, 3d ser., 3:152–158 (April 1946).

1771. TUESDAY. JUNE 4TH.

Rode over to the Spring. One Childs had built a little House, within a few Yards of the Spring, and there some of the lame and infirm People keep. The Spring arises at the Foot of a Steep high Hill, between a Cluster of Rocks very near the Side of a River. The Water is very clear, limpid and transparent, the Rocks And Stones and Earth at the Bottom are tinged with a reddish yellow Colour, and so is the little Wooden Gutter that is placed at the Mouth of the Spring to carry the Water off—indeed the Water communicates that Colour, which resembles that of the Rust of Iron, to whatever Object it washes. Mrs. Child furnished me with a Glass Mugg, broken to Pieces and painted[1] together again, and with that I drank pretty plentifully of the Water. It has the Taste of fair Water with an Infusion of some Preparation of steel in it, which I have taken, heretofore—Sal Martis, somewhat like Copperas. They have built a shed over a little Reservoir made of Wood, about 3 feet deep and into that have conveyed the Water from the Spring, and there People bath, Wash and plunge, for which Childs has 8d. a time. I plunged in twice—but the 2d time was superfluous and did me more hurt than good, it is very cold indeed.

Mrs. Child directed me to one Greens about half a Mile from the Spring, as a Place to lodge at, and when I got there I found it was my old Acquaintance John Green who lived with Coll. Chandler at Worcester while I lived with Putnam and married A. Ward, daughter of Captn. Ward and Sister of Sam. Ward who married Dolly Chandler.

Green told me, to day, that he had lived in Woodstock 13 Years and had nothing but bad luck, all the Time. Now he was about to try whether Change of Place, would alter his fortune. I asked what bad

Luck? He said he had fail'd in Trade like a fool—and after Dinner he [said] [2] that the richest Men were such as had fail'd in Trade. His Uncle John Chandler broke once, and very nigh breaking another Time. His Uncle Tommy Green broke once. John Spooner broke once. So I dont entirely despair.—This News I was not att all surprized to hear, for I thought fifteen Year ago, that Jno. Green would turn out so. He was a boaster of his Vices—a great affecter of licentiousness—and at last got in Love, like a fool, with a Girl, much too good for him. He says that McClelan of Woodstock is the richest Man in that Town, by a great Run of surprizing Luck in Trade in English, W. India Goods and Potash.

Dined at Greens, and after 2 Hours by Sun took my Horse and went to the Spring again, and drank of the Water. Then I rode up the Mountain, at the Foot of which this Spring ooses. The Hill is high And the Prospect from it, extensive, but few cultivated Spots appear, the Horison is chiefly Wilderness. The Mountain seems to be a Body of Oar, Iron Oar, I suppose, and the Water filtrating thro that Mountain of Mineral's imbibes its salubrious Quality. What Particles it is impregnated with, I cant tell—But it is saturated with something. The Bottom and sides of the Cistern are painted a deep yellow, and a plentifull Dust or flour remains after the Water is drawn off. They say, that this yellow Sediment is the best thing for Scrophulous Humours, or any other Breakings out, Eruptions, Sores, Ulcers, Cankers, &c.

Jno. Green and his Wife reminded me to day of the old Story of Betsy Friswell, who staid at Mrs. Putnams when I was there and afterwards fell in Love, with Green. She fell in Love [at] [3] Worcester, but restrained and suppressed her Passion, till sometime after Green made his Appearance at Woodstock Meeting and the sight of him revived all her old Thoughts and Emotions, and quite overcame her. She went into Fits &c. and her Brother prevailed on Green to go and see her, and she asked him, whether she should live or die, for her life and death were in his Power. If he would have her she should live, if not, she should die. He said He could not—he was engaged—or could not like her well enough—and She went into Fits, immediately, and languished away and died. This Anecdote was very familiar to me, when I first left Worcester. I have told it 100 times, with much Pleasure and Laughter, but had entirely forgot it, so that I could not for some Time recollect the Name of Betsy Friswell. But I never heard before the melancholly Circumstance that the poor Girl died.

The Place where I now sit, in the Chamber in Greens House, has the Command of a great View, this is a Mountainous Country. This House stands upon very high Land, and here is a fine spacious Road laid out, very wide and of great Length and quite strait, which lies right before me now, with the Meeting House in the Middle of it, more than half a Mile off.

Coll. Abijah Willard and Sam Ward and another bought of Wm. Brown of Salem, or Virginia, 7000 Acres of Land in this Town, and they are about erecting Iron Mills here, Furnaces, &c. and there is a Talk of making this a Shire Town, &c. Unimproved Land is to be bought in this Town in great Plenty for 6s. an Acre.

At Night, Green call'd to his Wife, come put by your Work and come in, and takes his Family Bible, and reads a Chapter and then makes a long Prayer of half an Hour, and we all go to bed.

[1] Thus in MS, and probably exactly what JA meant. CFA silently corrected this word to "puttied."
[2] MS: "had."
[3] MS: "and."

1771. WEDNESDAY JUNE 5TH.

Rode to the Spring, drank and plunged. Dipped but once. Sky cloudy.

Activity and Industry, care, and Œconomy, are not the Characteristicks of this Family. Green was to set out upon a Journey to Providence to day to get Stores &c. and Stock for Trade, but he lounged and loitered away, hour after Hour till 9 O Clock before he mounted. The Cow, whose Titts strutt with Milk, is unmilked till 9 O Clock. My Horse would stand by the [Head?] Hour after Hour if I did not put him out my self, tho I call upon the father and the Sons to put him out.

Looking into a little Closet in my Chamber this Morning I found a pretty Collection of Books, the Preceptor, Douglass's History, Paradise lost, the musical Miscellany in two Volumes, the Life of the Czar, Peter the great &c.

I laid hold of the 2d Volume of the Preceptor, and began to read the Elements of Logick, and considered the four fold Division of the Subject, simple Apprehension, or Perception, Judgment or Intuition, Reasoning, and Method. This little Compendium of Logick, I admired at Colledge. I read it over and over. I recommended it to others, particularly to my Chum David Wyer,[1] and I took the Pains to read a great Part of it to him and with him.

By simple Apprehension or Perception we get Ideas, by Sensation and by Reflection, the Ideas we get are Simple, &c.

Mem.—I hope I shall not forget to purchase these Preceptors, and to make my Sons transcribe this Treatise on Logick entirely with their own Hands, in fair Characters, as soon as they can write, in order to imprint it on their Memories. Nor would it hurt my Daughter to do the same. I have a great Opinion of the Exercise of transcribing, in Youth.

About 11. O Clock arrived, Dr. McKinstry of Taunton and spoke for Lodgings for himself and Co[lborn] Barrell and his Wife.—It is not you? Is it? says he.—Persons in your Way are subject to a certain weak Muscle and lax Fibre, which occasions Glooms to plague you. But the Spring will brace you.—I Joy and rejoice at his Arrival. I shall have Opportunity to examine him about this mineral, medicinal Water.

I have spent this day in sauntering about, down in the Pasture to see my Horse, and over the fields in the Neighbourhood. Took my Horse after noon and rode away East, a rugged rocky Road, to take View of the Lands about the Town—and went to the Spring. 30 People have been there to day, they say. The Halt, the Lame, the vapoury, hypochondriac, scrophulous, &c. all resort here. Met Dr. McKinstry at the Spring. We mounted our Horses together, and turned away the Western Road toward Somers to see the Improvements, that I saw Yesterday from the Mountain by the Spring, and returned, to our Lodgings.—The Dr. I find is a very learned Man. He said that the Roman Empire came to its Destruction as soon as the People got set against the Nobles and Commons as they are now in England, and they went on Quarrelling, till one Brutus carried all before him and enslaved em all.—Cæsar, you mean Dr.—No I think it was Brutus, want it?—Thus We see the Dr. is very Book learnt. And when we were drinking Tea, I said, 500 Years hence there would be a great Number of Empires in America, independent of Europe and of each other.—Oh says he I have no Idea that the World will stand so long—not half 500 Years. The World is to conform to the Jewish Calculations, every seventh day was to be a day of Rest, every 7th Year was to be a Jubilee, and the 7th. Thousand Years will be a Thousand Years of Rest and Jubilee—no Wars, no fightings, and there is but about 230 wanting to compleat the 6000 Years. Till that Time, there will be more furious Warrs than ever.

Thus I find I shall have in the Dr. a fund of Entertainment. He is superficial enough, and conceited enough, and enthusiastical enough to entertain.

[1] Wyer, who came from Falmouth (Portland, Maine), was in the Harvard class of 1758; he studied law and from 1762 practiced in Falmouth; admitted attorney in the Superior Court, 1765, and barrister two years later; died in 1776 (Superior Court of Judicature, Minute Books 76, 87; Stark, *Loyalists of Mass.*, p. 466).

1771. THURSDAY JUNE 6.

Spent this fine day in rambling on horseback and on foot with Dr. McKinstry East and West, North and South. Went with him twice to the Spring and drank freely of the Waters, and rode about to hire an Horse to carry me to Springfield and Northampton. At last obtained one. The Dr. is alert and chearfull and obliging and agreable.

In the afternoon Colburn Barrell and his Wife and Daughter came, and took Lodgings at our House. Drank Tea and spent the Evening with them. When the Dr. took his Hat to go out to a Neighbours to lodge, Colburn sprung out of his Chair and went up to the Dr., took him by the Hand And kissed him, before all the Company in the Room. This is Sandemanianism.[1]

Rode this day, beyond the Meeting House, and found my old Acquaintance the Parson, John Willard, at his own Door. He lives in a little, mean looking Hutt. How many of my Contemporaries at Colledge, worthy Men, live in poor and low Circumstances! Few of them have so much of this Worlds Goods as have fallen even to my Share, tho some of them have much more. Let me enjoy then what I have, and be gratefull.

Mr. Barrell confirms the Account of Mr. Otis's Behaviour in the House, which Mr. Chandler gave me at Worcester. But says he cannot reconcile this, to Mr. Otis's whole Conduct for a Course of Years.

[1] Colborn Barrell was an elder, or preacher, of the Sandemanian sect in Boston; from the custom mentioned here by JA, the Sandemanians were sometimes vulgarly called "Kissites" (Col. Soc. Mass., *Pubns.*, 6 [1904]:113, 131, 132, note).

1771. FRYDAY. JUNE 7TH.

Went to the Spring with the Dr. and drank a Glass and an half i.e. a Jill and an half. My Horse was brought very early—my own Mare I shall leave in a very fine Pasture, with Oats for her twice a Day that she may rest and recruit.

Barrell this Morning at Breakfast entertained Us with an Account of his extravagant Fondness for Fruit. When he lived at New market he could get no fruit but Strawberries, and he used frequently to eat 6 Quarts in a Day. At Boston, in the very hottest of the Weather he breakfasts upon Water Melons—neither Eats nor drinks any Thing else for Breakfast. In the Season of Peaches he buys a Peck, every Morning, and eats more than half of them himself. In short he eats so much fruit in the Season of it that he has very little Inclination to any other Food. He never found any Inconvenience or ill Effect from fruit—

enjoys as much Health as any Body. Father Dana is immoderately fond of fruit, and from several other Instances one would conclude it very wholsome.

Rode to Somers, over a very high large Mountain which the People here call Chesnut Hill. It is 5 miles over, very bad Road, very high Land. It is one of a Range of great Mountains, which runs North and South Parallell with Connecticutt River, about 10 miles to the East of it, as another similar Range runs on the Western Side of it. There is a Mountain which they call the bald Mountain which you pass by as you cross Chesnutt hill, much higher from whence you can see the great River, and many of the great Turns upon it, as they say.—Dined at Kibbys, met People going over to the Spring.

In Kibbys Barr Room in a little Shelf within the Barr, I spied 2 Books. I asked what they were. He said every Man his own Lawyer, and Gilberts Law of Evidence. Upon this I asked some Questions of the People there, and they told me that Kibby was a sort of Lawyer among them—that he pleaded some of their home Cases before Justices and Arbitrators &c. Upon this I told Kibby to purchase a Copy of Blackstones Commentaries.

Rode from Kibbys over to Enfield, which lies upon Connecticutt River, oated and drank Tea at Peases—a smart House and Landlord truly, well dressed, with his Ruffles &c., and upon Enquiry I found he was the great Man of the Town—their Representative &c. as well as Tavern Keeper, and just returned from the gen[eral] Assembly at Hartford.—Somers and Enfield are upon a Levell, a fine Champaign Country. Suffield lies over the River on the West Side of it.

Rode along the great River to Windsor, and put up at Bissalls—i.e. in East Windsor, for the Town of Windsor it seems lies on the West Side of the River.

The People in this Part of Connecticutt, make Potash, and raise a great Number of Colts, which they send to the West Indies, and barter away for Rum &c. They trade with Boston and New York but most to New York. They say there is a much greater Demand for Flaxseed of which they raise a great deal, at N. York, than there is at Boston, and they get a better Price for it. Kibby at Somers keeps a Shop, and sells W. India goods and English Trinketts, keeps a Tavern, and petty foggs it.

At Enfield you come into the great Road upon Connecticutt River, which runs back to Springfield, Deerfield, Northampton &c. Northward and down to Windsor and Hartford, Weathersfield and Middleton, Southward.

The Soil as far as I have ridden upon the River if I may judge by the Road is dry and sandy. But the Road is 3/4 of a mile from the River and the intervale Land lies between.

I begin to grow weary of this idle, romantic Jaunt. I believe it would have been as well to have staid in my own Country and amused myself with my farm, and rode to Boston every day. I shall not suddenly take such a Ramble again, merely for my Health. I want to see my Wife, my Children, my Farm, my Horse, Oxen, Cows, Walls, Fences, Workmen, Office, Books, and Clerks. I want to hear the News, and Politicks of the Day. But here I am, at Bissills in Windsor, hearing my Landlord read a Chapter in the Kitchen and go to Prayers with his Family, in the genuine Tone of a Puritan.

1771. SATURDAY JUNE 8TH.

Bissill says, there are Settlements, upon this River, for 300 Miles— i.e. from Seabrook [Saybrook] where it discharges itself. The River, in the Spring, when the Snow melts, swells prodigiously and brings down the Washings of Mountains and old Swamps, rotten Wood and Leaves &c. to inrich the Intervale Lands, upon its banks.

At eleven O Clock arrived at Wrights in Weathersfield. I have spent this Morning in Riding thro Paradise. My Eyes never beheld so fine a Country. From Bissills in Windsor to Hartford Ferry, 8 Miles, is one continued Street—Houses all along, and a vast Prospect of level Country on each Hand, the Lands very rich and the Husbandry pretty good. The Town of Hartford is not very compact, there are some very handsome and large Houses, some of brick. The State House is pretty large, and looks well. I stopped only to oat my Horse and get my Head and Face shaved, and then rode to Weathersfield 4 miles, on the West Side of the River.—Here is the finest Ride in America, I believe. Nothing can exceed the Beauty, and Fertility of the Country. The Lands upon the River, the flatt low Lands, are loaded with rich, noble Crops of Grass, and Grain and Corn. Wright says, some of their Lands, will yeild 2 Crops of English Grass, and two Ton and an half at each Crop, and plenty of after feed besides—but these must be nicely managed and largely dunged. They have in Weathersfield a large brick Meeting House, Lockwood the Minister. A Gentleman came in and told me, that there was not such another Street in America as this at Weathersfield excepting one at Hadley, and that Mr. Ingersol the Stamp Master told him, he had never seen in Phyladelphia nor in England, any Place equal to Hartford and Weathersfield.—One Joseph Webb, one

Deane[1] and one Verstille, are the principal Traders here, both in English and W. India Goods.

Dined at the Widow Griswalls [Griswolds] in Weathersfield about 3 Miles from Wrights, the Road and Country are equally pleasant all the Way. Sat down to Table with the old Woman and another Woman, and a dirty, long, greybearded Carpenter who was at Work for Landlady, and might be smelled from one Room to the other—So that these Republicans are not very decent or neat. Landlady and her Housewright very very chatty about Boston, Providence, Newport, Marthas Vineyard And Nantuckett. Landlady says the Deputy Governor calls here and always has some comical Story to tell her. He asked her tother day to come down and see his Wife make cheese. He has 22 Cows, and his Women make Cheese in the forenoon and then dress up and go out, or receive Company at home.

Rode to Middletown, and put up for the Sabbath at Shalers, near the Court House. Middleton I think is the most beautifull Town of all. When I first opened[2] into the Town which was upon the Top of a Hill, there opened before me the most beautifull Prospect of the River, and the Intervals and Improvements, on each Side of it, and the Mountains at about 10 Miles distance both on the East and West Side of the River, and of the main Body of the Town at a Distance. I went down this Hill, and into a great Gate, which led me to the very Banks of the River. The Road lies here along the Bank of the River and on the right Hand is a fine level Tract of Interval Land as rich as the Soil of Egypt. The Lotts are divided by no Fence, but here are Strips runing back at right Angles from the River, on one is Indian Corn, on another Parrallell to it is Rye, on another Barley, on another Flax, on another a rich Burden of Clover and other English Grasses, and after riding in this enchanting Meadow for some Time you come to another Gate, which lets you into the main Body of the Town, which is ornamented as is the Meadow I just mentioned, with fine Rows of Trees and appears to me as populous, as compact and as polite as Hartford.

The Air all along from Somers to Middleton appears to me to be very clear, dry, and elastic. And therefore, if I were to plan another Journey for my Health, I would go from Boston to Lancaster and Lunenbourg, thence to No. 4.[3] and thence down to N. Hampton, Deerfield, Hadley, Springfield, then to Endfield, and along the River down to Seabrook, and from thence over to Rhode Island and from thence to Braintree. And here I might possibly, i.e. at No. 4. look up some Land to purchase for my Benefit, or the Benefit of my Children. But I hope I shall not take another Journey merely for my Health very soon. I feel sometimes sick of this—I feel guilty—I feel as if I ought not to saunter and loyter and trifle away this Time—I feel as if I ought to be employed, for the Benefit of my fellow Men, in some Way or other.

In all this Ramble from Stafford, I have met with nobody that I knew, excepting Jo. Trumble, who with his father the Governor were crossing the ferry for the East Side when I was for the West.

Bespoke Entertainment for the Sabbath, at Shalers, and drank Tea. She brought me in the finest and sweetest of Wheat Bread, and Butter, as yellow as Gold, and fine Radishes, very good Tea and sugar. I regaled without Reserve. But my Wife is 150 Miles from me at least, and I am not yet homeward bound. I wish Connecticutt River flowed through Braintree. But the barren rocky Mountains of Braintree are as great a Contrast as can be conceived to the level smoth, fertile Plains of this Country. Yet Braintree pleases me more.

I long to be foul of Deacon Belchers Orchard. I am impatient to begin my Canal, and banks, to convey the Water all round, by the Road and the House. I must make a Pool in the Road by the Corner of my Land at the Yard in front of the House, for the cool Spring Water to come into the Road there—that the Cattle, and Hogs, and Ducks may regale themselves there.

Looking into the Almanac, I am startled. S[uperior] C[ourt] Ipswich is the 18th. day of June. I thought it a Week later 25. So that I have only next Week to go home 150 Miles. I must improve every Moment. It is 25 miles a day if I ride every day next Week.

---

[1] Silas Deane, lawyer, merchant, member of the Connecticut legislature, and subsequently a member of the Continental Congress and one of the American commissioners in Paris, with whose activities in Europe JA, as Deane's successor, was to be deeply involved.

[2] Thus in MS. JA doubtless meant "rode" or "came."

[3] JA probably means that he would travel via Lancaster and Lunenburg, Mass., to "No. 4," a settlement on the upper Connecticut River that is now Charlestown, N.H.

1771. SUNDAY, JUNE 9TH.

Feel a little discomposed this Morning. Rested but poorly last night. Anxious about my Return—fearfull of very hot or rainy weather. I have before me an uncomfortable Journey to Casco Bay—little short of 300 miles.

Looking into a little bedroom, in this House Shaylers, I found a few Books, the musical Miscellany, Johnsons Dictionary, the farmers Letters, and the Ninth Volume of Dr. Clarks sermons.[1] This last I took for my Sabbath Day Book, and read the Sermon on the Fundamentals of Christianity, which he says [are] the Doctrines concerning the Being and Providence of God, the Necessity of Repentance and Obedience to his Commands, the Certainty of a Life to come, a Resurrection from the dead and a future Judgment.

Read also another Sermon on the Reward of Justice. "There is, says the Dr., a Duty of Justice towards the Public. There is incumbent upon Men the very same Obligation, not to wrong the Community; as there is, not to violate any private Mans Right, or defraud any particular Person of his Property. The only Reason, why Men are not always sufficiently sensible of this; so that many, who are very just in their Dealings between Man and Man, will yet be very fraudulent or rapacious with Regard to the Public; is because in this latter Case, it is not so obviously and immediately apparent upon whom the Injury falls, as it is in the Case of private Wrongs. But so long as the Injury is clear and certain; the Uncertainty of the Persons upon whom the Injury falls in Particular, or the Number of the Persons among whom the damage may chance to be divided, alters not at all the Nature of the Crime itself."

Went to Meeting in the Morning, and tumbled into the first Pew I could find—heard a pretty sensible, Yalensian, Connecticuttensian Preacher. At Meeting I first saw Dr. Eliot Rawson, an old School fellow. He invited me to dine. His House is handsome without, but neither clean nor elegant within, in furniture or any Thing else. His Wife is such another old Puritan as his Cousin, Peter Adams's Wife at Braintree.[2] His Children are dirty, and ill governed. He first took me into his Physick Room, and shewed me a No. of Curiosities which he has collected in the Course of his Practice—first an odd kind of long slender Worm preserved in Spirits. He says he has had between 20 and 30 Patients with such Worms—several Yards long and some of them several Rods. He shewed me some fingers he cutt off and some Wens, and his Physick Drawers And his Machine to pound with his Pestle &c.

His dining Room is crouded with a Bed and a Cradle, &c. &c. We had a picked up Dinner. Went to Meeting with him in the Afternoon, and heard the finest Singing, that ever I heard in my Life, the front and side Galleries were crowded with Rows of Lads and Lasses, who performed all the Parts in the Utmost Perfection. I thought I was wrapped up. A Row of Women all standing up, and playing their Parts with perfect Skill and Judgment, added a Sweetness and Sprightliness to the whole which absolutely charmed me.—I saw at Meeting this Afternoon Moses Paine, who made a decent Appearance and the Dr.

tells me lives by his Trade of a shoemaker comfortably from Day to day.

The more I see of this Town the more I admire it. I regrett extremely that I cant pursue my Tour to New Haven.

The Dr. thinks Hancock vain. Told a Story.—"I was at school with him, and then upon a level with him. My father was richer than his. But I was not long since at his Store and said to Mr. Glover whom I knew, this I think is Mr. Hancock. Mr. H. just asked my Name and nothing more—it was such a Piece of Vanity! There is not the meanest Creature that comes from your Way, but I take Notice of him—and I ought. What tho I am worth a little more than they—I am glad of it, and that I have it that I may give them some of it." I told the Dr. that Mr. H. must have had something upon his Mind—that he was far from being Arrogant—&c.

Drank Tea with Landlady, and her Son Mr. Shaylor, in pretty, western Room. But they are not very sociable. In short, I have been most miserably destitute of Conversation here. The People here all Trade to N. York, and have very little Connection with Boston. After Tea went over to the Drs., and found him very social and very learned. We talked much about History &c. He says, that Boston lost the Trade of this Colony by the severe Laws vs. their old Tenor. But they may easily regain the Trade, for the People here are much disgusted with N. York for their Defection from the N[on] Importation Agreement, and for some frauds and unfair Practises in Trade. He says they have found out that N. York Merchants have wrote home to the Manufacturers in England to make their Goods narrower and of a meaner fabric that they might sell cheaper, and undersell Boston. The Dr. says that Coll. Josa. Quincy quarrells with his Workmen &c. but Norton is a clever Man, he called to see him and was much pleased, &c.

Landlady has an only Son Nat. Shaylor, and she is very fond and very proud of him. He lived with a Merchant—is now 25 or 26 and contents himself still to keep that Merchants Books without any Inclination to set up for himself. Is a great Proficient in Musick. Plays upon the Flute, Fife, Harpsicord, Spinnett &c. Associates with the Young and the Gay, and is a very fine Connecticutt young Gentleman. Oh the Misery, the Misfortune, the Ruin of being an only Son! I thank my God that I was not, and I devoutly pray, that none of mine may ever be!

[1] Samuel Clarke (1675–1729), rector of St. James's, Westminster, a prolific writer on metaphysical and theological subjects (*DNB*).

[2] This Peter Adams was a cousin of Deacon John Adams; his 2d wife was Elizabeth Rawson (A. N. Adams, *Geneal. Hist. of Henry Adams of Braintree*, p. 397).

1771. MONDAY JUNE 10TH.

Took my Departure from Middleton, homewards, the same Way I went down. Very hot. Oated at Hartford, and reached Bissills of Winser, 23 Miles before Dinner, just as they had got their Indian Pudding and their Pork and Greens upon the Table, one quarter after 12. After Dinner attempted to cutt off an Angle, by striking over by Goshen, i.e. Ellington, to Kibbys at Somers, but lost my Way, and got bewildered among Woods and cross Paths, and after riding 10 Miles to no Purpose returned to Bissells, and took the old Rout to Enfield, excessive hot. Lodged at Peases. But passed a very restless uncomfortable Night. Overcome with Fatigue and inflamed with Heat I could not sleep. And my Meditations on my Pillow were unhappy.

1771. TUESDAY JUNE 11.

Rode to Kibbys at Somers but got caught in the Rain—very heavy plentifull Showers—I was much wet. Thus I have hitherto had not very good Luck upon my homeward bound Voyage. Dined at Kibbys and then rode over the Mountain to Stafford, went to the Spring and drank of the Waters with a Gentleman from New Jersey, who was there, with a Servant. Dr. McKinstry was gone to Brookfield, to accompany Mr. Barrell so far in his Way home.

1771. WEDNESDAY JUNE 12.

Sat out upon my Return home, oated at Warreners, in Brimfield, caught in a cold Rain, obliged to stop at Cheneys in Western in order to dine. Landlord very sick of a Plurisie. While I was at Cheneys 5 Chaises went by. Jona. Amory and Wife, Deacon Newhall and Wife, Ned Paine and Wife and Sister and servants &c.—Oated at Spencer, drank Tea and putt up at Serjeants in Leicester—a very good House, neat and clean and convenient &c.

I have had a naked, barren Journey. My Brains have been as barren the whole Time, as a sandy Plain, or a gravelly Nole. My Soul has been starved. Came off, just when Company began to collect. This Week and the next would have brought together a curious Collection of Characters from all Parts of New England, and some perhaps from the Southern Provinces and some from the W. Indies.

1771. THURSDAY JUNE 13TH.

Remarkable, the Change of Thoughts, and feelings, and Reasonings which are occasioned by a Change of Objects. A Man is known by his

Company, and evil Communications corrupt good Manners. "Man is a Social Creature and his Passions, his feelings, his Imaginations are contagious." We receive a Tincture of the Characters of those we converse with.

Stopped at Mr. Putnams, and at the Court House, went in and bowed to the Court and shook Hands with the Bar, said How d'ye, and came off. Dined at Coll. Williams's, drank Tea at Munns, with Dr. Cooper and his Lady, Captn. Jona. Freeman and his Lady and Mr. Nat. Barrett and his Lady, who were upon their Return from a Tour to Lancaster.

Rode this day from Worcester to Munns in Company with one Green of Leicester, who was very social, and good Company, an honest, clever Man. By him I learn that Thomas Faxon of Braintree, has removed with his Family, to Leicester, and hired an House near the Meeting House. And I met Joseph Crane to day in Marlborough, going to Rutland. He is about removing his Family there. But I find that People in Rutland, and Leicester and Worcester, &c. are more disposed to emigrate still farther into the Wilderness, than the Inhabitants of the old Towns.

I hear much to day and Yesterday of the Harmony prevailing between the Governor and the House. Cushing is unanimous Commissary, not negatived, and Goldthwait is Truckmaster. Behold how good and pleasant it is, for Brethren to dwell together in Unity. It seems to be forgotten entirely, by what means Hutchinson procured the Government—by his Friendship for Bernard, and by supporting and countenancing all Bernards Measures, and the Commissioners and Army and Navy, and Revenue, and every other Thing we complain of.

I read to day an Address from the Convention of Ministers, and from the Clergy in the northern Part of the County of Hampshire and from the Town of Almesbury [Amesbury], all conceived in very high Terms, of Respect and Confidence and Affection.[1] Posterity will scarcely find it possible, to form a just Idea of this Gentlemans Character. But if this wretched Journal should ever be read, by my own Family, let them know that there was upon the Scene of Action with Mr. Hutchinson, one determined Enemy to those Principles and that Political System to which alone he owes his own and his Family's late Advancement— one who thinks that his Character and Conduct have been the Cause of laying a Foundation for perpetual Discontent and Uneasiness between Britain and the Colonies, of perpetual Struggles of one Party for Wealth and Power at the Expence of the Liberties of this Country, and of perpetual Contention and Opposition in the other Party to preserve them, and that this Contention will never be fully terminated but by Warrs, and Confusions and Carnage. Cæsar, by destroying the Roman Republic, made himself perpetual Dictator, Hutchinson, by countenancing and supporting a System of Corruption and all Tyranny, has made himself Governor—and the mad Idolatry of the People, always the surest Instruments of their own Servitude, laid prostrate at the Feet of both. With great Anxiety, and Hazard, with continual Application to Business, with loss of Health, Reputation, Profit, and as fair Prospects and Opportunities of Advancement, as others who have greedily embraced them, I have for 10 Years together invariably opposed this System, and its fautors. It has prevailed in some Measure, and the People are now worshipping the Authors and Abetters of it, and despizing, insulting, and abusing, the Opposers of it.—Edward and Alfred

> closed their long Glories with a Sigh to find
> th' unwilling Gratitude of base Mankind.

As I came over Sudbury Causey, I saw a Chaplain of one of the Kings Ships fishing in the River, a thick fat Man, with rosy Cheeks and black Eyes. At Night he came in with his fish. I was in the Yard and he spoke to me, and told me the News.—The Governor gave a very elegant Entertainment to the Gentlemen of the Army and Navy and Revenue, and Mrs. Gambier in the Evening a very elegant Ball—as elegant a cold Collation as perhaps you ever see—all in figures &c. &c. &c.

Read this days Paper.[2] The melodious Harmony, the perfect Concords, the entire Confidence and Affection, that seems to be restored greatly surprizes me. Will it be lasting. I believe there is no Man in so curious a Situation as I am. I am for what I can see, quite left alone, in the World.

[1] The three addresses mentioned here, with Hutchinson's answers, are all printed in the *Boston Evening Post*, 3 June 1771.
[2] The *Boston News Letter*, which printed this day the cordial answer of the Council to the Governor's address to both houses at the opening of the session, together with a detailed report of the military exercises and the dinner "at the charge of the Province" in honor of the King's 34th birthday, 4 June.

1771. FRYDAY JUNE 14.

A fine Morning.

MONDAY. JUNE 17TH. 1771.[1]

Sat out upon the Eastern Circuit. Stopped at Boston, at my Office, and no where else. Came over Charlestown Ferry and Penny Ferry, and dined at Kettles in Malden, by the Meeting House. Kettle is a D[eputy] Sherriff. The Meeting House is Mr. Thatchers.

I mounted my Horse and rode to Boston in a Cloth Coat and Waiscoat, but was much pinched with a cold, raw, harsh, N.E. Wind. At Boston I put on a thick Flannel Shirt, and that made me comfortable, and no more—So cold am I or so cold is the Weather, 17th. June.

Overtook Judge Cushing in his old Curricle and 2 lean Horses, and Dick his Negro at his Right Hand driving the Curricle. This is the Way of travelling in 1771. A Judge of the Circuits, a Judge of the Superiour Court, a Judge of the Kings Bench, Common Pleas, and Exchequer for the Province, travells, with a Pair of wretched old Jades of Horses, in a wretched old Dung Cart of a Curricle, and a Negro, on the same seat with him, driving.—But we shall have more glorious Times anon—When the Sterling Salaries are ordered out of the Revenue, to the Judges &c., as many most ardently wish—and the Judges themselves, among the rest I suppose. Stopped at Martins in Lynn with J. Cushing, oated, and drank a Glass of Wine—And heard him sigh and groan the Sighs and Groans of 77, tho he is yet active. He conversed in his usual, hinting, insinuating, doubting, scrupling Strain.

Rode with King a D. Sherriff who came out to meet the Judges, into Salem, put up at Goodhues. The Negro that took my Horse soon began to open his Heart.—He did not like the People of Salem, wanted to be sold to Captn. John Dean of Boston. He earned 2 Dollars in a forenoon, and did all he could to give Satisfaction. But his Mistress was cross, and said he did not earn Salt to his Porridge, &c. and would not find him Cloaths &c.

Thus I find Discontents in all Men. The Black thinks his Merit rewarded with Ingratitude, and so does the white. The Black estimates his own Worth, and the Merit of his Services higher than any Body else. So does the White. This flattering, fond Opinion of himself, is found in every Man.

I have hurt myself to day, by taking cold in the forenoon and by drinking too much Wine, at Kettles and at Martins. I drank 1/2 Pint at Kettles and 2 Glasses at Martins.

Just after I had drank Tea, and got my Fire made in my Chamber, my old Neighbour Jo. Barell came and lodged at Goodhues in the same Chamber with me. His Grief is intense indeed. He spent the whole Evening and a long Time after we got to Bed in lamenting the Loss of his Wife, in enumerating her Excellencies, &c.[2] Heartily wishes himself with her. Would have been very glad to have gone with her. He married from pure Regard, utterly vs. the Will of his Mother and all his Friends because she was poor—but she made him happy. She was the best of Women. The World has lost all its Charms to him. He never shall be happy but in another Wife, and the Chances are so much vs. his getting so good an one, that his Hopes are faint. He never will marry for Money. His Mother and sister shall never illtreat another Wife. His Children shall never be slighted. He would never part with his Children for a Thousand Indies. He never would have a Woman that should make them an Objection. He had tryed his Wife in Prosperity And Adversity, she had made him happy in both. Just as he had got over all his Difficulties, and Providence smiled upon his Business and affairs, she was taken from him.—This Killing of Wives Mr. Adams is a dreadfull Thing. There is not an Hour but I think of her. I wish I was with her. I'd run the risque out this Moment. I never dined from her 3 Times in 6 years and 9 months, except on her Washing days. I never spent 3 Evenings from her in the whole Time. I am made for that sort of Life. She begged of me, but just before she dyed, to be married again immediately. She knew I must be unhappy she said, without a Wife to take Care of me. She beckoned to me, but a few Minutes before she died, when her Hands were as cold as clods. She whispered to me—I love you now—if I could but carry you and the Children with me I should go rejoicing.—

In this eloquent Strain of Grief did he run on. Millions of Thoughts, did this Conversation occasion me. I thought I should have had no Sleep all night—however I got to sleep and slept well.

[1] First entry in "Paper book No. 18" (our D/JA/18), a stitched gathering of leaves containing entries through 5 July 1771 and a date heading but no entry for 6 July.

[2] CFA quotes an obituary notice of Anna, wife of Joseph Barrell, from the *Boston Gazette*, 22 April 1771 (JA, *Works*, 2:280, note).

TUESDAY JUNE 18. 1771.

Rode with Mr. Barrell to Ipswich, and put up at Treadwells. Every Object recalls the Subject of Grief. Barrell all the Way to Ipswich was like the Turtle, bemoaning the Loss of his Mate. "Fine Season and beautifull Scenes, but they did not charm him as they used to. He had often rode this Way a Courting with infinite Pleasure," &c. I cant reallize that she has left me forever. When she was well I often thought I could reallize the Loss of her, but I was mistaken. I had no Idea of it.—In short, this Mans Mournings have melted and softened me, beyond Measure.

1771. SATURDAY. JUNE 22ND.

Spent this Week at Ipswich in the usual Labours and Drudgery of Attendance upon Court. Boarded at Treadwells. Have had no Time to write.

Landlord and Landlady are some of the grandest People alive.[1] Landlady is the great Grand Daughter of Governor Endicott, and has all the great Notions, of high Family, that you find in Winslows, Hutchinsons, Quincys, Saltonstals, Chandlers, Leonards, Otis's, and as you might find, with more Propriety, in the Winthrops. Yet she is cautious, and modist about discovering of it. She is a new Light— continually canting and whining in a religious Strain. The Governor was uncommonly strict, and devout, eminently so, in his day, and his great grand Daughter hopes to keep up the Honour of the family in hers, and distinguish herself among her Contemporaries as much.— "Terrible Things, Sin causes." Sighs and Groans. "The Pangs of the new Birth." "The death of Christ shews above all things the heignous Nature of sin!" "How awfully Mr. Kent talks about death! How lightly and carelessly. I am sure a Man of his Years who can talk so about Death, must be brought to feel the Pangs of the new Birth here, or made to repent of it forever." "How dreadfull it seems to me to hear him—I, that am so afraid of death, and so concerned lest I ant fit and prepared for it.—What a dreadfull Thing it was, that Mr. Gridley died so—too great, too big, too proud to learn any Thing. Would not let any Minister pray with him. Said he knew more than they could tell him— asked the News and said he was going where he should hear no News," &c.

Thus far Landlady. As to Landlord, he is as happy and as big, as proud, as conceited, as any Nobleman in England. Always calm and good natured, and lazy, but the Contemplation of his farm, and his Sons and his House, and Pasture and Cows, his sound Judgment as he thinks and his great Holiness as well as that of his Wife, keep him as erect in his Thoughts as a Noble or a Prince. Indeed the more I con- sider of Mankind, the more I see, that every Man, seriously, and in his Conscience believes himself, the wisest, brightest, best, happiest &c. of all Men.

I went this Evening, spent an Hour, and took a Pipe with Judge Trowbridge at his Lodgings. He says, "you will never get your Health, till your Mind is at ease. If you tire yourself with Business, but especially with Politicks, you wont get well," I said, I dont meddle with Politicks, nor think about em.—"Except, says he, by Writing in the Papers."—I'le be sworn, says I, I have not wrote one Line in a Newspaper these two Years, &c.—The Judge says, he had an Hint, that Foster Hutchinson was appointed Judge because of the Judgment of the Court in the Case of Spear vs. Keen.[2] The Merchants took the Alarm, and said that instead of Lawyers they ought to have Merchants upon the Bench, and Mr. Hutchinson being both a Lawyer and a Merchant he was the Man, vs. the Governors Determination, a little time before.—But this is one Instance among 1000 of the Governors Disguise, before those that he induces to believe has his entire familiarity and Confidence. He made Mr. Goffe understand he intended to make Worthington or some other Lawyer, a Judge, when he fully designed to make his Brother, not indeed to please the Merchants, or because Foster was a Merchant, but because he was his Brother and that the family might have a Majority in that Court. He is impenetrable to those who dont desire to reach any Imperfection in him, and who are determined not to fathom him, where they may. The Bigotted, the Superstitious, the Enthusiastical, the Tools, the Interested, the Timid, are all dazzled with his Glare, and cant see clearly, when he is in the Horizon.

[1] Capt. Nathaniel and his (2d) wife, Hannah (Endicott) Treadwell (Thomas F. Waters, *Ipswich in the Massachusetts Bay Colony*, Ipswich, 1917, 2:75, 81–84).

[2] Foster Hutchinson, brother of the Governor, was appointed an associate justice of the Superior Court on 21 March (Whitmore, *Mass. Civil List*, p. 70). The case of Nathan Spear *v.* Josiah Keen concerned a debt of Keen to Spear for molasses and coopering. Spear won a judgment in the Inferior Court in January, but Keen appealed, and the Superior Court in February reversed the decision, JA serving as Keen's counsel. In 1773 Spear obtained a writ of review and Keen unaccountably defaulted. (Superior Court of Judicature, Minute Books 91, 95, 98; Records, 1771, fol. 211; 1773, fol. 105; Early Court Files, &c., Nos. 101970, 102329.) The bearing of the case on Foster Hutchinson's appointment nowhere appears.

SUNDAY JUNE 23D.

In the Morning my Horse was gone. Went to Meeting all day and heard old Mr. Rogers—a good, well meaning man, I believe. After Meeting rode to Newbury, and visited Brother Lowell, Brother Farnham, and then went and supped with Mr. Jonathan Jackson, in Company with Capt. Tracy, Mr. Hooper, Mr. Williams, Mr. Frasier[1] and Brother Lowell. Then went and lodged with Lowell.

[1] Moses Frazier, a merchant of Newburyport. His daughter Mary was to have an important connection with the Adams family as the girl who principally inspired JQA's poem "The Vision," written in 1788. See JQA, *Life in a New England Town*, *passim*; Currier, *Newburyport*, 2:540–547; Bemis, *JQA*, 1:24 and note, with references there.

MONDAY. JUNE 24. 1771.

Reached Portsmouth with Lowell, and walked half an Hour with him on the Town House Floor, with Mr. Livius and Mr. Jona. Warner, &c. Put up at Tiltons, and intend to visit the Governor this afternoon.

Had a good deal of Chat with Lowell on the Road. He practises much in New Hampshire, and gave me an Account of many strange Judgments of the Superior Court at Portsmouth—that an Infant, if allowed to trade by his Parents, is bound by his Contract, &c. And he gave me an Account also of the Politicks of the Province. A Controversy is arising or has arisen in the Wentworth Family. The old Governor by his Will gave all his Estate to his Wife, and she is since married to one Michael Wentworth, which has a little disappointed the Governor,[1] and he not long since asked the Advice of his Council whether he might not reassume the Lands which were formerly granted by the late Governor to himself, or at least reserved to himself, in each Grant of a Township, and grant them over again to a 3d. Person from whom he might take a Conveyance of them to himself. All the Council except Livius, advised him to the Reassumption, He having laid before them the Opinion of S. Fitch of Boston, that the Governor could not grant Land to himself. Livius dissented and entered his Protest and gave his Reasons, for which the Governor has displaced him, as a Judge of one of their Courts.

At Tiltons in Portsmouth I met with my Cousin Joseph Adams, whose Face, I was once as glad to see as I should have been to see an Angel. The Sight of him gave me a new feeling. When he was at Colledge, and used to come to Braintree with his Brother Ebenezer, how I used to love him.[2] He is broken to Pieces with Rheumatism and Gout now. To what Cause is his Ruin to be ascribed?

After Dinner a Gentleman came to Tiltons to enquire me out, and it proved to be Mr. Pickering a Lawyer.[3] He treated me with great Politeness, and seems a very sensible and well accomplished Lawyer.

After Dinner rode to York and put up at Ritchies, with Lowell and Bradbury.

[1] "The old Governor" was Benning Wentworth (1696–1770); his successor was his nephew, John Wentworth, JA's Harvard classmate (*DAB*, under both names).

[2] Joseph (1723–1801), a physician, and his brother Ebenezer (1726–1764) were sons of JA's uncle, Rev. Joseph Adams, of Newington, N.H. (A. N. Adams, *Geneal. Hist. of Henry Adams of Braintree*, p. 398).

[3] Doubtless John Pickering (1737–1805), later a state and federal judge famous for his eccentricities and still more famous for his highly political impeachment by Congress, 1803 (*DAB*).

TUESDAY JUNE 25TH. 1771.

At York Court, dined with the Judges, and spent the Evening at Ritchies with Bradbury and Hale of Portsmouth, a sensible young Lawyer. Bradbury says there is no need of Dung upon your Mowing Land if you dont feed it in the Fall nor Spring. Let the old Fog remain upon it, and die and rot and be washed into the Ground, and dont suffer your Cattle to tread upon it and so poach and break the soil, and you will never want any Dung.

Recipe to make Manure.

Take the Soil and Mud, which you cutt up and throw out when you dig Ditches in a Salt Marsh, and put 20 Load of it in a heap. Then take 20 Loads of common Soil or mould of Upland and Add to the other. Then to the whole add 20 Loads of Dung, and lay the whole in a Heap, and let it lay 3 months, then take your Spades And begin at one End of the Heap, and dig it up and throw it into another Heap, there let it lie, till the Winter when the Ground is frozen, and then cart it on, to your English Grass Land.—Ten or 20 Loads to an Acre, as you choose.—Rob. Temple learnt it in England, and first practised it at Ten Hills. From him the Gentry at Cambridge have learnt it, and they all Practise it.

I will bring up 20 or 30 Loads, of this Salt Marsh Mud, and lay it in my Cow Yard upon the Sea Weed that is there, bring up that which lies in the Road by James Bracketts as we go to Mr. Quincys. Q[uery]. Would not a Load of fresh meadow Mud, and a Load of Salt Meadow Mud with some Sand, and some dung &c. make a good Mixture.

If I can so fence and secure Deacon Belchers and Lt. Belchers Orchards, as not to feed them at all in the Fall, Winter nor Spring I could get a fine Crop of English Hay from thence. But I must keep up my Fences all Winter to keep off my Neighbours Creatures, Hogs, Horses, Oxen, Cows and Sheep.

WEDNESDAY JUNE 26TH: 1771.

Yesterday I had a good deal of Conversation with Judge Trowbridge. He seems alarmed about the Powers of the Court of Probate. He says if Judge Danforth was to die Tomorrow, and the Governor was to offer that Place to him, he would not take it, because he thinks it ought always to be given to some Judge of the Inferiour Court, and then, some one Lawyer might be found in each County who would take a Seat upon the Inferiour Bench, if he could be made a Judge of Probate at the same Time. He says he is utterly against Foster Hutchinsons holding the Probate Office in Boston, if he takes his Place upon the Superior Bench—and if the Governor is an integral Part, of the Court of Probate, the Supreme ordinary, i.e. if he is not, with the Members of the Council, only Primus inter Pares but has a Negative upon all their Decrees as Governor Shirley, Govr. Bernard and the late Secretary, were of Opinion, he thinks we may be in great Danger from the Court of Probate, and Judge Russell always opposed every Attempt to extend the Power of the Court of Probate.—He used to say We might have Bishops here, and the Court of Probate might get into their Hands, and therefore We ought to be upon our Guard.

FRYDAY JUNE 28TH. 1771.

At York. Yesterday I spent in Walking, one Way and another, to view the Town. I find that Walking serves me much. It sets my Blood in Motion much more than Riding.

Had some Conversation this Week with Chadburn of Berwick. He says, that Jo. Lee came to him, on the Election day Morning, and said "I know you are a peaceable Man. Why cant you vote for a few Gentlemen who would be agreable to the Governor and then perhaps some Gentlemen may not be negatived who would be agreable to you. Why cant you promote a Coalition?" Chadburn answered, I dont know who would be agreable to the Governor. I have not had a List.—Lee then mentioned Mr. Ropes, Lt. Govr. Oliver, and some of the Judges.—Why cant you choose some of those old Statesmen, who have [been] long and intimately acquainted with the Policy of the Province? &c.—Thus the Governors Emissaries are busy—instilling, insinuating, their Notions, and Principles, &c.

Had a little Chat this Week with Coll. Sparhawk of Kittery. He says "Now you are come away, they are become peaceable. You kept up a shocking Clamour while you was there."—This he said laughing, but there was rather too much Truth in it, to be made a Jest.—"They do you the Justice to say that no Man ever spoke more freely, than you did, and in Opposition to the rising Sun. But in order to take off from your Virtue, they say there is some private Pique between the Governor and you."—I told him there was none. He had always treated me well personally. If I had been actuated by private Pique, I would not have left the general Court but I would have remained there on Purpose to plague him. I could at least have been a Thorn in his Side—&c. But that I had been fully convinced in my own Mind these 10 Years that he was determined to raise himself and family, at all Hazards, and even on the Ruins of the Province, and that I had uniformly expressed that Opinion these 10 Years.

Sparhawk mentioned the Intrepidity of Sam Adams, a Man he says of great Sensibility, of tender Nerves, and harrased, dependant, in their Power. Yet he had born up against all—it must have penetrated him very deeply, &c.

TUESDAY JULY 2ND. 1771.

At Falmouth, at Mr. Jonathan Webbs, who has removed to an House very near the Court House.

Last Fryday Morning, I mounted with Brother Bradbury and his Brother Bradbury, at York for Falmouth, went over the Sands but could not ford Cape Nettick, and so was obliged to go round over the Bridge, by the Mill. Dined at Littlefields in Wells, drank Tea and lodged at Allens at Biddeford. Coll. Ting[1] and his Son in Law Jo. Tyler came along and lodged there, Tyng being the owner of the House and Farm there 47 Rods wide upon the River and 4 miles and an half long. Next day Saturday it rained, and Jona. Sewall, Mr. Lowell and Mr. Leonard Jarvis came in, and afternoon Judges Lynde and Cushing with their Servants. But the House had not Lodgings for them. The Judges went back to Lads [Ladds], Sewall and Lowell went to James Sullivans. Sunday Morning the Weather was fair, and We set off, for Scarborough, put up at Millikins, went to Meeting forenoon and afternoon, heard Mr. Briggs a young Gentleman and after Meeting rode to Falmouth, and I put up at Webbs where I have been ever-since reading the Atchievements of Don Quixotte.

This has been the most flat, insipid, spiritless, tasteless Journey that ever I took, especially from Ipswich. I have neither had Business nor Amusement, nor Conversation. It has been a moaping, melancholly Journey upon the whole. I slumber, and moap, away the Day. Tyng, Tyler, Sewall, Lowell, Jarvis were all Characters which might have afforded me Entertainment, perhaps Instruction, if I had been possessed of Spirits to enjoy it.

Saturday afternoon, I projected making a back Gammon Table, and about it Sewall, Lowell and Jarvis and Jo. Tyler went, got Pieces of Cedar, &c. and while they were playing I went to sleep.

Sunday Jarvis was telling of an Instance of Cruelty and Inhumanity in Hall the Wharfinger in Boston in ordering a poor Widow to be taken with a single Writ, when her Daughter was dying, and of his being Bail for her. Sewall said Hall would certainly be damned and you will certainly go to Heaven let you do what you will.

I feel myself weary of this wandering Life. My Heart is at Home. It would be more for my Health to ride to Boston every fair Morning, and to Braintree every fair Afternoon. This would be riding enough and I could there have one Eye to my office, and another to my farm. After my Return I shall try the Experiment.

In the Evening went to the Clubb, or friendly Society as they call themselves, where I found Wm. Cushing, Wyer, with whom I went, i.e. at his Invitation, Mr. Lyde, Child, Symmons, Jarvis, Dr. Coffin, Captn. Wait and Don Webb &c. Conversation decent, but upon Trifles and common Matters.

Saw Mr. Simmons at Court, a Gentleman from England who has been at Falmouth a No. of [years][2] as a Factor for several Merchants in England purchasing Deals.

[1] John Tyng, of Boston and Dunstable, "the last of the great magnates of the Massachusetts frontier" (Sibley-Shipton, *Harvard Graduates*, 7:595–601).

[2] CFA's conjecture for a word missing in the MS.

THURSDAY. JULY 4TH. 1771.

Dined with D. Wyer, in Company with his Father, Farnum, Sewall, Cushing, Sewall, Lowell &c. Conversation turns upon Revelations, Prophecies, Jews, &c.

Spent the Evening, with the Barr, at Shattucks the Tavern in high Spirits. Agreed unanimously to recommend Tim. Langdon, to be sworn.[1] All in good Spirits, very chearfull, and chatty—many good stories, &c. This day Argued the Cause of Freeman and Child, a Suit for £10 Penalty, for taking greater Fees in the Custom House than those allowed by the Province Law.[2]

[1] Timothy Langdon was duly admitted to practice and in the following June term at Falmouth was admitted attorney in the Superior Court (Superior Court of Judicature, Minute Book 92).

[2] An appeal by Child from the judgment of a lower court; the jury again found for Freeman, whose counsel were JA and Wyer (same; also JA's minutes on Freeman *v.* Child, Adams Papers, Microfilms, Reel No. 185).

FRYDAY. JULY 5. 1771.

Cadwallader Ford came to me this Morning, and congratulated me on the Verdict for Freeman.—Sir, says he, I shall think myself forever obliged to you, for the Patriotick manner in which you conducted that Cause. You have obtained great Honour in this County, by that Speech. I never heard a better &c.—All this is from old Cadwallader. Langdon told me, that a Man came running down, when I had done speaking, and said "That Mr. Adams has been making the finest Speech I ever heard in my Life. He's equall to the greatest orator that ever spoke in Greece or Rome."—What an Advantage it is to have the Passions, Prejudices, and Interests of the whole Audience, in a Mans Favour. These will convert plain, common Sense, into profound Wisdom, nay wretched Doggerell into sublime Heroics. This Cause was really, and in truth and without Partiality, or Affectation of Modesty, very indifferently argued by me. But I have often been surprized with Claps and Plauditts, and Hosannas, when I have spoke but indifferently, and as often met with Inattention and Neglect when I have thought I spoke very well.—How vain, and empty is Breath!

SATURDAY JULY 6. 1771.[1]

[1] Last entry in "Paper book No. 18," though followed by a large number of blank leaves. For reasons known only to himself JA now returned to "Paper book No. 16," in which he had written nothing since 16 Feb. 1771, and continued to keep his Diary therein until the end of Nov. 1772.

1771. [*ca.* 20] JULY.[1]

Tuesday went to Boston with my Wife, and the next day to Commencement at Cambridge, was only at 3 Chambers—Palmers, Frenches and Rogers's.

[1] Approximately dated from the reference to commencement at Harvard, which took place this year on Wednesday, 17 July.

1771. JULY 22D. MONDAY.

After rambling about my Farm and giving some Directions to my Workmen I went to Boston. There soon came into my Office, Ruddock and Story. It seems that Andrew Belchers Widow has sued Story as Deputy Register of the Admiralty under her Husband in his Lifetime, and Ruddock as his Bondsman, upon the Bond given for the faithfull Discharge of his Office. Three or £400 st. of the Kings third of a Seizure is not accounted for and Ruddock is in Trouble. This Ruddock is as unique a Character as any of his Age—a finished Example of self Conceit, and Vanity.—"I am plunged! I never was concerned in any Affair before, that I could not have any Thoughts of my own upon it. I know there are several Laws—by one Law the Sherriffs Bonds are not to be put in Suit, after 2 Years, and the Treasurers are limited to 3 Years, but whether these Precedents will govern this Case I cant tell. I consulted Mr. Pratt, once about an Affair: and he advised me to do something. I told him I was of a different opinion. Every Line in his face altered, when I said this.—You are certainly wrong said he. —Well, says I, you'l be my Lawyer, when We come to Court.—Yes said he.—But next Morning he told me 'Brother Ruddock I have been ruminating your Affair on my Pillow, and I find You was right, and I was wrong.' "[1]—Thus Mr. Justice Ruddock is mighty in Counsell.

"I told Andrew Belcher, if he would not do so and so, he should never be chosen Counsellor again. He would not do it, and the next Year he was left out. I told him further, that I would not except of any Post in the World to stop my Mouth about Liberty, but I would write home and get away his Post of Register of the Admiralty."—Thus Squire Ruddock thinks himself powerfull at Court. The Instances of this Mans Vanity are innumerable—his Soul is as much Swollen as his Carcass.

I dined at my Lodgings, came early to my Office, went home and drank Tea at 6 O Clock and returned to my Office, and here I am.— What a Multitude passes my Window every day! Mr. Otis's Servant brought his Horse to the Door at Seven, and he took a Ride. Treasurer Gray stalked along from New Boston,[2] where his Daughter Otis lives, down to the B[ritish] Coffeehouse where the Clubb meets, as I suppose about half after Seven.

Spent an Hour or two in the Evening at Mr. Cranch's. Mr. Jo. Greenleaf came in, and Parson Hilyard [Hilliard] of Barnstable—and we were very chatty.

Sister Cranch says, she has had an Opportunity of making many Observations, this Year at Commencement. And she has quite altered her Mind about dancing and dancing Schools, and Mr. Cranch seems convinced too, and says it seems, that all such as learn to dance are so taken up with it, that they cant be students. So that if they should live to bring up Billy to Colledge, they would not send him to dancing School—nor the Misses Betsy and Lucy neither.[3] —What a sudden, and entire Conversion is this! That Mrs. C. should change so quick is not so wonderfull, But that his mathematical, metaphysical, mechanical, systematical Head should be turned round so soon, by her Report of what she saw at Cambridge is a little remarkable. However the Exchange is for the better. It is from Vanity to Wisdom—from Foppery to Sobriety and solidity. I never knew a good Dancer good for any Thing else. I have known several Men of Sense and Learning, who could dance, Otis, Sewal, Paine, but none of them shone that Way, and neither of em had the more Sense or Learning, or Virtue for it.

I would not however conclude, peremptorily, against sending Sons or Daughters to dancing, or Fencing, or Musick, but had much rather they should be ignorant of em all than fond of any one of em.

[1] Here and below, Ruddock's monologue has been slightly repunctuated for clarity.

[2] The Beacon Hill area, later called the West End (Shurtleff, *Description of Boston*, p. 125).

[3] The Cranches' three children were (1) Elizabeth (1763–1811), who in 1789 married Rev. Jacob Norton of Weymouth (Weymouth Hist. Soc., *History of Weymouth*, Weymouth, 1923, 4:445); (2) Lucy (1767–1846), who in 1795 married John Greenleaf (Pattee, *Old Braintree and Quincy*, p. 240–241); and (3) William (1769–1855), Harvard 1787, for many years chief justice of the federal Circuit Court of the District of Columbia (*DAB*).

JULY 23D. TUESDAY.

The Court sat. Nothing remarkable. Dined at home at Brother Smiths, with Mr. Johnson. No Conversation memorable. Brother has 2 Dogs, 4 Rabbits, Six tame Ducks, a dozen Chickens, one Pidgeon, and some yellow Birds and other singing Birds, all in his little Yard.

It is a pitty that a Day should be spent, in the Company of Courts &c., and nothing be heard or seen, worth remembering. But this is the Case—of all that I have heard from Judges, Lawyers, Jurors, Clients, Clerks, I cant recollect a Word, a Sentence, worth committing to writing.

Took a Pipe in the Beginning of the Evening with Mr. Cranch and then supped with Dr. Warren.

The Indian Preacher cryed good God!—that ever Adam and Eve should eat that Apple when they knew in their own Souls it would make good Cyder.

JULY 24. WEDNESDAY.

Dined at home, i.e. at my Brother Smiths with one Payson, a Man who now lives at Milton where Coll. Gooch lived, and who married a Sister of David Wyers Wife. He had an Horse to sell, part English Bred, of Brig. Ruggles's raising—a young Horse, very firm and strong —good in a Chaise &c. We tryed him in a Saddle and in a Chaise too. Brother bought him. Spent the Evening at S. Quincys, with Deacon Storer and J. F. and H. Green about their Cases, in Consultation.

JULY 25. AND 26. THURSDAY AND FRYDAY.

Both these Days spent in the Tryal of Mr. Otis's Case vs. Mr. Robinson.[1]

[1] On 4 Sept. 1769 James Otis had published in the *Boston Gazette* a card denouncing the Commissioners of Customs in Boston for their abuse of "all true *North-Americans*, in a manner that is not to be endured." He was referring to statements by the Commissioners in their memorials and other papers that had recently made their way back to Boston and were soon to be published in *Letters to the Ministry from Governor Bernard ...*, Boston, 1769. To this he added another communication saying among other things that if Commissioner John Robinson "misrepresents me, I have a natural right ... to break his head." See entries of 2 and 3 Sept. 1769, above. It was Otis' head that got broken, in a fracas with Robinson and his friends at the British Coffee House in the evening of 5 Sept.; see *Boston Gazette*, 11 Sept. 1769.

Otis promptly engaged three lawyers— JA, S. S. Blowers, and Samuel Fitch— and sued for £3,000 damages. His case came up in the January sitting of the Suffolk Inferior Court but was continued from term to term until July 1771, when (as JA reports in the next entry) the jury awarded him £2,000. Both parties appealed to the Superior Court, Robinson through his father-in-law and attorney, James Boutineau, he himself having long since left Boston for London. The appeals were also continued. But at length in the August term of 1772, Otis in a long statement accepted Robinson's apology in open court in lieu of damages, and required only that Robinson's attorney pay £112 11s. 8d. for "the common costs of court," Otis' medical expenses, and his lawyers' fees in the amount of £30 each. (This statement is printed in full in Tudor, *James Otis*, p. 504–506, from Suffolk County Court House, Early Court Files, &c., No. 102135, where other relevant papers will be found.)

In JA's docket of Superior Court actions for this term (Adams Papers, Microfilms, Reel No. 184) appears the following:

"*Otis* vs. Robinson [and] Robinson vs. *Otis*

recd. a genteel Fee in these Cases from Mr. Otis in full."

JULY 27. SATURDAY.

The Jury this Morning delivered their Verdict, for £2000 Sterling Damages, and Costs.—I have spent this Morning in reading the Centinells. There is a profuse Collection of Knowledge in them, in Law, History, Government, that indicates to me the only Author, I think. A great Variety of Knowledge.[1]

The Subject of the Governors Independency, is a serious, a dangerous, and momentous Thing. It deserves the utmost Attention.

[1] A series of 40 more or less regular weekly essays on current constitutional and political questions appeared in Thomas' *Massachusetts Spy*, May 1771– March 1772, over the signature of "A Centinel." Though JA thought he knew who wrote them, no further evidence has yet been found on this point. They parallel JA's own thinking, show substantial learning in law and history, and Gov. Hutchinson evidently suspected that JA was the author (see 2 Feb. 1772, below); but for numerous reasons this is an unacceptable hypothesis.

1771. AUG. 8 [*i.e.* 9?]. FRYDAY.[1]

Have loitered at home the most of the past Week, gazing at my Workmen. I set 'em upon one Exploit, that pleases me much. I proposed ploughing up the Ground in the Street along my Stone Wall opposite to Mr. Jos. Fields, and carting the Mould into my Cow Yard. A few Scruples, and Difficulties were started but these were got over —and Plough, Cart, Boards, Shovells, Hoes, &c. were collected, and We found it easyly ploughed by one Yoke of Oxen, very easy to shovel into the Cart, and very easily spread in the Yard. It was broke entirely to Pieces, and crumbled like dry Snow or indian meal in the Cow Yard. It is a Mixture of Sand, of Clay, and of the Dung of Horses, neat Cattle, Sheep, Hogs, Geese &c. washed down the whole length of Pens hill by the Rains. It has been a Century a Washing down, and is probably deep. We carted in 8 Loads in a Part of an Afternoon with 3 Hands besides ploughing it up, and 8 Loads more the next forenoon, with 2 Hands. I must plough up a long ditch the whole length of my Wall from N. Belchers to my House, and cart in the Contents. I must plough up the whole Balk from my Gate to Mr. Fields Corner, and cart in the Sward. I must enlarge my Yard and plough up what I take in, and lay on that Sward; I must dig a Ditch in my fresh Meadow from N. Belchers Wall down to my Pond, and cart the Contents into my Yard. I must open and enlarge four Ditches from the Street down to Deacon Belchers Meadow, and cart in the Contents. I must also bring in 20 Loads of Sea Weed, i.e. Eel Grass, and 20 Loads of Marsh Mud, and what dead ashes I can get from the Potash Works and what Dung I can get from Boston, and What Rock Weed from Nat. Belcher or else where. All this together with what will be made in the Barn and Yard, by my Horses, Oxen, Cows, Hogs, &c. and by the Weeds, that will be carried in from the Gardens, and the Wash and Trash from the House, in the Course of a Year would make a great Quantity of Choice manure.

J.Q.[2] says Mr. O[tis] was quite wild at the Bar Meeting—cursed the Servants for not putting 4 Candles on the Table, swore he could yet afford to have 4 upon his own—&c.—&c.

[1] The 8th was a Thursday; with little doubt JA was writing on Friday the 9th. Except for the final short paragraph, this whole entry was omitted by CFA from his text of the Diary.

[2] Doubtless Josiah Quincy Jr. There is no record of this meeting in the Suffolk Bar Book (MHi). Apparently when JA was absent no minutes were kept.

AUGUST 13. OR 14TH. 1771.[1]

Spent the Evening at Cordis's, the British Coffee house.—In the front Room, towards the long Wharfe, where the Merchants Clubb has met this twenty Years. It seems there is a Schism in that Church— a Rent in that Garment—a Mutiny in that Regiment, and a large Detachment has decamped, and marched over the Way, to Ingersols.[2]

This Evening The Commissary and Speaker, and Speaker and Commissary, Mr. Cushing was present. The Clerk of the House Mr. Adams, Mr. Otis, Mr. John Pitts, Dr. Warren, Mr. Molineux, Mr. Josa. Quincy, and myself were present.

[1] Actually the 13th; see note on next entry.
[2] Cordis' British Coffee House and Ingersol's Bunch of Grapes tavern are located and described in Samuel A. Drake, *Old Boston Taverns and Tavern Clubs*, new edn., Boston, 1917, p. 102, 103–104.

AUG. 14. OR 15. WEDNESDAY.[1]

Slept last Night, at Mr. Cranches, arose about Sunrise, and repaired to my Office. A fine, sweet, fresh Morning.

[1] The 14th was a Wednesday.

AUG. 20. 1771. TUESDAY.

At the Office.

AUGUST 22D. AND 23. THURSDAY AND FRYDAY.

At the Office. Mr. Otis's Gestures and Motions are very whimsical, his Imagination is disturbed—his Passions all roiled. His Servant, he orders to bring up his Horse, and to hold him by the Head at the Stone of his Door, an Hour before He is ready to mount. Then he runs into one Door and out at another, and Window &c. &c. &c.

1771. NOVR. 5TH. TUESDAY.

At Salem. Fine Weather. Deacon Thurston of Rowley came in last Night, a venerable old Man, with his snowy, hoary Locks. Kent and the Deacon soon clashed upon Religion.—Dont you think Sir, says the Deacon, We are here Probationers for Eternity?—No by no means says Kent. We are here Probationers for the next State and in the next We shall be Probationers for the next that is to follow, and so on thro as many States as there are Stars or Sands, to all Eternity. You have gone thro several States already before this, one in the Womb, and one in your fathers Loyns.—Ay, says the Deacon, Where do you get this—dont you believe the Scriptures.

I put in my Oar—He made it Deacon out of the whole Cioth. It never existed out of his Imagination.

Kent. I get it from Analogy.

It is the delight of this Kents Heart to teaze a Minister or Deacon with his wild Conceits, about Religion.

1771. NOVR. 9. SATURDAY.

At Salem, all this Week at Court. Dined one day at C[hief] Justice Lyndes. All the rest of the Week till this day with the Court.

Dined this Day, spent the Afternoon, and drank Tea at Judge Ropes's, with Judges Lynde, Oliver and Hutchinson, Sewal, Putnam, and Winthrop.

Mrs. Ropes is a fine Woman—very pretty, and genteel.

Our Judge Oliver is the best bred Gentleman of all the Judges, by far. There is something in every one of the others indecent and disagreable, at Times in Company—affected Witticisms, unpolished fleers, coarse Jests, and sometimes rough, rude Attacks, but these you dont see escape Judge Oliver.

Drank Tea at Judge Ropes's. Spent the Evening at Colonel Pickmans. He is very sprightly, sensible and entertaining. Talks a great deal. Tells old Stories in abundance—about the Wit[ch]craft—Paper Money—Governor Belchers Administration, &c.

SUNDAY NOVR. 10. 1771.

Heard Mr. Cutler of Ipswich Hamlet.[1] Dined at Dr. Putnams with Coll. Putnam and Lady and 2 young Gentlemen Nephews of the Dr. and Coll.—and a Mrs. Scollay. Coll. Putnam told a Story of an Indian upon Connecticutt River who called at a Tavern in the fall of the Year for a Dram. The Landlord asked him two Coppers for it. The next Spring, happening at the same House, he called for another and had 3 Coppers to pay for it.—How is this, Landlord, says he, last fall you asked but two Coppers for a Glass of Rum, now you ask three.—Oh! says the Landlord, it costs me a good deal to keep Rum over Winter. It is as expensive to keep an Hogshead of Rum over Winter as a Horse.—Ay says the Indian, I cant see thro that, He wont eat so much Hay—*may be He drink as much Water.*—This was *sheer Wit, pure Satyre,* and *true Humour.* Humour, Wit, and Satyr, in one very short Repartee.

Kent brought with him, Utopia, or the happy Republic, a Philosophical Romance, by Sir Thos. More, translated by Bp. Burnet. There is a sensible Preface by the Translator prefixed, and some Testimonies concerning More by great and learned Men of different Nations and Religions. Cardinal Pool [Pole], Erasmus, Jo. Cochleus, Paulus Jovius, Jo. Rivius, Charles 5. &c. The Translation, I think is better than mine, which is by another Hand.[2] The Romance is very elegant and ingenious—the fruit of a benevolent and candid Heart, a learned and strong Mind. The good Humour, Hospitality, Humanity, and Wisdom of the Utopians, is charming—their Elegance, and Taste is engaging—their freedom from Avarice, and foppery, and Vanity is admirable.

[1] This was Manasseh Cutler, Yale 1765, later famous as a botanist and a framer of the Northwest Ordinance of 1787. "Nov. 10, *Lord's Day*. I preached at Salem, at Mr. Barnard's Meeting House. The Superior Court was then sitting. The most of the judges and gentlemen of the law were at that meeting" (William P. and Julia P. Cutler, *Life, Journals and Correspondence of Rev. Manasseh Cutler, L.L.D.*, Cincinnati, 1888, 1:36).

[2] No copy of More's *Utopia* has yet been located among JA's books.

1772. FEBY. 2D. SUNDAY.

Have omitted now for 3 months almost to keep any "Note of Time or of its Loss."

Thomas Newcomb dined with me. He says that Etter, the Stocking Weaver, told him about a fortnight ago, that he saw the Governor within these 3 Months, and told him, he hoped the People would be contented and easy now they had a Governor from among themselves. The Governor said, "there were some Discontents remaining occasioned by continual Clamours in the Newspapers, and that a great Part of those Clamours, came from his (Etters) Town, (Braintree)."

This was partly, I suppose, to pump Etter, and get something out of him, and partly to put Etter upon the right Scent, as the Governor thought, that he might hunt down the seditious Writer at Braintree. This Conversation shews that the Governor is puzzled And wholly ignorant of the real Writers that molest him. The Centinel has puzzled him.

Mr. Thomas Edwards our School Master and Mr. Joseph Crosby, a Senior Sophister at Colledge, spent the Evening with me. Our Conversation was upon Austin, Tudor, Bulkley, Moreton [Morton], Thayer, Angier[1]—Colonel Thayer, the Settlement of the Militia, Algebra, Fenning, Dr. Sanderson &c. &c. &c.

Edwards is ballancing in his Mind the several Professions, in order to choose one. Is at a Loss between Divinity and Law, but his Inclination is to the latter. Asked me to take him. I only answered there were such Swarms of young ones, that there was no Encouragement.

[1] All young lawyers or young men studying for the law.

1772. FEBY. 4TH. TUESDAY.

Took a Ride in the Afternoon with my Wife and little Daughter to make a visit to my Brother.[1] But finding him and Sister just gone to visit my Mother we rode down there, and drank Tea, altogether. Chatted about the new Promotions in the Militia, and speculated about the future Officers of this Company, upon supposition that the old Officers should resign—Billings, Brother, &c. &c.

It is curious to observe the Effect these little Objects of Ambition have upon Mens Minds. The Commission of a Subaltern, in the Militia, will tempt these little Minds, as much as Crowns, and Stars and Garters will greater ones. These are Things that strike upon vulgar, rustic Imaginations, more strongly, than Learning, Eloquence, and Genius, of which common Persons have no Idea.

My Brother seems to relish the Thought of a Commission, and if Rawson and Bass resign, I hope he will have one—under Billings.

[1] JA's youngest brother, Elihu (1741–1775), who lived on property he had inherited from his father in that part of Braintree later set off as Randolph. In 1765 he had married Thankful White.

1772. FEBY. 9. SUNDAY.[1]

"If I would but go to Hell for an eternal Moment or so, I might be knighted."—Shakespeare.

Shakespeare, that great Master of every Affection of the Heart and every Sentiment of the Mind as well as of all the Powers of Expression, is sometimes fond of a certain pointed Oddity of Language, a certain Quaintness of Style, that is ⟨considered as⟩ an Imperfection, in his Character. The Motto prefixed to this Paper, may be considered as an Example to illustrate this Observation.

Abstracted from the Point and Conceit in the Style, there is Sentiment enough in these few Words to fill ⟨Volumes⟩ a Volume. It is a striking Representation of that Struggle which I believe always happens, between Virtue and Ambition, when a Man first commences a Courtier. By a Courtier I mean one who applies himself to the Passions and Prejudices, the Follies and Vices of great Men in order to obtain their Smiles, Esteem and Patronage and consequently their favours and Preferments. Human Nature, depraved as it is, has interwoven in its very Frame, a Love of Truth, Sincerity, and Integrity, which must be overcome by Art, Education, and habit, before the Man can become entirely ductile to the Will of a dishonest Master. When such a Master requires of all who seek his favour, an implicit Resignation to his Will and Humour, and these require that he be soothed, flattered and assisted in his Vices, and Follies, perhaps the blackest Crimes, that Men can commit, the first Thought of this will produce in a Mind not yet entirely debauched, a Soliloqui, something like my Motto—as if he should say—The Minister of State or the

Governor would promote my Interest, would advance me to Places of Honour and Profitt, would raise me to Titles and Dignities that will be perpetuated in my family, in a Word would make the Fortune of me and my Posterity forever, if I would but comply with his Desires and become his Instrument to promote his Measures.—But still I dread the Consequences. He requires of me, such Complyances, such horrid Crimes, such a Sacrifice of my Honour, my Conscience, my Friends, my Country, my God, as the Scriptures inform us must be punished with nothing less than Hell Fire, eternal Torment. And this is so unequal a Price to pay for the Honours and Emoluments in the Power of a Minister or Governor, that I cannot prevail upon myself to think of it. The Duration of future Punishment terrifies me. If I could but deceive myself so far as to think Eternity a Moment only, I could comply, and be promoted.

Such as these are probably the Sentiments of a Mind as yet pure, and undefiled in its Morals. And many and severe are the Pangs, and Agonies it must undergo, before it will be brought to yield entirely to Temptation. Notwithstanding this, We see every Day, that our Imaginations are so strong and our Reason so weak, the Charms of Wealth and Power are so enchanting, and the Belief of future Punishments so faint, that Men find Ways to persuade themselves, to believe any Absurdity, to submit to any Prostitution, rather than forego their Wishes and Desires. Their Reason becomes at last an eloquent Advocate on the Side of their Passions, and [they] bring themselves to believe that black is white, that Vice is Virtue, that Folly is Wisdom and Eternity a Moment.

The Brace of Adams's.[2]

In the Spring of the Year 1771, several Messages passed between the Governor and the House of Representatives, concerning the Words that are ⟨commonly⟩ always used in Acts of Parliament, and which were used in all the Laws of this Province, till the Administration of Governor Shirley, "in General Court assembled and by the Authority of the same."[3] Governor Shirley in whose Administration those Words were first omitted in Consequence of an Instruction to him, saw and read these Messages in the Newspapers, and enquired of somebody in Company with him at his Seat in Dorchester,[4] who had raised those Words from Oblivion at this Time?—The Gentleman answered, the Boston Seat.—Who are the Boston Seat? says the Governor.—Mr. Cushing, Mr. Hancock, Mr. Adams and Mr. Adams says the Gentleman.—Mr. Cushing I know, quoth Mr. Shirley, and Mr. Hancock I

54

know, but where the Devil this Brace of Adams's came from, I cant conceive.

Q[uery]. Is it not a Pity, that a Brace of so obscure a Breed, should be the only ones to defend the Household, when the generous Mastiffs, and best blooded Hounds are all hushed to silence by the Bones and Crumbs, that are thrown to them, and even Cerberus himself is bought off, with a Sop?

The Malice of the Court and its Writers seems to be principally directed against these two Gentlemen. They have been stedfast and immoveable in the Cause of their Country, from the Year 1761, and one of them Mr. Samuel Adams for full 20 Years before. They have always since they were acquainted with each other, concurred in Sentiment that the Liberties of this Country had more to fear from one Man the present Governor Hutchinson than from any other Man, nay than from all other Men in the World. This Sentiment was founded in their Knowledge of his Character, his unbounded Ambition and his unbounded Popularity. This Sentiment they have always freely, tho decently, expressed in their Conversation and Writings, Writings which the Governor well knows and which will be remembered as long as his Character and Administration. It is not therefore at all surprizing that his Indignation and that of all his Creatures should fall upon those Gentlemen. Their Maker has given them Nerves that are delicate, and of Consequence their Feelings are exquisite, and their Constitutions tender, and their Health especially of one of them, very infirm: But as a Compensation for this he has been pleased to bestow upon them Spirits that are unconquerable by all the Art and all the Power of Governor Hutchinson, and his Political Creators and Creatures on both Sides of the Atlantic. That Art and Power which has destroyed a Thatcher, a Mayhew, an Otis, may destroy the Health and the Lives of these Gentlemen, but can never subdue their Principles or their Spirit. They have not the chearing salubrious Prospect of Honours and Emoluments before them, to support them under all the Indignities and Affronts, the Insults and Injuries, the Malice and Slander, that can be thrown upon Men, they have not even the Hope of those Advantages that the suffrages of the People only can bestow, but they have a Sense of Honour and a Love of their Country, the Testimony of a good Conscience, and the Consolation of Phylosophy, if nothing more, which will certainly support them in the Cause of their Country, to their last Gasp of Breath whenever that may happen.

[1] What follows is obviously a draft of an essay intended for a newspaper, but no printing has been found. For apparently related fragments, see entries of

Diary of John Adams

Jan.? 1770 and Aug.? 1770, above.
² Another piece evidently intended for newspaper publication but not found in print.
³ This dispute over the phrasing of the laws occurred, not in the spring of 1771, but in Nov. 1770. See Mass.,

House Jour., 1770–1771, p. 128, 134–135, 145–146, 159–163; Hutchinson, Massachusetts Bay, ed. Mayo, 3:225–227.
⁴ An error for Roxbury. Shirley died there in March 1771 (DAB).

1772. FEBY. 10. MONDAY.

Went to Boston to the Court of Admiralty, and returned at Night. I went upon the first Appeal that has been yet made and prosecuted before Judge Auchmuty, and as it is a new Thing the Judge has directed an Argument, and a Search of Books concerning the Nature of Appeals by the civil Law. I found Time to look into Calvins Lexicon Title Appellatio and Provocatio, and into Maranta, who has treated largely of Appeals. Borrowed Ayliff, but there is no Table and could find nothing about the Subject. Domat I could not find.

[NOTES FOR AN ORATION AT BRAINTREE, SPRING 1772.]¹

The Origin, the Nature, the Principles and the Ends of Government, in all Ages, the ignorant as well as the enlightened, and in all Nations, the barbarous as well as civilized, have employed the Wits of ingenious Men.²

The Magi, the Mufti, the Bramins, and Brachmans, Mandarines, Rabbies, Philosophers, Divines, Schoolmen, Hermits, Legislators, Politicians, Lawyers, have made these the subjects of their Enquiries and Reasonings. There is nothing too absurd, nothing too enthusiastical or superstitious, nothing too wild or whimsical, nothing too prophane or impious, to be found among such Thinkers, upon such Subjects. Any Thing which subtelty could investigate or imagination conceive, would serve for an Hypothesis, to support a System, excepting only what alone can support the System of Truth—Nature, and Experience.

The Science of Government, like all other Sciences, is best pursued by Observation And Experiment—Remark the Phenomina of Nature, and from these deduce the Principles and Ends of Government.

Men are the Objects of this Science, as much as Air, Fire, Earth and Water, are the Objects of Philosophy, Points, Lines, Surfaces and Solids of Geometry, or the Sun, Moon and Stars of Astronomy. Human Nature therefore and human Life must be carefully observed and studied. Here we should spread before Us a Map of Man—view him in different Soils and Climates, in different Nations and Countries, under different Religions and Customs, in Barbarity and Civility, in a

State of Ignorance and enlightened with Knowledge, in Slavery and in freedom, in Infancy and Age.

He will be found, a rational, sensible and social Animal, in all. The Instinct of Nature impells him to Society, and Society causes the Necessity of Government.

Government is nothing more than the combined Force of Society, or the united Power of the Multitude, for the Peace, Order, Safety, Good and Happiness of the People, who compose the Society. There is no King or Queen Bee distinguished from all others, by Size or Figure, or beauty and Variety of Colours, in the human Hive. No Man has yet produced any Revelation from Heaven in his favour, any divine Communication to govern his fellow Men. Nature throws us all into the World equall and alike.

Nor has any Form of Government the Honour of a divine original or Appointment. The Author of Nature has left it wholly in the Choice of the People, to make what mutual Covenants, to erect what Kind of Governments, and to exalt what Persons they please to power and dignities, for their own Ease, Convenience and Happiness.

Government being according to my Definition the collected Strength of all for the general Good of all, Legislators have devised a Great Variety of forms in which this Strength may be arranged.

There are only Three simple Forms of Government.

When the whole Power of the Society is lodged in the Hands of the whole Society, the Government is called a Democracy, or the Rule of the Many.

When the Sovereignty, or Supreme Power is placed in the Hands of a few great, rich, wise Men, the Government is an Aristocracy, or the Rule of the few.

When the absolute Power of the Community is entrusted to the Discretion of a single Person, the Government is called a Monarchy, or the Rule of one, in this Case the whole Legislative and Executive Power is in the Breast of one Man.

There are however two other Kinds of Monarchies. One is when the supreme Power is not in a single Person but in the Laws, the Administration being committed solely to the Prince.

Another Kind is a limited Monarchy, where the Nobles or the Commons or both have a Check upon all the Acts of Legislation of the Prince.

There is an indefinite Variety of other Forms of Government, occasioned by different Combinations of the Powers of Society, and different Intermixtures of these Forms of Government, one with another.

The best Governments of the World have been mixed.

The Republics of Greece, Rome, Carthage, were all mixed Governments. The English, Dutch and Swiss, enjoy the Advantages of mixed Governments at this Day.

Sometimes Kings have courted the People in Opposition to the Nobles. At other Times the Nobles have united with the People in Opposition to Kings. But Kings and Nobles have much oftener combined together, to crush, to humble and to Fleece the People.

But this is an unalterable Truth, that the People can never be enslaved but by their own Tameness, Pusillanimity, Sloth or Corruption.

They may be deceived, and their Symplicity, Ignorance, and Docility render them frequently liable to deception. And of this, the aspiring, designing, ambitious few are very sensible. He is the Statesman qualifyed by Nature to scatter Ruin and Destruction in his Path who by deceiving a Nation can render Despotism desirable in their Eyes and make himself popular in Undoing.

The Preservation of Liberty depends upon the intellectual and moral Character of the People. As long as Knowledge and Virtue are diffused generally among the Body of a Nation, it is impossible they should be enslaved. This can be brought to pass only by debasing their Understandings, or by corrupting their Hearts.

What is the Tendency of the late Innovations? The Severity, the Cruelty of the late Revenue Laws, and the Terrors of the formidable Engine, contrived to execute them, the Court of Admiralty? Is not the natural and necessary Tendency of these Innovations, to introduce dark Intrigues, Insincerity, Simulation, Bribery and Perjury, among Custom house officers, Merchants, Masters, Mariners and their Servants?

What is the Tendency, what has been the Effect of introducing a standing Army into our Metropolis? Have we not seen horrid Rancour, furious Violence, infernal Cruelty, shocking Impiety and Profanation, and shameless, abandoned Debauchery, running down the Streets like a Stream?

Liberty, under every conceivable Form of Government is always in Danger. It is so even under a simple, or perfect Democracy, more so under a mixed Government, like the Republic of Rome, and still more so under a limited Monarchy.

Ambition is one of the more ungovernable Passions of the human Heart. The Love of Power, is insatiable and uncontroulable.

Even in the simple Democracies of ancient Greece, Jealous as they were of Power, even their Ostracism could not always preserve them from the grasping Desires and Designs, from the overbearing Popularity, of their great Men.

Even Rome, in her wisest and most virtuous Period, from the Expulsion of her Kings to the Overthrow of the Commonwealth, was always in Danger from the Power of some and the Turbulence, Faction and Popularity of others.

There is Danger from all Men. The only Maxim of a free Government, ought to be to trust no Man living, with Power to endanger the public Liberty.

In England, the common Rout to Power has been by making clamorous Professions of Patriotism, in early Life, to secure a great Popularity, and to ride upon that Popularity, into the highest Offices of State, and after they have arrived there, they have been generally found, as little zealous to preserve the Constitution, as their Predecessors whom they have hunted down.

The Earl of Strafford, in early Life, was a mighty Patriot and Anti-courtier.

Sir Robert Walpole. Commited to the Tower the Father of Corruption.

Harley also, a great and bold Advocate for the Constitution and Liberties of his Country.

But I need not go to Greece or to Rome, or to Britain for Examples. There are Persons now living in this Province, who for a long Course of their younger Years, professed and were believed to be the Guardian Angells of our civil and Religious Liberties, whose latter Conduct, since they have climbed up by Popularity to Power, has exhibited as great a Contrast to their former Professions and Principles, as ever was seen in a Strafford, an Harley, or a Walpole.

Be upon your Guard then, my Countrymen.

We see, by the Sketches I have given you, that all the great Kingdoms of Europe have once been free. But that they have lost their Liberties, by the Ignorance, the Weakness, the Inconstancy, and Disunion of the People. Let Us guard against these dangers, let us be firm and stable, as wise as Serpents and as harmless as Doves, but as daring and intrepid as Heroes. Let Us cherish the Means of Knowledge—our schools and Colledges—let Us cherish our Militia, and encourage military Discipline and skill.

The English Nation have been more fortunate than France, Spain, or any other—for the Barons, the Grandees, the Nobles, instead of uniting with [the] Crown, to suppress the People, united with the People, and struggled vs. the Crown, untill they obtained the great Charter, which was but a Restoration and Confirmation of the Laws and Constitution of our Saxon King Edward the Confessor.

Liberty depends upon an exact Ballance, a nice Counterpoise of all the Powers of the state.[3]

When the Popular Power becomes grasping, and eager after Augmentation, or for Amplification, beyond its proper Weight, or Line, it becomes as dangerous as any other. Sweeden is an Example.

The Independency of the Governor, his Salary granted by the Crown, out of a Revenue extorted from this People.

The Refusal of the Governor to consent to any Act for granting a Salary to the Agent, unless chosen by the 3 Branches of the General Court.

The Instruction to the Governor, not to consent to any Tax Bill unless certain Crown Officers are exempted.

The Multiplication of Offices and Officers among Us.

The Revenue, arising from Duties upon Tea, Sugar, Molasses and other Articles, &c.

It is the popular Power, the democraticall Branch of our Constitution that is invaded.

If K[ing], Lords and Commons, can make Laws to bind Us in all Cases whatsoever, The People here will have no Influence, no Check, no Power, no Controul, no Negative.

And the Government we are under, instead of being a mixture of Monarchy, Aristocracy and Democracy, will be a Mixture only of Monarchy and Aristocracy. For the Lords and Commons may be considered equally with Regard to Us as Nobles, as the few, as Aristocratical Grandees, independent of Us the People, uninfluenced by Us, having no fear of Us, nor Love for Us.

Wise and free Nations have made it their Rule, never to vote their Donations of Money to their Kings to enable them to carry on the Affairs of Government, untill they had Opportunities to examine the

State of the Nation, and to remonstrate against Grievances and demand and obtain the Redress of them. This was the Maxim in France, Spain, Sweeden, Denmark, Poland, while those Nations were free. What Opportunities then shall we in this Province have to demand and obtain the Redress of Grievances, if our Governors and Judges and other Officers and Magistrates are to be supported by the Ministry, without the Gifts of the People.—Consider the Case of Barbadoes and Virginia. Their Governors have been made independent by the imprudent shortsighted Acts of their own Assemblies. What is the Consequence.

[1] At the annual town meeting in Braintree, 2 March 1772, it was "Voted, an oration relative to the civil & religious rights & Priviledges of the People be Delivd. on the Day the annual meeting for the choice of a Representative shall be appointed in May next." Also, "Voted, The Selectmen be desired to wait on John Adams Esqr. with the above vote and request his assistance therein, and in case of his refusal to engage some other Gentleman of the Town to assist in that affair" (*Braintree Town Records*, p. 435).
The annual election was held 18 May, and Ebenezer Thayer Jr. was reelected (same, p. 435-436), but no further mention of the oration has been found. It is in the highest degree likely, however, that the present notes are JA's first thoughts for the patriotic address the town had invited him to deliver. CFA evidently regarded this material as too fragmentary to preserve in print, but it embodies some very characteristic ideas and expressions. From the blank intervals in the MS, the discontinuity of the thought, and variations in ink, it is clear that the notes were written at different times over an extended period.
[2] This opening passage was much reworked in the MS, as were some passages below, but the alterations seem scarcely worth recording.
[3] This and the following paragraph were doubtless meant for insertion at some point earlier in JA's development of his theme.

FALMOUTH, CASCO BAY. JUNE 30TH. 1772. TUESDAY.

My Office at Boston will miss me, this day. It is the last day of Arresting for July Court. What equivalent I shall meet with here is uncertain.

It has been my Fate, to be acquainted, in the Way of my Business, with a Number of very rich Men—Gardiner, Bowdoin, Pitts, Hancock, Rowe, Lee, Sargeant, Hooper, Doane. Hooper, Gardiner, Rowe, Lee, and Doane, have all acquired their Wealth by their own Industry. Bowdoin and Hancock received theirs by Succession, Descent or Devise. Pitts by Marriage.[1] But there is not one of all these, who derives more Pleasure from his Property than I do from mine. My little Farm, and Stock, and Cash, affords me as much Satisfaction, as all their immense Tracts, extensive Navigation, sumptuous Buildings, their vast Sums at Interest, and Stocks in Trade yield to them. The Pleasures of Property, arise from Acquis[it]ion more than Possession, from what is to come rather than from what is. These Men feel their Fortunes. They feel the Strength and Importance, which their Riches give them in the World. Their Courage and Spirits are buoyed up, their Imaginations are inflated by them. The rich are seldom remarkable for Modesty, Ingenuity, or Humanity. Their Wealth has rather a Tendency to make them penurious and selfish.

I arrived in this Town on Sunday Morning, went to Meeting all day, heard Mr. Smith and Mr. Deane. Drank Tea with Brother Bradbury, and spent the Evening with him at Mr. Deanes. Sat in the Pew with Mr. Smith, Son of the Minister in the Morning, and with Wm. Tyng Esq. Sherriff and Rep[resentative] in the Afternoon.

Lodge at Mrs. Stovers, a neat, clean, clever Woman, the Wife of a Sea Captain at Sea.

Have spent my idle Time, in reading my Clasmate Heminways Vindication of the Power, Obligation and Encouragement of the unregenerate to attend the Means of Grace—and The clandestine Marriage by Colman and Garrick.

[1] Councillor James Pitts, a Boston land magnate and merchant, had married Elizabeth, a sister of James Bowdoin. Mr. Shipton points out that Pitts by no means acquired all his wealth through his marriage (Sibley-Shipton, *Harvard Graduates*, 9:76).

WEDNESDAY JULY 1. 1772.

> He, who contends for Freedom,
> can ne'er be justly deem'd his Sovereign's Foe:
> No, 'tis the wretch that tempts him to subvert it,
> The soothing Slave, the Traitor in the Bosom,
> Who best deserves that name; he is a worm
> That eats out all the Happiness of Kingdoms.[1]

> When Life, or Death,
> becomes the Question, all Distinctions vanish;
> Then the first Monarch and the lowest Slave
> on the same Level Stand, in this the Sons
> of equal Nature all.

[1] Note by CFA: "These lines are taken from a play, now little read: [James] Thomson's Edward and Eleanora, act i. sc. 2, and act ii. sc. 2" (JA, *Works*, 2:297).

1772. SEPTR. 22.[1]

At Boston. Paid Doctr. Gardiner and took up my last Note to him. I have now got compleatly thro, my Purchase of Deacon Palmer, Coll.

Quincy and all my Salt Marsh, being better than 20 Acres, and have paid £250 O.T. towards my House in Boston, and have better than £300 left in my Pockett. At Thirty Seven Years of Age, almost, this is all that my most intense Application to Study and Business has been able to accomplish, an Application, that has more than once been very near costing me my Life, and that has so greatly impaired my Health.

I am now writing in my own House in Queen Street, to which I am pretty well determined to bring my Family, this Fall.[2] If I do, I shall come with a fixed Resolution, to meddle not with public Affairs of Town or Province. I am determined, my own Life, and the Welfare of my whole Family, which is much dearer to me, are too great Sacrifices for me to make. I have served my Country, and her professed Friends, at an immense Expense, to me, of Time, Peace, Health, Money, and Preferment, both of which last have courted my Acceptance, and been inexorably refused, least I should be laid under a Temptation to forsake the Sentiments of the Friends of this Country. These last are such Politicians, as to bestow all their Favours upon their professed and declared Enemies. I will devote myself wholly to my private Business, my Office and my farm, and I hope to lay a Foundation for better Fortune to my Children, and an happier Life than has fallen to my Share.

This [is] the last Training Day for the Year—have been out to view the Regiment, the Cadets, the Grenadiers, the Train &c.—a great Show indeed.

Epitaph.[3]
Algernon Sidney fills this Tomb,
An Atheist for disdaining Rome
A Rebel bold for striving still
To keep the Laws above the Will
Of Heaven he sure must needs despair
If holy Pope be turnkey there
And Hell him ne'er will entertain
For there is all Tyrannick Reign
Where goes he then? Where he ought to go.
Where Pope, nor Devil have to do.

[1] There are no Diary entries between 1 July and 22 Sept. 1772. Part of the explanation certainly lies in the press of JA's legal business. His Office Book for 1770–1774 (MS in MQA) shows that he handled 66 cases in the July term of the Suffolk Inferior Court, and his docket of actions in the August term of the Suffolk Superior Court, which ran well over into September, lists no fewer than 78 continued and new cases in which he was concerned (Adams Papers, Microfilms, Reel No. 183).

[2] On 21 Aug. JA bought of Shrimpton

Hunt for £533 6s. 8d. a brick house and lot in South Queen Street "near the Scæne of my Business, opposite the Court House" (Suffolk Deeds, Liber 122, fol. 7). Late in November his family moved in, and it remained their residence until the summer of 1774. See entries of 21 and 28 [i.e. 27] Nov., below.

Queen Street was that part of present Court Street which curved around from present Washington Street (formerly Cornhill) to Hanover Street; its name was officially changed to Court Street in 1788 (*Boston Streets*, &c., 1910, p. 137, 385). JQA used the front room of this house for his own law office when he

began practice, 1790–1791 (JQA to JA, 9 Aug. 1790, Adams Papers).

According to a note prepared by HA2 for Samuel F. Bemis (Adams Papers Editorial Files), this property remained in the family until about 1900. After the Civil War the Adams Building, No. 23 Court Street, was erected on the site, and here JQA2 and CFA2 had their Boston offices for many years. The building was torn down when the land passed to the Old Colony Trust Company.

[3] Copied into the Diary at some point between 22 Sept. and 5 Oct. 1772. The rudimentary punctuation of the MS has been retained.

1772. OCTR. 5TH. MONDAY.

Rode to Plymouth with my Sister Miss Betsy Smith.[1] Most agreably entertained at the House of Coll. Warren. The Colonel, his Lady and Family are all agreable. They have 5 Sons, James, now at Colledge, Winslow, Charles, Henry and George—5 fine Boys.

[1] Elizabeth Smith, youngest sister of AA; she married, first (1777) Rev. John Shaw of Haverhill, and second (1795) Rev. Stephen Peabody of Atkinson, N.H.

1772. OCTR.

At Taunton. This Week has been a remarkable one.[1]

[1] From Tuesday through Friday, 13–16 Oct., JA attended the Superior Court at Taunton. He tried nine cases covering such varied subjects as prescriptive rights, the admissibility of evidence of a lost deed, guardianship, marine insurance, and breach of covenant of quiet enjoyment of real estate. Of these cases, he lost six, including two for verdicts of £91 and £102. (Superior Court of Judicature, Minute Book 84; Suffolk County Court House, Early Court Files, &c., vol. 979.)

OCTR. 19. 1772. BOSTON.

The Day of the Month reminds me of my Birth day, which will be on the 30th. I was born Octr. 19. 1735. Thirty Seven Years, more than half the Life of Man, are run out.—What an Atom, an Animalcule I am!—The Remainder of my Days I shall rather decline, in Sense, Spirit, and Activity. My Season for acquiring Knowledge is past. And Yet I have my own and my Childrens Fortunes to make. My boyish Habits, and Airs are not yet worn off.

1772. OCTR. 27. TUESDAY.

At the Printing Office this Morning. Mr. Otis came in, with his

Eyes, fishy and fiery, looking and acting as wildly as ever he did.—"You Mr. Edes, You John Gill and you Paul Revere, can you stand there Three Minutes."—Yes.—"Well do. Brother Adams go along with me."— Up Chamber we went. He locks the Door and takes out the Kee. Sit down Tete a Tete.—"You are going to Cambridge to day"—Yes.—"So am I, if I please. I want to know, if I was to come into Court, and ask the Court if they were at Leisure to hear a Motion—and they should say Yes—And I should say 'May it please your Honours—

" 'I have heard a Report and read an Account that your Honours are to be paid your Salaries for the future by the Crown, out of a Revenue raised from Us, without our Consent. As an Individual of the Community, as a Citizen of the Town, as an Attorney and Barrister of this Court, I beg your Honours would inform me, whether that Report is true, and if it is, whether your Honours determine to accept of such an Appointment?'

"Or Suppose the substance of this should be reduced to a written Petition, would this be a Contempt? Is mere Impertinence a Contempt?" [1]

In the Course of this curious Conversation it oozed out that Cushing, Adams, and He, had been in Consultation but Yesterday, in the same Chamber upon that Subject.

In this Chamber, Otis was very chatty. He told me a story of Coll. Erving, whose Excellency lies, he says, not in military Skill, but in humbugging. Erving met Parson Morehead [Moorehead] near his Meeting House. You have a fine Steeple, and Bell, says he, to your Meeting House now.—Yes, by the Liberality of Mr. Hancock and the Subscriptions of some other Gentlemen We have a very hansome and convenient House of it at last.—But what has happened to the Vane, Mr. Morehead, it dont traverse, it has pointed the same Way these 3 Weeks.—Ay I did not know it, i'l see about it.—Away goes Morehead, storming among his Parish, and the Tradesmen, who had built the Steeple, for fastening the Vane so that it could not move. The Tradesmen were alarmed, and went to examine it, but soon found that the fault was not in the Vane but the Weather, the Wind having sat very constantly at East, for 3 Weeks before.

He also said there was a Report about Town that Morehead had given Thanks publicly, that by the Generosity of Mr. Hancock, and some other Gentlemen, they were enabled to worship God as *genteely* now as any other Congregation in Town.

After We came down Stairs, something was said about military Matters.—Says Otis to me, Youl never learn military Exercises.—Ay why not?—That You have an Head for it needs no Commentary, but not an Heart.—Ay how do you know—you never searched my Heart.— "Yes I have—tired with one Years Service, dancing from Boston to Braintree and from Braintree to Boston, moaping about the Streets of this Town as hipped as Father Flynt at 90, and seemingly regardless of every Thing, but to get Money enough to carry you smoothly through this World."

This is the Rant of Mr. Otis concerning me, and I suppose of 2 thirds of the Town.—But be it known to Mr. Otis, I have been in the public Cause as long as he, 'tho I was never in the General Court but one Year. I have sacrificed as much to it as he. I have never got [my] [2] Father chosen Speaker and Councillor by it, my Brother in Law chosen into the House and chosen Speaker by it, nor a Brother in Laws Brother in Law into the House and Council by it. Nor did I ever turn about in the House, betray my Friends and rant on the Side of Prerogative, for an whole Year, to get a father into a Probate Office, and a first Justice of a Court of Common Pleas, and a Brother into a Clerks Office.

There is a Complication of Malice, Envy and Jealousy in this Man, in the present disordered State of his Mind that is quite shocking.

I thank God my mind is prepared, for whatever can be said of me. The Storm shall blow over me in Silence.

Rode to Cambridge and made a Mornings Visit to Judge Trowbridge in his solitary, gloomy State. He is very dull, talks about retiring from Court. Says he cant fix his Attention as he could—is in doubt whether he ought to sit in a Capital Case, least he should omit something that is material—&c. &c.

Was inquisitive however, about Politicks and what the Town of Boston was likely to do about the Judges Salaries. Said he heard they were about to choose a Committee to wait upon the Court, to enquire of them &c. &c. Comparing this with Otis's distracted Proposal to me, about a Motion or Petition, I concluded that something of this Kind had been talked of in Town, 'tho I never heard a Hint of it from any but these two.[3]

Trowbridge thought there never was a Time when every Thing was so out of Joint. Our general Court gave Cushing for a fortnights Work as much as the Judges for a Years. The Ministry gave £600 a Year to the Admiralty Judges, for doing no more Business than the Superior Court did in one Term, 'tho the latter had a Controul over the former. For his Part he could not look upon it in any other Light than as an Affront. This is nearly the same that he said to Coll. Warren.

Attended Court, all Day, dined with the Judges &c. at Bradishes. Brattle was there and was chatty. Fitch came in blustering when Dinner was half over.

[1] Minimum punctuation for clarity has been supplied in the dialogue here and below.

[2] MS: "Mr."

[3] For JA's part in the controversy over the judges' salaries, see entry of 4 March 1773, below.

1772. NOVR. 21.

Next Tuesday I shall remove my Family to Boston, after residing in Braintree about 19 Months. I have recovered a Degree of Health by this Excursion into the Country, tho I am an infirm Man yet. I hope I have profited by Retirement and Reflection!—and learned in what manner to live in Boston! How long I shall be able to stay in the City, I know not; if my Health should again decline, I must return to Braintree and renounce the Town entirely. I hope however to be able to stay there many Years! To this End I must remember Temperance, Exercise and Peace of Mind. Above all Things I must avoid Politicks, Political Clubbs, Town Meetings, General Court, &c. &c. &c.

I must ride frequently to Braintree to inspect my Farm, and when in Boston must spend my Evenings in my Office, or with my Family, and with as little Company as possible.

NOVR. 21ST. 1772.

Eleven Years have passed since I minuted any Thing in this Book.[1] What an admirable Advantage it would have been if I had recorded every Step in the Progress of my Studies for these Eleven Years.

If I had kept an exact Journal of all my Journeys on the Circuits, of all the Removes of my Family, my Buildings, Purchases, the gradual Increase of my Library, and Family, as well as of the Improvement of my Mind by my Studies, the whole would have composed entertaining Memoirs, to me in my old Age, and to my Family after my Decease.

One Thing in this Book shall be a Lesson to me. The Gentleman to whom the Letter is directed, an extract of which is in the Beginning of this Book, Eleven Years ago I thought the best Friend, I had in the World.[2] I loved him accordingly and corresponded with him, many Years, without Reserve: But the Scæne is changed. At this Moment I look upon him [as] the most bitter, malicious, determined and implacable Enemy I have. God forgive him the Part he has acted, both in public and private Life! It is not impossible that he may make the same Prayer for me.

I am now about removing, a Second Time from Braintree to Boston. In April 1768 I removed to Boston, to the white House in Brattle Square, in the Spring 1769, I removed to Cole Lane, to Mr. Fayerweathers House. In 1770 I removed to another House in Brattle Square, where Dr. Cooper now lives, in 1771, I removed from Boston to Braintree, in the Month of April, where I have lived to this Time. I hope I shall not have Occasion to remove so often for 4 Years and an half to come.

The numerous Journeys and Removes, that I have taken in this Period, have put my Mind into an unsettled State. They have occasioned too much Confusion and Dissipation. I hope to pass a more steady, regular Life for the future in all Respects.

When I chance to meet with any of my own Compositions, of Ten Years old, I am much inclined to think I could write with more Accuracy and Elegance then than I can now, and that I had more Sense and Knowledge then, than I have now. My Memory, and Fancy were certainly better then, and my Judgment, I conjecture quite as good.

[1] This entry derives from D/JA/4, JA's desultory record of reading and studies, kept only for a brief period and long since abandoned; in the MS it follows immediately an entry dated 20 Nov.

1761, q.v. above.
[2] Jonathan Sewall. The letter in question, at the beginning of D/JA/4, is dated Oct. 1759 (vol. 1:123–124, above).

1772. NOVR. 28 [*i.e.* 27?]. FRYDAY.[1]

This Week vizt. last Tuesday my Family and Goods arrived at Boston where we have taken Possession of my House in Queen street where I hope, I shall live as long as I have any Connections with Boston.

This Day Majr. Martin came into the Office and chatted an Hour very sociably and pleasantly. He says that Politicks are the finest Study and science in the World, but they are abused. Real Patriotism or Love of ones Country is the greatest of moral Virtues, &c. He is a Man of Sense and Knowledge of the World. His Observation upon Politicks is just, they are the grandest, the Noblest, the most usefull and important Science, in the whole Circle.

A Sensible Soldier is as entertaining a Companion as any Man whatever. They acquire an Urbanity, by Travel and promiscuous Conversation, that is charming. This Major Martin has conversed familiarly in Scotland, in England, and in America, and seems to understand every Subject of general Conversation very well.

I have now got through the Hurry of my Business. My Father in Law[2] Mr. Hall and my Mother are well settled in my Farm at Braintree, the Produce of my Farm is all collected in, my own Family is removed and well settled in Boston, my Wood and Stores are laid in for the Winter, my Workmen are nearly all paid. I am disengaged from public Affairs, and now have nothing to do but to mind my Office, my Clerks and my Children.

But this Week which has been so agreable to me, in the Course of my own Affairs, has not been so happy for my Friends. My Brother in Law has failed in Trade, is confined to his House, unable to answer the Demands upon him, by some Thousands. A Miserable Prospect before him for himself, his Wife, Children, Father, Mother, and all his Friends.[3] Beware of Idleness, Luxury, and all Vanity, Folly and Vice!

The Conversation of the Town and Country has been about the strange Occurrence of last Week, a Piracy said to have been committed on a Vessell bound to Cape Cod, 3 Men killed, a Boy missing, and only one Man escaped to tell the News—a misterious, inexplicable Affair![4] About Wilkes's probable Mayoralty, and about the Salaries to the Judges. These are the 3 principal Topicks of Conversation at present.

My Workmen have this day loaded my Brothers Boat with Horse dung from Bracketts stable. This is the 3d. Freight—the first was 15. Load, the second 12 and this last 11, in all 38 Loads.

[1] Friday was the 27th.
[2] That is, stepfather.
[3] This "Brother in Law" has not been certainly identified.
[4] The Ansell Nickerson murder case, an "Affair" in which JA was to be involved as one of Nickerson's counsel and which remains to this day "misterious." The *Boston Evening Post* of 23 Nov. 1772 gives the facts as they were first reported:

"On Sunday the 15th Current, Captain Joseph Doane, jun. sailed from Chatham Harbour on the Back of Cape-Cod, and soon after, viz. about 10 o'Clock in the Forenoon saw a Schooner with a Signal of Distress, and, going on board, found one Man only in her who appeared to be in a great Fright, and gave the following Account.—That the Day before the said Schooner, Thomas Nickerson, Master, sailed from Boston, bound to Chatham—That about 2 o'Clock the next Morning they saw a Topsail Schooner, who brought them to, and sent a Boat on board, and after questioning them returned again—Soon after four Boats with armed Men came back from the Schooner, and the Man who gave the Account fearing he should be Impressed, got over the Stern and held with his Hands by the Taffarill, with his Feet on the Moulding, under the Cabin Windows. That whilst he was thus hanging over the Stern he judges by what he heard that the Master, with his own Brother, and a Brother-in-Law, named Newcomb, were murdered and thrown overboard, and a Boy named Kent, carried away alive, as they said, in order to *make Punch for them*—That he heard a Talk of burning the Vessel, but it was finally agreed to leave her to drive out to Sea with her Sails standing. That after perpetrating this inhuman Deed they plundered the Vessel of a considerable Quantity of Cash, knocked out the Head of a Barrel of Rum, and after wasting the greatest Part of it, went off with the Money and other Booty; tho' they left behind a Quarter of fresh Beef & a number of small Stores.—That when they left the Vessel he came upon Deck, he found none of the Crew, but saw the Marks of Blood, and supposes they were murdered."

Nickerson was brought to Boston, examined by the Governor and other officials, and committed to jail pending his trial by a special court of admiralty. Public opinion was soon sharply divided between whigs who, remembering the Corbet case, were willing to believe the British navy was responsible for the atrocity, and tories who, like Hutchinson, found "Every part of [Nickerson's] account ... incredible" and thought him guilty of a shocking multiple crime for the sake of "the money which the crew had received at Boston" (Hutchinson, *Massachusetts Bay*, ed. Mayo, 3:300–302).

On 16 Dec. the court sat. Nickerson's counsel, JA and Josiah Quincy Jr., requested and obtained a delay in order to gather further evidence. The trial took place in the summer, extending from 28 July to 6 Aug., and the prisoner, who stoutly maintained his innocence throughout, was found not guilty (*Boston Gazette*, 9 Aug. 1773).

Hutchinson says the verdict was owing to a technicality: Nickerson could be tried in America only for piracy (if for murder, he would have had to be sent to England, where evidence would be impossible to obtain). But four of the eight judges held that in order to prove the piracy, the murders would also have to be proved. Hutchinson did not agree, but the equal division of the judges resulted in acquittal.

JA's civil law authorities and other notes for his argument in the Nickerson case will be found among his legal papers (Adams Papers, Microfilms, Reel No. 185). In his Autobiography he wrote: "I know not to this day what Judgment to form of his Guilt or Innocence. And this doubt I presume was the Principle of Acquittal." On 30 July 1773 Nickerson signed a promissory note to JA for his legal fees and expenses in the amount of £6 13s. 4d. lawful money. The note remains in the Adams Papers. It is not receipted.

1772 DECR. 16. WEDNESDAY.[1]

Dined with the Reverend Mr. Simeon Hayward [Howard] of West Boston, in Company with Dr. Chauncey, Captn. Phillips, Dr. Warren, Mrs. Hayward, Miss Betsy Mayhew and a young Gentleman whose Name I dont know. Had a very agreable Conversation.

Mr. Hayward was silent. Dr. Chauncey very sociable—glories much in his inflexible Adherence to rules of Diet, Exercise, Study, Sleep &c. If he had not lived as regularly as the sun moves in the Heavens, he should long ago have mouldered to dust, so as not to be distinguished from common Earth. Never reads nor studies after 8 O Clock. He would not, for all the Commissions in the Gift of all the Potentates upon Earth, become the Tool of any Man alive. Told us of his Writing to England and Scotland, and of the Politicks he wrote—among the rest that in 25 Years there would be more People here than in the 3 Kingdoms &c.—the greatest Empire on Earth. Our Freeholds would preserve us for Interest would not lie. If ever he should give the Charge at an Ordination, he would say We, Bishops, &c. &c. He told us of Mr. Temples keeping a fair Journal of all the Proceedings of the Board of

Commissioners &c. and that the Ministry provided for him, to prevent his raising a Clamour.

Captn. Phillips would not have got his Appointment, if Mr. Temple had not been his Friend, &c.

Phillips says they are all still and quiet at the southward, and at New York they laugh at Us.

Brother Elihu	10 Cords and 6 feet of Wood
bought of Crane	6
brought by Bracket	5
12	1

¹ First entry in "Paper Book No. 19" (our D/JA/19), a gathering of leaves stitched into a cover of marbled paper and containing irregular entries through 18 Dec. 1773.

1772 DECR. 20. SUNDAY.

Heard Dr. Chauncey in the Morning upon these Words "As Paul reasoned of Righteousness, Temperance, and Judgment to come Fælix trembled." The Dr. dilated upon the Subject of Pauls Discourse, the great moral Duties of Justice and Temperance as they are connected with the future Judgment. Upon the Apostles manner, he reasoned &c., and upon the Effect, that such Reasoning had upon Fælix, it made him tremble.

In the Afternoon Dr. Cooper sounded harmoniously, upon the deceitfullness of Sin. The Drs. Air and Action are not gracefull—they are not natural and easy. His Motions with his Head, Body and Hands are a little stiff and affected. His Style is not simple enough for the Pulpit. It is too flowery, too figurative—his Periods too much or rather too apparently rounded and laboured.—This however Sub Rosâ, because the Dr. passes for a Master of Composition, and is an excellent Man.

1772. DECR. 23. WEDNESDAY.

Major Martin at the Office. He is very gracious with the first Man in the Province. The Governor spoke very handsomely, of all my Council.—"He did you Justice," &c. &c. The Major is to dine with me tomorrow. He wishes for Warr, wants to be a Colonell—to get 1000 st. a Year for 8 or 10 Years that he may leave Something to his Children, &c. &c.—"An Ensign in the Army is Company for any Nobleman in England. A Colonel in the Army with 1000 a Year will spend an Evening with an Ensign, who can but just live upon his Pay and make him pay his Clubb. The Company that the Officers are obliged to keep, makes them poor, as bare as a scraped Carrot"—&c. &c.[1]

The Manners of these Gentlemen are very engaging and agreable.

Took a Walk this Morning to the South End, and had some Conversation with my old Friends Crafts and Trot. I find they are both cooled—both flattened away. They complain especially Crafts that they are called Tories—&c. &c. Crafts has got Swifts Contests and Dissentions of the Nobles and Commons of Athens and Rome, and is making Extracts from it—about Clodius and Curio, popular Leaders &c. &c.

My Wife says her Father never inculcated any Maxim of Behaviour upon his Children, so often as this—never to speak ill of any Body. To say all the handsome Things she could of Persons but no Evil—and to make Things rather than Persons the Subjects of Conversation.— These Rules, he always impressed upon Us, whenever We were going abroad, if it was but to spend an Afternoon.—He was always remarkable for observing these Rules in his own Conversation.—Her Grandfather Quincy was remarkable for never praising any Body, He did not often speak evil, but he seldom spoke well.

[1] Initial quotation marks have been supplied twice in this paragraph.

1772. DECR. 24. THURSDAY.

Major Martin, Mr. Blowers and Mr. Williams dined with me—all agreable.

This Day I heard that Mr. Hancock had purchased 20 Writs ⟨of *Mr. Goldthwait*⟩, for this Court, of Mr. S. Quincy.—Oh the Mutability of the legal, commercial, social, political, as well as material World! For about 3 or 4 Years I have done all Mr. Hancocks Business, and have waded through wearisome, anxious Days and Nights, in his Defence.— But Farewell!—

1772 DECR. 29 [*i.e.* 28?].

Spent the last Sunday Evening with Dr. Cooper at his House with Justice Quincy and Mr. Wm. Cooper. We were very social and we chatted at large upon Cæsar, Cromwell &c.

Yesterday Parson Howard and his Lady, lately Mrs. Mayhew, drank Tea with Mrs. Adams.

Heard many Anecdotes from a young Gentleman in my Office of Admirall Montagu's Manners. A Coachman, a Jack Tar before the Mast, would be ashamed—nay a Porter, a Shew Black or Chimney Sweeper would be ashamed of the coarse, low, vulgar, Dialect of this

Sea Officer, tho a rear Admiral of the Blue, and tho a Second Son of a genteel if not a noble Family in England. An American Freeholder, living in a log House 20 feet Square, without a Chimney in it, is a well bred Man, a polite accomplished Person, a fine Gentleman, in Comparison of this Beast of Prey.

This is not the Language of Prejudice, for I have none against him, but of Truth. His brutal, hoggish Manners are a Disgrace to the Royal Navy, and to the Kings Service.

His Lady is very much disliked they say in general. She is very full of her Remarks at the Assembly and Concert. Can this Lady afford the Jewells and Dress she wears?—Oh that ever my son should come to dance with a Mantua Maker.[1]

As to the Admiral his continual Language is cursing and damning and God damning, "my wifes d——d A—se is so broad that she and I cant sit in a Chariot together"—this is the Nature of the Beast and the common Language of the Man. Admiral Montagu's Conversation by all I can learn of it, is exactly like Otis's when he is both mad and drunk.

The high Commission Court, the Star Chamber Court, the Court of Inquisition, for the Tryal of the Burners of the Gaspee, at Rhode Island, are the present Topick of Conversation. The Governor of that Colony, has communicated to the assembly a Letter from the Earl of Dartmouth. The Colony are in great Distress, and have applied to their Neighbours for Advice, how to evade or to sustain the Shock.[2]

[1] The last two sentences are apparently examples of Mrs. Montagu's social chat. CFA supplied quotation marks around them.

[2] The *Gaspee*, a British revenue schooner, was burned by citizens of Providence when she went aground in Narragansett Bay while pursuing a suspected smuggler, 9 June 1772. A naval officer was wounded in the fracas, and a special royal commission was appointed to investigate, with authority to transport any suspect to England for trial. This measure aroused deep indignation throughout the colonies. For the documents see *Records of the Colony of Rhode Island*, ed. John R. Bartlett, 7 (Providence, 1862):55–192; also Eugene Wulsin, "The Political Consequences of the Burning of the Gaspee," *Rhode Island History*, 3:1–11, 55–64 (Jan., April 1944).

1772. DECR. 29. TUESDAY.

This Afternoon I had a Visit from Samuel Pemberton Esqr. and Mr. Samuel Adams. Mr. P. said they were a Subcommittee deputed by the Standing Committee of the Town of Boston, to request that I would deliver an Oration in Public upon the ensuing 5th. of March. He said that they two were desirous of it, and that the whole Committee was unanimously desirous of it.

I told them, that the feeble State of my Health rendered me quite willing to devote myself forever to private Life. That, far from taking any Part in Public, I was desirous to avoid even thinking upon public Affairs—and that I was determined to pursue that Course, and therefore that I must beg to be excused.

They desired to know my Reasons. I told them that so many irresistable Syllogisms rushed into my Mind, and concluded decisively against it, that I did not know which to mention first. But I thought the Reason that had hitherto actuated the Town, was enough—vizt. the Part I took in the Tryal of the Soldiers. Tho the Subject of the Oration, was quite compatible with the Verdict of the Jury, in that Case, and indeed, even with the absolute Innocence of the Soldiers yet I found the World in general were not capable or not willing to make the Distinction. And therefore, by making an Oration upon this Occasion, I should only expose myself to the Lash of ignorant and malicious Tongues on both Sides of the Question. Besides that I was too old to make Declamations.

The Gentleman desired I would take Time to consider of it. I told them, No, that would expose me to more difficulties—I wanted no Time—it was not a thing unthought of, by me, tho this Invitation was unexpected. That I was clearly, fully, absolutely, and unalterably determined against it, and therefore that time and thinking would answer no End.

The Gentlemen then desired that I would keep this a Secret and departed.

1772. DECR. 30. WEDNESDAY.

Spent this Evening with Mr. Samuel Adams at his House. Had much Conversation, about the State of Affairs—Cushing, Hancock, Phillips, Hawley, Gerry,[1] Hutchinson, Sewall, Quincy, &c. &c. Adams was more cool, genteel and agreable than common—concealed, and restrained his Passions—&c. He affects to despize Riches, and not to dread Poverty. But no Man is more ambitious of entertaining his Friends handsomely, or of making a decent, an elegant Appearance than he. He has lately new covered and glased his House and painted it, very neatly, and has new papered, painted and furnished his Rooms. So that you visit at a very genteel House and are very politely received and entertained.

Mr. Adams corresponds with Hawley, Gerry and others. He corresponds in England and in several of the other Provinces. His Time is all employed in the public Service.

[1] Elbridge Gerry, who was to become one of JA's most intimate friends, correspondents, and colleagues, was just coming into political prominence as an active whig leader in Marblehead (*DAB*). He had recently begun a brisk correspondence with Samuel Adams; see Austin, *Gerry*, 1:8 ff.

1772 DECR. 31. THURSDAY.
To Mrs. Maccaulay.

Madam

It is so long since I received your obliging Favour, that I am now almost ashamed to acknowledge it.[1] The State [of] my Health, obliged me to retreat into the Country, where Nineteen Months Relaxation from Care, and rural Exercises, have restored me to such a State, that I have once more ventured into the Town of Boston, and the Business of my Profession.

The Prospect before me, however, is very gloomy. My Country is in deep Distress, and has very little Ground of Hope, that She will soon, if ever get out of it. The System of a mean, and a merciless Administration, is gaining Ground upon our Patriots every Day. The Flower of our Genius, the Ornaments of the Province, have fallen, melancholly Sacrifices, to the heart piercing Anxieties, which the Measures of Administration have occasioned. A Mayhew, a Thatcher, an Otis to name [no] more, have fallen, the two first by Death and the last by a Misfortune still much worse, Victims to the Enemies of their Country. The Body of the People seem to be worn out, by struggling, and Venality, Servility and Prostitution, eat and spread like a Cancer. Every young rising Genius, in this Country, is in a situation much worse than Hercules is represented to have been in, in the Fable of Prodicus.—Two Ladies are before him: The one, presenting to his View, not the Ascent of Virtue only, tho that is steep and rugged, but a Mountain quite inaccessible, a Path beset with Serpents, and Beasts of Prey, as well as Thorns and Briars, Precipices of Rocks over him, a Gulph yawning beneath, and the Sword of Damocles [over] his Head.— The other displaying to his View, Pleasures, of every Kind, Honours, such as the World calls by that Name, and showers of Gold and Silver.

If We recollect what a Mass of Corruption human Nature has been in general, since the Fall of Adam, we may easily judge what the Consequence will be.

Our Attention is now engaged by the Vengeance of Despotism that [*sentence unfinished*]

This Evening at Mr. Cranch's, I found that my constitutional or habitual Infirmities have not entirely forsaken me. Mr. Collins an English Gentleman was there, and in Conversation about the high Commissioned Court, for enquiring after the Burners of the Gaspee at Providence, I found the old Warmth, Heat, Violence, Acrimony, Bitterness, Sharpness of my Temper, and Expression, was not departed. I said there was no more Justice left in Britain than there was in Hell—That I wished for War, and that the whole Bourbon Family was upon the Back of Great Britain—avowed a thoughrough Dissaffection to that Country—wished that any Thing might happen to them, and that as the Clergy prayed of our Enemies in Time of War, that they might be brought to reason or to ruin.

I cannot but reflect upon myself with Severity for these rash, inexperienced, boyish, raw, and aukward Expressions. A Man who has no better Government of his Tongue, no more command of his Temper, is unfit for every Thing, but Childrens Play, and the Company of Boys.

A Character can never [be] supported, if it can be raised, without a good a great Share of Self Government. Such Flights of Passion, such Starts of Imagination, tho they may strike a few of the fiery and inconsiderate, yet they lower, they sink a Man, with the Wise. They expose him to danger, as well as familiarity, Contempt, and Ridicule.

[1] Dated London, 19 July 1771 (Adams Papers). It is uncertain whether the present partial draft was finished and sent. The next letter from JA that Mrs. Macaulay acknowledged was dated 19 April 1773 and has not been found (Catharine Macaulay to JA, Aug. 1773, Adams Papers).

1773 JANUARY THE FIRST, BEING FRYDAY.

I have felt very well and been in very good Spirits all Day. I never was happier, in my whole Life, than I have been since I returned to Boston. I feel easy, and composed and contented. The Year to come, will be a pleasant, a chearfull, a happy and a prosperous Year to me. At least such are the Forebodings of my Mind at Present. My Resolutions to devote myself to the Pleasures, the studies, the Business and the Duties of private Life, are a Source of Ease and Comfort to me, that I scarcely ever experienced before.—Peace, be still, my once Anxious Heart.—An Head full of Schemes and an Heart full of Anxiety, are incompatible with any Degree of Happiness.

I have said Above that I had the Prospect before me of an happy and prosperous Year, and I will not retract it, because, I feel a great Pleasure in the Expectation of it, and I think, that there is a strong Probability and Presumption of it. Yet Fire may destroy my Substance, Diseases may desolate my family, and Death may put a Period to my

Hopes, and Fears, Pleasures and Pains, Friendships and Enmities, Virtues and Vices.

This Evening my Friend Mr. Pemberton invited me and I went with him, to spend the Evening with Jere. Wheelwright. Mr. Wheelwright is a Gentleman of a liberal Education about 50 Years of Age, and constantly confined to his Chamber by Lameness. A Fortune of about two hundred a Year enables him to entertain his few Friends very handsomely, and he has them regularly at his Chamber every Tuesday and Fryday Evening. The Speaker, Dr. Warren and Mr. Swift were there— And We Six had a very pleasant Evening. Our Conversation turned upon the Distress of Rhode Island, upon the Judges Dependency, the late numerous Town Meetings, upon Brattles Publication in Drapers Paper of Yesterday,[1] and upon each others Characters. We were very free, especially upon one another. I told Cushing as Ruggles told Tyler, that I never knew a Pendulum swing so clear. Warren told me, that Pemberton said I was the proudest and cunningest Fellow, he ever knew. We all rallied Pemberton, upon the late Appointment of Tommy Hutchinson to be a Judge of the common Bench, and pretended to insist upon it that he was disappointed, and had lost all his late Trimming, and Lukewarmness and Toryism. Warren thought I was rather a cautious Man, but that he could not say I ever trimmed. When I spoke at all I always spoke my Sentiments. This was a little soothing to my proud Heart, no doubt.

Brattle has published a Narration of the Proceedings of the Town of Cambridge at their late Meeting, and he has endeavoured to deceive the World.

[1] See the following entry and note 2 there.

1773 MARCH 4TH. THURSDAY.

The two last Months have slided away. I have written a tedious Examination of Brattle's absurdities. The Governor and General Court, has been engaged for two Months upon the greatest Question ever yet agitated. I stand amazed at the Governor, for forcing on this Controversy. He will not be thanked for this. His Ruin and Destruction must spring out of it, either from the Ministry and Parliament on one Hand, or from his Countrymen, on the other. He has reduced himself to a most ridiculous State of Distress. He is closetting and soliciting Mr. Bowdoin, Mr. Dennie, Dr. Church &c. &c., and seems in the utmost Agony.[1]

The Original of my Controversy with Brattle is worthy to be comitted to Writing, in these Memorandums.—At the Town Meeting in Cambridge, called to consider of the Judges Salaries, he advanced for Law, that the Judges by this Appointment, would be compleatly independent, for that they held Estates for Life in their offices by common Law and their Nomination and Appointment. And, he said "this I averr to be Law, and I will maintain it, against any Body, I will dispute it, with Mr. Otis, Mr. Adams, Mr. John Adams I mean, and Mr. Josiah Quincy. I would dispute it with them, here in Town Meeting, nay, I will dispute it with them in the Newspapers."

He was so elated with that Applause which this inane Harrangue procured him, from the Enemies of this Country, that in the next Thurdsdays Gazette, he roundly advanced the same Doctrine in Print, and the Thursday after invited any Gentleman to dispute with him upon his Points of Law.

These vain and frothy Harrangues and Scribblings would have had no Effect upon me, if I had not seen that his Ignorant Doctrines were taking Root in the Minds of the People, many of whom were in Appearance, if not in Reality, taking it for granted, that the Judges held their Places during good Behaviour.

Upon this I determined to enter the Lists, and the General was very soon silenced.—Whether from Conviction, or from Policy, or Contempt I know not.[2]

It is thus that little Incidents produce great Events. I have never known a Period, in which the Seeds of great Events have been so plentifully sown as this Winter. A Providence is visible, in that Concurrence of Causes, which produced the Debates and Controversies of this Winter. The Court of Inquisition at Rhode Island, the Judges Salaries, the Massachusetts Bay Town Meetings, General Brattles Folly, all conspired in a remarkable, a wonderfull Manner.

My own Determination had been to decline all Invitations to public Affairs and Enquiries, but Brattles rude, indecent, and unmeaning Challenge of me in Particular, laid me under peculiar Obligations to undeceive the People, and changed my Resolution. I hope that some good will come out of it.—God knows.

[1] JA alludes to the bitter dispute between Hutchinson and the House of Representatives over the issue whether "Parliament was our Sovereign Legislature, and had a Right to make Laws for Us in all Cases whatsoever"—a dispute evoked by Hutchinson's speech of 6 Jan., which was answered in an elaborate paper by the House on 26 Jan. For further details, especially on JA's part in the answer, see his Autobiography and his letter to William Tudor, 8 March 1817 (LbC, Adams Papers; inserted by CFA in his text of the Diary, *Works*, 2:310–313); Hutchinson, *Massachusetts Bay*, ed. Mayo, 3:266–280. The documents are printed in Mass., *Speeches of the Governors*, p. 336–364.

[2] At a special town meeting in Cambridge, 14 Dec. 1772, Gen. William Brattle opposed the town's vote of instructions condemning the ministerial proposal to have the Superior Court judges paid by the crown and thus rendered independent of the Province. Brattle published his reasons in the *Boston News Letter*, 31 Dec. JA answered him in the *Boston Gazette*, 11 Jan. 1773, and followed with six more weekly pieces, citing innumerable British legal authorities from Bracton onward, to Brattle's sole rejoinder in the same paper, 25 Jan. All these articles, preceded by the Cambridge instructions, are reprinted in JA, *Works*, 3:511–574. The nub of the controversy, as JA phrased it in his Autobiography, was that since "the Judges Commissions were during pleasure" (*durante beneplacito*), the judges would become "entirely dependent on the Crown for Bread [as] well as office." The position of Brattle and other tory advocates of the measure was that under the common law the judges held office during good behavior (*quamdiu bene se gesserint*), and by the proposed mode of payment would be rendered independent of both royal and popular influence.

1773. MARCH 5TH. FRYDAY.

Heard an Oration, at Mr. Hunts Meeting House,[1] by Dr. Benja. Church, in Commemoration of the Massacre in Kings Street, 3 Years ago. That large Church was filled and crouded in every Pew, Seat, Alley, and Gallery, by an Audience of several Thousands of People of all Ages and Characters and of both Sexes.

I have Reason to remember that fatal Night. The Part I took in Defence of Captn. Preston and the Soldiers, procured me Anxiety, and Obloquy enough. It was, however, one of the most gallant, generous, manly and disinterested Actions of my whole Life, and one of the best Pieces of Service I ever rendered my Country. Judgment of Death against those Soldiers would have been as foul a Stain upon this Country as the Executions of the Quakers or Witches, anciently. As the Evidence was, the Verdict of the Jury was exactly right.

This however is no Reason why the Town should not call the Action of that Night a Massacre, nor is it any Argument in favour of the Governor or Minister, who caused them to be sent here. But it is the strongest of Proofs of the Danger of standing Armies.

[1] The Old South Church, whose minister was John Hunt.

1773. MARCH 22D. MONDAY.

This Afternoon received a Collection of Seventeen Letters, written from this Prov[ince], Rhode Island, Connecticutt and N. York, by Hut[chinson], Oli[ver], Moff[at], Paxt[on], and Rome, in the Years 1767, 8, 9.

They came from England under such Injunctions of Secrecy, as to the Person to whom they were written, by whom and to whom they are sent here, and as to the Contents of them, no Copies of the whole or any Part to be taken, that it is difficult to make any public Use of them.

These curious Projectors and Speculators in Politicks, will ruin this Country—cool, thinking, deliberate Villain[s], malicious, and vindictive, as well as ambitious and avaricious.

The Secrecy of these epistolary Genii is very remarkable—profoundly secret, dark, and deep.[1]

[1] The letters were furnished (from a source never divulged) by Benjamin Franklin, London agent of the Massachusetts House of Representatives, in a letter to Speaker Thomas Cushing, London, 2 Dec. 1772 (Franklin, *Writings*, ed. Smyth, 6:265–268; a variant version, copied in JA's hand, is in the Adams Papers, Microfilms, April 1773, and is printed in JA's *Works*, 1:647–648). JA also made a copy of the Hutchinson letter that gave greatest offense to whig feelings. It was originally written, as we now know all the purloined letters were, to Thomas Whately, dated at Boston, 20 Jan. 1769, and contained the following passage as copied and attested by JA:

"This is most certainly a Crisis. I really wish that there may not have been the least degree of Severity, beyond what is absolutely necessary to maintain, I think I may say to you, *the dependance* which a Colony ought to have upon the Parent State, but if no measures shall have been taken to secure this dependance or nothing more than some Declaratory Acts or Resolves, *it is all over with Us*. The Friends of Government will be utterly disheartned and the friends of Anarchy will be afraid of nothing be it ever so extravagant. . . .

"I never think of the measures necessary for the Peace and good Order of the Colonies without pain. There must be an Abridgment of what are called English Liberties. I relieve myself by considering that in a Remove from the State of nature to the most perfect State of Government there must be a great restraint of natural Liberty. I doubt whether it is possible to project a System of Government in which a Colony 3000 miles distant from the parent State shall enjoy all the Liberty of the parent State. I am certain I have never yet seen the Projection. I wish the Good of the Colony, when I wish to see some further Restraint of

Liberty rather than the Connection with the parent State should be broken for I am sure such a Breach must prove the Ruin of the Colony."

The letters were handed about too freely and over too long a time to be kept a secret, and on 15 June they were by order of the House turned over to the printers (Mass., *House Jour.*, 1773–1774, p. 56). They appeared in a pamphlet published by Edes and Gill under the title *Copy of Letters Sent to Great-Britain, by His Excellency Thomas Hutchinson, the Hon. Andrew Oliver, and Several Other Persons, Born and Educated Among Us*, 1773, which was several times reprinted in America and England, and they ran all summer serially in Thomas' *Massachusetts Spy*. They led to a petition by the Massachusetts House for the removal of Hutchinson and Oliver from their posts, to a duel in London, to the famous denunciation of Franklin by Alexander Wedderburn in the Privy Council, and to Franklin's loss of his office as postmaster general in America. Franklin's account of the affair, published posthumously, is in his *Writings*, ed. Smyth, 6:258–289; Hutchinson's in his *Massachusetts Bay*, ed. Mayo, 3:282–298, supplemented by "Additions to Thomas Hutchinson's *History of Massachusetts Bay*," Amer. Antiq. Soc., *Procs.*, 59 (1949):60–65. Mr. Malcolm Freiberg in an article entitled "Missing: One Hutchinson Autograph Letter" points out and discusses the significance of the variations between the texts of the critical paragraphs in Hutchinson's letter quoted above as on the one hand printed by his adversaries and as on the other hand preserved in his letterbook in the Massachusetts Archives (*Manuscripts*, 8:179–184 [Spring 1956]). But it should be noted that Hutchinson himself did not raise questions about the validity of the printed text and indeed quoted that text (*Massachusetts Bay*, ed. Mayo, the most controversial passage of all from 3:293–294).

1773. APRIL 7TH: WEDNESDAY.

At Charlestown. What shall I write?—say?—do?
Sterility, Vacuity, Barrenness of Thought, and Reflection.
What News shall we hear?

1773 APRIL 24TH. SATURDAY.

I have communicated to Mr. Norton Quincy, and to Mr. Wibird the important Secret. They are as much affected, by it, as any others. Bone of our Bone, born and educated among us! Mr. Hancock is deeply affected, is determined in Conjunction with Majr. Hawley to watch the vile Serpent, and his deputy Serpent Brattle.

The Subtilty, of this Serpent, is equal to that of the old one.

Aunt is let into the Secret, and is full of her Interjections!

But, Cushing tells me, that Powell told him, he had it from a Tory, or one who was not suspected to be any Thing else, that certain Letters were come, written by 4 Persons, which would shew the Causes and the Authors of our present Grievances. This Tory, we conjecture to be Bob. Temple, who has received a Letter, in which he is informed of these Things. If the Secret ⟨*should leak?*⟩[1] out by this means, I am glad it is not to be charged upon any of Us—to whom it has been committed in Confidence.

Fine, gentle Rain last night and this morning, which will lay a foundation for a crop of Grass.

My Men at Braintree have been building me a Wall, this Week against my Meadow. This is all the Gain that I make by my Farm to repay me, my great Expence. I get my Land better secured—and manured.

[1] These two words are heavily inked out in the MS without replacement.

1773. AP. 25. SUNDAY.

Heard Dr. Chauncy in the Morning and Dr. Cooper this Afternoon. Dr. Cooper was up[on] Rev. 12.9. And the great Dragon was cast out, that old Serpent called the Devil and Satan, which deceiveth the whole World: he was cast out into the Earth and his Angells were cast out with him. Q[uery]. Whether the Dr. had not some political Allusions in the Choice of this Text.

81

1773. MAY 24TH [*i.e.* 25TH]. TUESDAY.[1]

Tomorrow is our General Election. The Plotts, Plans, Schemes, and Machinations of this Evening and Night, will be very numerous. By the Number of Ministerial, Governmental People returned, and by the Secrecy of the Friends of Liberty, relating to the grand discovery of the compleat Evidence of the whole Mystery of Iniquity, I much fear the Elections will go unhappily. For myself, I own I tremble at the Thought of an Election. What will be expected of me? What will be required of me? What Duties and Obligations will result to me, from an Election? What Duties to my God, my King, my Country, my Family, my Friends, myself? What Perplexities, and Intricacies, and Difficulties shall I be exposed to? What Snares and Temptations will be thrown in my Way? What Self denials and Mortifications shall I be obliged to bear?

If I should be called in the Course of Providence to take a Part in public Life, I shall Act a fearless, intrepid, undaunted Part, at all Hazards—tho it shall be my Endeavour likewise to act a prudent, cautious and considerate Part.

But if I should be excused, by a Non Election, or by the Exertions of Prerogative from engaging in public Business,[2] I shall enjoy a sweet Tranquility, in the Pursuit of my private Business, in the Education of my Children and in a constant Attention to the Preservation of my Health. This last is the most selfish and pleasant System—the first, the more generous, tho arduous and disagreable.

But I was not sent into this World to spend my days in Sports, Diversions and Pleasures.

I was born for Business; for both Activity and Study. I have little Appetite, or Relish for any Thing else.

I must double and redouble my Diligence. I must be more constant to my office and my Pen. Constancy accomplishes more than Rapidity. Continual Attention will do great Things. Frugality, of Time, is the greatest Art as well as Virtue. This Economy will produce Knowledge as well as Wealth.

Spent this Evening at Wheelwrights, with Parson Williams of Sandwich, Parson Lawrence of Lincoln, Mr. Pemberton and Swift.

Williams took up the whole Evening with Stories about Coll. Otis and his Son the Major.[3] The Major employed the Treasurer and Parson Walter to represent him to the Governor as a Friend to Government, in order to get the Commission of Lieutenant Colonel. The Major quarrells and fights with Bacon.—They come to you lie and you lie—

and often very near to blows, sometimes quite. The Major has Liberty written over his Manufactory House, and the Major inclosed the exceptionable Passages in the Governors Proclamation in Crotchetts. Col. Otis reads to large Circles of the common People, Allens Oration on the Beauties of Liberty and recommends it as an excellent Production.—

Stories of Coll. Otis's Ignorance of Law, about Jointenancies—criticizing upon the Word Household Goods in a Will of the Parsons Writing, and saying it was a Word the Law knew nothing of, it should have been Household Stuff.

Coll. Otis's orthodoxy, and yet some Years ago, his arguing in the Strain of Tindal against Christianity.

Yet some Years ago Otis and Williams were very friendly.

These Prejudices against Otis and his Family are very carefully cultivated, by the Tories in that County and by the Judges of the Superior Court. They generally keep Sabbath there. The C[hief] J[ustice] went to spend the Evening with him this Year when I was at Sandwich—in order to keep up his Spirits and fill his Head with malicious stories.

After I got home, my Wife surprized me. She had been to Justice Quincys. Mr. Hancock came in, and gave before a large Company of both Sexes, to Mr. Cooper a particular Account of all the Plans of Operation for tomorrow, which he and many others had been concerting. Cooper no doubt carried it directly to Brattle, or at least to his Son Thomas. Such a leaky Vessell is this worthy Gentleman.

[1] Tuesday was the 25th.

[2] On the first day of the new General Court, 26 May, JA was elected by the House a member of the Council, but together with Jerathmeel Bowers and William Phillips he was negatived by Gov. Hutchinson (Mass., *House Jour.*, 1773–1774, p. 6, 7; Hutchinson, *Massachusetts Bay*, ed. Mayo, 3:284 and note).

[3] Col. James Otis Sr. and Maj. Joseph Otis, of Barnstable, father and brother, respectively, of James Otis the lawyer and orator.

1773 JUNE 8TH.

Parson Turners Sermon, the spirited Election, Parson Haywards Artillery sermon, the 17 Letters, Dr. Shipleys sermon, the Bp. of St. Asaph, before the Society for propagating the Gospell, discover the Times to be altered. But how long will the Tides continue to set this Way?

1773 JULY 16.[1]

Drank Tea at Dr. Coopers with Mr. Adams, Mr. S. Elliot, Mr. T.

Chase, and with Mr. Miffling [Mifflin], of Phyladelphia, and a French
Gentleman. Mr. Miffling is a Grandson, his Mother was the Daughter,
of Mr. Bagnall of this Town, who was buried the day before Yesterday.
Mr. Miffling is a Representative of the City of Phyladelphia—a very
sensible and agreable Man. Their Accademy emits from 9 to 14
Graduates annually. Their Grammar School has from 90 to 100
schollars in all. Mr. Miffling is an easy Speaker—and a very correct
Speaker.

[1] Perhaps an error for 15 July, since the following entry is correctly dated Friday,
16 July.

1773. JULY 16. FRYDAY.

Mr. F. Dana came to me with a Message from Mr. Henry Merchant
[Marchant] of Rhode Island—And to ask my Opinion, concerning the
Measures they are about to take with Rome's and Moffats Letters.[1]
They want the originals that they may be prosecuted as Libells, by their
Attorney General, and Grand Jury. I told him, I thought they could
not proceed without the originals, nor with them if there was any
material obliteration or Erasure, 'tho I had not examined and was not
certain of this Point, nor did I remember whether there was any
Obliteration on Romes and Moffats Letters.

Mr. Dana says the Falshoods and Misrepresentations in Romes
Letter are innumerable, and very flagrant.

Spent the Evening with Cushing, Adams, Pemberton and Swift at
Wheelwrights—no body very chatty but Pemberton.

[1] Thomas Moffatt, a Scottish physician, and George Rome, a loyalist, both
of Newport, R.I. Letters written by each
of them were among those transmitted
by Franklin to Cushing (note by CFA
in JA, *Works*, 2:321; Hutchinson,
Massachusetts Bay, ed. Mayo, 3:283
and note).

1773. JULY [19 or 26.] MONDAY.
To Tho. Hutchinson.[1]

Sir

You will hear from Us with Astonishment. You ought to hear from
Us with Horror. You are chargeable before God and Man, with our
Blood.—The Soldiers were but passive Instruments, were Machines,
neither moral nor voluntary Agents in our Destruction more than the
leaden Pelletts, with which we were wounded.—You was a free
Agent. You acted, coolly, deliberately, with all that premeditated
Malice, not against Us in Particular but against the People in general,

which in the Sight of the Law is an ingredient in the Composition of Murder. You will hear further from Us hereafter.

Chrispus Attucks

[1] Doubtless intended for a newspaper, but no printing has been found.

AUGUST 23D. 1773. MONDAY.

Went this Morning to Mr. Boylstones, to make a wedding Visit to Mr. Gill and his Lady.[1] A very cordial, polite, and friendly Reception, I had. Mr. Gill shewed me Mr. Boylstones Garden, and a large, beautifull and agreable one it is—a great Variety of excellent fruit, Plumbs, Pears, Peaches, Grapes, Currants &c. &c.—a figg Tree, &c.

Mr. and Mrs. Gill both gave me a very polite Invitation, to sup and spend the Evening there with Mr. Linch and his Lady,[2] which I promised to do. At Noon, I met Mr. Boylstone upon Change, and he repeated the Invitation, in a very agreable Manner.

In the Evening I waited on my Wife there and found Mr. Linch and his Lady and Daughter, Mr. Smith, his Lady and Daughter, and Miss Nabby Taylor—and a very agreable Evening we had. Mr. Linch is a solid, sensible, tho a plain Man—an hearty friend to America, and her righteous Cause. His Lady has the Behaviour and Appearance of a very worthy Woman, and the Daughter seems to be worthy of such Parents.

[1] Moses Gill (1734–1800), afterward lieutenant governor of Massachusetts, married as his 2d wife Rebecca, sister of Nicholas and Thomas Boylston, cousins of JA's mother (Francis E. Blake, *History of the Town of Princeton, Mass.*, Prince-ton, 1915, 1:270–277).

[2] Thomas Lynch Sr. (1727–1776), of South Carolina, a member of the first and second Continental Congresses; his wife was the former Hannah Motte (*DAB*).

MONDAY. AUG. 30 1773.

Spent the Evening with my Wife at her Uncle Smiths, in Company with Mr. Lynch, his Lady and Daughter, Coll. Howorth, his Sister and Daughter, Mr. Ed. Green and his Wife, &c. The young Ladies Miss Smith and Miss Lynch entertained us upon the Spinnet &c.

Mr. Lynch still maintains the Character. Coll. Howorth attracted no Attention, untill he discovered his Antipathy to a catt.

1773. DECR. 17TH.[1]

Last Night 3 Cargoes of Bohea Tea were emptied into the Sea. This Morning a Man of War sails.

This is the most magnificent Movement of all. There is a Dignity, a Majesty, a Sublimity, in this last Effort of the Patriots, that I greatly admire. The People should never rise, without doing something to be remembered—something notable And striking. This Destruction of the Tea is so bold, so daring, so firm, intrepid and inflexible, and it must have so important Consequences, and so lasting, that I cant but consider it as an Epocha in History.

This however is but an Attack upon Property. Another similar Exertion of popular Power, may produce the destruction of Lives. Many Persons wish, that as many dead Carcasses were floating in the Harbour, as there are Chests of Tea:—a much less Number of Lives however would remove the Causes of all our Calamities.

The malicious Pleasure with which Hutchinson the Governor, the Consignees of the Tea, and the officers of the Customs, have stood and looked upon the distresses of the People, and their Struggles to get the Tea back to London, and at last the destruction of it, is amazing. Tis hard to believe Persons so hardened and abandoned.

What Measures will the Ministry take, in Consequence of this?—Will they resent it? will they dare to resent it? will they punish Us? How? By quartering Troops upon Us?—by annulling our Charter?—by laying on more duties? By restraining our Trade? By Sacrifice of Individuals, or how.

The Question is whether the Destruction of this Tea was necessary? I apprehend it was absolutely and indispensably so.—They could not send it back, the Governor, Admiral and Collector and Comptroller would not suffer it. It was in their Power to have saved it—but in no other. It could not get by the Castle, the Men of War &c. Then there was no other Alternative but to destroy it or let it be landed. To let it be landed, would be giving up the Principle of Taxation by Parliamentary Authority, against which the Continent have struggled for 10 years, it was loosing all our labour for 10 years and subjecting ourselves and our Posterity forever to Egyptian Taskmasters—to Burthens, Indignities, to Ignominy, Reproach and Contempt, to Desolation and Oppression, to Poverty and Servitude.

But it will be said it might have been left in the Care of a Committee of the Town, or in Castle William. To this many Objections may be made.

Deacon Palmer and Mr. Is. Smith dined with me, and Mr. Trumble came in. They say, the Tories blame the Consignees, as much as the Whiggs do—and say that the Governor will loose his Place, for not taking the Tea into his Protection before, by Means of the Ships of War, I suppose, and the Troops at the Castle.

I saw him this Morning pass my Window in a Chariot with the Secretary. And by the Marching and Countermarching of Councillors, I suppose they have been framing a Proclamation, offering a Reward to discover the Persons, their Aiders, Abettors, Counsellors and Consorters, who were concerned in the Riot last Night.

Spent the Evening with Cushing, Pemberton and Swift at Wheelwrights. Cushing gave us an Account of Bollans Letters—of the Quantity of Tea the East India Company had on Hand—40,00000[2] weight, that is Seven Years Consumption—two Millions Weight in America.[3]

[1] Little remains among JA's papers or elsewhere to fill the three-and-a-half-month gap between the preceding Diary entry and this one. In his Autobiography JA says that he spent all his leisure time in the fall, winter, and spring of 1773–1774 collecting "Evidence and Documents" and writing "a State of the Claim of this Province to the Lands to the Westward of New York." This took the form of a report to the General Court, now lost. What is known of this scholarly investigation, which led JA to ransack the famous Mather and Prince libraries, is summarized in a note on a passage dated Fall 1773 in his Autobiography, Part One, below.

From his legal papers and the Superior Court Minute Books it appears that JA handled cases in that court in its August term in Boston, in its September term in Worcester, and in its October terms in both Taunton and Cambridge, as well as in the Inferior Court at Boston in October.

[2] Thus in MS. See William Bollan to the Massachusetts Council, 1 Sept. 1773 (MHS, *Colls.*, 6th ser., 9 [1897]:309–310).

[3] Two letters from JA to James Warren, one of the present date and the other of 22 Dec., elaborate JA's views on what has become known as the Boston Tea Party (MHi: Warren-Adams Coll.; printed in JA, *Works*, 9:333–336).

1773. DECR. 18. SATURDAY.

J. Quincy met me this Morning and after him Kent, and told me that the Governor said Yesterday in Council, that the People had been guilty of High Treason, and that he would bring the Attorney General on Monday to convince them that it was so—and that Hancock said, he was for having a Body Meeting[1] to take off that Brother in Law of his.[2]

[1] That is, a mass meeting, which anyone could attend (including persons from nearby towns), as distinguished from a town meeting. The term is fully explained in Tudor, *James Otis*, p. 418, note.

[2] This can only mean Jonathan Sewall, the attorney general. Sewall's wife was the former Esther Quincy. Hancock was betrothed to her sister Dorothy.

1774. FEBY. 28.[1]

I purchased of my Brother, my fathers Homestead, and House where I was born. The House, Barn and thirty five acres of Land of which the Homestead consists, and Eighteen acres of Pasture in the North Common, cost me 440£. This is a fine addition, to what I had there before, of arable, and Meadow. The Buildings and the Water, I wanted, very much.

That beautifull, winding, meandering Brook, which runs thro this farm, always delighted me.

How shall I improve it? Shall I try to introduce fowl Meadow And Herds Grass, into the Meadows? or still better Clover and Herdsgrass?

I must ramble over it, and take a View. The Meadow is a great Object—I suppose near 10 Acres of [it]—perhaps more—and may be made very good, if the Mill below, by overflowing it, dont prevent. Flowing is profitable, if not continued too late in the Spring.

This Farm is well fenced with Stone Wall against the Road, against Vesey, against Betty Adams's Children, vs. Ebenezer Adams, against Moses Adams, and against me.

The North Common Pasture has a numerous Growth of Red Cedars upon it, perhaps 1000, which in 20 years if properly pruned may be worth a Shilling each. It is well walled in all round. The Prunings of those Cedars will make good Browse for my Cattle in Winter, and good fuel when the Cattle have picked off all they will eat. There is a Quantity of good Stone in it too.

¹ First entry in "Paper book No. 20" (our D/JA/20), a gathering of leaves stitched into a marbled paper cover and containing irregular entries through 25 June 1774.

1774 MARCH 2D. WEDNESDAY.

Last evening at Wheelwrights, with Cushing, Pemberton and Swift. Lt. Govr. Oliver, senseless, and dying, the Governor sent for and Olivers Sons. Fluker [Flucker] has laid in, to be Lieutenant Governor, and has perswaded Hutchinson to write in his favour. This will make a difficulty. C[hief] J[ustice] Oliver, and Fluker will interfere.

Much said of the Impeachment vs. the C.J.—and upon the Question whether the Council have the Power of Judicature in Parliament, which the Lords have at home, or whether the Governor and Council have this Power? ¹

It is said by some, that the Council is too precarious a Body to be intrusted with so great a Power. So far from being independent, and having their Dignities and Power hereditary, they are annually at the Will, both of the House and the Governor, and therefore are not sufficiently independent, to hold such Powers of Judicature over the Lives and Fortunes of Mankind. But the answer is this, they may be intrusted with the Powers of Judicature, as safely as with the Powers of Legislature, and it should be remembered that the Council can in no

Case here be Tryers of Fact as well as Law, as the Lords are at home when a Peer is impeached, because the Council are all Commoners and no more. The House of Representatives are the Tryers of the Facts and their Vote Impeaching is equivalent to a Bill of Indictment, and their Vote demanding Judgment is equivalent to a Verdict of a Jury, according to Selden. Is not the Life, and Liberty and Property of the subject, thus guarded, as secure as it ought to be, when No Man can be punished, without the Vote of the Rep[resentative]s of the whole People, and without the Vote of the Council Board if he can without the Assent of the Governor.

But it is said, that there is no Court of Judicature in the Province, erected by the Charter, only. That in the Charter a Power is given to the general Court to erect Courts. That General Court has not made the Governor and Council a Court of Judicature, and therefore it is not one, only in Cases of Marriage and Probate.

To this it may be answered by enquiring, how the Council came by their Share in the Legislative? The Charter says indeed that the General Court shall consist of Governor, Council and House, and that they shall make Laws, but it no Where says, the Council shall be an integral Part of this General Court—that they shall have a Negative Voice.

It is only from Analogy, to the British Legislative, that they have assumed this Importance in our Constitution.

Why then may they not derive from the same analogy, the Power of Judicature?

About 9 at Night I step'd over the Way, and took a Pipe with Justice Quincy and a Mr. Wendel of Portsmouth. Mr. Wendell seems a Man of Sense and Education, and not ill affected to the public Cause.

[1] According to his Autobiography, it was JA who suggested and who furnished the legal authorities for impeachment proceedings against Chief Justice Peter Oliver for his willingness to accept his salary from the crown. The proceedings failed in a formal sense but had the effect wanted, which was to exclude Oliver from the bench. See Sibley-Shipton, *Harvard Graduates*, 8:748–754, and references there.

1774 MARCH 5TH.

Heard the oration pronounced, by Coll. Hancock, in Commemoration of the Massacre—an elegant, a pathetic, a Spirited Performance. A vast Croud—rainy Eyes—&c.

The Composition, the Pronunciation, the Action all exceeded the Expectations of every Body. They exceeded even mine, which were very considerable. Many of the Sentiments came with great Propriety from him. His Invective particularly against a Prefference of Riches to Virtue, came from him with a singular Dignity and Grace.[1]

Dined at Neighbour Quincys, with my Wife. Mr. John Dennie and Son there. Dennie gave a few Hints of vacating the Charter and sending Troops, and depriving the Province of Advantages, quartering Troops &c.—But all pretty faint.

The Happiness of the Family where I dined, upon account of the Colls. justly applauded Oration, was complete. The Justice and his Daughters were all joyous.

[1] Hancock's *Oration* was promptly printed, "at the request of the inhabitants of the Town of Boston," by Edes and Gill and was several times reprinted; Evans 13314–13317. In his Autobiography JA remembered that "Mr. Samuel Adams told me that Dr. [Benjamin] Church and Dr. [Joseph] Warren had composed Mr. Hancocks oration on the fifth of March, which was so celebrated, more than two thirds of it at least."

1774 SUNDAY MARCH 6TH.

Heard Dr. Cooper in the Morning. Paine drank Coffee with me.

Paine is under some Apprehensions of Troops, on Account of the high Proceedings, &c. He says there is a ship in to day, with a Consignment of Tea from some private Merchants at home—&c.

Last Thursday Morning March 3d. died Andrew Oliver Esquire Lieutenant Governor. This is but the second death which has happened among the Conspirators, the original Conspirators against the Public Liberty, since the Conspiracy was first regularly formed, and begun to be executed, in 1763 or 4. Judge Russell who was one, died in 1766. Nat. Rogers, who was not one of the original's, but came in afterwards, died in 1770.

This Event will have considerable Consequences.—Peter Oliver will be made Lieutenant Governor, Hutchinson will go home, and probably be continued Governor but reside in England, and Peter Oliver will reside here and rule the Province. The Duty on Tea will be repealed. Troops may come, but what becomes of the poor Patriots. They must starve and mourn as usual. The Hutchinsons and Olivers will rule and overbear all Things as usual.

An Event happened, last Fryday that is surprising. At a General Council, which was full as the General Court was then sitting, Hutchinson had the Confidence to Nominate for Justices of the Peace, George Bethune, Nat. Taylor, Ned. Lloyd [Lyde], Benj. Gridly and Sam Barrett—and informed the Board that they had all promised to take the oath.

The Council had the Pusillanimity to consent by their Silence at least to these Nominations.

Nothing has a more fatal Tendency than such Prostitution of the Council. They tamely, supinely, timorously, acquiesce in the Appointment of Persons to fill every executive Department in the Province, with Tools of the Family who are planning our Destruction.

Neighbour Quincy spent the Evening with me.

1774. MONDAY MARCH 7.

This Morning brought us News from S. Carolina of the Destruction of the Tea there, and from England of a Duel between Mr. Temple and Mr. Whately, and Mr. Franklins explicit Declaration, that he alone sent the Governors Letters to Boston and that both Temple and Whately were ignorant and innocent of it [1] —and that 3 Regiments are ordered to Boston and N. York, that the Judges opinions are required, and the Board of Trade in Motion, and great Things are to be laid before Parliament &c. &c. Twenty Eight Chests of Tea arrived Yesterday, which are to make an Infusion in Water, at 7 o Clock this Evening.

This Evening there has been an Exhibition in Kingstreet of the Portraits of the soldiers and the Massacre—and of H———n and C. J. Oliver, in the Horrors—reminded of the Fate of Empson and Dudley, whose Trunks were exposed with their Heads off, and the Blood fresh streaming after the Ax.

[1] The duel between John Temple and William Whately (brother and executor of Thomas Whately, recipient of the controversial letters) was reported in the *Boston Gazette* of this day, where also will be found Franklin's public letter of 25 Dec. 1773 declaring that he alone was "the person who obtained and transmitted to Boston the letters in question." See entry of 22 March 1773, above.

1774. TUESDAY MARCH 8.

Last Night 28 Chests and an half of Tea were drowned.[1]

[1] On orders, according to the *Boston Gazette*, 14 March, of "His Majesty OKNOOKORTUNKOGOG King of the Narranganset Tribe of Indians," whose tribesmen "are now returned to Naragansett to make Report of their doings to his Majesty, who we hear is determined to honour them with Commissions for the Peace."

1774. WEDNESDAY MARCH 9TH.

Returned from Charlestown Court with Coll. Tyng of Dunstable, who told me some Anecdotes of Bernard and Brattle, Otis, Hutchinson, &c. Bernard said "he never thought of Pratt"—he would find a Place for him now, upon that Bench. Brattle shall be Colonel and Brigadier, &c.—Bernard said—Afterwards this Miff broke out into a Blaze.[1]

Jemmy Russell was as sociable, and familiar, with Dix and Gorham, and Stone, and All the Members of the House as possible—an Artfull fellow! deeply covered.—He told a saying of the Admiral, at the Funeral Yesterday. "There never was any Thing in Turkey nor in any Part of the World, so arbitrary and cruel as keeping old Mr. Clark, at the Castle all this winter, an old Man, from his family." [2]

This day the General Court prorogued in Anger by the Governor.

[1] The ambiguous punctuation of the MS has been retained. Presumably Tyng's anecdotes continue through the next paragraph.

[2] Richard Clarke, one of the con- signees of the tea in Nov. 1773; his daughter Susanne was the wife of John Singleton Copley (Col. Soc. Mass., *Pubns.*, 8 [1906]:78–90).

1774. FRYDAY MARCH 11TH.

Dined at Charlestown with Mr. Thomas Russell, with Mr. Temple,[1] Mr. Jacob Rowe, Mr. Nicholls, Mr. Bliss, and several other Gentlemen and Ladies, to me unknown. No Politicks, but Mr. Temples Duell, and the Pieces in the London Papers, relative to it. A young Brother of Mr. Russell came in. Conversation about making Porter here—our Barley, Hops &c.

The Right of private Judgment and the Liberty of Conscience was claimed by the Papists and allowed them in the reign of James 2d.— But has been prohibited by Law ever since. The Advocates for the Administration now in America, claim the Right of private Judgment to overthrow the Constitution of this Province, the Priviledges of all America, and british Liberties into the Bargain—sed Non allocatur.

[1] Robert Temple, brother of John Temple the duelist.

SATURDAY. MARCH 12.

There has been and is a Party in the Nation, a very small one indeed, who have pretended to be conscienciously perswaded, that the Pretender has a Right to the Throne. Their Principles of Loyalty, hereditary Right, and passive obedience have led them to this Judgment, and Opinion. And as long as they keep these Opinions to themselves, there is no Remedy against them. But as soon as they express these opinions publicly, and endeavour to make Proselytes, especially if they take any steps to introduce the Pretender, they become offenders, and must suffer the Punishment due to their Crimes. Private Judgment might be alledged in Excuse for many Crimes—a poor Enthusiast [may?] bring himself to believe it lawfull for him to steal from his rich Neighbour, to supply his Necessities, but the Law will not allow of this Plea. The Man must be punished for his Theft.

Ravaillac and Felton probably thought, they were doing their Duty, and nothing more, when they were committing their vile assassinations: But the Liberty of private Conscience, did not exempt them from the most dreadfull Punishment that civil Authority can inflict or human Nature endure.

Hutchinson and Oliver might be brought by their interested Views and Motives, sincerely to think that an Alteration in the Constitution of this Province, and an "Abridgment of what are called English Liberties,"[1] would be for the Good of the Province, of America, and of the Nation. In this they deceived themselves, and became the Bubbles of their own Avarice and Ambition. The rest of the World are not thus deceived. They see clearly, that such Innovations will be the Ruin not only of the Colonies, but of the Empire, and therefore think that Examples ought to be made of these great offenders, in Terrorem.

The Enmity of Govr. Bernard, Hutchinson and Oliver, and others to the Constitution of this Province is owing to its being an Obstacle to their Views and Designs of Raising a Revenue by Parliamentary Authority, and making their own Fortunes out of it.

The Constitution of this Province, has enabled the People to resist their Projects, so effectually, that they see they shall never carry them into Execution, while it exists. Their Malice has therefore been directed against it, and their Utmost Efforts been employed to destroy it.

There is so much of a Republican Spirit, among the People, which has been nourished and cherished by their Form of Government, that they never would submit to Tyrants or oppressive Projects.

The same Spirit spreads like a Contagion, into all the other Colonies, into Ireland, and into Great Britain too, from this single Province, of Mass. Bay, that no Pains are too great to be taken, no Hazards too great to be run, for the Destruction of our Charter.

[1] Closing quotation marks supplied. The quoted phrase is from Hutchinson's letter to Thomas Whately, 20 Jan. 1769; see entry of 22 March 1773 and note, above.

1774 SUNDAY. MARCH 13.

Heard Mr. Lothrop [Lathrop] in the Forenoon and Dr. Cooper in the Afternoon. Last evening Justice Pemberton spent with me. He says that Moses Gill has made many Justices by lending Money.

MONDAY. MARCH 27 [*i.e.* 28?]. 1774.

Rode with Brother Josiah Quincy to Ipswich Court. Arrived at Piemonts in Danvers, in good order and well conditioned. Spent the evening, and lodged, agreably. Walked out in the Morning to hear the Birds sing. Piemont says there is a Report that the Sons of Liberty have received some Advices from England which makes them look down—that they have received a Letter from Mr. Bollan that they must submit—and other Letters which they keep secret.

TUESDAY MARCH 28 [*i.e.* 29?] 1774.

Rode to Ipswich and put up at the old Place, Treadwells. The old Lady has got a new Copy of her GranGranfather Govr. Endicott's Picture, hung up in the House. The old Gentleman is afraid they will repeal the Excise upon Tea and then that we shall have it plenty, wishes they would double the Duty, and then we should never have any more.

The Q[uestion] is who is to succeed Judge Ropes—whether Brown or Pynchon or Lee or Hatch.[1] The Bar here are explicit vs. the 2 last, as unfit. Lowell says Pynchon would take it, because he wants to make Way for Wetmore who is about marrying his Daughter.

Pynchon says Judge Ropes was exceedingly agitated all the time of his last Sickness—about the public Affairs, in general, and those of the Superiour Court in particular—afraid his Renunciation would be attributed to Timidity—afraid to refuse to renounce—worried about the Opinion of the Bar, &c.

Mr. Farnum is exceedingly mollified—is grown quite modest, and polite in Comparison of what he used to be, in Politicks. Lowell is so too—seems inclined to be admitted among the Liberty Men.

At a Meeting of the Bar a Doubt of Brother Lowell was mentioned upon the Law of the Prov[ince] for the Relief of poor Prisoners for Debt. Questions were asked whether appealing an Action was not fraud, whether trading without insuring was not fraud &c. A Question also about the Duty of the Sheriff? Whether a Party Plaintiff could controul the Kings Precept, &c., by ordering the Sheriff not to serve it &c. Mr. Wetmore was agreed to be recommended for the Oath &c.

[1] Nathaniel Ropes, a justice of the Superior Court, died on 18 March; he was succeeded by William Browne, a classmate of JA's at Harvard (Whitmore, *Mass. Civil List*, p. 70).

1774. WEDNESDAY. MARCH 30TH.

A dull Day. My Head is empty, but my Heart is full. I am wanted at my Office, but not wanted here. There is Business there, but none here. My Wife perhaps wants to see me. I am anxious about her. I cannot get the Thoughts of her State of Health out of my Mind. I think she must remove to Braintree—and the Family, at least for the Season.

1774. THURSDAY MARCH 31.

Let me ask my own Heart, have I patience, and Industry enough to write an History of the Contest between Britain and America? It would be proper to begin at the Treaty of Peace in 1763, or at the Commencement of Govr. Bernards Administration, or at the Accession of George 3d. to the Throne—The Reign, or the Peace.

Would it not be proper, to begin, with those Articles in the Treaty of Peace which relate to America?—The Cession of Canada, Louisiana, and Florida, to the English.

Franklin, Lee, Chatham, Campden [Camden], Grenville and Shelburne, Hilsborough, Dartmouth, Whately, Hutchinson, Oliver, J[udge] Oliver, Barnard [Bernard], Paxton, Otis, Thatcher, Adams, Mayhew, Hancock, Cushing, Phillips, Hawley, Warren, with many other Figures would make up the Groope.[1]

[1] Loosely inserted in the Diary at this point is an itemized bill to JA from an unidentified person for "29 Entries ... 24 bills," &c., in the amount of £19 9s. 6d., docketed on the verso: "John Adams Esqe. Accot: for April Ct. 1774."

[NOTES ON THE NAME OF THE MERRIMACK RIVER, SPRING 1774.][1]

The River has been universally called and known by the Name of Merrimack and by no other, from the Mouth of it at the Sea, thro Pennicook, Suncook, Nottingham, Litchfield, and all the other Towns and Places, quite up to the Crotch made by Winnipissioke Pond and Pemiggewasset River. Pemiggewasset and Winnipissioke, joining make the Crotch, and from that Crotch to the Sea it has always been called and known by the Name of Merrimack River, and is so to this day, and in all the Records of New Hampshire laying out Towns and Countys and in all Records of Towns and Counties[2] and in all Deeds and Conveyances from private Persons of Lands upon this River, it has been uniformly and invariably, called Merrimack and by no other Name.

[1] Immediately following the entry of 31 March (except for the inserted receipt mentioned above) is a series of extracts from Massachusetts provincial statutes, 1730–1734, relating mainly to the establishment of towns on the Merrimack River and to the boundary controversy between Massachusetts and New Hampshire which was then current (see Hutchinson, *Massachusetts Bay*, ed. Mayo,

2:290–297. In addition there are extracts from three treasury supply acts, 1733–1735, reciting the wages to be paid the garrison "at the Block House above Northfield" in the northwestern part of the Province. Then follows the paragraph concerning the name of the Merrimack River which is printed here. Probably all this material was put down while JA was investigating Massa-chusetts' northern and western boundaries for his report to the General Court this spring; see entry of 17 Dec. 1773, note 1, above, and Autobiography, Part One, under Fall 1773, below. All of it except the single paragraph that JA himself may have composed is omitted in the present text.

² MS: "Countries."

JUNE 20TH. 1774. MONDAY.

At Piemonts in Danvers, bound to Ipswich. There is a new, and a grand Scene open before me—a Congress.

This will be an assembly of the wisest Men upon the Continent, who are Americans in Principle, i.e. against the Taxation of Americans, by Authority of Parliament.

I feel myself unequal to this Business. A more extensive Knowledge of the Realm, the Colonies, and of Commerce, as well as of Law and Policy, is necessary, than I am Master of.

What can be done? Will it be expedient to propose an Annual Congress of Committees? to Petition.—Will it do to petition at all?—to the K[ing]? to the L[ords]? to the C[ommon]s?

What will such Consultations avail? Deliberations alone will not do. We must petition, or recommend to the Assemblies to petition, or—

The Ideas of the People, are as various, as their Faces. One thinks, no more petitions, former having been neglected and despized. Some are for Resolves—Spirited Resolves—and some are for bolder Councils.

I will keep an exact Diary, of my Journey, as well as a Journal of the Proceedings of the Congress.¹

¹ On 13 May Gen. Thomas Gage arrived in Boston to relieve Gov. Hutchinson and to enforce the "Coercive Acts," passed by Parliament as punishment for the destruction of the tea; Hutchinson sailed for London on 1 June, the day the Boston Port Act went into effect (Hutchinson, *Massachusetts Bay*, ed. Mayo, 3:329). On 25 May the new General Court met, and JA was once again elected by the House a member of the Council, only to be negatived, with twelve others, by Gage next day (Mass., *House Jour.*, May–June 1774, p. 6–7). On instructions from the crown, Gage adjourned the legislature from Boston to Salem, 7 June (same, p. 8). Ten days later the *Journal* records: "Upon a Motion, *Ordered*, that the Gallaries be clear'd and the Door be shut," and a committee on the state of the Province reported that "in Consideration of the unhappy Differences" between Great Britain and the colonies, "it is highly expedient and necessary that a Meeting of Committees from the several Colonies on this Continent be had on a certain Day, to consult upon the present State of the Colonies and the Miseries to which they are reduced by the Operation of certain Acts of Parliament respecting America" (same, p. 44). The House adopted these recommendations in virtually the same language and proceeded to elect "a Committee on the Part of this Province, to consist of five Gentlemen, any three of whom to be a Quorum," to meet with "Committees or Delegates" from the

other colonies at Philadelphia or any other suitable place on 1 Sept. Those chosen were James Bowdoin, Thomas Cushing, Samuel Adams, JA, and Robert Treat Paine; £500 was appropriated for their expenses; and Gage immediately, but too late, dissolved the General Court (same, p. 44–45).

1774. JUNE 25TH. SATURDAY.

Since the Court[1] adjourned without Day this afternoon I have taken a long Walk, through the Neck as they call it, a fine Tract of Land in a general Field—Corn, Rye, Grass interspersed in great Perfection this fine season.

I wander alone, and ponder.—I muse, I mope, I ruminate.—I am often In Reveries and Brown Studies.—The Objects before me, are too grand, and multifarious for my Comprehension.—We have not Men, fit for the Times. We are deficient in Genius, in Education, in Travel, in Fortune—in every Thing. I feel unutterable Anxiety.—God grant us Wisdom, and Fortitude!

Should the Opposition be suppressed, should this Country submit, what Infamy and Ruin! God forbid. Death in any Form is less terrible.

[1] Essex Superior Court, sitting at Ipswich.

BOSTON. AUGUST 10. WEDNESDAY.[1]

The committee for the Congress took their departure from Boston, from Mr. Cushing's house, and rode to Coolidge's, where they dined in company with a large number of gentlemen, who went out and prepared an entertainment for them at that place. A most kindly and affectionate meeting we had, and about four in the afternoon we took our leave of them, amidst the kind wishes and fervent prayers of every man in the company for our health and success. This scene was truly affecting, beyond all description affecting. I lodged at Colonel Buck's.[2]

[1] This entry and the one immediately following (first entry under 15 Aug.) are transcribed from JA, *Works*, 2:340–341, no MS source for them having been found.

JA's correspondence and Autobiography supply the information that from Ipswich he had gone "for the tenth and last time on the Eastern Circuit" in Maine, where, on a hill above Casco Bay, took place the affecting separation between him and Jonathan Sewall—"the sharpest thorn on which I ever sat my foot" (JA, Preface to *Novanglus and Massachusettensis*, Boston, 1819, p. vi). By mid-July JA was back in Braintree with his family, but he was soon caught up in work for the distressed town of Boston, being appointed on 26 July to a committee to receive donations for the relief of the inhabitants (which proved a burdensome assignment) and to another committee appointed to consider "proper Measures to be adopted for the common Safety" (Boston Record Commissioners, *18th Report*, p. 185).

[2] Robert Treat Paine's entry in his Diary (MHi) for this day adds a few details:

"At 11 o'clock the honble. Thos. Cushing Esq. and the other Commission[ers] of Congress for this Province sat out in a Coach and four and four Servants, the honble. James Bowdoin not being able to go on Account of the Indisposition of his Family; We dind at Coolidge at Watertown in Company with between 50 and 60 Gentlemen from Boston who rode out to take their leave of us and give us their best Wishes for our Success on the Embassy. Thence we rode to Col. Buckminster at Framingham and lodged, a very hot day."

JA omits the next three days in his Diary, but Paine recorded that the party set out at 5 in the morning of the 11th,

breakfasted at Westborough, and proceeded through Worcester, dining "in good season," and then on to Spencer, where they lodged. On the 12th they again started at 5, breakfasted at Brookfield, dined at Palmer, and lodged at Springfield. They did not leave Springfield until 10 the next morning, dined at Suffield, and lodged at Hartford, the weather remaining "hot and very dry and dusty." The 14th being a Sunday, they went to meeting and rested.

15. MONDAY.

Mr. Silas Deane, of Wethersfield, came over to Hartford to see us. He is a gentleman of a liberal education, about forty years of age; first kept a school, then studied law, then married the rich widow of Mr. Webb, since which he has been in trade. Two young gentlemen, his sons-in-law, Messrs. Webbs, came over with him. They are genteel, agreeable men, largely in trade, and are willing to renounce all their trade.

Mr. Deane gave us an account of the delegates of New York. Duane and Jay are lawyers. Livingston, Low, and Alsop are merchants. Livingston is very popular. Jay married a Livingston, Peter's daughter, and is supposed to be of his side.[1]

Mr. Deane says the sense of Connecticut is, that the resolutions of the Congress shall be the laws of the Medes and Persians; that the Congress is the grandest and most important assembly ever held in America, and that the *all* of America is intrusted to it and depends upon it.

[1] The New York delegates to the first Continental Congress, chosen by popular election in New York City, 28 July, were John Alsop, James Duane, John Jay, Philip Livingston, and Isaac Low (Force, *Archives*, 4th ser., 1:320). CFA in a note on this passage points out JA's error concerning Jay's wife; she was the daughter of William Livingston, himself a delegate from New Jersey and a brother of both Peter and Philip.

1774 AUG. 15. MONDAY.[1]

Last Evening, after spending the Evening at the Meeting House to hear the Singing, We were invited into Mr. Church's. Mr. Seymour, Mr. Paine [Payne], Lawyers, and Mr. Bull, Merchant, came to see us and invited us to dine with them this Day with the Principal Gentlemen of the Place.

This Morning Mr. Deane, and two young Gentlemen, Messrs. Webbs, came to see us from Weathersfield.—Mr. Deane says there is

30,000 Bushells of Flax Seed sent to New York yearly, in Exchange for Salt. That it would be no Loss to stop this, as the Seed may be made into Oil more profitably. They have many Oil Mills in the Colony.

Connecticutt sends great Quantities of Provisions, Cattle and Horses to the West Indies, and bring[s] great Quantities of Rum as well as Sugar and Molasses, to N. York. Some Lumber they send, Staves, Hoops, Heading &c. There is a Stream of Provisions continually running from Connecticutt.

Mr. Deane, and Messrs. Webbs, are intimately acquainted and closely connected with People at N. York.

We dined at the Tavern, with upwards of thirty Gentlemen of the first Character in the Place, at their Invitation. The Secretary Willis [Wyllys], the Treasurer,[2] Judge Talcott, Mr. Alsop, Merchant, Mr. Paine and Mr. Seymour Lawyers, two Mr. Bulls, and many others. The Company appeared to be determined to abide by the Resolutions of the Congress.

After Dinner at 4 o Clock We satt out, for Middleton. A Number of Gentlemen in Carriages and a No. on Horse back insisted upon attending us, which they did to our Brother Deanes in Weathersfield. There We stopd, and were most cordially and genteelly entertained with Punch, Wine, and Coffee.

We went up the Steeple of Weathersfield Meeting House from whence is the most grand and beautifull Prospect in the World, at least that I ever saw. Then We rode to Middleton and lodged at Bigelows. There Mr. Hobby and another Gentleman came to see us.

[1] Second (and in part duplicative) entry of this date, but the first entry in JA's paper booklet "21," a gathering of leaves stitched into a marbled paper cover and containing entries through 3 Sept. 1774.
[2] John Lawrence.

1774 AUG. 16. TUESDAY.

This Morning Dr. Elliot Rawson, Mr. Allsop, Mr. Mortimer, and others the Committee of Correspondence, Mr. Henshaw, and many other Gentlemen, came to pay their Respects to Us, and to assure us that they thought, We had their all in our Hands, and that they would abide by whatever should be determind on, even to a total Stoppage of Trade to Europe and the West Indies.

This morning rode to Wallingford, to Johnsons where We dine.

We wrote a Card to Dr. Dana, to dine with us. He came and informed us that he had wrote some Cards to Us to put up with him this Night. The Doctor dined with us and was very social and agreable.

At four We made for N[ew] Haven. 7 Miles out of Town at a Tavern We met a great Number of Carriages and of Horse Men who had come out to meet us. The Sherriff of the County and Constable of the Town and the Justices of Peace were in the Train, as We were coming We met others to the amount of I know not what Number but a very great one. As We came into the Town all the Bells in Town were sett to ringing, and the People Men, Women and Children, were crouding at the Doors and Windows as if it was to see a Coronation. At Nine O Clock the Cannon were fired, about a Dozen Guns I think.

These Expressions of Respect to Us, are intended as Demonstrations of the Sympathy of this People with the Massachusetts Bay and its Capital, and to shew their Expectations from the Congress and their Determination to carry into Execution whatever shall be agreed on.

No Governor of a Province, nor General of an Army was ever treated with so much Ceremony and Assiduity, as We have been, throughout the whole Colony of Connecticutt, hitherto, but especially all the Way from Hartford to N. Haven, inclusively.

Nothing shews to me, the Spirit of the Town of New Haven, in a stronger Point of Light, than the Politeness of Mr. Ingersoll Judge of Admiralty for the Pensilvanian middle District, who came over with his Neighbours this Evening, and made his Compliments very respectfully to Tom. Cushing, Sam. Adams, John Adams and Bob. Paine.

The Numbers of Gentlemen who have waited on Us from Hartford to this Place, the Heat of the Weather and the shortness of the Time, have made it impossible for me to learn the Names.

1774 AUG. 17. WEDNESDAY AT N[EW] HAVEN.

We are told here that New York are now well united and very firm.

This Morning Roger Sherman Esqr., one of the Delegates for Connecticutt, came to see us at the Tavern, Isaac Bears's. He is between 50 and 60—a solid sensible Man. He said he read Mr. Otis's Rights &c. in 1764 and thought that he had conceeded away the Rights of America. He thought the Reverse of the declaratory Act was true, vizt. that the Parliament of G.B. had Authority to make Laws for America in no Case whatever. He would have been very willing the Massachusetts should have rescinded that Part of their Circular Letter, where they allow Parliament to be the Supream Legislative, over the Colonies in any Case.[1]

Mr. Jones, Mr. Douglass, and several other Gentlemen accompanied us, to take a View of the Town. It is very pleasant. There are 3 Congregational Meeting Houses and one Episcopal Church, near together. Went to view the Grave Stone of Dixwell the Regicide, in the Burying Yard.

Went to Colledge and saw their Library, their Apparatus and Chappell &c.

Mr. Dwight and Mr. Davenport, two of the Tutors, waited on us with great Civility.

We dined with Mr. Douglass, with Mr. Badcock [Babcock], son of Dr. Badcock of Westerly, Mr. Odle [Odell], Mr. Smith, Mr. Sherman and a No. of Ladies. Were very genteelly entertained, and spent the whole Afternoon in Politicks, the Depths of Politicks. Mr. Douglass shew[ed] us his Garden, which is a very good one—fine fruit, and Musk Mellens and Water Mellens such as I never saw before, a Musk Mellen 17 Inches long and a Water Mellen, whose Inside looked as if it was painted.

An Enquiry was started, who were the Members of the H. of Commons who had Plantations in the West Indies, and who were returned by the Interest of the West India Planters?

No one could tell. None could pretend to foresee the Effect of a total Non Exportation to the West Indies.

Jamaica was said to be the most independent Part of the World. They had their Plantane for Bread. They had vast forrests, and could make their own Heading, Staves and Hoops. They could raise their own Provisions.

This Afternoon and Evening We had a plentifull Rain.

[1] See entry of 1 July 1770 and note, above.

1774 AUG. 18. THURSDAY.

Mr. Badcock is of the same Mind with Major Hawley, that a Non Importation and Non Consumption Agreement will not be faithfully observed—That the Congress have not Power to inforce Obedience to their Laws—That they will be like a Legislative without an Executive.

We had a good deal of Chatt last Evening with Mr. Bears our Landlord. By his Account, the Parade which was made, to introduce Us into Town, was a Sudden Proposal, in order to divert the Populace from erecting a Liberty Pole &c. Ingersols Friends were at the Bottom of it.

Breakfasted at Bryants in Milford, where there are two Meeting Houses and a Church. We visited the burying Yard and the Tomb of Paines Great Grandfather R. Treat 30 years Governor and Deputy

Governor died 1710, 87 Years of Age. There is an old venerable Monument over him, with an Inscription.

About 10 We passed the Housatonnoc River, at Stratford, a River which runs up 150 Miles and more, tho it is not navigable above 10 miles. We stoped at Curtis's. The People here all say, Boston is suffering Persecution, that now is the Time for all the rest to be generous, and that Boston People must be supported.

Dined at Fairfield, at Bulkeleys. Mr. Elliot [Eliot] the new Minister of this Town came to see us. This is a County Town, and has an elegant Court House, Meeting House and Church, as well as many very elegant private Houses.

Mr. Burr came to see us.

After noon We rode to Quintards of Norwalk, where we are to put up, having rode 36 Miles, and having 50 Miles to N. York.

1774. AUG. 19. FRYDAY.

Rode to Fitch's of Stamford, where we breakfasted. Rode to Havilands of Rye, the first Town in the Province of N. York. The Barber says that Religion dont flourish in this Town. The congregational Society have no Minister. The Church minister has 45£ from the Society. They have a School for Writing and Cyphering, but no Grammar School. There is no Law of this Province that requires a Minister or school Master.

1774 AUG. 20. SATURDAY.

Lodged at Cocks at Kingsbridge, a pretty Place—Uncas River running before the Door and verdant Hills all round. This Place is about 15 Miles from N. York. Uncas River is the Bound between the County of Westchester and the County of N. York. This Place is 10 Miles from Hell Gate, which is supposed to be occasioned by a large Cavern under the Rocks, into which the Water rushes at certain Times of the Tide. This Whirlpool is 5 Miles from the City.

We breakfasted at Days, and arrived in the City of New York at 10 O Clock—at Hulls, a Tavern, the Sign the Bunch of Grapes. We rode by several very elegant Country Seats, before we came to the City.

This City will be a Subject of much Speculation to me.

From Hulls We went to private Lodgings at Mr. Tobias Stoutenberg's, in Kings Street, very near the City Hall one way and the French Church the other.[1] Mr. McDougal and Mr. Platt came to see us. Mr. Platt asked us to dinner next Monday. Mr. McDougal stayed longer, and talk'd a good deal. He is a very sensible Man, and an open one. He has none of the mean Cunning which disgraces so many of my Country men. He offers to wait on us this afternoon to see the City.

After Dinner, Mr. McDougal and Mr. Platt came and walked with Us, to every Part of the City. First We went to the Fort where We saw the Ruins of that magnificent Building the Governors House.[2] From the Parade before the Fort you have a fine Prospect of Hudsons River and of the East River or the Sound and of the Harbour—of Long Island, beyond the Sound River, and of New Jersey, beyond Hudsons River. The Walk round this Fort is very pleasant, tho the Fortifications are not strong. Between the Fort and the City is a beautifull Elipsis of Land, railed in with solid Iron, in the Center of which is a Statue of his Majesty on Horse back, very large, of solid Lead, gilded with Gold, standing on a Pedastal of Marble very high.[3] We then walked up the broad Way, a fine Street, very wide, and in a right Line from one End to the other of the City. In this rout We saw the old Church, and the new Church. The new is a very magnificent Building—cost 20,000£ York Currency. The Prison is a large and an handsome stone building. There are two setts of Barracks. We saw the New York Colledge which is also a large Stone Building. A new Hospital is building of Stone. We then walked down to a ship Yard, where a Dutch East India Ship is building of 800 Tons burden. Then We walked round thro another Street which is the Principal Street of Business. Saw the several Marketts. After this We went to the Coffee House, which was full of Gentlemen, read the News Papers, &c. Here were introduced to Us Mr. Morine [John Morin] Scott and a Mr. Litchfield, who invited us to Hulls Tavern, where we went and staid till 11 0 Clock. We supped together, and had much Conversation. Mr. Scott is a Lawyer, of about 50 years of Age, a sensible Man, but not very polite. He is said to be one of the readiest Speakers upon the Continent. It was he who harrangued the People, and prevailed upon them to discard the Resolves of their Committee of 51, as void of Vigour, Sense and Integrity.

Mr. Scott was censuring McDougal in a friendly free Way for not insisting upon choosing Delegates by Ballot, &c.

Mr. Platt said but little. But McDougal was talkative, and appears to have a thorough Knowledge of Politicks. The two great Families in this Province, upon whose Motions all their Politicks turn, are the Delanceys and Livingstones. There is Virtue and Abilities as well as fortune, in the Livingstones, but not much of either of the three in the Delanceys, according to him.

The Streets of this Town are vastly more regular and elegant than those in Boston, and the Houses are more grand as well as neat. They are almost all painted—brick buildings and all.

In our Walks they shewed us the House of Mr. William Smith, one of their Council and the famous Lawyer—Mr. Thomas Smith &c., Mr. Rivington's Store &c.

¹ R. T. Paine's Diary (MHi) gives the spelling "Stoutenburgh's" and says that it was "at Corner of Nassau Street."

² On 29 Dec. 1773 the Governor's House in Fort George, at the lower end of Broadway, had been gutted by fire

(Stokes, *Iconography of Manhattan Island*, 3:974; 4:844).

³ A plan of the Fort and of the Bowling Green, in which the statue stood, is in same, 1: pl. 46–A.

1774. AUG. 21. SUNDAY.

Went to Meeting at the old Presbyterian Society, where Dr. Pemberton formerly preached. We heard Dr. Rogers [Rodgers] on "seek first the Kingdom of God and his Righteousness and all other Things shall be added unto you." After Service, Mr. Peter Vanbrugh Livingston and Mr. Thos. Smith came to our Lodgings introduced to Us by Mr. McDougall.

Mr. Livingston is an old Man, extreamly Stanch in the Cause, and very sensible. He tells us, that Dr. Chandler and Dr. Cooper and other Episcopal Clergymen, were met together about the Time of the News of the Boston Port Bill, and were employed night and Day writing Letters and sending Dispatches to the other Colonies, and to England. This he thinks was to form an Union of the Episcopal Party thro the Continent in Support of ministerial Measures. He says they never have been able to obtain a Charter for their Burying Yard or the Ground on which their Presbyterian Church stands. They have solicited their Governors, and have solicited at Home, without success.

In the afternoon We went to the same Meeting and heard Mr. Treat from "These shall go away into everlasting Punishment." Both these Clergymen are good Speakers, and without Notes.

The Psalmody is an exact Contrast to that of Hartford. It is in the *Old Way*, as we call it—all the drawling, quavering, Discord in the World.

After Meeting Mr. McDougal introduced me and Mr. Paine to Mr. Wm. Smith, the Historian of N. York, a Gentleman a little turn'd of 40—a plain, composed Man to appearance. He very politely invited us to Tea at his House, but we were engaged. He then enquired where we lodged, and said he would wait on us.

After Meeting We went to Mr. McDougals, where we saw his Lady, a charming Woman, and his Daughter an agreable Miss. Mrs. Climer

[Clymer] was there from Philadelphia, who enquired very kindly after Mr. Hancock and his Aunt and Mr. Jona. Mason and his Family. This is a very facetious and social Lady.—At Mr. McDougals Coll. Folsom and Major Sullivan, the Delegates from N. Hampshire, came to see us. They were hastening over the ferry for fear of the small Pox, neither of them having had that Distemper.

Att Mr. McDougalls, a Number of Gentlemen came to see us. Mr. Low, a Relation of the Delegate from N. York of that Name, Mr. Lamb, Mr. Hewes a School Master, and many others, whose Names I cant recollect.

We then went to Mr. David Vanhorns, who sent his Compliments to Mr. McDougal, and requested him to introduce Us to his House as he was sick and unable to come out. He seems well affected to the public Cause, and speaks very sensibly about it.

1774. AUG. 22. MONDAY.

This Morning We took Mr. McDougal into our Coach and rode three Miles out of Town, to Mr. Morine Scotts to break fast. A very pleasant Ride! Mr. Scott has an elegant Seat there, with Hudsons River just behind his House, and a rural Prospect all round him.[1] Mr. Scott, his Lady and Daughter, and her Husband Mr. Litchfield were dressed to receive Us. We satt in a fine Airy Entry, till called into a front Room to break fast. A more elegant Breakfast, I never saw—rich Plate—a very large Silver Coffee Pott, a very large Silver Tea Pott—Napkins of the very finest Materials, and toast and bread and butter in great Perfection. After breakfast, a Plate of beautifull Peaches, another of Pairs and another of Plumbs and a Muskmellen were placed on the Table.

Mr. Scott, Mr. William Smith and Mr. William Livingston, are the Triumvirate, who figured away in younger Life, against the Church of England—who wrote the independent Reflecter, the Watch Tower, and other Papers.[2] They are all of them Children of Yale Colledge. Scott and Livingston are said to be lazy. Smith improves every Moment of his Time. Livingstone is lately removed into N. Jersey, and is one of the Delegates for that Province.

Mr. Scott is an eminent Lawyer. He drew the Answer of the Council to Governor Coldens Reasons in favour of an Appeal in the Case of Forsey vs. Cunningham. He is said to be one of the readyest Speakers on the Continent.

Scott told me that the State of the New York Claim, Massachusetts Claim, N. Hampshire Claim and Canada Claim, which is printed in the Journal of the House in New York 1773, to the Lands contested between Connecticutt and Hudsons River was principally drawn by Mr. Duane who has unhappily involved almost all his Property in those Lands.[3] He has purchased Patents of Government and Claims of Soldiers &c. to the amount of 100,000 Acres. Mr. Duane is an Episcopalian, so are all the Delegates from N. York, excepting Mr. Livingston.

Mr. Jay is a young Gentleman of the Law of about 26, Mr. Scott says an hard Student and a good Speaker.

Mr. Alsop is a Merchant, of a good Heart, but unequal to the Trust in Point of Abilities, as Mr. Scott thinks.

Mr. Low, the Chairman of the Committee of 51, they say will profess Attachment to the Cause of Liberty but his Sincerity is doubted.

Mr. Wm. Bayard, Mr. McEvers, and Mr. Beech, are Gentlemen who were very intimate with General Gage when he was here. Mr. Bayard has a son and a Son in Law in the Army, and a son in the Service of the East India Company. These are connected with Mr. Apthorp and his Contracts and are Lookers up to Government for favours—are Correspondents of General Gages—and will favour his Measures, tho they profess attachment to the American Cause.

Mr. McDougal gave a Caution to avoid every Expression here, which looked like an Allusion to the last Appeal. He says there is a powerfull Party here, who are intimidated by Fears of a Civil War, and they have been induced to acquiesce by Assurances that there was no Danger, and that a peacefull Cessation of Commerce would effect Relief.

Another Party he says are intimidated least the levelling Spirit of the New England Colonies should propagate itself into N. York.

Another Party are prompted by Episcopalian Prejudices, against New England.

Another Party are Merchants largely concerned in Navigation, and therefore afraid of Non Importation, Non Consumption and Non Exportation Agreements.

Another Party are those who are looking up to Government for Favours.

About 11 O Clock four of the Delegates for the City and County of N. York came to make their Compliments to us—Mr. Duane, Mr. Livingston, Mr. Low and Mr. Alsop. Mr. Livingston is a down right strait forward Man. Mr. Alsop is a soft sweet Man. Mr. Duane has a sly, surveying Eye, a little squint Eyed—between 40 and 45 I should guess—very sensible I think and very artfull. He says their private Correspondence and their Agents Letters (Mr. Bourke) are that the Nation is against us, that we cannot depend upon any Support of any kind from thence, that the Merchants are very much against us, that their Pride is touched and what they call their Rights by our turning away their Ships from our Ports.[4]

A Question arose whether it was a Prerogative of the Crown at common Law to licence Wharfes. I thought it was by Statutes at home which were never extended to America before the Boston Port Bill. Mr. Duane was of my Opinion. Mr. Livingston thought it was a Prerogative of the Crown at Common Law. Said it had been so understood here—that all the public Wharfes in this Town were by Charter from the Governor. He questioned whether the officers of the Customs were obliged to attend any Wharfes, but licenced ones.

Mr. Morin Scott called upon Us at our Lodgings, and politely insisted upon our taking a Seat in his Chariot, to Mr. Platts. We accepted the Invitation and when We came there were shewn into as elegant a Chamber as ever I saw—the furniture as rich and splendid as any of Mr. Boylstones. Mr. Low, Mr. Peter Vanbrugh Livingston, Mr. Phillip Livingston, Dr. Treat a Brother of the Minister, and Mr. McDougal, Mr. Scott and Mr. Litchfield dined with us and spent the Afternoon.

P. V. Livingston is a sensible Man, and a Gentleman—he has been in Trade, is rich, and now lives upon his Income. Phill. Livingston is a great, rough, rappid Mortal. There is no holding any Conversation with him. He blusters away. Says if England should turn us adrift we should instantly go to civil Wars among ourselves to determine which Colony should govern all the rest. Seems to dread N. England—the Levelling Spirit &c. Hints were thrown out of the Goths and Vandalls—mention was made of our hanging the Quakers, &c. I told him, the very Existence of the Colony was at that Time at Stake—surrounded with Indians at War, against whom they could not have defended the Colony, if the Quakers had been permitted to go on.

[1] John Morin Scott's house "stood in (modern) West 43d St., between Eighth and Ninth Aves." (Stokes, *Iconography of Manhattan Island*, 4:864).

[2] On these activities see a study that derives its title from an epithet in this paragraph: Dorothea R. Dillon, *The New York Triumvirate: A Study of the Legal and Political Careers of William Livingston, John Morin Scott, and William Smith, Jr.*, N.Y., 1949, ch. 2.

[3] The reference is to the protracted and many-sided dispute over the "New Hampshire Grants," in which Duane was heavily involved both as a land speculator and the principal adviser to the New York government on its title. See Edward P. Alexander, *A Revolutionary Conservative: James Duane of New York*, N.Y., 1938, ch. 5, especially p. 88, note.

[4] Parentheses supplied. Edmund Burke had been agent of the New York Assembly since 1770. The letters from

Diary of John Adams

Burke alluded to here were probably those of 6 April and 4 May 1774 describing the debates in Parliament on the so-called Intolerable Acts (Ross J. S. Hoffman, ed., *Edmund Burke, New York Agent, with His Letters to the New York Assembly* ..., Phila., 1956, p. 245–262).

1774 AUG. 23. TUESDAY.

We went upon the new Dutch Church Steeple and took a View of the City. You have a very fine View of the whole City at once—the Harbour, East River, North River, Long Island, N. Jersey &c. The whole City is upon a Levell—a Flatt. The Houses in general are smaller than in Boston and the City occupies less Ground.

We breakfasted with Mr. Low, a Gentleman of Fortune and in Trade.[1] His Lady is a Beauty. Rich Furniture again, for the Tea Table. Mr. Lott, the Treasurer of the Province, did us the Honour to break fast with us, and politely asked us to dine or to break fast with him—but we were engaged for all the Time we were to stay.

The Conversation turned upon the Constitution of the City; the Mayor and Recorder are appointed by the Governor, the Aldermen and Common Council are annually elected by the People. The Aldermen are the Magistrates of the City and the only ones. They have no Justices of the Peace in the City, so that the Magistracy of the City are all the Creatures of the People. The City cannot tax itself. The Constables, Assessors &c. are chosen annually. They Petition the Assembly every Year to be impowered by Law to assess the City for a certain Sum.

The whole Charge of the Province is annually between 5 and 6000£ York Money. Mr. Cushing says the Charge of the Massachusetts is about 12,000 L.M., which is 16,000 York Currency. The Support of Harvard Colledge, and of Forts and Garrisons and other Things makes the Difference.

About Eleven o Clock Mr. Low, Mr. Curtenius, Mr. Pascall Smith, Mr. Van Shaw [Van Schaack] and others, a Deputation from the Committee of Correspondence from this City, waited on Us, with an Invitation to dine with them Thursday next which we accepted.

One of the Gentlemen said, he was in England at the Time of a former Non Importation Agreement and it was not much felt among the Merchants or Manufacturers. Another of them replyed the true Cause of that was the German Contract and the Demand from Russia.

Mr. Ebenezer Hazard waited on me with a Letter requesting my assistance in making his Collection of American State Papers. I recommended him to Mr. S. Adams, and Dr. Samuel Mather. I advised him to publish from Hackluyt, the Voyage of Sebastian Cabot, in this Collection. He thought it good Advice.

Hazard is certainly very capable of the Business he has undertaken—he is a Genius.[2]

Went to the Coffee House, and saw the Virginia Paper. The Spirit of the People is prodigious. Their Resolutions are really grand.[3]

We then went to Mr. Peter Vanbrugh Livingstons where at 3 O Clock we dined, with Scott, McDougal, Phillip Livingston, Mr. Thomas Smith, and a young Gentleman Son of Mr. Peter Livingston.

Smith and young Livingston seem to be modest, decent and sensible Men.

The Way we have been in, of breakfasting, dining, drinking Coffee &c. about the City is very disagreable on some Accounts. Altho it introduces us to the Acquaintance of many respectable People here, yet it hinders us from seeing the Colledge, the Churches, the Printers Offices and Booksellers Shops, and many other Things which we should choose to see.

With all the Opulence and Splendor of this City, there is very little good Breeding to be found. We have been treated with an assiduous Respect. But I have not seen one real Gentleman, one well bred Man since I came to Town. At their Entertainments there is no Conversation that is agreable. There is no Modesty—No Attention to one another. They talk very loud, very fast, and alltogether. If they ask you a Question, before you can utter 3 Words of your Answer, they will break out upon you, again—and talk away.

[1] This was Cornelius Low, according to R. T. Paine's Diary (MHi) under this date; not Isaac Low, mentioned earlier as one of the New York delegates to the Congress.

[2] Hazard, at this time a partner with Garret Noel in a bookselling business in New York (see 25 Aug., below), was just launching his project for a comprehensive collection of documents relating to the early history of America. He circulated printed appeals for aid and suggestions widely among the colonies and ultimately published, by subscription, *Historical Collections; Consisting of State Papers . . . Intended as Materials for an History of the United States*, Phila., 1792–1794; 2 vols. A text of his printed proposals, bearing the very date of the present diary entry, is in DLC:Jefferson Papers, and is reprinted in Jefferson, *Papers*, ed. Boyd, 1:144–145; see also 5:562–563, and Fred Shelley, "Ebenezer Hazard: America's First Historical Editor," *WMQ*, 3d ser., 12:44–73 (Jan. 1955).

[3] JA was doubtless reading the resolutions or "Association" of the Virginia Convention that had met at Williamsburg, 1–6 Aug., to elect and instruct delegates to the first Continental Congress. This spirited paper was printed in Purdie and Dixon's *Virginia Gazette*, 11 Aug., and has been reprinted in Jefferson, *Papers*, ed. Boyd, 1:137–140.

1774 AUG. 24. WEDNESDAY.

This Day Cushing and Paine went over to Long Island to dine with

Phill. Livingston. Adams and I sent our Excuse that we were not very well. It was raw and wett.

1774 AUG. 25. THURSDAY.

Mr. Mathew Cushing came and escorted Us into Trinity Church and Church Yard. Under the Chancell of this Church Mr. Pratt was buried. This is an old Building. We then went into St. Pauls. This is a new Building which Cost 18,000£ Y[ork] Money. It has a Piazza in Front and some Stone Pillars, which appear grand, but the Building taken all together does not strike me, like the Stone Chappell or like Dr. Coopers Meeting, Either on the Inside or Outside.

We then went to see Mr. Cushing work his new constructed Pumps, which work easier he says, and convey more Water than any other.

We then went to Colledge, were introduced to Mr. Harper [Harpur], who shew[ed] Us the Library, the Books and Curiosities. We were then introduced to Dr. Clossie [Clossy] who was exhibiting a Course of Experiments to his Pupils to prove the Elasticity of the Air.

There is but one Building at this Colledge and that is very far from full of Schollars. They never have had 40 Schollars at a Time.

We then made a Visit of Ceremony to Mr. William Smith, a Councillor at Law, and a Councillor by Mandamus. This Gentleman has the Character of a great Lawyer, a sensible and learned Man and yet a consistent unshaken Friend to his Country and her Liberties. He entertained us with an Account of his Negociating between the Governor (Colden), the General (Gage) and the People in the year 1765, when the People attacked the Fort, to obtain the Stamped Papers—in which he acted an intrepid, an honest and a prudent Part. Mr. McDougal told me of the Part he acted in the Affair of the Prosecution of him for a Libel. The Governor asked him if he would not act for the Crown. Mr. Smith said he would not do the dirty Jobbs of Government—He would not hold any Thing under the Crown upon such Terms.

Mr. Smith expressed his Sentiments of General Gage and his new Station and Character very freely. He said he had a great personal Regard for the General—that he was a good natured, peacable and sociable Man here. But that he was altogether unfit for a Governor of the Massachusetts. That he would loose all the Character he had acquired as a Man, a Gentleman and a General and dwindle down into a mere Scribbling Governor, a mere Bernard, or Hutchinson.

Mr. Smith received us very politely.

We afterwards made a Visit to Friend Holt, the Liberty Printer, and to Noel and Hazards. We afterwards dined in the Exchange Chamber, at the Invitation of the Committee of Correspondence, with more than 50 Gentlemen, at the most splendid Dinner I ever saw—a Profusion of rich Dishes &c. &c. I had a great deal of Conversation with Mr. Duane who is a sensible, an Artfull, and an insinuating Man. He talked of Mr. Pratt—said he had the greatest Memory of any Man he ever saw, that he had read a great deal—but that he had not a clear Head. One of the Bar used to say that Mr. Pratt thickened the clear. That he knew Mr. Pratt try 8 criminals in a forenoon, upon different Indictments, and with the same Jury, that he took no Notes, but summed the Evidence with great Exactness, remembered every Circumstance of every Testimony, and the Names of all the Witnesses, altho the Witnesses were dutch People and their Names such as Mr. Prat never could have heard.

After Dinner the Connecticutt Delegates came in. In the Evening several Gentlemen came to our Lodgings and among others Mr. Sears.

1774 AUG. 26. FRYDAY.

This Morning We went to see the City Hall, the Chamber where the Supream Court sitts, and that where the Mayor and Recorder sit. Afterwards We went down to the new Dutch Church, which is a much more elegant Building than St. Pauls—it is the most elegant Building in the City. The Pillars are smaller than Dr. Coopers, and the Pews are all painted, but the Building is not so handsome. At Nine o Clock We crossed Powlus Hook Ferry, to N. Jersey—then Hackinsack Ferry, then Newark Ferry and dined at Elizabeth Town. After Dinner We rode twenty miles, crossed Brunswick Ferry and put up at Farmers, in the City of Brunswick. That Part of the Province of New Jersey which We have passed is all upon a Level—as fine a Road as ever was trod. Yet the Lands seem to be good.

1774 AUG. 27. SATURDAY.

Went to view the City of Brunswick, there is a Church of England, a Dutch Church and a Presbyterian Church in this Town, there is some little Trade here—small Craft can come up to the Town. We saw a few small sloops. The River is very beautifull. There is a stone Building for Barracks which is tolerably handsome. It is about the Size of Boston Goal. Some of the Streets are paved and there are 3 or 4 handsome Houses. Only about 150 Families in the Town. Rode ten Miles to Jones's, where We stopped to blow our Horses.

This whole Colony of N. Jersey is a Champaign.

About 12 O Clock We arrived at the Tavern in Prince Town, which holds out the Sign of Hudibrass, near Nassau Hall Colledge. The Tavern Keepers Name is Hire.

The Colledge is a stone building about as large as that at New York. It stands upon rising Ground and so commands a Prospect of the Country.

After Dinner Mr. Pidgeon a student of Nassau Hall, Son of Mr. Pidgeon of Watertown from whom we brought a Letter, took a Walk with us and shewed us the Seat of Mr. Stockton a Lawyer in this Place and one of the Council, and one of the Trustees of the Colledge.[1] As we returned we met Mr. Euston [Houston], the Professor of Mathematicks and natural Philosophy, who kindly invited Us to his Chamber. We went. The Colledge is conveniently constructed. Instead of Entries across the Building, the Entries are from End to End, and the Chambers are on each side of the Entries. There are such Entries one above another in every Story. Each Chamber has 3 Windows, two studies, with one Window in each, and one Window between the studies to enlighten the Chamber.

Mr. Euston then shewed us the Library. It is not large, but has some good Books. He then led us into the Apparatus. Here we saw a most beautifull Machine, an Orrery, or Planetarium, constructed by Mr. Writtenhouse of Philadélphia.[2] It exhibits allmost every Motion in the astronomical World. The Motions of the Sun and all the Planetts with all their Satellites. The Eclipses of the Sun and Moon &c. He shewed us another orrery, which exhibits the true Inclination of the orbit of each of the Planetts to the Plane of the Ecliptic. He then shewed Us the electrical Apparatus, which is the most compleat and elegant that I have seen. He charged the Bottle and attempted an Experiment, but the State of the Air was not favourable. By this Time the Bell rang for Prayers. We went into the Chappell, the President[3] soon came in, and we attended. The Schollars sing as badly as the Presbyterians at New York. After Prayers the President attended Us to the Balcony of the Colledge, where We have a Prospect of an Horizon of about 80 Miles Diameter. We went into the Presidents House, and drank a Glass of Wine. He is as high a Son of Liberty, as any Man in America. He says it is necessary that the Congress should raise Money and employ a Number of Writers in the Newspapers in England, to explain to the Public the American Plea, and remove the Prejudices of Britons. He says also We should recommend it to every Colony to form a Society for the Encouragement of Protestant Emigrants from the 3 Kingdoms. The Dr. waited on us to our Lodgings and took a Dish of Coffee. He is one of the Committee of Correspondence, and was upon the Provincial Congress for appointing Delegates from this Province to the general Congress. Mr. William Livingston and He laboured he says to procure an Instruction that the Tea should not be paid for. Livingston he says is very sincere and very able in the public Cause, but a bad Speaker, tho a good Writer.

Here we saw a Mr. Hood a Lawyer of Brunswick, and a Mr. Jonathan Dickenson Serjeant,[4] a young Lawyer of Prince town, both cordial Friends to American Liberty. In the Evening, young Whitwell, a student at this Colledge, Son of Mr. Whitwell at Boston to whom we brought a Letter, came to see us.

By the Account of Whitwell and Pidgeon, the Government of this Colledge is very Strict, and the Schollars study very hard. The President says they are all Sons of Liberty.

[1] The home of Richard Stockton, an eminent lawyer and afterward a signer of the Declaration of Independence, was called Morven. It is now the official residence of the governor of New Jersey. See Alfred Hoyt Bill, *A House Called Morven*, Princeton, 1954.

[2] This famous orrery, constructed by David Rittenhouse of Norriton and Philadelphia, was acquired by the College of New Jersey in 1770–1771; it has recently been restored and placed on view in the University Library. See Howard C. Rice Jr., *The Rittenhouse Orrery*, Princeton, 1954, and illustrations there.

[3] John Witherspoon, D.D., president of the College of New Jersey since 1768, and subsequently a signer of the Declaration of Independence from New Jersey.

[4] Jonathan Dickinson Sergeant, an active young patriot in New Jersey and closely associated with the College; he afterward moved to Philadelphia (*DAB*).

1774 AUG. 28. SUNDAY.

Heard Dr. Witherspoon all Day. A clear, sensible, Preacher. Mr. Mason came to see us. We sent a Card to Mr. Serjeant a Lawyer. He dined, drank Coffee and spent the Evening with Us. He is a young Gentleman of about 25 perhaps. Very sociable. He gave us much Light concerning the Characters of the Delegates from N. York, Philadelphia, Virginia &c. and concerning the Characters of the Principal Lawyers, in all these Provinces.

Smith he says is the oracle of New York for Chamber Council. Scott is a Character very much like that of old Mr. Auchmuty. Set up all Night at his Bottle. Yet argue to Admiration next Day. An admirable Speaker according to him. Duane is a plodding Body, but has a very effeminate, feeble Voice. He says the Virginians speak in Raptures about Richard Henry Lee and Patrick Henry—one the Cicero and the other the Demosthenes of the Age. Jo Reed is at the Head of his Profession in Philadelphia. Fisher is next. Walln[1] and Dickenson have retired.

[1] Nicholas Waln, a Quaker lawyer who had studied with Joseph Galloway and at the Middle Temple, in 1772 renounced the world in order to live a devotional life (E. Alfred Jones, *Ameri-* *can Members of the Inns of Court*, London, 1924, p. 212-213; Frederick B. Tolles, *Meeting House and Counting House*, Chapel Hill, 1948, p. 122-123, 238-239).

1774 AUG. 29. MONDAY.

Rode to Trenton upon Delaware River, to break fast. At Williams's the Tavern at Trenton Ferry, We saw four very large black Walnut Trees standing in a Row behind the House. It seems that these Trees are plenty in these Southern Provinces—all the black Walnut Timber which is used by our Cabinet Makers in Boston is brought from the Southern Provinces.

This Town of Trenton is a pretty Village—it appears to be the largest Town that we have seen in the Jerseys, larger than Elizabeth Town, Brunswick or Prince town.

We then crossed the Ferry over Delaware River to the Province of Pensylvania. We then rode across an Elbow, and came to the Delaware again—a beautifull River navigable up as far as Trenton. The Country on each Side is very level.

We arrived at Bristol about Eleven O Clock, a Village on the Delaware, opposite to which is Burlington. The Scenes of Nature are delightfull here. This is 20 Miles from Philadelphia. Here We saw two or 3 Passage Waggons—a Vehicle with four Wheels contrived to carry many Passengers and much Baggage.

We then rode to the red Lion and dined. After Dinner We stopped at Frankfort [Frankford] about five Miles out of Town. A Number of Carriages and Gentlemen came out of Phyladelphia to meet us. Mr. Thomas Mifflin, Mr. McKean of the Lower Counties, one of their Delegates,[1] Mr. Rutledge of Carolina, and a Number of Gentlemen from Philadelphia. Mr. Folsom and Mr. Sullivan, the N. Hampshire Delegates. We were introduced to all these Gentlemen and most cordially wellcomed to Philadelphia.[2] We then rode into Town, and dirty, dusty, and fatigued as we were, we could not resist the Importunity, to go to the Tavern, the most genteel one in America.[3] There we were introduced to a Number of other Gentlemen of the City—Dr. Shippen, Dr. Knox, Mr. Smith, and a Multitude of others, and to Mr. Linch and Mr. Gadsden of S. Carolina. Here we had a fresh Welcome to the City of Philadelphia, and after some Time spent in Conversation a curtain was drawn, and in the other Half of the Chamber a Supper appeared as elegant as ever was laid upon a Table. About Eleven o Clock we retired.[4]

By a Computation made this Evening by Mr. McKean, there will be at the Congress about 56 Members, twenty two of them Lawyers. Mr. McKean gave me an Account this Evening of the Behaviour of Ruggles at the former Congress 1765. He was treated pretty cavalierly, his Behaviour was very dishonourable.

A Gentleman who returned into Town with Mr. Paine and me in our Coach, undertook to caution us against two Gentlemen particularly.[5] One was Dr. Smith the Provost of the Colledge, who is looking up to Government for an American Episcopate and a Pair of lawn Sleeves. Soft, polite, insinuating, adulating, sensible, learned, industrious, indefatigable, he has had Art enough and Refinement upon Art to make Impressions even on Mr. Dickinson and Mr. Reed.

[1] That is, a delegate from Delaware.

[2] According to JA's much later and doubtless somewhat embellished recollections of this meeting, the purpose of the deputation from Philadelphia was to warn the Massachusetts delegates against proposing "any bold measures" or hinting anything in favor of American independence (JA to Timothy Pickering, 6 Aug. 1822, MHi; JA, *Works*, 2:512, note).

[3] Opened in 1773 or 1774 and furnished "in the style of the best London taverns," the City Tavern stood on the west side of Second Street between Walnut and Chestnut Streets (Scharf and Westcott, *History of Philadelphia*, 1:291, note).

[4] R. T. Paine's Diary (MHi) under this date says, "thence [i.e. from the City Tavern] we went to Mrs. Yards and lodged." In his Autobiography JA recalled that Sarah Yard's "Stone House opposite the City Tavern," from the fact that the Massachusetts delegates lodged there, "was by some Complimented with the Title of Head Quarters, but by Mr. Richard Henry Lee, more decently called Liberty Hall." For an interval of a few days (31 Aug.–3 Sept.) JA and his colleagues took rooms at Miss Jane Port's in Arch Street between Front and Second, but then moved back to Mrs. Yard's, which was thereafter JA's "Head Quarters" in Philadelphia until the spring of 1777 (entry of 1 Sept. 1774; Account, Jan.–Sept. 1777, below; Paine, Diary, 3 Sept. 1774).

[5] This "Gentleman" may with some confidence be identified as Dr. Benjamin Rush. In his *Autobiography* (p. 110) Rush wrote:

"I went as far as Frankford to meet the delegates from Massachusetts, and rode back into town in the same carriage with John Adams, and two of his colleagues. This gentleman's dress and manners were at that time plain, and his conversation cold and reserved. He asked me many questions relative to the state of public opinion upon politicks, and the characters of the most active citizens on both sides of the controversy."

This memorable meeting began a friendship between JA and Rush that ended only with the latter's death in 1813.

1774. AUG. 30. TUESDAY.

Walked a little about Town. Visited the Markett, the State house, the Carpenters Hall where the Congress is to Sit, &c.—then call'd at Mr. Mifflins—a grand, spacious, and elegant House. Here We had much Conversation with Mr. Charles Thompson [Thomson], who is it seems about marrying a Lady a Relation of Mr. Dickensons with 5000£. st[erling]. This Charles Thompson is the Sam. Adams of Phyladelphia—the Life of the Cause of Liberty, they say.

A Friend Collins came to see us and invited us to dine on Thursday. We returned to our Lodgings and Mr. Lynch, Mr. Gadsden, Mr. Middleton, and young Mr. Rutledge came to visit us. Mr. Linch introduced Mr. Middleton to us. Mr. Middleton was silent and reserved, young Rutledge was high enough. A Promise of the King was mentioned. He started, "I should have no Regard to his Word. His Promises are not worth any Thing," &c. This is a young, smart, spirited Body.

Mr. Blair came to visit us, with another Gentleman. Mr. Smith, an old Gentleman, was introduced to us, by his Son. Another Mr. Smith came in with our Mr. Paine.

The Regularity and Elegance of this City are very striking. It is situated upon a Neck of Land, about two Miles wide between the River De la ware and the River Schuilkill. The Streets are all exactly straight and parrallell to the River. Front Street is near the River, then 2 street, 3d, 4th, 5th, 6th, 7th, 8th, 9th. The cross Streets which intersect these are all equally wide, straight and parallell to each other, and are named from forrest and fruit Trees, Pear Street, Apple Street, Walnut street, Chestnut Street, &c.

Towards the Evening, Mr. Thomas Smith, son of the old Gentleman who made us a Visit who is a Brother of Mr. Smith the Minister of Casco Bay, and Dr. Shippen and his Brother and Mr. Reed, went with Us to the Hospital. We saw, in the lower Rooms under Ground, the Cells of the Lunaticks, a Number of them, some furious, some merry, some Melancholly, and among the rest John Ingham, whom I once saved at Taunton Court from being whipped and sold for Horse stealing. We then went into the Sick Rooms which are very long, large Walks with rows of Beds on each side, and the lame and sick upon them—a dreadfull Scene of human Wretchedness. The Weakness and Languor, the Distress and Misery, of these Objects is truely a Woefull Sight.

Dr. Shippen then carried Us into his Chamber where he shewed Us a Series of Anatomical Paintings of exquisite Art. Here was a great Variety of Views of the human Body, whole, and in Parts. The Dr. entertained us with a very clear, concise and comprehensive Lecture upon all the Parts of the human Frame. This Entertainment charmed me. He first shewed us a Set of Paintings of Bodies entire and alive—then of others with the Skin taken off, then with the first Coat of Muscles taken off, then with the second, then with all—the bare bones. Then he shewed Us paintings of the Insides of a Man, seen before, all the Muscles of the Belly being taken off. The Heart, Lungs, Stomach, Gutts.[1]

[1] When William Shippen Jr. returned home in 1762 from his medical studies in London and Edinburgh, he was put in charge of a "set of Anatomical Paintings & Castings in plaister of Paris representing different views of the Several parts of the Human body," the gift of the philanthropic Dr. John Fothergill of London to the recently established Pennsylvania Hospital. The paintings were the work of the Dutch medical artist Van Rymsdyk; they were long one of the points of interest for tourists in Philadelphia and are still on display at the Hospital, which remains, though much expanded, on its original site at Pine and 8th Streets. See Betsy Copping Corner, *William Shippen, Jr., Pioneer in American Medical Education*, Phila., 1951, p. 98–100.

AUG. 30.[1]

Sent to be washed at Philadelphia. 6 shirts 5 Stocks—2 Caps in [and?] Pair worsted stockings in one silk Handkerchief.

[1] This homely entry is on the front flyleaf of the present booklet.

1774 AUG. 31. WEDNESDAY.

Breakfasted at Mr. Bayards of Philadelphia, with Mr. Sprout a presbyterian Minister.[1]

Made a Visit to Governor Ward of Rhode Island at his Lodgings. There We were introduced to several Gentlemen.

Mr. Dickenson, the Farmer of Pensylvania, came to Mr. Wards Lodgings to see us, in his Coach and four beautifull Horses. He was introduced to Us, and very politely said he was exceedingly glad to have the Pleasure of seeing these Gentlemen, made some Enquiry after the Health of his Brother and Sister, who are now in Boston. Gave us some Account of his late ill Health and his present Gout. This was the first Time of his getting out.

Mr. Dickenson has been Subject to Hectic Complaints. He is a Shadow—tall, but slender as a Reed—pale as ashes. One would think at first Sight that he could not live a Month. Yet upon a more attentive Inspection, he looks as if the Springs of Life were strong enough to last many Years.

We dined with Mr. Lynch, his Lady and Daughter at their Lodgings, Mrs. McKenzies. And a very agreable Dinner and Afternoon we had notwithstanding the violent Heat. We were all vastly pleased with Mr. Lynch. He is a solid, firm, judicious Man.

He told us that Coll. Washington made the most eloquent Speech at the Virginia Convention that ever was made. Says he, "I will raise 1000 Men, subsist them at my own Expence, and march my self at their Head for the Relief of Boston." [2]

He entertained us with the Scandalous History of Sir Egerton

Leigh—the Story of his Wifes Sister, and of his Dodging his Uncle, the Story the Girl swore to before the Lord Mayor, and all that.

There is not says Lynch a greater Rascall among all the Kings Friends. He has great Merit, in this Reign.

Mr. Lynch says they shall export this Year 12,000 Wt. of Indigo and 150,000 Tierces of Rice from S. Carolina. About 300 Ships are employed.

Mrs. Lynch enquired kindly after Mrs. Adams's Health, and Mrs. Smith and family and Mr. Boylstone And Mrs. and Mr. Gill &c.

¹ James Sproat (1722–1793), a Yale graduate (1741), who was for many years minister of the Second Presbyterian Church in Philadelphia (Sprague, *Annals Amer. Pulpit*, 3:125–129). JA and other New Englanders so often spelled his name "Sprout" as to suggest that it was so pronounced.

² The story of Washington's "eloquent Speech," though repeatedly told at this time and later, is according to Douglas Freeman "unfounded" (Freeman, *Washington*, 3:377 and note).

[MISCELLANEOUS EXPENSES, AUGUST–SEPTEMBER 1774.]¹

a Guinea to the lame Man

pd. the Barber 2£:5s:0d. Philadel.   1£:16s. L.M.

6 Dollars.—pd. 2 Washings.—pd. for Leather Straps at Watertown.

¹ These items are written inside the front cover of JA's paper booklet "22"; see note on entry of 4 Sept., below.

1774 SEPTR. 1. THURSDAY.

This Day, We breakfasted at Mr. Mifflins, Mr. C. Thompson came in, and soon after Dr. Smith. The famous Dr. Smith, the Provost of the Colledge. He appears a plain Man—tall, and rather Aukward—there is an Appearance of Art.

We then went to return Visits to the Gentlemen who had visited us. We visited a Mr. Cadwallader a Gentleman of large Fortune, a grand and elegant House And Furniture. We then visited Mr. Powell, another splendid Seat. We then visited the Gentlemen from S. Carolina and about twelve were introduced to Mr. Galloway, the Speaker of the House in Pensylvania. He looks like Ben. Davis the Sandimanian.

We dined at Friend Collins's—Stephen Collins's—with Govr. Hopkins, Govr. Ward, Mr. Galloway, Mr. Rhoades, &c.

In the Evening all the Gentlemen of the Congress who were arrived in Town, met at Smiths the new City Tavern and spent the Evening together. 25 Members were come. Virginia, N. Carolina, Maryland, and the City of N. York were not arrived.

Mr. William Livingston from the Jerseys, lately of New York, was there. He is a plain Man, tall, black, wears his Hair—nothing elegant or genteel about him. They say he is no public Speaker, but very sensible, and learned, and a ready Writer.

Mr. Rutledge the Elder, was there, but his Appearance is not very promising. There is no Keenness in his Eye. No Depth in his Countenance. Nothing of the profound, sagacious, brilliant, or sparkling in his first Appearance.

Yesterday We removed our Lodgings to the House of Miss Jane Port, in Arch Street, about half Way between Front Street and Second Street.

I find that there is a Tribe of People here, exactly like the Tribe in the Massachusetts, of Hutchinsonian Addressers. There is indeed a Sett in every Colony. We have seen the Revolutions of their Sentiments. Their Opinions have undergone as many Changes as the Moon. At the Time of the Stamp Act, and just before it, they professed to be against the Parliamentary Claim of Right to tax Americans, to be Friends to our Constitutions, our Charter &c. Bernard was privately, secretly endeavouring to procure an Alteration of our Charter. But he concealed his Designs untill his Letters were detected. Hutchinson professed to be a stanch Friend to Liberty, and to our Charter, untill his Letters were detected—a great Number of good People thought him a good Man, and a Sincere Friend to the Congregational Interest in Religion and to our Charter Priviledges. They went on with this · machiavilian Dissimulation, untill those Letters were detected—after that they waited untill the Boston Port Bill was passed, and then, thinking the People must submit immediately and that Lord North would carry his whole System triumphantly, they threw off the Mask. Dr. Smith, Mr. Galloway, Mr. Vaughan and others in this Town, are now just where the Hutchinsonian Faction were in the Year 1764 [1765], when We were endeavouring to obtain a Repeal of the Stamp Act.

1774. FRYDAY. SEPTR. 2.

Dined at Mr. Thom. Mifflins with Mr. Lynch, Mr. Middleton, and the two Rutledges with their Ladies. The two Rutledges are good Lawyers. Govr. Hopkins and Govr. Ward were in Company. Mr. Lynch gave us a Sentiment "The brave Dantzickers, who declare they will be free in the face of the greatest Monarch in Europe."—We were very sociable, and happy.

After Coffee We went to the Tavern, where we were introduced to Peyton Randolph Esqr., Speaker of Virginia, Coll. Harrison, Richard

Henry Lee Esq., and Coll. Bland. Randolph is a large, well looking Man. Lee is a tall, spare Man. Bland is a learned, bookish Man.

These Gentlemen from Virginia appear to be the most spirited and consistent, of any. Harrison said he would have come on foot rather than not come. Bland said he would have gone, upon this Occasion, if it had been to Jericho.

1774. SATURDAY. SEPTR. 3.

Breakfasted at Dr. Shippens. Dr. Witherspoon was there. Coll. R. H. Lee lodges there. He is a masterly Man.

This Mr. Lee is a Brother of the Sherriff of London,[1] and of Dr. Arthur Lee, and of Mrs. Shippen. They are all sensible, and deep thinkers.

Lee is for making the Repeal of every Revenue Law, the Boston Port Bill, the Bill for altering the Massachusetts Constitution, and the Quebec Bill, and the Removal of all the Troops, the End of the Congress, and an Abstinence from all Dutied Articles the Means—Rum, Mollosses, Sugar, Tea, Wine, Fruits, &c.

He is absolutely certain, that the same Ship which carries home the Resolution will bring back the Redress. If we were to suppose that any Time would intervene, he should be for Exceptions.

He thinks We should inform his Majesty, that We never can be happy, while the Lords Bute, Mansfield and North are his Confidents and Councillors.

He took his Pen and attempted a Calculation of the Numbers of People represented by the Congress which he made about 2200000, and of the Revenue now actually raised which he made 80,000£ st.

He would not allow Ld. North to have great Abilities. He had seen no symptoms of them. His whole Administration had been blunder.

He said the Opposition had been so feeble and incompetent hitherto that it was Time to make vigorous Exertions.

Mrs. Shippen is a religious and a reasoning Lady. She said she had often thought, that the People of Boston could not have behaved through their Tryals, with so much Prudence and firmness at the same Time, if they had not been influenced by a Superiour Power.

Mr. Lee think's that to strike at the Navigation Acts would unite every Man in Britain against us, because the Kingdom could not exist without them, and the Advantages they derive from these Regulations and Restrictions of our Trade, are an ample Compensation for all the Protection they have afforded us, or will afford us.

Dr. Witherspoon enters with great Spirit into the American Cause. He seems as hearty a Friend as any of the Natives—an animated Son of Liberty.

This Forenoon, Mr. Cæsar Rodney, of the lower Counties on Delaware River, two Mr. Tilghmans from Maryland, were introduced to us.

We went with Mr. Wm. Barrell to his Store and drank Punch and eat dryed smoaked Sprats with him, read the Papers and our Letters from Boston.

Dined with Mr. Joseph Reed the Lawyer, with Mrs. Deberdt and Mrs. Reed, Mr. Willing, Mr. Thom. Smith, Mr. De hart, and &c.

Spent the Evening at Mr. Mifflins with Lee and Harrison from Virginia, the two Rutledges, Dr. Witherspoon, Dr. Shippen, Dr. Steptoe, and another Gentleman. An elegant Supper, and We drank Sentiments till 11 O Clock. Lee and Harrison were very high. Lee had dined with Mr. Dickenson, and drank Burgundy the whole Afternoon.

Harrison gave us for a Sentiment "a constitutional Death to the Lords Bute, Mansfield and North." Paine gave us "May the Collision of british Flint and American Steel, produce that Spark of Liberty which shall illumine the latest Posterity." [2] Wisdom to Britain and Firmness to the Colonies, may Britain be wise and America free. The Friends of America throughout the World. Union of the Colonies. Unanimity to the Congress. May the Result of the Congress, answer the Expectations of the People. Union of Britain and the Colonies, on a Constitutional Foundation—and many other such Toasts.

Young Rutledge told me, he studied 3 Years at the Temple. He thinks this a great Distinction. Says he took a Volume of Notes, which J. Quincy transcribed. Says that young Gentlemen ought to travel early, because that freedom and Ease of Behaviour, which is so necessary, cannot be acquired but in early Life. This Rutledge is young—sprightly but not deep. He has the most indistinct, inarticulate Way of Speaking. Speaks through his nose—a wretched Speaker in Conversation. How he will shine in public I dont yet know. He seems good natured, tho conceited. His Lady is with him in bad Health.

His Brother still maintains the Air of Reserve, Design and Cunning—like Duane, and Galloway, and Bob Auchmuty.

Cæsar Rodney is the oddest looking Man in the World. He is tall—thin and slender as a Reed—pale—his Face is not bigger than a large Apple. Yet there is Sense and Fire, Spirit, Wit and Humour in his Countenance.

He made himself very merry with Ruggles and his pretended Scruples and Timidities, at the last Congress.

Mr. Reed told us, at dinner, that he never saw greater Joy, than he saw in London when the News arrived that the Nonimportation agreement was broke. They were universally shaking Hands and Congratulating each other.

He says that George Haley is the worst Enemy to America that he knew there—swore to him that he would stand by Government in all its Measures, and was allways censuring and cursing America.

[1] William Lee, a Virginia merchant in London and a follower of John Wilkes, was in 1773 elected a sheriff of London (DAB).

[2] Closing quotation mark editorially supplied. It would seem a fair assumption that the "Sentiments" which follow were not offered by Paine exclusively but by various members of the party.

1774. SEPTR. 4. SUNDAY.[1]

Went to the Presbyterian Meeting and heard Mr. Sprout in the forenoon. He uses no Notes—dont appear to have any. Opens his Bible and talks away. Not a very numerous, nor very polite Assembly.

Dined at our Lodgings at Mrs. Yards, with Major De boor[2] a French Gentleman, a Soldier, Mr. Webb, and another.

Went in the Afternoon to Christ Church, and heard Mr. Coombs [Coombe]. This is a more noble Building, and a genteeler Congregation. The Organ and a new Choir of Singers, were very musical. Mr. Coombs is celebrated here as a fine Speaker. He is sprightly, has a great deal of Action, speaks distinctly. But I confess, I am not charmed with his oratory. His Style was indifferent, his Method, confused. In one Word, his Composition was vastly inferiour to the ordinary Sermons of our How, Hunt, Chauncey, Cooper, Elliot, and even Stillman. Mr. Mifflin spent the Sunday Evening with Us, at our Lodgings.

[1] First regular entry in JA's Diary booklet "No. 22" (our D/JA/22), a gathering of leaves stitched into a marbled paper cover and containing entries through 9 Nov. 1774.

[2] CFA corrects to "De Bure," but apparently simply by conjecture. This officer remains unidentified.

1774. SEPTR. 5. MONDAY.

At Ten, The Delegates all met at the City Tavern, and walked to the Carpenters Hall, where they took a View of the Room, and of the Chamber where is an excellent Library. There is also a long Entry, where Gentlemen may walk, and a convenient Chamber opposite to the Library. The General Cry was, that this was a good Room, and the Question was put, whether We were satisfyed with this Room, and it passed in the Affirmative. A very few were for the Negative and they were chiefly from Pensylvania and New York.[1]

Then Mr. Lynch arose, and said there was a Gentleman present who had presided with great Dignity over a very respectable Society, greatly to the Advantage of America, and he therefore proposed that the Hon. Peytoun Randolph Esqr., one of the Delegates from Virginia, and the late Speaker of their House of Burgesses, should be appointed Chairman and he doubted not it would be unanimous.—The Question was put and he was unanimously chosen.

Mr. Randolph then took the Chair, and the Commissions of the Delegates were all produced and read.[2]

Then Mr. Lynch proposed that Mr. Charles Thompson a Gentleman of Family, Fortune, and Character in this City should be appointed Secretary, which was accordingly done without opposition, tho Mr. Duane and Mr. Jay discovered at first an Inclination to seek further.[3]

Mr. Duane then moved that a Committee should be appointed, to prepare Regulations for this Congress. Several Gentlemen objected. I then arose and asked Leave of the President to request of the Gentleman from New York, an Explanation, and that he would point out some particular Regulations which he had in his Mind. He mentioned particularly the Method of voting—whether it should be by Colonies, or by the Poll, or by Interests.

Mr. Henry then arose, and said this was the first general Congress which had ever happened—that no former Congress could be a Precedent—that We should have occasion for more general Congresses, and therefore that a precedent ought to be established now. That it would be great Injustice, if a little Colony should have the same Weight in the Councils of America, as a great one, and therefore he was for a Committee.

Major Sullivan observed that a little Colony had its All at Stake as well as a great one.

This is a Question of great Importance.—If We vote by Colonies, this Method will be liable to great Inequality and Injustice, for 5 small Colonies, with 100,000 People in each may outvote 4 large ones, each of which has 500,000 Inhabitants. If We vote by the Poll, some Colonies have more than their Proportion of Members, and others have less. If We vote by Interests, it will be attended with insuperable Difficulties, to ascertain the true Importance of each Colony.—Is the Weight of a Colony to be ascertained by the Number of Inhabitants merely—or by the Amount of their Trade, the Quantity of their Exports and Imports, or by any compound Ratio of both. This will lead us into such a Field of Controversy as will greatly perplex us. Besides I question whether it is possible to ascertain, at this Time, the Numbers of our

People or the Value of our Trade. It will not do in such a Case, to take each other's Words. It ought to be ascertained by authentic Evidence, from Records.[4]

[1] "The City have offered us the Carpenters Hall, so called, to meet in, and Mr. Galloway offers the State House and insists on our meeting there, which he says he has a right to offer as Speaker of that House. The last is evidently the best place, but as *he* offers, the other party oppose" (Silas Deane to Mrs. Deane [1–3 Sept. 1774], Burnett, ed., *Letters of Members*, 1:4–5; see also p. 8–10).

Carpenters' Hall was so new that some details in it were not yet completed. The second floor had, however, been rented and occupied by the Library Company of Philadelphia since 1773. The most authoritative historical and descriptive account of Carpenters' Hall is by Charles E. Peterson, in *Historic*

Philadelphia (Amer. Philos. Soc., *Trans.*, 43 [1953]:96–128), which is copiously illustrated.

[2] Printed in full in *JCC*, 1:15–24. The North Carolina delegates had not yet come in, and Georgia sent no delegates to the first Continental Congress.

[3] For an account of Thomson's assumption of his duties, supposedly written by Thomson himself, see Burnett, ed., *Letters of Members*, 1:10, note. Galloway's unhappy comments on the selection of both the meeting place and the secretary are in his letter of this date to Gov. William Franklin (*Archives of the State of New Jersey*, 1st ser., 10 [1886]: 477–478).

[4] This speech was unquestionably made by JA himself.

1774. SEPTR. 6. TUESDAY.

Went to congress again. Received by an express an Intimation of the Bombardment of Boston—a confused account, but an alarming one indeed.—God grant it may not be found true.[1]

[1] R. T. Paine's Diary (MHi) has this account under this date:

"About 2 o Clock a Letter came from Israel Putnam into Town forwarded by Expresses in about 70 hours from Boston, by which we were informed that the Soldiers had fired on the People and Town at Boston, this news occasioned the Congress to adjourn to 8 o Clock PM. The City of Phila. in great Concern, Bells muffled rang all PM."

This alarm sprang from the bloodless seizure by Gage's troops, in the early

hours of 1 Sept., of powder stored in a public magazine in that part of Charlestown which is now Somerville, bordering Cambridge (*Commonwealth Hist. of Mass.*, 2:548; see entry of 8 Sept., below). The whole countryside from Boston almost to New York City was roused by the report, and the ever-curious Ezra Stiles made an elaborate and valuable investigation of the spread of the false rumor of bloodshed (Stiles, *Literary Diary*, 1:477–485). See also entry of 6 Nov., below.

[NOTES OF DEBATES IN THE CONTINENTAL CONGRESS, 6 SEPTEMBER 1774.][1]

Mr. Henry. Government is dissolved. Fleets and Armies and the present State of Things shew that Government is dissolved.—Where are your Land Marks? your Boundaries of Colonies.

We are in a State of Nature, Sir. I did propose that a Scale should be laid down. That Part of N. America which was once Mass. Bay, and that Part which was once Virginia, ought to be considered as having a Weight. Will not People complain, 10,000 ⟨People⟩ Virginians have not outweighed 1000 others.

I will submit however. I am determined to submit if I am overruled.

A worthy Gentleman (Ego)[2] near me, seemed to admit the Necessity of obtaining a more Adequate Representation.

I hope future Ages will quote our Proceedings with Applause. It is one of the great Duties of the democratical Part of the Constitution to keep itself pure. It is known in my Province, that some other Colonies are not so numerous or rich as they are. I am for giving all the Satisfaction in my Power.

The Distinctions between Virginians, Pensylvanians, New Yorkers and New Englanders, are no more.

I am not a Virginian, but an American.

Slaves are to be thrown out of the Question, and if the freemen can be represented according to their Numbers I am satisfyed.

Mr. Lynch. I differ in one Point from the Gentleman from Virginia, that is in thinking that Numbers only ought to determine the Weight of Colonies. I think that Property ought to be considered, and that it ought to be a compound of Numbers and Property, that should determine the Weight of the Colonies.

I think it cannot be now settled.

Mr. Rutledge. We have no legal Authority and Obedience to our Determinations will only follow the reasonableness, the apparent Utility, and Necessity of the Measures We adopt. We have no coercive or legislative Authority. Our Constitutents are bound only in Honour, to observe our Determinations.

Govr. Ward. There are a great Number of Counties in Virginia, very unequal in Point of Wealth and Numbers, yet each has a Right to send 2 Members.

Mr. Lee. But one Reason, which prevails with me, and that is that we are not at this Time provided with proper Materials. I am afraid We are not.

Mr. Gadsden. I cant see any Way of voting but by Colonies.

Coll. Bland. I agree with the Gentleman (Ego)[3] who spoke near me, that We are not at present provided with Materials to ascertain the Importance of each Colony. The Question is whether the Rights and Liberties of America shall be contended for, or given up to arbitrary Power.

Mr. Pendleton. If the Committee should find themselves unable to ascertain the Weight of the Colonies, by their Numbers and Property, they will report this, and this will lay the Foundation for the Congress to take some other Steps to procure Evidence of Numbers and Property at some future Time.

Mr. Henry. I agree that authentic Accounts cannot be had—if by Authenticity is meant, attestations of officers of the Crown.

I go upon the Supposition, that Government is at an End. All Distinctions are thrown down. All America is all thrown into one Mass. We must aim at the Minutiæ of Rectitude.

Mr. Jay. Could I suppose, that We came to frame an American Constitution, instead of indeavouring to correct the faults in an old one— I cant yet think that all Government is at an End. The Measure of arbitrary Power is not full, and I think it must run over, before We undertake to frame a new Constitution.

To the Virtue, Spirit, and Abilities of Virginia We owe much—I should always therefore from Inclination as well as Justice, be for giving Virginia its full Weight.

I am not clear that We ought not to be bound by a Majority tho ever so small, but I only mentioned it, as a Matter of Danger, worthy of Consideration.[4]

[1] First entry in D/JA/22A, a collection of loose folded sheets of various sizes in which from time to time JA entered minutes of the debates in the first Continental Congress. These entries are mostly undated but have been inserted below under their most likely dates. Burnett, who prints the present notes in full, gives the evidence for assigning them to 6 Sept. (*Letters of Members,* 1:14–15).

[2-3] This word inserted above the line in MS. Parentheses have been supplied by the editors.

[4] Congress resolved this day that since it did not have and could not not "at present . . . procure proper materials for ascertaining the importance of each Colony," "each Colony or Province shall have one Vote" (JCC, 1:25).

1774 SEPTR. 7. WEDNESDAY.

Went to congress again. Heard Mr. Duchè read Prayers. The Collect for the day, the 7th of the Month, was most admirably adapted, tho this was accidental, or rather Providential. A Prayer, which he gave us of his own Composition, was as pertinent, as affectionate, as sublime, as devout, as I ever heard offered up to Heaven. He filled every Bosom present.[1]

Dined with Mr. Miers Fisher, a young Quaker and a Lawyer. We saw his Library, which is clever.

But this plain Friend, and his plain, tho pretty Wife, with her Thee's and Thou's, had provided us the most Costly Entertainment— Ducks, Hams, Chickens, Beef, Pigg, Tarts, Creams, Custards, Gellies, fools, Trifles, floating Islands, Beer, Porter, Punch, Wine and a long &c.

We had a large Collection of Lawyers, at Table. Mr. Andrew Allen, the Attorney General, a Mr. Morris, the Prothonotary, Mr. Fisher, Mr. McKean, Mr. Rodney—besides these We had Mr. Reed, Govr. Hopkins and Governor Ward.

We had much Conversation upon the Practice of Law, in our different Provinces, but at last We got swallowed up, in Politicks, and the great Question of Parliamentary Jurisdiction. Mr. Allen asks me, from whence do you derive your Laws? How do you intitle yourselves to English Priviledges? Is not Lord Mansfield on the Side of Power?

[1] This dramatic performance by Jacob Duché, assistant rector of Christ Church and St. Peter's in Philadelphia, following as it did the as yet uncontradicted rumor of the bombardment of Boston, had a profound effect on many besides JA; see Burnett, ed., *Letters of Members*, 1:19, and references there. What JA called the "Collect" was the thirty-fifth Psalm. JA wrote home at some length about the sensation produced by the eloquence of Duché, who, however, became a loyalist in 1777 and achieved notoriety by urging George Washington to have the Declaration of Independence withdrawn (JA to AA, 16 Sept. 1774, Adams Papers; printed in *Works*, 2:368, note; *DAB*, under Duché).

1774. SEPTR. 8. THURSDAY.

Attended my Duty on the Committee all Day, and a most ingenious, entertaining Debate We had.[1] —The happy News was bro't us, from Boston, *that no Blood had been spill'd* but that Gen. Gage had taken away the Provincial Powder from the Magazine at Cambridge. This last was a disagreable Circumstance.

Dined at Mr. Powells, with Mr. Duchè, Dr. Morgan, Dr. Steptoe, Mr. Goldsborough, Mr. Johnson, and many others.—A most sinfull Feast again! Every Thing which could delight the Eye, or allure the Taste, Curds and Creams, Jellies, Sweet meats of various sorts, 20 sorts of Tarts, fools, Trifles, floating Islands, whippd Sillabubs &c. &c.— Parmesan Cheese, Punch, Wine, Porter, Beer &c. &c.

At Evening We climbed up the Steeple of Christ Church, with Mr. Reed, from whence We had a clear and full View of the whole City and of Delaware River.

[1] On the 6th Congress voted to appoint a committee "to State the rights of the Colonies in general, the several instances in which these rights are violated or infringed, and the means most proper to be pursued for obtaining a restoration of them" (JCC, 1:26). This committee was named on the 7th and consisted of two delegates from each colony, those from Massachusettts being the two Adamses (same, p. 27–28). Its deliberations are reported by JA from time to time in entries and minutes of debates, beginning this day, below; see especially a note on the entry of 14 Oct., the day on which a "Declaration of Rights" was adopted.

Diary of John Adams

In the Committee for States Rights,[2] Grievances and Means of Redress.

Coll. Lee. The Rights are built on a fourfold foundation—on Nature, on the british Constitution, on Charters, and on immemorial Usage. The Navigation Act, a Capital Violation.

Mr. Jay. It is necessary to recur to the Law of Nature, and the british Constitution to ascertain our Rights.

The Constitution of G.B. will not apply to some of the Charter Rights.

A Mother Country surcharged with Inhabitants, they have a Right to emigrate. It may be said, if We leave our Country, We cannot leave our Allegiance. But there is no Allegiance without Protection. And Emigrants have a Right, to erect what Government they please.

Mr. J. Rutledge. An Emigrant would not have a Right to set up what constitution they please. A Subject could not alienate his Allegiance.

Lee. Cant see why We should not lay our Rights upon the broadest Bottom, the Ground of Nature. Our Ancestors found here no Government.

Mr. Pendleton. Consider how far We have a Right to interfere, with Regard to the Canada Constitution.

If the Majority of the People there should be pleased with the new Constitution, would not the People of America and of England have a Right to oppose it, and prevent such a Constitution being established in our Neighbourhood.

Lee. It is contended that the Crown had no Right to grant such Charters as it has to the Colonies—and therefore We shall rest our Rights on a feeble foundation, if we rest em only on Charters—nor will it weaken our Objections to the Canada Bill.

Mr. Rutledge. Our Claims I think are well founded on the british Constitution, and not on the Law of Nature.

Coll. Dyer. Part of the Country within the Canada Bill, is a conquered Country, and part not. It is said to be a Rule that the King can give a Conquered Country what Law he pleases.

Mr. Jay. I cant think the british Constitution inseperably attached to the Person of every Subject. Whence did the Constitution derive its Authority? From compact. Might not that Authority be given up by Compact.

Mr. Wm. Livingston. A Corporation cannot make a Corporation. Charter Governments have done it. K[ing] cant appoint a Person to make a Justice of Peace. All Governors do it. Therefore it will not do for America to rest wholly on the Laws of England.

Mr. Sherman. The Ministry contend, that the Colonies are only like Corporations in England, and therefore subordinate to the Legislature of the Kingdom.—The Colonies not bound to the King or Crown by the Act of Settlement, but by their consent to it.

There is no other Legislative over the Colonies but their respective Assemblies.

The Colonies adopt the common Law, not as the common Law, but as the highest Reason.

Mr. Duane. Upon the whole for grounding our Rights on the Laws and Constitution of the Country from whence We sprung, and Charters, without recurring to the Law of Nature—because this will be a feeble Support. Charters are Compacts between the Crown and the People and I think on this foundation the Charter Governments stand firm.

England is Governed by a limited Monarchy and free Constitution.

Priviledges of Englishmen were inherent, their Birthright and Inheritance, and cannot be deprived of them, without their Consent.

Objection. That all the Rights of Englishmen will make us independent.

I hope a Line may be drawn to obviate this Objection.

James was against Parliaments interfering with the Colonies. In the Reign of Charles 2d. the Sentiments of the Crown seem to have been changed. The Navigation Act was made. Massachusetts denied the Authority—but made a Law to inforce it in the Colony.

Lee. Life and Liberty, which is necessary for the Security of Life, cannot be given up when We enter into Society.

Mr. Rutledge. The first Emigrants could not be considered as in a State of Nature—they had no Right to elect a new King.

Mr. Jay. I have always withheld my Assent from the Position that every Subject discovering Land [does so] [3] for the State to which they belong.

Mr. Galloway. I never could find the Rights of Americans, in the Distinctions between Taxation and Legislation, nor in the Distinction between Laws for Revenue and for the Regulation of Trade. I have looked for our Rights in the Laws of Nature—but could not find them in a State of Nature, but always in a State of political Society.

I have looked for them in the Constitution of the English Government, and there found them. We may draw them from this Soursce securely.

Power results from the Real Property, of the Society.

The States of Greece, Macedon, Rome, were founded on this Plan. None but Landholders could vote in the Comitia, or stand for Offices.

English Constitution founded on the same Principle. Among the Saxons the Landholders were obliged to attend and shared among them the Power. In the Norman Period the same. When the Landholders could not all attend, the Representation of the freeholders, came in. Before the Reign of H[enry] 4., an Attempt was made to give the Tenants in Capite a Right to vote. Magna Charta. Archbishops, Bishops, Abbots, Earls and Barons and Tenants in Capite held all the Lands in England.

It is of the Essence of the English Constitution, that no Law shall be binding, but such as are made by the Consent of the Proprietors in England.

How then did it stand with our Ancestors, when they came over here? They could not be bound by any Laws made by the British Parliament—excepting those made before. I never could see any Reason to allow that we are bound to any Law made since—nor could I ever make any Distinction between the Sorts of Laws.

I have ever thought We might reduce our Rights to one. An Exemption from all Laws made by British Parliament, made since the Emigration of our Ancestors. It follows therefore that all the Acts of Parliament made since, are Violations of our Rights.

These Claims are all defensible upon the Principles even of our Enemies—Ld. North himself when he shall inform himself of the true Principles of the Constitution, &c.

I am well aware that my Arguments tend to an Independency of the Colonies, and militate against the Maxim that there must be some absolute Power to draw together all the Wills and strength of the Empire.[4]

[1] From JA's separate sheets of minutes of debates (D/JA/22A).

[2] Thus in MS, but surely an inadvertence and a very curious one. CFA silently corrected the phrase to read: "stating rights. . . ." The committee had been appointed "to State the rights of the Colonies in general," &c.

[3] Editorial conjecture for an omission in the MS.

[4] Compare the language and arguments in Galloway's pamphlet, printed prior to the sitting of the Congress but not published, entitled *Arguments on Both Sides in the Dispute between Great-Britain and Her Colonies*, reprinted in *Archives of the State of New Jersey*, 1st ser., 10 (1886):478–492, especially p. 484 ff.; and see Julian P. Boyd, *Anglo-American Union: Joseph Galloway's Plans to Preserve the British Empire, 1774–1788*, Phila., 1941, p. 33–34. Brief as they are, JA's notes show that Galloway's speech in committee was a

summary of his arguments carefully prepared earlier. See also JA's notes on

Galloway's speech in Congress, 28 Sept., below.

1774 SEPTR. 9. FRYDAY.

Attended my Duty upon Committees.[1] Dined at home.

[1] "*9th.* The Committee met, agreed to found our rights upon the laws of Nature, the principles of the English Constitution, and charters and compacts; ordered a Sub-Committee to draw up a Statement of Rights" (Samuel Ward, Diary, Burnett, ed., *Letters of Members,*

1:27). JA was a member of the sub-committee, whose proceedings he later described at some length but not entirely accurately in his Autobiography. See also Ward's Diary entry of 10 Sept., Burnett, ed., *Letters of Members,* 1:28.

1774 SEPTR. 10. SATURDAY.

Attended my Duty upon the Sub Committee. Dined at home. Dr. Morgan, Dr. Cocks [Cox?], Mr. Spence [Spencer?], and several other Gentlemen, Major Sullivan and Coll. Folsom dined with us upon Salt Fish. Rambled in the Evening with Jo. Reed, and fell into Mr. Sprouts Meeting where We heard Mr. Spence preach.

Mr. Reed returned with Mr. Adams and me to our Lodgings, and a very social, agreable and communicative Evening We had.

He says We never were guilty of a more Masterly Stroke of Policy, than in moving that Mr. Duchè might read Prayers, it has had a very good Effect, &c. He says the Sentiments of People here, are growing more and more favourable every day.

1774. SEPTR. 11. SUNDAY.

There is such a quick and constant Succession of new Scenes, Characters, Persons, and Events turning up before me that I cant keep any regular Account.

This Mr. Reed is a very sensible and accomplished Lawyer of an amiable Disposition—soft, tender, friendly, &c. He is a friend to his Country and to Liberty.

Mr. Reed was so kind as to wait on us to Mr. Sprouts Meeting, where we heard Mr. Spencer. These Ministers all preach without Notes.

We had an Opportunity of seeing the Custom of the Presbyterians in administering the Sacrament. The Communicants all came to a Row of Seats, placed on each Side of a narrow Table spread in the Middle of the Alley reaching from the Deacons Seat to the front of the House. Three setts of Persons of both sexes, came in Succession. Each new sett had the Bread and the Cup given to them by a new

Minister—Mr. Sprout first, Mr. Treat next and Mr. Spencer last. Each Communicant has a token, which he delivers to the Deacons or Elders, I dont know which they call em.

As We came out of Meeting a Mr. Webster join'd us, who has just come from Boston, and has been a generous Benefactor to it, in its Distresses. He says he was at the Town Meeting, and he thinks they managed their Affairs with great Symplicity, Moderation, and Discretion.[1]

Dined at Mr. Willings, who is a Judge of the Supream Court here, with the Gentlemen from Virginia, Maryland and New York. A most splendid Feast again—Turtle and every Thing else.

Mr. Willing told us a Story of a Lawyer here, who the other Day, gave him upon the Bench the following Answer, to a Question Why the Lawyers were so increased.

"You ask me why Lawyers so much are increas'd
Tho most of the Country already are fleec'd
The Reason I'm sure is most strikingly plain
The Sheep are oft sheered yet the Wool grows again
And tho you may think e'er so odd of the Matter
The oft'ner they're fleeced, the Wool grows the better
Thus downy-chin'd Boys as oft I have heard
By frequently shaving obtain a large Beard."

By Mr. Peters, written at the Bar and given to a Judge Mr. Willing, who had asked the Question at Dinner, in Pleasantry.

Mr. Willing is the most sociable, agreable Man of all. He told us of a Law of this Place, that whereas oysters, between the Months of May and Septr. were found to be unwholesome food, if any were brought to Markett they should be forfeited and given to the Poor.

We drank Coffee, and then Reed, Cushing and I strolled, to the Moravian Evening Lecture where we heard soft, sweet Music and a dutchified english Prayer and Preachment.

[1] JA's informant was evidently Pelatiah Webster, a Philadelphia merchant and writer on finance and political economy (*DAB*). In the Boston town meeting of 30 Aug. various projects were discussed and approved "for employing the Poor" who were "now out of Business by the Operation of the Port Bill" (Boston Record Commissioners, *18th Report*, p. 188–189).

1774. SEPTR. 12. MONDAY.

Attended my Duty on the Committee, untill one O Clock, and then went with my Colleagues and Messrs. Thompson and Mifflin to the Falls of Schuylkill, and viewed the Museum at Fort St. Davids, a great

Collection of Curiosities.[1] Returned and dined with Mr. Dickinson at his Seat at Fair Hill, with his Lady, Mrs. Thompson, Miss Norris and Miss Harrison. Mr. Dickinson has a fine Seat, a beautyfull Prospect, of the City, the River and the Country—fine Gardens, and a very grand Library. The most of his Books, were collected by Mr. Norris, once Speaker of the House here, father of Mrs. Dickinson.[2] Mr. Dickinson is a very modest Man, and very ingenious, as well as agreable. He has an excellent Heart, and the Cause of his Country lies near it. He is full and clear for allowing to Parliament, the Regulation of Trade, upon Principles of Necessity and the mutual Interest of both Countries.

[1] The Society of Fort St. David was one of several early "fishing companies" or clubs, with a house near the Falls of Schuylkill. Its site and pre-Revolutionary "Museum," which consisted principally of Indian antiquities, are described in a letter written in 1830 and printed in *PMHB*, 21:417-418 (Oct. 1897).

[2] There is an illustrated account of Fairhill, the Norris-Dickinson villa, in Thompson Westcott, *The Historic Mansions and Buildings of Philadelphia*, Phila., 1877, p. 481 ff. The estate lay between the Frankford and Germantown Roads, north of the city. R. T. Paine, who was one of the party, described it as "a convenient, decent, elegant Philosophical Rural Retreat" (Diary, MHi, 12 Sept. 1774).

1774. SEPTR. 13. TUESDAY.

Attended my Duty all Day, on the Sub Committee. Agreed on a Report.[1]

1. and 2. Phil. and Mary. C. 10. ss. 7.[2]

[1] To the full committee on stating the rights of the Colonies, &c. See the following entry and note 2 there.

[2] The statute cited in this detached note is "An Acte wherby certayne Offences bee made Tresons," 1554-1555, of which the 7th section is a "General Saving" or exemption: "Saving to every P[er]son and P[er]sones Bodyes Politike and Corporate their heires and successours, other then Thoffendours and their heires and suche P[er]son and P[er]sons as claime to any of their uses, all suche Rightes Titles Interestes Possessions [&c.], whiche they or any of them shall have at the day of the committing suche Treasons or at any tyme afore, in as large and ample maner as yf this Acte hadd never bene hadd nor made" (*The Statutes of the Realm*, London, 1810-1828, 4:257). Members of the first Continental Congress could hardly help exhibiting some interest in the British statutes relating to treason.

1774. SEPT. 14. WEDNESDAY.

Visited Mr. Gadsden, Mr. Deane, Coll. Dyer, &c. at their Lodgings. Gadsden is violent against allowing to Parliament any Power of regulating Trade, or allowing that they have any Thing to do with Us.— Power of regulating Trade he says, is Power of ruining us—as bad as acknowledging them a Supream Legislative, in all Cases whatsoever.

A Right of regulating Trade is a Right of Legislation, and a Right of Legislation in one Case, is a Right in all.—This I deny.[1]

Attended the Congress and Committee all the forenoon.[2] Dined with Dr. Cox. Dr. Morgan, Dr. Rush, Mr. Bayard, old Mr. Smith dined with us. Dr. Rush lives upon Water Street and has from the Windows of his back Room and Chamber, a fine Prospect of Delaware River, and of New Jersey beyond it. The Gentlemen entertained us, with Absurdities in the Laws of Pensylvania, New Jersey and Maryland. This I find is a genteel Topic of Conversation here.—A mighty Feast again, nothing less than the very best of Claret, Madeira, and Burgundy. Melons, fine beyond description, and Pears and Peaches as excellent.

This Day Mr. Chase introduced to us, a Mr. Carrell [Carroll] of Anapolis, a very sensible Gentleman, a Roman catholic, and of the first Fortune in America. His Income is Ten thousand Pounds sterling a Year, now, will be fourteen in two or 3 years, they say, besides his father has a vast Estate, which will be his, after his father.

[1] That is, presumably, Gadsden denies it (Parliament's right of legislating for the Colonies in any case whatever). CFA supplied quotation marks around the last three sentences in this paragraph (JA, *Works*, 2:379).

[2] Samuel Ward's Diary is more informative: "*14th*. The Sub-Committee met, and reported to the great Committee, who appointed next morning for the consideration of the report [on stating the rights of the Colonies]. A Sub-Committee appointed to state the infringements of our rights" (Burnett, ed., *Letters of Members*, 1:30). On the same day, in Congress: "The delegates from the Province of Massachusetts-bay, agreeable to a request from the joint committees of every town & district in the county of Middlesex ... communicated to the Congress the proceedings of those committees at Concord, on the 30th & 31st days of August last, which were read" (JCC, 1:31). The Middlesex Resolves were printed as a broadside (Ford, *Massachusetts Broadsides*, No. 1702; Evans 13439); text also available in Force, *Archives*, 1:750–752.

1774. SEPT. 16. FRYDAY [*i.e.* THURSDAY, 15 SEPTEMBER].[1]

Dined with Mr. Wallace, with a great deal of Company at a paultry elegant Feast again.

[1] JA clearly dated this entry one day late, since (1) R. T. Paine's Diary (MHi) records dining with "Mr. Wallace" on Thursday the 15th; and (2) Paine and other members record attending "a grand Dinner to the Congress at the State House," at which "about 500 dind at once," on Friday the 16th (same; also Burnett, ed., *Letters of Members*, 1:32). This leaves a gap in JA's record for 16 Sept. According to Samuel Ward's Diary, "*16th*. The large Committee met, resumed the business and adjourned" (Burnett, ed., *Letters of Members*, 1:32; and see note on next entry).

1774. SEPT. 17. SATURDAY.

This was one of the happiest Days of my Life. In Congress We had generous, noble Sentiments, and manly Eloquence. This Day convinced me that America will support the Massachusetts or perish with her.[1]

Dined with old Mr. Smith, with much Company. Visited the bettering House, a large Building—very clean, neat, and convenient for the Poor. Viewed the Gardens, &c.

[1] On the 16th "Paul Revere arrived Express from Boston" (R. T. Paine, Diary, MHi), bringing the "Resolutions entered into by the delegates from the several towns and districts in the county of Suffolk"—the well-known Suffolk Resolves—which, with other relevant papers, were presented to Congress by the Massachusetts delegates on the 17th, recorded in the Journal, and unanimously approved and supported in resolutions ordered to be printed (*JCC*, 1:31-40; Burnett, ed., *Letters of Members*, 1:33-35, including an extract from JA's letter to AA, 18 Sept., the original of which is in the Adams Papers).

1774. SEPTR. 18. SUNDAY.

Went to Church, and heard Mr. Coombs read Prayers, and Mr. Duchè preach. A fine Preacher, indeed. Dined at home.

Went to Dr. Allisons Meeting in the Afternoon. Heard Mr. ——— a very ingenious Preacher, of Benevolence and Humanity. Spent the Evening at home with General Lee, Capt. Dagworthy, Mr. McDougall and others. Wrote many Letters to go by Mr. Paul Revere.

1774 MONDAY SEPTR. 19.

Dined with Dr. Rush in Company with Dr. Shippen, and many others. Folsom and Sullivan from N. Hampshire. Mr. Blair &c. &c.

1774 TUESDAY SEPTR. 20.

Had Cards a Week ago to dine with Mr. Maese [Mease]—but forgot it, and dined at home. After We had dined after 4 O Clock, Mr. Maes's Brother came to our Lodgings after Us. We went, after Dinner, and found Mr. Dickinson, Mifflin, Dr. Rush, Mr. West, Mr. Biddle, and Captn. All and Mr. Maes's Brother—a very agreable Company. Our Regret at the Loss of this Company was very great.

Mr. Dickenson was very agreable.

A Question was started about the Conduct of the Bostonian Merchants since the Year 1770, in importing Tea and paying the Duty. Mr. Hancock it is said has received the Freight of many Chests of Tea. I think the Bostonian Merchants are not wholly justifiable—yet their Conduct has been exaggerated. Their fault and guilt has been magnified. Mr. Hancock I believe is justifiable, but I am not certain, whether he is strictly so. He owned a Ship in Partnership with Geo. Hayley, who is agreed here to be a ministerial Man, and Haley I suppose sent the Tea in the Ship.

1774. WEDNESDAY. SEPTR. 21.

Captn. Callender came to breakfast with Us. Coll. Dagworthy and his Brother Captn. Dagworthy breakfasted with Us. Mrs. Yard entertained Us, with Muffins, Buck Wheat Cakes and common Toast. Buckwheat is an excellent grain, and is very plenty here.—Attended Congress from 9 to after 3.[1]—Rode out of Town six Miles to Mr. Hills where we dined with Mr. Hill and Lady, Mr. Dickinson and his Lady, Mr. Thompson and his Lady, old Mr. Meredith, father of Mrs. Hill, Mr. Johnson of Maryland and Mr. Jo Reed.

[1] JA means that he attended the committee on stating the rights of the Colonies, not Congress. According to Samuel Ward's Diary, the committee met on the 19th, 20th, and 21st, while Congress adjourned from day to day, awaiting the committee's report (Burnett, ed., *Letters of Members*, 1:36, 37).

1774. THURSDAY. SEPTR. 22.

Dined with Mr. Chew, Chief Justice of the Province, with all the Gentlemen from Virginia, Dr. Shippen, Mr. Tilghman and many others. We were shewn into a grand Entry and Stair Case, and into an elegant and most magnificent Chamber, untill Dinner. About four O Clock We were called down to Dinner. The Furniture was all rich.[1]—Turttle, and every other Thing—Flummery, Jellies, Sweetmeats of 20 sorts, Trifles, Whip'd Syllabubbs, floating Islands, fools—&c., and then a Desert of Fruits, Raisins, Almonds, Pears, Peaches—Wines most excellent and admirable. I drank Madeira at a great Rate and found no Inconvenience in it.

In the Evening General Lee and Coll. Lee, and Coll. Dyer and Mr. Deane, and half a Score friends from Boston came to our Lodgings. Coll. Lee staid till 12 o Clock and was very social and agreable.[2]

[1] Presumably this was Benjamin Chew's town house, Third Street between Walnut and Spruce; not his famous country mansion still standing on Germantown Avenue.

[2] On this day "The Committee appointed to state the rights of the colonies &c." brought in a report, but consideration of it was deferred to the 24th. See entry of 8 Sept., above, and JCC, 1:42.

1774. FRYDAY. SEPT. 23.

Walked along Second Street Southward, untill I got out of the City into the Country. The Uniformity of this City is dissagreable to some.—I like it.

Dined with the late C[hief] Justice Allen—with all the Gentlemen from North Carolina, and Mr. Hambleton [Hamilton], late Governor—and Mr. Andrew Allen Attorney General.

We had much Conversation, about Mr. Franklin. The C[hief] J[ustice] and Attorney General had much droll Chat together.

1774 SATURDAY. SEPTR. 24.

Dined with Mr. Charles Thompson, with only Mr. Dickenson, his Lady and Niece in Company. A most delightfull Afternoon we had. Sweet Communion indeed we had—Mr. Dickinson gave us his Thoughts and his Correspondence very freely.

1774. SUNDAY. SEPT. 25.

Went in the Evening to Quaker Meeting and afterwards went to Supper at Stephen Collins's.

1774. MONDAY. SEPTR. 26.

Dined at old Dr. Shippens with Mr. And Mrs. Blair, young Dr. Shippen, the Jersey Delegates and some Virginians. Afterwards went to the Hospital and heard another Lecture upon Anatomy, from young Dr. Shippen.

1774. TUESDAY. SEPTR. 27.

Dined at Mr. Bayards, with Dr. Cox, Dr. Rush, Mr. Hodge, Mr. Deane, Coll. Dyer. Dr. Cox gave us a Toast "May the fair Dove of Liberty, in this Deluge of Despotism, find Rest to the Sole of her Foot in America."

[NOTES OF DEBATES IN THE CONTINENTAL CONGRESS, 26–27 SEPTEMBER 1774.][1]

Mr. Lee made a Mo[tion] for a Non Importation.

Mr. Mifflin. The 1st of Novr. ought to be fixed, for no honest orders were sent after the first of June. Orders are generally sent in April and May. But the Intention was known, of a Non Importation.

Coll. Bland. I think the Time ought to be fixed, when Goods are shipp'd in Great Britain, because a ship may have a long Voyage.

Mr. Gadsden. For the 1st of Novr.—We may be deceived and defrauded, if we fix it to the Time when Goods are shipped.

Coll. Lee. Invoices have been antedated.

Mr. John Rutledge. I think all the Ways and Means should be proposed.

Mr. Mifflin. Proposes Stoppage of Flax seed and Lumber to the West

Indies—and Non Importation of dutied Articles—to commence 1st. Aug. 1775.

Mr. Chace [Chase]. Force, I apprehend is out of the Question, in our present Enquiry.

In 1770, the annual Tax was 13 millions. Last Year it was only 10 millions.

Land Tax, Malt Tax, perpetual Funds, amount to only 10 millions. They are compelled to raise 10 millions in time of Peace.

The Emigrations from G. Britain prove that they are taxed as far as they can bear.

A total Non Import and Non Export to G. Britain and W. Indies must produce a national Bankruptcy, in a very short Space of Time.

The foreign Trade of G. Britain is but four Million and an half. As great a Man as ever Britain produc'd, calculated the Trade with the Colonies at two Millions. I believe the Importation to the Colonies now represented, may be three millions.

A Non Exportation amounts to 3 millions more, and the Debt due to four Million. Two thirds in the Colonies, are cloathed in British Manufactures. Non Exportation of vastly more importance than a Non Importation—it affects the Merchants as well as Manufacturers, the Trade as well as the Revenue.

60 thousand Hdds. of Tobacco—225 british Ships employed.

I am for a Non Exportation of Lumber to W. Indies immediately.

The Importance of the Trade of the West Indies to G. Britain almost exceeds Calculation.

The Sugar carries the greatest Revenue—the Rum a great deal.

If you dont stop the Lumber immediately, you cant stop it at all. If it takes Place immediately, they cant send home their next Years Crop.

A Non Exportation at a future day, cannot avail us.

What is the Situation of Boston and the Massachusetts.

A Non Exportation at the Virginia Day, will not opperate before the fall 1766 [1776].

I [It?] would not affect the Trade of the Colonies to the Mediterranean or other Parts of the World.

I am for a more distant Day than the first of November.

Mr. Linch. We want not only Redress, but speedy Redress. The Mass. cant live without Government I think one Year. Nothing less than what has been proposed, by the Gentleman last speaking, will put the Colonies in the State I wish to see them in. I believe the Parliament would grant us immediate Relief. Bankrupcy would be the Consequence if they did not.

Mr. Gadsden. By saving our own Liberties, we shall save those of the West Indies. I am for being ready, but I am not for the sword. The only Way to prevent the sword from being used is to have it ready.

'Tho the Virginians are tied up, I would be for doing it without them.

Boston and New England cant hold out—the Country will be deluged in Blood, if We dont Act with Spirit. Dont let America look at this Mountain, and let it bring forth a Mouse.

Mr. Chace. We cant come into a Non Exportation immediately without Virginia.

Mr. Cushing. For a Non Importation, Non Exportation and Non Consumption, and immediately.

Coll. Bland. It has been our Glory [*sentence unfinished*]

Mr. Hooper. We make some Tobacco. I was instructed to Protest vs. Petitioning alone.

Tar, Pitch, and Turpentine We can ship nowhere but to Great Britain. The whole of the Subsistence of the People in the Southern Parts, are from naval Stores.

G. Britain cannot do without Naval Stores, from N. Carolina.

Mr. Ed. Rutledge. A Gentleman from the other End of the Room talked of Generosity. True Equality is the only public Generosity. If Virginia raises Wheat instead of Tobacco they will not suffer. Our Rice is an enumerated Commodity. We shall therefore loose all our Trade.

I am both for Non Im and Exportation to take Place immediately.

Mr. Henry. We dont mean to hurt even our Rascalls—if We have any. I move that December may be inserted instead of November.

Mr. Jay. Negociation, suspension of Commerce, and War are the only three things. War is by general Consent to be waived at present.

I am for Negociation and suspension of Commerce.

Coll. Lee. All Considerations of Interest and Equality of Sacrifice should be laid aside.

Produce of the other Colonies, is carried to Markett, in the same Year when it is raised, even Rice.

Tobacco is not untill the next Year.

Mr. Sullivan. We export Masts, Boards, Plank, Fish, Oil and some Potash. Ships, we load with Lumber for the West Indies, and thence carry Sugar to England and pay our Debts that Way.

Every kind of Lumber, We export to West Indies.

Our Lumber is made in Winter. Our Ships sale in Jany. or Feby. for W. Indies.

Coll. Dyer. They have now drawn the Sword, in order to execute their Plan, of subduing America. And I imagine they will not sheath it, but that next Summer will decide the Fate of America.

To withdraw all Commerce with Great Britain at once, would come upon them like a Thunder Clap. By what I heard Yesterday, G. Britain is much more in our Power, than I expected—the Masts from the Northward—the Naval Stores from N. Carolina.

We are struggling for the Liberties of the West Indies and of the People of G. Britain as well as our own—and perhaps of Europe.

Stopping the Flax Seed to Ireland would greatly distress 'em.

Govr. Ward.

Mr. Cushing. Whoever considers the present State of G. Britain and America must see the Necessity of spirited Measures. G.B. has drawn the sword against Us, and nothing prevents her sheathing it in our Bowells but Want of Sufficient Force.

I think it absolutely necessary to agree to a Non Importation Non Exportation immediately.[1]

[1] This entry is from JA's loose sheets of minutes of debates (D/JA/22A). Though undated, it clearly pertains to the discussion of "the means most proper to be pursued for a restoration of our rights," first taken up in Congress on Saturday, 24 Sept., resumed on Monday and Tuesday the 26th and 27th, when a resolution was unanimously adopted not to import or consume British goods "from and after" 1 Dec. 1774, though the details remained to be worked out. Several more days were required to reach an agreement not to export goods to Great Britain and the West Indies. This was voted on 30 Sept., but for the benefit of the southern Colonies it was not to go into effect for a year. The present minutes obviously belong to the first stage of the debate, and since they cover two successive days must pertain to speeches made on 26–27 Sept. See JCC, 1:42–43, 51–52; Burnett, ed., *Letters of Members*, 1:48; also JA's Notes under 6? Oct., below.

1774. WEDNESDAY. SEPT. 28.

Dined with Mr. R. Penn. A magnificent House, and a most splendid Feast, and a very large Company.[1] Mr. Dickinson and General Lee were there, and Mr. Moiland [Moylan], besides a great Number of the Delegates.—Spent the Evening at Home, with Coll. Lee, Coll. Washington and Dr. Shippen who came in to consult with us.[2]

[1] The house of Richard Penn, grandson of the founder of Pennsylvania, was on the south side of High (later Market) Street between Fifth and Sixth. It became the headquarters of Sir William Howe during the British occupation of Philadelphia and of Benedict Arnold while military governor of the city; after the Revolution it was the residence of Robert Morris, who largely rebuilt it after a fire. Considered "the best *Single house* in the City," it was acquired by the City Corporation to serve as an executive mansion when Congress moved to Philadelphia in 1790, and was consequently the Philadelphia home of President and Mrs. Washington, 1790–1797, and of President and Mrs. Adams, 1797–1800. See an illustrated article by Harold D. Eberlein, "190, High Street (Market

Street below Sixth)," Amer. Philos. Soc., *Trans.*, 43 (1953):161–178.

² George Washington's Diary has the following entry under this day: "Dined at Mr. Edward Shippen's. Spent the afternn. with the Boston Gentn." (*The Diaries of George Washington*, ed. John C. Fitzpatrick, Boston and N.Y., 1925, 2:165). To this first intimate contact between JA and his fellow delegates on the one hand, and the silent member from Virginia on the other, much has been attributed, probably justly. With little doubt it markedly influenced Washington's view of the conduct of the leaders of the patriotic movement in Massachusetts. See Washington's letter to Robert Mackenzie, a British officer in Boston, 9 Oct. 1774 (*Writings*, ed., Fitzpatrick, 3:244–247), and a communication by CFA on the background of Washington's nomination as commander in chief, in MHS, *Procs.*, 1st ser., 4 (1858–1860):68–75.

[NOTES OF DEBATES IN THE CONTINENTAL CONGRESS, 28 SEPTEMBER 1774.][1]

Mr. Galloway. The Proposal I intended to make having been opposed, I have waited to hear a more effectual one. A general Non Importation from G. Britain and Ireland has been adopted, but I think this will be too gradual in its Operation for the Relief of Boston.

A General Non Exportation, I have ever looked on as an indigested Proposition. It is impossible America can exist, under a total Non Exportation. We in this Province should have tens of Thousands of People thrown upon the cold Hand of Charity.—Our Ships would lie by the Walls, our Seamen would be thrown out of Bread, our Shipwrights &c. out of Employ and it would affect the landed Interest. It would weaken us in another Struggle which I fear is too near.

To explain my Plan I must state a Number of facts relative to Great Britain, and relative to America.

I hope no facts which I shall state will be disagreable.

In the last War, America was in the greatest Danger of Destruction. This was held up by the Massa[chusetts] and by the Congress in 1754. They said We are disunited among ourselves. Their is no indifferent Arbiter between us.

Requisitions came over. A No. of the Colonies gave most extensively and liberally, other[s] gave nothing, or late. Pensylvania gave late, not for Want of Zeal or Loyalty, but owing to their Disputes, with Proprietors—their disunited State.

These Delinquencies were handed up to the Parent State, and these gave Occasion to the Stamp Act.

America with the greatest Reason and Justice complained of the Stamp Act.

Had they proposed some Plan of Policy—some Negociation but set afoot, it would have terminated in the most happy Harmony between the two Countries.

They repealed the Stamp Act, but they passed the declaratory Act.

Without some Supream Legislature, some common Arbiter, you are not, say they, part of the State.

I am as much a friend of Liberty [as] exists—and No Man shall go further, in Point of Fortune, or in Point of Blood, than the Man who now addresses you.

Burlamaqui, Grotius, Puffendorf, Hooker.—There must be an Union of Wills and Strength. Distinction between a State and a Multitude. A State is animated by one Soul.

As We are not within the Circle of the Supream Jurisdiction of the Parliament, We are independent States. The Law of Great Britain dont bind us in any Case whatever.

We want the Aid and Assistance and Protection of the Arm of our Mother Country. Protection And Allegiance are reciprocal Duties. Can We lay claim to the Money and Protection of G. Britain upon any Principles of Honour or Conscience? Can We wish to become Aliens to the Mother State.

We must come upon Terms with G. Britain.

Some Gentlemen are not for Negociation. I wish I could hear some Reason against it.

The Minister must be at 20, or 30 millions [expense]² to inforce his Measures.

I propose this Proposition. The Plan.—2 Classes of Laws. 1. Laws of Internal Policy. 2. Laws in which more than one Colony were concerned, raising Money for War.—No one Act can be done, without the Assent of Great Britain.—No one without the Assent of America. A British American Legislature.

Mr. Duane. As I mean to second this Motion, I think myself bound to lay before the Congress my Reasons. N. York thought it necessary to have a Congress for the Relief of Boston and Mass.—and to do more, to lay a Plan for a lasting Accommodation with G. Britain.

Whatever may have been the Motive for departing from the first Plan of the Congress, I am unhappy that We have departed from it.— The Post Office Act was before the Year 1763.—Can we expect lasting Tranquility. I have given my full Assent to a Non Im and Exportation Agreement.

The Right of regulating Trade, from the local Circumstances of the Colonies, and their Disconnection with each other, cannot be exercised by the Colonies.

Mass. disputed the Navigation Act, because not represented, but made a Law of their own, to inforce that Act.

Virginia did the same nearly.

I think Justice requires that we should expressly ceed to Parliament the Right of regulating Trade.

In the Congress in 1754 which consisted of the greatest and best Men in the Colonies, this was considered as indispensable.

A civil War with America, would involve a national Bankruptcy.

Coll. Lee. How did We go on for 160 Years before the Year 1763? —We flourished and grew.

This Plan would make such Changes in the Legislatures of the Colonies that I could not agree to it, without consulting my Constituents.

Mr. Jay. I am led to adopt this Plan.

It is objected that this Plan will alter our Constitutions and therefore cannot be adopted without consulting Constituents.

Does this Plan give up any one Liberty?—or interfere with any one Right.

Mr. Henry. The original Constitution of the Colonies, was founded on the broadest and most generous Base.

The Regulation of Our Trade, was Compensation enough for all the Protection we ever experienced from her.

We shall liberate our Constituents from a corrupt House of Commons, but thro them into the Arms of an American Legislature that may be bribed by that Nation which avows in the Face of the World, that Bribery is a Part of her System of Government.

Before We are obliged to pay Taxes as they do, let us be as free as they. Let us have our Trade open with all the World.

We are not to consent by the Representatives of Representatives.

I am inclined to think the present Measures lead to War.

Mr. Ed. Rutledge. I came with an Idea of getting a Bill of Rights, and a Plan of permanent Relief.

I think the Plan may be freed from almost every objection. I think it almost a perfect Plan.

Mr. Galloway. In every Government, Patriarchal, Monarchical, Aristocratical or democratical, there must be a Supream Legislature.

I know of no American Constitution. A Virginia Constitution, a Pensylvanian Constitution We have. We are totally independent of each other.

Every Gentleman here thinks, that Parliament ought to have the Power over Trade, because Britain protects it and us.

Why then will we not declare it.

Because Parliament and Ministry is wicked, and corrupt and will take Advantage of such Declaration to tax us—and will also Reason from this Acknowledgment, to further Power over us.

Answer. We shall not be bound further than We acknowledge it.

Is it not necessary that the Trade of the Empire should be regulated by some Power or other? Can the Empire hold together, without it.—No.—Who shall regulate it? Shall the Legislature of Nova Scotia, or Georgia, regulate it? Mass. or Virginia? Pensylvania or N. York. It cant be pretended. Our Legislative Powers extend no farther than the Limits of our Governments. Where then shall it be placed. There is a Necessity that an American Legislature should be set up, or else that We should give the Power to Parliament or King.

Protection.—Acquiescence. Mass. Virginia.

Advantages derived from our Commerce.

[1] From JA's loose sheets of minutes of debates (D/JA/22A). The speech by Galloway proposing a plan for a union between Great Britain and the Colonies, here minuted by JA, was published by Galloway himself in his pamphlet, *Historical and Political Reflections on the Rise and Progress of the American Rebellion*, London, 1780, and is reprinted from that source in JCC, 1:44–48. Julian P. Boyd has pointed out the discrepancies—inevitable under the circumstances—between the speech as minuted by JA in 1774 and as written up and published by its author in 1780 for a very different audience (*Anglo-American Union*: *Joseph Galloway's Plans to Preserve the British Empire, 1774–1788*, Phila., 1941, p. 35–36). For the plan itself and its eventual rejection by Congress (22 Oct. 1774), see JCC, 1:48–51; Burnett, ed., *Letters of Members*, 1:51–59, 80.

[2] Word omitted in MS.

1774. THURSDAY. SEPT. 29.

Dined at Home, with the Delegates from North Carolina and a No. of other Gentlemen.

1774 FRYDAY [30 SEPTEMBER].

Dined at Mr. Jonathan Smiths—Dr. Allison, Mr. Sprout and many other Gentlemen.[1]

[1] On this day Congress adopted, in principle, a nonexportation agreement, to go into effect on 10 Sept. 1775. (JCC, 1:51–52). On the same day JA introduced a series of resolves in support of Massachusetts' resistance to royal authority. Among them was one calling for an immediate cessation of exports if "Hostilities should be further pursued against that Province." These resolves are not mentioned in the Journal, but some of their language was incorporated in similar resolves adopted on 7 and 8 Oct. (same, p. 57–58). The MS of JA's motion, endorsed, apparently in the hand of Charles Thomson, "J. Adams' Motion Sept. 30th," is in the Adams Papers under that date. The text is printed in JA, *Works*, 2:391, note, which, however, omits some important matter that is canceled in the MS but will be printed in Series III of the present work.

[NOTES ON MEASURES TO BE TAKEN UP BY CONGRESS, SEPTEMBER–OCTOBER 1774.][1]

Non Importation, Non Consumption, Non Exportation to Britain, and W. Indies.

Petition to the King—Address to the People of England—Address to the People of America.

Societies of Arts and Manufactures in every Colony.

A Militia Law in every Colony. Encouragement of Militia and military Skill.

Raising 500,000£ st. and 20,000 Men.

Offering to raise a sum of Money, and appropriate it to the Support of the Navy.

Sending home Agents from the Congress to negociate—and propose an American Legislature—⟨to impose⟩[2]

Petitions

1. Petition to the King.—⟨Send⟩
Agents to carry it.

2. Offers to raise Money 200,000£ say, and appropriate it to the Support of the Navy.

Agents to negotiate this—and propose an American Legislature—to lay Taxes in certain Cases and make Laws in certain others.

Addresses

3. Address to the People of England—and America—commercial Struggle

4. Societies of Arts and Manufactures, in every Colony.
Auxiliary to.[3]

5. N. Importation, N. Consumption, N. Exportation.

Preparations for War, procuring Arms and Ordnance, and military Stores

6. Raising Money and Men.

7. A Militia Law in every Colony. Encouragement of Militia and military skill.

[1] These two undated and hitherto unpublished lists are separated from each other by several intervening pages in JA's loose notes of debates in the first Continental Congress (D/JA/22A). The items in the first list (up to the subhead "Petitions" in this entry) are obviously simply rearranged in a classified form in the second, but in view of JA's clerical caprices their respective locations in the MS provide no real clues as to when they were written. It is very likely, however, that the first list was inspired by the debate "on the means most proper to be pursued for a restoration of our rights," which began on 24 Sept., was

continued on the 26th and 27th, was taken up again on 6 Oct., and from that point on was blended with plans for both an "Association" (approved 18 Oct., and signed 20 Oct.) and a "Declaration of Rights" (agreed to on 14 Oct.). See JCC, 1:42, 43, 55, 63–73, 75–81.

[The editors are indebted to Mr. Lucius Wilmerding Jr. of Princeton, N. J., for correcting their erroneous interpretation of the above document as annotated in the original edition of the present work. The two last measures in the list as first arranged could not have been JA's, and they are conciliatory rather than hostile.

The idea of colonial contributions to support the British navy was urged by James Duane in September; see Burnett, ed., *Letters of Members*, 1:39, 43. An "American Legislature" was a feature of Joseph Galloway's Plan of Union proposed and defeated on 28 Sept.; see above, p. 141–144; JCC, 1:43–51; Burnett, 1:51. Whether JA or another member proposed, or intended to propose, "Raising 500,000£ st. and 20,000 Men" is still a question.]

[2] Possibly "impress."

[3] Thus in MS. The intent of this fourth measure was included in the Association of 20 Oct. (JCC, 1:78).

1774. SATURDAY [1 OCTOBER].

Dined with Mr. Webster. Spent the Evening with Stephen Collins. Went to see the Election at the State House. Mr. Dickinson was chosen.[1]

[1] As one of the representatives of Philadelphia co. to the Pennsylvania Assembly, which in turn, 15 Oct., elected him to the Continental Congress. In a letter to AA of 7 Oct. JA wrote at some length on the favorable turn of the Pennsylvania elections for the patriotic party (Adams Papers; printed in JA-AA, *Familiar Letters*, p. 44–45).

In Congress this day JA was chosen to a committee to prepare "a loyal address to his majesty ... dutifully requesting the royal attention to the grievances that alarm and distress his majesty's faithful subjects in North-America" (JCC, 1:53; see also p. 102–104, 113, 115–122, and entry of 11 Oct., below).

1774. SUNDAY. OCTR. 2.

Went to Christ Church and heard Mr. Coombs upon "Judge not according to the Appearance, but judge righteous Judgment." Went to Mr. Sprout's in the Afternoon and heard Mr. Tenant [Tennent].

Spent the Evening at home with Mr. Macdougal, Mr. Cary of Charlestown, Mr. Reed and Coll. Floyd.

1774 MONDAY OCTR. 3. 1774.

Breakfasted at home with Coll. Dagworthy of Maryland, Captn. Dagworthy his Brother, Major De Bois, Mr. Webb, Dr. Clopton &c. The hurry of Spirits I have been in, since my Arrival in this City, has prevented my making Remarks in my Journal as I wished to have done. The quick Succession of Objects, the Variety of Scenes and Characters, have rendered it impracticable. Major De Bois says he will drink Dispute this Morning. The Congress not come to Decision, yet.

Dined at home. This Day Charles Thompson and Thos. Mifflin were chosen Burgesses for this City. The Change in the Elections for this City and County is no small Event. Mr. Dickinson and Mr. Thompson, now joined to Mr. Mifflin, will make a great Weight in favour of the American Cause.

1774 TUESDAY. OCTR. 4.

Dined with Mr. Alexander Wilcox, with all the Delegates from N. York, and several other Gentlemen.—This Evening General Lee came to my Lodgings and shewed me an Address from the C[ongress] to the People of Canada which he had.[1]

[1] It was not, however, until 21 Oct. that Congress resolved to prepare an address to the people of Quebec, which was brought in by a committee (on which JA did not serve) two days later, debated, and recommitted; a new draft was brought in, read, debated, amended, and approved on 26 Oct., the last day of the session (JCC, 1:101, 103, 105–113).

1774. WEDNESDAY OCTR. 5TH.

Dined with Dr. Cadwallador, in Company with Governor Hamilton, Gen. Lee, Mr. Henry, Mr. Pendleton, Mr. De Hart, and many others —Mr. Maese and others.—Spent the Evening at Home with Mr. McDougal, and Mr. Sherman—in sad and solemn Consultation about the Miseries and Distresses of our dear Town of Boston.

1774 THURSDAY. OCTR. 6.

Dined with Mr. Hodge, Father in Law to Mr. Bayard.

[NOTES OF DEBATES IN THE CONTINENTAL CONGRESS, 6? OCTOBER 1774.][1]

Mr. Gadsden. There are Numbers of Men who will risque their all. I shudder at the thought of the Blood which will be spilled, and would be glad to avoid it.

Mr. Pendleton. How is the Purchaser to know whether the Molosses, Sugar, or Coffee, has paid the Duty or not? It cant be known. Shant We by this hang out to all the World our Intentions to smuggle?

Don't We complain of these Acts as Grievances, and shant we insist on the Repeal.

But this will give an Advantage to the West Indians and will make it their Interest to oppose our obtaining Redress.

Coll. Dyer. This Subject as every Part of our Deliberations are important. The Q[uestion] is how far to extend the Non Importation of dutiable Articles.

Mr. Chace. I am against the Question before you.—What are the Ways and Means of obtaining Redress. In the manner it is penn'd it would not answer the End. How shall the Buyer know whether the Duties have been paid or not.

Our Enemies will think that We mean to strike at the Right of Parliament to lay duties for the Regulation of Trade.

I am one of those who hold the Position, that Parliament has a Right to make Laws for us in some Cases, to regulate the Trade—and in all Cases where the good of the whole Empire requires it.

My Fears were up when We went into the Consideration of a Bill of Rights. I was afraid We should say too little or too much.

It is said this is not a Non Importation Resolution. But it is, for there is no Importation of goods but according to the Law of the Land.

Mr. Linch. I came here to get Redress of Grievances, and to adopt every Means for that End, which could be adopted with a good Conscience.

In my Idea Parliament has no Power to regulate Trade. But these Duties are all for Revenue not for Regulation of Trade.

Many Gentlemen in this Room know how to bring in Goods, sugars and others, without paying Duties.

Will any Gentleman say he will never purchase any Goods untill he is sure, that they were not smuggled.

Mr. Mifflin. We shall Agree I suppose, to a Non Exportation of Lumber to the West Indies. They cannot send their Sugars to England, nor to America. Therefore they cant be benefited.

Mr. Low. Gentlemen have been transported by their Zeal, into Reflections upon an order of Men who deserve it the least of any Men in the Community.

We ought not to deny the just Rights of our Mother Country. We have too much Reason in this Congress, to suspect that Independency is aimed at.

I am for a Resolution against any Tea, Dutch as well as English.

[We] ought to consider the Consequences possible as well as [pro]bable of every Resolution We take and provide ourselves [with] a Retreat or Resource.[2]

[Wha]t would be the Consequence of an Adjournment of the [Con]gress for 6 months? or a Recommendation of a [new] Election of another to meet at the End of 6 Months? [Is not it] possible they may make it criminal, as Treason, [Mi]sprision of Treason, or Felony or a Præmunire? [Bo]th in the Assemblies who choose and in the Mem[bers] who shall accept the Trust.

[Wou]ld the assemblies or Members be intimidated? [Wou]ld they regard such an Act?[3]

Will, Can the People bear a total Interruption of the West India Trade? Can they live without Rum, Sugar, and Molasses? Will not their Impatience, and Vexation defeat the Measure?

This would cutt up the Revenue by the Roots—if Wine, Fruit, Molasses and Sugar, were discarded, as well as Tea.

But, a Prohibition of all Exports to the West Indies, will annihilate the Fishery—because, that cannot afford to loose the West India Fish[4] —and this would throw a Multitude of Families in our fishing Towns into the Arms of Famine.

[1] From JA's loose minutes of debates in the first Continental Congress (D/ JA/22A). Though the principles of nonimportation and nonexportation had been agreed on by the end of September, the specific terms of what came to be called the Continental Association remained subject to debate until the adoption of that paper on 18 Oct. (JCC, 1:75). From the language in a resolve of 6 Oct. (same, p. 57), it is likely though by no means certain that JA is here reporting the debates of that day.

[2] Missing words and parts of words, lost through the crumbling of the paper along one edge, have been supplied from CFA's printed text (JA, *Works*, 2:394).

[3] In the MS a substantial space follows this paragraph, which ordinarily indicates a shift from one speaker to another. The substance of the remarks that follow also suggests that a New Englander rather than a New Yorker was speaking, but the question cannot now be resolved.

[4] CFA silently but no doubt rightly altered this word to "market."

1774 FRYDAY OCTR. 7.

Dined with Mr. Thos. Smith, with a large Company, the Virginians and others.

1774 SATURDAY OCTR. 8.

Dined with Mr. George Clymer—Mr. Dickinson and a large Company again.

1774. SUNDAY [9 OCTOBER].

Went to hear Dr. Allison, an Aged Gentleman. It was Sacrament Day and he gave us a sacramental Discourse. This Dr. Allison is a Man of Abilities and Worth, but I hear no Preachers here like ours in Boston, excepting Mr. Duchè. Coombs indeed is a good Speaker, but not an original, but a Copy of Duchè.

The Multiplicity of Business and Ceremonies, and Company that we are perpetually engaged in, prevents my Writing to my Friends in Mass. as I ought, and prevents my recording many Material Things in my Journal.

Phyladelphia with all its Trade, and Wealth, and Regularity is not Boston. The Morals of our People are much better, their Manners are more polite, and agreable—they are purer English. Our Language is better, our Persons are handsomer, our Spirit is greater, our Laws are wiser, our Religion is superiour, our Education is better. We exceed them in every Thing, but in a Markett, and in charitable public foundations.

Went in the Afternoon to the Romish Chappell and heard a good discourse upon the Duty of Parents to their Children, founded in Justice and Charity. The Scenery and the Musick is so callculated to take in Mankind that I wonder, the Reformation ever succeeded. The Paintings, the Bells, the Candles, the Gold and Silver. Our Saviour on the Cross, over the Altar, at full Length, and all his Wounds a bleeding. The Chanting is exquisitely soft and sweet.[1]

[1] JA set down his reflections on this experience at greater length in a letter to AA of this date (Adams Papers; printed in JA-AA, *Familiar Letters*, p. 45–47).

1774 MONDAY. OCTR. 10TH.

The Deliberations of the Congress, are spun out to an immeasurable Length. There is so much Wit, Sense, Learning, Acuteness, Subtilty, Eloquence, &c. among fifty Gentlemen, each of whom has been habituated to lead and guide in his own Province, that an immensity of Time, is spent unnecessarily.

Johnson of Maryland has a clear and a cool Head, an extensive Knowledge of Trade, as well as Law. He is a deliberating Man, but not a shining orator—His Passions and Imagination dont appear enough for an orator. His Reason and Penetration appear, but not his Rhetoric.

Galloway, Duane, and Johnson, are sensible and learned but cold Speakers. Lee, Henry, and Hooper [are][1] the orators. Paca is a deliberater too. Chase speaks warmly. Mifflin is a sprightly and spirited Speaker. John Rutledge dont exceed in Learning or oratory, tho he is a rapid Speaker. Young Edward Rutledge is young, and zealous—a little unsteady, and injudicious, but very unnatural and affected as a Speaker. Dyer and Sherman speak often and long, but very heavily and clumsily.

[1] MS: "and."

1774 TUESDAY OCTR. 11.

Dined with Mr. McKean in Markett Street, with Mr. Reed, Rodney, Chace, Johnson, Paca, Dr. Morgan, Mr. R. Penn, &c.

Spent the Evening with Mr. Henry at his Lodgings consulting about a Petition to the King.[1]

Henry said he had no public Education. At fifteen he read Virgill and Livy, and has not looked into a Latin Book since. His father left him at that Age, and he has been struggling thro Life ever since. He has high Notions. Talks about exalted Minds, &c. He has a horrid Opinion of Galloway, Jay, and the Rutledges. Their System he says would ruin the Cause of America. He is very impatient to see such Fellows, and not be at Liberty to describe them in their true Colours.

[1] See entry of 1 Oct., note, above. The committee to prepare an address or petition to the King brought in its report on 21 Oct., but after debate it was recommitted and John Dickinson, who had come into Congress as recently as 17 Oct., was added to the committee (*JCC*, 1:102; Burnett, ed., *Letters of Members*, 1:lix). A revised draft was reported on 24 Oct. and approved the next day (*JCC*, 1:103–104). There is good reason to believe that JA was very dissatisfied with the version adopted, though he signed it with the other delegates on the 26th, the last day of the session (same, p. 113, 115–122). Dickinson later claimed the authorship of the approved text wholly for himself, saying that "the draft brought in by the original committee was written in language of asperity very little according with the conciliatory disposition of Congress" (Stillé, *Dickinson*, p. 140–148). See also JA to Jefferson, 12 Nov. 1813, where the original, rejected draft is said to have been composed by R. H. Lee (DLC:Jefferson Papers; printed from LbC, Adams Papers, in JA, *Works*, 10:78–80).

1774. WEDNESDAY. OCTR. 12.

Dined with Captn. Richards with Dr. Coombs.

1774 THURSDAY. OCTR. 13.

Dined with Mr. Dickenson with Chase, Paca, Low, Mifflin, Mr. Penn and General Lee, at six o Clock.

From 10 O Clock untill half after four, We were debating, about the Parliamentary Power of regulating Trade. 5 Colonies were for allowing it, 5. against it, and two divided among themselves, i.e. Mass. and Rhode Island.[1]

Mr. Duane has had his Heart sett upon asserting in our Bill of Rights, the Authority of Parliament to regulate the Trade of the Colonies. He is for grounding it on Compact, Acquiescence, Necessity, Protection, not merely on our Consent.

[1] This vote does not appear in the Journal of Congress. The fullest account of the debates of 12-13 Oct., mainly concerned with what came to be called the Declaration of Rights, is in Duane's Notes, printed in Burnett, ed., *Letters of Members*, 1:72-74, 75.

1774. FRYDAY. OCTR. 14.

Went in the Morning to see Dr. Chevott [Chovet] and his Skelletons and Wax Work—most admirable, exquisite Representations of the whole Animal Æconomy.

Four compleat Skelletons. A Leg with all the Nerves, Veins and Arteries injected with Wax. Two compleat Bodies in Wax, full grown. Waxen Representations of all the Muscles, Tendons &c., of the Head, Brain, Heart, Lungs, Liver, Stomack, Gutts, Cawl-Bladder, Testicles. This Exhibition is much more exquisite than that of Dr. Shippen, at the Hospital. The Doctor reads Lectures, for 2 half Jos. a Course, which takes up Four Months. These Wax Works are all of the Drs. own Hands.[1]

Dined with Dr. Morgan, an ingenious Physician and an honest Patriot. He shewed us some curious Paintings upon Silk which he brought from Italy which are Singular in this Country, and some Bones of an Animal of enormous Size, found upon the Banks of the River Ohio. Mr. Middleton, the two Rutledges, Mr. Mifflin and Mr. Wm. Barrell dined with Us. Mrs. Morgan is a sprightly, pretty lady.[2]

In the Evening We were invited to an Interview at Carpenters Hall, with the Quakers and Anabaptists. Mr. Bacchus is come here from Middleborough, with a design to apply to the Congress, for a Redress of the Grievances of the Antipædobaptists in our Province. The Cases from Chelmsford, the Case of Mr. White of Haverhill, the Case of Ashfield and Warwick, were mentioned by Mr. Bacchus.

Old Israel Pemberton was quite rude, and his Rudeness was resented. But the Conference which held till 11 O Clock, I hope will produce good.[3]

[1] On Abraham Chovet (1704-1790) see *DAB*; also Peter Stephen Du Ponceau's reminiscences of Chovet and his anatomical waxworks, *PMHB*, 63:323-329 (July 1939).

[2] On this day Congress adopted a Declaration of Rights, one of the ultimate products of the committee "to State the rights of the Colonies in general," appointed 7 Sept. (see entry of 8 Sept., above), and of the discussions in Congress, beginning 24 Sept., of "the means most proper to be pursued for a restoration of our rights" (*JCC*, 1:42). An undated committee (or subcommittee) draft of this declaration, with a caption reading "Heads of Grievances and Rights," is in the Adams Papers under the assigned date of 14 Oct. 1774; it was correctly identified by CFA and printed in JA, *Works*, 2:535-542; but the usual attribution of it to John Sullivan (same, p. 377 and note; *JCC*, 1:63) cannot be corroborated. The paper is not in Sullivan's hand, though neither has the hand so far been identified as

that of any other member of the committee on rights. The report as submitted, or at any rate as approved by Congress, varies widely from the so-called Sullivan draft, containing among other alterations a new and important paragraph written by JA, denying Parliament any authority over the Colonies except, "from the necessity of the case, ... the regulation of our external commerce" (JA, *Works*, 2:538–539). This paragraph, numbered "4," was the subject of long and vigorous debate; see same, 2:374–375; JA to Edward Biddle?, 12 Dec. 1774 (Dft, Adams Papers, printed in *Works*, 9:350); JCC, 1:63–73; Burnett, ed., *Letters of Members*, 1:72–75. Writing from memory in his Autobiography, JA said that "When Congress had gone through the Articles, I was appointed to put them into form and report a fair Draught for their final Acceptance." This may very well have been so, but there is no contemporary evidence to verify JA's statement unless his mention of staying home on Sunday to put "the Proceedings of the Congress into Order" (entry of 16 Oct., below) alludes to this assignment.

³ In his Autobiography JA elaborates from memory on this conference of the Massachusetts delegates with certain Baptist leaders from New England and several prominent Philadelphia Quakers. But the fullest account is in Alvah Hovey, *A Memoir of the Life and Times of the Rev. Isaac Backus, A.M.*, Boston, 1859, chs. 15–16. James Manning, president of the newly established Rhode Island College (now Brown University), and Isaac Backus (somewhat quaintly spelled "Bacchus" by JA), Baptist minister at Middleborough, Mass., had been sent to Philadelphia by an association of their churches to see what could be done for the relief of Baptists who under Massachusetts law were obliged to pay taxes for the support of "established" ministers not of their own choosing—or who at any rate had great difficulty obtaining exemption from such taxation. On the advice of conservative Quakers, who were not disinclined to embarrass the radical Massachusetts delegates, Manning and Backus requested the conference JA describes. Backus' Diary (quoted by Hovey) gives the names of

many who attended and reports the proceedings in full. The discussion was warm and lasted four hours. Backus and Manning pointed out that in a number of instances the Baptists in Massachusetts had been victims of taxation without representation, and Backus recorded that at one point Robert Treat Paine remarked, "There was nothing of conscience in the matter; it was only a contending about paying a little money" (Hovey, *Backus*, p. 211). Paine's Diary (MHi) is, as usual, laconic on the incident, but on his way home later this month Paine told Ezra Stiles about it, and from this and other evidence Stiles concluded that the Baptists, and Manning especially, were in alliance with the Anglicans and hostile to the patriotic cause (Stiles, *Literary Diary*, 1:168–170, 472–475, 491, 528; 2:23, 51).

The most protracted of the cases of religious scruple mentioned by JA, all of which can be traced in the histories of the towns concerned, was that of Ashfield. In 1767 certain Baptists of that "new plantation" refused to contribute to the building of a Congregational meetinghouse where they had settled first and had their own place of worship. When property of theirs was distrained to satisfy the tax requirement, they petitioned the General Court and ultimately carried their case to the King in Council. A mass of petitions, legislative acts and resolves, and other documents concerning the troubles in Ashfield from 1767 to 1774 will be found in Mass., *Province Laws*, 4:1015–1016, 1035–1046; 5:111–113, 143, 228–230, 278–279, 331–334, 371–375; 18:333–334, 450–451. Despite his lack of sympathy with the Baptists' position, Ezra Stiles acknowledged in a long and informative letter of 20 Nov. 1772 that injustice had been done at Ashfield (*Literary Diary*, 1:472, note). Backus' account of the Ashfield case was published in an anonymous pamphlet entitled *An Appeal to the Public for Religious Liberty*, Boston, 1773, p. 33 ff., and copies of this tract were handed out to those who attended the conference at Carpenters' Hall. Chagrined as they were by the surprise sprung upon them by the Baptist and Quaker lobbyists, the Massachusetts delegates promised to do what they could to redress the grievances complained of, but on their own ground, i.e. in Massachusetts. Accordingly, in Nov. 1774, Backus submitted a memorial of grievances to the Provincial Congress sitting in Cambridge. A Baptist leader who obtained his information from one of the members reported: "It was generally agreed not to do anything about it, but throw it out; when Mr. Adams got up and said, he was apprehensive, if they threw it out, it might cause a division among the provinces; and it was his advice to do something with it" (Hezekiah Smith to James Manning, 20 Jan. 1775, Hovey, *Backus*, p. 222). The action taken, however, consisted only of a resolution, 9 Dec. approving of religious liberty for all denominations and advising the petitioners to lay their complaints before the next "general assembly [when it] shall be convened in this colony" (Mass. Provincial Congress, *Jours.*, p. 65, 67).

1774 SATURDAY. OCTR. 15.

Dined at Mr. Wests with the Rutledges and Mr. Middleton. An elegant House, rich furniture, and a splendid Dinner.

1774 SUNDAY. OCTR. 16.

Staid at Home all day. Very busy in the necessary Business of putting the Proceedings of the Congress into Order.[1]

[1] That is, the final version of the Declaration of Rights? See entry of 14 Oct., note 2, above. So far as the Journal shows, the Declaration had been approved on 14 Oct., but there is evidence to show that some points relative to it were debated in Congress as late as the 17th; see Duane's Notes in Burnett, ed., *Letters of Members*, 1:77–79; and JA's Notes on the "Canada Bill," under 17? Oct., below.

1774. MONDAY OCTR. 17.

Dined at Home.

[NOTES OF DEBATES IN THE CONTINENTAL CONGRESS, 17? OCTOBER 1774.][1]
CANADA BILL.

Proof of Depth of Abilities, and Wickedness of Heart.
Precedent. Lords refusal of perpetual Imprisonment.
Prerogative to give any Government to a conquered People.
Romish Religion.
Feudal Government.
Union of feudal Law and Romish Superstition.
Knights of Malta. Orders of military Monks.
Goths and Vandals—overthrew the roman Empire.
Danger to us all. An House on fire.

[1] From JA's loose sheets of minutes of debates (D/JA/22A). In the MS these undated notes follow minutes of debates on Galloway's plea for a plan of union (Debates, 28 Sept., above), but their physical location is a very doubtful

clue to their date. The question of including the "Canada Bill" (Quebec Act) among the colonists' grievances was repeatedly debated, but the parallels in substance and even in phrasing between the present rough notes and Duane's Notes tentatively assigned by Burnett to 17 Oct. strongly suggest that both pertain to the same day's debate. See JCC, 1:66; Burnett, ed., *Letters of Members*, 1:77–79. It seems likely that JA's notes are the heads of his own arguments exclusively, but Duane's summary of JA's speech is too meager and cryptic to make this conjecture certain.

1774 TUESDAY. OCT. 18.

Dined at Stephen Collins's.

1774 WEDNESDAY. OCTR. 19.

Dined at Home.

1774 THURSDAY OCTR. 20.

Dined with the whole Congress at the City Tavern, at the Invitation of the House of Representatives of the Province of Pensylvania, the whole House dined with Us, making near 100 Guests in the whole—a most elegant Entertainment. A Sentiment was given, "May the Sword of the Parent never be Stain'd with the Blood of her Children." Two or 3 broadbrims,[1] over against me at Table—one of em said this is not a Toast but a Prayer, come let us join in it—and they took their Glasses accordingly.[2]

[1] Quakers.
[2] On this day the Association of the Colonies, or nonimportation and nonexportation agreement, was read in Congress and signed by the members, including JA (JCC, 1:75–81, 127–128 [Nos. 2–5], and facsimile of the Association as signed, in pocket of back cover of that volume).

1774 FRYDAY. OCT. 21.

Dined at the Library Tavern with Messrs. Marcoo's [Markoes] and a dozen Gentlemen from the W. Indies and N. Carolina. A fine bowling Green here—fine Turtle, and admirable Wine.[1]

[1] On this day Congress approved an "address to the people of Great-Britain" and a "memorial to the inhabitants of the British Colonies"; and Galloway, McKean, JA, and Hooper were named "a committee to revise the minutes of the Congress" (JCC, 1:81–101). The committee to prepare an address to the King also reported, but its report was recommitted; see entry of 11 Oct. and note, above.

1774. SATURDAY. OCTR. 22.

Dined in the Country, with Mr. Dickinson, with all the Delegates from N. England. Mr. Duane, Mr. Reed, Mr. Livingstone &c.

1774. SUNDAY. OCTR. 23.

Heard Mr. Piercy, at Mr. Sprouts. He is Chaplain to the Countess of Huntingdon. Comes recommended to Mr. Cary of Charlestown, from her, as a faithful servant of the Lord. No Genius—no Orator.

In the Afternoon I went to the Baptist Church and heard a trans Alleganian—a Preacher, from the back Parts of Virginia, behind the Allegany Mountains.[1] He preached an hour and an half. No Learning—No Grace of Action or Utterance—but an honest Zeal. He told us several good Stories. One was, that he was once preaching in Virginia and said that those Ministers who taught the People that Salvation was to be obtained by good Works, or Obedience, were leading them to ruin. Next Day, he was apprehended, by a Warrant from a Magistrate, for reviling the Clergy of the Church of England. He asked for a Prayer Book and had it. Turned to the 18 or 20th. Article, where the same sentiment is strongly expressed. He read it to the Magistrate. The Magistrate as soon as he heard it, dash'd the Warrant out of his Hand, and said sir you are discharged.

In the Evening I went to the Methodist Meeting and heard Mr. Webb, the old soldier, who first came to America, in the Character of Quarter Master under Gen. Braddock. He is one of the most fluent, eloquent Men I ever heard. He reaches the Imagination and touches the Passions, very well, and expresses himself with great Propriety. The Singing here is very sweet and soft indeed. The first Musick I have heard in any Society, except the Moravians, and once at Church with the organ.

Supped and spent the Remainder of the Evening, at Mr. Jo. Reeds with Coll. Lee, Dr. Shippen, Mr. Cary, Dr. Loring &c.

[1] His name is given in R. T. Paine's Diary (MHi) as "Fristo"; probably William Fristoe, a self-taught Baptist preacher of western Virginia, of whom there is a brief account in Sprague, *Annals Amer. Pulpit*, 6:125, note.

1774. MONDAY. OCTR. 24.

In Congress, nibbling and quibbling—as usual.[1]

There is no greater Mortification than to sit with half a dozen Witts, deliberating upon a Petition, Address, or Memorial. These great Witts, these subtle Criticks, these refined Genius's, these learned Lawyers, these wise Statesmen, are so fond of shewing their Parts and Powers, as to make their Consultations very tedius.

Young Ned Rutledge is a perfect Bob o' Lincoln—a Swallow—a Sparrow—a Peacock—excessively vain, excessively weak, and excessively variable and unsteady—jejune, inane, and puerile.

Mr. Dickinson is very modest, delicate, and timid.[2]

Spent the Evening at home. Coll. Dyer, Judge Sherman and Coll. Floyd came in and spent the Evening with Mr. Adams and me. Mr. Mifflin and General Lee came in. Lee's Head is running upon his new Plan of a Battallion.

[1] On this day Congress heard, debated, and recommitted the proposed address to the people of Quebec, and heard a revised draft of the address to the King, which was agreed to next day (*JCC*, 1:103–104).

[2] This comment was probably evoked by Dickinson's diluted revision of the address to the King; see entry of 11 Oct. and note, above.

1774 TUESDAY [25 OCTOBER].

Dined with Mr. Clymer. General Lee &c. there.

1774. WEDNESDAY [26 OCTOBER].

Dined at Home. This Day the Congress finished. Spent the Evening together at the City Tavern—all the Congress and several Gentlemen of the Town.[1]

[1] Among other things Congress this day debated and approved the address to the people of Quebec, signed the address to the King, voted a resolution of thanks to the Pennsylvania Assembly "for their politeness to this Congress," and "then dissolved itself" (*JCC*, 1:104–114). It had already, on 22 Oct., arranged for the printing of its Journal and resolved "that another Congress should be held on the tenth day of May next, unless the redress of grievances, which we have desired, be obtained before that time," recommending Philadelphia as the best meeting place (same, p. 102).

1774. THURSDAY. OCTR. 27.

Went this Morning with Mr. Tudor to see the Carpenters Hall, and the Library, and to Mr. Barrells and Bradfords, and then to the State House to see the Supream Court sitting. Heard Mr. Wilcox and Mr. Reed argue a Point of Law concerning the Construction of a Will. Three Judges, Chew, Willing and Moreton.

1774. FRYDAY. OCTR. 28.

Took our Departure in a very great Rain, from the happy, the peacefull, the elegant, the hospitable, and polite City of Phyladelphia.—It is not very likely that I shall ever see this Part of the World again, but I shall ever retain a most greatefull, pleasing Sense, of the many Civilities I have received, in it. And shall think myself happy to have an opportunity of returning them.—Dined at Andersons,[1] and reached Priestly's of Bristol at Night, twenty miles from Phyladelphia, where We are as happy as We can wish.

[1] The Red Lion, in the rural community then called Byberry, now part of Philadelphia City. See R. T. Paine, Diary (MHi), under this date.

1774. SATURDAY. OCTR. 29.

Rode to Prince Town, where We dine, at the sign of Hudibrass.—Vacation at Nassau Hall. Dr. Witherspoon out of Town. Paine recollected the Story of Mr. Keiths Joke upon him at Howlands of Plymouth, the Time of the Stamp Act. Paine said he would go to making brass Buckles. Keith said he might do that to great Advantage for his Stock would cost him nothing.

Lodged at Farmers in Brunswick.

1774. SUNDAY. OCTR. 30.

My Birthday. I am 39 Years of Age.—Rode to Elizabeth Town in New Jersey, where We are to dine. Rode down to Elizabeth Town Point, and put our Carriage and all our Horses into two Ferry Boats. Sail'd or rather rowed, Six Miles to a Point on Staten Island where We stoped and went into a Tavern. Got to Hulls in New York, about 10 O Clock, at night.

1774 MONDAY. OCT. 31.

Mr. McDougall, Mr. Scott, Captn. Sears, Mr. Platt, Mr. Hewes came to see us. All but the last dined with us. Walked to see the new Hospital, a grand Building. Went to the Coffee House. Mr. Cary and Dr. Loring dined with us.

The Sons of Liberty are in the Horrors here. They think they have lost ground since We passed thro this City. Their Delegates have agreed with the Congress, which I suppose they imagine, has given additional Importance to their Antagonists.[1]

[1] CFA provides a useful interpretive note on this paragraph, too long to quote here (JA, *Works*, 2:402).

1774. TUESDAY. NOVR. 1.

Left Brother Paine at New York to go by the Packett to New Port. Rode to Cocks at Kings bridge to break fast, to Havilands at Rye to Dinner, and to Knaps at Horse Neck in Greenwich to lodge.

1774. WEDNESDAY. NOVR. 2.

Rode to Bulkleys at Fairfield to dinner, and to Captn. Benjamins of Stratford to lodge.

1774. THURSDAY. NOVR. 3.

We design to Great Swamp to day. 42 miles.

At Newhaven, Coll. Dyer, Deane and Sherman, Mr. Parsons, the new Speaker Williams, Mr. Trumbull and many other Gentlemen came to see us at Beers's as soon as we got in. Coll. Dyer presented the Compliments of the Governor and Council to the Massachusetts Delegates and asked our Company, to spend the Evening. I begged Coll. Dyer to present my Duty to the Governor and Council, and my Gratitude for the high Honour they did us, but that We had been so long from home and our affairs were so critical, We hoped they would excuse us if we passed thro the Town as fast as possible.

Mr. Sherman invited us to dine, but Mr. Babcock claimed a Promise, so we dined with him.

2 or 3 Carriages accompanied us, a few Miles out of Town in the Afternoon.

We had the most pressing Invitations from many Gentlemen to return thro N. London, Windham &c. &c. &c., but excused ourselves. The People had sent a Courier to N. Haven on Purpose to wait for our Arrival and return to inform the People we were coming.

Twenty miles from Middletown We met two Gentlemen from thence who came on Purpose to meet us and invite us to dine tomorrow at Middletown. We excused ourselves with great Earnestness.

1774. FRYDAY. NOVR. 4.

Dined at Hartford, at Bulls, where we had the Pleasure of seeing Mr. Adams's Minister Mr. How, who is supposed to be courting here. Lodged at Dr. Chafy's [Chaffee's] in Windsor. Very cordially entertained.

1774 SATURDAY. NOVR. 5.

Break fasted at Austins of Suffield. Went to see a Company of Men exercising upon the Hill, under the Command of a green coated Man, lately a Regular. A Company of very likely stout men.

Dined at Parsons's of Springfield. Captn. Pynchon and another Pynchon, and Mr. Bliss, came in to see Us, and at last Coll. Worthington. Worthington behaved decently and politely. Said he was in Hopes we should have staid the Sabbath in Town and he should have had the Pleasure of waiting on us, &c.

Captn. Pynchon was of the late provincial Congress and gave us some Account of their Proceedings.

Arrived, about 7 O Clock at Scotts of Palmer alias Kingston, where We are to lodge. Scott and his Wife are at this instant, great Patriots. Zealous Americans. Scotts faith is very strong that they will repeal all the Acts, this very winter. Dr. Dana told Us all America, and G. Britain and Europe ow'd us Thanks and that the Ministry would lay hold of our Consent that they should regulate Trade, and our Petition and grant us Relief this Winter.—But neither the Doctors nor Scotts Faith are my Faith.

1774. SUNDAY. NOVR. 6.

Went all day to hear Mr. Baldwin a Presbyterian Minister at Kingston. We put up at Scotts. Mr. Baldwin came in the Evening to see us.

Hor. B. 3. O. 2. Pueros ab ineunte Ætate assuefaciendos esse rei militari et Vitæ laboriosæ.[1]

We walked to Meeting above 2 Miles at Noon. We walked 1/4 of a Mile and staid at one Quintouns an old Irishman, and a friendly cordial Reception we had. The old Man was so rejoiced to see us he could hardly speak—more glad to see Us he said than he should to see Gage and all his Train.—I saw a Gun. The young Man said that Gun marched 8 Miles towards Boston on the late Alarm. Almost the whole Parish marched off, and the People seemed really disappointed, when the News was contradicted.[2]

[1] Not a quotation from Horace's Book III, Ode ii, but a comment on it. In effect: "[Horace says] that boys from an early age should be accustomed to military activity and a strenuous life."

[2] See entry of 6 Sept. and note, above.

1774. MONDAY. NOVR. 7.

Dined at Rice's of Brookfield. Major Foster came to see us, and gave us an Account of the Proceedings of the Prov[incial] Congress.

Lodged at Hunts in Spencer.

1774. TUESDAY. NOVR. 8.

Breakfasted at Coll. Henshaws of Leicester. Dined at Woodburns of Worcester. Furnival made the two young Ladies come in and sing Us the New Liberty Song.

Lodged at Coll. Buckminsters of Framingham.

1774. WEDNESDAY. NOVR. 9.

Break fasted at Reeve's of Sudbury.

1775. APRIL 30TH. SUNDAY.[1]

Heard Mr. Strong all Day. At Night, a Man came in and inform'd us of the Death of Josa. Quincy.—Proh Dolor![2]

[1] First diary entry in a stitched booklet with marbled paper covers labeled by JA: "Account. 1775." Not numbered by CFA in the sequence of JA's MS Diaries, this booklet has been assigned the number D/JA/22B by the present editors. It contains only two diary entries (30 April, 3 Sept. 1775) among numerous account entries, mostly for travel expenses during the period May–Dec. 1775, with two detached pages of travel expenses for Jan.–Feb. 1777 laid in.

No diary entries survive for the period 10 Nov. 1774–29 April 1775. On 23 Nov. 1774 JA was "desired to favor" the Provincial Congress, then sitting in the Cambridge meetinghouse, "with his presence, as soon as may be" (Mass. Provincial Congress, *Jours.*, p. 49). Five days later he was elected as an additional delegate from Braintree to that body (*Braintree Town Records*, p. 453). Presumably he attended from that time until the Congress dissolved itself, 10 December. JA was not a member of the second Provincial Congress, which convened at Cambridge on 1 Feb., but on 6 March he was elected a selectman of Braintree and named on a committee to "prepare a covenant similar to the association of the Continental Congress," to be adopted by the town "if they think proper" (same, p. 455); for the "covenant" as adopted, 15 March, see same, p. 457–461.

JA's principal activity during the early months of 1775 was the composition of his newspaper essays signed "Novanglus" in reply to the loyalist essays of "Massachusettensis," who JA long believed was Jonathan Sewall but who was actually Daniel Leonard of Taunton. Leonard's first essay appeared in Mills and Hicks' *Boston Post Boy* (at the time called the *Massachusetts Gazette and Boston Post Boy*), 12 Dec. 1774. Sixteen more numbers followed, the last being published on 3 April 1775. Several collected editions were published later. JA's answers were printed in Edes and Gill's *Boston Gazette*, 23 Jan.–17 April, and were discontinued then only

because the outbreak of hostilities caused the *Gazette* to suspend publication for a time. Only fragments of the "Novanglus" papers survive in MS. The history of the collected editions, the last of which appeared in 1819, is complex. See JA's account in his Autobiography, his preface to *Novanglus and Massachusettensis* . . . (Boston, 1819), and CFA's note preceding the "Novanglus" essays as reprinted in JA, *Works*, 4:4.

On 2 Dec. 1774 the Provincial Congress, sitting in Cambridge, had reelected JA and his three colleagues in the first Continental Congress (Samuel Adams, Thomas Cushing, and R. T. Paine) to the next Congress, and had added John Hancock to the delegation in the place of James Bowdoin, who had never attended (Mass. Provincial Congress, *Jours.*, p. 55; see also p. 86). JA probably set off from Braintree on 26 April; he traveled with one servant and arrived in Hartford on the 29th, where the present entry was written and where he joined the other Massachusetts delegates, who then traveled together the rest of the way. Paine's Diary (MHi) has the following entry under 10 May: "Proceeded [from Bristol] to Philadelphia, met 5 Miles out of Town by a Great No. of Gentlemen and military Companys, one of Rifle Men escorted by Music to City Tavern, dind at Mrs. Yards where we put up. PM met in Congress at the State House, Chief of the Members arrived. Chose a President Mr. Randolph, and Secr[etar]y." The Salem tory Samuel Curwen, who was about to sail from Philadelphia for England, left a much fuller account of the arrival of the Massachusetts delegates in the city (Curwen, *Journal and Letters*, 4th edn., 1864, p. 29).

It is extremely unfortunate that JA appears to have kept neither a personal diary nor any minutes of the debates of this session of Congress, which lasted until 1 Aug. 1775. One must suppose that extreme pressure of business was the primary cause of this neglect. In his correspondence JA repeatedly remarked that he and the other delegates had far more than they could possibly do. "We have been all so assiduous . . . in this exhausting debilitating Climate," he told his wife just before adjournment, "that Our Lives are more exposed than they would be in Camp" (30 July, Adams Papers). His own health was poor and his spirits depressed throughout most of the session. His letters complain of "Smarting Eyes" and other ailments for which he could find no real relief, and still more often of "The Fidgets, the Whims, the Caprice, the Vanity, the Superstition, the irritability of some of us" (to AA, 24 July, Adams Papers). Yet during these few summer weeks Congress established an army, appointed and instructed a commander in chief and a corps of general officers, began the long struggle to organize an adequate supply system, issued the first Continental money, established a postal system, and at least proposed a plan of confederation among the colonies. All this and more business was actually transacted besides issuing various declarations of principle appealing to American, - British, and world opinion, including one document that nearly rent Congress asunder, the second or "Olive Branch" Petition to the King, signed by all the members on 8 July (see JCC, 2:158–162), but by some with reluctance and by a few with disgust. JA was one of these few. In his Autobiography he characterized this project of John Dickinson's as a "Measure of Imbecility [that] embarrassed every Exertion of Congress," and it is clear that this was his view of it from the outset. His feelings about Dickinson as a man and his conciliatory program overflowed in a letter addressed to James Warren on 24 July that fell into British hands, was published, and raised a small tempest; see note on entry of 16 Sept., below.

It would be inappropriate here, even if feasible, to list JA's numerous committee assignments and reports during the May–July session of Congress. They must be traced in the Journal (JCC, vol. 2), which is supplemented by JA's contemporary correspondence and the retrospective narrative in his Autobiography (which is, however, to be used with caution because constructed largely from memory and colored by later political events). Special attention may be drawn to his role in the selection, 15 June, of Washington as commander in chief. See JCC, 2:91; note on entry of 28 Sept. 1774, above; Burnett's note and references in *Letters of Members*, 1:130–132 (which reprints JA's account); and Freeman, *Washington*, vol. 3: ch. 18.

[2] Josiah Quincy died within sight of Gloucester, Mass., 26 April 1775, on his return from a mission to England, the purpose of which was to explain the position of the American patriots to the British government. See Josiah Quincy, *Josiah Quincy, Jr.*, p. 287–288. In reporting this "melancholy Event" to JA, 4 May, AA said that Quincy "wrote in minuts which he left behind that he had matters of concequence intrusted with him, which for want of a confident must die with him" (Adams Papers).

[ACCOUNT WITH MASSACHUSETTS AS A DELEGATE TO THE CONTINENTAL CONGRESS, APRIL–AUGUST 1775.] [1]

Mass. Bay Dr. to John Adams

	£	s	d
To the Hire of two Horses at £10 each	20:	0:	0
To the Hire of a Sulky £8:0s:0d [2]	8:	0:	0
To the Wages of a servant from the 26 of April to the 14th. of August at £3 per Month 10:16:0	10:16:		0
To Cash paid Mrs. Yard in Philadelphia for Board and Lodging for myself and Servant &c. Pensylvania Currency £38:13s:6d [3]	30:18:10		

I. CONGRESS VOTING INDEPENDENCE, BY EDWARD SAVAGE

	£	s	d
To Cash paid Hannah Hiltzheimer for keeping my Horses	4:16:	3	
To Cash paid Dibley & Stringer for keeping my Horses Pen. Currency £8:13s:8 1/2d	7: 0:	0	
To Cash paid Messrs. Marshalls for Sundry Medicines	0: 8:	0	
	79:19:	1 [4]	

Cr.

	£	s	d
By Cash recd.	100: 0:	0	
carried with me, when I went	50: 0:	0	
borrowed out of Money for the Sufferers, at one Time[5]	31: 0:	0	
at another	12: 0:	0	

	£	s	d
To Cash paid Daniel Smith for Sundries as pr Rect.	2: 8:	0 [6]	
To Cash paid J Young for Sundries	3: 0:	0 [7]	
To Cash paid at Horse Neck for a Saddle[8]	3: 0:	0	
To cash paid for a light Suit of Cloaths	4: 0:	0	
To Cash paid for my Expences, keeping two Horses and a servants Expences, upon the Road from Braintree to Phyladelphia, and from thence to Braintree together with Sundry miscellaneous Expences, while there	26:12:11		
To 2 Days Spent, in riding after Mr. Cushing before I went away, to get the Money granted me for my Expences Self and Horse	0:18:	0 [9]	

To the Hire of an Horse and Man to go to Providence, after my Money which Mr. Cushing said was carried there[10]

To the Hire of the second Horse and Man to the same Place for the same Purpose, not having obtaind it the first Time.

To Cash paid Mr. Joseph Bass for a Surtout and Pair of Leather Breeches before I went—the Breeches were not brought out of Boston, the 19th of April and there they now are in Mr. Whitwells shop as he told me at Hartford [3:16: 0][11]

To Cash pd. the owner of a sulky for the Damage

£   s   d

done to it, by the Horse taking fright and running
vs. a Rock and dashing the Top in Pieces   [12: 0: 0] [12]

[1] From D/JA/22B, as are the other accounts which follow in 1775 unless otherwise indicated. This is JA's running record of expenses; he later prepared a fair copy and submitted it to the General Court, together with a file of receipted bills as vouchers, in order to obtain reimbursement. The fair copy, which is in M-Ar: vol. 210, varies in some respects from the rough record; see the notes below. The supporting vouchers are also in M-Ar: vol. 210, but in disorder. Since they throw some light on modes of travel and living on the eve of the Revolution, and since we have no diary entries for this period, the more interesting among them are printed below as separate entries, usually under the dates they were receipted.

[2] Fair copy in M-Ar adds: "from April to December." The sulky belonged to AA's father, Rev. William Smith, and met with an unhappy fate. See last entry in the present document, and JA to AA, 8 May 1775 (Adams Papers; JA-AA, *Familiar Letters*, p. 54–55).

[3] The ratio of Philadelphia currency to New England "lawful money" was as 5 is to 4. This must be kept in mind when comparing the receipted bills below with the corresponding account entries.

[4] Error for £81 19s. 1d.

[5] JA had been a member of the committee to receive donations for the sufferers under the Boston Port Act since the summer of 1774; see note on entry of 10 Aug. 1774, above. Returning from Philadelphia in Aug. 1775, he brought with him donations from Berks and Bucks cos., Penna., in the amount of £208 15s. 11d.; see his receipt from Moses Gill, 12 Sept. 1775 (Adams Papers).

[6] Fair copy has, instead, £3 0s. 0d. Smith's receipted bill, printed below under 10 July, is in the amount of £2 17s. 2d., Philadelphia currency, so that neither figure given by JA is exactly right.

[7] This item is omitted in the fair copy, though JA submitted a supporting voucher for it, printed below under 31 July.

[8] Fair copy adds: "after my Sulky was overset and destroyed."

[9] This entry does not appear in the fair copy. The entries that follow are separated from those that precede by a blank page in the MS, and no sums are attached to them.

[10] This and the following entry obviously repeat the preceding entry in more specific language; neither of them is in the fair copy.

[11] The figure is supplied from the fair copy.

[12] The figure is supplied from the fair copy, which also has a total, £134 8s. 0d., followed by the signed statement: "A true Account, Errors excepted John Adams." This is correct for JA's account as he submitted it for payment. For the settlement, see JA's Account for Aug.–Dec. 1775, below, and note 4 there.

[DANIEL SMITH'S BILL FOR ENTERTAINMENT.] [1]

Jno. Adams Esqr.   Dr.
To Daniel Smith

1775			£	s	d
May 13th.	To Bottle Brandy			2	6
26.	To Bottle do.			2	6
July 10.	To Quart Spirits			2	6
			£0	7	6
	To 5 dinner Clubs with the Delegates			2 9	8
				2 17	2

Recd. the Contents   Danl. Smith

[1] M-Ar: vol. 210. Endorsed by JA: "Mr. Smiths Acct." See JA's Account with Massachusetts, April–Aug. 1775 above, and note 6 there.

[J. YOUNG JR.'S BILL FOR RIDING EQUIPMENT.] [1]

John Adams Esqr. B[ough]t of J. Young Junr.

1775

June 14.	To a new Pad and Double raind Curb Bridle	£	14 6
15.	Mendg. an old Bridle		1
July 3.	To a Cover for sword Scabboard		3
14.	To a small pad for housings		2
31.	To a Portmanteau & Strap's	1	7
	To a Pair Pistol Bags	1	
	To a Male pylion		6
		£3:13:6	

Recd. the Contents in full   J. Young jr.

[1] M-Ar: vol. 210.

[SARAH YARD'S BILL FOR BOARD.] [1]

Mr. John Adams   Dr.   To Mrs. Yard.

1775

Augt. 1st.	To your Board & Lodging from the 10th May to this day 11 1/2 Wks. à 30s. per Wk.	£17: 5
	To your Servants Board for 7 Wks. 4 days à 15s.	5:12: 6
	To your Proportion to the Parlour and Candles 11 1/2 Wks. à 4s.	2: 6
	To your proportion of the Liquor	13:10
		£38:13: 6

Receiv'd the Above in full—Sarah Yard

```
        38  13  6
         7  14  8  1/2
        ─────────────
        £30. 18. 9  1/2
L.M. £30:18s:10d            39:  2
                           38:13:  6
                           ────────
                              8:  6
```

[1] M-Ar: vol. 210. The arithmetic at the foot of the paper is in JA's hand.

According to its Journal, Congress adjourned on 1 Aug. to meet again on 5

Sept. (JCC, 2:239). But it should be noted that R. T. Paine's Diary (MHi) has under 1 Aug. only the notation "Very hott," but on the following day: "D[itt]o. Congress adj[ourne]d. . . . 1/2 past 12 Clock Sat out, Stopt at Red Lyon. . . . thence to Trenton. Lodged." Clearly Congress met at least briefly on the 2d; see also Francis Lewis to Philip Schuyler, 2 Aug. (Burnett, ed., *Letters of Members*, 1:187). From Paine's use of the second person plural in entries recording his return to Massachusetts, it seems likely that the other delegates accompanied him, but there is nothing to confirm that JA did so, and he certainly reached Braintree well before Paine reached Taunton on the 10th, because on that day JA attended a meeting of the Massachusetts Council, to which he had been elected by the new House on 21 July (Mass., *House Jour.*, 1775–1776, 1st sess., p. 6, 60). [See a correction in *Adams Family Corr.*, 1:272–273.]

[DIBLEY & STRINGER'S BILL FOR CARE OF JOHN ADAMS' HORSES.][1]

John Adams Esqre.   Dr. to Wm. Dibley & Stringer

1775			£	s	d
June 28		To hay for two Horses 3/ Oats 2/		5:	
	29	To Ditto to July 2d. 3 days hay 9/ Oats 9/		18:	
July	2	To hay 3/ Oats 1/4		4:	4
	3	To ditto 3/ Oats 1/4		4:	4
	4	To Shoeing		4:	6
	4	To hay 5 days to July 9th. at 3/ a day		15:	
		To Oats 5 days to July 9th. at 1/4		6:	8
	5	To Triming Horse		5:	
	9	To hay 1/6 to Oats 1/6		3:	
	10	To hay 10 days to 20 July at 3/	1:10:		
	-	To Oats 10 days to 20 July at 1/4		13:	4
	20	To hay 4 days to 24 July at 3/		12:	
		To Oats 4 days to 24 July at 2/		8:	
	24	To Oats 8			8
	30	hay 3/ Oats 3/		6:	
	31	To hay 3/ Oats 3/ Aug. 1 to hay 3/ Oats 3/		12:	
Aug.	2	To hay 3/ Oats 3/		6:	
Aug.	3[2]	To Oats		1:	
		To Mr. Wrights Bill for Pasture.		10:	4 1/2
			£8:	5:	2 1/2
	Shoeing			8:	6
			8:13:		8 1/2

Received August 1st. 1775 the within Account is full to the third Instant   Wm. Dibley

[1] M-Ar: vol. 210. Endorsed by JA: "Dibley & Stringers Acct."
[2] If this date is correct, JA did not leave Philadelphia until 3 Aug., which would make his return to Braintree, where he evidently arrived on the 9th, a fast trip indeed. See note on Mrs. Yard's Bill, preceding.

[ACCOUNT WITH JOSEPH BASS.]

		£	s	d
May 31. 1775	pd. Jos. Bass a Dollar	0:	6:	0
	pd. him before 2 Dollars	0:	12:	0
	pd. him before at Braintree a Guinea	1:	8:	0

Jos. Bass Dr. to John Adams

Aug. 14. 1775.

To ballance of your Acct. left at Phyladelphia, as you recollect it if wrong to be rectified — 2: 8: 0

To a Guinea paid you before we went away from Braintree — 1: 8: 0

To Cash left with Mrs. Yard to pay Dr. Shippen for innoculating you — 2: 0: 0

To Cash paid you this Day — 5: 0: 0

10:16: 0

By your Service from 26th. of April to the fourteenth of Aug. 1775. — 10:16: 0

Braintree Aug. 14. 1775.[1] Received of John Adams Five Pounds lawfull Money, which together with five Pounds sixteen shillings of lawfull Money received before, is in full for my Service from the 26th. of April to this day. Joseph Bass jr.

[1] The itemized accounts with Bass above are in D/JA/22B. The receipt, in JA's hand and signed by Bass, is in M-Ar: vol. 210.

[SAMUEL COOKE'S BILLS FOR BOARD.][1]

The Honble. John Adams Esqr. to Saml. Cook — Dr.

1775

Augst. 24th. To Boarding your Lady & Self 3 days — £0:12:

To 3 days Keeping yr. Horse — 3:

£0:15:

Received the Contents in full for my Brother Saml. Cooke

The Honble. John Adams to Samll. Cooke junr. — Dr.

To boardg: 6 days @ 2/ — £0:12. 0

To breakfasting & dining 4 persons @ 9/ — 3.

To keeping your horse 4 nights @ 1/ — 4.

£0. 19

Received the above in full Saml. Cooke junr.

¹ M-Ar: vol. 210, where it is followed by the second (undated) bill from Cooke, printed here without a separate caption. Cooke's was presumably in Watertown, where JA was attending the Massachusetts Council. AA was with him there from the 22d through the 24th (AA to Mercy Otis Warren, 27 Aug., MHi). In a list of Council members and their expenses authorized for payment on 11 Sept. JA is stated to have attended Council nine days during the first session of the new General Court (M-Ar: vol. 164).

1775. AUG. 28.¹

Took with me £70:0:0 consisting in £62:10 Pen. Currency in Paper Bills and £20 L.M of Mass. in silver and Gold.

¹ This was the day JA set off from Braintree, but he went only as far as Watertown, where he stayed until at least the 30th, attending Council, before starting for Philadelphia. See Mass. Council Records, 17:61, 68, 69 (M-Ar). With Samuel Adams he left Watertown probably on 1 Sept., since they spent Sunday the 3d in Woodstock, Conn.; see entry of that date, below. In a letter to James Warren, 17 Sept., JA described at length and in his own inimitable manner his cousin Sam's ungainly horsemanship (MHi; printed in *Warren-Adams Letters*, 1:110–111).

[ACCOUNT WITH MASSACHUSETTS AS A DELEGATE TO THE CONTINENTAL CONGRESS, AUGUST–DECEMBER 1775.]¹

1775 Aug. 28th.	£	s	d
pd. at Davis's at Roxbury for Oats	0:	0:	8
pd. at Watertown for Horses Servant &c	1:	14:	2
pd. at Baldwins for Oats	0:	0:	8
pd. at Buckminsters at Framingham	0:	5:	0
pd. at Bowmans at Oxford	0:	2:	4
pd. at Shermans in Grafton at Breakfast	0:	1:	8
Septr. 4. pd. at Hides in Woodstock for board and Lodgings for Selves and Servants and Horse keeping from Saturday to Monday.	1:	13:	0
pd. at Clarks at Pomfret	0:	2:	0
pd. at Carys of Windham	0:	7:	4
pd. at Lebanon Grays	0:	9:	10
pd. at Taynters in Colchester	0:	6:	0
pd. at Smiths of Haddam	0:	4:	0
pd. at Camps in Durham	0:	8:	6
pd. at Beers's of N. Haven	0:	6:	0
pd. at Bryants of Milford	0:	8:	10
pd. at Stratford Ferry	0:	2:	0
pd. at Stratfield for Oats	0:	0:	6
pd. at Penfields of Fairfield	0:	14:	7
pd. at Betts's of Norwalk	0:	6:	0

	£	s	d
pd. at Fitch's of Stamford	0:	6:	11
pd. at Knaps of Horse Neck	0:	16:	0
pd. at Bulls of White Plains	0:	3:	8
pd. at Jasper the Ferryman, at Dobbs Ferry			
for Dinners and Ferryge	0:	4:	0
pd. at Mrs. Watsons at Hackin Sack	0:	8:	10
pd. at Piersons of Newark	0:	2:	10
pd. at Elizabeth Town for Shewing Horse	0:	0:	10
pd. at Grahams Elizabeth Town	0:	18:	4
pd. for Man and Horse to Newark after our Men			
and to the Horsler	0:	5:	8
pd. at Woodbridge Dawsons	0:	1:	6
pd. at Brunswick, Farmers, and at the Ferry	0:	8:	0
pd. at Jones's at Ten mile run	0:	0:	10
pd. at Princetown	0:	8:	6
pd. at Trenton	0:	3:	0
pd. at Priestly's in Bristol	0:	12:	0
pd. at Wilsons'	0:	2:	8
pd. at Shammony [Neshaminy] Ferry	0:	0:	6

Cr.

	£ : s : d
Recd. of Mr. S. Adams, for his Share of our Expences on the Road from Woodstock to Philadelphia [2]	5: 6: 4

		£ : s : d
1775 Sept. 14.	pd. for Paper Wax &c	0: 2: 0
Octr.	pd. for Tavern Expences on Committees	0: 6: 0
1775 Octr. 16.	pd. for Papers, Pamphlets Wax, mending a Pistoll, a Bridle &c	0: 12: 0
	pd. for Tobacco, Plans of Boston Harbour, &c &c	0: 14: 0
1775 Nov. 1.	pd. Mr. John Wright his Account for pasturing my Horses, 9 dollars	2: 14: 0
Nov. 13.	Cash paid for Sundry Medicines	0: 12: 0
Novr. 15.	pd. Mr. McLane for a Leathern Breeches and Waistcoat	2: 16: 0
Novr. 27.	pd. Mrs. Lucy Leonard for Mrs. Yard £20 P. Curren[cy]	16: 0: 0
Decr. 8 1775.	pd. Mr. Aitkens Acct.	0: 16: 0
	pd. Washerwoman	1: 4: 0

	£	s	d
pd. John Stille's Acct.	3:	0:	0
pd. Mr. Marshalls Acct	0:	4:	0
pd. James Starrs Acct	0:	8:	10
pd. Mr. Smiths Acct	0:	10:	4
pd. Bass	2:	8:	0
pd. Lucy Leonards Acct	0:	16:	0
Mr. Wm. Barrells Acct.	2:	3:	0
Hiltsheimers Acct.	0:	8:	0
Joseph Fox's Acct.	0:	10:	0
Wm. Shepards Acct.	10:	14:	0
one Pr. of Gloves	0:	6:	0
Mrs. Yards Acct.	23:	18:	6 [8]

Decr. 9. 1775. borrowed of the Hon. Saml. Adams Esqr. for which I gave him my Note of Hand	25: 0: 0

1779 [*i.e.* 1775]. Decr. 9. pd. at Andersons the red Lyon	0: 3: 4
pd. at Bassinetts at Bristow	0: 8: 2
Decr. 10. pd. at Shammony Ferry and at Trenton Ferry	0: 1: 6
pd. at Williams's	0: 3: 0
pd. at Hiers Princetown	0: 11: 8
pd. at Farmers	0: 4: 0
pd. at Ferry	0: 1: 6
Decr. 12. pd. at Dawsons at Woodbridge	0: 7: 6
pd. at Grahams Elizabeth Town	0: 3: 0
pd. at Piersons Newark	0: 3: 0
pd. at Hackinsack, Phillipsborough and White Plains including the Ferriage of North River	1: 04: 0
Decr. 13. pd. at Knaps at Horse Neck	0: 6: 0
14. pd. at Betts's Norwalk	0: 8: 0
pd. for shewing Horses at White Plains and this Place	0: 4: 0
pd. at Fairfield for Horse shewing Dinner &c	0: 7: 0
Decr. 16. pd. at Bryants Milford	0: 8: 6
pd. at Bears's N. Haven	0: 5: 0
pd. at Robinsons Wallingford and at another Tav. for Oats	0: 6: 0

	£	s	d
pd. at Colliers in Hartford for Entertainment and Horse shoeing	0:	11:	0
pd. Mr. Nicholas Brown for a Girt and for transporting my wrecked Sulky from Horse Neck to Hartford 90 miles	1:	5:	6
pd. for Oats and Hay at Woodbridges East Hartford	0:	1:	0
pd. at Fellows, Bolton for Dinners Oats and Hay &c	0:	2:	6
pd. at Windham for Horse shewing and Entertainment	0:	7:	0
pd. at 2 Taverns for Oats	0:	1:	4
pd. at Providence for Entertainment	0:	12:	4
pd. at Moreys Norton	0:	2:	8
Decr. 21st. pd. at Coll. Howards Bridgewater	0:	6:	0
pd. Bass's Accounts' first	1:	7:	0
2d.	1:	11:	6
3d.	11:	5:	0

Hire of one Horse from Aug. to 21. Decr.
Hire of another for the Same Time [4]

[1] This is JA's running record of his expenses for his service in the third session of the Continental Congress. A fair copy, containing rather negligible differences in phrasing, was prepared and submitted by JA to the legislature in order to obtain reimbursement; this is in M-Ar: vol. 210 and is supported by receipted bills for many of the charges listed. The more interesting of these bills (filed in the same volume) are printed below under the dates they were receipted.

[2] They arrived in Philadelphia on 12 Sept.; Congress, which had been adjourning from day to day for want of a quorum, met for business on 13 Sept. (Ward, Diary, in Burnett, ed., *Letters of Members*, 1:192–193).

[3] As shown in Mrs. Yard's receipted bill (printed below under 9 Dec.), this amount is in Pennsylvania currency, which JA should have converted to New England lawful money when entering it here. The fair copy of JA's expense account in M-Ar has the correct amount

£19 2s. 9d. inserted by another hand at this point. See the following note.

[4] The fair copy enters the cost of these last two items as £20 and reckons the total amount expended as £127 7s. 10d. It then subjoins two "credit" items —the £5 6s. 4d. borrowed of Samuel Adams, and "By Cash recd. of the Treasurer," £130—making a total credit of £135 6s. 4d., so that JA found the "Ballance due to the Colony" to be £7 18s. 6d. (The Treasurer's warrant is recorded in the Minutes of the Council, 22 Aug., in M-Ar: vol. 86.) This "Ballance" was deducted when JA's still outstanding account for April–Aug. 1775 (q.v. above) was at length settled, 16–18 Sept. 1776, together with a further deduction of £4 15s. 9d., owing to an "Error of Mrs. Yard's Balance Decr. 1775" (see note 3 above), so that he was finally reimbursed in the amount of £121 13s. 9d. (M-Ar: vol. 210, p. 290, 280–280A; Mass., *House Jour.*, 1775–1776, 3d sess., p. 175, 196, 281; same, 1776–1777, p. 104, 108).

1775 SEPTEMBER 3D.

At Woodstock. Heard Mr. Learned [Leonard] from Is. 32:16. The Work of Righteousness is Peace, and the Effect of Righteousness, Quietness and assurance forever.

1775. SEPTR. 15. FRYDAY.[1]

Archibald Bullock and John Houstoun Esquires, and the Revd. Dr. Zubly, appear as Delegates from Georgia.[2]

Dr. Zubly is a Native of Switzerland, and a Clergyman of the Independent Perswasion, settled in a Parish in Georgia. He speaks, as it is reported, Several Languages, English, Dutch, French, Latin &c. —is reported to be a learned Man. He is a Man of a warm and zealous Spirit. It is said that he possesses considerable Property.

Houstoun is a young Gentleman, by Profession a Lawyer, educated under a Gentleman of Eminence in South Carolina. He seems to be sensible and spirited, but rather inexperienced.

Bullock is cloathed in American Manufacture.

Thomas Nelson Esquire, George Wythe Esqr., and Francis Lightfoot Lee Esq. appeared as Delegates from Virginia.

Nelson is a fat Man, like the late Coll. Lee of Marblehead. He is a Speaker, and alert and lively, for his Weight.

Wythe is a Lawyer, it is said of the first Eminence.

Lee is a Brother of Dr. Arthur, the late Sheriff of London,[3] and our old Friend Richard Henry, sensible, and patriotic, as the rest of the Family.

Deane says, that two Persons, of the Name of De Witt of Dutch Extraction, one in Norwich the other in Windham, have made Salt Petre with Success—and propose to make a great deal. That there is a Mine of Lead at Middletown, which will afford a great Quantity. That Works are preparing to smelt and refine it, which will go in a fortnight. There is a Mine at Northampton, which Mr. W. Bowdoin spent much Money in working, with much Effect, tho little Profit.

Langdon and Bartlett came in this Evening, from Portsmouth. 400 Men are building a Fort on Pierce's Island to defend the Town vs. Ships of War.

Upon recollecting the Debates of this Day in Congress, there appears to me a remarkable Want of Judgment in some of our Members. Chace is violent and boisterous, asking his Pardon. He is tedious upon frivolous Points. So is E. Rutledge. Much precious Time is indiscreetly expended. Points of little Consequence are started, and debated [with] warmth. Rutledge is a very uncouth, and ungracefull Speaker. He shruggs his Shoulders, distorts his Body, nods and wriggles with his Head, and looks about with his Eyes, from side to side, and Speaks thro his Nose, as the Yankees Sing. His Brother John dodges his Head too, rather disagreably, and both of them Spout out their Language in a rough and rapid Torrent, but without much Force or Effect.

Dyer is long winded and roundabout—obscure and cloudy. Very talkative and very tedious, yet an honest, worthy Man, means and judges well.

Sherman's Air is the Reverse of Grace. There cannot be a more striking Contrast to beautifull Action, than the Motions of his Hands. Generally, he stands upright with his Hands before him. The fingers of his left Hand clenched into a Fist, and the Wrist of it, grasped with his right. But he has a clear Head and sound Judgment. But when he moves a Hand, in any thing like Action, Hogarths Genuis could not have invented a Motion more opposite to grace. It is Stiffness, and Aukwardness itself. Rigid as Starched Linen or Buckram. Aukward as a junior Batchelor, or a Sophomore.

Mr. Dickinsons Air, Gate, and Action are not much more elegant.

[1] First entry in booklet "24" as numbered by CFA (our D/JA/24), the first of a series of small memorandum books bound in red-brown leather covers, presumably purchased from Robert Aitken in Philadelphia (see his receipted bill, 8 Dec., below), in which JA kept his Diary and notes of debates for a year. D/JA/24 contains entries through 10

Dec. 1775.

[2] The Georgia delegates had actually appeared in Congress on 13 Sept., and their credentials were read that day (*JCC*, 2:240–242). The present entry is therefore at least in part retrospective.

[3] The "late [i.e. former] Sheriff" was still another brother, William Lee; see entry of 3 Sept. 1774, above.

1775 SEPT. 16. SATURDAY.

Walking to the Statehouse this Morning, I met Mr. Dickinson, on Foot in Chesnut Street. We met, and passed near enough to touch Elbows. He passed without moving his Hat, or Head or Hand. I bowed and pulled off my Hat. He passed hautily by. The Cause of his Offence, is the Letter no doubt which Gage has printed in Drapers Paper.[1]

I shall for the future pass him, in the same manner. But I was determined to make my Bow, that I might know his Temper.

We are not to be upon speaking Terms, nor bowing Terms, for the time to come.

This Evening had Conversation with Mr. Bullock of Georgia.—I asked him, whether Georgia had a Charter? What was the Extent of the Province? What was their Constitution? How Justice was administered? Who was Chancellor, who Ordinary? and who Judges? He says they have County Courts for the Tryal of civil Causes under £8.—and a C[hief] Justice, appointed from Home and 3 other Judges appointed by the Governor, for the decision of all other Causes civil and criminal, at Savanna. That the Governor alone is both Chancellor and Ordinary.

Parson Gordon of Roxbury, spent the Evening here.—I fear his indiscreet Prate will do harm in this City. He is an eternal Talker, and somewhat vain, and not accurate nor judicious. Very zealous in the Cause, and a well meaning Man, but incautious, and not sufficiently tender of the Character of our Province, upon which at this Time much depends. Fond of being thought a Man of Influence, at Head Quarters, and with our Council and House, and with the general Officers of the Army, and also with Gentlemen in this City, and other Colonies.—He is a good Man, but wants a Guide.[2]

[1] That is, JA's letter to James Warren, Philadelphia, 24 July 1775, which brought more notoriety to its writer than anything else he had yet written. Entrusted (with others) to a well-meaning but meddlesome young Boston lawyer, Benjamin Hichborn, it was captured by a British naval vessel at a ferry crossing in Rhode Island. JA had written the letter in a mood of exasperation with John Dickinson's "pacific System" and alluded to Dickinson as "A certain great Fortune and piddling Genius [who] has given a silly Cast to our whole Doings" (Tr, enclosed in Gage to Lord Dartmouth, 20 Aug. 1775, Dartmouth MSS, deposited in William Salt Library, Stafford, England). This and other reckless expressions in the same letter and in another of the same date to AA, amounting, as some thought, to "an Avowal of Independency," and likewise intercepted, amused and outraged the British by turns. Literally dozens of MS copies of the letters are recorded in the Adams Papers Editorial Files, but the originals, supposedly sent by Vice-Admiral Samuel Graves to the Admiralty Office in London, have never come to light. Nor did JA himself retain copies. In consequence there is no way of knowing whether or how far the texts were tampered with, as JA asserted, when they were printed in Margaret Draper's *Massachusetts Gazette and Boston Weekly News Letter*, 17 Aug. 1775. From this source they were widely reprinted. The most readily available published texts are in JA, *Works*, 1:178–180; also at 2:411, note, from early transcripts in the Adams Papers. The story of the interception, Hichborn's escape from a British vessel in Boston Harbor, his efforts to clear himself with JA and others, and the sensation produced by the published letters both in America and England, is too long to tell here and more properly belongs elsewhere. But see, besides JA's account in his Autobiography, *Warren-Adams Letters*, 1:88–89, 106, 118; Gage, *Corr.*, 1:412–413; Stiles, *Literary Diary*, 1:650–652 (an acute analysis of the offending passages in JA's letters); Hichborn to JA, 28 Oct., 25 Nov.–10 Dec. 1775, 20 May 1776 (Adams Papers); Jeremy Belknap, "Journal of My Tour to the Camp," MHS, *Procs.*, 1st ser., 4 (1858–1860):79–81. Allen French deals incidentally but helpfully with the Adams letters in his article "The First George Washington Scandal," MHS, *Procs.*, 65 (1932–1936):460–474, a study of Benjamin Harrison's letter to Washington, 21–24 July 1775, which was also captured on the person of Hichborn and which, when published, was embellished with a forged paragraph on "pretty little Kate the Washer-woman's Daughter."

Despite the buzzing of tongues and waggling of ears that ensued, it was JA's considered opinion that the interception and publication of his letters "have had no such bad Effects, as the Tories intended, and as some of our shortsighted Whiggs apprehended: so far otherwise that I see and hear every day, fresh Proofs that every Body is coming fast into every political Sentiment contained in them" (to AA, 2 Oct. 1775, Adams Papers). To Hichborn, who was still offering abject apologies, JA wrote on 29 May 1776 that he (JA) was not "in the least degree afraid of censure on your Account," and indeed thought his own aims had been more promoted than injured by Hichborn's gaucherie (LbC, Adams Papers).

² William Gordon, a dissenting clergyman who had come from England and was settled as minister of the third Congregational society in Jamaica Plain (Roxbury). Appointed chaplain to the Massachusetts Provincial Congress, he was an incurably political parson, corresponded widely with military and political leaders, and began at an early date to collect materials for a history of the Revolution. The four-volume work which resulted, entitled *The History of the Rise, Progress, and Establishment, of the Independence of the United States* (London, 1788), though suffering from defects common to its kind, notably plagiarism, is more valuable than has sometimes been recognized, because Gordon knew many of the persons he wrote about and made the earliest use of the manuscript files of Washington, Gates, and others. See *DAB*; "Letters of the Reverend William Gordon" (including some from the Adams Papers), ed. Worthington C. Ford, MHS, *Procs.*, 63 (1929–1930):303–613. JA's marginalia in his own copy of Gordon's *History* (in the Boston Public Library) have been printed by Zoltán Haraszti in the *Boston Public Library Quarterly*, 3:119–122 (April 1951).

[JACOB BENINGHOVE'S BILL FOR TOBACCO.] ¹

Philadelphia 16th Septr. 1775

Mr. John Adams   To Jacob Beninghove

	s	d
To 1 Carrot pigtail Tobacco	2	6
To 6 lb. Cutt Do. @ 12d per [lb.]	6	0
To Earthen pott	0	4
	8	10

¹ M-Ar: vol. 210; accompanied by a duplicate; neither is receipted.

1775 SEPTR. 17TH. SUNDAY.

Mr. Smith, Mr. Imlay and Mr. Hanson, breakfasted with us. Smith is an Englishman, Imlay and Hanson N. Yorkers.

Heard Sprout [Sproat], on 3 Tit. 5. Not by Works of Righteousness, which We have done, but according to his Mercy he saved us, through the Washing of Regeneration and the Renewing of the holy Ghost.

There is a great deal of Simplicity and Innocence in this worthy Man, but very little Elegance or Ingenuity.—In Prayer, he hangs his Head in an Angle of 45° over his right Shoulder. In Sermon, which is delivered without Notes, he throws himself into a Variety of indecent Postures. Bends his Body, Points his Fingers, and throws about his Arms, without any Rule or Meaning at all. He is totally destitute of the Genius and Eloquence of Duffil [Duffield], has no Imagination, No Passions, no Wit, no Taste and very little Learning, but a great deal of Goodness of Heart.

1775 SEPTR. 18. MONDAY.

This Morning John McPherson Esq. came to my Lodging, and requested to speak with me in Private. He is the Owner of a very handsome Country Seat, about five Miles out of this City: is the Father of Mr. McPherson, an Aid de Camp to General Schuyler. He has been a Captain of a Privateer, and made a Fortune in that Way the last War. Is reputed to be well skilled in naval Affairs.—He proposes great Things. Is sanguine, confident, positive, that he can take or burn every Man of War, in America.—It is a Secret he says. But he will communicate it to any one Member of Congress upon Condition, that it be not divulged during his Life at all, nor after his Death but for the Service of this Country. He says it is as certain as that he shall die, that he can burn any Ship.[1]

In the afternoon Mr. S.A. and I made visit at Mrs. Bedfords to the Maryland Gentlemen. We found Paca and Chase and a polite Reception from them. Chase is ever social and talkative. He seems in better Humour, than he was before the Adjournment. His Colony have acted with Spirit in Support of the Cause. They have formed themselves into a System and enjoyed an Association, if that is not an Absurdity.

[1] On Capt. McPherson and his scheme, see JCC, 3:296, 300, 301; Samuel Ward, Diary, 20 Oct. 1775, in Burnett, ed., *Letters of Members*, 1:238, with references there.

1775 SEPTR. 19. TUESDAY.

This Morning Mr. Henry Hill with his Brother Nat. Barrett came to visit us. Paine introduced him to Mrs. Yard as one of the Poor of Boston. He is here with his Wife, on a Visit to her Brother. P. cries You H. Hill, what did you come here for? Who did you bring with you? ha! ha! ha!

1775. SEPTR. 20. WEDNESDAY.

Took a Walk in Company with Govr. Ward, Mr. Gadsden and his Son, and Mr. S. Adams, to a little Box in the Country, belonging to old Mr. Marshall, the father of three Sons who live in the City.[1] A fine facetious old Gentleman, an excellent Whigg. There We drank

Coffee. A fine Garden. A little Box of one Room. Very chearfull and good humoured.

¹ This was Christopher Marshall (1709-1797), the well-known Philadelphia diarist and patriot. See *Extracts from the Diary of Christopher Marshall, . . . 1774-1781*, ed. William Duane, Albany, 1877, p. 43.

1775. SEPTR. 21. THURSDAY.

The famous Partisan Major Rogers came to our Lodgings to make Us a Visit.¹ He has been in Prison—discharged by some insolvent or bankrupt Act. He thinks We shall have hot Work, next Spring. He told me an old half Pay Officer, such as himself, would sell well next Spring. And when he went away, he said to S.A. and me, if you want me, next Spring for any Service, you know where I am, send for me. I am to be sold.—He says the Scotch Men at home, say d—n that Adams and Cushing. We must have their Heads, &c. Bernard used to d—n that Adams—every dip of his Pen stung like an horned Snake, &c. Paxton made his Will in favour of Ld. Townsend, and by that Maneuvre got himself made a Commissioner. There was a great deal of Beauty in that Stroke of Policy. We must laugh at such sublime Strokes of Politicks, &c. &c. &c.

In the Evening Mr. Jona. Dickinson Sergeant of Prince Town, made a Visit to the Sec.² and me. He says he is no Idolater of his Name Sake. That he was disappointed when he first saw him. Fame had given him an exalted Idea: but he came to N. Jersey upon a particular Cause, and made such a flimsy, effeminate, Piece of Work of it, that he sunk at once in his Opinion.

Serjeant is sorry to find a falling off in this City—not a third of the Battalion Men muster, who mustered at first.

D. he says sinks here in the public opinion. That many Gentlemen chime in with a spirited Publication in the Paper of Wednesday, which blames the conduct of several Gentlemen of Fortune, D., Cad., R., and J. Allen &c.³

¹ On the advent and intentions of Rogers in Philadelphia, see references in Burnett, ed., *Letters of Members*, 1: 201, note, and the notice of Rogers in *DAB*.

² Samuel Adams had been elected secretary of state by the new Massachusetts government in August (Wells, *Samuel Adams*, 2:321).

³ Probably John Dickinson, [   ] Cadwalader, Samuel Rhoads, and James Allen. The "Publication in the Paper of Wednesday" appeared in the *Pennsylvania Journal*, 20 Sept., and was a long unsigned account and defense of a demonstration, 6 Sept., by a group of "Associators" who wished to punish a tory lawyer, Isaac Hunt, and a violently tory physician, the younger John Kearsley. Certain "men of fortune" interfered with these proceedings, and, according to Christopher Marshall, Mayor Samuel Rhoads ordered out troops to disperse the crowd (*Extracts from the Diary of Christopher Marshall, . . . 1774-1781*, ed. William Duane, Albany, 1877, p. 41-42).

1775. FRYDAY. SEPTR. 22.

Mr. Gordon spent the Evening here.

1775. SATURDAY. SEPTR. 23.

Mr. Gordon came and told us News, opened his Budget.—Ethan Allen with 500 green mountain Boys, were entrenched half Way between St. Johns and Montreal, and had cutt off all Communication with Carlton, and was kindly treated by the French. A Council of War had been held, and it was their opinion that it was practicable to take Boston and Charlestown: but as it would cost many Lives, and expose the Inhabitants of Boston to destruction it was thought best to postpone it for the present.

Major Rogers came here too this Morning. Said he had a Hand and an Heart: tho he did not choose by offering himself to expose himself to Destruction.

I walked, a long Time this Morning, backward and forward, in the Statehouse Yard with Paca, McKean and Johnson. McKean has no Idea of any Right or Authority in Parliament. Paca contends for an Authority and Right to regulate Trade, &c.

Dyer and Serjeant of Princetown, spent the Evening here. S. says that the Irish Interest in this City has been the Support of Liberty. Maes [Mease] &c. are leaders in it. The Irish and the Presbyterian Interest coalesce.

[NOTES OF DEBATES IN THE CONTINENTAL CONGRESS]
1775. SATURDAY. SEPT. 22D. [*i.e.* 23D].[1]

S[*amuel*] A[*dams*] moved, upon Mifflins Letter, that a Sum be advanced from the Treasury for Mifflin and Barrell.[2]

Mr. E. Rutledge wished the Money might be advanced upon the Credit of the Qr. Mr. General. Wished that an Enquiry might be made whether Goods had been advanced. If so, it was against the association.

Lynch wish'd the Letter read.—*S. Adams* read it.

Jay. Seconded the Motion of E. Rutledge that a Committee be appointed to enquire if Goods are raised vs. the association.

Gadsden wished the Mo[tion] put off. We had other Matters of more importance.

Willing. Thought that Goods might be purchased upon four Months Credit. We should not intermix our Accounts.

Paine. We have not agreed to cloath the Soldiers, and the Qr. Mr.

Genl. has no Right to keep a Slop Shop any more than any Body else. It is a private Matter. Very indigested Applications are made here for Money.

Deane. The Army must be cloathed, or perish. No preaching vs. a Snow Storm. We ought to look out, that they be kept warm and that the Means of doing it be secured.

Lynch. We must see that the Army be provided with Cloathing. I intended to have moved this very day that a Committee be appointed to purchase woolen Goods in this City and N. York, for the use of the Army.

E. Rutledge. I have no objection to the Committee. I meant only that the poor Soldiers should be supplied with Goods and Cloathing as cheap as possible.

Lewis. Brown of Boston bought Goods at N. York and sent em up the North River, to be conveyed by Land to Cambridge.

Dyer. Wanted to know whether the Soldiers would be obliged to take these Goods. Goods cheaper in York than here.

Sherman. The Sutlers, last War, sold to the Soldiers who were not obliged to take any Thing. Many will be supplied by Families with their own Manufacture. The Qr. Mr. General did not apply to Congress, but to his own private Correspondents.

Deane. The Soldiers were imposed on by Sutlers last War. The Soldiers had no Pay to receive.

Lynch. A Soldier without Cloathing is not fit for Service, but he ought to be cloathed, as well as armed, and we ought to provide as well as it can be done, that he may be cloathed.

Nelson. Moved that 5000£ st. be advanced to the Qr. Mr. Genl. to be laid out in Cloathing for the Army.

Langdon. Hoped a Committee would be appointed.

Sherman liked Nelsons motion with an Addition that every Soldier should be at Liberty to supply himself in any other Way.

Reed. Understood that Mass. Committee of Supplies had a large Store that was very full.

Sherman. For a Committee to enquire what Goods would be wanted for the Army, and at what Prices they may be had and report.

Gadsden. Liked that best.

Johnson. Moved that the Sum might be limit[ed] to 5000£ st. We dont know what has been supplied by Mass., what from Rhode Island, what from N. York, and what from Connecticutt.

S. Adams. Liked Nelson's Motion.

Ward. Objected to it, and preferred the Motion for a Committee.

Nelson. The Qr. Mr. is ordered by the General to supply the Soldiers, &c.

Paine. It is the Duty of this Congress to see that the Army be supplied with Cloathing at a reasonable Rate. I am for a Committee. Qr. Mr. has his Hands full.

Zubly. Would it not be best to publish Proposals in the Papers for any Man who was willing to supply the Army with Cloathing, to make his offers.

Harrison. The Money ought to be advanced, in all events. Content with a Committee.

R. R. Livingston.

Willing. Proposed that We should desire the Committee of this City, to enquire after these Goods and this will lead them to an Enquiry, that will be beneficial to America.

Chase. The City of Philadelphia has broke the association by raising the Price of Goods 50 per Cent. It would not be proper to purchase Goods here. The Breach of the association here is general, in the Price of Goods, as it is in N. York with Respect to Tea. If We lay out 5000£ here we shall give a Sanction to the Breaches of the association. The Breach is too general to be punished.

Willing. If the Association is broke in this City, dont let us put the Burden of Examining into it upon a few, but the whole Committee. N. York have broke it, entirely. 99 in 100 drink Tea. I am not for screening the People of Philadelphia.

Sherman. I am not an Importer, but have bought of N. York Merchants for 20 years, at a certain Advance on the sterling Cost.

R. R. Livingston. Thought We ought to buy the Goods where they were dearest, because if We bought em at N. York where they were cheapest, N. York would soon be obliged to purchase in Phil. where they are dearest and then the loss would fall upon N. York. Whereas in the other Way the Loss would be general.

Jay. We had best desire the Committee of this City to purchase the Quantity of Goods at the Price stated by the Association and see if they were to be had here at that Price.

This Debate terminated in a Manner that I did not foresee.—A Committee was appointed to purchase 5000£ st.s worth of Goods, to be sent to the Qr. Mr. and by him be sold to the Soldiers at first Cost and Charges. Qr. Mr. to be allowed 5 Pr. Cent for his Trouble.

Mr. Lynch, and Coll. Nelson and Coll. Harrison indulged their Complaisance and private Friendship for Mifflin and Washington so far as to carry this.

It is almost impossible to move any Thing but you instantly see private Friendships and Enmities, and provincial Views and Prejudices, intermingle in the Consultation. These are degrees of Corruption. They are Deviations from the public Interest, and from Rectitude. By this Vote however, perhaps the poor Soldiers may be benefited, which was all I wished, the Interest of Mr. Mifflin being nothing to me.

[1] First entry in booklet "23" as labeled by CFA (our D/JA/23), a small memorandum book bound in red-brown leather, containing exclusively notes on the proceedings of Congress, from the present date through 21 Oct. 1775. All accounts of debates through the latter date derive from this booklet, though in the present text they have been interspersed chronologically among JA's regular diary entries.

Saturday fell on 23 Sept. 1775, and there is other evidence to show that the debate recorded here occurred on the 23d. See *JCC*, 3:260, and Samuel Ward, Diary, 23 Sept., in Burnett, ed., *Letters of Members*, 1:205.

[2] Thomas Mifflin had been appointed Continental quartermaster general on 14 Aug. (*DAB*). His letter under discussion has not been found in the Papers of the Continental Congress or in any other likely repository.

1775. SEPTR. 24. SUNDAY.

Dyer is very sanguine that the 2 De Witts, one of Windham, the other of Norwich, will make Salt Petre in large Quantities. He produces a Sample, which is very good.

Harrison is confident that Virginia alone will do great Things from Tobacco Houses. But my faith is not strong, as yet.

Ld. North is at his old Work again. Sending over his Anodynes to America—deceiving one credulous American after another, into a Belief that he means Conciliation, when in Truth he means nothing but Revenge. He rocks the cradle, and sings Lullaby, and the innocent Children go to Sleep, while he prepares the Birch to whip the poor Babes. One Letter after another comes that the People are uneasy and the Ministry are sick of their Systems. But nothing can be more fallacious. Next Spring We shall be jockied by Negociation, or have hot Work in War. Besides I expect a Reinforcement to Gage and to Carlton, this fall or Winter.

Heard Mr. Smith of Pequay [Pequea], at about 40 Miles towards Lancaster, a Scotch Clergyman, of great Piety as Coll. Roberdeau says: The Text was Luke 14:18. And they all with one Consent began to make excuse.—This was at Duffills Meeting. In the afternoon, heard our Mr. Gordon, in Arch Street. The Lord is nigh unto all that call upon him.

Call'd upon Stephen Collins who has just returned.

Stephen has a Thousand Things to say to Us, he says. A Thousand observations to make.

One Thing he told me, for my Wife, who will be peeping here, sometime or other, and come across it. He says when he call'd at my House, an English Gentleman was with him, a Man of Penetration, tho of few Words. And this silent, penetrating Gentleman was pleased with Mrs. Adams, and thought her, the most accomplished Lady he had seen since he came out of England.—Down Vanity, for you dont know who this Englishman is.

Dr. Rush came in. He is an elegant, ingenious Body. Sprightly, pretty fellow. He is a Republican. He has been much in London. Acquainted with Sawbridge, McCaulay, Burgh, and others of that Stamp. Dilly sends him Books and Pamphletts, and Sawbridge and McCaulay correspond with him.[1] He complains of D[ickinson]. Says the Committee of Safety are not the Representatives of the People, and therefore not their Legislators; yet they have been making Laws, a whole Code for a Navy. This Committee was chosen by the House, but half of them are not Members and therefore not the Choice of the People. All this is just. He mentions many Particular Instances, in which Dickenson has blundered. He thinks him warped by the Quaker Interest and the Church Interest too. Thinks his Reputation past the Meridian, and that Avarice is growing upon him. Says that Henry and Mifflin both complained to him very much about him. But Rush I think, is too much of a Talker to be a deep Thinker. Elegant not great.

In the Evening Mr. Bullock and Mr. Houstoun, two Gentlemen from Georgia, came into our Room and smoked and chatted, the whole Evening. Houstoun and Adams disputed the whole Time in good Humour. They are both Dabbs at Disputation I think. H. a Lawyer by Trade is one of Course, and Adams is not a Whit less addicted to it than the Lawyers. The Q. was whether all America was not in a State of War, and whether We ought to confine ourselves to act upon the defensive only. He was for acting offensively next Spring or this fall if the Petition was rejected or neglected. If it was not answered, and favourably answered, he would be for acting vs. Britain and Britains as in open War vs. French and frenchmen. Fit Privateers and take their Ships, any where.

These Gentlemen give a melancholly Account of the State of Georgia and S. Carolina. They say that if 1000 regular Troops should land in Georgia and their commander be provided with Arms and Cloaths enough, and proclaim Freedom to all the Negroes who would join his Camp, 20,000 Negroes would join it from the two Provinces in a fortnight. The Negroes have a wonderfull Art of communicating Intelligence among themselves. It will run severall hundreds of Miles in a Week or Fortnight.

They say, their only Security is this, that all the Kings Friends and Tools of Government have large Plantations and Property in Negroes. So that the Slaves of the Tories would be lost as well as those of the Whiggs.

I had nearly forgot a Conversation with Dr. Coombe concerning assassination, Henry 4., Sully, Buckingham &c. &c. Coombe has read Sullys Memoirs with great Attention.

[1] See L. H. Butterfield, "The American Interests of the Firm of E. and C. Dilly, with Their Letters to Benjamin Rush, 1770–1795," Bibliog. Soc. Amer., *Papers,* 45 (1951):283–332.

1775. SEPTR. 25. MONDAY.

Rode out of Town and dined with Mr. Macpherson. He has the most elegant Seat in Pensilvania, a clever Scotch Wife and two pretty daughters. His Seat is on the Banks of Schuylkill.[1]

He has been Nine Times wounded in Battle. An old Sea Commander, made a Fortune by Privateering. An Arm twice shot off, shot thro the Leg. &c.—He renews his Proposals of taking or burning Ships.

Spent the Evening with Lynch at the City Tavern. He thinks the Row Gallies and Vesseau de Frize inadequate to the Expence.[2]

[1] In what is now Fairmount Park. See "Mount Pleasant and the Macphersons," in Thomas A. Glenn, *Some Colonial Mansions and Those Who Lived in Them,* 2d ser., Phila., 1900, p. 445–483.

[2] These were defenses of Philadelphia on the Delaware River; see entry of 28 Sept. and note, below.

[NOTES OF DEBATES IN THE CONTINENTAL CONGRESS] 1775 MONDAY. SEPT. 24 [*i.e.* 25].

An Uneasiness, among some of the Members concerning a Contract with Willing & Morris, for Powder, by which the House, without any Risque at all will make a clear Profit of 12,000£ at least.

Dyer and Deane spoke in public, Lewis to me in private about it. All think it exorbitant.

S. Adams desired that the Resolve of Congress, upon which the Contract was founded might be read: he did not recollect it.[1]

De Hart. One of the Contractors, Willing, declared to this Congress that he looked upon the Contract to be that the first Cost should be insured to them, not the 14£ a Barrell for the Powder.

R. R. Livingston. I never will vote to ratify the Contract in the sense that Morris understands it.

Willing. I am as a Member of the House, a Party to that Contract, but was not privy to the Bargain. I never saw the Contract, untill I saw it in Dr. Franklins Hand. I think it ensures only the first Cost. My Partner thinks it ensures the whole. He says that Mr. Rutledge said at the Time, that Congress should have nothing to do with Sea risque. The Committee of this City offered 19£. I would wish to have nothing to do with the Contract: but to leave it to my Partner, who is a Man of Reason and Generosity, to explain the Contract with the Gentlemen who made it with him.

J. Rutledge. Congress was to run no Risque only vs. Men of War and Customhouse officers. I was surprized this Morning to hear that Mr. Morris understood it otherwise. If he wont execute a Bond, such as We shall draw, I shall not be at a loss what to do.

Johnson. An hundred Ton of Powder was wanted.

Ross. In Case of its Arrival Congress was to pay £14. If Men of War, or Custom house officers, should get it, Congress was to pay first Cost only as I understood it.

Zubly. We are highly favoured. 14£ We are to give if We get the Powder: and 14£ if We dont get it. I understand Persons enough will contract to supply Powder at 15£ and run all risques.

Willing. Sorry any Gentleman should be severe. Mr. Morris's Character is such that he cannot deserve it.

Lynch. If Morris will execute the Bond, well, if not the Committee will report.

Deane. It is very well that this matter has been moved and that so much has been said upon it.

Dyer. There are not Ten Men in the Colony I come from, who are worth so much Money as will be made clear [2] by this Contract.

Ross. What has this Matter to [do with] the present debate, whether Connecticutt Men are worth much or no. It proves there are no Men there whose Capital or Credit are equal to such Contracts. That is all.

Harrison. The Contract is made and the Money paid. How can We get it back?

Johnson. Let us consider the Prudence of this Contract. If it had not been made Morris would have got 19£, and not have set forward a second Adventure.

Gadsden. Understands the Contract as Morris does, and yet thinks it a prudent one, because Morris would have got 19£.

J. Adams. — — — — &c. &c. &c.

Cushing. I move that We take into Consideration a Method of keeping up an Army in the Winter.

Gadsden. Seconds the Motion and desires that a Motion made in Writing some days ago, and postponed may be read as it was. As also Passages of G. Washingtons Letter.

S. Adams. The General has promised another Letter in which We shall have his Sentiments. We shall have it tomorrow perhaps.

Lynch. If We have, We shall only loose the Writing of a Letter.

J. Adams moved that the Generals Advice should be asked concerning Barracks &c. and that a Committee be appointed to draught a Letter. *Lynch* seconded the Motion.

A Committee was appointed. Lynch, J. Adams, and Coll. Lee the Men.[3]

Sherman moved that a Committee be appointed of one Member from each Colony, to receive, and examine all Accounts.

S. Adams seconded the Motion.

Harrison asked is this the Way of giving Thanks?

S. Adams. Was decent to the Committee for Rifle Mens Accounts, meant no Reflections upon them, was sorry that the worthy Gentleman from Virginia, conceived that any was intended. He was sure there was no foundation for it.

Paine. Thought that Justice and Honour required that We should carefully examine all Accounts, and see to the Expenditure of all public Monies.

That the Minister would find out our Weakness, and would foment divisions among our People.

He was sorry that Gentlemen could not hear Methods proposed, to settle and pay Accounts in a manner that would give Satisfaction to the People, without seeming to resent them.

Harrison. Now the Gentlemen have explained themselves he had no Objection, but when it was proposed to appoint a new Committee in the Place of the former one, it implied a Reflection.

Deane. ———.

Willing. These Accounts are for Tents, Arms, Cloathing, &c. as well as Expences of the Riflemen, &c.

Nelson moved that 20,000 dollars be voted into the Hands of the other Committee to settle the Accounts.

S. Adams. Seconded the Motion, but still hoped that some time or other, a Committee would be appointed of one Member from each Colony, to examine all Accounts because he thought it reasonable.[4]

[1] See JCC, 2:253–255.

[2] "made clear" here means "cleared."

[3] See JCC, 3:261, which indicates that two letters from Washington were involved, apparently those dated 4 and 31 Aug. (*Writings*, ed. Fitzpatrick, 3:390–399, 461–463). The committee reported a draft answer on 26 Sept., which was agreed to and sent over Pres. Hancock's name the same day (JCC, 3:263; Burnett, ed., *Letters of Members*, 1:207–209).

[4] According to the Journal, such a committee was in fact appointed this day (JCC, 3:262).

1775 SEPTR. 26. TUESDAY.

Wrote to Mrs. A. and Mr. and Mrs. W.[1]

[1] The letter to AA is in the Adams Papers and is unpublished; those to James and Mercy Warren are in MHi and are printed in *Warren-Adams Letters*, 1:115–118.

1775. SEPTR. 27. WEDNESDAY.

Mr. Bullock and Mr. Houstoun, the Gentlemen from Georgia, invited S.A. and me to spend the Evening with them in their Chamber, which We did very agreably and socially. Mr. Langdon of N. Hampshire was with us.

Mr. Bullock after Dinner invited me to take a ride with him in his Phaeton which I did. He is a solid, clever Man. He was President of their Convention.

[NOTES OF DEBATES IN THE CONTINENTAL CONGRESS]
1775. SEPTR. 27.

Willing in favour of Mr. Purveyances Petition.[1] *Harrison* vs. it.

Willing thinks the Non Exportation sufficiently hard upon the Farmer, the Merchant and the Tradesman, but will not arraign the Propriety of the Measure.

Nelson. If We give these Indulgences, I know not where they will end. Sees not why the Merchant should be indulged more than the Farmer.

Harrison. It is the Merchant in England that is to suffer.

Lynch. They meant gain and they ought to bear the Loss.

Sherman. Another Reason. The Cargo is Provisions and will probably fall into the Hands of the Enemy.

R. R. Livingston. There is no Resolve of Congress vs. exporting to foreign Ports. We shall not give Licence to deceit, by clearing out for England.

Lynch. Moves that the Committee of this City, be desired to enquire whether Deans Vessell taken at Block Island and another at Cape Codd, were not sent on Purpose to supply the Enemy.

Reed. The Committee of this City have enquired of the owners of one Vessell. The owners produc'd their Letter Books, and were ready to swear. The Conduct of the Captain is yet suspicious. Thinks the other Enquiry very proper.

Lee. Thinks Lynches Motion proper. Thinks the conduct detestible Parricide—to supply those who have Arms in their Hands to deprive us of the best Rights of human Nature. The honest Seamen ought to be examined, and they may give Evidence vs. the guilty.

Hancock. Deane belongs to Boston. He came from W. Ind[ies] and was seized here, and released. Loaded with flour and went out.

[1] A memorial of Samuel and Robert Purviance, the well-known Baltimore merchants, is summarized under this date in JCC, 3:264. It was tabled.

1775. SEPT. 28. THURSDAY.

The Congress, and the Assembly of this Province were invited to make an Excursion upon Delaware River in the new Row Gallies built by the Committee of Safety of this Colony. About Ten in the Morning We all embarked. The Names of the Gallies are the Washington, the Effingham, the Franklin, the Dickenson, the Otter, the Bull Dog, and one more, whose Name I have forgot. We passed down the River by Glocester where the Vesseau de Frize are. These a[re] Frames of Timber to be fill'd with Stones and sunk, in three Rowes, in the Channell.[1]

I went in the Bull Dog Captn. Alexander Commander. Mr. Hillegas, Mr. Owen Biddle, and Mr. Rittenhouse, and Capt. Faulkner [Falconer] were with me. Hillegas is one of our Continental Treasurers, is a great Musician—talks perpetually of the Forte and Piano, of Handell &c. and Songs and Tunes. He plays upon the Fiddle.

Rittenhouse is a Mechannic, a Mathematician, a Philsosopher and an Astronomer.

Biddle is said to be a great Mathematician. Both are Members of the American Philosophical Society. I mentioned Mr. Cranch to them for a Member.

Our Intention was to have gone down to the Fort[2] but the Winds and Tide being unfavourable We returned by the City and went up the River to Point no Point, a pretty Place.[3] On our Return Dr. Rush, Dr. Zubly and Counciller Ross, Brother of George Ross, joined us.[4]

Ross is a Lawyer, of great Eloquence, and heretofore of extensive Practice. A great Tory, they say, but now begins to be converted. He said the Americans were making the noblest and firmest Resistance to Tyranny that ever was made by any People. The Acts were founded in

Wrong, Injustice and Oppression. The great Town of Boston had been remarkably punished without being heard.

Rittenhouse is a tall, slender Man, plain, soft, modest, no remarkable Depth, or thoughtfullness in his Face—yet cool, attentive, and clear.

[1] JA had furnished a brief description of the "Row Gallies" or "gondolas" in a letter to Col. Josiah Quincy, 29 July (MHi; printed in JA, *Works*, 9: 362). Immediately after the evacuation of Boston by the British, JA wrote to Cotton Tufts advising that *vaisseaux de frise* be used to defend Boston Harbor: "They are large Frames of great Timber, loaded with stone and sunk—great Timbers barbed with Iron, pointed and feathered, are placed in such a Posture as to intangle a Vessell, and shatter her, and sink her" (29 March 1776, NhHi). See drawings in *PMHB*, 65 (1941):

354; also David B. Tyler, *The Bay and River Delaware*, Cambridge, Md., 1955, p. 32–33.

[2] Later named Fort Mifflin and located on Mud (sometimes called Fort) Island, just below the mouth of the Schuylkill.

[3] Near the mouth of Frankford Creek in the region called Richmond. JA described it in detail in a letter to AA, 25 May 1777 (Adams Papers; printed in JA, *Letters*, ed. CFA, 1:230–231).

[4] Rush gave his recollections of this jaunt on the Delaware in a letter to JA, 13 April 1790 (Adams Papers; printed in Benjamin Rush, *Letters*, 1:545).

[NOTES OF DEBATES IN THE CONTINENTAL CONGRESS]
OCT. 3 [*i.e.* 4].[1]

Johnson. I should be for the Resolutions about Imports and Exports, standing, till further order.

I should be vs. giving up the Carriage. The Grower, the Farmer gets the same, let who will be the Exporter. But the Community does not. The Shipwright, Ropemaker, Hempgrower, all Shipbuilders, the Profits of the Merchant are all lost, if Foreigners are our sole Carriers, as well as Seamen, &c. I am for the Report standing, the Association standing.

J. Rutledge. The Question is whether We shall shut our Ports entirely, or adhere to the Association. The Res[olutions] we come to, ought to be final.

Lee. N. Carolina is absent. They are expected every Hour. We had better suspend a final Determination. I fear our determination to stop Trade, will not be effectual.

Willing. N.C. promised to put themselves in the same situation with other Colonies.[2] N. York have done the same. Our Gold is lok'd up, at present. We ought to be decisive. Interest is near and dear to Men. The Committee of Secrecy [3] find Difficulties. Merchants dare not trade.

Deane. Sumptuary Laws, or a Non Imp[ortation] were necessary, if We had not been oppressed. A N[on] Export[ation] was attended with Difficulty. My Colony could do as well as others. We should have acquiesced in an immediate Non Export. or a partial one. Many voted for it as an Object in Terrorem. Merchants, Mechanicks, Farmers, all call for an Establishment.

Whether We are to Trade with all Nations except B[ritain], Ireland and West Indies, or with one or two particular Nations, We cannot get ammunition without allowing some Exports, for The Merchant has neither Money nor Bills, and our Bills will not pass abroad.

R. R. Livingston. We should go into a full Discussion of the Subject. Every Gentleman ought to express his Sentiments. The 1st Q. is how far we shall adhere to our Association—What advantages we gain, What Disadvantages we suffer, by it. An immediate Stoppage last year would have had a great Effect: But at that time the Country could not bear it. We are now out of Debt, nearly.

The high Price of Grain in B. will be an advantage to the Farmer. The Price of Labour is nearly equal in Europe. The Trade will be continued and G.B. will learn to look upon America as insignificant. If We export to B. and dont import, they must pay Us in Money. Of great Importance that We should import. We employ our Ships and Seamen. We have nothing to fear but Disunion among ourselves. What will disunite us, more than the Decay of all Business. The People will feel, and will say that Congress tax them and oppress them worse than Parliament.

Ammunition cannot be had unless We open our Ports. I am for doing away our Non Exportation Agreement entirely. I see many Advantages in leaving open the Ports, none in shutting them up. I should think the best way would be to open all our Ports. Let us declare all those Bonds illegal and void. What is to become of our Merchants, Farmers, Seamen, Tradesmen? What an Accession of Strength should We throw into the Hands of our Enemies, if We drive all our Seamen to them.

Lee. Is it proper that Non Export. Ag[reemen]t should continue. For the Interest [4] of Americans to open our Ports to foreign Nations, that they should become our Carriers, and protect their own Vessells.

Johnson. Never had an Idea that We should shut our Export. Agreement closer than it is at present. If We leave it as it is, We shall get Powder by Way of N. York, the lower Counties and N. Carolina. In Winter our Merchants will venture out to foreign Nations. If Parliament should order our Ships to be seized, We may begin a Force in Part to protect our own Vessells, and invite Foreigners to come here and protect their own Trade.

J. Rutledge. We ought to postpone it, rather than not come to a decisive Resolution.

Lee. We shall be prevented from exporting if B. Power can do it. We ought to stop our own Exports, and invite foreign Nations to come and export our Goods for Us.

I am for opening our Exportations to foreigners farther than We have.

Willing. The Gents. favorite Plan is to induce foreigners to come here. Shall We act like the Dog in the Manger, not suffer N.Y. and the lower Counties and N. Carolina to export because We cant. We may get Salt and Ammunition by those Ports. Cant be for inviting foreigners to become our Carriers. Carriage is an amazing Revenue. Holland and England have derived their maritime Power from their Carriage. The Circulation of our Paper will stop, and [lose?] its Credit without Trade. 7 Millions of Dollars have been struck by the Continent and by the separate Colonies.

Lee. The End of Administration will be answered by the Gentns. Plan. Jealousies and Dissensions will arise and Disunion and Division. We shall become a Rope of Sand.

Zubly. The Q. should be whether the Export should be kept or not.

Chace. I am for adhering to the Association and think that We ought not to determine these Questions this day. Differ from R. Livingston,[5] our Exports are to be relaxed except as to Tobacco and Lumber. This will produce a Disunion of the Colonies. The Advantage of cultivating Tobacco is very great. The Planters would complain. Their Negro females would be useless without raising tobacco.

That Country must grow rich that Exports more than they import. There ought not to be a partial Export to Great Britain. We affect the Revenue and the Remittance, by stopping our Exports. We have given a deadly Blow to B. and Ireland, by our Non Export. Their People must murmur, must starve. The Nation must have become Bankrupt before this day if We had ceased Exports at first. I look upon B., I. and W.I. as our Enemies, and would not trade with them, while at War.

We cant support the War and our Taxes, without Trade. Emissions of Paper cannot continue. I dread an Emission for another Campaign. We cant stand it without Trade.

I cant agree that N.Y., the lower Counties and N. Carolina, should carry on Trade. Upon giving a Bond, and making Oath, they may export. I am vs. these Colonies trading according to the restraining Act. It will produce Division. A few Weeks will put us all on a footing. N. York &c. are now all in Rebellion as the Ministry call it, as much as Mass. Bay.

We must trade with foreign Nations, at the Risque indeed. But We may export our Tobacco to France, Spain or any other foreign Nation.

If We treat with foreign Nations, We should send to them as well as they to Us.

What Nation or Countries shall We trade with. Shall We go to there Ports and pay duties, and let them come here and pay none.

To say you will trade with all the World, deserves Consideration.

I have not absolutely discarded every Glimpse of a Hope of Reconciliation. Our Prospect is gloomy. I cant agree, that We shall not export our own Produce. We must treat with foreign Nations upon Trade. They must protect and support Us with their Fleets.

When you once offer your Trade to foreign Nations, away with all Hopes of Reconciliation.

E. Rutledge. Differs with all who think the Non Exportation should be broke, or that any Trade at all should be carried on.

When a Commodity is out of Port, the Master may carry it where he pleases.

My Colony will receive your Determination upon a general Non Export. The People will not be restless. Proposes a general Non Export, untill next Congress.

Our People will go into Manufactures, which is a Source of Riches to a Country. We can take our Men from Agriculture, and employ them in Manufactures.

Agriculture and Manufactures cannot be lost. Trade is precarious.

R. R. Livingston. Not convinced by any Argument. Thinks the exception of Tobacco and Lumber, would not produce Disunion. The Colonies affected can see the Principles, and their Virtue is such that they would not be disunited.

The Americans are their own Carriers now, chiefly. A few British Ships will be out of Employ.

I am vs. exporting Lumber. I grant that if We trade with other Nations, some of our Vessells will be seized and some taken. Carolina is cultivated by rich Planters—not so in the northern Colonies. The Planters can bear a Loss and see the Reason of it. The northern Colonies cant bear it.

Not in our Power to draw People from the Plough to Manufactures.

We cant make Contracts for Powder, without opening our Ports. I am for exporting where B. will allow Us, to Britain itself. If We shut up our Ports, We drive our Sailors to Britain. The Army will be supplied, in all Events.

Lee makes a Motion for 2 Resolutions. The Trade of Virginia and Maryland may be stopped by a very small naval Force. N. Carolina is badly off. The Northern Colonies are more fortunate.

The Force of G.B. on the Water being exceedingly great, that of

America, almost nothing—they may prevent allmost all our Trade, in our own Bottoms.

G.B. may exert every Nerve next Year, to send 15, 20, or even 30,000 Men to come here.

The Provisions of America, are become necessary to several Nations. France is in Distress for them. Tumults and Attempts to destroy the Grain in the Year [Ear]. England has turned Arable into Grass—France into Vines. Grain cant be got from Poland, nor across the Mediterranean. The Dissentions in Poland continue. Spain is at War with the Algerians, and must have Provisions. It would be much safer for them to carry our Provisions than for Us. We shall get necessary Manufactures and Money and Powder.

This is only a temporary Expedient, at the present Time, and for a short Duration—to End when the War ends. I agree We must sell our Produce. Foreigners must come in 3 or 4 Months. The Risque We must pay, in the Price of our Produce. The Insurance must be deducted. Insurance would not be high to foreigners on account of the Novelty. It is no new Thing. The B. Cruizers will be the Danger.

[1] The debates recorded here, in the next entry, and in others farther on, took place in a committee of the whole on "the state of the trade of the thirteen Colonies," which sat repeatedly during this session to discuss a report of a committee on American trade appointed 22 September. From time to time the committee of the whole reported recommendations for action but as late as 23 Dec. had not finished its deliberations. See JCC, 3:259, 268–269, 276, 291–293, 307–308, 314–315, 361–364, 455. JA's own views on the momentous questions at issue (e.g. the problem of obtaining powder and other essential munitions, of commercial relations with foreign powers, of building a navy) do not appear in his notes of the debates, but he wrote frequently to James Warren about them while the debates were going on; see his letters of 7, 19 (bis), 20, and 28 Oct. (MHi; printed in *Warren-Adams Letters*, 1:126–129, 145–147, 155–156, 166–167).

Since JA took these notes hastily and never revised them, there are passages among them that remain cryptic. For example, Samuel Chase's rambling speech appears to argue on both sides of more than one of the questions at issue.

[2] The ports of New York, Delaware ("the three lower Counties"), North Carolina, and Georgia had not been closed by the so-called Restraining Acts of March–April 1775 (15 Geo. 3, chs. 10, 18). But as Chase predicted in the course of this debate, they were soon to be (by the Prohibitory Act of Dec. 1775; 16 Geo. 3, ch. 5), and all the mainland colonies "put ... on a footing." Thus much of the warm discussion in committee of the whole was irrelevant and immaterial.

[3] The committee agreed to ˙and appointed, 18–19 Sept., "to contract and agree for the importation and delivery" of powder and other munitions (JCC, 2:253–255).

[4] That is, "It is for the Interest. . . ."

[5] Here supply "who holds that" or some equivalent phrase.

[NOTES OF DEBATES, CONTINUED] OCTR. 5.

Gadsden. I wish we may confine ourselves to one Point. Let the

Point be whether We shall shut up all our Ports, and be all on a footing. The Ministry will answer their End, if We let the Custom houses be open, in N.Y., N.C., the lower Counties and Georgia. They will divide us. One Colony will envy another, and be jealous. Mankind act by their feelings. Rice sold for £3—it wont sell now for 30s. We have rich and poor there as in other Colonies. We know that the excepted Colonies dont want to take Advantage of the others.

Zubly. Q. whether the Custom houses be stopped, and the Trade opened to all the World. The object is so great that I would not discuss it, on Horse back, riding Post haste. It requires the debate of a Week. We are lifting up a Rod—if you dont repeal the Acts, We will open our Ports.

Nations as well as Individuals are sometimes intoxicated. It is fair to give them Notice. If We give them Warning, they will take Warning. They will send Ships out. Whether they can stop our Trade, is the Question. N. England I leave out of the Question. N.Y. is stopped by one Ship. Philadelphia says her Trade is in the Power of the fleet. V[irginia] and Maryland, is within the Capes of Virginia. N. Carolina is accessible. Only one good Harbour, Cape Fear. In G[eorgia] We have several Harbours, but a small naval Force may oppose or destroy all the naval Force of Georgia.

The Navy can stop our Harbours and distress our Trade. Therefore it is impracticable, to open our Ports.

The Q. is whether we must have Trade or not. We cant do without Trade. We must have Trade. It is prudent not to put Virtue to too serious a Test. I would use American Virtue, as sparingly as possible lest We wear it out.

Are We sure one Cano will come to trade? Has any Merchant received a Letter from Abroad, that they will come. Very doubtfull and precarious whether any French or Spanish Vessell would be cleared out to America. It is a Breach of the Treaty of Peace. The Spaniards may be too lazy to come to America. They may be supplied from Sicily. It is precarious, and dilatory—extreamly dangerous—and pernicious.

I am clearly vs. any Proposition to open our Ports to all the World. It is not prudent to threaten.

The People of England will take it we design to break off, to separate. We have Friends in Eng. who have taken this up, upon virtuous Principles.

Lee. I will follow Mr. Gadsden and simplify the Proposition, and confine it to the Q. whether the Custom houses shall be shut? If they are open, the excepted Colonies may trade, others not, which will be unequal. The Consequence Jealousy, Division and Ruin. I would have all suffer equally. But We should have some Offices, set up, where Bond should be given that Supplies shall not go to our Enemies.

[NOTES OF DEBATES, CONTINUED] OCTR. 6.

Chase. I dont think the Resolution goes far enough.[1] Ld. Dunmore has been many Months committing Hostilities vs. Virginia, and has extended his Piracies to Maryland.[2] I wish he had been seized, by the Colony, Months ago. They would have received the Thanks of all North America.

Is it practicable now? Have the Committee any naval Force? This order will be a mere Piece of Paper. Is there a Power in the Committee to raise and pay a naval Force? Is it to be done at the Expence of the Continent. Have they Ships or Men.

Lee. I wish Congress would advise Virginia and Maryland to raise a Force by Sea to destroy Ld. Dunmores Power. He is fond of his Bottle and may be taken by Land, but ought to be taken at all Events.

Zubly. I am sorry to see the very threatening Condition that Virginia is likely to be in. I look on the Plan We heard of yesterday to be vile, abominable and infernal—but I am afraid it is practicable. Will these Mischiefs be prevented by seizing Dunmore. Seizing the K's Representatives will make a great Impression in England, and probably Things will be carried on afterwards with greater Rage.

I came here with 2 Views. One to secure the Rights of America. 2. A Reconciliation with G. Britain.

Dyer. They cant be more irritated at home than they are. They are bent upon our Destruction. Therefore that is no Argument vs. seizing them. Dunmore can do no Mischief in Virginia[3]—his Connections in England are such that he may be exchanged to Advantage. Wentworth is gone to Boston. Franklyn is not dangerous. Pen is not. Eden is not.[4]

Johnson. Dunmore a very bad Man. A defensive Conduct was determined on, in the Convention of Virginia. I am for leaving it to Virginia.

We ought not to lay down a rule in a Passion. I see less and less Prospect of a Reconciliation every day. But I would not render it impossible. If We should render it impossible, our Colony would take it into their own Hands and make Concessions inconsistent with the Rights of America. N.C., V., P., N. York, at least have strong Parties, each of them of that Mind. This would make a Disunion. Five or six Weeks will give Us the final Determination of the People of G. Britain. Not a Governor in the Continent has the real Power, but some have

List of Stores sent on board the Boston

6 doz of Poultry — 5 bushels of Corn
1 barrel of Apples.
6 or 7 doz of Syder
2 fatt Sheep
2 hogs.
1 Ten gallo. Keg of old Spirit
1 barrel of 2 or 3 doz Medena Wine
1 bed & beding —
12 or 14 doz of Eggs
7 Loves of Sugar
30 — Brown Do
1 Case Rum
2 doz & 4 bottle Port Wine
1 double Matrass, bolster & Pillow
2 quire Paper, 2 mem? Books, 1 box Wafers
some Quills & Ink
1 bag Indian Meal
6d Chocolate
2w Tea
   Pepper & Mustard
   Pipes & Tobacco
   Money in the Shoes.
28 Guineas ————— at 21/ — £29 – 8
12 half Joes ——— · 36/ ·— 21 · 12
                                 51
46½ Guineas — 21/ — 48 · 16 · 6
      Change ————— · 3 · 6
                         £ 100

3. LIST OF STORES SENT ON BOARD THE CONTINENTAL FRIGATE
Boston, FEBRUARY 1778

For the Hon John Adams Esqr

1 Bushel Indian Meal
1 Cask Rum
1 Ream Paper
2 Account Books
1/2 hundred Quills
30 lb Brown Sugar
1 Box Wafers
1 Bottle Ink
1 doz Pipes
2 lb Tobacco
2 Bottles Mustard
2 lb Tea
2 lb Chocolate. There is 52 lb 6 ℔ in the whole
a Mattrass & Bolster
a Leaden Cask —

City March 2 1779

These certify that the Box or Cask which
accompany this contains only a Quantity
of Books belonging to the Honorable
John Adams one of the late Commissioners
from the United States of America and
that they are intended for Nantes in this
Way to America — All concerned are requested
to permit them to pass.

the Shadow of it. A Renunciation of all Connection with G.B. will be understood by a step of this Kind. 13 Colonies connected with G.B. in 16 Months have been brought to an Armed Opposition to the Claims of G.B. The line We have pursued has been the Line We ought to have pursued. If what we have done had been proposed two Years ago, 4 Colonies would not have been for it.

Suppose we had a dozen Crown Officers in our Possession. Have We determined what to do with them? Shall we hang them.

Lee. Those who apply general Reasons to this particular Case will draw improper Conclusions. Those Crown Officers who have advised his Lordship vs. his violent Measures, have been quarrell'd with by him.

Virginia is pierced in all Parts with navigable Waters. His Lordship knows all these Waters and the Plantations on them. Shuldam is coming to assist him in destroying these Plantations. We see his Influence with an abandoned Administration, is sufficient to obtain what he pleases.

If 6 Weeks may furnish decisive Information, the same Time may produce decisive destruction to Maryland and Virginia. Did We go fast enough when We suffered the Troops at Boston to fortify.

Zubly. This is a sudden Motion. The Motion was yesterday to apprehend Govr. Tryon.[5] We have not yet conquered the Army or Navy of G.B. A Navy, consisting of a Cutter, rides triumphant in Virginia. There are Persons in America who wish to break off with G.B. A Proposal has been made to apply to France and Spain—before I agree to it, I will inform my Constituents. I apprehend the Man who should propose it would be torn to pieces like De Wit.

Wythe. It was from a Reverence for this Congress that the Convention of Virginia, neglected to arrest Lord Dunmore. It was not intended suddenly, to form a Precedent for Govr. Tryon. If Maryland have a Desire to have a Share in the Glory of seizing this Nobleman, let them have it.

The 1st. objection is the Impracticability of it.—I dont say that it is practicable, but the attempt can do no harm.

From seizing Cloathing in Delaware, seizing the Transports &c., the Battles of Lexington, Charlestown, &c., every Man in Great Britain will be convinced by Ministry and Parliament that We are aiming at an Independency on G.B. Therefore We need not fear from this Step disaffecting our Friends in England. As to a Defection in the Colonies, I cant answer for Maryland, Pensylvania, &c. but I can for Virginia.

Johnson. I am not vs. allowing Liberty to arrest Ld. Dunmore—there is Evidence that the Scheme he is executing was recommended by himself. Maryland does not regard the Connection with G.B. as the first good.

Stone. If We signify to Virginia, that it will not be disagreable to us, if they secure Ld. Dunmore, that will be sufficient.

Lewis moves an Amendment, that it be recommended to the Council of Virginia, that they take such Measures to secure themselves, from the Practices of Lord Dunmore, either by seizing his Person, or otherwise as they think proper.

Hall. A Material Distinction between a peremptory order to the Council of Virginia, to seize his Lordship, and a Recommendation to take such Measures as they shall judge necessary, to defend themselves against his Measures.

Motion to export Produce for Powder.[6]

Sherman. I think We must have Powder, and We may send out Produce for Powder. But upon some Gentlemens Principles We must have a general Exportation.

Paine. From the observations some Gentlemen have made I think this Proposition of more Importance than it appeared at first. In Theory I could carry it further, even to Exportation and Importation to G.B. A large Continent cant Act upon Speculative Principles, but must be govern'd by Rules. Medicines, We must have—some Cloathing, &c. I wish We could enter upon the Question at large, and agree upon some System.

Chase. By that Resolution We may send to G.B., Ireland and W. Indies.

Lee. Suppose Provisions should be sold in Spain for Money, and Cash sent to England for Powder.

Duane. We must have Powder. I would send for Powder to London, or any where. We are undone if We hant Powder.

Dean. I hope the Words "Agreable to the Association" will be inserted. But I would import from G.B. Powder.

R. R. Livingston. We are between Hawk and Buzzard. We puzzle ourselves between the commercial and warlike opposition.

Rutledge. If Ammunition was to be had from England only, there would be W[eigh]t in the Gentlemans Arg[ument].—The Captn. Reed[7] told us Yesterday that he might have bro't 1000 Blls. of Powder. Why? Because he was not searched. But if he had attempted to bring Powder, he would have been search'd.—I would let the Ass[ociation] stand as it is, and order the Committee to export our Provisions consistent with it.

Lee. When a Vessell comes to England vs. our Association, she must be observed and watched. They would keep the Provisions, but not let us have the Powder.

Deane. I have not the most distant Idea of infringing the Association.

Duane. The Resolution with the Amendment amounts to nothing. The Committee may import now consistent with the Association. I apprehend that by breaking the Association We may import Powder, without it not. We must have Powder. We must fight our Battles in two or three Months, in every Colony.

J. Rutledge. They may export to any other Place and thence send Money to England.

New York Letter, concerning a Fortification on the high Lands, considered.[8]

Dyer. Cant say how far it would have been proper to have gone upon Romains Plan in the Spring, but thinks it too late now. There are Places upon that River, that might be thrown up in a few days, that would do. We must go upon some Plan that will be expeditious.

Lee. Romain says a less or more imperfect Plan would only be beginning a Strong hold for an Enemy.

Deane. An order went to N. York. They have employed an Engineer. The People and he agree in the Spot and the Plan. Unless We rescind the whole, We should go on. It ought to be done.

[1] *"Resolved,* That it be recommended to the several provincial Assemblies or Conventions, and councils or committees of safety, to arrest and secure every person in their respective colonies, whose going at large may, in their opinion, endanger the safety of the colony, or the liberties of America" (JCC, 3:280).

[2] The activities of John Murray, 4th Earl of Dunmore, last royal governor of Virginia, after his expulsion from Williamsburg in June 1775, are documented in Jefferson, *Papers,* ed. Boyd, vol. 1; see the index under Dunmore.

[3] This passage is cryptic. Dyer may have said (or meant) that Dunmore could do no *more* mischief in Virginia in consequence of an order to seize him than he was already doing.

[4] John Wentworth, governor of New Hampshire; Sir William Franklin, governor of New Jersey; John Penn, lieutenant governor of Pennsylvania; Robert Eden, governor of North Carolina.

[5] William Tryon, of New York Province.

[6] *"Resolved,* That the Committee appointed by this Congress for the importation of powder, export, agreeable to the continental Association, as much provisions or other produce of these colonies, as they shall judge expedient for the purchase of arms and ammunition" (JCC, 3:280).

[7] Probably Thomas Read, brother of the Delaware delegate George Read and a naval officer in the service of Pennsylvania. See Burnett, ed., *Letters of Members,* 1:216 and note.

[8] The letter was from the New York Committee of Safety, 19 September. The New York Provincial Congress had engaged the engineer and cartographer Bernard Romans to draw plans for fortifications on the Hudson at the Highlands above New York City. See JCC, 2:59–60; 3:280–282; Force, *Archives,*

4th ser., 3:732, 1279–1280; Romans'
plans are reproduced in same, following
col. 736. See also JA's Notes of Debates, 7 Oct., below.

[NOTES OF DEBATES, CONTINUED] OCTR. 7.

Chase. It is the maddest Idea in the World, to think of building an American Fleet.[1] Its Latitude is wonderfull. We should mortgage the whole Continent. Recollect the Intelligence on your Table—defend N. York—fortify upon Hudsons River.

We should provide for gaining Intelligence—two swift sailing Vessells.

Dyer. The Affair of Powder from N. York should be referr'd to the Committee.

Hopkins. No Objection to putting off the Instruction from Rhode Island, provided it is to a future day.

Paine. Seconds Chace's Motion, that it be put off to a future day Sine die.

Chace. The Gentleman from Maryland never made such a Motion. I never used the Copulative. The Gentleman is very sarcastic, and thinks himself very sensible.

Zubly. If the Plans of some Gentlemen are to take Place, an American Fleet must be a Part of it—extravagant as it is.

Randolph moves that all the orders of the day should be read every Morning.

Deane. I wish it may be seriously debated. I dont think it romantic, at all.

J. Rutledge. Move that some Gentn. be appointed to prepare a Plan and Estimate of an American Fleet.

Zubly seconds the Motion.

Gadsden. I am against the Extensiveness of the Rhode Island Plan, but it is absolutely necessary that some Plan of Defence by Sea should be adopted.

J. Rutledge. I shall not form a conclusive opinion till I hear the Arguments. I want to know how many Ships are to be built and what they will cost.

S. Adams. The Committee cant make an Estimate untill they know how many Ships are to be built.

Zubly. Rhode Island has taken the lead. I move that the Delegates of R.I. prepare a Plan, give us their opinion.

J. Adams. The Motion is entirely out of order. The Subject is put off for a Week, and now a Motion is to appoint a Committee to consider the whole subject.

Zubly, Rutledge, Paine, Gadsden, lightly skirmishing.

Deane. It is like the Man that was appointed to tell the Dream and the Interpretation of it. The Expence is to be estimated, without knowing what Fleet there shall be, or whether any att all.

Gadsden. The design is to throw it into Ridicule. It should be considered out of Respect to the Colony of R. Island who desired it.

Determined against the appointment of a Committee.

Report of the Committee for fortifying upon Hudsons River considered.

J. Rutledge. I think We should add to the Report, that they take the most effectual Measures to obstruct the Navigation of Hudsons River by Booms or otherwise.

Gadsden seconds the Motion.

Deane doubts the Practicability of obstructing it with Booms, it is so wide.

The Committee said 4 or 5 Booms chained together, and ready to be drawn across, would stop the Passage.[2]

The Congress of N.Y. is to consult the Assembly of Connecticutt and the Congress of N. Jersey, the best Method of taking Posts and making Signals, and assembling Forces for Defence of the River.

Gadsden. Moves that all the Letters, laid before us from England, should be sent to the Convention of N. York. Tryon is a dangerous Man, and the Convention of that Colony should be upon their guard.

Lee. I think the Letters should by all means be sent.

Rutledge. Dr. F. desired they might not be printed. Moves that Gen. Wooster with his Troops may be ordered down to N. York.

Duane. Moves that Woosters Men may be employed in building the Fortifications.

Dyer 2ds the Motion allowing the Men what is usual.

Sherman. Would have the order conditional, if Schuyler dont want them. Understands that N.Y. has the best Militia upon the Continent.

R. Livingston. They will be necessary at the Highlands.

Dyer thinks they ought to have the usual allowance for Work.

S. Adams. Understands that the Works at Cambridge was done without any Allowance, but that G[eneral] W[ashington] has ordered that for future works they be allowed half a Pistareen a day.

Langdon would not have the order to Wooster, but to Schuyler for he would not run any risque of the northern Expedition.

Rutledge thinks Schuyler cant want them. He waited only for Boats to send 500 Men more.

Sherman. Would it not be well to inform Schuyler of our endeavours to take the Transports and desire him to acquaint Coll. Arnold of it.

Rutledge. He may cooperate with Arnold in taking the Transports. I hope he is in Possession of Montreal before now.

Deane. I wish that whatever Money is collected, may be sent along to Schuyler.

E. Rutledge. We have been represented as beggarly fellows, and the first Impressions are the strongest. If We eat their Provisions and dont pay, it will make a bad Impression.

Ross. Produces a Resolve of the Assembly of Pensylvania that their Delegates lay the Connecticutt Intrusion before Congress, that something may be done to quiet the Minds.[3]

J. Rutledge moves that the Papers be referr'd to the Delegates of the two Colonies.

Willing. Thinks them Parties and that they must have an Umpire.

Sherman. Thinks they may agree on a temporary Line.

Lee. Moves that Parliamentary or ministerial Post may be stopp'd, as a constitutional Post is now established from N.H. to G.[4]

Langdon 2d[s] the Motion.

Willing. Thinks it is interfering with that Line of Conduct which we have hitherto prescribed to ourselves—it is going back beyond the Year 1763.

Lee. When the Ministry are mutilating our Correspondence in England, and our Enemies here are corresponding for our ruin, shall We not stop the ministerial Post.

Willing. Looks upon this to be one of the offensive Measures which are improper at this Time—it will be time enough to throw this aside when the Time comes that we shall throw every Thing aside—at present We dont know but there may be a Negociation.

Dyer. We have already superceeded the Act of Parliament effectually.

Deane is for a Recommendation to the People to write by the constitutional Post, not forbid a Man to ride.

S. Adams thinks it a defensive Measure, and advising People not to write by it, looks too cunning for me. I am for stopping the Correspondence of our Enemies.

Langdon. Administration are taking every Method to come at our Intentions, why should not we prevent it.

Duane. I shall vote vs. it. It may be true that We are come to the Time when We are to lay aside all. I think there should be a full Representation of the Colonies. N.C. should be here.

Deane 2d[s] the Motion for postponing it.

Zubly. The Necessity of this Measure does not appear to me. If We have gone beyond the Line of 1763 and of defence without apparent Necessity it was wrong, if with Necessity right. I look upon the Invasion of Canada [as] a very different Thing. I have a Right to defend myself vs. Persons who come vs. me, let em come from whence they will. We in G. have gain[ed] Intelligence by the K's Post that We could not have got any other Way. Some Gentlemen think all Merit lies in violent and unnecessary Measures.

S. Adams. The Gentlemans Argument would prove that We should let the Post go into Boston.

Moreton. Would not this stop the Packett. Would it not be ordered to Boston. Does the Packett bring any Intelligence to Us that is of Use?

Lee. No Intelligence comes to Us, but constant Intelligence to our Enemies.

Stone. Thinks it an innocent Motion, but is for postponing it, because he is not at present clear. He thinks that the setting up a new Post has already put down the old one.

Paine. My opinion was that the Ministerial Post will die a natural death. It has been under a Languishment a great while. It would be Cowardice to issue a Decree to kill that which is dying. It brought but one Letter last time, and was obliged to retail Newspapers, to bear its Expences. I am very loath to say that this Post shall not pass.

Lee. Is there not a Doctor Ld. North who can keep this Creature alive.

R. R. Livingstone. I dont think that Tory Letters are sent by the Royal Post. I consider it rather as a Convenience than otherwise. We hear 5 times a Week from N.Y.

The Letters upon our Table advise us to adopt every conciliatory Measure, that we may secure the Affections of the People of England.

[1] On 3 Oct. "One of the Delegates for Rhode Island laid before the Congress a part of the Instructions given them by the House of Magistrates, Aug. 26, 1775," stating that "this Assembly is persuaded, that the building and equipping an American fleet, as soon as possible, would greatly and essentially conduce to the preservation of the lives, liberty and property of the good people of these Colonies," and urging, therefore, that such a fleet be built "at the Continental expence" (JCC, 3:274). This momentous proposal was debated for the first time on 7 Oct., and in the present notes JA has recorded the earli-

est formal discussion of the idea of an American navy. The time not yet being quite ripe, Congress deferred further discussion until the 16th, and continued to postpone action until mid-December (same, p. 281, 420). Meanwhile a very urgent practical problem arose, and though it bore directly on the question of establishing a naval armament, Congress for a time kept the general and the particular problems strictly separate. The particular problem sprang from the news, received 5 Oct., that two vessels loaded with powder and munitions had sailed from England for Quebec. A committee of three was immediately appointed "to prepare a plan for intercepting" these valuable prizes; it brought in recommendations which were adopted the same day; and next day it brought in further recommendations (for a pair of swift armed vessels) which were adopted on 13 Oct. (same, p. 276–279, 293–294). Still no "navy"! The Journal does not name the members of the committee that prepared these reports, but in his Autobiography and elsewhere JA says they were Silas Deane, John Langdon, and himself; see especially JA to Langdon, 24 Jan. 1813 (LbC, Adams Papers; printed in JA, *Works*, 10:27–28). A new committee was appointed on the 13th to carry out the resolutions adopted that day; it consisted of Deane, Langdon, and Gadsden (JCC, 3:294). But on the 30th Congress enlarged both the membership and duties of the committee and named JA as one of the additional members (same, p. 311–312). At first called the committee to fit out armed vessels, it was soon referred to as "the naval committee," because it was actually organizing a naval force; see List of Persons Suitable for Naval Commands, Nov. 1775, below, and note there. In his Autobiography JA left a graphic account of the sessions of this committee, held every evening "in a public house in the City" and constituting, JA thought, "the pleasantest part of my Labours for the four Years I spent in

Congress." Early in 1776 the nominally limited functions of this special committee were absorbed by the new and permanent Marine Committee, which in December had developed out of the Rhode Island instruction quoted at the beginning of this note. The Marine Committee consisted of one member from each colony, and since JA was absent when it was formed he was not a member.

Dry as these details are, they are essential for understanding and correcting JA's various accounts of the origins of the American navy and for filling in the gaps left by the meager record in the Journal. For further clarification and references see Charles O. Paullin, *The Navy of the American Revolution*, Cleveland, 1906, chs. 1 and 3; and two exhaustively documented notes in Burnett, ed., *Letters of Members*, 1:216, and 2:318. The pertinent documents will be published in *The Naval Documents of the American Revolution*, in preparation by the Office of Naval History of the United States Navy, under the editorship of William Bell Clark.

[2] See JCC, 3:282. It is by no means clear from the MS whether or not this and the following paragraph are part of Deane's speech.

[3] The Pennsylvania Assembly's resolve, 30 Sept. 1775, is printed in JCC, 3:283. It was at first referred to the Pennsylvania and Connecticut delegates in Congress, but nothing conclusive came of it. On the Wyoming Valley controversy at this stage, see Jefferson, *Papers*, ed. Boyd, 1:248, and references there.

[4] Nothing on this subject appears in the Journal under this date, but just possibly (as suggested by CFA) the discussion arose in connection with a paragraph in the report of the committee on fortifying the Hudson recommending the establishment of posts "to be ready to give intelligence to the country, in case of any invasion" (JCC, 3:282).

[NOTES OF DEBATES, CONTINUED] OCTR. 10.

Who shall have the Appointment of the Officers in the 2 Battallions to be raised in New Jersey?[1]

Sherman. Best to leave it to the Provincial Conventions.

Ward seconds the Motion.

Chace. This is persisting in Error in Spight of Experience. We have found by Experience that giving the Choice of Officers to the People, is attended with bad Consequences. The French Officers are allowed to exceed any in Europe, because a Gentleman is hardly entituled to the Smiles of the Ladies without serving a Campaign. In my Province, We want Officers. Gentlemen have recommended Persons from personal Friendships, who were not suitable. Such Friendships will have more Weight, in the Colonies.

Dyer. We must derive all our Knowledge, from the Delegates of that Colony. The Representatives at large are as good Judges and would give more Satisfaction. You cant raise an Army if you put Officers over the Men whom they dont know. It requires Time to bring People off from ancient Usage.

E. Rutledge. We dont mean to break in upon what has been done. In our Province we have raised our Compliment of Men in the Neighbouring Colonies. I am for it that We may have Power to reward Merit.

Ward. The Motion is intended for a Precedent. In the Expedition to Carthagena and Canada, the Crown only appointed a Lieutenant in my Colony. The Men will not enlist. When the Militia Bill was before Us. I was vs. giving the Choice to the Men. I dont know any Man in the Jerseys.

Duane. A Subject of Importance—a Matter of Delicacy. We ought to be all upon a Footing. We are to form the grand Outlines of an American Army—a general Regulation. Will such a Regulation be salutary? The public Good alone, will govern me. If We were to set out anew, would the same Plan be pursued. It has not been unprecedented, in this Congress. Mr. Campbell, Allen, Warner, were promoted here. We ought to insist upon it. We shall be able to regulate an Army better. Schuyler and Montgomery would govern my Judgment. I would rather take the opinion of Gen. Washington than of any Convention. We can turn out the unworthy and reward Merit. The Usage is for it.

Governors used to make Officers—except in Con. and Rhode Island. But We cant raise an Army? We are then in a deplorable Situation indeed. We pay. Cant We appoint with the Advice of our Generals.

Langdon. Looks upon this [as] a very extraordinary Motion, and big with many Mischiefs.

Deane. It is the Peoples Money, not ours. It will be fatal. We cant sett up a Sale for Offices, like Lord Barrington.

E. Rutledge. The appointment hitherto has been as if the Money belonged to particular Provinces not to the Continent. We cant reward Merit. The Governor appointed Officers with Us.

Ross. My Sentiments coincide with those of the Gentlemen from N.Y. and C[arolina] and would go farther and appoint every Officer, even an Ensign. We have no Command of the Army! They have different Rules and Articles.

Jay. Am of opinion with the Gentleman who spoke last. The Union depends much upon breaking down provincial Conventions. The whole Army refused to be mustered by your Muster Master.

[1] On 9 Oct. Congress recommended to the New Jersey Convention that it immediately raise two battalions "at the expence of the Continent," but did not mention the appointment of any field officers. During the two following days the question was debated whether New Jersey or the Continental Congress should appoint these officers. The matter was finally settled on 7 Nov., when Congress elected precisely the officers nominated by the Convention. See *JCC*, 3: 285–286, 287, 288, 335; William Livingston to Alexander Stirling, 8 Nov. 1775 (Burnett, ed., *Letters of Members*, 1:250).

[NOTES OF DEBATES, CONTINUED] OCT. 12.

Report, on Trade, considered in a Committee of the whole.[1]

Lee. It has been moved to bring the debate to one Point, by putting the Q. whether the Custom houses shall be shut up, and the officers discharged from their several Functions. This would put N. York, N.C., lower Counties and Georgia upon the same Footing with the other Colonies.

I therefore move you, that the C[ustom] Houses be shut, and the officers discharged. This will remove Jealousies and Divisions.

Zubly. The Measure, We are now to consider, extreamly interesting. I shall offer my Thoughts. If We decide properly, I hope We shall establish our Cause—if improperly, We shall overthrow it, altogether.

1st Prop[osition]. Trade is important. 2. We must have a Reconciliation with G.B. or the Means of carrying on the War. An unhappy day when We shall[2]

A Republican Government is little better than Government of Devils. I have been acquainted with it from 6 Years old.

We must regulate our Trade so as that a Reconciliation be obtained or We enable[d] to carry on the War.

Cant say, but I do hope for a Reconciliation, and that this Winter may bring it. I may enjoy my Hopes for Reconciliation, others may enjoy theirs that none will take Place.

A Vessell will not go, without Sails or Oars. Wisdom is better than

Weapons of War. We dont mean to oppose G.B. merely for Diversion.
If it is necessary that We make War, and that we have the Means of
it, This Continent ought to know what it is about. The Nation dont.
We ought to know what they mean to be about. We ought to have Intelligence of the Designs. K. of Prussia and Count Daune march'd and
counter march'd untill they could not impose upon Each other any
more. Every Thing We want for the War are Powder and Shot.

2d Thing necessary that We have Arms and Ammunition.

3. We must have Money. The Cont[inent']s Credit must be supported. We must keep up a Notion that this Paper is good for Something. It has not yet a general Circulation. The Mississippi Scheme
in France and the South Sea Scheme in England were written for our
Learning. An hundred Million fell in one day. 20 Men of War may
block up the Harbour of N. York, Del[aw]are River, Cheasapeak Bay,
the Carolinas and Georgia.

Whether We can raise a Navy is an important Question. We may
have a Navy—and to carry on the War We must have a Navy. Can We
do this without Trade? Can we gain Intelligence without Trade. Can
We get Powder without Trade? Every Vessell you send out is thrown
away. N. England where the War is may live without Trade. [The?]
Money circulates there—they may live. Without Trade our People
must starve. We cannot live. We cannot feed or cloath our People.
My Resolution was that I would do and suffer any Thing rather than
not be free. But I resolved not to do impossible Things.

If We must trade, We must trade with Somebody, and with Somebody that will trade with us, either with foreigners or G.B. If with
foreigners, We must either go to them or they must come to us. We
cant go to them if our Harbours are shut up. I look upon the Trade
with foreigners as impracticable. St. Lawrence being open is a Supposition.

N. England People last War went to C[ape] Francois.

Spaniards are too lazy to come to Us.

If We cant trade with foreigners we must trade with G. Britain. Is
it practicable. Will it quit cost. Will it do more hurt than good. This
is breaking our Association. Our People will think We are giving Way
and giving all up. They will say one mischivous Man has overset the
whole Navigation. I speak from Principle. It has been said here that
the Association was made in terrorem.

Gadsden. 2ds. Lees Motion, and affirms that We can carry on Trade
from one End of the Continent to the other.

Deane. Custom house Officers discharged! Were they ever in our

Pay, in our service. Let em stand where they are. Let this Congress establish what Offices they please. Let the others die. I think that all the Colonies ought to be upon a footing. We must have Trade. I think We ought to apply abroad. We must have Powder and Goods. We cant keep our People easy without.

Lee. The Gentleman agrees that all ought to be upon a Footing. Let him shew how this can be done without shutting the Customhouses.

Jay. This should be the last Business We undertake. It is like cutting the Foot to the shoe, not making a shoe for the Foot. Let Us establish a System first.

I think We ought to consider the whole, before We come to any Resolutions. Now Gentlemen have their Doubts whether the N. Exportation was a good Measure. I was last Year, clear vs. it. Because the Enemy have burn'd Charlestown, would Gentlemen have Us burn N. York? Let us lay every Burden as equal on all the Shoulders that We can. If Prov[idence] or Ministry inflict Misfortunes on one, shall We inflict the same on all? I have one Arm sore—why should not the other Arm be made sore too? But Jealousies will arise. Are these reasonable? Is it politick? We are to consult the general Good of all America. Are We to do hurt to remove unreasonable Jealousies. Because Ministry have imposed hardships on one, shall We impose the same on all. It is not from affection to N. York, that I speak. If a Man has lost his Teeth on one side of his Jaws, shall he pull out the Teeth from the other that both sides may be upon a Footing? Is it not realizing the Quarrell of the Belly and the Members? The other Colonies may avail themselves of the Custom houses in the exempted Colonies.

Lee. All must bear a proportional share of the Continental Expence. Will the exempted Colonies take upon themselves the whole Expence. V. pays a sixth Part, the lower Counties an 8oth.—yet lower Counties may trade, V. not. The Gentleman exercised an Abundance of Wit to shew the Unreasonableness of Jealousies. If this ministerial Bait is swallowed by America another will be thrown out.

Jay. Why should not N.Y. make Money, and N. Jersey not. One Colony can cloath them.

McKean. I have 4 Reasons for putting the favoured Colonies upon a footing with the rest. 1st. is to disappoint the Ministry. Their design was insidious. 2. I would not have it believed by Ministry or other Colonies that those Colonies had less Virtue than others. 3. I have a Reconciliation in View, it would be in the Power of those Colonies, it might become their Interest to prolong the War. 4. I believe Parliament has done or will do it for us, i.e. put us on the same footing. I would choose that the exempted Colonies should have the Honour of it. Not clear that this is the best Way of putting them upon a Footing. If We should be successfull in Canada, I would be for opening our Trade to some Places in G.B., Jamaica, &c.

J. Rutledge. Wonders that a Subject so clear, has taken up so much Time. I was for a general Non Exportation. Is it not surprizing, that there should so soon be a Motion for breaking the Association. We have been reproached for our Breach of Faith in breaking the Non Imp[ortation]. I have the best Authority to say that if We had abided by a former Non Imp. We should have had redress. We may be obliged hereafter to break the Association, but why should We break it before We feel it. I expected the Delegates from the exempted Colonies would have moved to be put upon the same footing.

Dont like shutting the C. Houses and discharging the Officers—but moves that the Res[olution] be, that People in York, N. Car., Georgia and lower Counties dont apply to the Custom house.

Zubly. Georgia is settled along Savanna River, 200 miles in Extent, and 100 mile the other Way. I look upon it the Association alltogether will be the Ruin of the Cause. We have 10,000 fighting Indians near us. Carolina has already smuggled Goods from Georgia.

Chase. I will undertake to prove that if the Revd. Gentlemans Positions are true and his Advice followed, We shall all be made Slaves. If he speaks the Opinion of Georgia I sincerely lament that they ever appeared in Congress. They cannot, they will not comply!—Why did they come here? Sir We are deceived. Sir We are abused! Why do they come here? I want to know why their provinc[ial] Congress came to such Resolutions. Did they come here to ruin America. That Gentlemans Advice will bring Destruction upon all N. America. I am for the Resolution upon the Table. There will be Jealousies, if N.Y. and the other exempted Colonies are not put upon a footing.

It is not any great Advantage to the exempted Colonies. What can they export that will not be serviceable to G.B. and the West Indies.

The exports of N. Car. are of vast Importance to G.B. If these Colonies are in Rebellion, will not their Effects be confiscated, and seized even upon the Ocean.

Arms and Ammunition must be obtained by what is call'd Smuggling. I doubt not We shall have the Supply. Leaving open N. York &c. will prevent our getting Arms and Ammunition.

Houstoun. Where the Protection of this Room did not extend, I would not set very tamely.

Chase. I think the Gentleman ought to take offence at his Brother Delegate.

Wythe. Agrees with the Gentleman from N. York that We dont proceed regularly. The Safety of America depends essentially on a Union of the People in it. Can We think that Union will be preserved if 4 Colonies are exempted. When N. York Assembly did not approve the Procedings of the Congress it was not only murmured at, but lamented as a Defection from the public Cause. When Attica was invaded by the Lacedemonians, Pericles ordered an Estate to be ravaged and laid waste because he tho't it would be exempted, by the Spartan King.

Nothing was ever more unhappily applied, than the fable of the Stomach and the Limbs.

Sherman. Another Argument for putting [*sentence unfinished*]

¹ This and the following entry continue the debate on trade policy of which JA had recorded earlier stages in his Notes of Debates, 4 and 5 Oct., above.

² No punctuation in MS, but the meaning is clear: " . . . when we shall have those means."

[NOTES OF DEBATES, CONTINUED] OCTR. 13.

R. Livingston. Hopes the whole Matter will be putt off. Is willing as it seems the general sense, that all should be put upon a Footing.

Gadsden. Hopes it will not be putt off. S. Carolina will be in the utmost Confusion if this matter is not decided. Let the Continent determine.

Stone. Can see no particular Inconvenience to Carolina. 2ds. the Motion of Mr. Livingston, for postponing the Question, and gives his Reasons.—The Powder Committee must take Clearances. If they are allowed to take Clearances, and no other, then whenever they take a Clearance it will be known, that it is for Powder, and the Vessell will be watched.

Lee. I see very clearly, that the best Time for putting a Question is when it is best understood. That Time is the present. As to Powder, Time may be allowed for the Committee to clear Vessells.

J. Rutledge. Thinks this Motion extraordinary. This Subject has been under Consideration 3 Weeks. It is really trifling. The Committee may have Time allowed to clear Vessells for Powder. But I had rather the Continent should run the Risque of sending Vessells without clearances. What Confusion would ensue if Congress should break up without any Resolution of this sort. The Motion seems intended to defeat the Resolution entirely. Those who are against it, are for postponing.

Jay. We have complied with the restraining Act. The Question is whether we shall have Trade or not? And this is to introduce a most destructive Scheme, a scheme which will drive away all your Sailors, and lay up all your Ships to rot at the Wharves.[1]

[1] JA's notes of this debate are continued under 20 Oct., below, the next time Congress sat as a committee of the whole on "the state of the trade of the confederated colonies."

[JOHN TYLER'S BILL FOR REPAIRING A PISTOL.] [1]

To Cleaning a pistol	o: 2: o
To one side pin	o: o: 9
To two small screws to the Lock	o: 1: o
To a new tumbler to ..... Do.	o: 3: o
	£ o: 6: 9

[16 October 1775] Recd of Mr. Jno. Adams the Contents in full of all Demands

Pr me
Jno. Tyler

[1] M-Ar: vol. 210. Endorsed by JA. Date supplied from an entry in JA's Account with Massachusetts, Aug.–Dec. 1775, above.

[NOTES OF DEBATES IN THE CONTINENTAL CONGRESS]
OCT. 20.[1]

Deane. Their Plunder only afforded one Meal of fresh meat for the privates. All the rest was reserved for the Officers and their Friends among the Inhabitants. I would have Traders prohibited from importing unnecessary Articles, and from exporting live Stock, except Horses.

Gadsden. If we give one leave when there is 100 who have an equal Right, it will occasion Jealousy. Let each Colony export to the Amount of so many thousand Pounds, and no more.

Chase. We have Letters, from Guadaloupe, Martinique and the Havanna that they will supply us with Powder for Tobacco.

Gadsden. France and Spain would be glad to see G.B. despotic in America. Our being in a better State than their Colonies, occasions complaints among them, Insurrections and Rebellions, but these Powers would be glad We were an independent State.

Chase. The Proposition is for exporting for a special Purpose, importing Powder. I would not permit our Cash to go for Rum. Live Stock is an inconsiderable Part of our Cargoes.

I dont wish to intermix any Thing in this debate. I would restrain the Merchant from importing any Thing but Powder &c.

Molasses was an Article of importance in the Trade of the Northern Colonies. But now they cant carry on the African Trade, and the Rum is pernicious. If you give a Latitude for any Thing but Arms and Ammunition, We shant agree what Articles are necessary and what unnecessary. Each Colony should carry on this Trade, not individuals. I would not limit the Quantity of Ammunition to be imported by each Colony. An 100 Ton a Colony would supply the W. Indies mediately and the Army and Navy. 20 Ton would be a considerable Adventure for a Colony. Debts are due from the B[ritish] W. India Islands to the Inhabitants of these Colonies. I am not for permitting Vessells to go in Ballast and fetch Cash. I wish to import Cash from every Place as much as possible.

Deane. It cannot be done with secrecy or dispatch. I rather think it would be as well to leave it to Traders.

Zubly. It is of great Weight that there be no favourites.

Dyer. There will be such continual Applications to the Assemblies, by their Friends among the Traders, it will open a compleat Exportation. It would compleatly supply the W. Indies.

Jay. We have more to expect from the Enterprise, Activity and Industry of private Adventurers, than from the Lukewarmness of Assemblies. We want French Woolens, dutch Worsteds, Duck for Tents, German Steel, &c. Public Virtue is not so active as private Love of Gain. Shall We shutt the Door vs. private Enterprise.

Lee. The Gentleman may move for those Things as Exceptions to the general Rule.

Randolph. We are making Laws contradictory in Terms. We say nobody shall export and yet Somebody shall. Against all Rule.

Lee. It is a common Rule in making Laws, to make a Rule and then make a Proviso for special Cases.

Dyer. The Rule and the Proviso are passed at once in the same Act, 'tho. If I give my Voice for an Unconditional Proposition, what security have I that the Condition or Proviso will be added afterwards. The greatest Impropriety, in the World.

Chase. Both Sides are right, and it arises from this, that one Proposition is to be made public the other kept secret. We have very little Confidence in each other.

Zubly. If half the Law is to be public and the other half secret, will not half the People be governed by one half and the other half by the other. Will they not clash?

Jay. Least your Produce falls into the Hands of your Enemies, you publish a Law that none go from the Continent. Yet to get Powder, We keep a secret Law that Produce may be exported. Then comes the Wrangles among the People. A Vessell is seen loading. A fellow runs to the Committee.

Lee. The Inconvenience may arise in some Measure, but will not the People be quieted, by the Authority of the Conventions. If We give public Notice, our Enemies will be more active to intercept Us. On the Contrary the People may be quieted by the Committees of Safety.

Wythe. The only Persons who can be affected by this Resolution are those, whom on the other side the Water will be called Smugglers. Consider the danger these Smugglers will run—lyable to seizure by C. House officers, by Men of War at Sea, and by Custom house officers in the Port they go to. What can they bring. Cash, Powder, or foreign Manufactures. Cant see the least Reason for restraining our Trade, as little can be carried on. My Opinion is We had better open our Trade altogether. It has long been my Opinion, and I have heard no Arguments vs. it.

Zubly. We cant do without Trade. To be, or not to be is too trifling a Question for many Gentlemen. All that Wise Men can do among many Difficulties, is to choose the least.

Stone. Cannot agree to the Proposition made by the gentleman from Maryland. Not for binding the People closer, than they are bound already. The Proposition is the same with that which was made that our Vessells should be stopp'd and foreigners invited to come here for our Produce and protect their own Trade. This appears to be a destructive System.

It was a laborious Task to get America into a general Non Exportation to G.B., I., and W. Indies.

Shall We now combine with Britain, to distress our People in their Trade, more than by the Association. People have look'd up to this, and are unwilling to go further. The restraining Bill a most cruel, unjust, unconstitutional Act: Yet We are going to greater Cruelties than they. We are all to be in the same Circumstances of Poverty and Distress. Will the West Indies be supplied by a circuitous Trade. I think not. How can the West Indies get Supplies from France, Holland or Spain? The whole Produce will not be carried. It is said the Men of War will take the Produce. This Argument will operate against exporting for Powder. The Army will be supplied. It is impossible to prevent their getting Supplies at least of Bread. It appears to me, this is not a temporary Expedient, but will have a perpetual Influence. It is a destructive, ruinous Expedient and our People never will bear it. Under the faith that your Ports would be kept open to foreigners, People have made Contracts with foreigners. You are giving a Sanction to the Act of Parliament, and going further. Under such a Regulation We never can exist.

I would export Produce to foreign W. Indies, or any where for Powder. But the Mode of doing it, will defeat it. The Assemblies never will turn Merchants successfully. I would have private Adventurers give Bond, to return Powder, or the Produce itself.

Chase. Differs from his Colleague. A different Proposition from that for restraining our People and inviting foreigners. This Proposition invites your People.

If you carry on your Exports, without the Protection of a foreign Power you destroy America.

If you Stop Provisions and not other Produce you create a Jealousy. If you export Provisions and not other Produce you create a Jealousy. Dont think the Risque will prevent Supplies to the W. I. Islands.

We must prevent em Lumber as well as Provisions. Great Quantities will be exported, notwithstanding the Risque. All the fleet of B. cannot stop our Trade. We can carry it all on. We must starve the W. I. Islands and prevent em exporting their Produce to G.B. There will be great Quantities of Provisions and Lumber exported. It will enhance the Expence to carry em to Spain or France first and thence to the W. Indies, but the Price will be such that the W. Indies will get em.—I hold it clearly We can do without Trade. This Country produces all the Necessaries, many of the Conveniences and some of the Superfluities of Life. We cant grow rich. Our Provisions will be cheap. We can maintain our Army and our Poor. We shant loose our Sailors —The Fishermen will serve in another Capacity. We must defend the Lakes, and Cities.

Merchants will not grow rich—there is the Rub. I have too good an opinion of the Virtue of our People to suppose they will grumble.

If We drop our commercial System of Opposition We are undone.— We must fail.—We must give up the Profits of Trade or loose our Liberties.

Let the Door of Reconciliation be once shutt, I would trade with foreign Powers and apply to them for Protection.

Leave your Ports open, and every Man that can will adventure. The Risque will not prevent it.

It was strongly contended at the first Congress that Trade should be stopp'd to all the World, that all Remittances should cease. You would have saved a civil War if you had, but it could not be carried—the Gentleman from S. Carolina could not prevail to stop our Exports to B., I. and W.I.

Our Vessells will all be liable to Seizure—our Trade must be a smuggling Trade. Yet We can trade considerably, and many Vessells will escape. No Vessell can take a Clearance. Many Vessells will go out unless you restrain them. All America is in suspence. The common sense of the People have pointed out this Measure. They have stopped their Vessells.

Lee. We possess a fine Climate and a fertile Soil. Wood, Iron, Sheep &c. We make 11. or 12,00000 thousand [2] Pounds Worth of Provisions more than is necessary for our own Consumption. Dont think it necessary to combat the Opinion of some Gentlemen that We cannot live without Trade.

Money has debauched States as well as Individuals, but I hope its Influence will not prevail over America vs. her Rights and dearest Interests.

We shall distress the W. Indies so as immediately to quit Coin for Corn. 4 Millions go yearly from the W. Indies to B. and a Million at least returns. If our Provisions go from these Shores, then they will go where the best Price is to be had. W. Indies and our Enemies will get em.

If it was not proper a year ago, it may be now. This Proposition is not perpetual. When We get Powder We may make ourselves strong by sea and carry on Trade.

J. Rutledge. A Question of the greatest Magnitude that has come before this Congress. If it is necessary to do without Trade our Constituents will submit to it. The Army will be supplied with Flower from England, where it is now cheaper than here. But they would be supplied here, if they were to demand it, upon Pain of destroying our Towns. W. Indies are supplied and have laid up Stores, and some of them have been raising Provisions on their own Lands. It will bear hard upon the Farmer as well as the Merchant. Dont think the Reasons the same now as last Year. It would then have destroyed the Linen Manufactory, and the W.I.—but now they have had Notice of it they are prepared against it.

[1] This and the following entry continue the debates in the committee of the whole on the state of American trade; see entries of 4, 5, 12, 13 Oct., above, and 21, 27 Oct., below.

[2] Thus in MS. Corrected by CFA, no doubt properly, to "eleven or twelve hundred thousand."

[NOTES OF DEBATES, CONTINUED] OCTR. 21.

Zubly. We cant do without Powder, Intelligence, Druggs. Georgia must have an Indian War, if they cant supply the Indians. The Creeks and Cherrokees are in our Province. We must have Indian Trade. Four Millions have been spent in 6 Months. We have been successfull. But We have gain'd little. All the Power of G.B. it is true, has gained very little. N. England has been at great Expence, so has N. York. Pensylvania has spent hundred thousand Pounds of their Money to fortify their River. Virginia as much. N. Carolina a great deal. S. Carolina have issued a Million.

18 Millions of Dollars is an enormous Sum of Money. Whenever your Money fails, you fail too. We are to pay Six Millions, now, 12 Millions more presently, and have no Trade. I would bear the Character of a Madman, or that of an Emissary of Lord North, rather than believe it possible to pay 18 Millions of Dollars without Trade. Can We make bricks without Straw? We can live upon Acorns, but will We?

Wythe. The Rule that the Question should be put upon the last Motion that is made and seconded—this is productive of great Confusion in our Debates—6 or 7 Motions at once.

Commerce, whether we consider it, in an Economical, a moral, or political Light appears to be a great Good. Civility and Charity, as well as Knowledge are promoted by it. The Auri Sacra Fames is a fine Subject for Philosophers and Orators to display themselves upon. But the abuse of a Thing is not an Argument vs. it. If the Gentleman was possessed of Philosophers Stone or Fortunatus's Cap, would he not oblige the Continent with the Use of it.

Why should not America have a Navy? No maritime Power, near the Sea Coast, can be safe without it. It is no Chimæra. The Romans suddenly built one in their Carthaginian War. Why may We not lay a Foundation for it. We abound with Furs [Firs], Iron ore, Tar, Pitch, Turpentine. We have all the materials for construction of a Navy. No Country exceeds us in Felicity of Climate or Fertility of Soil. America is one of the Wings upon which the British Eagle has soared to the Skies. I am sanguine, and enthusiastical enough to wish and to hope, that it will be sung that America inter Nubila condit. British Navy will never be able to effect our Destruction. Before the days of Minus, Natives round the Archipelago carried on piratical Wars. The Moors carry on such Wars now, but the Pillars of Hercules are their Ne Plus ultra. We are too far off, for Britain to carry on a Piratical War. We shall sometime or other rise superiour to all the difficulties they may thro in our Way.—I wont say there is none that doeth good in Britain, no not one, but I will say she has not righteous Persons enough to save their State. They hold those Things honorable which please em and those for just which profit em.

I know of no Instance where a Colony has revolted and a foreign Nation has interposed to subdue them. But many of the Contrary. If France and Spain should furnish Ships and Soldiers, England must pay them! Where are her Finances. Why should We divert our People from Commerce and banish our Seamen.

Our Petition may be declared to be received graciously, and promised to be laid before Parliament. But We can expect no success from it. Have they ever condescended to take Notice of you. Rapine, Depopulation, Burning, Murder. Turn your Eyes to Concord, Lexington, Charlestown, Bristol, N. York—there you see the Character of Ministry and Parliament.

We shall distress our Enemies by stopping Trade. Granted. But how will the small Quantities we shall be able to export, supply our Enemies. Tricks may be practised.

If desire of Gain prevails with Merchants so does Caution against Risques.

Gadsden. I wish We could keep to a Point. I have heard the two Gentlemen, with a great deal of Pleasure. I have argued for opening our Ports, but am for shutting them untill We hear the Event of our Petition to the King, and longer untill the Congress shall determine otherwise. I am for a Navy too, and I think that shutting our Ports for a Time, will help us to a Navy. If We leave our Ports open, warm Men will have their Ships seized, and moderate ones will be favoured.

Lee. When you hoist out a Glimmering of Hope that the People are to be furnished from abroad, you give a Check to our own Manufactures. People are now everywhere attending to Corn and Sheep and Cotton and Linen.

Chase. A Glove has been offered by the Gentleman from Georgia and I beg leave to discharge my Promise to that Gentleman to answer his Arguments.

My Position was this—that that Gentlemans System would end in the total destruction of American Liberty. I never shall dispute self evident Propositions.

The present State of Things requires Reconciliation, or Means to carry on War. Intelligence We must have. We must have Powder and shot. We must support the Credit of our Money.

You must have a Navy to carry on the War. You cant have a Navy says the Gentleman. What is the Consequence? I say, that We must submit.

G.B. with 20 ships can distroy all our Trade, and ravage our sea Coast—can block up all your Harbours—prevent your getting Powder. What is the Consequence? That We should submit. You cant trade with nobody, you must trade with Somebody. You cant trade with any Body but G.B.—therefore I say We must submit. We cant trade with foreigners, the Gentleman said. The whole Train of his Reasoning proved that We must break our whole Association as to Exports and Imports. If We trade with G.B. will she furnish us with Powder and Arms.

Our Exports are about 3 Millions. Would B. permit us to export to her, and receive Cash in return? It would impoverish and ruin G.B. They will never permit a Trade on our Side without a Trade on theirs!

Gentn. from N. York, would not permit Tobacco and Naval Stores to be sent to G.B.—nothing that will support their naval Power or Revenue. But will not this break the Union? Would 3 Colonies stop their Staple when the other Colonies exported theirs.

1500 Seamen are employed by the Tobacco Colonies—125 Sail of british Ships.

But you may drop your Staple, your Tobacco. But it is difficult to alter old Habits. We have a great Number of female Slaves, that are best employed about Tobacco. N.C. cannot, will not give up their Staple.

The Gentleman from G. was for trading with G.B. and all the World. He says We cant trade with any Nation but Britain, therefore We must trade with B. alone.

What Trade shall we have, if We exclude B., I., W.I., british and foreign. Eastern Provinces may carry it on with a small Fleet, if their Harbours were fortified. S[outhern] Colonies cannot. Eastern Colonies cant carry on their Trade to that Extent without a naval Power to protect em not only on the Coast but on the Ocean, and to the Port of their Destination. The same force, that would assist the Eastern Colonies, would be of little service to us in summer Time. It must be a small, narrow and limited Trade.

The best Instrument We have is our Opposition by Commerce. If We take into Consideration G.B. in all her Glory—Commons voted 18.18.20 milions[1] last War, 80,000 seamen, from her Trade alone. Her strength is all Artificial—from her Trade alone.

Imports from G.B. to the united Colonies are 3 Millions per annum —15 Millions to all the World—1/5th. 3/4 is british Manufactures.

A Thousand british Vessels are employed in American Trade. 12 Thousand Sailors—all out of employ. What a Stroke! I dont take into view I[reland] or W. Indies.

Colonies generally indebted about one years Importation. The Revenue of Tobacco alone half a Million, if paid. N[orth] Britain enter less than the Quantity and dont pay what they ought. It employs a great Number of Manufacturers. Reexported abroad is a Million. It is more. 80,000 Hdds. are reexported and pays british Debts. The Reexport employs Ships, Sailors, Freight, Commissions, Insurance.

Ireland. The flaxseed 40,000£. st. Linen brought 2,150000£ from I. to England. Yard 200,000. Ireland can raise some flaxseed, but not much.

W. Indies. Glover, Burk, and other Authors. They depend for Indian Corn and Provisions, and Lumber, and they depend upon Us for a great Part of the Consumption of their Produce. Indian Corn and Fish are not to be had but from the Colonies, except Pilchards and Herrings. Jamaica can best provide for her Wants, but not entirely. Ireland can send em Beef and Butter but no Grain. B. can send em Wheat, Oats not Corn, without which they cannot do.

Stop Rum and Sugar, how do you affect the Revenue and the Trade?

They must relax the Navigation Act to enable foreign Nations to supply the W. Indies. This is dangerous as it would force open a Trade between foreigners and them.

Britain can never support a War with Us, at the Loss of such a valuable Trade.

Affrican Trade dependent upon the W. India Trade.—700,000£.

25,000 Hdds. of Sugar are imported directly into these Colonies and as much more, from Britain, manufactured.

Jamaica alone takes 150,000£ st. of our Produce.

National Debt 140,0000,[2] ten Millions the Peace Establishment. 20 Million the whole Current Cash of the Nation. Blackstone. I never read any Body that better understood the subject. For the State of the Revenue, He calculates the Taxes of Ireland and England.

Taxes of B. perpetual and annual. Funds three—the Aggregate, general and South Sea. Taxes upon every Article of Luxuries and Necessaries. These funds are mortgaged for the civil List 800,000 as well as the Interest of the Debt.

[1] Thus in MS. JA may have meant to write "18 or 20 millions." The erratic punctuation and capitalization in this paragraph make it impossible to follow Chase's thought with certainty, and the editors' slight regularization of the passage may not be absolutely correct.

[2] Thus in MS. CFA corrects to "one hundred and forty millions."

OCTR. 25TH. 1775. WEDNESDAY.

Mr. Duane told me at the Funeral of our late virtuous and able President [1] that he, Mr. Duane, had accustomed him self to read the

Year Books. Mr. De Lancey who was C[hief] J[ustice] of N. York he said advised him to it, as the best Method of imbibing the Spirit of the Law. De Lancey told him that he had translated a Pile of Cases from the Year Books, altho he was a very lazy Man.

Duane says that Jefferson is the greatest Rubber off of Dust that he has met with, that he has learned French, Italian, Spanish and wants to learn German.[2]

Duane says, he has no Curiosity at all—not the least Inclination to see a City or a Building &c.

That his Memory fails, is very averse to be burthened. That in his Youth he could remember any Thing. Nothing but what he could learn, but it is very different now.

Last Evening Mr. Hewes of N. Carolina, introduced to my Namesake and me, a Mr. Hog from that Colony, one of the Proprietors of Transylvania, a late Purchase from the Cherokees upon the Ohio. He is an associate with Henderson who was lately one of the Associate Judges of N. Carolina, who is President of the Convention in Transylvania.

These Proprietors have no Grant from the Crown nor from any Colony, are within the Limits of Virginia and North Carolina, by their Charters which bound those Colonies on the South Sea. They are charged with Republican Notions—and Utopian Schemes.[3]

[1] "This Ev'ning the honble. Peyton Randolph Esqr. late President of the Congress died suddenly of a paryletick fit at the house of Mr. Henry Hill near Schuylkill" (R. T. Paine, Diary, MHi, 22 Oct. 1775; see also Samuel Ward to Henry Ward, 24 Oct., in Burnett, ed., *Letters of Members*, 1:240). Next day (Monday) Congress appointed a committee "to superintend the funeral," which took place on Tuesday the 24th, with Jacob Duché delivering a sermon at Christ Church and the entire Congress attending as mourners.

[2] Though this is the first mention of Jefferson in JA's Diary, it by no means implies that the two men were unacquainted. They had served together in Congress for about six weeks in the preceding summer and had been colleagues on one important committee, that which prepared a reply to Lord North's conciliatory proposal in July 1775; see Jefferson, *Papers*, ed. Boyd, 1:225–233, and notes there. But since JA kept no diary during that session, we do not have his first impressions of the Virginia delegate whose career was to be so closely entwined with his own.

[3] James Hogg had just arrived as a "delegate" representing the Transylvania Company, which, having purchased a vast tract of land from the Cherokee Indians, was endeavoring to establish a fourteenth colony in what is now Kentucky and Tennessee. Hogg's very interesting report on his "embassy" to Philadelphia is printed in Force, *Archives*, 4th ser., 4:543–546; see especially col. 544 on his meeting with "the famous *Samuel* and *John Adams*." See also additional references in a footnote on the present entry as printed by Burnett in *Letters of Members*, 1:210, under the erroneous date of 28 Sept.—an error that must be nearly unique in this invaluable work but that is attributable to the inconspicuousness of the date headings in JA's Diary as printed by CFA.

[NOTES OF DEBATES IN THE CONTINENTAL CONGRESS]
1775. OCTR. 27.[1]

R. R. Livingston. Cloathing will rise tho Provisions will fall. Labourers will be discharged. One Quarter Part of R. Island, N. York, and Pensylvania depend upon Trade, as Merchants, Shopkeepers, Shipwrights, Blockmakers, Riggers, Smiths, &c. &c. &c.

The 6 Northern [Colonies][2] must raise 9 millions of Dollars to support the Poor.

This Vote will stop our Trade for 14 months, altho it professes to do it only to the 20th of March. For the Winter when the Men of War cannot cruise upon the Coast is the only Time that We can trade.

Wealthy Merchants, and monied Men cannot get the Interest of Money.

More Virtue is expected from our People, than any People ever had. The low Countries did not reason as We do about speculative opinions, but they felt the oppression for a long Course of Years, rich and poor.

Zubly. Concludes that the Sense and Bent of the People, is vs. stopping Trade by the Eagerness with which they exported before the 10th. of September.

We cant get Intelligence, without Trade. All that are supported by Trade, must be out of Business.

Every Argument which shews that our Association will materially affect the Trade of G.B. will shew that We must be affected too, by a Stoppage of our Trade.

G.B. has many Resources. I have bought 2 Barrells of Rice in Carolina for 15s. and Negro Cloth was 3s. instead of 18d.

The W. Indies will get supplies to keep soul and Body together. The ingenious Dutchmen will smuggle some Indian Corn from America.

Is it right to starve one Man because I have quarelled with another. I have a great Scruple whether it is just, or prudent. In Decr. 1776, We shall owe between 20 and 30 Millions of Money.

J. Rutledge. Am for adhering to the Association and going no further. The Non Export. in Terrorem—and generally agreed.

The Consequences will be dreadfull, if We ruin the Merchants.

Will not the Army be supplied if Vessells go from one Province to another.

We may pass a Resolution that no live Stock shall be exported.[3]

[1] First entry in booklet "25" as numbered by CFA (our D/JA/25). This is a memorandum book with red-brown leather covers containing a handful of scattered entries in 1775–1776, the last being dated 13 Oct. 1776, followed by notes on French grammar and vocabulary and a list of Philadelphia ad-

dresses of delegates to the Continental Congress.

The present entry concludes JA's notes of debates in committee of the whole on American trade. See 4, 5, 12, 13, 20, 21 Oct., above.

² MS: "Dollars"—an obvious inadvertence.

³ Congress sat again on 31 Oct. as a committee of the whole on the state of American trade and agreed to "certain resolutions." Three of these were adopted and the rest deferred on 1 Nov. (JCC, 3:314–315; see also an earlier version of the committee's report, same, p. 292–293).

1775. OCTR. 29. SUNDAY.

Paine brought in a large Sample of Salt Petre, made in this City, by Mr. Ripsama. It is very good, large and burns off, when laid upon a Coal like moist Powder. I tried it.

Heard Mr. Carmichael, at Mr. Duffils, on "Trust in the Lord and do good, so shall you dwell in the Land and verily thou shallt be fed."

[NOTES OF DEBATES IN THE CONTINENTAL CONGRESS]
1775. OCTR. 30TH. MONDAY.[1]

Ross. We cant get Seamen to man 4 Vessells. We could not get Seamen to mann our Boats, our Gallies.

Wythe, Nelson, and *Lee* for fitting out 4 Ships.

[1] From D/JA/25, which then has a gap until 24 Jan. 1776. The present fragment is from a debate on resolutions, agreed to this day, to fit out four armed vessels for Continental service. Another resolution added JA to the committee to execute this business. See JCC, 3:311–312, and entry of 7 Oct. and note, above.

[WILLIAM SMITH'S BILL FOR SUNDRY MEDICINES.][1]

Philadelphia Novr. 13th. [1775]

Mr. John Adams
Bought of William Smith.

At the Rising Sun in Second Street between Market and Chestnut Streets.

2 ozs. Cinnamon	£0: 6: 0
1 oz. Turkey Rhubarb	2: 6
1 oz. Cloves	2:
1 oz. Pink Root	1:
	£ 11: 6

Recd. the Contents for Dr. Wm. Smith per Malachy Salter Junr.

[1] M-Ar: vol. 210. A printed form filled in.

[ANN SMITH'S BILL FOR LAUNDRY.][1]

John Adams Esqr. to An Smith Dr.

	£	s	d
Novr. 29 For washing of Seven doz. and 4 pieces of Lining at 3/6 per doz.	1	5	4
For mending	0	3	9
	1	9	1

Received the Contents per Me Ann Smith

¹ M-Ar: vol. 210. Endorsed by JA.

[LIST OF PERSONS SUITABLE FOR NAVAL COMMANDS.
NOVEMBER 1775.] [1]

Captn. Isaac Sears
Thos. Randall
John Hanson
Christopher Miller
John Harrison.
Dudley Saltonstall
Eseck Hopkins.
Abraham Whipple.
  Souther.
James Dougherty
Thomas More.
  Reed.
Charles Alexander.
Michael Corbitt.
  Davinson.
Clement Lempriere. S.C.
  Obrian.
  Carghill.
John Lawrence.
  Alexander [2]
  Faulkner.
Simeon Sampson. P. [3]

¹ This list, not printed by CFA in his edition of the Diary, was written inside the back cover of D/JA/24. Since the names were obviously put down at different times, the list may be supposed a running memorandum of persons suggested for commands in the naval force for which Congress was being forced to plan in the last months of 1775; see entries of 7 and 30 Oct. and notes, above.

On 2 Nov. Congress voted $100,000 for the work of the committee on armed vessels or "naval committee," and authorized it "to agree with such officers and seamen, as are proper to man and command said vessels" (JCC, 3:316). Probably the present list of qualified officers was begun at that moment. On 5 Nov. JA wrote to Elbridge Gerry, a member of the Massachusetts House: "I must . . . intreat you to let me know the Names, Places of Abode, and Characters, of such Persons belonging to any of the seaport Towns in our Province, who are qualified for Officers and Commanders of Armed Vessells" (NHpR). Gerry must have brought this and JA's related inquiries before the House, for a partial copy of his letter is among the papers of that body, docketed "Mr. Speaker Mr. Gerry Colo. Orne," evidently a committee to whom it was referred (M-Ar: vol. 207). On the same day (5 Nov.) JA had addressed a very similar appeal to James Warren, speaker of the House (MHi; *Warren-Adams Letters*, 1:174–175), and Warren replied in detail on 14–16 Nov., naming Simeon Sampson and Daniel Souther as good officer candidates (Adams Papers; same, p. 181–186). Souther was well up on JA's list, but Sampson is the last name there and may have been added upon receipt of Warren's letter. If this is so, it fixes an approximate closing date for the list, say soon after 20 November.

On 22 Dec. the committee reported to Congress the names of the officers it had already appointed (JCC, 3:443). Of the five senior officers—Esek Hopkins, "commander in chief of the fleet," and Saltonstall, Whipple, Biddle, and John Burroughs Hopkins, captains—three are on JA's list. Others from that list obtained Continental commands later on, and still others served as privateers or in state naval forces, but detailed annotation of these names must be left to naval historians.

[2] Doubtless a repeated entry for Charles Alexander, above.

[3] An alphabetical arrangement, with the names filled in and corrected and the colonies with which they were associated, follows. Since many of the names are common ones, some of the identifications must be considered tentative: Charles Alexander, Penna. James? Cargill, Mass. Michael Corbet, Mass. Samuel Davison, Penna. James Dougherty, probably Penna. Nathaniel Falconer, Penna. John Hanson, Md. John Harrison, Md. Ezek Hopkins, R.I. John Lawrence, probably Conn. Clement Lempriere, S.C. Christopher Miller, N.Y. Thomas Moore, Md. Jeremiah O'Brien, Mass. Thomas Randall, N.Y. or Penna. Thomas Read, Del. Dudley Saltonstall, Conn. Simeon Sampson, Mass. (the "P." following his name must stand for Plymouth, his home port.) Isaac Sears, Mass. Daniel Souther, Mass. Abraham Whipple, R.I.

[JOHN STILLE'S BILL FOR CLOTHING.] [1]

John Adams Esqr. To John Stille   Dr.
1775 June 24th.

To makeing Suit of Nankeen	1:	6:	0
3 3/4 Y[ard]s of Linnen @ 3/6	0:13:	1	1/2
Buttons	0:	2:	7
Thread 1/6 Silk 3/ hair 2/ Buckram /3 Staying			
1/6	0:	8:	3

                                                            £2: 9:11 1/2

Novem 7th.

To makeing 2 pair of Draws	0:	4:	0
3 Y[ard]s of Superfine White flannel at 7/	1:	1:	

                                                            £3:14:11 1/2

Received December 7th: 1775 the Above Contents in full John Stille

[1] M-Ar: vol. 210. Endorsed by JA.

[ROBERT AITKEN'S BILL FOR BOOKS.] [1]

John Adams Esqr. Bought of R. Aitken

1775

Decr. 8	To 3 red Memdm. books @ 1/3 [2]	3	9
	To 2 Sticks Sealing wax 1/	2	
	To Marshall Saxe's Reveries I paid to Mrs. Hall for you	13	
	⟨To 1 Sett *political Disquisitions* 3 Vols.	1 10	⟩
		0 18 9	

Decr. 8th. 1775 Recd. of the Above account in full For Robt. Aitken

Frans: Sellers

> N.B. I am not certain whither it was the Political Disquisitions or some other book you had from me, when you got them you proposed paying me but for want of Change at that time, it was not done, & I omitted setting any of your Accot. down in my book. I therefore beg you will set the matter right. R. Aitken.[3]

[1] M-Ar: vol. 210.

[2] These are doubtless the three booklets in red-brown leather covers (D/JA/23-25) in which, for the most part, JA kept his Diary from Sept. 1775 to Sept. 1776.

[3] James Burgh, author of *Political Disquisitions* . . . , London, 1774-1775, had already presented to JA an inscribed set of the first two volumes of this work critical of British political institutions. The inscription is dated 7 March 1774. When the third volume was published in the following year, Burgh sent JA a complete set, inscribing this also. Both sets survive in the Boston Public Library. See JA to Burgh, 28 Dec. 1774 (Adams Papers, an incomplete draft; printed in JA, *Works*, 9:350-352).

[DANIEL SMITH'S BILL FOR ENTERTAINMENT.] [1]

Jno. Adams		Dr.	
		s	d
1775	To Club Venison Dinner	10	10
	2 Bottles Cyder	2	
		S 12 10	

[8 December 1775] Recd. the Contents Danl. Smith

[1] M-Ar: vol. 210. Date supplied from an entry in JA's Account with Massachusetts, Aug.–Dec. 1775, above.

1775. DECR. 9TH.[1]

Having Yesterday as[ked and] obtained Leave of Congress to go home, this Morning I mounted, with my own Servant only, about twelve o Clock, and reached the red Lyon about two where I dine. The Roads very miry and dirty, the Weather pleasant, and not cold.[2]

[1] This is the first regular entry since 29 Oct. in JA's Diary. Why he failed to keep a record of either personal or congressional affairs during the last six weeks he attended Congress is unexplained except by the number of committees on which he sat and the amount of writing that some of them, notably the so-called naval committee, required. His correspondence also fell off. On 25 Nov. he wrote to Mercy Warren: "I wish it was in my Power to write to you oftener than I do, but I am really engaged in constant Business [from] seven to ten in the Morning in Committee, from ten to four in Congress and from Six to Ten again in Committee. Our Assembly

is scarcly numerous enough for the Business. Every Body is engaged all Day in Congress and all the Morning and evening in Committees" (Adams Papers).

In respect to JA's activities in Congress the gap in the Diary is at least partially supplied by his Autobiography, which states that he sought a leave at this time because he was "worn down with long and uninterrupted Labour."

[2] JA's itinerary and expenses on this return trip from Philadelphia are recorded in meticulous detail in his Account with Massachusetts, Aug.–Dec. 1775, q.v. above. He arrived in Braintree on 21 December.

[SARAH YARD'S BILL FOR BOARD.][1]

John Adams to Mrs. Yard Dr.

To Board from Septr. 12 to Decr. 8 at 30s. per Week	18:17: 0
To a Servants Board for same Time at 15s. per Week	9: 8: 6
To Clubb in Punch and Wine at Dinner and in your own Room	11: 0: 0
To Sperma Ceti Candles at .05s. per Week	3: 0: 0
To Firewood for 8 Weeks at 7s:6 per Week	1:10: 0
To Cash paid for the Post	0: 3: 0
	43:18: 6
	20: 0: 0
	23:18: 6

By Cash recd. the Above in fool Sarah Yard

December 9th 1775
Philad

[1] M-Ar: vol. 210. In JA's hand except the dated acknowledgment of payment, which was written and signed by Mrs. Yard. At foot of page are some arithmetical calculations by JA, apparently irrelevant, and a highly relevant

notation by the legislative committee appointed to report on JA's accounts converting £23 18s. 6d. Philadelphia currency to £19 2s. 9d. lawful money; see JA's Account with Massachusetts, Aug.–Dec. 1775, above, and note 3 there.

1775. DECR. 10. SUNDAY.

Rode from Bristol to Trenton, breakfasted, rode to Princetown, and dined with a Captain Flahaven, in Ld. Sterlings Regiment, who has been express to Congress from his Lordship.

Flahaven's Father lives in this Province. He has lived in Maryland. Says that the Virginia Convention granting the Scotch Petition to be neutral has done all the Mischief and been the Support of Lord Dunmore. He says the Scotch are in some Parts of Virginia powerfull—that in Alexandria he has heard them cursing the Congress and vilifying not only their public Proceedings but their private Characters. He has heard them decrying the Characters of the Maryland Delegates particularly Chase and the Virginia Delegates particularly Lee, Henry and Washington.

Last Evening, when I dismounted at Bristow, the Taverner shewed me into a Room, where was a young Gentleman very elegantly dress'd, with whom I spent the Evening. His name I could not learn. He told me, he had been an Officer in the Army but had sold out. I had much Conversation with him and some of it very free.

He told me, We had two valuable Prizes among the Prisoners, taken at Chambly and St. Johns—a Mr. Barrington Nephew of Lord Barrington, and a Captain Williams who he says is the greatest Officer in the Service. He gives a most exalted Character of Williams as a Mathematician, Phylosopher, Engineer, and in all other Accomplishments of an Officer.

In the Evening Mr. Baldwin came to see me. We waited on Dr. Witherspoon the President of the Colledge where we saw Mr. Smith and two other of the light Horse from Philadelphia going to the Camp with a Waggon.

[JOSEPH BASS' BILLS TO JOHN AND SAMUEL ADAMS.] [1]
John Adams Esqr. to Joseph Bass Dr.

AD 1775			
Sepr. 11	For bording at Mr. Dibleys	0: 8: 5	
Oct.	For one pr. of Quality binding	0 4 0	
	Paid to the Sadler	0 2: 3	
	Paid for triming of the horses	0 5: 0	
	For one Quir of paper	0 3: 6	
	For one Dito	0 3: 6	
	For one stick of sealing wax	0: 1: 0	
	For one Comb	0 2 6	
	For one Quier of paper	0 3: 6	

             £ s d

Pen. Curr. £1 13 8 = 1: 7: 0

               L.M.

Recd. the above Joseph Bass

Mr. Adamses bill

Mr. Adams Dr. to Joseph Bass

	£	s	d
To my Wages from 28th. Aug. to 21. Decr. 1775 @			
£3 per Month	11:	5:	0

Recd. the above in full Joseph Bass

Honl. Samuel Adams, & John Adams Esqr. to Joseph Bass Dr.

AD 1775		£	s	d
Nor. 8	For travling Charges to Philidelpha	19:18:	0	
	To one doz of pipes	0:15:	0	
	For hors hier	1:	3:	9
Nor. 28	For one doz of pipes	0:18:	0	
	To half a doz Dito	0:	3:	0
	To two pound of tobacow	0:18:	0	

Old Ten[or] £23:15: 9

Recd. one half of Mr. J. Adams £1:11s:6 L.M.

Joseph Bass

[1] M-Ar: vol. 210. Endorsed by JA.

1776 JANY. 3D. WEDNESDAY.[1]

[1] This heading without text is the last entry in D/JA/24.

After a week in Braintree JA resumed his seat, 26 Dec., in the Massachusetts Council, which was sitting in Watertown. A payroll record in the Council Papers (M-Ar: vol. 164) indicates that he attended sixteen days between then and 24 Jan., the day before he set out once more for Congress, and was paid £5 10s. 10d. for travel and services. His work on committees was as intense as it had been in Congress; see the Council Journal for this session as printed in Force, *Archives*, 4th ser., 4:1219–1312. One of his committee assignments led to a very characteristic composition from JA's pen, a proclamation "By the Great and General Court of the Colony of Massachusetts-Bay," dated 23 Jan. 1776 and designed to be read "at the opening of the several Courts of Justice through this Colony, and at Town-Meetings" (Ford, *Mass. Broadsides*, No. 1973, with facsimile facing p. 272; MS in M-Ar: vol. 138; see Council Journal, Force, *Archives*, 4th ser., 4:1246, 1268–1270; Mass., *House Jour.*, 1775–1776, 3d sess., p. 189–192). Others took him to headquarters in Cambridge for consultations with Gen. Washington and formal councils of war. His surviving correspondence with Washington, together with the Council Journal, shows that he was repeatedly at headquarters in January, and the next entry in the Diary records that he dined with a party of officers, including the commander in chief, and their ladies at Cambridge on the day before he started for Philadelphia.

1776. JANUARY 24. WEDNESDAY.[1]

Began my Journey to Phildelphia, dined at C[olonel] Mifflins at

Cambridge with G. Washington, and Gates and their Ladies, and half a Dozen Sachems and Warriours of the french Cocknowaga Tribe, with their Wives and Children. Williams is one, who was captivated in his Infancy, and adopted. There is a Mixture of White Blood french or English in most of them. Louis, their Principal, speaks English and french as well as Indian. It was a Savage feast, carnivorous Animals devouring their Pray. Yet they were wondrous polite. The General introduced me to them as one of the Grand Council Fire at Philadelphia, upon which they made me many Bows, and a cordial Reception.[2]

[1] First entry in D/JA/25 since 30 Oct. 1775. The following entries, through 29 Jan., are from the same booklet.

On 15 Dec. 1775 the General Court elected the two Adamses, Hancock, and Paine to another year's term as delegates to the Continental Congress, but replaced Thomas Cushing with Elbridge Gerry—an action that disturbed conservatives both in Massachusetts and in Congress. See Mass., *House Jour*, 1775–1776, 3d sess., p. 44; Samuel Adams to James Warren, 8 March 1776, *Warren-Adams Letters*, 1:211–212. But JA was pleased by it and had the company of Gerry on the road to Philadelphia, where the two arrived in Congress on 8 Feb. and took their seats in Congress next day (JA to AA, 11 Feb. 1776, Adams Papers; see also *JCC*, 4:122).

[2] On the Caughnawagas, who had come to offer their services to the Americans, see Washington to Philip Schuyler, 27 Jan. 1776 (*Writings*, ed. Fitzpatrick, 4:280–281).

1776. JANY. 25. THURSDAY.

About 10 Mr. Gerry called me, and we rode to Framingham, where We dined. Coll. Buckminster after Dinner shewed us, the Train of Artillery brought down from Ticonderoga, by Coll. Knox.[1] It consists of Iron—9 Eighteen Pounders, 10 Twelves, 6. six, four nine Pounders, Three 13. Inch Mortars, Two Ten Inch Mortars, one Eight Inch, and one six and an half. Howitz,[2] one Eight Inch and an half and one Eight.

Brass Cannon. Eight Three Pounders, one four Pounder, 2 six Pounders, one Eighteen Pounder, and one 24 Pounder. One eight Inch and an half Mortar, one Seven Inch and an half Dto. and five Cohorns.

After Dinner, rode to Maynards, and supped there very agreably.

[1] The documents relative to Knox's transportation of the great train of artillery from Fort Ticonderoga to the American camp outside Boston are printed by Alexander C. Flick in N.Y. State Hist. Assoc., *Quart. Jour.*, 9:119–135 (April 1928). They include Knox's own inventory of the guns, with which JA's list closely corresponds and which has been helpful in interpreting JA's confusing punctuation in this passage.

[2] A singular or plural form according to *OED*. Knox's list has the more conventional term "Howitzers."

1776 JANY 26. FRYDAY.

Stopped at Sternes's [Stearns's] in Worcester, and dined with Mr.

Lincoln at Mr. Jonathan Williams's.[1] In Putnams Office where I formerly trimm'd the Midnight Lamp, Mr. Williams keeps Laws Works and Jacob Behmens, with whose Mistical Reveries he is much captivated.[2]

[1] This Jonathan Williams (d. 1780), Harvard 1772, had been a law clerk in JA's office. He was a cousin of the better-known Jonathan Williams (1750–1815), Benjamin Franklin's great-nephew, who a little later crossed JA's path when serving as American agent at Nantes and who became first superintendent of the military academy at West Point; see *DAB*. On JA's law clerk see "Suffolk Bar Book," MHS, *Procs.*, 1st ser., 19 (1881–1882):151; *Harvard Quinquennial Cat.*; John Thaxter to JA, 7 Aug. 1780, Adams Papers.

[2] William Law, author of *A Serious Call to a Devout and Holy Life*, 1728, and other religious works, was an English disciple of the German mystic Jakob Boehme or Behmen; see *DNB* under Law.

1776. SUNDAY. JANY. 28.

Mr. Upham informs that this Town of Brookfield abounds with a Stone, out of which Allum, Coperas and Sulphur are made. Out of one Bushell of this Stone, he made five Pounds of Coperas. He put the Stone into a Tub, poured Water on it, let it Stand 2 or 3 days, then drew it off, and boiled the Liquor away—let it stand and it shot into a Kind of Christals. Adding Chamberly [1] and Alkaline Salts to the Coperas and that makes Allum.

We made some Sulphur, by Sublimation. We put 4 Quarts of the Stone into an Iron Kettle, laid a Wooden Cover over the Kettle leaving an Hole in the Middle. Then We put an Earthern Pot over the Top of the Kettle, and cemented it with Clay—then made a fire under the Kettle, and the Sulphur sublimated. We got about a Spoonfull.[2]

We have found a Bed of yellow Ocre in this Town. I got 12,00 Wt. We make Spanish Brown by burning the yellow Ocre.

[1] Chamber-lye (variously spelled, 1500–1800): "Urine; *esp.* as used for washing, etc." (*OED*).

[2] JA could hardly have participated in these experiments, and so it must be assumed that this and the following paragraph are direct discourse by Upham. CFA supplied quotation marks around this passage.

1776 MONDAY. JAN. 29.

Rode to Springfield, dined at Scotts. Heard that the Cannon at Kingsbridge in N. York were spiked up. That dry Goods, English Goods were sent round to N. York from Boston, and from N. York sold all over N.E. and sent down to Camp. That Tryon has issued Writs for the Choice of a new Assembly, and that the Writs were likely to be obeyed, and the Tories were likely to carry a Majority of Members.

[NOTES OF DEBATES IN THE CONTINENTAL CONGRESS]
1776. FEB. [16].[1]

In Committee of the whole.

Cant we oblige B. to keep a Navy on foot the Expence of which will be double to what they will take from Us. I have heard of Bullion Sp[anish] Flotas being stoppd least they should be taken—But perishable Commodities never were stopped. Open your Ports to Foreigners. Your Trade will become of so much Consequence, that Foreigners will protect you.[2]

Wilson. A Gentleman from Mass. thinks that a middle Way should be taken. That Trade should be opened, for some Articles, and to some Places, but not for all Things and to all Places.

I think the Merchants ought to judge for themselves of the danger and Risque. We should be blamed if We did not leave it to them.

I differ from the Gentleman of Massachusetts. Trade ought in War to be carried on with greater Vigour. By what means did B. carry on their Tryumphs last War? The United Provinces their War vs. Spain.

If We determine that our Ports shall not be opened, our Vessells abroad will not return. Our Seamen are all abroad—will not return, unless We open our Trade. I am afraid it will be necessary to invite Foreigners to trade with Us, altho We loose a great Advantage, that of trading in our own Bottoms.

Sherman. I fear We shall maintain the Armies of our Enemies at our own Expence with Provisions. We cant carry on a beneficial Trade, as our Enemies will take our Ships. A Treaty with a foreign Power is necessary, before We open our Trade, to protect it.

Rutledge.[3]

Harrison. We have hobbled on, under a fatal Attachment to G.B. I felt it as much as any Man but I feel a stronger to my Country.

Wythe. The Ports will be open the 1st. March. The Q. is whether We shall shutt em up. Fæce Romuli non Republica Platonis. Americans will hardly live without Trade. It is said our Trade will be of no Advantage to Us, because our Vessells will be taken, our Enemies will be supplied, the W.I. will be supplied at our Expence. This is too true, unless We can provide a Remedy. Our Virginia Convention have resolved, that our Ports be opened to all Nations that will trade with us, except G.B., I. and W.I. If the Inclination of the People, should become universal to trade, We must open our Ports. Merchants will not export our Produce, unless they get a Profit.

We might get some of our Produce to Markett, by authorizing Adventurers to Arm themselves, and giving Letters of Mark—make Reprisals.

2d. by inviting foreign Powers to make Treaties of Commerce with us.

But other Things are to be considered, before such a Measure is adopted. In what Character shall We treat, as subjects of G.B.—as Rebells? Why should We be so fond of calling ourselves dutifull Subjects.

If We should offer our Trade to the Court of France, would they take Notice of it, any more than if Bristol or Liverpool should offer theirs, while We profess to be Subjects.—No. We must declare ourselves a free People.

If We were to tell them, that after a Season, We would return to our Subjection to G.B., would not a foreign Court wish to have Something permanent.

We should encourage our Fleet. I am convinced that our Fleet may become as formidable as We wish to make it. Moves a Resolution.[4]

¹ First entry in booklet "26" (our D/JA/26), a pocket memorandum book stitched in red-brown leather covers and containing scattered notes of debates in Congress from February to April (possibly early May) 1776.

The day on which the present debate took place can be assigned with some confidence because Richard Smith summarized in his Diary under 16 Feb. a debate of "4 or 5 Hours ... in Grand Comee. [committee of the whole] on Trade," which corresponds at essential points with JA's fragmentary notes (Burnett, ed., *Letters of Members*, 1: 350–352; see JCC, 4:154). See note 4, below.

² JA does not indicate whose speech this was.

³ Following [Edward] Rutledge's name there is a blank in the MS amounting to two-thirds of a page. JA probably intended to supply notes on Rutledge's speech but failed to do so.

⁴ "Wyth ... offered Propositions whereof the first was that the Colonies have a Right to contract Alliances with Foreign Powers. an Objection being offered that this was Independency there ensued much Argument upon that Ground. a leading Question was given

Whether this Proposn. shall be considered by the Comee. it was carried in the Affirmative 7 Colonies to 5. then it was debated and postponed" (Richard Smith, Diary, 16 Feb., Burnett, ed., *Letters of Members*, 1:350–351). See also JA's Memorandum of Measures to Be Pursued in Congress, Feb.? 1776, following.

From this point until he sailed for France in Feb. 1778, JA's Diary is so fragmentary that it is scarcely practical to indicate, even in summary form, the events in his personal and political life which he failed to record. In compensation, however, one may turn to his Autobiography, where the record for the year 1776 is remarkably full, for when he came to deal with that climactic year he read the published *Journals of Congress* closely, quoted from them copiously, and commented on them with characteristic freedom. (His own extensive collection of the *Journals*, Phila., 1777–1788, and early reprints, survives in the Boston Public Library; see *Cat. of JA's Library*, p. 60–61.) What is more, he occasionally dipped into his files of old correspondence, as he had not done at all up to this point in the Autobiography, to support his commentary. The result is that about half of the entire text of Part One of the Autobiography is devoted to the first ten months of 1776 alone, ending with his departure from Congress in October of that year.

[MEMORANDUM OF MEASURES TO BE PURSUED
IN CONGRESS, FEBRUARY? 1776.][1]

Mem.

The Confederation to be taken up in Paragraphs.[2]

An Alliance to be formed with France and Spain.[3]

Embassadors to be sent to both Courts.

Government to be assumed in every Colony.[4]

Coin and Currencies to be regulated.[5]

Forces to be raised and maintained in Canada and New York. St. Lawrence and Hudsons Rivers to be secured.

Hemp to be encouraged and the Manufacture of Duck.[6]

Powder Mills to be built in every Colony, and fresh Efforts to make Salt Petre.[7]

An Address to the Inhabitants of the Colonies.[8]

The Committee for Lead and Salt to be fill'd up, and Sulphur added to their Commission.

Money to be sent to the Paymaster, to pay our Debts, and fullfill our Engagements.

Taxes to be laid, and levied, Funds established. New Notes to be given on Interest, for Bills borrowed.

Treaties of Commerce with F. S. H. D. &c.[9]

Declaration of Independency, Declaration of War with the Nation, Cruising on the british Trade, their East India Ships and Sugar Ships.[10]

Prevent the Exportation of Silver and Gold.

[1] Regrettably it is impossible to date this important memorandum with certainty. In the MS (D/JA/25) it appears on two facing pages between the entries of 26 and 28 Jan. 1776, which, disregarding other considerations, should indicate that it was written during JA's return journey to Philadelphia. This may be the case, but for reasons pointed out elsewhere the editors have learned to distrust the physical position of undated entries in the Diary as clues to their dates of composition. JA's list displays such familiarity with issues current in Congress that it is extremely doubtful that he could have prepared it on his way back to Philadelphia. It is far more likely that he drew it up after he had resumed his seat on 9 Feb. and had tested the temper of his fellow delegates and, through them, the temper of the country, especially those sections of it beyond New England — which he now felt certain, to use Jefferson's phrase, was ready to fall "from the parent stem" (*Papers*, ed. Boyd, 1:313). What he found was that, except for Virginia, most of the other colonies were not matured to that point of ripeness, and his task was, in conjunction with others of his mind in Congress, to bring them to that point. As the notes below indicate, many of the measures listed can be identified as resolutions introduced in Congress by JA and other leaders of the independence party during the weeks

immediately following his return; others were not put forward until late spring or early summer, or at least did not get beyond the talking stage and so are not recorded in the Journal.

The most plausible supposition is that JA compiled his list of agenda, which has the appearance of being composed at one sitting, after conferring with Samuel Adams, Richard Henry Lee, and others with advanced views and agreeing with them on what measures should be pressed, soon after taking his seat, very probably between 10 and 15 Feb. and certainly before 23 Feb. (see note 7, below). If this is a sound conjecture, this paper may be regarded as minutes of a caucus among members who favored American independence.

² On 21 July 1775 Franklin had laid before Congress a draft plan of "Articles of Confederation and Perpetual Union," but the subject was so touchy that no record of it was made in the official Journal. Copies of Franklin's plan circulated in the colonies and even reached print, but without noticeable effect (Burnett, *Continental Congress*, p. 91–92; Jefferson, *Papers*, ed. Boyd, 1:179–180). On 23 Dec. 1775 Jefferson, as chairman of a committee to ascertain the unfinished business before Congress, entered the "Report of the Proposed Articles of Confederation (adjourned from August last)" as the first item, but it was struck from his list, probably by the committee before reporting (JCC, 3:454–456; Jefferson, *Papers*, ed. Boyd, 1:274–275). According to Richard Smith's Diary there were "considerable Arguments" on the floor of Congress, 16 Jan. 1776, "on the Point Whether a Day shall be fixed for considering the Instrument of Confederation formerly brought in by a Comee. it was carried in the Negative [and so not recorded in the Journal]. Dr. Franklin exerted Himself in Favor of the Confederation as did Hooper, Dickinson and other[s] agt. it" (Burnett, ed., *Letters of Members*, 1:313; and see Samuel Adams to JA, 15–16 Jan. 1776, Adams Papers; same, p. 311–312). The Journal of Congress is silent on this subject until 7 June, when the Virginia Resolutions "respecting independency" were brought in, one of which proposed "That a plan of confederation be prepared and trans-

mitted to the respective Colonies for their consideration and approbation," and after debate extending over several days a committee was appointed "to prepare and digest the form of a confederation to be entered into between these colonies" (JCC, 5:425, 431, 433). For later developments see entries of 25 July and following, below.

³ A proposal approaching this was made by George Wythe on 16 Feb. 1776; see JA's Notes of Debates of that date, preceding, and note 4 there.

⁴ JA's main objective (and accomplishment) in the spring of 1776. See his Notes of Debates, 13–15 May, below, and notes there.

⁵ On 19 April 1776 a committee, of which JA was a member, was appointed by Congress "to examine and ascertain the value of the several species of gold and silver coins, current in these colonies, and the proportions they ought to bear to Spanish milled dollars" (JCC, 4:294). Its report, largely the work of George Wythe, was brought in on 22 May and tabled (same, p. 381–383). For its later history see Jefferson, *Papers*, ed. Boyd, 1:511–518).

⁶ This proposal was introduced by JA and adopted by Congress in an enlarged form in March; see JA's Draft Resolutions for Encouraging Agriculture and Manufactures, Feb.–March, below.

⁷ These proposals, together with the next but one in the present list of agenda, emerged in a series of four important resolutions, adopted by Congress on 23 Feb., to promote the production of military supplies, and ordered to be published (JCC, 4:170–171). Richard Smith in his Diary noted that "these were presented by John Adams" (Burnett, ed., *Letters of Members*, 1:361). They were printed in the *Pennsylvania Gazette* of 28 Feb. 1776.

⁸ A committee of five members had been appointed on 24 Jan. to draft such an address (JCC, 4:87). All of its members were conservatives (Dickinson, Wilson, Hooper, Duane, and Alexander), and the draft they submitted on 13 Feb., largely the work of Wilson, was a conservative paper that disavowed independence as an American aim (same, p. 134–146; C. Page Smith, *James Wilson, Founding Father, 1742–1798*, Cha-

pel Hill, 1956, p. 74–76). This address was in fact part of a campaign by conservative leaders, begun two weeks earlier, to smoke out those in Congress who were secretly working for independence; see Burnett, ed., *Letters of Members*, 1: 304, 311, 326, 334, 348. Proceeding on the assumption that the present notes were the product of a caucus of delegates determined on strong measures, this item could appear among their agenda only because they wished either to alter the proposed address drastically or to suppress it entirely. When it was presented on 13 Feb., they succeeded in tabling it, and it was never resurrected. But while these facts are all consonant with the date of mid-February suggested for JA's memorandum, they do not help to date it any more precisely.
⁹ France, Spain, Holland, Denmark.
¹⁰ On 23 March Congress after some days of debate passed a series of resolutions authorizing "the inhabitants of these colonies . . . to fit out armed vessels to cruize on the enemies of these United Colonies" and establishing regulations concerning prizes taken by such privateers (*JCC*, 4:229–233). The committee that reported a draft of these resolutions (in the form of a "Declaration") consisted of Wythe, Jay, and Wilson, but their report was amended in Congress, and JA with little doubt contributed to its final form as published (except for a secret paragraph) in the *Pennsylvania Gazette*, 27 March; see his Autobiography under 19, 22, 23 March 1776. On the day of its adoption JA told a friend that it amounted to at least "three Quarters of a war" against Great Britain (to Horatio Gates, NHi; Burnett, ed., *Letters of Members*, 1: 405–406).

[DRAFT RESOLVES CONCERNING THE SECRET COMMITTEE
OF CORRESPONDENCE AND A PLAN OF CONFEDERATION,
FEBRUARY? 1776.] ¹

Resolved that the Committee of Secret Correspondence be directed to lay their Letters before this Congress.

Resolved that   be a Committee to prepare a Draught of firm Confederation, to be reported as soon as may be to this Congress, to be considered and digested and recommended to the several Assemblies and Conventions of these united Colonies, to be by them adopted, ratified and confirmed.

¹ It is impossible to date with certainty these draft resolutions, which JA perhaps introduced in an unrecorded session of a committee of the whole. In the MS they follow his notes of debates assigned to 16 Feb. and precede the quotation from Jeremiah which follows the present entry. But it was not until 10 May that Congress "*Resolved*, That the Committee of Secret Correspondence be directed to lay their proceedings before Congress on Monday next, withholding the names of the persons they have employed, or with whom they have corresponded" (*JCC*, 4:345). And it was not until 11–12 June (as a result of the Virginia Resolutions of 7 June) that a committee was agreed to and appointed to prepare a plan of confederation (same, 5:431, 433; see Memorandum of Measures to Be Pursued in Congress, preceding, and note 2 there).

[FEBRUARY? 1776.]

3. Jer. 12. Go proclaim these Words towards the North. Return thou

backsliding Israel and I will not cause my anger to fall upon you, for I am merciful and will not be angry forever.[1]

[1] On 17 Feb. Congress *"Resolved, That a committee of three be chosen to prepare instructions for the committee appointed to go to Canada"*; and the members chosen were JA, Wythe, and Sherman (JCC, 4:159). They reported a draft on 9 March, which after amendments and additions was finally adopted and spread on the Journal on 20 March (same, p. 193, 215–219). Doubtless JA recorded this appropriate Scriptural passage while engaged in this assignment, which he considered to be of the utmost importance; see his Autobiography under 17 Feb., 20 March 1776.

[FEBRUARY? 1776.]

Any Goods or Commodities, except Staves for Sale, may be exported, from the united Colonies to any other Part of the World, not subject to the Crown of G.B.[1]

[1] Written on an otherwise blank front leaf in D/JA/26, this is evidently tentative phrasing for an article in the report of the committee of the whole on American trade. From 16 Feb. on, this committee discussed from time to time the opening of American ports, and on 6 April Congress voted certain regulations including the present one, though in different language (JCC, 4:154, 257).

[DRAFT RESOLUTIONS FOR ENCOURAGING AGRICULTURE AND MANUFACTURES, FEBRUARY–MARCH 1776.][1]

Resolved, That it be recommended to the several Assemblies, Conventions, Councils of Safety and Committees of Correspondence and Inspection, that they use their utmost Endeavours, by all reasonable Means to promote the Culture of Flax, Hemp, and Cotton and the Growth of Wool in these united Colonies.

Resolved That it be recommended to the Assemblies, Conventions, and Councils of Safety, that they take the earliest Measures for erecting in each and every Colony a Society for the Encouragement of Agriculture, Arts, Manufactures and Commerce, and that a Correspondence be maintained between such Societies, that the [2] numerous natural Advantages of this Country for supporting its Inhabitants may not be neglected.

Resolved that it be recommended to the said Assemblies, Conventions and Councils of Safety that they [3] consider of Ways and Means of introducing the Manufactures of Duck and Sail Cloth [4] into such Colonies where they are not now understood and of [5] increasing and promoting them where they are.

Resolved that   be a Committee, to receive all Plans and Proposals for encouraging and improving the Agriculture, Arts, Manufactures and Commerce both foreign and domestic of America, to correspond with the several Assemblies, Conventions, Councils and

Committees of Safety, Committees of Correspondence and of Observation in these united Colonies upon these interesting Subjects.[6]
That these be published.

[1] The first three of these four resolutions were voted by Congress on 21 March and, as JA wished, were ordered to be published (*JCC*, 4:224). They were printed in the *Pennsylvania Gazette* of 27 March. In copying them into his Autobiography JA said that these were "three Resolutions, which I claim," though we have no clue as to when they were written or introduced except for the fact that in the MS they immediately precede the entry that JA himself dated 1 March. It should also be noted that well up on his list of Measures to be Pursued in Congress (Feb.? 1776, above) is the item: "Hemp to be encouraged and the Manufacture of Duck."

[2] The text as adopted by Congress inserts at this point: "rich and."

[3] Text as adopted inserts at this point: "forthwith."

[4] Text as adopted inserts at this point: "and steel"—the only substantive change between the resolutions as drafted and as adopted.

[5] Text as adopted inserts at this point: "encouraging."

[6] After reporting the adoption of the first three resolutions above, Richard Smith adds in his Diary that "a Clause was erased for a standing Comee. of Congress to correspond with and assist these Societies" (Burnett, ed., *Letters of Members*, 1:402). Thus was defeated the earliest in a long series of proposals by two successive generations of Adamses to associate the American government with the promotion of useful arts.

1776 MARCH 1.

How is the Interest of France and Spain affected, by the dispute between B. and the C[olonies]? Is it the Interest of France [to] stand neuter, to join with B. or to join with the C. Is it not her Interest, to dismember the B. Empire? Will her Dominions be safe, if B. and A[merica] remain connected? Can she preserve her Possessions in the W.I. She has in the W.I. Martinico, Guadaloupe, and one half of Hispaniola. In Case a Reconciliation should take Place, between B. and A. and a War should break out between B. and France, would not all her Islands be taken from her in 6 Months?

The Colonies are now much more warlike and powerfull than they were, during the last War. A martial Spirit has seized all the Colonies. They are much improved in Skill and Discipline. They have now a large standing Army. They have many good officers. They abound in Provisions. They are in the Neighbourhood of the W.I. A British Fleet and Army united with an American Fleet and Army and supplied with Provisions and other Necessaries from America, might conquer all the french Islands in the W.I. in six Months, and a little ⟨less⟩ more Time than that would be required, to destroy all their Marine and Commerce.[1]

[1] This entry and that dated 4 March which follows are presumably private reflections by the diarist. At any rate they have no discernible connection with proceedings in Congress of 1 or 4 March. No committee of the whole sat on either of those days.

MONDAY MARCH 4. 1776.

Resentment is a Passion, implanted by Nature for the Preservation of the Individual. Injury is the Object which excites it. Injustice, Wrong, Injury excites the Feeling of Resentment, as naturally and necessarily as Frost and Ice excite the feeling of cold, as fire excites heat, and as both excite Pain. A Man may have the Faculty of concealing his Resentment, or suppressing it, but he must and ought to feel it. Nay he ought to indulge it, to cultivate it. It is a Duty. His Person, his Property, his Liberty, his Reputation are not safe without it. He ought, for his own Security and Honour, and for the public good to punish those who injure him, unless they repent, and then he should forgive, having Satisfaction and Compensation. Revenge is unlawfull.

It is the same with Communities. They ought to resent and to punish.

[NOTES ON RELATIONS WITH FRANCE, MARCH–APRIL 1776.][1]

Is any Assistance attainable from F.?

What Connection may We safely form with her?

1st. No Political Connection. Submit to none of her Authority—receive no Governors, or officers from her.

2d. No military Connection. Receive no Troops from her.

3d. Only a Commercial Connection, i.e. make a Treaty, to receive her Ships into our Ports. Let her engage to receive our Ships into her Ports—furnish Us with Arms, Cannon, Salt Petre, Powder, Duck, Steel.

[1] These notes, very likely prepared for a speech in Congress or in committee of the whole, follow the entry of 4 March after a short interval of space in the MS. The subject of overtures to France was recurrently debated throughout March and April.

[DRAFT RESOLUTION CONCERNING INSTRUCTIONS TO
DELEGATES, MARCH–APRIL 1776.][1]

Whereas, the present State of America, and the cruel Efforts of our Enemies, render the most perfect and cordial Union of the Colonies and the utmost Exertions of their Strength, necessary for the Preservation and establishment of their Liberties, therefore

Resolved. That it be recommended to the several Assemblies and Conventions of these united Colonies, who have limited the Powers of their Delegates in this Congress, by any express Instructions, that they repeal or suspend those Instructions for a certain Time, that this Congress may have Power, without any unnecessary Obstruction or Embarrassment, to concert, direct and order, such further Measures, as may seem to them necessary for the Defence and Preservation, Support and Establishment of Right and Liberty in these Colonies.[2]

[1] This draft follows the preceding entry after a short interval of space and is the last entry in D/JA/26. There is no other clue to its date. CFA suggested that "This is perhaps the first draught of the well known motion made in Committee of the Whole, on the sixth of May, which was reported to the House, on the tenth," recommending the establishment of governments in the colonies "sufficient to the exigencies of their affairs" (JA, *Works*, 2:489, note; JCC, 4:342). But it seems to be, rather, a different device to achieve the same end, i.e. to draw the teeth from the instructions still controlling the delegations from the middle colonies. There can be no doubt that JA proposed to introduce it into the debates of the committee of the whole during March or April, but

whether he did or not remains a question. For the source of JA's language see the next note.

[2] Compare the instructions issued to the Massachusetts delegates by the General Court on 18 Jan. 1776 (while JA was attending as a member of the Council): "Resolved that they or any one or more of them are hereby fully impowered, with the delegates from the other American Colonies to concert, direct and order such further measures as shall to them appear best calculated for the Establishment of Right and Liberty to the American Colonies upon a Basis permanent and secured against the power and arts of the British Administration" (Adams Papers). JA was simply proposing to extend the Massachusetts Instructions throughout the Continent.

[RESIDENCES OF DELEGATES IN PHILADELPHIA, APRIL? 1776.][1]

Coll. Whipple lodges at Mrs.   in Walnut Street.

Mr. Hancock, Messrs. Adams's, Paine and Gerry at Mrs. Yards in 2d Street.

Mr. Hopkins at

Mr. Sherman, Coll. Wolcott and Coll. Huntington at Mr. Duncans in 3d.

Mr. Duane at the Collectors in Markett Street, next door to Coll. Reads.

Gen. Livingston, Mr. De Hart in Second Street.
Mr. Serjeant at Dr. Ewing's.

Mr. Moreton at
Mr. Wilson at

Mr. Johnson at
Mr. Alexander at
Mr. Goldsborough at
Mr. Tilghman at his Brothers.

Coll. R. H. Lee at
Coll. F. L. Lee at the Corner opposite Mr. George Clymers.
Mr. Wythe in Chesnutt Street.
Coll. Harrison at Randolphs.
Mr. Braxton at

Mr. Hewes, at, in 3d Street—lives alone.

Mr. Rutledge at Mrs. Yards.
Mr. Lynch at
Mr. Lynch Junr. at

[1] This imperfect but interesting list, hitherto unpublished, was written in the final leaves of D/JA/25. JA evidently put down all the names at one sitting but left ample space for additional names and addresses to be supplied later. A comparison with the attendance records of members compiled by Burnett (*Letters of Members*, 1:xli–lxvi) shows that, apart from the (doubtless inadvertent) omission of the Delaware delegation, JA's list closely approximates the membership of Congress known from other evidence to have been present in late April. One could be more confident and precise about the date if the attendance records of certain members of the New York and South Carolina delegations were less obscure.

[NOTES OF DEBATES IN THE CONTINENTAL CONGRESS, 13–15 MAY 1776.][1]

Mr. Duane moves that the Delegation from N. York might be read.[2]

When We were invited by Mass. Bay to the first Congress an Objection was made to binding ourselves by Votes of Congress.

Congress ought not to determine a Point of this Sort, about instituting Government. What is it to Congress, how Justice is administered. You have no Right to pass the Resolution—any more than Parliament has.

How does it appear that no favourable Answer is likely to be given to our Petitions? Every Account of foreign Aid, is accompanied with an Account of Commissioners.[3]

Why all this Haste? Why this Urging? Why this driving?—Disputes about Independence are in all the Colonies. What is this owing to, but our Indiscretion?

I shall take the Liberty of informing my Constituents that I have not been guilty of a Breach of Trust. I do protest vs. this Piece of Mechanism, this Preamble.

If the Facts in this Preamble should prove to be true, there will not be one Voice vs. Independence.

I suppose the Votes have been numbered and there is to be a Majority.[4]

McKean. Construes the Instructions from N. York as Mr. Sherman does, and thinks this Measure the best to produce Harmony with G. Britain. There are now 2 Governments in direct Opposition to each other. Dont doubt that foreign Mercenaries are coming to destroy Us. I do think We shall loose our Liberties, Properties and Lives too, if We do not take this Step.

S. Adams. We have been favoured with a Reading of the Instructions from N. York. I am glad of it. The first Object of that Colony is no doubt the Establishment of their Rights. Our Petitions have not been heard—yet answered with Fleets and Armies and are to be answered with Mirmidons from abroad. The Gentleman from N. York, Mr. Duane, has not objected to the Preamble, but this—he has not a Right to vote for it.[5] We cant go upon stronger Reasons, than that the King has thrown us out of his Protection. Why should We support Governments under his Authority? I wonder the People have conducted so well as they have.

Mr. Wilson. Was not present in Congress when the Resolution pass'd, to which this Preamble is proposed. I was present and one of the Committee, who reported the Advice to Mass. Bay.[6] N. Hampshire, Carolina and Virginia, had the same Advice, and with my hearty Concurrence.

The Claims of Parliament will meet with Resistance to the last Extremity. Those Colonies were Royal Governments. They could not subsist without some Government.

A Maxim, that all Government originates from the People. We are the Servants of the People sent here to act under a delegated Authority. If we exceed it, voluntarily, We deserve neither Excuse nor Justification.

Some have been put under Restraints by their Constituents. They cannot vote, without transgressing this Line. Suppose they should hereafter be called to an Account for it. This Province has not by any public Act, authorized us to vote upon this Question. This Province has done much and asked little from this Congress. The Assembly, largely increased, will [not][7] meet till next Monday. Will the Cause suffer much, if this Preamble is not published at this Time? If the Resolve is published without the Preamble. The Preamble contains a Reflection upon the Conduct of some People in America. It was equally irreconcileable to good Conscience Nine Months ago, to take the Oaths of Allegiance, as it is now. Two respectable Members last February, took the Oath of Allegiance in our Assembly. Why should We expose any Gentlemen to such an invidious Reflection?

In Magna Charta, there is a Clause, which authorises the People to seize the K[ing]'s Castles, and opposes his Arms when he exceeds his duty.

In this Province if that Preamble passes there will be an immediate Dissolution of every Kind of Authority. The People will be instantly in a State of Nature. Why then precipitate this Measure. Before We are prepared to build the new House, why should We pull down the old one, and expose ourselves to all the Inclemencies of the Season.[8]

R. H. Lee. Most of the Arguments apply to the Resolve and not to the Preamble.

---

[1] First entry in D/JA/27, a pocket memorandum book stitched into red-brown leather covers and containing scattered notes of proceedings in Congress from this date through 2 Aug. 1776. On the date of the present debate see the next note.

[2] That is, the instructions to the New York delegates issued by the New York Provincial Convention, 12 April 1775. The delegates were instructed "to concert and determine upon such measures, as shall be judged most effectual for the preservation and re-establishment of American rights and priviledges, *and for the restoration of harmony between Great Britain and the Colonies*" (JCC, 2:15–16; italics added). The New York delegates were not released from this instruction until 9 July, after independence had been voted and the Declaration adopted (same, 5:560).

On 10 May, according to the Journal, "Congress then resumed the consideration of the report from the committee of the whole [on the state of the United Colonies], which being read was agreed to as follows:

"*Resolved*, That it be recommended to the respective assemblies and conventions of the United Colonies, where no government sufficient to the exigencies of their affairs have been hitherto established, to adopt such government as shall, in the opinion of the representatives of the people, best conduce to the happiness and safety of their constituents in particular, and America in general.

"*Resolved*, That a committee of three

be appointed to prepare a preamble to the foregoing resolution:

"The members chosen, Mr. J[ohn] Adams, Mr. [Edward] Rutledge, and Mr. R[ichard] H[enry] Lee" (same, 4:342).

The resolution for instituting new governments, which JA in his Autobiography pronounced "an Epocha, a decisive Event," had been debated in committee of the whole for some time, though it is not clear just how long. The assumption, frequently encountered, that it formed part of the report of a committee of the whole on 6 May cannot be verified. As for its authorship, we have the statement by JA in his Autobiography that "In the Beginning of May I procured the Appointment of a Committee, to prepare a resolution recommending to the People of the States to institute Governments. The Committee of whom I was one requested me to draught a resolve which I did and by their Direction reported it." Though JA was undoubtedly a prime mover of this business, this account, written from memory, misleadingly blends the resolution adopted on the 10th with the preamble adopted on the 15th.

The committee to prepare a preamble reported a draft on 13 May, "which was read, and postponed till to morrow"; two days later it was taken "into consideration [and] agreed to" in the form spread on the Journal (JCC, 4:351, 357–358). Both the resolution and the preamble were published in the *Pennsylvania Gazette* of 22 May.

The debate recorded in the present

notes was clearly over the preamble, the language of which was much stronger than that of the resolution it accompanied, since it called for the total suppression "of every kind of authority" under the British crown. This debate must have taken place between 13 and 15 May. Carter Braxton, a conservative member from Virginia, wrote on 17 May to Landon Carter that the resolution and preamble, taken together, fall "little short of Independence. It was not so understood by Congress but I find those out of doors on both sides the question construe it in that manner. The assumption of Governt. was necessary and to that resolution little objection was made, but when the Preamble was reported much heat and debate did ensue for two or three Days" (Burnett, ed., *Letters of Members*, 1:453-454).

[2] See James Duane to John Jay, 11 May 1776 (same, p. 443).

[4] Carter Braxton said on 17 May that the vote on the preamble was "I think ... 6 to 4" (same, p. 454). James Allen, a member of the Pennsylvania

Assembly, recorded in his Diary on 15 May that it "was carried by a majority of 7 Colonies to 4" (*PMHB*, 9:187 [July 1885]). If Allen was right, this would mean that one colony was divided. (Georgia had no delegates present until 20 May.)

[5] Dash supplied in this sentence for clarity.

[6] "Advice" to throw off royal authority and assume the powers of government, June 1775; see *JCC*, 2:81, 83-84, and JA's Autobiography under 7 June 1775. Similar advice was given to other colonies when they sought it of Congress later in the same year.

[7] Inadvertent omission in the MS.

[8] Wilson proved a true prophet. The current measures of Congress effectually destroyed the proprietary government of Pennsylvania, a primary target of the independence party in Congress, and led directly to the formation of a new state government. See J. Paul Selsam, *The Pennsylvania Constitution of 1776*, Phila., 1936, ch. 3.

[NOTES OF DEBATES IN THE CONTINENTAL CONGRESS ON THE ARTICLES OF CONFEDERATION][1] JULY 25. 1776.[2]

Art. 14. of the Confederation.[3]

Terms in this Article, equivocal and indefinite.

Jefferson. The Limits of the Southern Colonies are fixed. . . .[4] Moves an Amendment, that all Purchases of Lands, not within the Boundaries of any Colony shall be made by Congress, of the Indians in a great Council.—*Sherman* seconds the Motion. . . .[5]

Chase. The Intention of this Article is very obvious, and plain. The Article appears to me to be right, and the Amendment wrong. It is the Intention of some Gentlemen to limit the Boundaries of particular States. No colony has a Right to go to the S[outh] Sea. They never had —they cant have. It would not be safe to the rest. It would be destructive to her Sisters, and to herself.

Art. 16 [*i.e.* 15]. . . .[6]

Jefferson. What are reasonable Limits? What Security have We that the Congress will not curtail the present Settlements of the States. I have no doubt, that the Colonies will limit themselves.

Wilson. Every Gentleman has heard much of Claims to the South

Sea. They are extravagant. The Grants were made upon Mistakes. They were ignorant of the Geography. They thought the S. Sea within 100 Miles of the Atlantic Ocean. It was not conceived that they extended 3000 Miles. Ld. Cambden considers the Claims to the South Sea, as what never can be reduced to Practice. Pensilvania has no Right to interfere in those claims. But she has a Right to say, that she will not confederate unless those Claims are cut off. I wish the Colonies themselves would cutt off those Claims. . . .

Art. 16.[7]

Chase moves for the Word deputies, instead of Delegates, because the Members of the Maryland Convention are called Delegates, and he would have a Distinction.—Answer. In other Colonies the Reverse is true. The Members of the House are called deputies.

Jefferson objects to the first of November.—*Dr. Hall* moves for May, for the time to meet.—*Jefferson* thinks that Congress will have a short Meeting in the Fall and another in the Spring.—*Hayward* thinks the Spring the best Time.—*Wilson* thinks the fall—and November better than October, because September is a busy Month, every where.

Dr. Hall. Septr. and Octr. the most sickly and mortal Months in the Year. The Season is forwarder in Georgia in April, than here in May.

Hopkinson moves that the Power of recalling Delegates be reserved to the State not to the Assembly, because that may be changed.

Art. 17.[8]

Each Colony shall have one Vote.

[1] This being the first entry since May, we have nothing in JA's Diary or his notes of proceedings in Congress to indicate the part he played in the final struggle for political independence or the nature of his labors in Congress in the weeks that followed. Among his many assignments that summer, the most taxing was his service at the head of the Board of War and Ordnance, a standing committee appointed on 13 June (JCC, 5:438), to which all routine military business was thereafter referred. In his Autobiography, under date of 15 June 1776, JA lists the duties of the Board, and he did not exaggerate in saying that "From this time, We find in Almost every days Journal References of various Business to the Board of War, or their Reports upon such Things as were referred to them." The MS reports of the Board of War from the summer of 1776 to Oct. 1777 fill a volume in PCC, No. 147.

[2] A summary account of efforts, July 1775–June 1776, to arrive at a plan of confederation has been given above in a note on JA's paper called Measures to be Pursued in Congress, Feb.? 1776. On 12 June a committee consisting of one member (not including JA) from each colony was appointed "to prepare and digest the form of a confederation to be entered into between these colonies"; exactly a month later this committee reported a draft composed by John Dickinson, which was read and ordered to be printed exclusively for the use of members (JCC, 5:433, 546–556). On 22 July the printed draft was taken

up in a committee of the whole, which debated the articles at intervals from then until 20 Aug., when a revised text or second draft was reported to Congress by the committee and a second confidential printing was ordered for later consideration (same, p. 600, 674–689). JA's Notes of Debates which follow record in a fragmentary way the discussions in committee of the whole from 25 July to 2 Aug., inclusive. They are paralleled and supplemented by similar notes taken by Jefferson on the debates in committee on two critical articles in Dickinson's plan during the three days 30 July–1 Aug. (Jefferson, *Papers*, ed. Boyd, 1:320–327).

³ Article XIV of the Dickinson draft dealt with the mode of purchasing land from the Indians (JCC, 5:549).

⁴ The suspension points, both here and below in this series of notes on the debates concerning confederation, are in the MS.

⁵ For the full text of Jefferson's amendment, written on a slip affixed to the MS of the Dickinson draft, see Jefferson, *Papers*, ed. Boyd, 1:181–182. The whole of Article XIV was omitted in the revised text, or second draft, of 20 Aug. (JCC, 5:679–680).

⁶ Article XV dealt with boundaries of colonies or states, but was dependent on a clause in Article XVIII granting Congress the power to fix these boundaries (same, p. 549). Debate on this subject was resumed in committee of the whole on 2 Aug., q.v., below.

⁷ Article XVI in the Dickinson draft dealt with the mode of choosing and recalling delegates, the times Congress would convene, &c. (JCC, 5:549–550).

⁸ Article XVII in the Dickinson draft reads: "In determining Questions *(in Congress)* each Colony shall have one Vote" (same, p. 550). Jefferson's Notes of Proceedings do not indicate that this important article came up at all until 30 July. If it did come up on the 25th, it was quickly passed over, but see 30 July and 1 Aug., below.

[NOTES OF DEBATES ON THE ARTICLES OF CONFEDERATION, CONTINUED] JULY. 26.

Rutledge and *Linch* oppose giving the Power of regulating the Trade and managing all Affairs of the Indians, to Congress.[1] The Trade is profitable they say.

Gwinnett is in favour of Congress having such Power.

Braxton is for excepting such Indians as are tributary to any State. Several Nations are tributary to Virginia.

Jefferson explains it to mean the Indians who live in the Colony. These are Subject to the Laws in some degree.

Wilson. We have no Right over the Indians, whether within or without the real or pretended Limits of any Colony.... They will not allow themselves to be classed according to the Bounds of Colonies. Grants made 3000 miles to the Eastward have no Validity with the Indians. The Trade of Pensilvania has been more considerable with the Indians than that of the neighbouring Colonies.

Walton. The Indian Trade is of no essential service to any Colony. It must be a Monopoly. If it is free it produces Jealousies and Animosities, and Wars. Carolina very passionately considers this Trade as contributory to her Grandeur and Dignity. Deerskins are a great Part of the Trade. A great difference between S. Carolina and Georgia.

Carolina is in no danger from the Indians at present. Georgia is a frontier and Barrier to Car. G. must be overrun and extirpated before Car. can be hurt. G. is not equal to the Expence of giving the Donations to the Indians, which will be necessary to keep them at Peace. The Emoluments of the Trade are not a Compensation for the Expence of donations.

Rutledge differs from Walton in a Variety of Points.—We must look forward with extensive Views. Carolina has been run to an amazing expence to defend themselves vs. Indians. In 1760 &c. fifty thousand Guineas were spent. We have now as many Men on the frontiers, as in Charlestown. We have Forts in the Indian Countries. We are connected with them by Treaties.

Lynch. Congress may regulate the Trade, if they will indemnify Car. vs. the Expence of keeping Peace with the Indians, or defending Us vs. them.

Witherspoon. Here are two adjacent Provinces, situated alike with respect to the Indians, differing totally in their Sentiments of their Interests.

Chase. S. Carolina claims to the S. Sea. So does North, Virginia, and Massachusetts Bay. S. Carolina says they have a Right to regulate the Trade with the Indians. If so 4 Colonies have all the Power of regulating Trade with the Indians. S.C. alone could not stand alone vs. the Indian Nations.

Sherman moves that Congress may have a Superintending Power, to prevent Injustice to the Indians or Colonies.

Willson. No lasting Peace will be with the Indians, unless made by some one Body. No such language as this ought to be held to the Indians. We are stronger, We are better. We treat you better than another Colony. No Power ought to treat, with the Indians, but the united States. Indians know the striking Benefits of Confederation—they have an Example of it in the Union of the Six nations. The Idea of the Union of the Colonies struck them forcibly last Year. None should trade with Indians without a Licence from Congress. A perpetual War would be unavoidable, if every Body was allowed to trade with them.

Stone. This Expedient is worse than either of the Alternatives. What is the meaning of this Superintendency? Colonies will claim the Right first. Congress cant interpose untill the Evil has happened. Disputes will arise when Congress shall interpose.

[1] The debate in committee of the whole this day relates to a clause in Article XVIII of the Dickinson draft granting Congress the power of "regulat-

ing the Trade, and managing all Affairs with the Indians," which was incorporated in the second draft of 20

Aug. with a minor modification (JCC, 5:550, 682).

[NOTES OF DEBATES ON THE ARTICLES OF CONFEDERATION, CONTINUED] JULY 30. 1776.

Dr. Franklin. Let the smaller Colonies give equal Money and Men, and then have an equal Vote. But if they have an equal Vote, without bearing equal Burthens, a Confederation upon such iniquitous Principles, will never last long.[1]

Dr. Witherspoon. We all agree that there must and shall be a Confederation, for this War. It will diminish the Glory of our Object, and depreciate our Hope. It will damp the Ardor of the People. The greatest danger We have is of Disunion among ourselves. Is it not plausible, that the small States will be oppressed by the great ones. The Spartans and Helotes—the Romans and their Dependents.

Every Colony is a distinct Person. States of Holland.[2]

Clark. We must apply for Pardons, if We dont confederate. . . .

Wilson. . . . We should settle upon some Plan of Representation.[3]

Chase. Moves that the Word, White, should be inserted in the 11. Article. The Negroes are wealth. Numbers are not a certain Rule of wealth. It is the best Rule We can lay down. Negroes a Species of Property—personal Estate. If Negroes are taken into the Computation of Numbers to ascertain Wealth, they ought to be in settling the Representation. The Massachusetts Fisheries, and Navigation ought to be taken into Consideration. The young and old Negroes are a Burthen to their owners. The Eastern Colonies have a great Advantage, in Trade. This will give them a Superiority. We shall be governed by our Interests, and ought to be. If I am satisfied, in the Rule of levying and appropriating Money, I am willing the small Colonies may have a Vote.[4]

Wilson. If the War continues 2 Years, each Soul will have 40 dollars to pay of the public debt. It will be the greatest Encouragement to continue Slave keeping, and to increase them, that can be to exempt them from the Numbers which are to vote and pay. . . . Slaves are Taxables in the Southern Colonies. It will be partial and unequal. Some Colonies have as many black as white. . . . These will not pay more than half what they ought. Slaves prevent freemen cultivating a Country. It is attended with many Inconveniences.[5]

Lynch. If it is debated, whether their Slaves are their Property, there is an End of the Confederation. Our Slaves being our Property, why should they be taxed more than the Land, Sheep, Cattle, Horses, &c. Freemen cannot be got, to work in our Colonies. It is not in the Ability, or Inclination of freemen to do the Work that the Negroes do. Carolina has taxed their Negroes. So have other Colonies, their Lands.

Dr. Franklin. Slaves rather weaken than strengthen the State, and there is therefore some difference between them and Sheep. Sheep will never make any Insurrections.

Rutledge. . . . I shall be happy to get rid of the idea of Slavery. The Slaves do not signify Property. The old and young cannot work. The Property of some Colonies are to be taxed, in others not. The Eastern Colonies will become the Carriers for the Southern. They will obtain Wealth for which they will not be taxed.

[1] The committee of the whole was now debating Article XVII of Dickinson's draft, which provided that each colony or state would have a single vote in Congress. (See entry of 25 July and note 8 there.) Compare Franklin's speech as recorded here and also Witherspoon's (which follows) with Jefferson's report of the same speeches in his *Papers*, 1:324–325.

[2] JA omits but Jefferson reports an important speech by JA himself on this topic this day, immediately following Witherspoon's (same, p. 325–326).

[3] Here follows a short interval of space in the MS, the only indication provided by the diarist that in what follows the committee had shifted to a different and equally important issue, namely the provision in Article XI of Dickinson's draft that the money contributions of the states should be "in Proportion to the Number of Inhabitants of every Age, Sex and Quality, except Indians not paying Taxes" (*JCC*, 5:548).

There is reason to believe that JA failed to note not only a change of subject but also a change in date between what precedes and what follows this break in his MS notes. That the method

of establishing tax quotas was debated on 31 as well as 30 July seems clear from Jefferson's Notes (*Papers*, ed. Boyd, 1:320), but JA passes over the 31st silently. More telling is the reference by Hooper, under 1 Aug., below, to the "Rule that was laid down Yesterday, that the Riches of a Country are in Proportion to the Numbers of Inhabitants." This almost certainly refers to the opening of JA's own remarks reported by Jefferson; see the following note.

Debate on Article XVII was resumed on 1 Aug., q.v., below.

[4] Compare Chase's speech as reported by Jefferson in his *Papers*, 1:320–321. The Chase amendment was not agreed to by the committee; see entry of 1 Aug., below, and note 2 there.

JA omits but Jefferson reports a speech by JA himself following Chase's (Jefferson, *Papers*, ed. Boyd, 1:321–322). For reasons mentioned in the preceding note it is likely that this speech was given on 31 July, though since Jefferson divides his report of the debates on confederation by topic rather than by date, this supposition cannot be verified.

[5] Compare Wilson's speech as reported by Jefferson in his *Papers*, 1:322.

[NOTES OF DEBATES ON THE ARTICLES OF CONFEDERATION, CONTINUED] AUG. 1. 1776.

Hooper.[1] N.C. is a striking Exception to the general Rule that was laid down Yesterday, that the Riches of a Country are in Proportion to the Numbers of Inhabitants. A Gentleman of 3 or 400 Negroes, dont raise more corn than feeds them. A Labourer cant be hired for less than £24 a Year in Mass. Bay. The neat profit of a Negro is not more than 5 or 6£ pr. An[num]. I wish to see the day that Slaves are not necessary. Whites and Negroes cannot work together. Negroes are Goods and Chattells, are Property. A Negro works under the Impulse of fear—has no Care of his Masters Interest.[2]

17. Art.

Dr. Franklin moves that Votes should be in Proportion to Numbers.

Mr. Middleton moves that the Vote should be according to what they pay.

Sherman thinks We ought not to vote according to Numbers. We are Rep[resentative]s of States not Individuals. States of Holland. The Consent of every one is necessary. 3 Colonies would govern the whole but would not have a Majority of Strength to carry those Votes into Execution.

The Vote should be taken two Ways. Call the Colonies and call the Individuals, and have a Majority of both.

Dr. Rush. Abbe Reynauld [Raynal] has attributed the Ruin of the united Provinces to 3 Causes. The principal one is that the Consent of every State is necessary. The other that the Members are obliged to consult their Constituents upon all Occasions.

We loose an equal Representation. We represent the People. It will tend to keep up colonial Distinctions. We are now a new Nation. Our Trade, Language, Customs, Manners dont differ more than they do in G. Britain.

The more a Man aims at serving America the more he serves his Colony.

It will promote Factions in Congress and in the States.

It will prevent the Growth of Freedom in America. We shall be loth to admit new Colonies into the Confederation. If We vote by Numbers Liberty will be always safe. Mass. is contiguous to 2 small Colonies, R.[I.] and N.H. Pen. is near N.Y. and D. Virginia is between Maryland and N. Carolina.

We have been to[o] free with the Word Independence. We are dependent on each other—not totally independent States.

Montesquieu pronounced the Confederation of Licea the best that ever was made. The Cities had different Weights in the Scale.

China is not larger than one of our Colonies. How populous.

It is said that the small Colonies deposit their all. This is deceiving Us with a Word.

I would not have it understood, that I am pleading the Cause of Pensilvania. When I entered that door, I considered myself a Citizen of America.[3]

Dr. Witherspoon. Rep[resentatio]n in England is unequal. Must I have 3 Votes in a County because I have 3 times as much Money as my Neighbour. Congress are to determine the Limits of Colonies.

G[overnor] Hopkins. A momentous Question. Many difficulties on each Side. 4 larger, 5 lesser, 4 stand indifferent. V. M. P. M.[4] make more than half the People. 4 may alw[5]

C., N.Y., 2 Carolinas, not concerned at all. The dissinterested Coolness of these Colonies ought to determine. I can easily feel the Reasoning of the larger Colonies. Pleasing Theories always gave Way to the Prejudices, Passions, and Interests of Mankind.

The Germanic Confederation. The K. of Prussia has an equal Vote. The Helvetic Confederacy. It cant be expected that 9 Colonies will give Way to be governed by 4. The Safety of the whole depends upon the distinctions of Colonies.

Dr. Franklin. I hear many ingenious Arguments to perswade Us that an unequal Representation is a very good Thing. If We had been born and bred under an unequal Representation We might bear it. But to sett out with an unequal Representation is unreasonable.

It is said the great Colonies will swallow up the less. Scotland said the same Thing at the Union.

Dr. Witherspoon. Rises to explain a few Circumstances relating to Scotland. That was an incorporating Union, not a federal. The Nobility and Gentry resort to England.

In determining all Questions, each State shall have a Weight in Proportion to what it contributes to the public Expences of the united States.

[1] Hooper is continuing the discussion of Article XI, on the method of apportioning taxes.

[2] In a vote in committee of the whole this day Chase's motion to insert "white" before "Inhabitants" in Article XI lost by seven states to five, the vote being strictly sectional, though Georgia's vote was divided and therefore not counted (Jefferson, *Papers*, ed. Boyd, 1:323).

After the present paragraph there is an interval of space in the MS amounting to half a page, and thereafter the committee resumed discussion of Article XVII, broken off on 30 July, q.v., above.

[3] Compare Rush's speech as reported by Jefferson in his *Papers*, 1:326.

[4] Virginia, Massachusetts, Pennsylvania, Maryland.

[5] Sentence breaks off thus in MS,

but compare Jefferson's summary of Hopkins' remarks: "the 4. largest ... therefore would govern the others as they should please" (*Papers*, ed. Boyd, 1:326).

[NOTES OF DEBATES ON THE ARTICLES OF CONFEDERATION, CONTINUED] AUG. 2d.

Limiting the Bounds of States which by Charter &c. extend to the South Sea.[1]

Sherman thinks the Bounds ought to be settled. A Majority of States have no Claim to the South Sea. Moves this Amendment, to be substituted in Place of this Clause and also instead of the 15th Article—

No Lands to be seperated from any State, which are already settled, or become private Property.

Chase denys that any Colony has a Right, to go to the South Sea....

Harrison. How came Maryland by its Land? but by its Charter: By its Charter Virginia owns to the South Sea. Gentlemen shall not pare away the Colony of Virginia. R. Island has more Generosity, than to wish the Massachusetts pared away. Delaware does not wish to pare away Pensilvania.

Huntington. Admit there is danger, from Virginia, does it follow that Congress has a Right to limit her Bounds? The Consequence is not to enter into Confederation. But as to the Question of Right, We all unite against mutilating Charters. I cant agree to the Principle. We are a Spectacle to all Europe. I am not so much alarmed at the Danger, from Virginia, as some are. My fears are not alarmed. They have acted as noble a Part as any. I doubt not the Wisdom of Virginia will limit themselves. A Mans Right does not cease to be a Right because it is large. The Q[uestion] of Right must be determined by the Principles of the common Law.

Stone. This Argument is taken up upon very wrong Ground. It is considered as if We were voting away the Territory of particular Colonies, and Gentlemen work themselves up into Warmth, upon that Supposition. Suppose Virginia should. The small Colonies have a Right to Happiness and Security. They would have no Safety if the great Colonies were not limited. We shall grant Lands in small Quantities, without Rent, or Tribute, or purchase Money. It is said that Virginia is attacked on every Side. Is it meant that Virginia shall sell the Lands for their own Emolument?

All the Colonies have defended these Lands vs. the K. of G.B., and at the Expence of all. Does Virginia intend to establish Quitrents?

I dont mean that the united States shall sell them to get Money by them.

Jefferson. I protest vs. the Right of Congress to decide, upon the Right of Virginia. Virginia has released all Claims to the Lands settled by Maryland &c.

[1] This is a close paraphrase of a clause in Article XVIII of Dickinson's draft, which listed the powers to be granted to Congress (JCC, 5:550–551). The debate in committee this day actually continued that begun on 25 July (q.v., above) concerning Article XV, further consideration of which was postponed until after discussion of Article XVIII. This controversial clause was omitted in the second draft of the Articles as submitted to Congress on 20 August. See JCC, 5:680 and note 2; p. 682 and note 1.

On 9 Aug. Samuel Chase wrote to Philip Schuyler: "when we shall be confederated States, I know not. I am afraid the Day is far distant. three great Difficulties occur—The Mode of Voting, whether by Colonies, or by an equal Representation; The Rule by which each Colony is to pay its Quota, and the Claim of several Colonies to extend to the South Seas. a considerable Diversity of opinion prevails on each Head" (Burnett, ed., *Letters of Members*, 2:44). Congress did not again take up the text of the Articles and attempt to complete them until 8 April 1777 (JCC, 7:240). Their subsequent history to the point of ultimate ratification, 1 March 1781 (see same, 19:208–223), may be best traced in Burnett, *Continental Congress*, chs. 13, 25, or in the standard work on the subject, Merrill Jensen, *The Articles of Confederation*, Madison, 1940.

SEPT. 10.

Took with me to N.Y. 51 dollars and 5s. 8d. Pen. Currency in Change.[1]

[1] An isolated entry in D/JA/25; an identical entry appears in D/JA/27 and is the last in that booklet.

This is the only allusion in JA's Diary to his journey from Philadelphia to Staten Island and back, in company with Benjamin Franklin and Edward Rutledge, a committee appointed by Congress on 6 Sept. to confer with Admiral Lord Howe in his capacity as a commissioner to accommodate the dispute between Great Britain and America (JCC, 5:728, 730–731, 737–738). The conference took place on 11 Sept. but accomplished nothing because, as the committee reported to Congress on 17 Sept., "it did not appear ... that his Lordship's commission contained any other authority of importance than ... that of granting pardons ... and of declaring America, or any part of it, to be in the king's peace" (same, 5:766). But the circumstances were dramatic, and the incident attracted much atten-

tion and comment. JA's account of it in his Autobiography is justly famous (printed in his *Works*, 3:75–81, without the supporting letters that appear in the MS). Much the fullest account of the conference itself is that by Henry Strachey, secretary to the British commissioners (the Howe brothers), first printed accurately by Paul L. Ford (from a MS now in NN) in an article entitled "Lord Howe's Commission to Pacify the Colonies," *Atlantic Monthly*, 77:758–762 (June 1896). See also Burnett, ed., *Letters of Members*, 2:15 and note, 66 and note; Benjamin Rush, *Autobiography*, 119–121, 140; Ambrose Serle, *American Journal*, ed. Edward H. Tatum Jr., San Marino, Calif., 1940, p. 100–101.

On 19 Nov. Congress resolved that there was due to Rutledge, Franklin, and JA, "a committee to Staten Island, for their expences there and back, 71 [and] 30/90 dollars" (JCC, 6:964).

1776 OCTR. 13. SUNDAY.

Sat out from Phyladelphia towards Boston, oated at the Red Lyon, dined at Bristol, crossed Trenton ferry, long before Sun set, drank Coffee at the Ferry House on the East Side of Delaware, where I putt up—partly to avoid riding in the Evening Air, and partly because 30 miles is enough for the first day, as my Tendons are delicate, not having been once on Horse back since the Eighth day of last February.[1]

[1] On 25 July JA addressed a letter to John Avery, deputy secretary of state, requesting leave of the General Court to return home. "I have attended here, so long and so constantly, that I feel myself necessitated to ask the Favour, on Account of my Health, as well as on many other Accounts" (M-Ar: vol. 195; printed in JA, *Works*, 9:426–427). He went on to propose to the legislature "an Alteration in their Plan of Delegation in Congress," the point of which was to have nine members chosen annually, so that "four, or Six, might be at home, at a Time, and every Member might be relieved, once in three or four Months." Whether or not this plan was adopted, he said, he was obliged to request an immediate replacement for himself. On 24, 26, and 27 July JA wrote three letters to James Warren, speaker of the House, to the same effect, particularizing the ailments of the Massachusetts delegates, discussing eligible replacements, and saying in the last of these letters: "Go home I will, if I leave the Massachusetts without a Member here" (all three letters in MHi and printed in *Warren-Adams Letters*, 1:263–266). Elbridge Gerry was on leave at this time, and on 12 Aug. Samuel Adams also departed for Massachusetts, leaving only Paine, who was quite ill, and JA on duty until Gerry's return on 2 Sept. (Burnett, ed., *Letters of Members*, 2:li–lii). In letters to his wife and to James Warren during August that are too numerous to list, JA repeatedly implored them to send horses so that he could make his way home. Meanwhile the General Court was in adjournment, and even after it convened on 28 Aug. it took no action on JA's request, service in Congress being relished by none who were eligible to serve (James Warren to JA, 19 Sept.,

Adams Papers; *Warren-Adams Letters*, 1:274). And toward the close of August, despite his irritation with his principals at home, JA himself thought it best to stay on in Philadelphia during the military crisis round New York. So it was that, although his old servant Bass arrived on 5 Sept. with horses procured by AA, JA did not apply to Congress for a leave of absence until 10 October. Three days later he set out. See AA to JA, 29 Aug.; JA to AA, 4, 5 Sept., 11 Oct. (all in Adams Papers); JA to Warren, 4 Sept. (MHi; *Warren-Adams Letters*, 1:273). The date of his arrival in Braintree after an absence of about ten months is not known. On 3 Jan. 1777 the General Court authorized payment to JA of £226 6s. 2d. "in full Satisfaction of his Services & Expences as a Delegate at the Continentale Congress for the Year 1776" (Resolves of 1776–1777, ch. 719; Mass., *Province Laws*, 19:744).

The present entry is the last in D/JA/25, though there follow in this booklet 37 pages of notes on the French language, copied from an unidentified French grammar. It is possible that these were copied into the Diary in the spring of 1776. An alliance with France was being discussed when JA returned to Congress in February, and on the 18th of that month he wrote to AA: "I wish I understood French as well as you. I would have gone to Canada [on the committee of Congress to visit the army there], if I had"; and he went on to adjure her to teach the children French, which will soon "become a necessary Accomplishment of an American Gentleman and Lady" (Adams Papers; printed in JA–AA, *Familiar Letters*, p. 136). On the other hand, the exercises may have been copied during the comparative leisure JA enjoyed after his return from Congress in the fall of 1776.

[ACCOUNT WITH MASSACHUSETTS AS A DELEGATE TO THE CONTINENTAL CONGRESS, JANUARY–SEPTEMBER 1777.][1]

		£	s	d

1777. Bought two Horses for my Journey to Baltimore, one of the Honourable Mr. Spooner for £15 another of John Gill for £20—I bought these Horses, because I had none of my own, but one, which I was obliged to leave at home for the Use of my Family, and I thought it would be a Saving to the public to buy a Couple of cheap Horses rather than to hire as I must have done at a dear rate. The public will allow me for the Hire of these Horses what they think just.[2] — 35: 0: 0

		£	s	d
January	Paid Mr. Vesey for shoeing my Horses 8s each	0	16	0
	Paid for a small Pair of Holsters for Pistolls and for Pistol Balls 4s	0	4	0
January 29.	Paid Isaac Greentrees Account at Philadelphia for keeping my Servant and Horses	2	8	0
	Cash paid Mr. Lovell, being Monies advanced by him, for me upon the Road	32	16	10
February 10.	Cash paid the Washerwoman at Baltimore for washing Linnen for me and my Servant one dollar	0	8	0
Feb. 24. 1777.	Cash paid John Turner for his Account £2:15s. 9d Pensilvania Currency	2	4	6
	To cash paid Turner 5s: Pen. Cur.	0	4	0
Feb. 27.	Cash paid Washerwoman for Washing for me and my Man	0	8	0
28	Cash paid for David Rusks Account, for keeping my Horses, &c. 37 dollars[3]	11	2	0
Feb. 29.	Cash paid Elizabeth Ross my Landlady in Baltimore for my own and my servants Board £9.12s:6d Pen. Cur.	7	14	0
Feb. 28.	Cash to M. K. Goddard for a Blank Book 25s P. Cur.	1	0	0
29.	Cash paid for a Quire of Paper 3s Pen. Cur.	0	2	6

		£	s	d
24	Cash paid Sam. & Robert Purveyance for a Bll. of flour shipped home to my family not to be charged to the public 2:13:1 Pen. cur.[4]	2:	2:	6
March 2	To cash paid the Hostler for trimming my Horses &c.	0:	3:	0
	To cash paid Wadsworth for my share towards Wood, Candles, Wine, cutting Wood &c.	0:	6:	0
	To cash paid Mrs. Ross for Board since the Date of her Account	0:	6:	0
		62:	4:	4

		Cr		
	By Articles in Mr. Lovell's Account which are not to be charged to the public			
	Cash paid for an Hanger	7:	10:	0
	Cash paid to Turner	3:	12:	0
	Cash paid for a Pistoll Belt	0:	4:	0
1777	By a Grant of Cash which I recd. of the Treasury	150:	0:	0[5]
Feb. 24.	By the Article of a Barrell of flour	2:	2:	6
Feb. 28.	By an abatement			

1777 March 7.	Cash paid Coll. Whipple, for my share of Expence for myself, my servant and Horses, on our Journey from Baltimore to Philadelphia, crossing the Susquehannah River at the Bald Fryars[6] £7. Pen. cur. 18 dollars & 2/3	5:	12:	0
10.	To cash paid the Newspaper Carrier,	0:	2:	0
15.	To cash paid John Turner for sundry Necessaries as per Acct.	0:	10:	8
April 11.	To cash paid for a Box of Dr. Ryans Pills to be sent to my Family. not to be charged to the public	0:	8:	0

		£	s	d
	Paid John Turner to pay Henry Moses for a Pair of Pistoll Holders	1:	4:	0
April 15.	Paid Jos. Fox for shoeing two Horses 30s Pen. cur.	1:	4:	0
	Paid Robertson for a Quart of Spirits 7s:6d Pen. cur.	˙0:	6:	0
April 17.	Paid John Turners Account 3 dollars	0:	18:	0
24.	Paid for one half Gallon of Wine 3 dollars	0:	18:	0
28.	Paid my Washerwoman 3 dollars	0:	18:	0
30	Paid Mrs. Yards Account for mine and servants Board [7]	4:	16:	0
May 2.	Paid General Wolcot, my Proportion towards four Gallons of Spirit which, he, Coll. Whipple, Mr. Lovell and myself, purchased together.	1:	2:	0
5.	Paid for Washing 5s:10d Pen. Cur.	0:	4:	8
13	Paid for one Gallon of Rum 40s Pen. Cur.	1:	12:	0
15	Paid Thos. Tufts for mending the Lock of my Chest	0:	1:	0
	Paid for Candles 2s:6d Pen. cur.	0:	2:	0
24.	Paid the Washerwoman 4 dollars	1:	4:	0
30	Paid John Burn the Barber £3. Pen. Cur.	2:	8:	0
July 4.	Paid for one Gallon of Rum Six Dollars £2:5s Pen. Cur.	1:	16:	0
22	Paid for a Girth of Leather 2 dollars	0:	12:	0
	Paid for Candles and black ball	0:	5:	0
		25:	11:	4
Money Spent in miscellaneous Expenses as on the other Page [*i.e. the following memorandum*]		7:	7	
		32:	18:	4

1777 July 23. I cast up the foregoing Account, and found it amounted to £87:15s:8d. At the same Time I counted over all the Money which I had left of the hundred Pounds I brought with me and found it amounted to £4:17s:4d which added to £87:15s:8d makes £92:13s:0d which being deducted from £100:0s:0d the sum I

brought with me from Home, (having left £50, with my Family)
leaves £7:7s:od—so that I have spent seven Pounds, seven shillings,
which I have kept no Account of—all this is gone in miscellaneous
Expences, on Committees, and for a Variety of miscellaneous Articles, without which it is impossible to live and of which it is impossible to account.

		£	s	d
1777 July 23d.	Paid William Dibley his Account for keeping my Horses £23:12s:6 P.C. 63 dollars	18:18:	o	
July 24.	Paid My Servant John Turners Account for his Wages, and 10 Weeks Board and some Disbursements for me, as per his Acct. and Rect. £31:6s:6d P. Cur. 83 dollars	24:18:	o	
	Paid Isaac Shoemakers £2:3s:9d P.C. 5 dollars & 5/6	1:15:	o	
	Paid Isaac Greentree for Horsekeeping £3:11s:od Pen. cur.	2:17:	o	
July 25	Paid Wm. Davey for keeping my Horses 6 Weeks £2:5s:od Pen. cur.	1:16:	o	
Aug. 11.	Paid John Turners Acct. £2:9s:9d Pen. Cur.	2: 2:	o	
	Paid John Coltons Acct. £2:12s:6d	2: 2:	o	
	Paid John Turner towards his Expences home	3: 2:	o	
Aug. 19.	Paid Washerwomans Account for washing for me and my Servant £4:11s:2d P.C. L.M.	3:13:	o	
Aug. 26.	Paid Byrnes Account £3 P.C.	2: 8:	o	
Aug. 30	Paid Captain Robert Duncans Account for mine and my Servants Board to 31st. Aug. £77.18s:4d P.C.	62: 8:	o	
Sept. 1.	Paid for two Pounds of Candles.	0: 4:	o	
14.	Paid Mr. Samuel McLane his Account £6:1os P.C.	5: 4:	o	
	Paid for a Pair of Straps	0: 6:	o	

1777 July 22.   By 1000 Dollars recd. of Mr. John Gibson in Part of a Note of Hand from

| | £ | s | d |

Mr. Hillegas to Mr. Hancock for
25,000 Dollars for which I gave a
Rect. on the back of the Note and
also a loose Rect. to Mr. Gibson   300: 0: 0 [8]

---

[1] This record of JA's expenses for his service in the Continental Congress during 1777 is in the back pages of one of his letterbooks (Lb/JA/3; Adams Papers, Microfilms, Reel No. 91), and is printed here because it is much more complete than an account for the same year, begun on a loose sheet inserted in D/JA/22B but broken off after a few entries. Even the present version is incomplete, extending only to mid-September though JA attended Congress two months longer. The explanation is in a letter from JA to Speaker James Warren, 15 Jan. 1778 (NN: Emmet Coll.). This letter enclosed a summary account of JA's claim against Massachusetts for 1777 and apologized for its want of fullness and lack of supporting vouchers. But, as the writer explained, owing to the sudden departure of Congress from Philadelphia when Howe's army was approaching the city from the Chesapeake, "I was obliged to leave a small Trunk of my Baggage together with my Account Book and all my Receipts behind me, in the Care of a Reverend Gentleman in the City." See Diary entries of 15, 19 Sept., below. On 15 Nov. 1776 JA had been elected to serve another year in Congress, together with his colleagues Hancock, Samuel Adams, Paine, and Gerry, and two additional members, James Lovell and Francis Dana (Mass., *House Jour.*, 1776–1777, p. 157). This enlargement of the delegation partly answered JA's pleas of the preceding summer, and a resolution voted by the General Court on 4 Feb. 1777 (laid before Congress on 12 March) went further by declaring that "any two or more of said Delegates, representing this State in Congress, being the major part present, be and hereby are vested with all the powers with which any three ... were vested" previously (enclosure in John Avery to JA, 17 Feb., Adams Papers; full text in JCC, 7:169–170).

[2] On 12 Dec. 1776 Congress had adjourned at Philadelphia as Howe's army drove Washington's army through New Jersey to the Delaware, and on 20 Dec. it convened in Baltimore (JCC, 6:1027–1028). So that when JA set out with James Lovell on 9 Jan. 1777, they took a circuitous, backcountry route. Upon leaving Hartford they crossed the hills of western Connecticut and reached the Hudson at Fishkill "After a March like that of Hannibal over the Alps." At Fishkill they found they had to travel north in order to cross the ice-choked Hudson, which they did at Poughkeepsie. Traversing Orange co., N.Y., and Sussex co., N.J., they reached Easton at the Forks of the Delaware by 24 January. A day or two later JA had his first view of the Moravian community at Bethlehem, Penna., and he and Lovell arrived at Baltimore on 1 February. JA described the journey in letters to AA dated 9, 13, 14, [17 or 18], 19, 20, 24 Jan.; 2, 7 Feb. 1777 (Adams Papers; printed in JA-AA, *Familiar Letters*, p. 233–242).

[3] In the fragmentary account in D/JA/22B this entry (the last in that fragment) reads: "Cash paid David Rusk for my Board and my servants, and for Stabling for my Horses 37 dollars." This indicates that JA lodged with Rusk before going to Mrs. Ross's; see Diary entry of 6 Feb., below.

[4] A receipt for this purchase from the Purviances is in Adams Papers under this date.

[5] This was an advance partial payment to JA for his service in Congress during 1777, authorized by a vote of the House on 4 Jan. (Mass., *House Jour.*, 1776–1777, p. 213).

[6] A ford a few miles south of the Pennsylvania-Maryland boundary, near present Conowingo. It is shown on a remarkable MS map of the country between the Chesapeake and Philadelphia

enclosed in a letter from James Lovell to AA, 29 Aug. (Adams Papers), and is described in *The Revolutionary Journal of Baron Ludwig von Closen, 1780–1783*, ed. Evelyn M. Acomb, Chapel Hill, 1958, p. 125. Evidently the crossings below this point were ice-bound.

⁷ JA probably left Baltimore on 2 March and arrived in Philadelphia by the 5th, the day to which Congress had, at its last sitting in Baltimore (27 Feb.), adjourned, though a quorum of members did not assemble until 12 March (*JCC*, 7:168–169). JA lodged at Mrs. Yard's in Second Street until 14 March, but on that day moved to Capt. Robert Duncan's on the south side of Walnut Street between Second and Third, because he got cheaper terms there; his fellow boarders included William Whipple of New Hampshire and Oliver Wolcott of Connecticut (JA to AA, 14, 16 March, Adams Papers). Here he stayed until 12 Sept.; see Diary, 15 Sept., below.

⁸ This is a credit item in favor of Massachusetts. John Gibson was auditor general and Michael Hillegas was treasurer of the United States. In his summary account submitted to the General Court, JA's total expenses, together with pay at 24s. a day for 322 days, came to £792 18s. 8d., from which he deducted £450 (£150 advance pay and £300 from the Continental Treasury are here listed), so that the balance due him amounted to £342 18s. 8d. (enclosure in JA to Speaker Warren, 15 Jan. 1778, NN:Emmet Coll.). Payment to him in this amount was authorized by a resolve of 27 Jan. 1778 (Resolves of 1777–1778, ch. 685; Mass., *Province Laws*, 20:261).

1777. THURSDAY FEBY. 6TH.[1]

Lodged last night for the first Time in my new Quarters, at Mrs. Ross'es in Markett Street, Baltimore a few Doors below the fountain Inn.

The Gentlemen from Pensilvania and Maryland, complain of the growing Practice of distilling Wheat into Whisky. They say it will become a Question whether the People shall eat bread or drink Whisky.

The Congress sits in the last House at the West End of Market Street, on the South Side of the Street. A long Chamber, with two fire Places, two large Closets, and two Doors. The House belongs to a Quaker, who built it for a Tavern.[2]

[1] First entry in "Paper book" No. 28 (our D/JA/28), a stitched gathering of leaves without cover containing entries extending to 21 Nov. 1777 but with a gap from the beginning of March to mid-September.

[2] A memorial tablet now marks the site of this building at the corner of Liberty and Baltimore (formerly Market) Streets. See Edith Rossiter Bevan, "The Continental Congress in Baltimore, Dec. 20, 1776 to Feb. 27, 1777," *Md. Hist. Mag.*, 42:21–28 (March 1947), a useful compendium of information on Congress' brief stay in Baltimore.

7TH FRYDAY.

Dined, about half a Mile out of Town at Mr. Lux's, with Dr. Witherspoon, Mr. S. Adams, Mr. Lovell, Mr. Hall, Dr. Thornton, a Mr. Harrison, Dr.   and Mr. George Lux, and two Ladies Mrs. Lux and her Sister. This Seat is named Chatworth, and an elegant one it is. Has a large Yard, inclosed with Stone in Lime, and before the Yard two fine Rows of large Cherry Trees, which lead out to the public Road. There is a fine Prospect about it. Mr. Lux and his Son are sensible Gentlemen. I had much Conversation with George about the new form of Government adopted in Maryland.

George is the young Gentleman, by whom I sent Letters to my friends from Philadelphia, when the Army was at Cambridge, particularly to Coll. Warren, whom and whose Lady Lux so much admired.

The whole Family profess great Zeal in the American Cause. Mr. Lux lives like a Prince.[1]

[1] The seat of William Lux, a merchant, shipowner, and Continental marine agent in Baltimore, was called Chatsworth. JA and Samuel Adams had written letters introducing Lux's son George to James Warren in July 1775. See Charles O. Paullin, ed., *Out-Letters of the Continental Marine Committee and Board of Admiralty*, N.Y., 1914, 1:131; Bevan, "Continental Congress in Baltimore," p. 27 and note; *Warren-Adams Letters*, 1:93–94.

1777. FEB. 8. SATURDAY.

Dined at the Presidents, with Mr. Lux, Messrs. Samuel and Robert Purveyance, Capt. Nicholson of the Maryland Frigate,[1] Coll. Harrison, Wilson, Mr. Hall—upon New England Salt fish. The Weather was rainy, and the Streets the muddiest I ever saw.—This is the dirtyest Place in the World—our Salem, and Portsmouth are neat in Comparison. The Inhabitants, however, are excusable because they had determined to pave the Streets before this War came on, since which they have laid the Project aside, as they are accessible to Men of War. This Place is not incorporated. It is neither a City, Town, nor Burrough, so that they can do nothing with Authority.

[1] JA doubtless means the frigate *Virginia*, built in Maryland and commanded by James Nicholson; see *JCC*, 5:423, and the next entry in this Diary. On Nicholson see *DAB*.

1777. FEBY. 9. SUNDAY.

Heard Mr. Allison. In the Evening walked to Fells Point, the Place where the Ships lie, a kind of Peninsula which runs out, into the Bason which lies before Baltimore Town. This Bason 30 Years ago was deep enough for large Tobacco ships, but since then has fill'd up, ten feet. Between the Town and the Point, We pass a Bridge over a little Brook which is the only Stream which runs into the Bason, and the only flux of Water which is to clear away the Dirt which flows into the Bason from the foul streets of the Town and the neighbouring Hills and Fields. There is a breast Work thrown up upon the Point, with a

Number of Embrasures for Cannon facing the Entrance into the Harbour. The Virginia Frigate Capt. Nickolson, lies off in the Stream. There is a Number of Houses upon this Point. You have a fine View of the Town of Baltimore from this Point.

On my Return, I stopped and drank Tea at Captn. Smiths, a Gentleman of the new Assembly.[1]

[1] William Smith; he was to be elected to Congress on 15 Feb. (Burnett, ed., *Letters of Members*, 2:xlix–l; *Biog. Dir. Cong.*; entry of 23 Feb., below).

On the following day JA resigned his seat, which he had never been able to occupy, as chief justice of Massachusetts, thus ending a dilemma that had made him uncomfortable for many months. On 28 Oct. 1775 he was notified that the Council had chosen him "to be first or Chief Justice of the Superior Court of Judicature" (Perez Morton to JA, 28

Oct. 1775, Adams Papers). Difficulties in filling up the high court proved insuperable for some time, and there was also much criticism in Congress during 1776 of plural officeholding, which JA found embarrassing. See his Autobiography, where he discusses the matter at length (*Works*, 3:25–28). His letter of resignation was enclosed in one to John Avery, 10 Feb. 1777 (LbC, Adams Papers; enclosure printed in *Works*, 3: 25, note).

1777 FEB. 16.

Last Evening I supped with my Friends Dr. Rush and Mr. Sergeant at Mrs. Page's over the Bridge. The two Coll. Lees, Dr. Witherspoon, Mr. Adams, Mr. Gerry, Dr. Brownson, made the Company. They have a Fashion in this Town of reversing the Picture of King G. 3d, in such Families as have it. One of these Topsy Turvy Kings was hung up in the Room, where we supped, and under it were written these Lines, by Mr. Throop, as we were told.

> Behold the Man who had it in his Power
> To make a Kingdom tremble and adore
> Intoxicate with Folly, See his Head
> Plac'd where the meanest of his Subjects tread
> Like Lucifer the giddy Tyrant fell
> He lifts his Heel to Heaven but points his Head to Hell.

FEB. 17. MONDAY.

Yesterday, heard Dr. Witherspoon upon redeeming Time. An excellent Sermon. I find that I understand the Dr. better, since I have heard him so much in Conversation, and in the Senate. But I perceive that his Attention to civil Affairs, has slackened his Memory. It cost him more Pains than heretofore to recollect his Discourse.

Mr. H[ancock] told C.W. [Colonel Whipple?] Yesterday, that he had determined to go to Boston in April. Mrs. H. was not willing to go

till May, but Mr. H. was determined upon April.—Perhaps the Choice
of a Governor, may come on in May.—What aspiring little Creatures
we are! how subtle, sagacious and judicious this Passion is! how clearly
it sees its Object, how constantly it pursues it, and what wise Plans it
devises for obtaining it!

1777. FEB. 21. FRYDAY.

Dined Yesterday at Mr. Samuel Purveyances. Mr. Robert his Brother
and Lady, the President and Lady, the two Coll. Lees and their Ladies, Mr. Page and his Lady, Coll. Whipple, Mrs. K. Quincy, a young
Gentleman and a young Lady made the Company.[1] A great Feast. The
Virginia Ladies had Ornaments about their Wrists, which I dont remember to have seen before. These Ornaments were like Miniature
Pictures, bound round the Arms with some Chains.

This Morning received a long Card from Mr. H. expressing great
Resentment about fixing the Magazine at Brookfield, against the Book
binder and the General.[2] The Complaisance to me and the Jealousy
for the Massachusetts in this Message, indicate to me, the same Passion
and the same design, with the Journey to B[oston] in April.

[1] Samuel and Robert Purviance were
prominent merchants who had come to
Baltimore from Ireland via Philadelphia
in the 1760's and were now engaged in
supplying the Continental forces; correspondence on their business activities
and especially on Samuel Purviance's
leading role in the Baltimore Committee
of Correspondence, is printed in Robert
Purviance, *A Narrative of Events Which
Occurred in Baltimore Town during the
Revolutionary War*, Baltimore, 1849,
which is in some sense a family memoir.
Among the other guests were Richard
Henry and Francis Lightfoot Lee and
Mann Page Jr., all delegates in Congress
from Virginia; and "Mrs." (i.e. Mistress,
actually Miss) Katharine Quincy, sister
of Mrs. President Hancock.

[2] Hancock's "long Card" to JA has not
been found; "the Book binder" was
Henry Knox, recently commissioned brigadier general (*DAB*). On the controversy
over locating the Continental magazines,
see Hancock to Washington, 29 Jan.
1777, in Burnett, ed., *Letters of Members*, 2:226, and references there.

1777. FEB. 23.

Took a Walk with Mr. Gerry, down to a Place called Ferry Branch,
a Point of Land which is formed by a Branch of the Patapsco on one
Side and the Basin before the Town of Baltimore on the other. At the
Point is a Ferry, over to the Road which goes to Anapolis. This is a
very pretty Walk. At the Point you have a full view of the elegant,
splendid Seat of Mr. Carroll Barrister.[1] It is a large and elegant House.
It stands fronting looking down the River, into the Harbour. It is one
Mile from the Water. There is a most beautifull Walk from the House
down to the Water. There is a descent, not far from the House. You

have a fine Garden—then you descend a few Steps and have another fine Garden—you go down a few more and have another. It is now the dead of Winter, no Verdure, or Bloom to be seen, but in the Spring, Summer, and fall this Scæne must be very pretty.

Returned and dined with Mr. William Smith a new Member of Congress. Dr. Lyon, Mr. Merriman, Mr. Gerry, a son of Mr. Smith, and two other Gentlemen made the Company. The Conversation turned, among other Things, upon removing the Obstructions and opening the Navigation of Susquehannah River. The Company thought it might easily be done, and would open an amazing Scæne of Business. Philadelphia will oppose it, but it will be the Interest of a Majority of Pensilvania to effect it.

This Mr. Smith is a grave, solid Gentleman, a Presbyterian by Profession—a very different Man from the most of those We have heretofore had from Maryland.

The Manners of Maryland are somewhat peculiar. They have but few Merchants. They are chiefly Planters and Farmers. The Planters are those who raise Tobacco and the Farmers such as raise Wheat &c. The Lands are cultivated, and all Sorts of Trades are exercised by Negroes, or by transported Convicts, which has occasioned the Planters and Farmers to assume the Title of Gentlemen, and they hold their Negroes and Convicts, that is all labouring People and Tradesmen, in such Contempt, that they think themselves a distinct order of Beings. Hence they never will suffer their Sons to labour or learn any Trade, but they bring them up in Idleness or what is worse in Horse Racing, Cock fighting, and Card Playing.

[1] Charles Carroll, "Barrister," was so designated to distinguish him from his distant relative Charles Carroll of Carrollton; see W. Stull Holt, "Charles Carroll, Barrister: The Man," *Md. Hist. Mag.*, 31:112–126 (June 1936). Both served as Maryland delegates in Congress, though not concurrently (Burnett, ed., *Letters of Members,* 2:xlv–xlvi). The Barrister's seat was called Mount Clare and is now a museum in Carroll Park, Baltimore. There is an illustrated article by Lilian Giffen, " 'Mount Clare,' Baltimore," *Md. Hist. Mag.*, 42:29–34 (March 1947).

1777. FEB. 28. FRYDAY.

Last Evening had a good deal of free Conversation, with Mr. R. Purveyance. He seems to me to have a perfect Understanding of the affairs of this State. Men and Things are very well known to him.

The object of the Men of Property here, the Planters &c., is universally, Wealth. Every Way in the World is sought to get and save Money. Landjobbers—Speculators in Land—little Generosity to the Public—little public Spirit.

FEB. 29.

SEPTR. 15. 1777. MONDAY.[1]

Fryday the 12, I removed from Captn. Duncans in Walnutt Street to the Revd. Mr. Sprouts in Third Street, a few doors from his Meeting House.[2] Mr. Merchant from Rhode Island boards here, with me.[3] Mr. Sprout is sick of a Fever. Mrs. Sprout, and the four young Ladies her Daughters, are in great Distress on Account of his Sickness, and the Approach of Mr. Howes Army. But they bear their Affliction with christian Patience and philosophic Fortitude. The young Ladies are Miss Hannah, Olive, Sally and Nancy. The only Son is an Officer in the Army. He was the first Clerk in the American War office.

We live in critical Moments! Mr. Howes Army is at Middleton and Concord. Mr. Washingtons, upon the Western Banks of Schuylkill, a few Miles from him. I saw this Morning an excellent Chart of the Schuylkill, Chester River, the Brandywine, and this whole Country, among the Pensilvania Files. This City is the Stake, for which the Game is playd. I think, there is a Chance for saving it, although the Probability is against Us. Mr. Howe I conjecture is waiting for his Ships to come into the Delaware. Will W. attack him? I hope so—and God grant him Success.

[1] In the MS there is only a half-page interval of space between the false entry of "Feb. 29" and the present entry six and a half months later. During that period JA was steadily in attendance at Congress in Philadelphia. His principal work, as in the summer and fall of 1776, was presiding over the Board of War and Ordnance, which handled the lion's share of Congress' routine work. Hundreds of communications, relating to military operations, recruits, defenses, prisoners, supplies, courts martial, and the rank of officers (a perpetual problem, made worse by the influx of foreign volunteers), to mention no others, were referred to the Board for recommendations or action during these months. Although there was discussion throughout the year of converting the Board into a professional body under the supervision of Congress, this step was not taken until after JA had left Congress in November. See Samuel Adams to JA, 9 Jan. 1777, Adams Papers; Burnett, ed., *Letters of Members*, 2:210, and notes and references there.

As early as May JA complained of "drooping" health, a lingering cold, and weakened eyes (to AA, 15, 21 May, Adams Papers). As summer came on, he had a strong additional reason for wishing to visit Braintree: AA was expecting a baby in July. On 11 July she was delivered of a daughter who was to have been named Elizabeth but who "never opened its Eyes in this World." See JA to AA, 4 June, 28 July; AA to JA, 9, 10-11, 16 July; John Thaxter to JA, 13 July (Adams Papers).

[2] This was to be a short stay. The American army had been defeated at Chadd's Ford on the Brandywine, 11 September. See entry of 19 Sept., below.

[3] Henry Marchant, of Newport, R.I., a delegate to the Continental Congress, 1777-1780, 1783-1784 (*Biog. Dir. Cong.*).

1777. SEPT. 16. TUESDAY.

No Newspaper this Morning. Mr. Dunlap has moved or packed up his Types. A Note from G. Dickinson that the Enemy in N. Jersey are 4000 strong.[1] How is about 15 miles from Us, the other Way. The City seems to be asleep, or dead, and the whole State scarce alive. Maryland and Delaware the same.

The Prospect is chilling, on every Side. Gloomy, dark, melancholly, and dispiriting. When and where will the light spring up?

Shall We have good News from Europe? Shall We hear of a Blow struck by Gates? Is there a Possibility that Washington should beat How? Is there a Prospect that McDougal and Dickinson should destroy the Detachment in the Jersies?

From whence is our Deliverance to come? Or is it not to come? Is Philadelphia to be lost? If lost, is the Cause lost? No—the Cause is not lost—but it may be hurt.

I seldom regard Reports, but it is said that How has marked his Course, from Elke, with Depredation. His Troops have plunderd Henroosts, dairy Rooms, the furniture of Houses and all the Cattle of the Country. The Inhabitants, most of whom are Quakers, are angry and disappointed, because they were promised the Security of their Property.

It is reported too that Mr. How lost great Numbers in the Battle of the Brandywine.

[1] Gen. Philemon Dickinson, at Trenton, to Congress, 15 Sept. 1777, in PCC, No. 78, VII.

1777. SEPTR. 18. THURSDAY.

The violent N.E. Storm which began the Day before Yesterday continues. We are yet in Philadelphia, that Mass of Cowardice and Toryism. Yesterday was buryed Monsr. Du Coudray, a French Officer of Artillery, who was lately made an Inspector General of Artillery and military Manufactures with the Rank of Major General. He was drowned in the Schuylkill, in a strange manner. He rode into the Ferry Boat, and road out at the other End, into the River, and was drowned. His Horse took fright. He was reputed the most learned and promising Officer in France. He was carried into the Romish Chappell, and buried in the Yard of that Church.

This Dispensation will save Us much Altercation.[1]

[1] Much altercation had, however, preceded this event. On Philippe Tronson du Coudray, a French artillery officer and prolific writer on artillery science, see Lasseray, *Les français sous les treize étoiles*, 2:444–454. By agreement with

Silas Deane in France, Du Coudray expected to be appointed major general and to take command of the Continental artillery upon his arrival in America in April 1777. This prospect outraged Generals Knox, Greene, and Sullivan and led them to threaten resignation of their commands. JA, distressed about what to do with Du Coudray, was much more distressed by the American generals' behavior. See JA to Nathanael Greene, 7 July 1777, LbC, Adams Papers; RC printed by Bernhard Knollenberg, with valuable comments, in *R.I. Hist.*, 1:78–81 (July 1942). Lafayette described Du Coudray's death as "peut-être un heureux accident" (Lasseray, 2:452).

1777. SEPTR. 19. FRYDAY.

At 3 this Morning was waked by Mr. Lovell, and told that the Members of Congress were gone, some of them, a little after Midnight. That there was a Letter from Mr. Hamilton Aid de Camp to the General, informing that the Enemy were in Poss[essio]n of the Ford and the Boats, and had it in their Power to be in Philadelphia, before Morning, and that if Congress was not removed they had not a Moment to loose.[1]

Mr. Merchant and myself arose, sent for our Horses, and, after collecting our Things, rode off after the others. Breakfasted at Bristol, where were many Members, determined to go the Newtown Road to Reading. We rode to Trenton where We dined. Coll. Harrison, Dr. Witherspoon, all the Delegates from N.Y. and N.E. except Gerry and Lovell. Drank Tea at Mr. Spencers, lodged at Mr. S. Tuckers, at his kind Invitation.

[1] Alexander Hamilton to John Hancock, 18 Sept. 1777 (Hamilton, *Works*, ed. Hamilton, 1:34–35). Congress had already agreed on the 14th that if it proved necessary to leave Philadelphia, "Lancaster shall be the place at which they shall meet" (*JCC*, 8:742; see also p. 754). For some further details on JA's departure and his circuitous route to Lancaster in order to avoid British scouting parties, see his letter to AA, 30 Sept. (Adams Papers; JA–AA, *Familiar Letters*, p. 314–315).

SEPTR. 20. SATURDAY.

Breakfasted at Mrs. J. B. Smiths. The old Gentleman, his Son Thomas the Loan Officer, were here, and Mrs. Smith's little Son and two Daughters. An elegant Break fast We had of fine Hyson, loaf Sugar, and Coffee &c.

Dined at Williams's, the Sign of the Green Tree. Drank Tea, with Mr. Thompson and his Lady at Mrs. Jacksons. Walked with Mr. Duane to General Dickinsons House, and took a Look at his Farm and Gardens, and his Greenhouse, which is a Scæne of Desolation. The floor of the Greenhouse is dug up by the Hessians, in Search for Money. The Orange, Lemon and Lime Trees are all dead, with the Leaves on. There is a spacious Ball Room, above stairs a drawing

Room and a whispering Room. In another Apartment, a huge Crash of Glass Bottles, which the Hessians had broke I suppose.—These are thy Tryumphs, mighty Britain.—Mr. Law, Mr. Hancock, Mr. Thompson, Mr.   were here. Spent the Evening at Williams's and slept again at Tuckers.

Mrs. Tucker has about 1600£ st. in some of the Funds in England, which she is in fear of loosing. She is accordingly, passionately wishing for Peace, and that the Battle was fought once for all &c. Says that, private Property will be plundered, where there is an Army whether of Friends or Enemies. That if the two opposite Armys were to come here alternately ten times, she would stand by her Property untill she should be kill'd. If she must be a Beggar, it should be where she was known &c. This kind of Conversation shews plainly enough, how well she is pleased, with the State of Things.

1777 SEPTR. 21. SUNDAY.

It was a false alarm which occasioned our Flight from Philadelphia. Not a Soldier of Howes has crossed the Schuylkill.[1] Washington has again crossed it, which I think is a very injudicious Maneuvre. I think, his Army would have been best disposed on the West Side of the Schuylkill. If he had sent one Brigade of his regular Troops to have heald[2] the Militia it would have been enough. With such a Disposition, he might have cutt to Pieces, Hows Army, in attempting to cross any of the Fords. How will not attempt it. He will wait for his Fleet in Delaware River. He will keep open his Line of Communication with Brunswick, and at last, by some Deception or other will slip unhurt into the City.

Burgoine has crossed Hudsons River, by which Gen. Gates thinks, he is determined at all Hazards to push for Albany, which G. Gates says he will do all in his Power to prevent him from reaching. But I confess I am anxious for the Event, for I fear he will deceive Gates, who seems to be acting the same timorous, defensive Part, which has involved us in so many Disasters.—Oh, Heaven! grant Us one great Soul! One leading Mind would extricate the best Cause, from that Ruin which seems to await it, for the Want of it.

We have as good a Cause, as ever was fought for. We have great Resources. The People are well tempered. One active masterly Capacity would bring order out of this Confusion and save this Country.

[1] The British occupied Philadelphia on 27 September.
[2] Thus in MS. CFA corrected to "headed," which may or may not be what the diarist intended.

1777. MONDAY. SEPTR. 22.

Breakfasted at Ringolds in Quaker Town, dined at Shannons in Easton at the Forks, slept at Johnsons in Bethlehem.

[TRAVEL EXPENSES, SEPTEMBER 1777.] [1]

pd. at Quaker Town	2 1/2 dollars.
pd. at Johnsons at Bethlehem	8 dollars
at Hartmans Reading	4 dollars
at Parkers	£4:18s:6d P.C.

[1] Fragmentary record of expenses, written on the last leaf of D/JA/28, during JA's journey from Philadelphia to Lancaster via Trenton, Easton, Bethlehem, and Reading.

Congress sat in Lancaster for only one day, 27 Sept., adjourning on that day to meet at York on the 30th, and was able to proceed with business on 1 Oct. (JCC, 8:755–756). Its place of meeting was the York co. courthouse (Robert Fortenbaugh, *The Nine Capitals of the United States*, York, Penna., 1948, p. 39). JA was at Lancaster by the 27th and at York by the 30th, where he stayed at the house of Gen. Daniel Roberdeau, a Pennsylvania delegate (JA to AA, 9 Oct., Adams Papers).

1777. TUESDAY. SEPTR. 23.

Mr. Okeley [Okely], Mr. Hassey [Hasse] and Mr. Edwine [Ettwein] came to see me. Mr. Edwine shewed Us, the Childrens Meeting at half after 8 o'Clock. Musick, consisting of an Organ and Singing in the German Language. Mr. Edwine gave a Discourse in German and then the same in English.[1]

Mrs. Langley shewed Us the Society of Single Women. Then Mr. Edwine shewed Us the Water Works and the Manufactures. There are six Setts of Works in one Building. An Hemp Mill, an Oil Mill, a Mill to grind Bark for the Tanners.

Then the Fullers Mill, both of Cloth and Leather, the Dyers House, and the Shearers House. They raise a great deal of Madder. We walked among the Rowes of Cherry Trees, with spacious orchards of Apple Trees on each Side of the Cherry Walk. The Society of Single Men have turned out, for the sick.

[1] A Moravian account of this visit to Bethlehem by members of the Continental Congress is printed in *PMHB*, 13:71–73 (April 1889).

1777 WEDNESDAY SEPT. 24.

Fine Morning. We all went to Meeting last Evening, where Mr. Edwine gave the People a short discourse in German, and the Congregation sung and the organ playd. There were about 200 Women and as many Men. The Women sat together in one Body and the Men in another. The Women dressed all alike. The Womens Heads resembled a Garden of white Cabbage Heads.

1777. THURSDAY. SEPTR. 25.

Rode from Bethlehem through Allan Town, Yesterday, to a German Tavern, about 18 Miles from Reading. Rode this Morning to Reading, where We breakfasted, and heard for certain that Mr. Howes Army had crossed the Schuylkill. Coll. Hartley gave me an Account of the late Battle, between the Enemy and General Wayne.[1] Hartley thinks that the Place was improper for Battle, and that there ought to have been a Retreat.

[1] Grey's surprise of Wayne at Paoli, 20 September.

1777 SATURDAY NOVR. 15TH.[1]

At Willis's at the Log Goal in New Jersey 28 miles from Easton.

1777 Tuesday Novr. 11. Sett off from York Town—reached Lancaster. 12. From Lancaster to Reading. Slept at Gen. Mifflins.[2] 13. Reached Strickser's. 14. Dined at Bethlehem. Slept at Easton at Coll. Hoopers. Supped at Coll. Deans.

Met Messrs. Elery and Dana and Coll. Brown on the 15 a few miles on this Side of Reading.

We have had 5 days of very severe Weather, raw, cold, frosty, snowy. This cold comes from afar. The Lakes Champlain and George have been boisterous, if not frozen. Will the Enemy evacuate Ti-[conderog]a? Are they supplied with Prov[isions] for the Winter? Can they bring em from Canada? by Water or Ice? Can they get them in the Neighbouring Country?

Can We take Mt. Independence in the Winter?

[1] In Congress, 7 Nov., *"Ordered, That Mr. Samuel Adams, and Mr. J[ohn] Adams, have leave of absence to visit their families"* (JCC, 9:880). The Adamses had waited to make this application until they supposed the text of the Articles of Confederation, debate over which had occupied Congress intermittently since early April, was complete. Actually a final text was not agreed to and spread on the Journal until 15 Nov. (same, p. 907–928); in this form it was to be printed and submitted to the states for adoption. Meanwhile, on the 11th, the Adamses set off from York, as appears from the retrospective entries incorporated in the present entry.

Some of the varied reasons for JA's retirement from Congress at this time are given in his Autobiography, at the beginning of Part Two, entitled "Travels and Negotiations." The reasons were largely personal. After four years of almost continuous service in Congress he needed to repair his health; and his business, farm, and family required his attention.

[2] At Reading JA paid Gen. Mifflin "92 dollars in Behalf of Mr. Hiltsheimer . . . for keeping one Horse to the 11. Aug. and another to the 19. Septr." This was a charge incurred in Philadelphia which

JA had failed to pay because of his hurried departure. Mifflin's receipt for this payment, dated 13 Nov. 1777, is in the Adams Papers.

MONDAY. NOVR. 17. 1777.

Rode Yesterday from Logg Jail, Willis's, breakfasted at Hoffmans, at Sussex Ct. House, and supped and lodged at David McCamblys, 34 miles from Willis's.—The Taverners all along are complaining of the Guard of Light Horse which attended Mr. H[ancock]. They did not pay, and the Taverners were obliged to go after them, to demand their Dues. The Expence, which is supposed to be the Countrys, is unpopular. The Torys laugh at the Tavern keepers, who have often turned them out of their Houses for abusing Mr. H. They now scoff at them for being imposed upon by their King, as they call him.—Vanity is allways mean. Vanity is never rich enough to be generous.

Dined at Brewsters, in Orange County, State of New York. Brewsters Grandfather, as he tells me, was a Clergyman and one of the first Adventurers to Plymouth. He died at 95 Years of Age, a Minister on Long Island, left a son, who lived to be above 80 and died leaving my Landlord, a son who is now I believe between 60 and 70. The Manners of this Family are exactly like those of the N.E. People. A decent Grace before and after Meat—fine Pork and Beef and Cabbage and Turnip.

TUESDAY NOVR. 18. 1777.

Lodged at Brooks's, 5 Miles from the North River. Rode to the Continental Ferry, crossed over, and dined at Fish Kill, at the Drs. Mess, near the Hospital, with Dr. Sam. Adams, Dr. Eustis, Mr. Wells, &c. It was a feast—Salt Pork and Cabbage, roast Beef and Potatoes, and a noble suit Pudding, Grog and a Glass of Port.

Our best Road home is through Litchfield and Springfield.[1]

Morehouses is a good Tavern, about 24 Miles, 3 or 4 Miles on this Side of Bulls Iron Works. 50 Miles to Litchfield.

Captn. Storms 8 Miles.—Coll. Vandeboroughs 5.—Coll. Morehouses 9.—Bulls Iron Works 4. No Tavern.—Cogswells Iron Works 10—a Tavern.—Litchfield, 8.—Cross Mount Tom to get to Litchfield.

[1] The notes on JA's itinerary which follow in this and succeeding entries are not to be taken literally as a record of the places that he passed through or stopped at. With the exception of the places where he states that he "dined," "lodged," or "breakfasted," the notes are simply information—some of it not wholly reliable—that he gathered concerning the distances and inns ahead.

WEDNESDAY NOVR. 19. 1777.

Dined at Storms, lodged last night and breakfasted this Morning at Loudouns at Fish Kill. Here We are at Coll. Morehouses's a Member of Assembly for Dutchess County.

THURSDAY NOVR. 20.

To Harrwington [Harwinton], Phillips's 5 Miles.—To Yales in Farmington 5.—To Humphreys in Simsbury 7 miles.—To Owens in Simsbury 7 miles.—To Sheldons in Suffield 10.—Kents in Suffield 5.— To Springfield 10.

NOVR. 21.

To Hays's, Salmon Brook 5. miles.—To Southwick, Loomis, 6.—To Fowlers 3. miles.—To Westfield, Claps, 4 miles.—To Captn. Claps, 4 miles this Side N.H.—To North Hampton, Lymans or Clarks.[1]

[1] The date of JA's arrival in Braintree, 27 Nov., is recorded in his summary account rendered to the State of Massachusetts, enclosed in a letter to Speaker James Warren, 15 Jan. 1778 (NN:Emmet Coll.).

1778 FEBRUARY 13. FRYDAY.[1]

Captain Samuel Tucker, Commander of the Frigate Boston, met me, at Mr. Norton Quincy's, where We dined, and after Dinner I sent my Baggage, and walked myself with Captain Tucker, Mr. Griffin a Midshipman, and my eldest Son, John Quincy Adams, between 10 and 11. Years of Age, down to the Moon Head, where lay the Bostons Barge.[2] The Wind was very high, and the Sea very rough, but by Means of a Quantity of Hay in the Bottom of the Boat, and good Watch Coats with which We were covered We arrived on board the Boston, about five O Clock, tolerably warm and dry.—On board I found Mr. Vernon, a Son of Mr. Vernon of the Navy Board, a little Son of Mr. Deane of Weathersfield, between 11. and 12. Years of Age, and Mr. Nicholas Noel, a french Gentleman, Surgeon of the Ship, who seems to be a well bred Man.[3]

Dr. Noel shewed me, a Book, which was new to me. The Title is, Les Elemens de la Langue Angloise, dévélopés d'une maniere nouvelle, facile et très concise, en forme de Dialogue, ou la pronunciation est enseignée par un Assemblage de Lettres qui forme des sons similaires en François, et ou la juste Mesure de chaque Syllable est determinée. Avec un Vocabulaire, des Phrases familieres, et des Dialogues, tres interessans, pour ceux qui souhaitent parler Anglois correctement, et en peu de Tems. Nouvelle Edition, revûe, corrigée et enrichè de plusieurs nouvelles Regles et Remarques, servant à écarter les Difficultés qui retardent le Progress des Etrangers. Par V. J. Peyton. Linguarum Diversitas alienat hominem ab homine, et propter solam linguarum diversitatem, nihil potest ad consociandos homines tanta Similitudo naturæ. St. August. De Civit. Dei. A Londres, Chez J. Nourse et Paul Vaillant, dans le Strand 1776.

[1] First entry in D/JA/47. This is a small quarto volume bound in marbled boards and may well be one of the two "Account Books" or "Memd. Book" purchased by the Navy Board for JA's use on his voyage and mission; see John Bradford to JA, 11? Feb. 1778 and enclosures (Adams Papers); the enclosures are reproduced in this volume. The book contains about a hundred pages of journal entries, 13 Feb. 1778–26 April 1779, and though not nearly filled it was doubtless left home when JA sailed for Europe again in Nov. 1779. Years later the blank leaves were fruitfully used for transcripts of JA's earliest Diary booklets, 1755–1761, made under the supervision of JQA; see Introduction.

When JA arrived home from Congress on 27 Nov. 1777, he had every expectation of a long leave and began to pick up the threads of his legal practice. But in York, Penna., on the following day Congress elected him a joint commissioner with Benjamin Franklin and Arthur Lee to represent the United States in France, Silas Deane having been recalled on 21 Nov. (JCC, 9:946–947, 975). JA's commission, erroneously dated 27 (instead of 28) Nov., was enclosed in a letter to him from Richard Henry Lee and James Lovell, "In Committee for foreign Affairs," York, 3 Dec. (Adams Papers; JA, *Works*, 7:6–7). "After much Agitation of mind and a thousand reveries," as he says in his Autobiography, JA announced his acceptance in a letter to President Henry Laurens, 23 Dec. (PCC, No. 84, I; Wharton, ed., *Dipl. Corr. Amer. Rev.* 2:458).

[2] In what is now Quincy Bay, though the name "Moon Head" is confusing and has been much disputed. There was and still remains a "Moon Head" on Moon Island off the tip of Squantum,

the peninsula that encloses Quincy Bay on the north. But this Moon Head could not have been accessible by foot and is thus ruled out as the place from which JA embarked. Family and local tradition in Quincy long designated a low eminence on the shore near Norton Quincy's house and just opposite Half Moon Island as the spot, but when some antiquarian-minded friends sent CFA a sketch of the ground in 1877 he declined to interpret what JA meant by Moon Head and in effect declared the problem insoluble (Cyrus Woodman to James Baxter, 10 Aug. 1877, enclosed in Baxter to CFA, 13 Aug., Adams Papers; CFA to Baxter, 15 Aug., LbC, Adams Papers). Two bits of evidence, hitherto overlooked, settle the question where JA embarked from, though not why he called it what he did. The first is in a letter from AA to John Thaxter, 15–18 Feb. 1778, in which she says that her husband and son "embarked from this Town, the place you well know, Hofs Neck" (MHi: Waterston Coll.). The second is a passage in JA's Autobiography that was not published by CFA: "In our Way [from Norton Quincy's house] We made an half of a few minutes at the House of Mr. Seth Spear on Hoffs neck, where some Sailors belonging to our barge had been waiting for us." He then relates the conversation that passed between him and Mrs. Spear, who predicted an unfavorable voyage. Clearly, then, the party embarked from Hough's Neck, the southern extremity of Quincy Bay. This point was directly on the way to Nantasket Roads, where the *Boston* was anchored. Capt. Tucker's logbook (see the following paragraph) has this entry for 13 Feb. 1778: "I haveing Some Capital business at Brantre Send my boat on Shore to Georges Island [in Nantasket Roads] and brought off a Pilot to Conduct me their att 10 AM Proceeded their finisht my business and Returned on board by 5 PM."

The original logbook of the *Boston,* a 24-gun Continental frigate, is in the Samuel Tucker Papers (MH) and forms a valuable supplement to JA's record of this voyage; it is printed with reasonable fidelity as an appendix to Sheppard, *Tucker,* p. 261–327. Tucker prepared what he called "An Abstract of a Journal Kept ... on Board the Contl. Frigate Boston," and presented it to JA in 1791 (Adams Papers, Microfilms, Reel No. 342). The "Abstract" differs in many · details from the logbook, a fact which accounts for the variations between material quoted from the log in our notes and quotations attributed to it in notes by CFA, who used the "Abstract" when editing JA's Diary (JA, *Works,* 3:95 ff.).

³ William Vernon Jr., College of New Jersey 1776, was going to France to gain experience in trade; after a brief stay at Bordeaux he entered the house of "Mr. Revellat aîné, one of the Principal Negociants" of Montauban in Guienne, declining an offer by JA to serve as his secretary (entry of 16 Feb., below; Vernon Jr. to JA, 10 April, 16 May, 26 Sept. 1778; JA to Vernon Jr., 12 May, 15 Sept. 1778, both LbC; JA to Vernon Sr., 2 Dec. 1778, LbC; all in Adams Papers). As for Jesse Deane, he was placed with JQA and other young Americans in M. Le Coeur's private boarding school in Passy. He stayed in Europe five years, spending the last two of them with his father in Ghent and London. Returning to America in 1783, he joined a business enterprise in Hartford, but was apparently not successful. See entry of 14 April, note, below; *Deane Papers,* index, under his name.

On Nicolas Noël, *chirurgien-major* in the French army, see Lasseray, *Les français sous les treize étoiles,* 2:342–345. The official ship's doctor was Benjamin Brown, later a member of Congress from Massachusetts (Sheppard, *Tucker,* p. 84 and *passim*).

1778. 14. FEB. SATURDAY.

A very fine Morning, the Wind at Northwest. At Daybreak orders were given for the Ship to unmoor.

My Lodging was a Cott, with a double Mattress, a good Bolster, my own Sheets, and Blanketts enough. My little Son, with me—We lay very comfortably, and slept well. A violent Gale of Wind in the Night.

FEB. 15. SUNDAY.

This Morning weigh'd the last Anchor, and came under Sail, before Breakfast. A fine Wind, and a pleasant Sun, but a sharp cold Air.— Thus I bid farewell to my native Shore.—Arrived, and anchored in the Harbour of Marblehead, about Noon. Major Reed, Captn. Gatchell Father in Law of Capt. Tucker came on board, and a Captain Stevens who came on Board to make me a present of a single Pistol.

1778. FEB. 16. MONDAY.

Another Storm for our Mortification—the Wind at N.E. and the Snow so thick that the Captain thinks he cannot go to Sea. Our Excursion to this Place, was unfortunate, because it is almost impossible, to keep the Men on Board. Mothers, Wives, Sisters come on bord, and beg for Leave for their Sons, Husbands, and Brothers to go on Shore for one Hour &c. so that it is hard for the Commander to resist their Importunity.

I am anxious at these Delays. We shall never have another Wind so good as We have lost. Congress, and the Navy Board, will be surprized at these Delays, and yet there is no Fault, that I know of. The Commander of the Ship is active and vigilant, and does all in his Power, but he wants Men—he has very few Seamen indeed. All is as yet Chaos on board. His Men are not disciplined. The Marrines are not. The Men are not exercised to the Guns. They hardly know the Ropes.

My Son is treated very complaisantly by Dr. Noel, and by a Captain and Lieutenant of Artillery, who are on board, all French Gentlemen. They are very assiduous in teaching him French. The Dr. Monsr. Noel, is a genteell well bred Man, and has received somewhere a good Education. He has Wounds on his Forehead, and on his Hands, which he says he received, last War, in the Light Horse Service.

The Name of the Captain of Artillery is Parison,[1] and that of the Lieutenant is Begard.

Since my Embarkation, Master Jesse Deane delivered me a Letter, from his Uncle Barnabas Deane dated 10. Feb. recommending to my particular Care and Attention, the Bearer, the only Child of his Brother Silas Deane Esq. now in France, making no doubt, as the Letter adds, that I shall take the same Care of a Child in his Situation, which I would wish to have done to a Child of my own, in the like Circumstance.—It is needless to mention his Youth and Helplessness, also how much he will be exposed to bad Company and to contract bad Habits, without some friendly Monitor to caution and keep him from associating with the common Hands on board.[2]

About the same Time, another Letter was delivered to me from Wm. Vernon Esq. of the Continental Navy Board, dated Feb. 9.—in these Words "I presume it is unnecessary to say one Word in order to impress your Mind with the Anxiety a Parent is under, in the Education of a Son, more especially when not under his immediate Inspection, and at 3000 Miles distance. Your parental Affection fixes this Principle. Therefore I have only to beg the Favour of you, Sir, to place my Son, in such a Situation, and with such a Gentleman as you would chuse for one of yours, whom you would wish to accomplish for a Merchant. If such a House could be found, either at Bourdeaux or Nantes, of protestant Principles, of general and extensive Business,

I rather think one of those Cities the best; yet if it should be your Opinion that some other Place might be more advantageous to place him at, or that he can be imployed by any of the States Agents, with a good Prospect of improving himself, in such manner, that he may hereafter be usefull to Society, and in particular to these American States, my Views are fully answered. I have only one Observation more to make, viz. in respect to the Æconomy of this Matter, which I am perswaded will engage your Attention, as the small Fortune that remains with me, I would wish to appropriate for the Education of my Son, which I know must be husbanded, yet I cant think of being rigidly parsimonious, nor must I be very lavish, lest my Money should not hold out.

"I imagine a Gratuity of one hundred Pounds Sterling may be given to a Merchant of Eminence to take him for two or three Years, and perhaps his yearly board paid for. I shall be entirely satisfyed in whatever may seem best for you to do, and ever shall have a gratefull Remembrance of your unmerited Favours, and sincerely hope in future to have it in my Power to make Compensation. I wish you Health and the Utmost Happiness, and am, with the greatest Regards &c." [3]

Thus I find myself invested with the unexpected Trust of a Kind of Guardianship of two promising young Gentlemen, besides my own Son. This benevolent office is peculiarly agreable to my Temper. Few Things have ever given me greater Pleasure than the Tuition of Youth to the Bar, and the Advancement of Merit.

[1] On "Pondicherry" Parison, "one of General Du Coudrais Captains," see entry of 19 Feb., below, and JA's Autobiography under date of 24–26 Feb. 1778.

[2] Deane's letter, here partly quoted and partly paraphrased, is in the Adams Papers, dated from Boston.

[3] This is the full text of Vernon's letter as found in the Adams Papers.

17. TUESDAY.

I set a Lesson to my Son in Chambauds French Grammar and asked the Favour of Dr. Noel to shew him the precise, critical Pronunciation of all the French Words, Syllables, and Letters, which the Dr. very politely did, and Mr. John is getting his Lessons accordingly, very much pleased.

The Weather is fair, and the Wind right, and We are again weighing Anchor in order to put to Sea.

Captn. Diamond and Captn. Inlaker came on Board, and breakfasted, two Prisoners taken with Manly in the Hancock and lately escaped from Hallifax.

Our Captn. is an able Seaman, and a brave, active, vigilant officer, but I believe has no great Erudition. His Library consists of Dyche's English Dictionary, Charlevoix's Paraguay, The Rights of the Xtian Church asserted vs. the Romish and other Priests, who claim an independent Power over it, The 2d Vol. of Chubbs posthumous Works, 1. Vol. of the History of Charles Horton, Esq. and 1 Vol. of the delicate Embarrassments a Novell.—I shall at some other Time take more Notice of some of these Books.

1778. FEB. 18. WEDNESDAY.

Last night, about Sunsett We sailed out of Marblehead Harbour, and have had a fine Wind, from that time to this, 24. Hours. The constant Rolling and Rocking of the Ship, last night made Us all sick —half the Sailors were so. My young Gentlemen, Jesse and Johnny, were taken about 12 O Clock last night and have been very seasick ever since. I was seized with it myself this Forenoon. My Servant Joseph Stevens[1] and the Captns. Will have both been very bad.

[1] Joseph Stephens (as he himself wrote his name), a former soldier and seaman, served JA in Europe in all kinds of capacities from 1778 to 1783, but was lost on a voyage home to America in the latter year.

FEB. 19. THURSDAY.

Arose at 4 O Clock. The Wind and Weather still fair. The Ship rolls less than Yesterday, and I have neither felt, nor heard any Thing of Sea Sickness, last night nor this Morning.

Monsr. Parison, one of General Du Coudrais Captains, dined with us, Yesterday, and made me a present of a Bottle of a nice French Dram, a Civility which I must repay. He seems a civil and sensible Man.

The Mal de Mer seems to be merely the Effect of Agitation. The Smoke and Smell of Seacoal, the Smell of stagnant, putrid Water, the Smell of the Ship where the Sailors lay, or any other offensive Smell, will increase the Qualminess, but do not occasion it.

C[aptain] Parison says, that the Roads from Nantes to Paris are very good, no Mountains, no Hills, no Rocks—all as smooth as the Ships Deck and a very fine Country: But the Roads from Bourdeaux to Paris, are bad and mountainous.

In the Morning We discovered three Sail of Vessells ahead. We went near enough to discover them to be Frigates, and then put away. We soon lost sight of two of them: but the third chased Us the whole Day. Sometimes We gained upon her, and sometimes she upon Us.[1]

[1] Tucker, Log (MH), 19 Feb.: "Att 6 A.M. Saw three Large Ships bearing East they Standing to the Northward I mistrusted they where a Cruizeing for me. I hauld my wind to the southward found they did not Persue. I then Consulted my Offercers to stand to the Northward after them. We agreed in opinions. Wore Ship Run one hour to the Northward then I Discoverd that one was a ship Not Less than ourselfs, one out of sight to the Northward and the other appeared to me and offercers to be a twenty gun ship. The man att the mast head Cauld out a ship on the weather Quarter—at that time the other two Under our Lee and Under short Sail. I then Consulted the Honble. John Addams Esq. and my offercers what was best to do not knowing how my ship may Sail. One and all Consented to stand to the southward from them. Att 10 A.M. I then wore ship to the southward and stood from them. The two that was Under my Lee before I wore Imediately wore and stood affter me. Att 12 on Meridian Lost sigh[t] of the small ship and the other was about three Leagues Under my Lee Quarter."

The vessel in pursuit was the *Apollo* (Ambrose Serle, *American Journal*, ed. Edward H. Tatum, Jr., San Marino, Calif., 1940, p. 315).

FEB. 20. FRYDAY.

In the Morning nothing to be seen, but soon after another Sail discovered ahead, which is supposed to be the same.[1]

[1] Tucker, Log (MH), 20 Feb.: "This 24 hours begins Very Pleasant the Ship Still in Chase. I being Poorly mand dare not attactk her and many other Principal Reasons. Att 2 P.M. Satt fore and main topmast stearing Sails found I Left the Ship att 6 P.M. It being dark Lost sight of the Ship in Small Sails and hauld my wind. The Cruizer supposing I bore away to stear the Course I was going When she saw me first Bore away and run ESE while I for six or Eight hours had being [been] Runing four Points more southerly att the Rate of seven knots brought her in my oppinion to bear of me ENE Distance about Eleven and half Leagues. Then the wind headed me. I fell off to ENE then Runing att the Rate of 6 knots for three hours. Saw the Same Ship Direct a head standing to southward & westward about 5 Leagues Distance. Hove in stays after makeing of her Plain and stood to the westward because I Could not Weather her on the former tack after Runing three hours to the westward. The wind favoured me. I then hove in Stays and Came to windward of the frigate about four miles and was Intirely Sattisfyd it was the Same Ship about four Miles Under my Lee Quarter. They again Tackt ship and Continued Chaseing that day—but I found I rather Left my Enemy."

FEB. 21. SATURDAY, 22. SUNDAY, AND 23D. MONDAY.

Exhibited such Scænes as were new to me. We lost Sight of our Enemy it is true but We found our selves in the Gulph Stream, in the Midst of an epouvantable Orage, the Wind N.E. then N., and then North West.

It would be fruitless to attempt a Description of what I saw, heard and felt, during these 3 days and nights. To describe the Ocean, the Waves, the Winds, the Ship, her Motions, Rollings, Wringings and Agonies—the Sailors, their Countenances, Language and Behaviour, is impossible. No Man could keep upon his Legs, and nothing could be kept in its Place—an universal Wreck of every Thing in all Parts of the Ship, Chests, Casks, Bottles &c. No Place or Person was dry.

On one of these Nights, a Thunder bolt struck 3 Men upon deck and wounded one of them a little, by a Scorch upon his Shoulder. It also struck our Main Topmast.[1]

[1] Tucker, Log (MH), 22 Feb.: ". . . heavy gales and a Dangerous Sea Running; one thing or another Continually giving away on board Ship. . . . Att half Past 3 A.M. Discoverd our fore sail was split in the Larbourd Leach but Could not Prevent it att that time for the Distress we wear at that time in; I Little Expected but to be Dismasted as I was almost Certain I heard the mainmast spring below the Deck. Afterwards Discoverd the truth of it. Still Continues an Extremity of Weather. So Ends this day. Pray god Protect Us and Carry Us through our Various troubles."

As for the seaman struck by lightning, "he lived three days and died raving mad" (William Jennison Jr., "Journal," *PMHB*, 15: 102 [April 1891]). Jennison was a lieutenant of marines aboard the *Boston,* and his journal adds a few details concerning this voyage not found elsewhere. See also JA's Autobiography under 20 Feb. 1778.

TUESDAY 24. WEDNESDAY 25. THURSDAY 26.

Tuesday We spyd a Sail and gave her Chase. We overhawled her, and upon firing a Gun to Leeward, and hoisting American Colours, she fired a friendly Gun and Hoisted the French Colours of the Province of Normandy. She lay to for us, and We were coming about to speak to her, when the Wind sprung up fresh of a sudden and carried away our Main top Mast. We have been employed ever since in getting in a New one, repairing the Sails and Rigging much damaged in the late Storm, and in cleaning the Ship and putting her in order. From the 36 to the 39. deg[rees] of Lat. are called the Squawly Latitudes, and We have found them to answer their Character.

I should have been pleased to have kept a minute Journal of all that passed, in the late Chases and turbulent Weather, but I was so wet, and every Thing and Place was so wett—every Table and Chair was so wrecked that it was impossible to touch a Pen, or Paper.

It is a great Satisfaction to me however, to recollect, that I was myself perfectly calm during the whole. I found by the Opinion of the People aboard, and of the Captain himself that We were in Danger, and of this I was certain allso from my own Observation, but I thought myself in the Way of my Duty, and I did not repent of my Voyage.

I confess I often regretted that I had brought my son. I was not so clear that it was my Duty to expose him, as myself, but I had been led to it by the Childs Inclination and by the Advice of all my Friends. Mr. Johnnys Behaviour gave me a Satisfaction that I cannot express—fully sensible of our Danger, he was constantly endeavouring to bear it with a manly Patience, very attentive to me and his Thoughts constantly running in a serious Strain.

1778. FEB. 26. THURSDAY.

I have made many Observations, in the late bad Weather, some of which I do not think it prudent to put in writing—a few I will set down. 1st. I have seen the inexpressible Inconvenience of having so small a Space between Decks, as there is in the Boston. As the main Deck was almost constantly under Water, the Sea rolling in and out at the Ports and Scuppers, We were obliged to keep the Hat[ch]ways down—whereby the Air became so hot and so dry in the 'Tween decks that for my own Part, I could not breathe, or live there. Yet the Water would pour down when ever an hatchway was opened, so that all was afloat. 2. The Boston is over metalled. Her Number of Guns and the Weight of their Metal is too great for her Tonnage. She has 5 Twelve Pounders, and 19. Nines. We were obliged to sail, day and Night during a Chaise with the Guns out, in order to be ready, and this exposed Us to certain Inconvenience and great Danger. They made the Ship labour and roll, so as to oblige Us to keep the Chain Pumps as well as the Hand Pumps, almost constantly going. Besides they Wring, and twist the Ship in such a Manner as to endanger the starting of a Butt, but still more to endanger the Masts and Rigging. 3. The Ship is furnished with no Pistolls, which she ought to be, with at least as many as there are Officers, because there is nothing but the Dread of a Pistoll will keep many of the Men to their Quarters in Time of Action. 4. This Ship is not furnished with good Glasses, which appears to me of very great Consequence. Our Ships ought to be furnished with the best Glasses that Art affords. Their Expence would be saved a Thousand Ways.

5. There is the same general Inattention, I find on Board the Navy to Œconomy that there is in the Army. 6. There is the same general Relaxation of order and Discipline. 7. There is the same Inattention to the Cleanliness of the Ship and the Persons and Health of the Sailors, as there is at land of the Cleanness of the Camp and the Health, and Cleanness of the soldiers. 8. The Practice of profane Cursing and Swearing, so silly as well as detestable, prevails in a most abominable Degree. It is indulged and connived at by Officers, and practised too in such a Manner that there is no Kind of Check against it. And I take upon me to say that order of every Kind will be lax as long as this is so much the Case.

This Morning Captn. Tucker made me a Present of Charlevoix's

History of Paraguay.[1] Yesterday Dr. Noel put into my Hand, a Pockett Volume, intituled, Le Geographe manuel, contenant La Description de tous les Pays du Monde, leurs qualités, leur climat, le caractère de leurs Habitans, leur Villes capitales, avec leur distances de Paris, et des Routes qui y menent tant par terre que par Mer; les Changes, et les Monnoies des principales Places de l'Europe, en Correspondance avec Paris; la manière de tenir les Ecritures de chaque Nation; la Reduction de toutes espèces de l'Europe au pied courant de France, &c. Par M. l'Abbé Expilly, de la Société royale des Sciences et belles Lettres de Nancy.[2] These manuals come out annually, and are to be had in any of the great Towns in France.

[1] Pierre François Xavier de Charlevoix, *The History of Paraguay*, Dublin, 1769, 2 vols., survives among JA's books in the Boston Public Library (*Catalogue of JA's Library*).

[2] Abbé Jean Joseph Expilly's *Géographe manuel*, Paris, 1765, is also among the numerous European guidebooks and similar works among JA's books in the Boston Public Library (same).

FEB. 27. FRYDAY.

A Calm. As soft and warm as Summer. A Species of black Fish, which our officers call Beneaters,[1] appeared about the Ship.

One Source of the Disorders in this Ship, is the Irregularity of Meals. There ought to be a well digested System, for Eating, Drinking and sleeping. At Six, all Hands should be called up. At Eight, all Hands should breakfast. At one all Hands should dine. At Eight again all Hands should sup. It ought to be penal for the Cook to fail of having his Victuals ready punctually.—This would be for the Health, Comfort and Spirits of the Men, and would greatly promote the Business of the Ship.

I am constantly giving Hints to the Captain concerning Order, Œconomy and Regularity, and he seems to be sensible of the Necessity of them, and exerts himself to introduce them.—He has cleared out the Tween Decks, ordered up the Hammocks to be aired, and ordered up the sick, such as could bear it, upon Deck for sweet Air. This Ship would have bred the Plague or the Goal Fever, if there had not been great Exertions, since the storm, to wash, sweep, Air and purify, Cloaths, Cots, Cabins, Hammocks and all other Things, Places and Persons.

The Captn. Yesterday went down into the Cock Pit, and ordered up every Body from that Sink of Devastation and Putrefaction—ordered up the Hamocks &c. This was in Pursuance of the Advice I gave him in the Morning, "if you intend to have any Reputation for Œconomy, Discipline or any Thing that is good, look to your Cock Pit."

Yesterday the Captn. brought in a Curiosity which he had drawn up over the Side in a Buckett of Water, which the Sailors call a Portuguese Man of War, and to day I have seen many of them sailing by the Ship. They have some Appearances of Life and Sensibility. They spread a curious Sail and are wafted along very briskly. They have something like Gutts, hanging down, which are said to be in a degree poisonous to human Flesh. The Hulk is like blue Glass. I pierced it with the sharp Point of my Pen Knife and found it empty. The Air came out, and the Thing shrunk up almost to nothing.

¹ CFA silently corrects this word to "bonitos."

1778. FEB. 28. SATURDAY.

Last Night and this Day We have enjoyed a fine easy Breeze. The Ship has had no Motion but directly forward. I slept as quietly and as soundly as in my own Bed at home. Dr. Noel gave me a Phial of Balsamum fioraventi, for an Inflammation in my Eyes, which seems to be very good for them. It is very much compounded. It is very subtle and penetrating. Pour a few Drops into the Palms of your Hands, rub it over the Palm and the Fingers, and then hold the Insides of your Hands before your Eyes, and the Steam which evaporates enters the Eyes, and works them clear. This Balsam derives its Name from its Author.

The Ship is now in very good order, cleaned out, between Decks, on the Main Deck, in the Cabin and Quarter Deck. The Masts, Yards, Sails and Rigging are well repaired.

The Captn. has just now sent written Orders to the Steward of the Ship, to make weekly Returns to him of the State of Provisions and to be very frugal of Provisions and Candles, which appeared to be very necessary as near one half of the Ships Stores of Candles are expended.

This is Saturday Night: a Fortnight Yesterday, since I took Leave of my Family.—What Scænes have I beheld since?—What Anxiety have my Friends on Shore suffered on my Account? during the N.E. Storm which they must have had at Land!

What is this Gulph Stream? What is the Course of it? From what Point and to what Point does it flow? How broad is it? How far distant is it from the Continent of America? What is the Longitude and Latitude of it.

1778. MARCH 1. SUNDAY.

Discovered that our Mainmast was sprung in two Places—one beneath the Main Deck, where if the Mast had wholly failed in the late Storm it must have torn up the main Deck and the Ship must have foundered. This is one among many Instances, in which it has already appeared that our Safety has not depended on ourselves.

A fine Wind, all day and night. Somewhat Sea Sick. The Ship was very quiet and still—no Disturbance—little noise.

I hope for the future We shall carry less Sail, especially of nights, and at all Times when We are not in Chase.

MARCH 2. MONDAY.

A fine Wind still and a pleasant Morning. The Colour of the Water which is green, not blue as it has been for many Days past, the Appearance of large Flocks of Gulls, and various other Birds, convinced the knowing ones, to say that We were not far from the Grand Bank of N. Foundland. The Captain however thinks it 35 Leagues to the N. West of Us.—Our Mast was Yesterday repaired with two large Fishes, as they call em, i.e. large oaken Planks cutt for the Purpose and put on. It seems now as firm as ever.—The Sailors are very superstitious. They say the Ship has been so unfortunate that they really believe there is some Woman on board.—Women are the unluckyest Creatures in the World at Sea &c.

This Evening the Wind is very fresh, and the Ship sails at a great Rate. We are out of the Reach I hope of the Gulph Stream and of British Cruizers, two Evils, which I have a great Aversion to.

1778. MARCH 3. TUESDAY.

Our Wind continued brisk and fresh all the last Night, and this Morning. Our Course is about N.E. Showers in the Night and this Morning. The Flocks of Gulls, still pursuing Us.

This Morning, Mr. Parison breakfasted with Us. Our Captn. in gay Spirits, chattering in French, Spanish, Portuguese, German, Dutch, Greek, and boasting that he could speak some Words in every Language. He told Us he had ordered two more Fishes upon the Mainmast to cover the Flaws, above Deck.

The Captain, Lieutenants, Master, Mates and Midshipmen, are now making their Calculations, to discover their Longitude, but I conjecture they will be very wild.

The Life I lead is a dull Scæne to me. No Business; No Pleasure; No Study....[1] Our little World is all wet and damp: there is nothing I can eat or drink without nauseating. We have no Spirits for Conversation, nor any Thing to converse about. We see nothing but Sky, Clouds and Sea, and then Seas, Clouds and Sky.

I have often heard of learning a Language as French or English on the Passage, but I believe very little of any Thing was ever learned on a Passage. There must be more Health and better Accommodations.

My young Friend, Mr. Vernon, has never had the least Qualm of the Sea Sickness, since We came aboard. I have advised him to begin the Study of the French Tongue methodically, by reading the Grammar through. He has begun it accordingly, and we shall see his Patience and Perseverance.

Dr. Noel shewed me, "Dictionaire geographique portatif," which is a Translation of Echards Gazetteer, into French Par Monsr. Vosgien, Chanoine de Vaucouleurs.[2]

[1] Suspension points in MS.

[2] The *Dictionnaire géographique portatif ... par Monsieur Vosgien* [actually Jean Baptiste Ladvocat] went through many editions, as had its English original—Laurence Eachard, *The Gazetteer's: or, Newsman's Interpreter: Being a Geographical Index of All the Considerable Cities, Bishopricks, Universities ... in Europe*; see BM, *Catalogue*. The French extracts in the immediately following Diary entries are taken from this *Dictionnaire*. Except for copying errors they correspond quite closely with the text of the Paris edition of 1749.

1778. MARCH 4. WEDNESDAY.

Fair Weather, but an Adverse Wind, from the N.E., which ob-[liges] Us to go to the Southward of the S.E. which is out of our Course.

Nantes, ancienne, riche, et tres considerable Ville de Fran[ce,] la seconde de la Bretagne, avec un riche Evêché suffrag[an] de Tours, une Université, et un Hôtel des Monnoies. C'[est] une de Villes les plus commercantes du Royaulme. Les Marchands ont une Sociéte avec ceux de Bilbao, appellee la Contractation, et un Tribunal reciproque [en] forme de Jurisdiction consulaire. Ce fut dans cette Ville que Henri 4th. donna, en 1598, le celebre Edit [de] Nantes, revoqué en 1685. Elle est sur la Rive droit de la Loire, à 15. lieus S.O. d'Angers, 27. N. Par O. de [La] Rochelle, 87. S.O. de Paris, 23. S. de Rennes. Long. 16.6.12. Lat. 47.13.7. Le Païs Nantois, ou le C. de Nantes, est [une] Contree des deux côtés de la Loire. On y fait du S[el,] et il y a beaucoup de Bestiaux.[1]

[1] Text defective because the outer edge of a leaf, loosened from the binding, is badly chipped.

MARCH 5. THURSDAY.

This Morning We have the pleasantest Prospect [we] have yet seen
—a fine easy Breeze, from the Southward, w[hich] gives us an Opportunity of keeping our true Course—a so[ft], clear, warm Air—a
fair Sun—no Sea. We have a g[reat] Number of Sails spread and We
go at the Rate of 9 Kno[ts.] Yet the Ship has no perceptible Motion,
and makes no N[oise.] My little Son is very proud of his Knowledge
of all the Sails, and last Night the Captn. put him [to learn the
Mariners Compass.]¹

Oh that We might make Prize to day of an English Vessell, lately
from London, with all the Newspapers, and Magazines on board, that
We might obtain the latest Intelligence, and discover the Plan of
Operations for the ensuing Campaign.

Whenever I arrive at any Port in Europe, whether in Spain or
France, my first Enquiry should be concerning the Designs of the
Enemy.—What Force they mean to send to America? Where they are
to obtain Men? What is the State of the British Nation? What the State
of Parties? What the State of Finances, and of Stocks?

Then the State of Europe, particularly France and Spain? What the
real Designs of those Courts? What the Condition of their Finances?
What the State of their Armies, but especially of their Fleets. What
No. of Ships they have fitted for the Sea—what their Names, Number
of Men and Guns, weight of Metal &c.—where they lie? &c.

The Probability or Improbability of a War, and the Causes and
Reasons for and against each supposition.

The Supplies of Cloathing, Arms, &c. gone to America, during the
past Winter. The State of American Credit in France. What Remittances have been made from America, in Tobacco, Rice, Indigo, or
any other Articles?

We are now supposed to be nearly in the Lat. of Cape Finisterre,
so that We have only to sail an Easterly Course.

Finistere, Finis Terræ; c'est le Cap, le plus occid. non seulement
de la Galice et de L'Esp., mais encore de l'Europe; ce qui fait que les
Anc. qui ne connoissoient rien au-dela, lui ont donné son nom, qui
signifie l'Extrêmité de la Terre, ou le bout du monde. Il y a une Ville
de mesme nom.

This Day, We have enjoyed the clearest Horison, the softest
Weather, the best Wind, and the smoothest Sea, that We have seen
since We [came] on board. All Sails are spread and We have gone
[ten Knots upon an Avarage the whole day.]

March 1778

[1] Here and below, the missing fragments of text have been supplied from parallel passages in JA's Autobiography.

1778. MARCH 6. FRYDAY.

The Wind continued in the same Point, about S[outh] all Night, and the Ship has gone 9 Knotts upon an Average. This is great Favour.

I am now reading the Amphitrion of Moliere, which is his 6. Volume.[1] revai-je? do I dream?—have I dreamed?—I have I been in a dream? [2] J'ai revé. I have been in a dream. It is in the Preterit.

We shall pass to the Northward of the Western Islands, and are now supposed to be as near them as We shall be. They all belong to Portugal.

Açores, Iles sit. entre l'Afr. et l'Amer. environ a 200 li. O. de Lisbonne; Gonzalo Vello les decouvrit vers le milieu du 15 Siecle, et les nomma Açores, mot qui signifie des Eperviers, parce qu'on y rem. beaucoup de ces Oiseaux. Il y en a neuf. Angra, dans l'ile de Tercere, est la Capital de Toutes. Ortelius assure que ceux partent de l'Europe, pour aller en Amer., sont delivres de toute Sorte de Vermine, aussitot qu'ils ont passe les Acores, ce qu'on doit attribuer a la qualite de l'Air, qui y e[s]t tres salubre. Le ble, les Vignes, les Arbres fruitiers, et le betail, y sont en abond. Elles appart. aux Port.—long. 346–354. Lat. 39.

[1] In a bilingual edition which JA had purchased "Many Years before" and made his first use of on this voyage (Autobiography under this date).
[2] Thus in MS.

MARCH 7. SATURDAY.

The same prosperous Wind, and the same beautifull Weather continue. We proceed in our Course at the Rate of about 200 Miles in 24 Hours. We have passed all the Dangers of the American Coast. Those of the Bay of Biscay, remain. God grant Us, an happy Passage through them all.

Yesterday, the Ship was all in an Uproar, with Laughter. The Boatswains Mate asked one of his superiour Officers, if they might have a Frolick.—The Answer was, Yes.—Jere. accordingly, with the old Sailors, proposed to build a Galley, and all the raw Hands to the Number of 20 or 30 were taken in, and suffered themselves to be tyed together, by their Legs. When all of a sudden, Jere. and his knowing ones, were found handing Bucketts of Water over the Sides and pouring them upon the poor Dupes, untill they were wet to the Skin.—The Behaviour of the Gullies,[1] their Passions and Speeches and Actions, were diverting enough.—So much for Jere's Fun. This Frolick, I suppose, according to the Sailors Reasoning, is to conjure up a Prize.

This Morning the Captain ordered all Hands upon Deck and took an account of the Number of Souls on board which amounted to 172. Then he ordered the Articles of War to be read to them—after which he ordered all Hands upon the Forecastle and then all Hands upon the Quarter deck, in order to try Experiments, for determining whether any difference was made in the Ships sailing, by the Weight of the Men being forward or abaft. Then all Hands were ordered to their Quarters to exercise them at the Guns. Mr. Barron[2] gave the Words of Command and they spent an Hour perhaps in the Exercise, at which they seemed tolerably expert. Then the Captain ordered a Dance, upon the Main Deck, and all Hands, Negroes, Boys and Men were obliged to dance. After this the old Sailors set on Foot another Frolic, called the Miller, or the Mill. I will not spend Time to describe this odd Scæne: but it ended in a very high frolic, in which almost all the Men were powdered over, with Flour, and wet again to the Skin.—Whether these whimsical Diversions are indulged, in order to make the Men wash themselves, and shift their Cloaths, and to wash away Vermin I dont know. But there is not in them the least Ray of Elegance, very little Wit, and a humour of the coarsest Kind. It is not superiour to Negro and Indian Dances.

[1] Thus in MS. The meaning is clear, but there is no lexicographical authority for this word.

[2] William Barron, of a Virginia family that furnished a number of American naval officers, was first lieutenant of the *Boston* (Sheppard, *Tucker*, p. 280; *VMHB*, 1:66 [July 1893]). For his tragic fate, see entries of 14 and 27 March below.

1778. MARCH 8. SUNDAY.

The same Wind and Weather continues, and We go at 7 and 1/2 and 8 Knots. We are supposed to be past the Western Islands.

Mr. Barrons our first Lt. appears to me to be an excellent Officer—very dilligent, and attentive to his Duty—very thoughtfull and considerate about the Safety of the Ship, and about order, Œconomy and Regularity, among the officers, and Men. He has great Experience at Sea. Has used the Trade to London, Lisbon, Affrica, West Indies, Southern States &c.

This Morning, the Captain ordered all Hands upon Quarter Deck to Prayers. The Captains Clerk, Mr. Wm. Cooper, had prepared a Composition of his own, which was a very decent, and comprehensive Prayer, which he delivered, in a grave and proper manner. The Officers and Men all attended, in clean Cloaths, and behaved very soberly.

The Weather has been cloudy all Day. Towards night it became rainy and windy, and now the Ship rolls, a little in the old Fashion.— We are about 2000 Miles from Boston.

The late Storm shewed the Beauty of Boileaus Description d'une Tempête.

> Comme l'on voit les flots, soûlevez par l'orage,
> Fondre sur un Vaisseau qui s'oppose a leur rage,
> Le Vent avec fureur dans les voiles frêmit;
> La mer blanchit d'écume et l'air au loin gémit;
> Le matelot troublè, que son Art abandonne,
> Croit voir dans chaque flot la mort qui l'environne.
> Trad. de Longin.

1778. MARCH 9. MONDAY.

Last Night the Wind shifted to the N. West, and blew fresh. It is now still fairer for Us than before. The Weather is fine, and We go on our Voyage at a great Rate. Some Officers think We shall reach our Port by Thursday night: others by Saturday night: But these make no Account of Chases and Cruises, and make no Allowance for the Variability of the Winds.

SATURDAY. MARCH 14.

I have omitted inserting the Occurrences of this Week, on Account of the Hurry and Confusion, We have been in. Tuesday We spied a Sail, and gave her Chase. We soon came up with her, but as We had bore directly down upon her, she had not seen our broadside, and knew not her [i.e. our] Force. She was a Letter of Mark with 14 Guns, 8 Nines and 6 sixes. She fired upon Us, and one of her shot went thro our Mizen Yard. I happened to be upon the Quarter deck, and in the Direction from the Ship to the Yard so that the Ball went directly over my Head. We, upon this, turned our broadside which the instant she saw she struck. Captn. Tucker very prudently, ordered his officers not to fire.

The Prize is the Ship Martha, Captn. McIntosh from London to New York, loaded with a Cargo of great Value. The Captn. told me that Seventy thousand Pounds sterling was insured upon her at Lloyds, and that She was worth 80 thousands.[1]

The Captain is very much of a Gentleman. There are two Gentlemen with him Passengers, the one Mr. R. Gault, the other Mr. Wallace of N. York. Two young Jews were on board.

That and the next day was spent in dispatching the Prize, under the Command of the 3d Lt. Mr. Welch to Boston.[2]

After that We fell in Chase of another Vessell, and overtaking her, found her to be a french Snow, from Bourdeaux to Miquelon.

We then saw another Vessell, chased and came up with her which proved to be a French Brig from Marseilles to Nantes. This last cost Us very dear. Mr. Barrons our 1st. Lt. attempting to fire a Gun, as a signal to the Brig, the Gun burst, and tore the right Leg of this excellent Officer, in Pieces, so that the Dr. was obliged to amputate it, just below the Knee.

I was present at this affecting Scæne and held Mr. Barron in my Arms while the Doctor put on the Turnequett and cutt off the Limb.

Mr. Barrons bore it with great Fortitude and Magnanimity—thought he should die, and frequently intreated me, to take Care of his Family. He had an helpless Family he said, and begged that I would take Care of his Children. I promised him, that by the first Letters I should write to America, I would earnestly recommend his Children to the Care of the Public, as well as of Individuals. I cannot but think the Fall of this Officer, a great Loss to the united States. . . .[3] His Prudence, his Moderation, his Attention, his Zeal, were Qualities much wanted in our Navy. He is by Birth a Virginian.[4]

[1] See also the entry in Tucker's Log, 11 March, which is, however, not very informative, being largely given over to a list of the prisoners taken in the *Martha* (printed in Sheppard, *Tucker*, p. 273–275). JA elaborates a little on the incident in his Autobiography under date of 10 March.

Various romanticized versions of JA's part in the action were widely circulated after his death. CFA cites one of these in a note on this passage (JA, *Works*, 3:109), taken from Peleg Sprague's *Eulogy on John Adams and Thomas Jefferson*, Hallowell, Maine, 1826. Samuel Tucker was still living at this time; Sprague's fanciful narrative came to Tucker's attention, and he put the matter straight in a letter to James Hovey of Bristol, Maine, 22 Aug. 1826, which has come to rest in the Adams Papers:

"About the 20th of March I fell in with a very large Ship—armed but not a cruiser, but however she soon appeared in a posture of engageing, my Ship in readiness and men at their quarters, it became my duty to give Mr. Adams such information as was necessary. He followed me on deck, where we expostulated a few minutes on the subject of taking the Ship, finally after listening a minute or two, to my entreaties he took me by the hand, with a god bless you, and descended the gangway ladder into the cockpit, I stept aft and came alongside the Ship I hailed, his answer was a broadside and immediately struck his coulours, before I could, to a good advantage discharge a broadside into him, being very near and in such a position the smoke blew over my ship, and looking round on the Quarter deck and observing the Damage I had received from his fire, I discovered Mr. Adams Among my marines accoutred as one of them, and in the act of defence. I then went unto him and Said my dear Sir, how came you here, and with a smile

he replied; I ought to do my Share of fighting. This was Sufficient for me to judge of the bravery of my venerable and patriotic Adams and the foregoing is all that ever I related on that Subject to anyone and quite enough to convince them of the bravery of Such a Man, please to have this inserted in the Bath Maine Gazette, and in Compliance Youll Much oblige Yours with Respect,
Samuel Tucker

"N.B. You may Shew this to any American Republican or whomsoever you please."

[2] Tucker's orders to Hezekiah Welch, 11 March 1778, are printed in Sheppard, *Tucker*, p. 83.

[3] Suspension points in MS.

[4] Lt. Barron died eleven or twelve days later; see entry of 27 March, below, and Jennison, "Journal," *PMHB*, 15:103 (April 1891). There is evidence that JA kept his pledge to write on behalf of Barron's family: In Congress, 27 Nov. 1778, "A letter from Hon. J. Adams, Esq. respecting the late Lieutenant Barron's family, was read: *Ordered,* That it be referred to the Marine Committee" (*JCC,* 12:1165). No trace of this letter has so far been found, either in the Papers of the Continental Congress or in the pension application filed in 1837 by his only daughter and surviving heir, Ann Mortimer Barron of Norfolk, Va. (DNA:RG 15, R 1065). The pension claim was rejected, but Congress had already (30 June 1834) granted Ann Barron the half pay of a first lieutenant of a frigate for seven years (letters from General Reference Branch, National Archives, to the editors, 13 Jan., 16 May 1959). There is also evidence that JA endeavored to do something in behalf of Barron's orphaned children during his brief return to Massachusetts in 1779; see William Vernon Sr. to AA, 4 Feb. 1780 (Adams Papers). But in his Autobiography JA expressed regret that he had not done more.

1778. MARCH 19. THURSDAY.

I have scarcely been able to stand, or sit, without holding fast, with both my Hands, upon some lashed Table, some lashed Gun, the Side, or Beams of the Ship, or some other fixed Object: such has been the perpetual Motion of the Ship arising from violent Gales, and an heavy Sea.

In the Course of the last 5 days, We have seen a great Number of Vessells, two of which at least, if not four were supposed to be Cruizers. But here We are—at Liberty, as yet.

The Wind has been directly against Us, but this Morning has veered and We now steer, at least our Head lies by the Compass, South East. —Who knows but Providence has favoured Us by the last Gale, as it seemed to do by the first.—By the last Gale We have already escaped Cruizers as We did by the first—and possibly this violent Gale from the south East may have driven all the Cruizers from the Coast of Spain and the Southerly Part of the Bay of Biscay, and by this Means have opened a clear Passage for Us to Bourdeaux. This is possible— and so is the contrary. God knows—

MARCH 20 FRYDAY.

Yester Afternoon, the Weather cleared up, and the Wind came

about very fair. We had a great Run, last Night. This Morning spyed a Sail, under our leward Bow, chased and soon came up with her, a Snow from Amsterdam to Demarara, and Essequibo.

I made Enquiry to day of our Prisoner Captn. McIntosh, concerning the Trinity House. He says it is the richest Corporation in the Kingdom. That Lord Sandwich is an elder Brother of it. That any Master of a Vessell may be made a younger Brother of it, if he will. That there are many Thousands of younger Brothers. That this House gives permission to every Vessell to take out or to take in Ballast, and that a few Pence 6d. perhaps per Ton are paid them for such Licence. That they have the Care of all Lighthouses &c.

My principal Motive for omitting to keep a regular and particular Journal, has been the Danger of falling into the Hands of my Enemies, and an Apprehension that I should not have an Opportunity of destroying these Papers in such a Case.

We have now so fine a Wind, that a very few days will determine, whether We shall meet any capital Disaster, or arrive safe at Port.

21. SATURDAY.

Five Weeks Yesterday, since my Embarkation. This Morning an heavy Wind, and high Sea. We go E.S.E.

27. FRYDAY.

On Wednesday Evening Mr. Barons died, and Yesterday was committed to the Deep, from the Quarter Deck.

He was put into a Chest, and 10 or 12, twelve Pounds shot put in with him, and then nailed up. The Fragment of the Gun, which destroyed him was lashed on the Chest, and the whole launched overboard through one of the Ports, in Presence of all the Ships Crew, after the Buryal service was read by Mr. Cooper.[1]

In the Course of the last Week We have had some of the Worst Winds, that We have felt yet.

Monday last We made the Land upon the Coast of Spain.

Tuesday We run into the Bay of St. Anthonio. 4 or 5 Boats with 15 or 16 Men in each came to Us, out of which We took a Pilot.

Upon sight of the Spanish Shore, which I viewed as minutely as possible through the Glasses, I had a great Curiosity to go on Shore. There was a fine Verdure, near the sea, altho the Mountains were covered with Snow. I saw one Convent, but We did not come in Sight of the Town. The Moment we were about turning the Point of the

Rock to go into the Harbour, a Sail appeared. We put out to see who she was, found her a Spanish Brig, and after this upon repeated Efforts found it impracticable to get into the Harbour. In the Night the Wind caught us suddenly at N.W. and We were obliged to make all the Sail We could and put to sea. We steered our Course for Bourdeaux.

Yesterday was a Calm, the little Wind there was, directly against Us. This Morning the Wind is a little better. We are supposed to be within 30 Leagues of Bourdeaux River.

[1] See Tucker, Log, entry of 26 April (printed in Sheppard, *Tucker,* p. 280).

MARCH 28. SATURDAY.

Last night and this Morning We were in the thoroughfare of all the Ships from Bourdeaux. We had always a great Number in Sight. By Obs[ervation] to day, our Lat. is 46D.:3M. North, about 7 Minutes South of the Middle of the Isle of Rea. We are therefore about 20 Leagues from the Tower of Cordoan. We have no Wind, and nothing can be more tedious and disagreable to me, than this idle Life.

Last Evening We had two little Incidents which were disagreable. One was, the French Barber attempting to go below, contrary to orders, the Centinell cutt off his great Toe with his Cutlass, which raised at first a little, ill blood in the French People, who are on board, but on Enquiry finding the fellow deserved it, they acquiesced. The other unpleasant Incident was that one of our Prisoners of War, a little more elevated than usual grew out of Temper, and was very passionate with Mr. Vernon and afterwards, with C. Palmes—but it has all subsided.[1]

Mr. McIntosh is of North Britain, and appears to be very decided vs. America in this Contest, and his Passions are so engaged that they easily inkindle. . . .[2]

Mr. Gault is an Irish Gentleman and as decided vs. America, in her Claims of Independance at least, as the other. Mr. Wallace is more reserved, cautious, silent and secret.

Jealousies arise among our Men, that the Prisoners are plotting with some of our profligate People: but I believe this Jealousy is groundless.

All Day Yesterday, and all the forenoon of this Day We have been looking out for Land—about 4 o Clock We found it—the Isles of Rhee and Oleron, between which two is the Entrance into the Harbour of Rochelle, which is about half Way between Bourdeaux and Nantes. . . . The Land is extremely flat and low. We see the Tower. . . . The Water is shoal, 25 or 30 Fathoms, the bottom Sand—the Reverse of the Spanish Coast on the other Side of the Bay of Biscay.

This Afternoon, a clock calm, and Mr. Goss played upon his Fiddle the whole Afternoon, and the Sailors danced, which seemed to have a very happy Effect upon their Spirits and good Humour.

Numbers of small Birds from the Shore, came along to day, some of them fatigued, allighted on our Rigging, Yards &c. and one of them We caught. A little Lark he was called. These Birds loose the Shore and get lost, and then fly untill they are so fatigued that the instant they allight upon a Ship they drop to sleep.

[1] Richard Palmes, captain of marines on the *Boston*; see Sheppard, *Tucker*, p. 93–94; *Warren-Adams Letters*, 1:372. The incident is elaborated in JA's Auto-biography under this date.

[2] Suspension points here and below in this entry are in the MS.

1778. MARCH 29. SUNDAY.

Becalmed all last Night. This Morning a vast Number of Sails in Sight. St. Martins, and Oleron in Sight, many Towers and Windmills —Land very low and level.

A Pilot Boat, with two Sails and 4 Men, came on Board, and the Pilot instantly undertook to pilot Us to Bourdeaux. He says this ship may go up quite to the City, if she draws 20 feet of Water, at high Water.—We are now sailing very agreably towards our Port.

The Pilot says War is declared, last Wednesday, and that the Pavillions were hoisted Yesterday at every Fort and Light House.—Quære.[1]

There is a civil Frenchman on board, whose Name I never asked untill to day. His Name is Quillau, Fourier des Logis de Mr. Le Ct. D'Artois. He was not of M. De Coudrays Corps.

The French Gentlemen on board can scarcely understand our new Pilot. He speaks Gascoine, the Dialect of Bourdeaux, they say, which is not good French.

This Day Six Weeks We sailed from Nantaskett Road. How many Dangers, Distresses and Hairbreadth Scapes have We seen?

A Story.—Garrick had a Relation, convicted of a capital Offence. He waited on his Majesty, to beg a Pardon. The K. asked what was the Crime?—He has only taken *a Cup too much*, says Garrick, may it please your Majesty.—Is that all? said the K. Let him be pardoned.—*Gault*.

A Story. A Frenchman in London advertised an infallible Remedy against Fleas. The Ladies all flocked to purchase the Powder. But after they had bought it, one of them asked for Directions to Use it.—Madam says the Frenchman you must catch the Flea, and squese him between your Fingers untill he gape, then you must put a little of this Powder in his Mouth, and I will be responsible he never will bite you again.—

✠
D. PEDRO MARTIN CERMEÑO

GARCIA DE PAREDES, CAVALLERO DE LA ORDEN
de Alcantara, Administrador de Villafamès en la de
Montesa, Teniente General de los Reales Exercitos,
del Consejo de S. M. en el Supremo de Guerra, Go-
vernador, y Comandante General del Reyno de Galicia, y Presidente de su Real Audiencia.

Por quanto Dn Juan Adams Ministro Plenipo
tenciario delas Provincias Unidas de America destinado ala Cort
de Paris con dos Hijos suios, el Secret.º de Embajada, su oficial,
y cinco Dependientes, y Criados deambos, pasan a Francia, dirigien
dose por Madrid, y Bilbao, ó por la via que mas sele acomode:
Portanto mando alos Cavos Militares, y Ministros de Justicia
sugetos ami Jurisn. yalos que nolo son pido, yencargo, noles pongan
envarazo ensu Viage antesbien les den quantos auxilios necesitaren, ylos
Carros, Bagages, y viveres que pidieren pagandolos alos precios reglados
por convenir asi al R.l servicio: Coruña 18 de Diziembre de 1779—

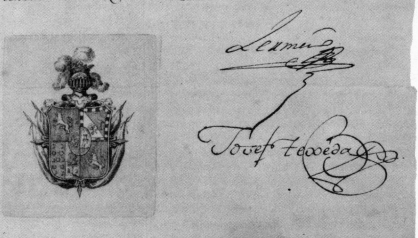

Lermé

Josef Texeda

8. TRADE CARD OF JOHN ADAMS' PARIS STATIONER,

But says the Lady, when I have him between my Fingers, why may I not rub him to death?—Oh Madam dat will do just as well den!— *Tucker.*

We have been becalmed all day in Sight of Oleron. The Village of St. Dennis was in Sight, and Multitudes of Wind Mills and Sand Hills all along the shore. Multitudes of Vessells in sight, French, Spanish, Dutch Vessells, and English Smugglers.

I feel a Curiosity to visit this Island of Oleron so famous in Antiquity for her Sea Laws, at least I take this to be the Place.

[1] A very proper query. France had recognized and formed an alliance with the United States by treaties of alliance and commerce signed at Versailles on 6 Feb.; the French ambassador in London, the Marquis de Noailles, had so notified the British government on 13 March; and diplomatic relations were at once broken off. But war was never formally declared between the two powers.

MARCH 30. MONDAY.

This Morning at 5, the Officer came down and told the Captain that a lofty Ship was close by Us, and had fired two heavy Guns. All Hands called. She proved to be an heavy loaded Snow.

The Weather cloudy, but no Wind. Still—except a small Swell.

The Tour of Cordovan, or in other Words Bourdeaux Lighthouse in Sight, over our larbord Bow.

The Captn. is now cleaning Ship and removing his Warlike Appearances.

This Day has been hitherto fortunate and happy.—Our Pilot has brought us safely into the River, and We have run up, with Wind and Tide as far as Pouliac, where We have anchored for the Night, and have taken in another Pilot.

This forenoon a Fisherman came along Side, with Hakes, Skates, and Gennetts. We bought a few, and had an high Regale.

This River is very beautifull—on both Sides the Plantations are very pleasant. On the South Side especially, We saw all along Horses, Oxen, Cowes, and great Flocks of Sheep grazing, the Husbandmen ploughing &c. and the Women, half a Dozen in a Drove with their Hoes. The Churches, Convents, Gentlemens seats, and the Villages appear very magnificent.

This River seldom Swells with Freshes, for the rural Improvements and even the Fishermens Houses, are brought quite down to the Waters Edge. The Water in the River is very foul to all Appearance, looking all the Way like a Mud Puddle. The Tide setts in 5 Knots. We outrun every Thing in sailing up the River.

The Buildings public and private, are of Stone, and a great Number of beautifull Groves, appear between the grand Seats, and best Plantations. A great Number of Vessells lay in the River....[1]

The Pleasure resulting from the Sight of Land, Cattle, Houses, &c. after so long, so tedious, and dangerous a Voyage, is very great: It gives me a pleasing Melancholly to see this Country, an Honour which a few Months ago I never expected to arrive at.—Europe thou great Theatre of Arts, Sciences, Commerce, War, am I at last permitted to visit thy Territories.—May the Design of my Voyage be answered.

[1] Suspension points in MS.

MARCH 31. TUESDAY.

Lying in the River of Bourdeaux, near Pouliac. A 24 Gun Ship close by Us, under French Colours, bound to St. Domingue.—A dark, misty Morning.

My first Enquiry should be, who is Agent for the united States of America at Bourdeaux, at Blaye, &c.—who are the principal Merchants on this River concerned in the American Trade? What Vessells French or American, have sailed or are about sailing for America, what their Cargoes, and for what Ports? Whether on Account of the united States, of any particular State, or of private Merchants french or American?

This Morning the Captain and a Passenger came on board the Boston, from the Julie, a large Ship bound to St. Domingue, to make Us a Visit. They invited Us on Board to dine. Captn. Palmes, M[aste]rs Jesse and Johnny and myself, went. We found half a Dozen genteel Persons on Board, and found a pretty ship, an elegant Cabin, and every Accommodation. The white Stone Plates were laid, and a clean Napkin placed in each, and a Cut of fine Bread. The Cloth, Plates, Servants, every Thing was as clean, as in any Gentlemans House. The first Dish was a fine french Soup, which I confess I liked very much.— Then a Dish of boiled Meat.—Then the Lights of a Calf, dressed one Way and the Liver another.—Then roasted Mutton then fricaseed Mutton. A fine Sallad and something very like Asparagus, but not it. —The Bread was very fine, and it was baked on board.—We had then Prunes, Almonds, and the most delicate Raisins I ever saw.—Dutch Cheese—then a Dish of Coffee—then a french Cordial—and Wine and Water, excellent Claret with our Dinner.—None of us understood French—none of them English: so that Dr. Noel stood Interpreter. While at Dinner We saw a Pinnace go on board the Boston with several, half a Dozen, genteel People on board.

On the Quarter Deck, I was struck with the Hens, Capons, and Cocks in their Coops—the largest I ever saw.

After a genteel Entertainment, Mr. Griffin, one of our petty Officers, came with the Pinnace, and C. Tuckers Compliments desiring to see me. We took Leave and returned where We found very genteel Company consisting of the Captn. of another Ship bound to Martinique and several Kings Officers, bound out. One was the Commandant.

C. Palmes was sent forward to Blaye, in the Pinnace to the Officer at the Castle in order to produce our Commission and procure an Entry, and pass to Bourdeaux. Palmes came back full of the Compliments of the Broker to the Captn. and to me. I shall not repeat the Compliments sent to me, but he earnestly requested that C. Tucker would salute the Fort with 13 Guns, &c.—which the Captn. did.

All the Gentlemen We have seen to day agree that Dr. Franklin has been received by the K[ing] in great Pomp and that a Treaty is concluded, and they all expect War, every Moment....[1]

This is a most beautifull River, the Villages, and Country Seats appear upon each Side all the Way. We have got up this Afternoon within 3 Leagues of the Town.

[1] Suspension points in MS.

1778 APRIL 1. WEDNESDAY.

This Morning Mr. J. C. Champagne, negociant and Courtier de Marine, at Blaye, came on board, to make a Visit and pay his Compliments.

He says, that of the first Grouths of Wine, in the Province of Guienne, there are four Sorts, Chateau Margeaux, Hautbrion, La Fitte, and Latour.

This Morning I took Leave of the Ship, and went up to Town with my Son, and servant, Mr. Vernon, Mr. Jesse, and Dr. Noel, in the Pinnace. When We came up to the Town We had the Luck to see Mr. McClary,[1] and Major Fraser [Frazer], on the Shore. Mr. McClary came on board our Boat, and conducted Us up to his Lodgings. Mr. Pringle was there. We dined there, in the Fashion of the Country. We had fish and Beans, and Salad, and Claret, Champain and Mountain Wine. After Dinner Mr. Bondfield, who is Agent here, invited me to take a Walk, which We did to his Lodgings, where We drank Tea.[2] Then We walked about the Town, and to see the new Comedie. After this We went to the Opera, where the Scenery, the Dancing, the Music, afforded to me a very chearfull, sprightly Amusement, having never seen any Thing of the Kind before. After this We returned to Mr. McClarys Lodgings, where We supped.

¹ That is, William McCreery, evidently from Baltimore, whom JA had known in America and who had recently "Setled in Bordeaux in the mercantile way" (AA to JA, 18 May 1778; JA, *Autobiography*, under the present date). JA and McCreery corresponded on commercial subjects for some years, though at first their letters rather amusingly centered on a pair of homespun breeches, lost by JQA in Bordeaux, that contained eight guineas sewed into the waistband. McCreery returned to America in 1781 (Franklin, *Writings*, ed. Smyth, 7:261, note). If he is the William McCreery who became a U.S. representative and senator from Maryland, the notice of him in *Biog. Dir. Cong.* is inadequate.

² John Bondfield was a merchant who served for many years as U.S. commercial agent at Bordeaux and whose surviving correspondence with JA and other American ministers in France is voluminous. JA says in his Autobiography under the present date that he had also known Bondfield in America, but his background is obscure. For a high opinion of his mercantile character see JA to William Vernon Jr., 12 May 1778 (LbC, Adams Papers). As late as 15 May 1789 Bondfield could write JA from Bordeaux: "I remain as when I had the Honor to see you at Bordeaux honor'd by the [American] Gentlemen at Paris with their Correspondence and publick and private Commissions and in my steddy Attention to every thing in my power to serve the States" (Adams Papers).

1778 APRIL 2. THURSDAY.

Walked round the Town, to see the Chamber and Council of Commerce, the Parliament which was sitting, where We heard the Council. Then We went round to the Ship Yards &c. Made many Visits—dined at the Hotel D'Angleterre. Visited the Customhouse, the Post office—visited the Commandant of the Chateau Trompette, a Work of Vaubans—visited the Premiere President of the Parliament of Bourdeaux. Went to the Coffee house. Went to the Commedie—saw Les deux Avares. Supped at Messrs. Reuiles De Basmarein and Raimbaux.¹

¹ The firm of Reculès de Basmarein et Raimbaux of Bordeaux were the "outstanding shipowners of France," and from them Lafayette had purchased the *Victoire*, in which he sailed to America just a year earlier (Gottschalk, *Lafayette*, 1:87–88, and ch. 7, *passim*).

APRIL 3. FRYDAY.

Waited on the Intendant, dined at Mr. Bondfields and supped at Mr. Le Texiers.—Our Company, on Thursday Evening, at Mr. Basmarains were—The Count of Virelade the Son of the Premiere President, Le Moine first Commissary of the Navy, Le Moine the Son, Commissary of the Navy, Cornie, Captain of a Frigate, Knight of St. Lewis, Jn. Bt. Nairac former Deputy of Commerce from La Rochelle, Paul Nairac, a Merchant, Elisee Nairac a Merchant, La tour Feger Esq. a Merchant, Menoire, Esq. a Merchant, Coutourier Esq. a Merchant,

Mr. Bondfield and Major Fraser. The Toasts were announced by 13 Shots, in honour of the 13 States. The K. of France 21 Shots. The Congress 13. G. Washington 3. Mr. De Sartine 3.[1] G[eneral] Gates 3. Marshall Broglie 3. The Count of Brolie his Brother 3. The Marquis De la Fayette 3. The Glory and Prosperity of the 13 united States 13. The Prosperity of France 3. Eternal Concord between the two Nations, now Friends and Allies, 3. The State of Massachusetts Bay and Mr. Adams its Representative. Mr. Destaing Vice Admiral. The City of Bourdeaux. Mrs. Adams 3. The French and American Ladies 21. The Departure of Mr. Adams, when he mounted his Coach, was saluted by 13. Shots. The Garden was beautifully illuminated, with an Inscription, God Save the Congress, Liberty and Adams.[2]

[1] Antoine Raymond Jean Gualbert Gabriel de Sartine, Comte d'Alby (1729–1801), French minister of marine, 1774–1780 (Hoefer, *Nouv. Biog. Générale*), with whom JA was to have extensive correspondence in his capacity as a joint commissioner to France.

[2] On this occasion JA learned something of the freedom of conversation between the sexes in France, and held his own, though not without a sense of shock; see his Autobiography under 2 April 1778.

1778 APRIL 4. SATURDAY.

About 10 O Clock We commenced our Journey to Paris, and went about 50 miles.

APRIL 5. SUNDAY.

Proceeded on our Journey, more than 100 Miles.

APRIL 6. MONDAY.

Arrived at Poictiers, the City so famous, for the Battle which was fought here. It is a beautifull situation and the Cultivation of the Plains about it is exquisite. The Houses are old and poor and the Streets very narrow. Afternoon passed thro Chatelerault, another City, nearly as large as Poictiers, and as old, and the Streets as narrow. When We stopped at the Post to change our Horses, about 20 young Women came about the Chaise, with their elegant Knives, scissors, tooth Picks &c. to sell. The Scæne was new to me, and highly diverting. Their eagerness to sell a Knife, was as great, as that of some Persons I have seen in other Countries to get Offices. We arrived in the Evening at Ormes, the magnificent Seat of the Marquis D'Argenson.— It is needless to make particular Remarks upon this Country. Every Part of it, is cultivated. The Fields of Grain, the Vineyards, the Castles, the Cities, the Parks, the Gardens, every Thing is beautifull: yet every Place swarms with Beggars.

1778. APRIL 7. TUESDAY.

Travelled from Les Ormes, the splendid Seat of the Marquis D'Argenson, to Mer. We went through Tours, and Amboise, and several other smaller Villages. Tours is the most elegant Place We have yet seen. It stands upon the River Loire, which empties itself at Nantes. We rode upon a Causey, made in the River Loire, for a great Number of Miles. The Meadows and River Banks were extremely beautifull.

APRIL 8. WEDNESDAY.

Rode through Orleans, &c. and arrived at Paris, about 9 O Clock. For 30 Miles from Paris or more the Road is paved, and the Scænes extreamly beautifull.

At Paris We went to several Hotels which were full—particularly the Hotell D'Artois, and the Hotell Bayonne. Then We were advised to the Hotell de Valois, where We found entertainment. But We could not have it without taking all the Chambers upon the floor which were four in Number, very elegant and richly furnished, at the small Price of two Crowns and an Half a Day, without any Thing to eat or drink. We send for Victuals to the Cooks. I took the Apartments only for two or three days.

At our Arrival last Night at a certain Barrier, We were stopped and searched, and paid the Duties for about 25 Bottles of Wine which we had left of the generous Present of Mr. Delap at Bourdeaux.

My little Son has sustained this long Journey of near 500 Miles at the Rate of an hundred Miles a day with the Utmost Firmness, as he did our fatiguing and dangerous Voyage.

Immediately on our Arrival, We were called upon for our Names, as We were at Mrs. Rives's at Bourdeaux.

We passed the Bridge, last Night over the Seine, and passed thro the Louvre. The Streets were crowded with Carriages, with Livery Servants.

1778 APRIL 9. THURSDAY.

This Morning the Bells, and Carriages, and various Cries in the Street make Noise enough, yet the City was very still last Night towards the Morning.

Le Hotell de Valois, en Rue de Richlieu, is the Name of the House and Street where I now am. Went to Passy, in a Coach, with Dr. Noel, and my Son.

Dr. Franklin presented to me the Compliments of Mr. Turgot, lately Comptroller of the Finances, and his Invitation to dine with him.[1] Went with Dr. Franklin and Mr. Lee and dined in Company with the Dutchess D'Anville, the Mother of the Duke De Rochefoucault, and twenty of the great People of France.—It is in vain to Attempt a Description of the Magnificence of the House, Gardens, Library, Furniture, or the Entertainment of the Table. Mr. Turgot has the Appearance of a grave, sensible and amiable Man. Came home and supped with Dr. Franklin on Cheese and Beer.[2]

[1] Anne Robert Jacques Turgot, Baron de l'Aulne (1727–1781), French statesman and *philosophe* (Hoefer, *Nouv. Biog. Générale*). It was a letter of Turgot's to Richard Price, concerning the new American state constitutions, written in 1778 and published in Price's *Observations on the Importance of the American Revolution*, London, 1784, that prompted JA to write a gigantic rebuttal entitled *A Defence of the Constitutions of Government of the United States of America*, London, 1787–1788; 3 vols. The personal and intellectual relations of JA and Turgot have been described, and JA's marginalia on Turgot's letter of 1778 printed, in Haraszti, *JA and the Prophets of Progress*, ch. 8, "Turgot's Attack on the American Constitutions." On the more immediate origins of JA's *Defence* see note on entry of 29 [i.e. 28] July 1786, below.

[2] This is the only intimation in the Diary that JA and JQA had joined Franklin's already numerous household in Passy, but a memorandum in JA's copy of the American Commissioners' accounts, 1777–1779 (in Lb/JA/35, Adams Papers, Microfilms, Reel No. 123), dated "Passi September 27 1778," states: "I arrived at Paris in the Evening of the 8th of April, and the next Morning, waited on Dr. Franklin at Passi, where I have resided from that Time."

Franklin's lodgings were in a separate building on the extensive grounds of the Hôtel de Valentinois, named for a former owner but acquired in 1776 by M. Le Ray de Chaumont (see next entry in this Diary), on the heights of Passy close to the Bois de Boulogne and overlooking the Seine and Paris to the east. The once semirural suburb of Passy is now engulfed by Paris, and blocks of apartments shut off the view that Franklin and his colleagues enjoyed; but see a plan of "Franklin's Passy," with explanatory text, in Bernard Faÿ, *Franklin, the Apostle of Modern Times*, Boston, 1929, facing p. 452, and a detail from an 18th-century map of the neighborhood in Howard C. Rice Jr., *The Adams Family in Auteuil, 1784–1785*, Boston, 1956. A contemporary description of the Valentinois gardens will be found in Dezallier, *Environs de Paris*, 1779, p. 16–18. The building occupied by Franklin and his entourage and by JA in succession to Silas Deane was variously called the "pavilion," the "basse cour," and the "petit hôtel"; a tablet now marks its site on a building at the corner of Rue Reynouard and Rue Singer. The American headquarters at Passy have been described by nearly all of Franklin's biographers, but perhaps in most detail by John Bigelow (who as American minister in Paris at one time hoped to acquire the site for a United States legation), in an article entitled "Franklin's Home and Host in France," *Century Mag.*, 35:741–754 (March 1888). The "petit hôtel" survived until at least 1866.

APRIL 10. FRYDAY.

Dined at Monsr. Brillon's, with many Ladies and Gentlemen....[1] Madam Brillon is a Beauty, and a great Mistress of Music, as are her two little Daughters.... The Dinner was Luxury as usual—a Cake was brought in, with 3 Flaggs, flying. On one, Pride subdued—on another, Hæc Dies, in qua fit Congressus, exultemus et potemus in ea. Supped in the Evening, at Mr. Chamonts.[2] In the evening 2 Gentlemen came in, and advised me, to go to Versailles tomorrow. One of them was the Secretary to the late Ambassador in London, the Count De Noailles.[3]

[1] Suspension points, here and below, in MS. The Brillons and particularly Mme. Brillon were among Franklin's most intimate French friends; see Bernard Faÿ, *Franklin, the Apostle of Modern Times*, Boston, 1929, p. 463–468.

[2] Jacques Donatien Le Ray de Chaumont the elder (1725–1803), capitalist, holder of numerous government sinecures, enthusiast in the American cause, and a heavy speculator in contracts for supplying the Continental army and outfitting American naval vessels. Upon Franklin's arrival in France in Dec. 1776 Chaumont offered him accommodations rent-free at the Hôtel de Valentinois, and there Franklin maintained his headquarters until he returned to America in 1785. JA's relations with Chaumont during his shorter stay in Passy were more troubled, as will appear from their correspondence and other evidence. On Chaumont and his family, which was to have continuing connections with America, see John Bigelow's article cited in note on preceding entry, and T. Wood Clarke,

Emigrés in the Wilderness, N.Y., 1941, especially chs. 2–3.

[3] Emmanuel Marie Louis, Marquis de Noailles (1743–1822), uncle of the Marquise de Lafayette; he had returned from London after notifying the British government of the Franco-American alliance (Hoefer, *Nouv. Biog. Générale*). His secretary in London, previously *chargé d'affaires* there, was Charles Jean Garnier (1738–1783?), a rather shadowy figure but one who, from several of JA's allusions to him, was regarded as influential in the French foreign office and an expert on British affairs. He was well known to English sympathizers with the American cause, and in 1779 JA thought he would be sent as a successor to Gérard, the first French minister in Philadelphia. See entries of 21 April, 8 May 1778, 9 Feb., 2 July 1779, below; also Doniol, *Histoire*, 5:658, and references there; R. H. Lee, *Arthur Lee*, 2:87. (Garnier's forenames and dates have been furnished by the Service des Archives Diplomatiques et de la Documentation, Paris.)

APRIL 11. SATURDAY.

Went to Versailles, with Dr. Franklin and Mr. Lee—waited on the Count De Vergennes, the Secretary of foreign Affairs—was politely received.—He hoped I should stay long enough to learn French perfectly—assured me, that every Thing should be done to make France agreable to me—hoped the Treaty would be agreable, and the Alliance lasting.—I told him I thought the Treaty liberal, and generous—and doubted not of its speedy Ratification. I communicated to him the Resolutions of Congress respecting the Suspension of Burgoines Embarkation, which he read through, and pronounced Fort bon.[1]

I was then conducted to the Count Maurepas, the Prime Minister, was introduced by Dr. F. as his new Colleague and politely received.

I was then shewn the Palace of Versailles, and happened to be present when the King passed through, to Council. His Majesty seeing my Colleagues, graciously smiled, and passed on. I was then shewn the Galleries, and Royal Apartments, and the K's Bedchamber. The Magnificence of these Scænes, is immense. The Statues, the Paintings, the every Thing is sublime.

We then returned, went into the City, and dined with the Count where was the Count De Noailles, his Secretary, and 20 or 30 others, of the Grandees of France. After Dinner, We went in the Coach, to see the Royal Hospital of Invalids, the Chappell of which is immensely grand, in Marble and Paintings and Statuary.

After this We went to the Ecole militaire, went into the Chapell and into the Hall of Council &c. Here We saw the Statues of the great Conde, Turenne, Luxembourg, and Saxe. Returned and drank Tea, at Mm. Brillons, who lent me Voyage picturesque de Paris,[2] and entertained Us, again, with her Music, and her agreable Conversation.

[1] These resolves, voted 8 Jan. 1778, are in JCC, 10:29–35.

[2] [Antoine Nicolas Dezallier d'Argenville,] *Voyage pittoresque de Paris, ou indication de tout ce qu'il y a de plus beau dans cette ville, en peinture, sculpture & architecture, par M. D****. JA acquired a copy of the 6th edition of this useful work when he returned to Paris in 1780; it is among his books in the Boston Public Library and has proved useful in annotating his Diary.

1778 APRIL 12. SUNDAY.

The Attention to me, which has been shewn, from my first Landing in France, at Bourdeaux, by the People in Authority of all Ranks and by the principal Merchants, and since my Arrival in Paris by the Ministers of State, and others of the first Consideration has been very remarkable, and bodes well to our Country. It shews in what Estimation the new Alliance with America is held.

On Fryday last, I had the Honour of a Visit from a Number of American Gentlemen—Mr. James Jay of New York Brother of the C[hief] Justice, Mr. Johnson Brother of Governor of Maryland,[1] Mr. , Mr. Amiel, Mr. Livingston, from Jamaica, Mr. Austin from Boston,[2] Dr. Bancroft. Mr. R. Issard [Izard] should be [*sentence unfinished*]

I must return the Visits of these Gentlemen.

This Day I had the Honour to dine with the Prince De Tingry, Le Duke De Beaumont, of the illustrious House of Montmorency, the Duke and Dutchess of [*sentence unfinished*]

Edisti satis, lusisti satis, atque bibisti
Tempus est abire tibi.—

Written under the Picture of Sir Rob. Walpole. Some one made an amendment of Bribisti instead of Bibisti.

[1] Joshua Johnson (1742–1802), born in Calvert co., Md., brother of Gov. Thomas Johnson of Maryland, was employed in London as factor of an Annapolis shipping firm until the Revolution. He then crossed to France en route to America, but having several small children he was discouraged by the prospect of a long sea voyage and settled as a merchant at Nantes, where he undertook various commissions for both Congress and the State of Maryland. JA and JQA visited the Johnsons in Nantes before returning to America in 1779. Johnson returned to London after the war and served as first U.S. consul there, 1790–1797. While on diplomatic service in London, JQA courted Johnson's daughter Louisa Catherine (1775–1852), and was married to her in 1797. See JA, Autobiography, under the present date; entry of 14 April 1779, below; *Md. Hist. Mag.*, 42:214–215 (Sept. 1947); JCC, 15:1126; *Archives of Maryland*, Baltimore, 1883– , 21:7, 140; 43:225; 47:79; Edward S. Delaplaine, *The Life of Thomas Johnson*, N.Y., 1927, p. 14; Bemis, JQA, 1:79–82; letter of Julia B. Carroll, Foreign Affairs Branch, The National Archives, to the editors, 22 Oct. 1959.

[2] Jonathan Loring Austin, Harvard 1766, who had brought the news of Burgoyne's surrender to France the previous fall and then served Franklin in various capacities; during the summer of 1778 he acted as secretary to JA (JA, Autobiography, under the present date; Wharton, ed., *Dipl. Corr. Amer. Rev.*, 1:620–621, 630–631; JA–Austin correspondence in Adams Papers).

1778. MONDAY. APRIL 13.

This Morning the Dutchess Dayen, and M. le Marquise De Fayette,[1] came to visit me, and enquire after the Marquise [Marquis].

Went to Versailles, was introduced, to the Levee of Mr. de Sartine, the Minister. A vast Number of Gentlemen were attending in one Room after another, and We found the Minister at last, entrenched as deep as We had formerly seen the Count Maurepas. The Minister politely received Us, and shewed Us, into his Cabinet, where were all the Books and Papers of his office.—After he had finished the Business of his Levee, he came into the Cabinet to Us, and asked whether I spoke French, and whether I understood French? The Answer was, un Peu, and Si on parle lentement, ou doucement.[2] He then made an Apology, to each of Us seperately, in the Name of his Lady, for her Absence, being gone into Paris to see a sick Relation. After this We were conducted down to dinner, which was as splendid as usual. All Elegance and Magnificence, a large Company, four Ladies only....[3] During Dinner Time many Gentlemen came in, and walked the Room, and leaned over the Chairs of the Ladies and Gentlemen, and conversed with them while at Table. After Dinner the Company all arose as usual, went into another Room, where a great

Additional Number of Gentlemen came in.—After some Time We came off, and went to make a Visit to Madam Maurepas, the Lady of the Prime Minister, but she was out and We left a Card. We then went to the office of the Secretary[4] of Mr. Vergennes and delivered him a Copy of my Commission—then went and made a Visit to Madam Vergennes, who had her Levee, and returned to Passi.

[1] The Duchesse d'Ayen and her daughter, Adrienne de Noailles, Marquise de Lafayette.

[2] According to JA's Autobiography under this date, the answer was made by Franklin.

[3] Suspension points in MS.

[4] Joseph Mathias Gérard de Rayneval (1746–1812), usually called Rayneval by JA, brother of Conrad Alexandre Gérard (1729–1790), the first French minister to the United States. The younger brother had just succeeded the elder as *premier commis* or secretary in the French foreign office, a circumstance that has led to their often being confused with each other. See *Despatches and Instructions of Conrad Alexandre Gérard,* ed. John J. Meng, Baltimore, 1939, p. 35, note, and *passim.*

AVRIL 14. MARDI.

Yesterday Morning sent for the Master of the Accademy in this Place, who came and shewed me his Conditions. [He] agreed to take my Son: who accordingly packed up his Things and went to School, much pleased with his Prospect because he understood that Rewards were given to the best Schollars, which he said was an Encouragement. Dancing, Fencing, Musick, and Drawing, are taught at this School, as well as French and Latin.[1]

[1] In a letter to his "Hond. Mamma," 20 April (Adams Papers), JQA described the regimen of M. Le Coeur's private boarding school. Among his American schoolmates were Jesse Deane, "Benny" Bache (Franklin's grandson), and Charles B. Cochran, the last of whom wrote JQA from Charleston, S.C., 5 June 1809, in a reminiscent vein about their school "Sur La Montagne de Crêve-Cœur" (Adams Papers). JQA replied from Ghent, 18 July 1814, with his recollections (RC, privately owned, printed in *AHR*, 15:572–574 [April 1910]).

AVRIL 15. MECREDI.

Went Yesterday to return the Visits, made me by American Gentlemen.

Dined this Day, with Madam Helvetius, one Gentleman, one Lady, Dr. F., his G. Son[1] and myself made the Company—an elegant Dinner. Mm. is a Widow—her Husband was a Man of Learning and wrote several Books. She has erected a Monument to her Husband, a Model of which she has. It is herself, weeping over his Tomb, with this Inscription. Toi dont L'Ame sublime et tendre, a fait ma Gloire, et mon Bonheur, J t'ai perdu: pres de ta Cendre, Je viens jouer de ma Douleur.

Here I saw a little Book of Fenelons, which I never saw before—

Directions pour la Conscience D'une Roi, composees pour l'Instruction du Louis de France, Duc de Bourgogne.

At Mm. Helvetius's, We had Grapes, preserved entire. I asked how? She said "Sans Air."—Apples, Pairs &c. are preserved here in great Perfection.

[1] William Temple Franklin (1762–1823), natural son of Benjamin Franklin's natural son William (Franklin, *Papers*, ed. Labaree and Bell, 1:lxii–lxiii). Temple, as he was usually called, was serving as his grandfather's secretary.

APRIL 16. JEUDI.

Dr. F. is reported to speak French very well, but I find upon attending to him that he does not speak it Grammatically, and indeed upon enquiring, he confesses that he is wholly inattentive to the Grammar. His Pronunciation too, upon which the French Gentlemen and Ladies compliment him, and which he seems to think is pretty well, I am sure is very far from being exact.

Indeed Dr. Franklin's Knowledge of French, at least his Faculty of speaking it, may be said to have begun with his Embassy to this Court. . . .[1] He told me that when he was in France before, Sir John Pringle was with him, and did all his Conversation for him as Interpreter, and that he understood and spoke French with great Difficulty, untill he came here last, altho he read it.

Dined, at Mr. La Freté's. The Magnificence of the House, Garden and Furniture is astonishing. Saw here an History of the Revolution in Russia in the Year 1762.[2]

This Family are fond of Paintings. They have a Variety of exquisite Pieces, particularly a Storm and a Calm.[3]

[1] Suspension points in MS.
[2] See entry of 29 May, below.
[3] This dinner party at Suresnes is described much more fully in JA's Autobiography under this date.

APRIL 17. VENDREDI.

Dined at home with Company—Mr. Platt and his Lady—Mr. Amiel and his Lady—Mr. Austin—Mr. Alexander &c.

After Dinner, went to the long Champ, where all the Carriages in Paris were paraded which it seems is a Custom on good Fryday.[1]

[1] See, further, JA's Autobiography under the present date.

1778 APRIL 18. SAMEDI.

This Morning the Father of General Conway came to visit me, and enquire after his Son as well as American Affairs. He seems a venerable Personage.

Dined at Mr. Bouffets, who speaks a little English. Mr. Bouffetts Brother, Mr. Veillard, M. Le Fevre, L'Abbe des Prades, Mr. Borry, &c. were there.

Called and drank Tea at Mm. Brillons. Then made a Visit to M. Boullainvilliers, and his Lady, who is a kind of Lord of the Manor of Passi, and is just now come out to his Country Seat.[1]

[1] "Le Château de M. le Marquis de Boulainviller, Prévôt de Paris, est la première maison considérable qui se trouve sur le chemin de Versailles" (Dezallier, *Environs de Paris*, p. 14, followed by a detailed description). The Boulainvilliers were close neighbors of the American Commissioners; see plan of "Franklin's Passy" in Bernard Faÿ, *Franklin, the Apostle of Modern Times,* Boston, 1929, facing p. 452.

AP. 19. DIMANCHE.

Dined at home, with Mr. Grand our Banker, his Lady, Daughter and Sons,[1] Mr. Austin, Mr. Chaumont, and a great deal of other Company.

Mr. David Hartley, a Member of the B[ritish] House of Commons came to visit Dr. F., a Mr. Hammond with him.[2]

Went with Mr. Chaumont in his Carriage to the Concert Spirituel. A vast Croud of Company of both Sexes, a great Number of Instruments. A Gentleman sung and then a young Lady.[3]

[1] The Grands, originally a Swiss family, were bankers in Paris and Amsterdam. In his Autobiography under the present date JA says that it was through the influence of Vergennes, Sartine, and Chaumont that Ferdinand Grand of Paris "obtained the Reputation and Emoluments of being the Banker to the American Ministers." The Grands had a country seat near the Hôtel de Valentinois in Passy and were hospitable to JA and particularly kind to JQA.
[2] David Hartley the younger (1732–1813), M.P. for Hull, was acting as an unofficial agent for Lord North; he had known Franklin intimately in England and was a tireless opponent of the American war, in Parliament and out (DNB). In his Autobiography under this date JA gives an unfavorable view of "This mysterious Visit" to Passy by the two Englishmen, the other of whom was William Hammond, father of George Hammond, later to be the first British minister to the United States. In 1783 Hartley was appointed by the Fox-North Coalition commissioner to negotiate and sign the Definitive Treaty; see entry of 27 April 1783 and notes, below.
[3] For an account of the *concerts spirituels* see Thiery, *Almanach du voyageur à Paris*, 1784, p. 212.

AP. 20. LUNDI.

My Son has been with me since Saturday.—The Concert Spirituel is in the Royal Garden, where was an infinite Number of Gentlemen and Ladies walking.

Dined with the Dutchess D'Anville, at her House with her Daughter and Granddaughter, Dukes, Abbotts, &c. &c. &c.[1]

Visited Mr. Lloyd and his Lady, where We saw Mr. Digges.[2]

[1] Including the philosopher Condorcet; see JA's Autobiography under this date.

[2] Thomas Digges (1742–1821) of Maryland, prior to the Revolution London agent for various shipping firms and afterward one of those colonial residents in London who worked, in greater or lesser measure, for the American cause. His recent arrival in Paris was for the purpose of presenting to the Commissioners David Hartley's five-point proposal for a peace conference. See William Bell Clark, "In Defense of Thomas Digges," *PMHB*, 77:381–438 (Oct. 1953), for a partial restoration of Digges' somewhat tarnished character. [This is an erroneous identification. The "Mr. Digges" mentioned by JA was actually George Digges, Thomas' younger brother. Thomas did not come to Paris until the following spring. A fuller note on George Digges will appear in *Adams Family Corr.*, vol. 3.]

1778 APRIL 21. MARDI.

Dined, this Day, at Mr. Chaumonts, with the largest Collection of great Company that I have yet seen. The Marquis D Argenson, the Count De Noailles, the Marshall de Maillebois, the Brother of the Count de Vergennes, and a great many others, Mr. Foucault and Mm., Mr. Chaumonts Son in Law and Daughter, who has a Fortune of 4 or 5000£. st. in St. Domingo, Mr. Chaumonts own Son and Miss Chaumont. Mr.[1]   the first officer under Mr. Sartine.

It is with much Grief and Concern that I have learned from my first landing in France, the Disputes between the Americans, in this Kingdom. The Animosities between Mr. D[eane] and Mr. L[ee]—between Dr. F[ranklin] and Mr. L.—between Mr. Iz[ard] and Dr. F.—between Dr. B[ancroft] and Mr. L.—between Mr. C.[2] and all. It is a Rope of Sand....[3]

I am at present wholly untainted with these Prejudices, and will endeavour to keep myself so. Parties and Divisions among the Americans here, must have disagreable if not pernicious Effects.

Mr. D. seems to have made himself agreable here to Persons of Importance and Influence, and is gone home in such Splendor, that I fear, there will be Altercations, in America about him.[4] Dr. F., Mr. D. and Dr. Bancroft, are Friends. The L's and Mr. Iz. are Friends. Sir J[ames] J[ay] insinuated that Mr. D. had been at least as attentive to his own Interest, in dabbling in the English Funds, and in Trade, and fitting out Privateers, as to the Public, and said he would give Mr. D. fifty thousand Pounds for his Fortune, and said that Dr. B. too had made a Fortune. Mr. McC[reery] insinuated to me, that the L's were selfish, and that this was a Family Misfortune. What shall I say? What shall I think?

It is said that Mr. L. has not the Confidence of the Ministry, nor of the Persons of Influence here—that he is suspected of too much Affection for England, and of too much Intimacy with Ld. Shel[burne]—that he has given offence, by an unhappy disposition, and by indiferent Speeches before Servants and others, concerning the French Nation and Government, despising and cursing them.—I am sorry for these Things, but it is no Part of my Business to quarrell with any Body without Cause. It is no Part of my Duty to differ with one Party or another, or to give offence to any Body. But I must do my duty to the Public, let it give offence to whom it will.

The public Business has never been methodically conducted. There never was before I came, a minute Book, a Letter Book or an Account Book—and it is not possible to obtain a clear Idea of our Affairs.[5]

Mr. D. lived expensively, and seems not to have had much order in his Business, public or private: but he was active, dilligent, subtle, and successfull, having accomplished the great Purpose of his Mission, to Advantage.... Mr. Gerard is his Friend, and I find that Dr. B. has the Confidence of Persons about the Ministry, particularly of the late Secretary to the Embassader to G.B.[6]

[1] CFA supplies, probably correctly, the name M. de Vilevault for the blank left by the diarist. See *Almanach royal,* 1778, p. 191.

[2] The Autobiography indicates that this was William Carmichael, a Marylander who had acted informally as secretary and performed other services for the American Commissioners in Europe before his return to America in Feb. 1778; he was later a member of the Continental Congress and American chargé d'affaires at Madrid (*DAB*).

[3] Suspension points, here and below, are in MS.

[4] Deane sailed for America from Toulon on 13 March with Gérard, the new minister to the United States, in the flagship of the Comte d'Estaing's squadron (Gérard, *Despatches and Instructions,* p. 41, note, 89–90).

[5] In a household account book of the American Commissioners, kept by Franklin's cook or major-domo at Passy, 1776–1778 (CtHi), the following entry appears at 30 May 1778: "achêté deux livres a Ecrire pour Monsieur Adam."

[6] JA's Autobiography under this date greatly elaborates on the characters and contentions of the persons spoken of here.

1778. AP. 22. WEDNESDAY.

Dined at home and spent the day with Mr. Lee.

AP. 23. THURSDAY.

Dined at home with Company.

AP. 24. FRYDAY.

Dined at Mr. Buffauts, with much Company.

AP. 25. SATURDAY.

Dined at Mr. Chaumonts with Company.

SUNDAY [26 APRIL].

Dined at home.

MONDAY. 27.

Dined with Mr. Boulainvilliers, at his House in Passi, with Generals and Bishops and Ladies &c.—In the Evening went to the French Comedy, and happened to be placed in the first Box, very near to the celebrated Voltaire who attended the Performance of his own Alzire. Between the Acts the Audience called out Voltaire and clapped and applauded him, the whole Time. The old Poet arose and bowed respectfully to the Audience. He has yet much Fire in his Eyes and Vigour in his Countenance, altho very old. After the Tragedy, the[y] Acted the Tuteur, a Comedy or a Farce of one Act. This Theatre does not exceed that at Bourdeaux.

I will attempt to keep my Journal in French, in order to familiarise myself to that Language.[1]

[1] In his Autobiography under this date JA says that he attended the theater primarily in order to improve his French. Another measure to the same end was, as he says here, to keep his journal in French, but "I found it took up too much of my time." The French entries that follow have been kept as literal as possible. They were omitted in CFA's text of the Diary because "not sufficiently good to merit publication" (*Works*, 3: 145, note). When JA set out seriously to learn French, he called on the services of the two inseparable French clerics Arnoux and Chalut; see entry of 4 July, below.

1778. AVRIL VINGT-HUIT. MARDI.

Dejeunois, chez nous, avec Messrs. Chaumont, Dubourg,[1] Chaumont le jeune, Franklin, Grandpere et Grandfils.

M. Dubourg disoit un Conte, touchant, C. Mazarine. Un Officier demandoit, de lui, de le faire un Capitaine, d'une Guarde de ⟨son⟩ sa Vie. Le Card. repondoit, qu'il n'avoit pas Besoin d'autre Guarde que de son Ange tutelaire.—Ah Monsr. dit l'officier—on, le poussera, avec, un peu de l'au benit.—Oh Monsr. repondoit, le Cardinal Je ne crains point cette eau benite.

Je crois qu'on riroit, si on verroit, mon francois.

Je dinai Aujourdhui, chez moi, avec Mr. Lee.— Apres diner, Mr. L. et moi, allames, a la Comedie itallien, ou nous avons vu Monsieur Harlequin, &c.

[1] Franklin's friend and editor, the physician Jacques Barbeu Dubourg (1709-

1779). JA tells more of Dubourg and of his anecdotes in his Autobiography under this date; see also Benjamin Rush, *Letters*, 1:77, note, and references there.

AVRIL VINGT NEUF. MERCREDI.

J'ai bien dormi, le derniere Soir. J'avois diné chez Le Marrechal De Maillebois avec Baucoup du Monde. Apres diner, went to the Accademy of Sciences and heard Mr. D'Alembert pronounce Eulogies upon divers Members deceased.[1]

[1] On this occasion occurred the famous encounter—and embrace—between Voltaire and Franklin, described more fully in JA's Autobiography under this date. Voltaire, who was 84, died on 30 May 1778.

AP. 30. JEUDI.

Dined with the Mareschall De Mouchy—with the Duke and Duchess D'Ayen, their Daughter the Marquise De la Fayette, the Viscountess De Maillbois, her sister, another sister unmarried, the Prussian Ambassador, an Italien Embassador, and a great deal of other great Company. The Nobleman with whom We dined is Phillip de Noailles, Marechal Duc De Mouchy, Grand d'Espagne de la premiere Classe, Chevalier des ordres du Roi et de la Toison D'or, Grand Croix de l'ordre de Malte, nommé Lieutenant General de Guienne en 1768 et Commandant en Chef dans le Gouvernement de ladite Province en 1775.

His being Commander in Chief in the Province of Guienne was the Cause of a great Compliment to me. He asked me how I liked Bourdeaux. I told him [I] found it a rich, elegant, Town flourishing in Arts and Commerce. He asked whether I was content with my Reception there. I said they had done me too much Honour. He replied he wished he had been there, to have joined them in doing me Honour.

He lives in all the Splendor and Magnificence of a Viceroy, which is little inferiour to that of a King.

1778 MAY 1. VENDREDI.

Aujourdhui J'ai été diner, chez Monsieur Le Duke D'Ayen, le Pere de Mm. Le Ms. [Madame la Marquise] De la Fayette. La Maison, Le Jardin, Les Promenades, Les Tableau's, Les Garnitures, son tres magnifiques.

Les Tableaux de la Famille de Noailles sont anciens, et nombreux.

Mm. la Dutchess D'Ayen, a cinque ou Six Enfans, contre la Coutume de ce Pays ci.

We were shewn, into the Library, and all the Rooms and first Suite of Chambers in the House. The Library is very large, and the Rooms very elegant and the Furniture very rich.

MAY 2. SATURDAY.

Dined at Mr. Izzards, with Mr. Lloyd and his Lady, Mr. Francois and much other Company. After Dinner went to the Comedie Francoise, and saw the Brutus of Voltaire and after it, the Cocher Supposé. —As I was coming out of the Box, a Gentleman seized me by the Hand.—I looked.—Governer Wentworth, Sir, says he.—Asked Questions about his Father and Friends in America &c.[1]

[1] John Wentworth, JA's Harvard classmate and former royal governor of New Hampshire, had arrived in Europe from Nova Scotia early in 1778 (Lawrence Shaw Mayo, *John Wentworth*, Cambridge, 1921, p. 164–167). His encounter with JA and its aftermath are amplified in JA's Autobiography under the present date, q.v. also on "Mr. Francois," i.e. Francès.

MAY 3. SUNDAY.

Mr. Izzard and Lady, Mr. Lloyd and Lady, Dr. Bancroft and much other Company dined, with Dr. Franklin and me at Passi. Mrs. Izzard at my particular Desire brought her little Son and two little Daughters. We had all our young Gentlemen, from the Accademy, which made a pretty Shew of young Americans.

MAY 4. MONDAY.

Dined at Mr. Chaumonts, with his Family, and some other Company.

MAY 5. TUESDAY.

Am to dine at home—a great Rarity and a great Blessing!

At Dinner, alone, my Servant brought me a Letter, A Messieurs, Messieurs, Franklin, Lée, et Adams, Deputés des Etats unies de l'Amerique a Passy. De Vergennes.—I opened, and found it in these Words

Versailles le 4. May 1778

J'ai pris les ordres du Roy, Messieurs, au Sujet de la presentation de M. Adams votre nouveau Collegue, et Sa Majesté le verra vendredi prochain, 8 de ce mois. J'espere que vous voudres bien me faire l'honneur de dinér ce jour la, chez moi; je serai ravi d'avoir cette Occasion de passer quelques Heures avec Vous, et de vous renouveller l'Assurance de la tres parfaite Consideration avec Laquelle jai l'honneur d'etre, Messieurs, Votre tres humble et tres obeissant Serviteur

De Vergennes

Mrs. Francklin, Lee et Adams.[1]

J'ai passé le tout de ce Jour, chez moi. Monsieur Lee vint chez moi, l'apres midi, et nous travaillions dans l'Examen du Papiers publiques. —En la Soiree Monsieur Chaumont, vint chez moi, et m'avertit de la Destination d'une Frigatte de trente deux Canons de Marseilles a Boston, et que Je puis ecrire, si Je voulois.

¹ RC not located. JA inserted an English translation in his Autobiography under the present date.

MAY 6. WEDNESDAY.

A Spanish Writer of certain Vissions of Hell, relates that a certain Devil who was civil and well bred, shewed him all the Departments, in the Place—among others the Department of deceased Kings. The Spaniard was much pleased at so illustrious a Sight, and after viewing them for some time, said he should be glad to see the Rest of them.— The Rest? said the Dæmon. Here are all the Kings, that ever reigned upon Earth from the Creation of it to this day, what the Devil would the Man have?—F[*ranklin*].

This was not so charitable as Dr. Watts, who in his view of Heaven says "here and there I see a King."—This seems to imply that K's are as good as other Men, since it is but here and there that We see a King upon Earth.

After Dinner went to the Review, where the King reviewed his Guards, French and Swiss, about 8000 of them. The Shew was splendid, as all other Shews are, in this Country. The Carriages of the Royal Family, were magnificent beyond my Talent at Description.— Returned and drank Coffee with Mr. Lee, walked home and drank Tea with Mr. Chaumonts Family, and spent the Rest of the Evening in reading Cardinal Richelieu.

1778. MAY. 7. THURSDAY.

J'allai, hier, apres midi, a la Revue, ou Le Roy, a fait une Revue de ses Guardes de Suiss et de francoise.

Ce Matin, [*sentence unfinished*]

MAY 8. FRYDAY.

This Morning Dr. Franklin, Mr. Lee, and Mr. Adams, went to Versailles, in Order that Mr. Adams might be presented to the King.— Waited on the Count De Vergennes, at his office, and at the Hour of Eleven the Count conducted Us, into the Kings Bed Chamber where he was dressing—one officer putting on his Sword, another his Coat &c.

The Count went up to the King, and his Majesty turned about, towards me, and smiled. Ce est il Monsieur Adams, said the King and then asked a Question, very quick, or rather made an Observation to me which I did not fully understand. The Purport of it was that I had not been long arrived.—The Count Vergennes then conducted me to the Door of another Room, and desired me to stand there which I did untill the King passed.—The Count told the King, that I did not yet take upon me to speak French. The King asked, whether I did not speak *at all* as yet—and passed by me, into the other Room.

This Monarch is in the 24th. Year of his Age, having been born the 23d of Aug. 1754. He has the Appearances of a strong Constitution, capable of enduring to a great Age. His Reign has already been distinguished, by an Event that will reflect a Glory upon it, in future Ages I mean, the Treaty with America.[1]

We afterwards made a Visit to Count Maurepas, to Mr. Sartine, to the Chancellor,[2] to Mr. Bertin &c.

The Chancellor, has the Countenance of a Man worn with severe Studies. When I was introduced to him he turned to Dr. F. and said Mr. Adams est un Person celebre en Amerique et en Europe.

We went afterwards to Dinner, with the Count de Vergennes. There was a full Table—no Ladies but the Countess. The Counts Brother, the Ambassador who lately signed the Treaty with Swisserland, Mr. Garnier the late Secretary to the Embassy in England, and many others, Dukes and Bishops and Counts &c.

Mr. Garnier and Mr. ⟨ ⟩ asked me, with some Appearance of Concern, whether there was any foundation for the Reports which the Ministry had spread in England, of a Dispute between Congress and Gen. Washington. A Letter they say has been printed, from an officer in Phila. to that Purpose.

Mr. Garnier is the 1st. french Gentleman who has begun a serious political Conversation with me of any length. He is a sensible Man.

[1] There are more details and reflections concerning this first audience with Louis XVI in JA's Autobiography under the present date.

[2] The Autobiography supplies the Chancellor's name, Miromenil (i.e. Miromesnil).

MAY 9. SATURDAY.

This Morning Mr. Joy, Mr. Johonnot, and Mr. Green, came to visit me—Joy who lived at Weymouth, Green Son of Mr. Rufus Green.[1]

Dined with Madam Bertin.[2]

[1] Michael Joy, Francis Johonnot, and William Greene, formerly of Massachusetts but more lately of London, who were traveling together in France (see note on the following entry). Greene kept a journal of this trip, in which he wrote of this visit to Passy: "Saturday, May 9, morning we took coach for Passy for which [we] gave six livres, we waited first on Mr. Adams, who receiv'd us very genteelly, but he has not wore off the natural restraint which always was in his behaviour, we tarried with him half an hour, from him we went to Dr. Franklin's apartment, he receiv'd us like children, and behaved to us with all the complaisance and tenderness imaginable, we were above half an hour in free discourse with this venerable man on our departure he desired our company to dinner the next day being Sunday" (MHS, Procs., 54 [1920–1921]:103).

[2] JA's Autobiography under this date more discreetly says, "The American Ministers dined with Madam Bertin, at Passi," and then goes on to tell more about their hostess.

1778. MAY. 10. SUNDAY.

Messieurs Brattle, Waldo, Joy, Johonnot, Green and Austin dined with Us, at Passi.[1] After dinner We walked in the Bois du Boulogne, as far as the new Seat of the Count D'Artois, where We saw Mr. Turgot, Mr. and Mm. La Fréte, and much other Company. Sunday in this Country is devoted to Amusements and Diversions. There are more Games, Plays, and Sports of every Kind on this day, than on any other, in the Week.

[1] The additional guests were Thomas Brattle (Harvard 1760), son of JA's old antagonist Gen. William Brattle, and Joseph Waldo (Harvard 1741); both had left Boston for England about the time hostilities broke out. (On Brattle see Sabine, Loyalists; on Waldo see Sibley-Shipton, Harvard Graduates, vol. 11 [in press].) A passage in JA's Autobiography under the present date makes clear why he received these former American acquaintances, and especially Waldo, with reserve: now that war between England and France was imminent, some if not all of them were suffering from second thoughts and would have been glad to accept appointments under Congress or the Commissioners, for which JA doubted their qualifications.

William Greene in his travel journal gives an entertaining account of this day which is too long to quote here. It is particularly revealing of Franklin's way of life at Passy and suggests why JA soon grew impatient with his colleague's habits. "In the afternoon," Greene remarks, "a number of ladies from the neighbourhood came in, and took us all to walk, in the Bois Boulogne. The old Doctor still so fond of the fair sex, that one was not enough for him but he must have one on each side, and all the ladies both old and young were ready to eat him up" (MHS, Procs., 54 [1920–1921]:104).

MAY 11. MONDAY.

Dined at Mr. Sorins, at Passi.

MAY 12. TUESDAY.

Dined, at Mr. Dupré's, at the Montagne. The Gardens and the Prospect are very fine. It lies adjoining to the Seat of the President of the Parliament of Paris. We met his Lady, who desired the Gentlemen to shew Us the Place, but not the Whole, for she wished to enjoy our Company, there, at her own Invitation, and she chose to reserve a Part of the Curiosities of the Place as an Inducement to Us to accept it.

From this Hill, We have a fine View of the Country, and of the Kings Castle at Vincennes. My little Son, and the other young Americans, at the Pension, dined with Us.

MAY 13. WEDNESDAY.

Dined at M. Chaumonts, with a great deal of Company. After Dinner took a Walk to Chaillot to see Mr. Lee, who had a large Company of Americans to dine with him, among the rest Mr. Fendell of Maryland and Dr. Smith Brother of Mr. Smith of N. York the Historian.[1]

[1] James Smith (1738–1812), College of New Jersey 1757; M.D., Leyden 1764; first professor of chemistry and materia medica at King's College (Princeton Univ., *Alumni Records*; Thomas, *Columbia Univ. Officers and Alumni*). JA later said that Smith, whose political position was ambiguous, gave the American Commissioners "a great deal of Vexation" and that he afterward furnished materials for one of the most unbridled published attacks on JA's career as a public man, namely John Wood's *History of the Administration of John Adams* ... , N.Y., 1802 (JA, *Autobiography*, under dates of 12, 21 April, 9 May 1778).

1778 MAY 14. THURSDAY.

MAY 15 FRYDAY.

Dined at Mr. Grands, with all the Americans, in Paris.[1]

[1] William Greene gives in his travel journal a detailed account of this "very jovial" dinner, a list of the "brilliant company" present, and even an explanation of the name of the Grands' residence in Passy, La Chaise: "One time when [Louis XV] was a hunting, he had occasion to ease himself, a person brought him a necessary chair, he said that house shou'd be called la Chaise, which it has been ever since, and the statue of Louis 15th on horse back stands always in the garden, the place where this happened, it is copper and small, it was put in the middle of the table" (MHS, *Procs.*, 54 [1920–1921]:108).

MAY 17 SUNDAY.

Dined at home. Dr. Dubourg, and Mr. Parker and another Gentleman dined with me.

MAY 18 MONDAY.

Dined at Mr. La Frété's Country Seat, at the Foot of Mount Calvare. The House, Gardens, and Walks are very spacious. It lies upon the Seine—nearly opposite to that Castle whimsically called Madrid, built by Francis 1.[1]—The Company Yesterday, were all single Personnes, except Mr. and Mm. La Frété and myself.

[1] Mont Calvaire, also called Mont Valérien, rises above the village of Suresnes, west of the Seine and across from the Bois de Boulogne. For a contemporary view of Mont Calvaire see Jefferson, *Papers*, ed. Boyd, 12: facing p. 482, with descriptive information and references in same, p. xxxv–xxxvi. Francis I's Madrid is described in Dezallier, *Environs de Paris*, 1779, p. 21–22. See also JA's Autobiography under this date.

MAY 19. TUESDAY.

Dined with Mr. Challut, one of the Farmers General.[1] We were shewn into the superbest Gallery that I have yet seen. The Paintings, Statues and Curiosities were innumerable. The old Marshall Richlieu dined there, and a vast Number of other great Company.

After dinner, M. Challut invited Dr. F. and me, to go to the Opera, and take a Seat in his Logis. We did. The Musick and dancing were very fine.

[1] M. Chalut de Vérin, brother of the Abbé Chalut with whom JA was to become very friendly (*Almanach royal*, 1778, p. 474; note on entry of 4 July, below; JA, Autobiography, under the present date).

1778 MAY 20. WEDNESDAY.

The french Opera is an Entertainment, which is very pleasing, for a few Times. There is every Thing, which can please the Eye, or the Ear. But the Words are unintelligible, and if they were not, they are said to be very insignificant. I always wish, in such an Amusement to learn Something. The Imagination, the Passions and the Understanding, have too little Employment, in the opera.

Dined at Dr. Dubourgs, with a small Company, very handsomely; but not amidst those Signs of Wealth and Grandeur, which I see every where else.

I saw however more of Sentiment, and therefore more of true Taste than I have seen in other Places, where there was ten times the Magnificence.—Among his Pictures were these.

Les Adieux D'Hector et D'Andromaque, in which the Passions were strongly marked.

La Continence de Scipio.

Le Medicin Erasistrate, decouvre L'Amour D'Antiochus.

Devellopement de la Decoration interieure et des Peintures des Plafonds de la Gallerie de Versailles.

We went and drank Tea, with Mm. Foucault, and took a View of Mr. Foucaults House—a very grand Hotell it is—and the Furniture is vastly rich. The Beds, the Curtains, the every Thing is as rich as Silk and Gold can make it.

I am wearied to death with gazing wherever I go, at a Profusion of unmeaning Wealth and Magnificence. The Adieu of Hector and Andromache gave me more Pleasure than the Sight of all the Gold of Ophir would. Gold, Marble, Silk, Velvet, Silver, Ivory, and Alabaster, make up the Shew everywhere.

A certain Taylor once stole an Horse, and was found out and committed to Prison, where he met another Person who had long followed the Trade of Horse Stealing. The Taylor told the other, his Story. The other enquired why he had not taken such a Road and assumed such a Disguise, and why he had not disguised the Horse?—I did not think of it.—Who are you? and what has been your Employment?—A Taylor. —You never stole a Horse before, I suppose in your Life.—Never.—G–d d—n you what Business had you with Horse stealing? Why did not you content your Self with your Cabbage?—F[*ranklin*].

MAY 21. THURSDAY.

Dined at home.

22 FRYDAY.

Dined at home with a great deal of Company. Went after Dinner to see the Misanthrope of Moliere, with Mr. Amiel. It was followed by the Heureusement,—Called at the Microcosme. Called at Mr. Amiels at the Pension.

1778. MAY 23. SATURDAY.

Dined at Home with Company.

SUNDAY 24.

Dined at Home.

MONDAY [25 MAY].

Dined at Home.

MAY 26. TUESDAY.

Dined at Mr. Bertins the Secretary of State at his Seat in the Country. Dr. F., his G. Son and I rode with Mm. Bertin, the Niece of the

Minister, in her Voiture with 4 Horses. This was one of the pleasantest Rides yet. We rode near the back side of Mount Calvare, which is perhaps the finest Height near Paris. Mount Martre is another very fine Elevation. The Gardens, Walks and Water Works of Mr. Bertin are very magnificent. He is a Batchelor. His House and Gardens are situated upon the River Seine. He has at the End of his Garden a Collection of Rocks, drawn together at a vast Expense, some Thousands of Guineas. I told him I would sell him a Thousand times as many for half a Guinea.

His Water Works are very curious. 4 Pumps, going by Means of two Horses. The Mechanism is simple and ingenious. The Horses go round as in a Mill. The four Pumps empty themselves into a square Pond which contains an Acre. From this Pond the Water flows through Pipes down to every Part of the Garden.

I enquired of a certain Abbe, who sat next me at Dinner, who were the purest Writers of french. He gave me in writing, L'Histoire universell du Bossuet. La Fontaine. Moliere. Racine. Rousseau. Le petit cærene [carême] de Massillon. Les sermons de Bourdaloue.

1778. MAY 29. FRYDAY.

Dined again at Monsieur La Fretes at the Foot of Calvare. Madam La Fretes four Sisters dined with Us.

Monsr. Rulier [Rulhière], who has always dined with me at that House, dined there to day—the same Gentleman who wrote the History of the Revolution in Russia. He has also written the Revolutions of Poland. I asked him who was the best Historian of France. He said Mezeray. He added, that the Observations upon the History of France by the Abby de Mably were excellent.[1] He told me I might read his History of the Revolution in Russia, when I would.

The Inclination and the Apparatus in this Country for Amusements is worthy of observation. There is scarcely a genteel House but is furnished with Accommodations for every Sort of Play. Every fashionable House at least has a Billiard Table, a Backgammon Table, a Chess Board, a Chequer Board, Cards &c.

---

[1] Gabriel Bonnot, Abbé de Mably (1709–1785), historian and philosopher, with whom the Adams family were to become very friendly later and whose *Observations sur le gouvernement et les loix des Etats-Unis d'Amérique*, Amsterdam, 1784, was addressed to JA. For an account of Mably's career and for JA's marginalia in his *De la législation, ou principes des loix*, Amsterdam, 1776, see Haraszti, *JA and the Prophets of Progress*, ch. 7, "The Communism of the Abbé de Mably." See, further, entry of 5 Jan. 1783 and note, below.

MAY 30. SATURDAY.

Dined at home with only Dr. F.'s new french Clerk. He has a smattering of Italian, German and English. He says that the best Italien Dictionary and Grammar are those of Veneroni. The best German Grammar and Dictionary are those of Gottsched.

The best french Prosody is the Poetique francoise de Marmontel.

1778. JUNE 2D. TUESDAY.

Went to Versailles, and found it deserted, the Court being gone to Marli.

We went to Marli, ⟨waited on⟩ met the Compte De Vergennes, and did some Business, then went to Mr. De Sartine, and dined with him. His Lady was at home, and dined with the Company. The Prince de Montbarry dined there.—Went with Madam Sartine to the Count D'Arandas, the Spanish Ambassadors Coffee, as they call it, where he gives Ice Cream and Cakes to all the World.

Marli is the most curious and beautifull Place I have yet seen. The Water Works here, which convey such a great Body of Water from the Seine to Versailles, and through the Gardens at Marli, are very magnificent. The Royal Palace here is handsome, the Gardens before it are grand. There are six Pavillions on each Side of the Garden, that is six Houses, for the Use of the Kings Ministers, while the Royal Family is at Marli, which is only for 3 Weeks. There is nothing prettier than the Play of the Fountains in the Garden. I saw a Rainbeau in all its Glory in one of them.

The Shades, the Walks, the Trees, are the most charming, that I have seen.[1]

[1] For a contemporary description of Marly and its grounds see Dezallier, *Environs de Paris,* 1779, p. 162–178.

1778 JUNE 7.

Went to Versailles in Company with Mr. Lee, Mr. Izzard and his Lady, Mr. Lloyd and his Lady and Mr. Francis. Saw the grand Procession of the Knights du St. Esprit or de le Cordon blue.

At 9 O Clock at Night went to the grand Couvert, and saw the King, Queen and Royal Family at Supper. Had a fine Seat and Situation close by the Royal Family, and had a distinct and full View of the royal Pair.[1]

[1] JA's narrative of and reflections on this visit to Versailles are greatly elaborated in his Autobiography under the present date. His personal accounts (printed at the end of 1778, below) show that the entertainment cost him 12 livres.

JUNE 8.

Dined with Mr. Alexander, and went to the Concert.[1]

[1] From this point until the following spring the Diary entries are very sporadic. In his Autobiography JA says that after residing a few months at Passy he grew "afraid to keep any Journal at all: For I had reason to believe, that the house was full of Spies, some of whom were among my own Servants, and if my Journal should fall into the hands of the Police, full of free remarks as it must be, to be of any value, it might do more Injury to my Country than mischief to me." When, however, JA reached the present point in composing his Autobiography, he filled the gaps in the Diary record to some extent by copying in letters from both the Commissioners' and his own letterbooks and by adding explanatory comments thereon. The inserted letters have been included in the text of the Autobiography in the present edition. His personal accounts in France, printed at the end of 1778, below, also give glimpses of his activities—sightseeing, attending court, book-buying, and the like—in the following months.

1778 JULY [4].

The Anniversary of the Declaration of American Independence. We had the Honour of the Company of all the American Gentlemen and Ladies, in and about Paris to dine, with Dr. Franklin and me, at Passi, together with a few of the French Gentlemen in the Neighbourhood, Mr. Chaumont, Mr. Brillon, Mr. Vaillard, Mr. Grand, Mr. Beaudoin, Mr. Gerard, the Abbys Challut and Arnold &c.[1]

I have omitted to keep any Journal for a long Time, in which I have seen a great many curious Things.

[1] On the inseparable Abbés Arnoux and Chalut, elderly but spritely enthusiasts for the American cause, who helped teach JA French and later became friendly with all the Adamses in France, see JA's Autobiography under date of 16 April 1778; AA to Mary (Smith) Cranch, 5 Sept. 1784 (MWA; AA, *Letters*, ed. CFA, 1848, p. 189–190).

JA and other Americans seldom succeeded in spelling the Abbés' names correctly.

The cost of this Fourth of July celebration, 600 livres and 7 sous, is entered in JA's retained record of the expenses of the American Commissioners in France, 1777–1779 (Lb/JA/35, Adams Papers, Microfilms, Reel No. 123).

6.

Dined with the Abby's Chaillut and Arnaud. The Farmer General, Mr. and Mrs. Izzard, Mr. Lee, Mrs. Gibbs and Mrs. Stevens, and Mr. and Mrs. Lloyd were there. After dinner the Abby invited Us to the French Comedy, where We saw the Malheureux imaginary and the Parti de Chasse d'Henri quatre.

7. MARDI.

Dined at St. Lu, with the Farmer general Challut. The Marshall Richelieu, and many Abbes, Counts, Marquisses &c.

14.

Dined at Chatou, with Mr. Bertine, Ministre D'Etat. Went to see the Park, where We rambled, untill We were weary.

1778 JULY 25.

It is an Amusement among some People, here, who understand a little English, to give Samples of English Sentences, hard to be pronounced.—"What think the chosen Judges? Thrust this Thistle through this Thumb. An Apple in each Hand and a third in my Mouth."—&c.[1]

[1] See further, on the difficulties of the French in pronouncing the name "Washington," JA's Autobiography under this date.

At this point, 25 July 1778, the second part of JA's Autobiography, entitled "Travels and Negotiations," breaks off.

The third part, entitled "Peace," does not resume the narrative of his life until 29 Sept. 1779, the date of JA's commissions from the Continental Congress to negotiate treaties of peace and commerce with Great Britain.

AUGUST 16.

Went to Church, to the Chappell of the Duch Embassador in Paris, where We had Prayer Books, Psalme Books in french and a Sermon. The Preacher spoke good French, I being judge, and with much grace. I shall go again.

17.

Dined at Chatou, with Mr. Bertin. After dinner went to view the Machine of Marli, which forces up from the River Seine, all the Water at Versailles and Marli. We walked up the Mountain to the Pavillion, and Dwelling House of Madam de Barry.[1] The Situation is one of the most extensive and beautiful, about Paris. The Pavillion is the most elegantly furnished of any Place I have seen. The House, Garden and Wallks are very magnificent. Mm. Barry was walking in the Garden. She sent Us word she should be glad to see Us—but We answered it was too late, We had so far to go.—Mr. Le Roy, of the Accademie of Sciences was with Us. As We returned We had an agreable Conversation, upon philosophical Subjects.

[1] Louvecienne (or Louveciennes), nearly adjoining but east of Marly. See Dezallier, *Environs de Paris*, 1779, p. 178–181.

18.

Went to Paris, with the Abbees Chalut and Arnaut. Went to see the

Church of St. Roche, the Splendor and Magnificence of which, is very striking to me.[1]

There I saw the Monument of the famous Mesnager. The Pomp of these Churches, I think exceeds the Magnificence of the Royal Palaces.

Mr. Challut says that the Rent of this Church is Eighty thousand Livres a Year, barely the Rent of the Pews and Chairs, and perhaps the Cellars. Out of this they maintain the officers of the Church, and the Servants and Labourers that attend it, and the organist &c.—but what becomes of the Remainder he did not say.

[1] A contemporary description of St. Roch will be found in Thiery, *Almanach du voyageur à Paris*, 1784, p. 544–549.

AUG. 30. 1778. SUNDAY.

This Evening had the English Gazette extraordinary, containing Extracts from Letters from Ld. How and Gen. Clinton—the first containing an account of the Arrival of the Toulon Fleet, and anchoring without Sandy Hook—the other, a Relation of the Action of the 28. June in the Jerseys. There are Letters in London, as M. J. Wharton[1] says, as late as the 14. July.

Elements of Spanish Grammar by Del Pino, and Dictionary of the Same.[2]

[1] Joseph Wharton of Philadelphia, who, according to his own testimony in an autobiographical letter written years later, had been supplying confidential information from London to Dr. Bancroft in Paris, and had fled to Paris this very month to avoid arrest by the British

(Joseph Wharton to JA, 4 June 1798, Adams Papers).

[2] This note cannot be dated. In the MS it follows the entry of 30 Aug. quite closely and is in turn followed by a half-page interval of space preceding the entry of 7 October.

1778 OCT. 7.

Captain Richard Grinnell of Newport Rhode Island says, that the English have this Year 17 Vessells, in the Brazil Whale Fishery off the River Plate, in S.A. in the Lat. 35 South and from thence to 40. just on the Edge of Soundings off and on, about the Longitude of 65[1] from London. That they sail in the Months of September and October.

Almost all the Officers and Men, belonging to these 17 Vessells are Americans from Nantuckett and Cape Cod, two or 3 from Rhode Island and Longisland.

The Names of the Captains are Aaron Sheffield of Newport R.I., Goldsmith Long Island, Richard Holmes New York, John Chadwick Nantucket, Francis Macy Nantucket, Reuben Macy Nantucket, John Meader Nantucket, Jonathan Meader Dto., Elisha Clarke Nantucket, Benjamin Clark Nantucket, William Ray Nantucket, Paul Pease Nantucket, Bunker Fitch Nantucket, Reuben Fitch Nantucket, Zebeda Coffin Nantucket, another Coffin Dto., John Lock Cape Codd,   Delano Nantucket, Andrew Swain Nantucket, William Ray Nantucket.—Holmes and Chadwick are returned home.

Some of these Vessells 4 or 5 go to Greenland.

The fleet sails to Greenland, the last of February or the Beginning of March.

There is another Whale Fishery discovered lately, in the Meditarranean on the Coast of Barbary, where they catch many fish.

There was last Year and this Year, a Publication made by the Ministry, A Letter from the Lords of the Admiralty to Mr. Dennis du Bert in Coleman Street, informing Mr. De Bert that there should be a Convoy appointed to convoy the Brazil fleet. But this is a Sham—a Deception. There was no Convoy last Year nor this. If a Convoy was to be appointed she could be of no service, as the Vessells are continually changing their Courses in Chase of Whales. That she would not go further than the Line as they would then judge themselves clear of American Privateers.

One Privateer from 12 to 20 Guns [and] 100 Men would be sufficient to take and destroy this whole Fleet.[2]

The Beginning of December would be the best Time to proceed from Hence—the same Time from Boston.

[1] Overwritten; perhaps "63."

[2] JA proposed precisely this project of Capt. Grinnell's to Capt. Daniel McNeill of the *General Mifflin* privateer, then apparently at Lorient, in writing him, 9 Oct., to find a place on his ship for Grinnell (LbC, Adams Papers). The Commissioners conducted a lengthy correspondence with the French ministry on this subject.

1778 OCT. 8. THURSDAY.

Captain Richard Grinnell was taken and carried into Guernsey by the Speedwell Cutter Captain Abraham Bushell of 12 Guns pierced for 14.

The Town of Guernsey the Capital of the Island, is fortified with one Fort upon an Island called Castle Island, within a Quarter of a Mile of the Town, right before it. There are between Eighty and an hundred Pieces of Cannon, in the Fort, but both Guns and Fort in bad Condition and Repair. Not more than 50 Soldiers at a Time in the Fort.

There are only five hundred Soldiers, highlanders, on the whole

Island. They have wrote to Scotland for another Regiment, which they say is coming.

The Militia keep watch round the Island. They are well armed, but are not exercised.

They have lately built new Batteries of four and six Guns in Places where Boats can land, and block Houses all round the Island, where Boats can Land.

The Island is not more than Ten Leagues from Cape La Hague, the french Coast. About five Thousand Souls, on the Island, very bitter against the French: but treat American Prisoners very well—more like Brothers than Prisoners.

There is a forty Gun Ship and two Frigates of 28 or 30 Guns in the Harbour before the Town of Guernsey, and several cruising round the Island as they say. Two Kings Cutters of 12 and 14 Guns, are here also.

They say there are forty six Privateers, from 8 to Twenty Guns belonging to this Island—about twenty more belonging to Jersey, Alderney and Sark.

The Proper Place to station a Frigate to intercept the Prizes, would be about 30 Leagues to the Westward of the Island, out of sight. Here a Frigate that could sail fast enough might retake many Prizes.

Captain Peter Collass of Boston, taken on board of Barns, by the Speedwell of Guernsey.[1]

Guernsey is about 20 miles in Circumference, 7 or 8 long and about 3 or 4 wide. There are breast Works all round the Island, and wherever there is a Cove or Bay where it is possible for Boats or Ships to come in there is a Battery of [2?] or 4 Guns, and they say they are building blockhouses all round the Island. They reckon they can muster between four and five Thousand Militia. They have five hundred Highlanders, all green, just off the Mountains. They have a Number of Invalids besides perhaps three or four hundred.

The Fort in the Harbour is on a Rock a Musquet shot from the Town, Eighty six Guns in the Fort, 42, 32, down to Twelves. Every Parish has a Field Piece or two. Of late they have received a No. of Field Pieces of a new Construction, 3 pounders, to be drawn by Men over Gutters, Ditches, &c. Guernsey, Jersey and Alderney have between fifty and sixty Privateers, small and great.

There is a Forty Gun Ship, a Frigate of 28 or 30 Guns, and two Cutters, of 10 or 12.

A 36 Gun Frigate to cruise about 10 or 12 Leagues to the Westward of the Island of Guernsey, might intercept their Prizes going in, provided she was a fast Sailer. She should keep out of Sight of the Island.

The Guernsey Men boasted that all the Islands had taken Prizes this War to an amount between three and four Millions.

¹ Capt. Peter Collas was a son-in-law of Franklin's favorite sister, Jane (Franklin) Mecom. He was captured by the British no less than five times during the war (*The Letters of Benjamin Franklin and Jane Mecom*, ed. Carl Van Doren, Princeton, 1950, p. 23–24). What follows is his testimony, as that above is Grinnell's, on the defenses of the Channel Islands. CFA silently supplied quotation marks around each of their statements.

MONDAY. OCT. 12.

Samuel Harding of Welfleet Cape Cod says that Mr. Robert Bartholomew or Bartlemé, and Incleby of London, are largely concerned in the Whale Fishery. Richard Coffyn and Shubael Gardiner of Nantuckett are concerned with them. Dennis Debert carries on the Business for Mr. Bartholomew. Mr. Nath. Wheatly of Boston is in Partnership with Mr. Bartholomew.—One Ship of forty Guns, or 20 Guns, would take all the Fishery.

There are about three Boats Crews on each Ship, which are twenty four Men.

1778 OCTR. 22. THURSDAY.

William Whitmarsh Jur., born in Braintree, maried and living in Marblehead, was taken Prisoner on board the Yankee Privateer, Captain Johnson. After having taken two Ships, the Prisonors rose upon them, and carried [them] to England. Carried to Chatham and put on board the Ardent 64 Gun Ship, Captn. Middleton. Next put on board the Mars 74, from thence on board the Vultur sloop for Spithead. At Spithead put on Board the Balfleur 90.—11 Oct. 1776 put on board the Rippon of 60 Guns Commodore Vernum [Vernon], bound to the East Indies. Sailed 24 Novr. from Spithead and arrived at Madrass 8 June 1777.—11 Aug. I left the Ship, and went Upon the Malabar Coast —from thence to a danish Island—thence to Bengal—thence to a danish Factory. Discharged from the danish Snow. In Novr. 17. I shipped on Board an East India man, homeward bound. Sailed in December to Madrass. Arrived in Jany. 1778—sailed 6th. February—arrived at Spithead 6 of Aug.—17 impressed. All the Men on board the Fleet were pressed, Midshipmen, Quarter Masters and all.—27. had a ticket of Liberty for 14 days.—11 September left London for Flushing. Arrived 27.—7 Oct. at Dunkirk.—Never entered, and never would.

9. "I HAVE TAKEN AN HOUSE ON THE KEYSERS GRAGT NEAR
THE SPIEGEL STRAAT" (AMSTERDAM, 1781)

10. KEIZERSGRACHT NO. 529 IN 1960

LE

POLITIQUE

HOLLANDAIS.

TOME I.

À AMSTERDAM,
chez J. A. CRAJENSCHOT.

A COLLECTION

O F

STATE-PAPERS,

Relative to the first Acknowledgment of the Sovereignty of the United States of AMERICA,
and the reception of their Minister Plenipotentiary, by their High Mightinesses the Sta-
tes-General of the United Netherlands.

AT THE HAGUE,
MDCCLXXXII.

This Collection was made, translated
and printed at the Hague by
John Adams.

Buth Hill Philadelphia March 31. 1790.

11. JOHN ADAMS PRINTS THE DOCUMENTS LEADING TO   12. THE PRO-AMERICAN JOURNAL BEGUN BY JOHN ADAMS'

1778 OCTR. 30. FRYDAY.

Last Saturday I dined with Mr. Grand in Company with Mr. Gebelin Author of the Monde Primitif.[1]

[1] Antoine Court de Gébelin (1725–1784) was the author of *Monde primitif, analysé et comparé avec le monde moderne,* a vast and learned but unfinished work on mythology and language of which JA owned a copy (9 vols., Paris, 1775–1782) that he read and heavily annotated in old age. See *Catalogue of JA's Library,* p. 65; Alfred Iacuzzi, *John Adams, Scholar,* N.Y., 1952, p. 230–232. Court de Gébelin is said to have served as one of the editors of the *Affaires de l'Angleterre et de l'Amérique,* a vehicle of American propaganda in which Franklin and JA were much interested (Hoefer, *Nouv. Biog. Générale;* see notes on entries of 11 Feb. and 3 March 1779, below).

NOV. 9.

Mr. Lee read me a Paragraph of a Letter, from London, "that Mr. D. Hartley would probably be here, in the Course of this Month."

At Dinner I repeated this Paragraph to Dr. Franklin, and said that I thought "Mr. H's Journey ought to be forbidden." The Dr. said "he did not see how his coming could be forbid." I replied "We could refuse to see him," and that I thought We ought to see nobody from England, unless they came with full Powers....[1] That little Emmissarys were sent by the King only to amuse a certain Sett of People, while he was preparing for his designs. That there had been enough of this.... The Dr. sayd "We could decline having any private Conversation with him."...

[1] Suspension points, here and below, in MS.

1778. NOVR: 26 JEUDI.

Went to see the Palace of Bourbon, belonging to the Prince of Condé. It is a City. The Apartements of the Prince, are very rich, and elegant. The Gallery has many fine Paintings. But I have no Taste for ringing the Changes of Mirrors, Gold, Silver, Marble, Glass, and Alabaster.—For myself I had rather live in this Room at Passy than in that Palace, and in my Cottage at Braintree than in this Hotel at Passy.

An unlucky Accident befell my Servant Stevens in falling from the Coach, and being dragged by the foot upon the Pavement. He was in great Danger but happily was not essentially hurt.

Dined with the Abbes C[halut] and A[rnoux]. Returned at Night and found M. Turgot, Abbe Condilac, Mad. Helvetius, and the Abbe &c.

NOVR. 30. 1778.

Orthodoxy is my Doxy, and Heterodoxy is your Doxy.— Definitions.
F[*ranklin*].

DECR. 2.

Captn. Bernard. Says There are Two hundred and Thirty Sail of
Merchand Ships lying at the Mother Bank, near Spithead, ready to sail
to the West Indies, loaded with all Kinds of Provisions and dry
Goods, and Warlike Stores. They are to be joined by about Thirty
Sail that now lay in the Downs. They are to sail the first Wind after the
two Fleets join. The Wind must be easterly. They all go to the Barbadoes, where the Fleet for the Windward Islands, seperates from that
to the Leward Islands. They are to be convoyed out of the Channell by
Twelve Ships of the Line, Six of them to go through the Voyage to the
W.I. Islands.—As they commonly exagerate, it is probable, that not so
many Men of War will go. There may be 8 or 9 Men of War, go out of
the Channell and perhaps two or three, go thro the Voyage. They cannot probably spare 6 Vessells of the Line without leaving the French
Masters of the Seas.

Account of Monies received

	£	s	d
1778. Feb. 12. Recd. of the Hon. the Navy Board at Boston, in Sterling.	100:	0:	0
	2400:	Liv.	

⟨April Recd. of Mr. Bondfield at Bourdeaux⟩³

⟨Feb.⟩ Ap. 18. ⟨drew an order on Mr. Grand, the Banker, in favour of Dr. Noel for two hundred and thirty one Livres and Six Sous, being the Ballance of Expences on the Road from Bourdeaux⟩

Account of Monies expended

	£	s	d
1778 Feb. To Sundry Expences at Boston, in making the necessary Preparations for my Voyage exclusive of the Articles furnished me by the Navy Board²—in Sterling.	10:	0:	0

Livres

⟨To Cash expended, at Bourdeaux, and on the Journey from thence to Paris near 500 Miles, in which is included the Expences of my self, Captain Palmes, sent to Paris by Captn. Tucker to receive the orders of the Commissioners, of Dr. Noel a French Surgeon of the Boston who went [as] our Interpreter, of Master Jesse Deane, and of my little Son, and my Domestic Servant 240: 0: 0

⟨Feb.⟩ April 18. ⟨Paid Dr. Noel by an order on the Banker 231 Livres and Six Sous, being for the Ballance of Expences on the Road from Bourdeaux to Paris.⟩ transferred to Pages 9 and 10.⁵   45: 0: 0⟩⁴

* For notes to Personal Receipts and Expenditures, see pages 343–344.

325

Account of Monies received

	£	s	d
deaux to Paris,⟩ transferred to Pages 9 and 10.[6]			
April 22. Recd. of Mr. Franklin twenty Louis D'ors — 480 Liv.			

Account of Monies expended

	£	s	d
paid for Padlocks and a few other little Necessaries, 7s. Sterling Liv. 8	0:	7:	0
Ap. 22. paid my Servant Joseph Stephens five Louis D'ors, as Per Rect.	120:	0:	0
1778. Ap. 23. paid for French Dictionaries & Grammars Liv. 36	1:	10:	0
Ap. 25. paid the Barber for a Wigg, one Louis D'or and 2 Crowns. Liv. 36	1:	10:	0
and half a Crown for a Bagg. Liv. 3	0:	2:	6
Ap. 27. Paid Joseph Stevens, 2 Louis D'ors Livres	48:	0:	0
To 8 English Guineas, lost in a Garment which was stole on the Road bet. Bourdeaux and Paris,—the Guineas were sewn up in the Garment, to conceal them from the Enemy in Case of Capture at Sea–sterling	8:	8:	0[7]
Decr. 19. Paid to Mr. Jonathan Williams for a Bill of Exchange, drawn by Mrs. Livres	192:	0:	0

A. in favr. of Codman and Smith, in-
dorsed to Mr. Williams 50£ sterling 50: 0: 0
         Liv. 1200
    In Livres, Sous and Deniers.8

Ap. 30. Paid the Washerwoman 7: 6: 0
 Paid for à Tickett. 6: 0: 0
May 1. & 2. Paid for two Ticketts and
 some Pamphlets 14: 0: 0
May 5. Paid Joseph Stevens for Sundry
 small Articles as per Rect. 44:12: 0
May 7. Paid Joseph Stevens 2 Louis D'ors
 equal to 48 Livres. Pr. Rect. 48: 0: 0
8. paid Mr. W. T. Franklin a Louis D'or to
 pay for Horses, servants &c. at the
 Hotell, where they dined when I was at
 Versailles to be presented to the K[ing] 24: 0: 0
May 9. Paid for two blank Paper Books9 16: 4: 0
10 pd. Washerwoman 4: 2: 0
 paid Mr. Lee a Crn. borrowed of him
 in Paris 6: 0: 0
May 14. Paid Mr. J. Hochereau his Ac-
 count10 40: 0: 0
 ditto for Almanack Royal11 6: 0: 0
1778. May 15. paid Mr. Hochereau another Acct. 42: 0: 0

1778. May 6. Recd. of Mr. W. T. Franklin
20 Louis D'ors 480: 0: 0

Account of Monies received	£	s	d	Account of Monies expended	£	s	d
				paid Mr. Lee 4 Louis D'ors for Articles of Dress purchased for me	96:	0:	0
				May 18. Paid for Pencils	3:	0:	0
				May 22. paid for a Tickett	6:	0:	0
				May 23 paid for a few necessary Books, And for some transient Expences 4. Louis D'ors	96:	0:	0
				May 31. paid for Tickett and transient Expences	24:	0:	0
				June 7 paid for Expences at Versailles, at the Ceremony of the Knights De St. Esprit and Seeing the King, Queen and Royal Family at the Grand Couvert	12:	0:	0
				June 16 Paid Denis Account two Louis D'ors.	48:	0:	0
				paid Mr. J. Williams for La Fontaines Works in 7 Vol.	24:	0:	0
				paid Joseph Stevens's Account	28:	9:	0
				17 paid for a Trunk a Louis	24:	0:	0
				paid the Comis for bringing it	0:	12:	0
				19 paid Chaubert the Shoemaker his Account 33 Livres.	33:	0:	0

1778. May 25. By Cash & Payments made to and for me at Bourdeaux, by Mr.

1778 May 25. To my Expences at Bourdeaux, and from thence to Paris in the

Bondfield, according to his Account, exhibited to me, in his Letter of 26 May.[12]
Livres
1404: 0: 0

Nota. B. this Article is to be substituted instead of the 2d Article in the first and 2 Pages of this Account, which is to be erased.[13]

Ap. 18. By an order drawn by me on Mr. Grand the Banker, in favour of Dr. Noel for Two hundred and thirty one Livres and Six Sous, being the Ballance of Expences from Bourdeaux to Paris. N.B. this Article is transfered from the two first Pages of this Book in order to have the whole of this Affair in one View.[14]
0231: 6: 0

1778. May 25. By Sundry Articles, shipped by Mr. Bondfield for my Family according to his Account, for which I am accountable.
888:12: 0

June 11. By an order drawn by me alone on Mr. Grand in favour of Mr. Le Cour for
365: 5: 0

June 12 By an order drawn by me alone on Mr. Grand in favour of Mr. Denis Hill
663: 5: 0

Hire of Carriages Horses and all other Expences for Captn. Palmes, Dr. Noel, and Jesse Deane, as well as my son, servant and self.
1404: 0: 0

Ap. 18. To Cash paid Dr. Noel by an order on the Banker for £231. 6s. od. being for the Ballance of Expences upon the Road from Bourdeaux to Paris.
0231: 6: 0

1778 May 25. Paid Mr. Bondfield, for the Articles shipped by him, as on the left Hand Page
888:12: 0

June 11. Paid Mr. Le Cœur, by an order as on the left Hand Page
365: 5: 0

12 Paid Dennis Hill by an order as on the left Hand Page
663: 5: 0

Account of Monies received	£	s	d

July 15 16. drew an order on Mr. Grand, in these Words viz. Mr. Grand, after considering of your Question concerning the Furniture which was made for Mr. Deane, and which he had used for Upwards of a Year, before I came into this Kingdom and after considering the Nature of the Contract, which Mr. Deane made, according to which fifteen hundred Livres I think are to be paid for the Use of them for the first Year: I have concluded, upon the whole that it is most for the Interest of the public, to pay for the Purchase than for the Loan: You will therefore be so good, as to pay for them as soon as you please. But I have one Request to make, which is, that in the Charge you make of this Article in the public Accounts, you would mention the Contract made with Mr. Deane, that I may not appear to be accountable, for more than my share of this Expence. I am &c.

Livres. 4294: 0: 0

1778 June 16. Recd. of Mr. Grand the

Account of Monies expended	£	s	d
16 Paid for Mr. Deanes Furniture as on the left Hand Page	4294:	0:	0

330

Banker for which I singly gave a Rect.
100 Louis   2400: 0: 0

1778 June 22 paid for two Pamphlets   3: 0: 0
paid for Ticketts and Coach hire   15: 0: 0
24 paid the Peruquiers Account   39:12: 0
25 paid Expences at Paris and at the Comedy   18: 0: 0
28 Paid Expences at Paris and at the Comedy   18: 0: 0
29 Paid Joseph Stevens his Account as pr his Rect.   96: 0: 0
30 paid Mr. Quillaus Account—32 Crowns   192: 0: 0
July 1. paid Expences at Paris   12: 0: 0
2 paid Expences at Paris   12: 0: 0
5 Expences at Paris   18: 0: 0
6 Dto.   12: 0: 0
9 paid Monsieur Quillau, his Memoire as per Rect   170: 0: 0
10 paid Joseph Stevens as per Rect   144: 0: 0
paid for Sundry Expences, myself 2 Louis   48: 0: 0
12 paid Expences at Paris   18: 0: 0
16 paid the Washerwoman 1 Louis   24: 0: 0
paid Expences at Paris   18: 0: 0
18. paid at the Bureau general des Gazettes etrangeres, for one Year and one Months Subscription for the Courier de L'Europe   52: 0: 0
19 paid Hocherau his Memoire   25: 0: 0

Account of Monies received

	£	s	d
1778 Aug. 6. drew an order on Mr. Grand for 100 Louis	2400:	0:	0

Account of Monies expended

	£	s	d
1778 July 21. paid Expences at Paris	13:	4:	0
22 paid Mr. Langlois Memoire	74:	0:	0
23 delivered 2 Louis to Captain Niles to be laid out in Tea for my family	48:	0:	0
paid Hochereau his Memoire	15:	0:	0
27 paid Hochereau his Memoir	61:	0:	0
paid Expences at Paris for Dr. Franklin and myself	18:	0:	0
29 paid Hochereau another Memoire	40:	0:	0
paid Expences in Town	18:	0:	0
paid Joseph Stephens his Account	28:	18:	0
31 paid Hochereau another Memoire	22:	10:	0
paid the Bureau des Gazettes etrangeres for the Gazette de la Haye	36:	0:	0
Aug. 2. Paid the Taylers Man, for bringing Cloathes	3:	0:	0
paid Expences at Paris	9:	0:	0
4 Paid Denny his Account	44:	4:	0
5 paid for the Gazette de France	12:	0:	0
1778. Aug. 7. paid the Maitre D'hotel his Account	52:	12:	0
8 paid for the Postage of 2 Packets of Letters from Bourdeaux, which came			

by the Way of St. Eustatia

paid transient Expences at Paris — 32: 0: 0

9 paid Expences at Paris — 18: 0: 0

10 paid Mr. Jonathan Williams, for Mr. Cranch, a private affaire, this Article to be charged to my private Account — 12: 0: 0

paid Mr. Amiel for Mr. Austin — 141: 9: 0

11 paid for the Marquise D'Argensons Work[16] — 72: 0: 0

12 deld. 8 Crowns to my servant to pay for several small Expences — 5: 0: 0

15 paid Jos. Stephens — 48: 0: 0

Expences in Town — 70: 0: 0

17 paid Expences at Lucienne for Dr. Franklin and myself — 15: 0: 0

paid Mr. Austin as on the other Side — 12: 0: 0

paid Hochereau his Memoire — 720: 0: 0

18 Paid Expences at Paris — 27: 0: 0

paid Hatters Account — 18: 0: 0

19 paid Bureau by an order, as on the other Side — 30: 0: 0

22 Expences at the Bois de Boulogne — 360: 0: 0

23. This day I accompanied the Abbeys Chalut and Arnold to Notre Dame—lenfans trouves,[17] a Charity [sermon?] at Passy, and the Spectacle at the Bois de — 12: 0: 0

17 drew an order on Mr. Grand in favour of Jon. Loring Austin for — 720: 0: 0

19 drew an Oder on Mr. Grand in favour of Monsieur Bureau fifteen Louis. — 360: 0: 0

Account of Monies received

	£	s	d
28. drew an Order on Mr. Grand in favour of Mr. Hill for	319	15	0
Septr. 13. drew an Ordre on Mr. Grand in favour of Mr. Hill for his Memoire	236	0	0
1778 September 9. drew an order on Mr. Grand for 229 Livres 6s: 9d, in favour of Mr. W. T. Franklin to pay Mr. Williams for some Goods shipped by Captn. Corbin Barnes for my family	229	6	9

Account of Monies expended

Boulonge, my Expences

	£	s	d
Aug. 30. Expences at Bois de Boulogne	48	0	0
31. paid Mr. Hochereau his Memoire	6	0	0
omitted Aug. 28. Paid Hill by an order on	12	0	0
Mr. Grand as in Page 20[18]	319	15	0
September 2. paid Expences at Paris	18	0	0
4 paid Mr. Hochereau his Memoire	22	4	0
5 paid M. Hochereau his Memoire	26	10	0
paid Expences at Paris	18	0	0
6. paid the Washerwomans Account	33	14	0
paid Joseph Stephens my servand	12	0	0
9 Expences at the Bois du Bouloge	6	0	0
omitted 13. Paid Hill by an order on Mr. Grand as in Page 20	236	0	0
13 paid the Taylors Servant, according to Custom	6	0	0
19 paid Dr. Bancroft for a Seal	99	0	0
paid Jos. Stevens	12	0	0
Expences at Paris	18	0	0
20 Expences in the Bois du Boulogne	1	4	0
21 paid Langlois Memoire	18	0	0
paid for mending my Watch	7	0	0
Expences at Paris	3	0	0

	£	s	d
omitted 1778 Septr. 9. Paid Mr. Williams by an order as on the left Hand	229	6	9
1778 Septr. 22. gave Mr. Austin four Crowns to be laid out in Tea for my family	24	0	0
paid Hochereau his Memoire	99	8	0
paid for Transient Expences	6	0	0
29 Expences in the Bois du Boulogne	6	0	0
Octr. 1. paid for Pen knives, a Walking Cane and a Watch String	18	0	0
2 paid M. Hochereau his Memoire	30	0	0
9 paid Jos. Stevens	18	0	0
10 Expences at Paris	12	0	0
12 paid Dennis Memoire	27	0	0
15. paid Hochereau	37	15	0
17 paid M. Hochereau	60	10	0
paid Joseph Stevens Expences at Paris	12	0	0
20. paid Mr. Hochereau his Memoire	12	0	0
23. paid Mr. Hochereau	137	10	0
1778. Octr. 25. *(Approved an account presented to me by Mr. Grand, for Linnen, Ruffles &c.*	43	10	0
	430	6	0⟩

Octr. 27. Paid Mr. Grand, his Account including the foregoing Article of the 25 of Octr. by a Rect. and an order to

Octr. 27. Recd. as by Article on the other side as per Mr. Grands Acct.   684: 17: 6

Account of Monies received

	£	s	d
Novr. 30. Drew an order on Mr. Grand the Banker in favour of Monsieur Hochereau to pay his Memoire	285:	0:	0
1778 Decr. 2 drew an Order on Mr. Grand in favour of Louis Tardy for the Amount of his Memoire	265:10:		0
Decr. 16. Recd. of Mr. Grand one hundred Lewis D'ors for which I gave a Rect	£2400:10:		0

Account of Monies expended

	£	s	d
place the whole to public Acct. as per Acct.	684:17:		6
Novr. 1. paid Mr. Hochereau his Memr.	165:10:		0
2 paid Joseph Stevens	12:	0:	0
3 paid Hochereau his Memoire	21:	0:	0
14 paid Jos. Stephens 1 Louis	24:	0:	0
paid Expences at Paris	3:	0:	0
30 paid Joseph Stevens's Tailers Bill	33:	0:	0
paid Monsr. Hochereaus Memoire by an order on Mr. Grand the Banker	285:	0:	0
paid Expences at Paris	6:	0:	0
1778 Decr. 1. Gave the Postilion of Mr. De Sartine who brought me Dispatches from America sent by his Master	12:	0:	0
Decr. 2. Paid Louis Tardy his Memoire by an Order on Mr. Grand	265:10:		0
9 Expences at Paris	12:	0:	0
15 Expences in Town	12:	0:	0
19 Expences	6:	0:	0
21 Paid Rouault his Memoire	14:	0:	0
23 paid Joseph Stevens	24:	0:	0
29 Expences in Town	4:	0:	0

	£	s	d
1779 Jany. 1. pd Stevens	12:	0:	0
paid penny Postman	4:	0:	0
3 Expences in Town	12:	0:	0
Expences to the Paroisse	3:	0:	0
1779. Jany 8 Expences at Paris	12:	0:	0
9 paid for Syrope de Tortue a Medicine	3:	0:	0
Paid a Barbers Boy for an Etrenne	3:	0:	0
20 Expences at Paris	9:	0:	0
25 Expences at Calvare	15:	0:	0
31 transient Expences	12:	0:	0
Feb. 2. given to a French Sailor who had been taken Prisoner in the Lexington and escaped to help him to his own Country of Flanders	6:	0:	0
6 Paid Visquenets Account	18:	0:	0
11 Expences at Paris	6:	0:	0
15 Expences at Paris	3:	0:	0
20 Expences at Paris	6:	0:	0
21 Paid a Bill of Exchange £100 st. 95 Louis and a Crown paid to Dr. Winship [Windship]	2286:	0:	0
1779 Feb. 25. Expences at Paris	6:	0:	0
27 Expences at St Dennis	12:	0:	0
March 3. Expences at Versailles	18:	0:	0
4 Expences at Calvare	6:	0:	0
Paid Pascall towards a Chaise	24:	0:	0

Account of Monies received

	£	s	d
1779 March 5. Recd. of Dr. Franklin an Order on Mr. Grand for 300 Louis	7200:	0:	0

Account of Monies expended

	£	s	d
5 Paid Hollevelles Memoire	209:	0:	0
Paid for an Inkhorn, some Purses and other Expences at Paris	24:	0:	0
6 Paid Brunell for a Caisse	24:	0:	0
Paid Mr. Chaumont for the Remr. of [Chalsons?] Account	125:	0:	0
Paid Mr. Desavots Memoire	60:	0:	0
8 paid Mr. Pascal the Remaining 3 Louis for the Post Chaise to Nantes	72:	0:	0
Pour le Garçon	1:	4:	0
Paid Dennis Memoire	63:	10:	0
Paid Barbers Rect for dressing my Wig	40:	0:	0
Paid Washerwomans Acct.	24:	1:	0
1779. March 12. To Expences from Paris to Nantes, Post Horses, &c. 5 days 18 Louis	432:	0:	0
March 14. and 15 Paid for the Hire of a Barge and Bargemen and Expences to Paimbeuf	24:	0:	0
15 Paid Bill of Exchange to J. Williams	240:	0:	0
16 Paid for an Hat	24:	0:	0
for another Hat	18:	0:	0
Expences at the Comedy	4:	0:	0
Paid for a Trunk to go to Brest	18:	0:	0

	£	s	d
Paid Jos. Stevens's Account	48	14	0
17 Paid the Barber	6	0	0
Paid the Coffee at Nantes.	15	0	0
Paid Washerwomans Acct.	5	11	6
Paid the Tavern keeper	72	6	0
22 Total of Expences from Nantes to Brest			
—15 Louis	360	0	0
Paid the Coffee for 3 Breakfasts	6	18	0
25 paid for a Portmanteau	15	0	0
paid Washerwoman	3	0	0
1779. March 26. paid Account at the Grand Monarch	20	16	0
27. Paid Expences at Brest	18	0	0
28 Dto.	6	0	0
29	12	0	0
30	18	0	0
April 1	9		
2	18	0	0
3	24	0	0
4. Lent to an American in Distress 2 Louis. J. W.	48	0	0
5 Paid Jo. Stevens Acct.	16	17	0
7 & 8 Paid Expences of Post Horses Postilion, and living from Brest to L'Orient	96	0	0
Expences at Lorient	50	0	0

Account of Monies received	£	s	d

Account of Monies expended	£	s	d
A Canister of Tea and small Loaf of Sugar to use on the Road	14:	5:	0
11 Expences from L'orient to Nantes	144:	0:	0
12 transient Expences at Nantes	9:	0:	0
13 transient Expences	6:	0:	0
14 Dto.	13:	0:	0
Ap. 15. pd. Washerwoman	2:	5:	0
transient Expences	6:		
16. Do.	7:10:	0	
17 Do.	12:	0:	0
pd. Washerwoman, and others	7:	0:	0
Nugents Dictionaries 2	9:	0:	0
19 transient Expences	15:	0:	0
Dto.	3:	0:	0
D'Olivets Phillippics	2:10:	0	
20 paid for Wine, Bread, fowls &c. for our Voyage down the River	9:	0:	0
paid the Barber	9:	0:	0
paid the Coffee	2:	0:	0
Min. of Things purchased at L'orient and Nantes to carry home for my familys Use. one Doz. cot. Han. £18.— half dozen Silk £27. 3 m. needles £9.— 1 m. Pins 6—Nankeen 30—coton 38.—			

1 dozen other Hank. 42.—a Peice of others 30.	200:	0:	0
May 1. Paid Expences at Nantes	32:	15:	0
2 Dto.	6:	0:	0
May 14 Paid Joseph Stevens two Months Wages, for his services from the 10 Feb.	108:	0:	0
Paid for Fresh fish on board ship	3:	0:	0
17. Paid Expences at L'orient	15:	0:	0
18 Dto.	9:	0:	0
19 Dto.	6:	0:	0
21. Paid for Hankerchiefs	34:	10:	0
Expences	3:	0:	
23. Dto.	6:		
25	3:		
May 26. Expences at L'orient	12:	0:	0
Paid Mr. Watkins for Materials he purchased for making me some Cloaths	38:	0:	0
Paid Dto. for making	8:	8:	0
Paid same at another Time for Do.	30:	0:	0
1779 June 9. Paid Bargemen Barber Cabbin Servants &c. on leaving the Allyance	24:	0:	0
10 Paid for Materials to make me some light Cloaths for the Voyage to Mr. Watkins	39:	0:	0
11 Transient Expences, at L'orient	12:	0:	0

May 22. Recd. of Mr. Schweighauser and Mr. Puchelberg his Partner at L'orient, for which I drew an order on Dr. Franklin in favour of Mr. Schweighauser.

Livres 2930:16: 0

341

Account of Monies received

	£	s	d
16 June. Puchelberg Acct.	1012	17:	0

Account of Monies expended

	£	s	d
12 Dto.	6:	0:	0
16 transient Expences	6:	0:	0
17. Coffee at L'orient	25:	1:	0
Garcon	1:	4:	0
Barber	12:	0:	0
Mr. Raimbault	104:	10:	0
Paid Salomon	159:	10:	0
Dr. Brooke for Medicine	19:	0:	0
17 June. Paid Captain Landais[19] a Louis he lent me at Nantes	24:	0:	0
Transient Expences	12:	0:	0
Paid Mr. Watkins for making and mending Cloaths	24:	0:	0
1779. Aug. 2. gave to the servants and Sailors 5 Crowns. Gave for the Hire of a Boat 5 dollars, to carry me, my Baggage &c. hence[20]			

[1] From D/JA/48, one of the two matching small quarto volumes bound in marbled boards probably purchased by the Navy Board in Boston and presented to JA when he sailed on his first mission to Europe; see entry of 13 Feb. 1778 and note 1 there. The present record of JA's receipts and expenditures, from the day before he sailed from Nantasket Roads until the day he returned there, occupies 24 leaves at the front of the volume. Doubtless JA left the volume home when he returned to Europe in Nov. 1779; most of its remaining leaves were used for transcripts of his early Diary when in 1829 JQA caused the earliest Diary booklets to be copied; see Introduction.

The record is valuable not only because it fills, at least in a manner, certain gaps in the Diary but also because it is a veritable guide to French currency and the exchange rate between French and British money during JA's first sojourn in Europe. In the early part of his record, JA, who was himself coping with the usual monetary problems of a traveler, gives his sums in both currencies, though it should be noted that the symbols for both (£ for pounds and livres, s. for shillings and sous [or sols], and d. for pence and deniers) were identical and were used interchangeably, each series having *proportionally* the same value. For a brief account of the French monetary system before and after the French Revolution, see JQA's *Report on Weights and Measures*, written and published as a U.S. Government document, Washington, 1821, p. 62–64. It is sufficient to say here that, as the figures in the present document show, 24 French livres equaled one British pound sterling (for which the French had an equivalent coin, called a louis d'or), and that 6 livres therefore equaled 5 shillings (for which the French had a coin called an écu or crown, as well as a half-crown piece worth 3 livres or 2s. 6d. sterling).

In printing this document the editors have omitted the totals that appear at the foot of the columns (which in the MS are on facing pages) on some pages in the MS. Since these are incomplete and were never added up to make a grand total, they would in our judgment prove more confusing than significant if set in type and dispersed here and there on the pages of the printed version.

[2] See note 1 on entry of 13 Feb. 1778, above, and facsimiles reproduced in this volume.

[3] A figure, apparently in British pounds, appears opposite this entry in the MS but is not wholly legible. See, however, the first entry under 25 May 1778 in this column, below.

[4] Repeated and corrected in the first entry under 25 May 1778 in this column, below.

[5] See a later entry dated 18 April 1778 in the Expenditures column, below.

[6] See a later entry dated 18 April 1778 in the Receipts column, below.

[7] See note 1 on Diary entry of 1 April 1778, above.

[8] From this point on, the sums are entered in French money only.

[9] Probably but not certainly the two folio letterbooks designated in the Adams Papers as Lb/JA/6–7, bound in white parchment and bearing handsome trade cards of Cabaret, "Au Griffon . . . Marchand Papetier Ordinaire des Bureaux du Roy," in Rue de Seine, Faubourg St. Germain, Paris.

[10] The Hochereau family were booksellers established in Paris from the beginning of the 18th century ([A. M. Lottin,] *Catalogue chronologique des libraires et des libraires-imprimeurs de Paris*, Paris, 1789, p. 80). From one or more of them JA bought books with great frequency during his first years abroad. Unfortunately, the "mémoires" or bills, which might indicate the titles of the books JA bought, have not been found. In rendering his accounts to Congress for this mission, JA included sums spent on such books as were essential to qualify himself in "the science of Negotiation," arguing that this was "one of the most necessary, and Useful Ways in which Money had ever been spent in that Country" (JA to the Board of Treasury, 19 Sept. 1779, LbC, Adams Papers; *Works*, 7:111–114). What is more, his argument prevailed; see the report of a committee on JA's accounts, 15 April 1780 (JCC, 16:368–369).

[11] This volume, *Almanach royal, année M. DCC. LXXVIII*, Paris, n.d., issued by the King's Printer, remains

among JA's books in the Boston Public Library and has proved useful to the editors in identifying French officials and others mentioned in the Diary.

[12] This letter has not been found, but JA's answer, 3 June (LbC, Adams Papers), elucidates this transaction. Bondfield had purchased various articles on JA's account to be sent to Braintree by Capt. Tucker in the *Boston*.

[13] Second entry in this column, above.

[14] Third entry in this column, above.

[15] Seemingly a mistake for June, but the payment by Grand of 4,294 livres to "Mrs. Poussin" for furniture was made on 17 July 1778, as recorded in the final accounts of the Commissioners (DNA:RG 39, Foreign Ledgers, Public Agents in Europe, 1776–1787, p. 87). A note is added in the official account: "N.B. the proportions of Mr. D. & Mr. A. must be settled by them."

[16] René Louis, Marquis d'Argenson, published anonymously *Considérations sur le gouvernement ancien et présent de la France*, Amsterdam, 1765, of which JA's copy remains among his books in the Boston Public Library (*Catalogue of JA's Library*).

[17] The "Hôpital des Enfans-Trouvés, près Notre-Dame" is described in Thiery, *Almanach du voyageur à Paris*, 1784, p. 331–332. Years later JA drew a political moral from what he saw on his visit to this foundling hospital; see his *Works*, 6:452.

[18] Entry of 28 Aug. 1778 in the Receipts column.

[19] On Pierre Landais see entries of 9 May and following, below.

[20] There is conflicting evidence on the exact date of JA's arrival home. La Luzerne and his party disembarked at Hancock's Wharf in Boston on 3 August. The present entry indicates that JA and JQA left the *Sensible* in Nantasket Roads on the 2d and were rowed to Braintree. This may be so, but on the other hand JA may have carelessly misdated this entry; see note on the Diary entry of 31 July, below.

1779. FEB. 2. TUESDAY.

Last Tuesday, I dined in Company with the Abbe Raynal, and Mr. Gebelin, and asked them to dine with me, on the then next Sunday. Accordingly the day before Yesterday, they both came.

M. Raynal is the most eloquent Man, I ever heard speak in French. His Voice is sharp and clear but pleasant. He talks a great deal, and is very entertaining.[1] M. Gebelin is much less addicted to talking. He is silent, soft, and still. His Mind always upon the Stretch.

[1] Guillaume Thomas François, Abbé Raynal (1713–1796), French *philosophe* and historian, is best remembered for his immensely popular *Histoire philosophique et politique des établissemens et du commerce des Européens dans les deux Indes*, first published at Amsterdam, 1770. The *Catalogue of JA's Library* records several works by Raynal owned by JA that have come to rest in the Boston Public Library, including the *Histoire des deux Indes* in both French and English editions.

FEB. 4.

Breakfasted with the Abbe Raynal, at his House at his particular Invitation, with a large Company of Gentlemen and Ladies. The Abbé is more than Sixty, seems worn with Studies, but he has Spirit, Wit, Eloquence and Fire enough.

February 1779

The Duke de Rochefoucault, Mr. Turgot, Abbe Rochon and De la Roche, dined here.

1779. FEB. 8.

In Conversation with Dr. Franklin, in the Morning I gave him my Opinion, of Mr. Deanes Address to the People of America, with great Freedom and perhaps with too much Warmth. I told him that it was one of the most wicked and abominable Productions that ever sprung from an human Heart. That there was no safety in Integrity against such a Man. That I should wait upon The Comte de Vergennes, and the other Ministers, and see in what light they considerd this Conduct of Mr. Deane. That if they, and their Representatives in America, were determined to countenance and support by their Influence such Men and Measures in America, it was no matter how soon the Alliance was broke. That no Evil could be greater, nor any Government worse, than the Toleration of such Conduct. No one was present, but the Doctor and his Grandson.[1]

In the Evening, I told Dr. Bancroft, to the same Effect, that the Address appeared to me in a very attrocious Light, that however difficult Mr. Lees Temper might be, in my Opinion he was an honest Man, and had the utmost fidelity towards the united States. That such a Contempt of Congress committed in the City where they set, and the Publication of such Accusations in the Face of the Universe, so false and groundless as the most heinous of them appeared to me, these Accusations attempted to be coloured by such frivolous Tittle Tattle, such Accusations made too by a Man who had been in high Trust, against two others, who were still so, appeared to me, Evidence of such a Complication of vile Passions, of Vanity, Arrogance and Presumption, of Malice, Envy and Revenge, and at the same Time of such Weakness, Indiscretion and Folly, as ought to unite every honest and wise Man against him. That there appeared to me no Alternative left but the Ruin of Mr. Deane, or the Ruin of his Country. That he appeared to me in the Light of a wild boar, that ought to be hunted down for the Benefit of Mankind. That I would start fair with him, Dr. Bancroft, and give him Notice that I had hitherto been loath to give up Mr. Deane. But that this Measure of his appeared to Me to be so decisive against him that I had given him up to Satan to be buffeted.

In all this it is easy to see there is too much Declamation, but the

345

substa[n]tial Meaning of it, is, as appears to me, exactly true, as such as I will abide by, unless, future Evidence which I dont expect should convince me, of any Error in it.[2]

[1] Silas Deane had arrived in Philadelphia on 12 July 1778, and had promptly requested an audience of Congress to enable him to defend his conduct in Europe, which had been severely impugned by his colleague Arthur Lee. Lee's charges, supported by relatives and friends, split Congress into warring factions, and Deane failed to get a satisfactory hearing. His patience at last exhausted, he took his case to the country by publishing in the *Pennsylvania Packet*, 5 Dec. 1778, an address "To the Free and Virtuous Citizens of America" (reprinted in *Deane Papers*, 3:66–76). Intended as the first in a series of public letters, this one contained violent counter-charges against Arthur and William Lee, treated certain members of Congress with great freedom, and led to a controversy that can hardly be said to be settled even yet by historians. The strength of JA's feelings about Deane's publication is revealed in his letter to Vergennes, drafted in his Diary and printed under 10–11 Feb., below.

[2] The final sentence of this heated entry is obviously defective but is here printed literally. It was silently (and plausibly) corrected by CFA to read: "... but the substantial meaning of it is such as appears to me exactly true, and such as I will abide by, unless future evidence, which I don't expect, should convince me of any error in it" (JA, *Works*, 3:187).

1779 FEB. 9.

Abbe C.[1]

Terruit Hispanos, Ruiter, qui terruit Anglos
Ter ruit in Gallos, territus ipse ruit.[2]

Cum fueris Romæ, Romano vivito more
Si fueris alibi, vivito sicut ibi.

Any Thing to divert Melancholly, and to sooth an aking Heart. The Uncandor, the Prejudices, the Rage, among several Persons here, make me Sick as Death.

Virtue is not always amiable. Integrity is sometimes ruined by Prejudices and by Passions. There are two Men in the World who are Men of Honour and Integrity I believe, but whose Prejudices and violent Tempers would raise Quarrells in the Elisian Fields if not in Heaven. On the other Hand there is another, whose Love of Ease, and Dissipation, will prevent any thorough Reformation of any Thing—and his ⟨Cunning and⟩ Silence and Reserve, render it very difficult to do any Thing with him. One of the other[s], whom I have allowed to be honest, has such a bitter, such a Sour in him, and so few of the nice feelings, that G[od] knows what will be the Consequence to himself and to others. Besides he has as much Cunning, and as much Secrecy.[3]

Called at Mr. Garniers—he not at home. At Mr. Grands. He and his Son began about the Address—bien faché. &c. I said, cooly, that I was astonished at the Publication of it without sending it to congress. That I believed Mr. Lee a Man of Integrity, and that all Suggestions of improper Correspondences in England, were groundless. That my Br[other] L[ee] was not of the sweetest disposition perhaps, but he was honest. That Virtue was not always amiable....[4] M. G. replyed, il est soupsonneux—il n'a du Confiance en Personne. Il croit que toute le Monde est—I cant remember the precise Word.... I believe this is a just Observation. He has Confidence in no body. He believes all Men selfish—And, no Man honest or sincere. This, I fear, is his Creed, from what I have heard him say. I have often in Conversation disputed with him, on this Point. However I never was so nearly in his Situation before. There is no Man here that I dare Trust, at present. They are all too much heated with Passions and Prejudices and party disputes. Some are too violent, others too jealous—others too cool, and too reserved at all Times, and at the same time, every day betraying Symptoms of a Rancour quite as deep.

The Wisdom of Solomon, the Meekness of Moses, and the Patience of Job, all united in one Character, would not be sufficient, to qualify a Man to act in the Situation in which I am at present—and I have scarcely a Spice of either of these Virtues.

On Dr. F. the Eyes of all Europe are fixed, as the most important Character, in American Affairs in Europe. Neither L. nor myself, are looked upon of much Consequence. The Attention of the Court seems most to F. and no Wonder. His long and great Rep[utation] to which L's and mine are in their infancy, are enough to Account for this. His Age, and real Character render it impossible for him to search every Thing to the Bottom, and L. with his privy Council, are evermore, contriving. The Results of their Contrivances, render many Measures more difficult.

[1] Chalut?

[2] A punning distich based on the life of the famous Dutch admiral M. A. de Ruyter (1607-1676), who had sailed up the Thames and Medway in 1667 but was mortally wounded fighting the French in the Mediterranean. Literally: "Ruyter, who terrified the Spaniards, who terrified the English, [and] thrice fell upon the French, himself has fallen, terrified himself."

[3] "It is almost needless to say that Mr. Arthur Lee, Mr. Izard, and Dr. Franklin, are the persons referred to" (note by CFA, in JA, *Works*, 3:188).

[4] Suspension points, here and below, in MS.

[DRAFT OF A LETTER TO VERGENNES, 10–11 FEBRUARY 1779.][1]

Confidential.

Sir

As your Excellency reads English perfectly well, my first Request is that you would not communicate this Letter, even to a Translator.

I have hitherto avoided, in my single Capacity, giving your Excellency, any Trouble at all either by Letter or by Conversation. But the present ⟨Crisis⟩ Emergency demands that I should ask the Favour of your Excellency to explain my Sentiments to you, either by Letter or in Person. If your Excellency will permit a personal Interview, ⟨*ignorant, and unpracticed as I am, in the French Language, I am sure that by my Countenance, my Gestures and my broken Syllables in French,*⟩ I am sure I can make my self understood by your Excellency. If you prefer a Correspondence in Writing, I will lay open my Heart in Writing, under my Hand.

It is the Address to the People in America under the Name of Mr. Silas Deane, that has occasioned this Boldness, in me....[2] It is to me, the most astonishing Measure, the most unexpected and unforeseen Event, that has ever happened, from the Year 1761, from which Year I have been as really engaged in this Controversy with G[reat] B[ritain] as I am now, to this Moment.

I hope your Excellency will not conclude from thence that I despair of ⟨*my*⟩ the Commonwealth. Far otherwise.—I perfectly know, that the Body of the People in the United States stand immoveable as Mount Atlas, against Great Britain.—The only Consequences of ⟨*these*⟩ an Address like this of Mr. Deanes ⟨*will*⟩ may be ⟨*a Prolongation of the War, and the necessity of hanging perhaps*⟩ ⟨*bringing to the last Punishment a few*⟩ ⟨*half a Dozen Tories the more. This last, I assure your Excellency is with me and still more with my Country men a great Evil. We wish to avoid it. But when I consider the honourable Testimonies of Confidence, which Mr. Deane carried with him to America—when I consider the Friendship which I have heard there was in France between Mr. Deane and the Plenipotentiary, and the Consul of France,*[3]⟩ ⟨*I confess I am afraid that,*⟩ ⟨*even*⟩ ⟨*the Honourable Testimonies from Your Excellency, and even, I dread to say it, from his Majesty*⟩ ⟨*I hope—I sincerely hope, that the Veneration which is due to the Plenipotentiary and the Consul of France has not been so employed*⟩ ⟨*have emboldened Mr. Deane to this Measure.—A Measure that must end in his Confusion and*⟩ ⟨*Ruin*⟩ ⟨*Shame.—I know it will not end in Submission to G.B. which is the greatest American Evil. But it may End in a Division of the States—for upon my Honour I think that this Address, itself is an open Contempt, and, as far as in Mr. Deane lies, a total subversion of our Constitution.—Your Excellency may depend upon this, that no Man knows of this Letter, but myself—and that no other Man shall know it from me.*

The Reason, of my presuming, to address myself to your Excellency, separately, is because, Mr. Franklin has unhappily, attached himself to Mr. Deane, and set himself against Mr. Lee, and therefore I have communicated this Letter to neither, and I am determined to communicate it to neither.

Dr. Franklin and Mr. Deane were upon better Terms with each other, than Dr. Franklin and Mr. Lee. I am extreamly sorry for this. But I am fully perswaded, that the Dr. is in this Instance mistaken and deceived.⟩ much Trouble to Individuals, but no final Detriment to the common Cause. But on the contrary that it will occasion so thorough an Investigation of several Things, as will rectify many Abuses.

It is my indispensable Duty, upon this Occasion to inform your Excellency, that Mr. Lee was, as long ago as 1770, appointed by the General House of Representatives of the Massachusetts Bay, of which I had then the Honour to be a Member, their Agent at the Court of London in Case of the Death or Absence of Dr. Franklin. ⟨*That from that*⟩ This Honourable Testimony was given to Mr. Lee, by an Assembly in which he had no Relation or Connection, on Account of his avowed and inflexible Attachment to the American Cause, and the Abilities of which he had given many Proofs in its Defence. From that Time he held a constant Correspondence with several of those Gentlemen who stood foremost in the Massachusetts Bay, against the Innovations and illegal Encroachments of Great Britain. This correspondence I had an Opportunity of seeing, and I assure your Excellency from my own Knowledge, that it breathed invariably the most inflexible Attachment, and the most ardent Zeal in the Cause of his Country. From the Month of Septr. 1774 to November 1777, while I had the Honour to be a Member of Congress, I had constantly an Opportunity to see his Letters to Congress, to their Committees and to several of their Individual Members. That through the whole of both these Periods, he ⟨*constantly*⟩ communicated the most constant and the most certain Intelligence, which was received from any Individual, within my Knowledge. And since I have had the Honour to be joined with him in the Commission, here, I have found in him the same Fidelity and Zeal.

I have not a Reason in the World, to believe or to suspect, that he has ever ⟨*written*⟩ maintained an improper Correspondence in England, or held any Conference or Negociation with any Body from England without communicating it to your Excellency and to his Colleagues.

I am confident therefore, that every Assertion and Insinuation and Suspicion against him, of Infidelity to the United States or to their Engagements with his Majesty are false and groundless, ⟨and⟩ that they may easily be made to appear to be so, and that they certainly will be proved to be so, to the Utter Shame and Confusion of all those who have rashly published them to the World, ⟨and particularly of Mr. Deane, who has been so forsaken by his Discretion as to have published to the World many such Insinuations⟩.

⟨The two Honourable Brothers of Mr. Lee, who are Members of Congress, I have long and intimately known. And of my own Knowledge I can say that no Men have discovered more Zeal, in Support of the Sovereignty of the United States, and in promoting from the Beginning a Friendship and Alliance with France, and there is nothing of which I am more firmly perswaded, than that every Insinuation that is thrown out of Mr. R. H. Lees holding improper Intercourse with a Dr. Berkenhout,[4] is a cruel and an infamous Calumny.⟩ [5]

[1] Written in JA's Diary (D/JA/47) beneath a date caption, "1779. Feb. 10," for a regular journal entry that was never written. Thus the letter draft may have been written on 10 or 11 Feb. or on both days. It bears no indication of the addressee's name, and three-quarters of the text is either lined out or crossed out, no doubt by JA himself. Three other versions of the letter are known, all of them dated 11 Feb. 1779: (1) LbC, Adams Papers; (2) RC, Archives Aff. Etr., Paris, Corr. pol., Etats-Unis, vol. 7; (3) Tr, MH: Arthur Lee Papers, enclosed to Lee in a letter from JA written at Lorient, 9 June 1779 (LbC, Adams Papers; JA, *Works*, 7:95–97). LbC is actually a second draft, replacing the first draft, printed here, which was meant to be wholly lined out; it is nearly identical in substance with the text finally sent to Vergennes, and since it is printed in JA's *Works* (7:79–80) and again in Wharton, ed., *Dipl. Corr. Amer. Rev.* (3:42–44), there is no need to list here the alterations JA made in revising his text. Roughly speaking, JA sent to Vergennes those parts of his letter which were not struck out in the first draft (that is, those portions which appear in roman type in the present text), and then added a brief and courteous closing paragraph. A notation at the foot of LbC indicates that the letter was

"Sent [to Vergennes] by a Comis, early in the Morning of the 12. Feb. 1779." The delay had doubtless helped to shorten the letter by removing some of the indiscretions and asperities of the first draft.

[2] Suspension points in MS.

[3] One and the same person, namely C. A. Gérard, who held a commission as consul general of France as well as minister plenipotentiary to the United States (Gérard, *Despatches and Instructions*, p. 130, note). Deane's sailing with Gérard in the flagship of the Comte d'Estaing's squadron had been intended by the French government as a special mark of favor to the recalled American commissioner (same, p. 89–90).

[4] Dr. John Berkenhout, a British secret agent, came to America to promote the aims of the Carlisle peace commission of 1778. Berkenhout had known Arthur Lee in London and thus contrived to meet Richard Henry Lee in Philadelphia, but with no further result than that, thanks to Deane, his relations with the Lees became a warm issue in the Deane-Lee controversy. See *Deane Papers*, 3:2–3, 72–73; Howard Peckham, "Dr. Berkenhout's Journal, 1778," *PMHB*, 65:79–92 (Jan. 1941).

[5] Vergennes' reply to the much curtailed version of this letter that JA finally sent him on 12 Feb., is in the Foreign Secretary's own hand and is

dated "a Versailles Le 13. fevrier 1779" (RC in Adams Papers, printed in JA's *Works*, 7:80–81, q.v.). See, further, entry of 12 Feb., below, and note 4 there.

1779. FEB. 11.

When I arrived in France, the French Nation had a great many Questions to settle.

The first was—Whether I was the famous Adams, Le fameux Adams? —Ah, le fameux Adams?—In order to speculate a little upon this Subject, the Pamphlet entituled Common sense, had been printed in the Affaires de L'Angleterre et De L'Amerique, and expressly ascribed to M. Adams the celebrated Member of Congress, le celebre Membre du Congress. It must be further known, that altho the Pamphlet Common sense, was received in France and in all Europe with Rapture: yet there were certain Parts of it, that they did not choose to publish in France. The Reasons of this, any Man may guess. Common sense undertakes to prove, that Monarchy is unlawful by the old Testament. They therefore gave the Substance of it, as they said, and paying many Compliments to Mr. Adams, his sense and rich Imagination, they were obliged to ascribe some Parts to Republican Zeal. When I arrived at Bourdeaux, All that I could say or do, would not convince any Body, but that I was the fameux Adams.—Cette un homme celebre. Votre nom est bien connu ici.—My Answer was—it is another Gentleman, whose Name of Adams you have heard. It is Mr. Samuel Adams, who was excepted from Pardon by Gen. Gage's Proclamation.—Oh No Monsieur, cette votre Modestie.[1]

But when I arrived at Paris, I found a very different Style. I found great Pains taken, much more than the Question was worth to settle the Point that I was not the famous Adams. There was a dread of a sensation—Sensations at Paris are important Things. I soon found too, that it was effectually settled in the English News Papers that I was not the famous Addams. No body went so far in France or Ingland, as to say I was the infamous Adams. I make no scruple to say, that I believe, that both Parties for Parties there were, joined in declaring that I was not the famous Adams. I certainly joined both sides in this, in declaring that I was not the famous Adams, because this was the Truth.

It being settled that he was not the famous Adams, the Consequence was plain—he was some Man that nobody had ever heard of before —and therefore a Man of no Consequence—a Cypher. And I am inclined to think that all Parties both in France and England—Whiggs and Tories in England—the Friends of Franklin, Deane and Lee, differing in many other Things agreed in this—that I was not the fameux Adams.

Seeing all this, and saying nothing, for what could a Man say?—seeing also, that there were two Parties formed, among the Americans, as fixed in their Aversion to each other, as both were to G.B. if I had affected the Character of a Fool in order to find out the Truth and to do good by and by, I should have had the Example of a Brutus for my Justification. But I did not affect this Character. I behaved with as much Prudence, and Civility, and Industry as I could. But still it was a settled Point at Paris and in the English News Papers that I was not the famous Adams, and therefore the Consequence was settled absolutely and unalterably that I was a Man of whom Nobody had ever heard before, a perfect Cypher, a Man who did not understand a Word of French—awkward in his Figure—awkward in his Dress—No Abilities—a perfect Bigot—and fanatic.

[1] A French translation of Thomas Paine's *Common Sense*, or rather of extracts from it, had been published in *Affaires de l'Angleterre et de l'Amérique*, vol. 1 (1776), No. 1, p. 84–87; No. 4, p. 33–85 (see note on entry of 3 March 1779, below). The introduction to the first extracts, in a "Lettre d'un Banquier de Londres à M.*** à Anvers ... le 4 Mai 1776," remarks (p. 83–84):

" ... je puis vous dire un mot aujourd'hui de la sensation que me paroît faire sur nos négocians, un écrit que l'on vient de recevoir d'Amérique, & qui a, dit-on, la plus grande vogue dans les Colonies.

"Il est intitulé le *Sens commun*, & on l'attribue à M. Adams, fameux proscrit, que le général Gage a exclu, ainsi que M. Hancoks, de son amnistie. Vous savez que M. Adams est un des députés de la baie de Massachusets au Congrès général, où on le regarde comme un des premiers pivots de la révolution. Vous allez voir quelques extraits de son Ouvrage. C'est M. Adams qui parle [&c.]."

FEB. 11. 1779.[1]

It is my indispensable Duty, to tell the Comte de Vergennes that I think one great Cause of this horrid Address of Mr. Deane is Mr. Franklins Certificate in his favour that he is an able and faithfull Negotiator, and that Mr. Franklin was deceived in this—that Mr. F.'s Knowledge actually in America, for a great Many Years has not been long[2]—that he was Upright in this but deceived. That there are such certain and Infallible Proofs of Vanity, Presumption, Ambition, Avarice, and Folly in Mr. Deane as render him very unworthy of Confidence and therefore that Dr. F. has been deceived.

[1] Second entry of this date. In the MS a blank of nearly half a page separates the two entries so dated.
[2] JA probably meant to write "wide" or "extensive"; or else he supposed, when completing this clause, that he had written "Residence" instead of "Knowledge" as subject of the clause.

FEB. 12.

My Mind has been in such a State, since the Appearance of Mr. Deanes Address to the People, as it never was before. I confess it appeared to me like a Dissolution of the Constitution. It should be remembered that it first appeared from London in the English Papers—then in the Courier De L'Europe—and We had not received the Proceedings of Congress upon it. A few days after, Dr. Franklin received from Nantes, some Philadelphia Papers, in which were the Pieces signed Senex and Common Sense,[1] and the Account of the Election of the New President Mr. Jay.[2] When it was known that Congress had not censured Mr. Deane, for appealing to the People, it was looked upon as the most dangerous Proof that had ever appeared, of the Weakness of Government, and it was thought that the Confederation was wholly lost by some. I confess it appeared terrible to me indeed. It appeared to me that it would wholly loose us the Confidence of the French Court. I did not see how they could ever trust any of Us again—that it would have the worst Effects upon Spain, Holland and in England, besides endangering a civil War in America. In the Agony of my Heart, I expressed myself to one Gentleman Dr. Bancroft, with perhaps too much warmth.

But this Day, Dr. Winship[3] arrived here, from Brest, and soon afterwards, the Aid du Camp of Le Marquis de Fayette, with Dispatches, from Congress, by which it appears that Dr. Franklin is sole Plenipotentiary, and of Consequence that I am displaced.

The greatest Relief to my Mind, that I have ever found since the Appearance of the Address. Now Business may be done by Dr. Franklin alone. Before it seemed as if nothing could be done.[4]

[1] Articles in the *Pennsylvania Packet*, beginning 15 Dec. 1778, for and against Deane; reprinted in *Deane Papers*, 3:81 ff.

[2] Henry Laurens resigned as president, 9 Dec. 1778, on the ground that Congress was not taking proper action on Deane's disrespect to Congress in his recent address to the public. Next day he was succeeded in office by John Jay, a partisan of Deane. See *JCC*, 12:1202–1206; Burnett, ed., *Letters of Members*, 3:528–529; entries of 20, 22 June, below.

[3] Amos Windship, Harvard 1771, surgeon on the *Alliance* (Harvard Univ. Archives; Diary entries in April–May, below).

[4] On 14 Sept. 1778 Congress dissolved the American Commission in France by electing Franklin sole minister plenipotentiary, but it did not get around to drawing up his instructions until 26 Oct., and these were not sent until Lafayette sailed for France in the *Alliance* in January (*JCC*, 12:908; Wharton, ed., *Dipl. Corr. Amer. Rev.*, 2:807–809). Before JA had been in Paris six weeks he had warmly recommended that a single minister be placed in charge of American affairs in France (to Samuel Adams, 21 May 1778, NN:Bancroft Coll.; copied into JA's Autobiography under its date). On 12 Feb., within a few hours of sending off his agitated letter to Vergennes (entry

of 10–11 Feb., above), he learned of "the new Arrangement," and in writing Vergennes again, 16 Feb. (as well as in private letters), he expressed satisfaction with what he called Congress' "masterly Measure," which obviated any need for him to pursue with Vergennes the question of Deane's conduct and its consequences (LbC, Adams Papers; Wharton, ed., *Dipl. Corr. Amer. Rev.*,

3:50–51). However, JA's notification by the Committee of Foreign Affairs did not recall him and gave him no instructions beyond a vague promise that something might follow, and "In the mean Time we hope you will exercise your whole extensive Abilities on the Subject of our Finances" (R. H. Lee and James Lovell to JA, 28 Oct. 1778, Adams Papers; same, 2:814–815).

FEBY. 13.

There is no such Thing as human Wisdom. All is the Providence of God. Perhaps few Men have guessed more exactly than I have been allowed to do, upon several Occasions, but at this Time which is the first I declare of my whole Life I am wholly at a Loss to foresee Consequences.

1779 MARCH 3.

Went to Versailles, in order to take Leave of the Ministry. Had a long Conversation, with the Comte De Vergennes, in french, which I found I could talk as fast as I pleased.

I asked him what Effect the Peace of Germany would have upon our War. He said he believed none, because neither the Emperor nor King of Prussia were maritime Powers.

I asked him, whether he thought that England would be able to procure any Ally among the northern Powers. That Congress would be anxious to know this.

He said I might depend upon it and assure Congress that in his Opinion England would not be able to procure any. That on the Contrary the northern Powers were arming, not indeed to war against England, but to protect their Commerce.

Quant a L'Espagne, Monsieur?—Ah! Je ne puis pas dire.

Called on Mr. De Sartine who was not at home. Called on Mr. Genet. Mr. Genets son went with me and my son to see the Menagerie.[1]

[1] The elder Genet was Edmé Jacques (1715–1781), publicist, chief clerk for many years of the bureau of interpreters in the French Ministry of Foreign Affairs, and an expert on England, where he had traveled and lived. His role at this time might be described as that of chief of the French information service (using that term in its modern meaning of propaganda). From early 1776 to late 1779 he edited the *Affaires de l'Angleterre et de l'Amérique*. This journal, the bibliography of which is unbelievably complex, bore an imprint "A Anvers" but was actually prepared in the French foreign office, with substantial help from Franklin and his circle and, after his arrival in France, from JA. A complete set consists of fifteen volumes bound in seventeen, though since each volume contains numerous imperfect and confusing paginations,

references must be to the eighty-two "cahiers" or numbers as originally issued at irregular intervals. Even such references may sometimes prove baffling. A very summary collation of the work was provided by Paul L. Ford in *PMHB*, 13:222–226 (July 1889), and in his *Franklin Bibliography*, Brooklyn, 1889, p. 153–154, Ford listed a number of pieces known or believed to have been contributed by Franklin to the *Affaires*. Ford did not know who the real editor was, but Minnigerode (see further on in this note) mentioned Genet as editor, and Gilbert Chinard supplied further information in a valuable but tantalizingly brief analysis of the *Affaires* in the *Newberry Library Bulletin*, 2d ser., No. 8 (March 1952), p. 225–236. Mr. Chinard shows that the documents selected for publication and the commentary on them reflect the mind of Vergennes and the windings of French policy respecting Great Britain and America in a most revealing way.

It is clear from extensive surviving correspondence between JA and Edmé Jacques Genet that JA became an active contributor to the *Affaires de l'Angleterre et de l'Amérique* during his first mission in France, 1778–1779. Some of his contributions are readily recognizable; others, drawn from letters and papers he received from America or elsewhere and then handed on to Genet, will not be identified until a very careful

comparison can be made between JA's files and the contents of the *Affaires*.

Quite unintentionally JA threw students off the trail by remarking in a warm tribute to Genet's work in behalf of the American cause written thirty years later that Genet "conducted the Mercure de France, in which he published many little speculations for me" (JA, *Corr. in the Boston Patriot*, p. 347). CFA repeated this statement without the explanation or amplification it requires (JA, *Works*, 7:59, note). JA's contributions to the political section of the *Mercure de France* belong to his second, or "peace," mission in Europe, beginning in 1780, after the *Affaires* had ceased publication. See note on entry of 5 Feb. 1780, below.

The younger Genet, Edmond Charles (1763–1834), precociously succeeded his father in the French foreign office and enjoyed a distinguished diplomatic career before coming to America as the first minister of the French Republic, 1793, and there achieving a great deal more notoriety than he desired.

On both Genets see a study by Meade Minnigerode with the curious title *Jefferson, Friend of France: The Career of Edmond Charles Genet*, N.Y. and London, 1928. This is based on family papers then still in the possession of descendants, but it says little about the elder Genet's work as a publicist.

1779. MARCH 4.

Walked with Mr. Jennings to Calvare, with my son.[1]

[1] Edmund Jenings (1731–1819) is an obscure but ubiquitous figure in the European scene during the American Revolution, and an important one in the history of JA's diplomatic missions. Born in Annapolis, he was named for his father, King's attorney and secretary of Maryland, and his grandfather, acting governor of Virginia early in the century. His sister Ariana married John Randolph the loyalist, and his family was also allied with the Grymes and Lee families of Virginia.

Jenings was educated at Eton, Cambridge, and the Middle Temple, and probably never returned to America

thereafter. Being in what were then always called easy circumstances, he practiced little law but lived a life of cultivated leisure in London and maintained a large correspondence with American friends and relatives, notably with the Lee brothers. By early 1778 he had left London for the Continent and during the next five years lived mostly at Brussels, though he appeared recurrently at Paris, Boulogne, and elsewhere. He was put forward by the Lees, unsuccessfully, for diplomatic appointments. Probably Arthur Lee introduced him as a trustworthy and useful man to JA, who addressed a "Secret and confidential" letter to him within a fortnight of JA's own arrival in Paris, proposing the republication in London of one of JA's early political tracts (20 April 1778, Adams Papers). It was in this role that Jenings was to prove remarkably assiduous and helpful to JA, for throughout the war he kept a channel open to the London press and, besides transmitting news and publications to JA, repeatedly placed pro-American writings, by both himself and JA, in British newspapers and journals. (For an example see the entry of 4 Dec. 1782, below, and note 1 there.)

JA thought so well of Jenings' abilities and character that he wished to have him appointed secretary to the American Peace Commission in Europe (letter to Henry Laurens, 15 Aug. 1782, LbC, Adams Papers; *Works*, 7:611), but to JA's annoyance William Temple Franklin was the choice of Franklin and Jay for this post. After the Preliminary Treaty was signed late in 1782, a bitter quarrel developed between Jenings and Henry Laurens over an anonymous letter that originated in the Dutch or Austrian Netherlands and had had been in circulation for six months or more, in which Laurens was cautioned against alleged misconduct by JA. Laurens came to believe that Jenings knew a great deal more about the letter than he admitted and might indeed have written it, with the aim of sowing distrust among the American Commissioners. The quarrel led to the printing of three pamphlets in London in 1783, two by Jenings in his own defense and one by Laurens, together with a vast amount of correspondence among all concerned, but the mystery of the anonymous letter remains as yet unsolved.

JA himself never doubted Jenings' integrity and took pains to defend him in all quarters; see especially his letter to Thomas Brand Hollis, 5 Sept. 1787 (LbC, Adams Papers), proposing to put his entire correspondence with Jenings in Brand Hollis' hands for reading. (JA had by this time recovered all the letters he had written to Jenings during the war, possibly with the intention of later publication.)

Jenings continued to live quietly in London from 1783 until his death. He called on JQA when the latter passed through London on his way to his first diplomatic post at The Hague, and expressed the loyal American sentiments he had always expressed to JQA's father (JQA, Diary, 25 Oct. 1794; *Memoirs*, 1:53-54). That he was something of a busybody seems clear, but until much more explicit evidence of misconduct or disloyalty on his part is brought to light, the damning charges of Laurens, repeated by Francis Wharton (*Dipl. Corr. Amer. Rev.*, 4:285, note), cannot be accepted.

The personal data on Jenings in this note were largely furnished by Mr. John M. Jennings, Director of the Virginia Historical Society, where an Edmund Jenings letterbook, 1756-1769, and other papers of his are preserved. Much scattered information on him will be found in the biographies and published correspondence of Arthur, Richard Henry, and William Lee. The privately printed pamphlets exchanged by Jenings and Laurens, which are so rare as to have been seldom examined by scholars, are entered in Sabin 35984, 35985, 39258; no library in the United States is known to possess all three.

1779 MARCH 12. FRYDAY.[1]

About one O Clock arrived at Nantes at L'hotelle de la Comedie, Rue,[2] after a Journey of near five days, having sett off from Passy Monday the 8th. This Journey, which was by Versailles, is thro the most barren and least cultivated Part of France.

After Dinner, I had the Honour to be visited by the following American Gentlemen. Mr. Williams, Mr. Williams my Pupil,[3] Mr. Lloyd, Mr. Ridley,[4] Mr. Wharton, Mr. Lee, Mr. Daubrèe [Dobrée], Mr.

Maese [Mease], Captn. Jones,[5] Lt. Brown, Mr. Ingraham [Ingram], Mr. Cummings, Mr. Bradford, Mr. [*blank in MS*]

Mr. Jno. Lloyd is a sensible Man. He says that the french officers of Marine, consider Convoys as a disgracefull Service. They hate to be ordered to convoy Merchant Vessells. That when a Convoy is ordered, the officer is negligent and the Merchant dares not complain. The Marine officers and Police officers, and Custom house officers are connected together, and if a Merchant complains he is marked out as an obnoxious Person and Advantages are taken of him, so that he hold his Tongue.

[1] First entry in "P[aper] B[ook] No. 29" (our D/JA/29), which consists of two gatherings of unstitched leaves without covers. These were evidently put together for JA to carry in his pocket, for use when his larger bound journal was packed up and inaccessible. Having made this single entry, JA did not recur to this "paper book" again until 28 April; the intervening entries were written in D/JA/47.

[2] Thus in MS, but see the following entry.

[3] On the two Jonathan Williamses, who were both from Boston and cousins, see note on 26 Jan. 1776, above.

[4] Matthew Ridley, a Maryland merchant and agent for his state in Europe (Kathryn Sullivan, *Maryland and France, 1774–1789*, Phila., 1936, ch. 6). Ridley was a correspondent of JA's and kept valuable diaries of his European sojourn, which are with other papers of his in MHi.

[5] John Paul Jones had recently secured, through the good offices of the French government, the vessel he named the *Bonhomme Richard*, and was fitting her out for a cruise later this year that was to become famous. Several of the persons mentioned here were Jones' officers or associates in this venture.

1779. APRIL 14. WEDNESDAY.[1]

At Nantes, Hotel de la Comedie, Rue Bignonestar....[2] Walked, this Morning with my Son over all the Bridges. There are several Islands in the River and they have built Bridges from one to another, and Houses upon the Islands. There are fine Meadows on each Side, and the mixed Appearance of Houses, Meadows, Water and Bridges is very uncommon and amuzing. The first Island is built on with very fine Houses, all stone. The Stone of this Place is very durable, which that of Paris is not.

I dined on Monday with Mr. Schweighauser, Tuesday with Mr. Johnson. Last Evening at the Comedie, where We had the Barbier de Seville, L'Epreuve nouvelle. The Stage here is not like that of Paris. A poor Building. The Company, on the Stage, great Part of it, and not very clean nor sweet. The Actors indifferent.

Last Evening I supped for the first Time, with the Company in the House. Had a good deal of Conversation, with a Gentleman, on the Subject of the Alliance and the War. He said it is not for Us Merchants to judge of the Interests of the State, the Court must conduct all political Affairs, but it would have been better for Us, the Trade, if this Alliance had not been, provided that would have avoided a War. We have had so many Vessells taken, that many Houses and Individuals are ruined.

I told him that much of this Trade, had grown out of the Connection with America—that the Commerce of France was on a more respectable foot than it would have been, if Harmony had continued between G.B. and America, even after all their Losses. That the Loss to trade was not so great, because if half their Cargoes arrived, they sold them for near as much as the whole would have produced if it had all arrived—besides that a great deal was insured in England. That there would have been a War between England and France if Harmony had continued between England and America, for the two Nations were seldom at Peace more than 10 or 12 Years together. That if a War had happened in that Case, the maritime Power as well as Commerce of France would have been in danger of entire destruction. That it was essential to the Interest of France that there should be a separation between E. and A.—He asked what Subject there was or would have been for War, between E. and F.—I told him a subject could never be wanting. The Passions of the two Nations were so strong vs. each other that they were easily enkindled, and the English would have been so hauty that France could not have born it.—He seemed pleased with the Conversation and convinced by the Argument: But I find there is more coolness both in the Marine and the Trade, than there was a Year ago. Americans were more caressed and courted then than now. Yet they all think they must go on, and they think justly.

I have neglected my Journal.

Drank Tea and spent the Evening at Mr. Johnsons,[3] with him and the two Messrs. Williams.

Had some Conversation with Mr. Johnson on the subject of a free Port. The Q[uestion] was between Nantes and L'orient. Johnson is in favour of Nantes. The Advantages of the River, and of the foreign Merchants settled there, are his chief Argument. You have the Productions and Manufactures of Paris, and the whole Country, at Nantes by Water, by means of the Loire.

[1] JA had come to Nantes expecting to sail to America in the Continental frigate *Alliance*, commanded by Capt. Pierre Landais. But that vessel was still at Brest, "embarrassed" with forty unruly British prisoners. JA proceeded on 22 March to Brest and with some difficulty arranged for an exchange of prisoners, which later took place near Nantes, whither he himself had returned on 11 April. On 22 April he and JQA boarded the *Alliance* at Saint

Nazaire. See JA to John Jay, 3 Aug. 1779 (PCC, No. 84, I); printed from LbC, Adams Papers, in JA, *Works*, 7: 97–99; also the later entries in JA's Personal Receipts and Expenditures, printed at the end of 1778, above.

[2] Suspension points in MS. The street was Rue de Bignon-Lestard, later incorporated in other streets (Edouard Pied, *Notices sur les rues ... de la ville de Nantes*, Nantes, 1906, p. 133).

[3] JA to TBA, 25 Oct. 1797: "I congratulate you, on your new Acquisition of a Sister. I suppose this match grew out of a Spark that was kindled at Nantes in 1779 when your Brother was with me frequently in the Family of Mr. Johnson. But through whatever course it came down from Heaven, I pray for its Blessings on it" (original owned by Dr. Herbert E. Klingelhofer, Bethesda, Md., 1959). But it should be pointed out that JQA was nearly twelve and Louisa Catherine Johnson was only four in April 1779.

1779. APRIL 15. THURSDAY.

Dined at home.

16.

Dined with Mr. Williams. Mr. Johnson there. Walked after dinner along the River, and about the Town.

17.

Yesterday and to day in the forenoon, assisted my Son in translating Cicero's first Phillippick against Cataline.

Nantes is pleasantly situated on the River, and there are several agreable Prospects. The Views from the front Windows in the Row of Houses along the River is very beautiful. Mr. Schweighausser crauled up three Pair of Stairs to visit me this Morning.

AP. 18. SUNDAY.

Dined at Mr. Schweighaussers.

About six O Clock in the Evening, Captain Landais came into my Chamber. The Alliance is safe arrived at St. Lazar,[1] with her Prisoners.

[1] JA first wrote "Isle de Lazare" and then altered it to the present reading. But he certainly meant Saint Nazaire, at the mouth of the Loire.

1779. APRIL 22ND. THURSDAY.

Yesterday Morning, embarked at Nantes, with Mr. Hill, the first Lieutenant, and Mr. Parks, who is Captain of Marines, and my Son. We stopped and dined at Portlaunay, after Dinner crossed over to Pelerine [Le Pellerin], where We went to the House of a Mr. Charmichael, a Scotch Man who lives by salting Beef and making Bacon for the Navigation of this River. This Man I suppose was a Jacobite who fled in 1745. We reached no farther than Paimboeuf where we went ashore and slept at a Tavern.

This Day We arrived safe, on board the Alliance and sent off to the Cartel Ship all the British Prisoners. Thus by my Excursion to L'orient and Brest, I have accomplished successfully, the Expedition of the Frigate [at]¹ Brest and the Exchange of the Prisoners, and have happily joined the ship and got my Son and Baggage, on board. The Frigate lyes at St. Lazare, where are several french Vessells of War, but none so large as the Alliance.

My Idea of the Beauty, and Wealth and Convenience of Nantes and Paimbœuf, and indeed of the Country, on both Sides of the River is much hightened, since my Return from Brest, having taken a more leisurely View of it.

I thought it my Duty to come down, altho the Weather was disagreable and the Wind contrary and very strong, because I found the British Prisoners had not been discharged from the Frigate, and could not be untill an order went down, and because I feared that other Business would be neglected and my not being ready alledged as an Excuse for it. But I was obliged to leave Jos. Stevens, sick of the Measles at the Tavern. This was a painful Circumstance to me, altho I took all the Precautions in my Power, by speaking to Mr. Schweighausser, Mr. Daubray, Captain Landais, Dr. Winship, to look to him, and engaged a carefull Woman to Nurse him. I hope he will be well in a few days. He must have taken the Infection, at Brest, where he imprudently exposed himself I fear, on Shore. The Distemper it seems is prevalent in this Kingdom, at present. The Queen of France is said to be ill of it.

I have now had an Opportunity of seeing Bourdeaux, Nantes, L'orient, and Breast, and the Intermediate Countries. I could wish to have seen Rochfort, and Rochelle. At Brest I visited the Commandant, whose Name I have forgot, The Comte D'orvilliere [d'Orvilliers] who is the Marine General, and Monsieur De la Porte who is the Intendant of the Marine. At L'orient I did not visit the Intendant, nor Commandant—nor at Nantes.

The Zeal, The Ardor, the Enthusiasm, the Rage, for the new American Connection I find is much damped, among the Merchants since the Loss of so many of their East and West India Ships. The Adventurers to America, have lost so many Ships, and have received so small Returns for those which went Safe, that they are discouraged, and I cannot learn that any Expeditions are formed or forming for our Country.—But all their Chagrine cannot prevent the Court from continuing the War. The Existence of french Commerce and Marine both, are at Stake, and are wholly undone without American Independance.

The Pleasure of returning home is very great, but I confess it is a Mortification to leave France. I have just acquired enough of the Language to understand a Conversation, as it runs at a Table at Dinner, or Supper, to conduct all my Affairs myself, in making Journeys through the Country, with the Port Masters, Postillions, Tavern keepers, &c. &c. I can go to a Shop, and examine the Goods, and understand all the Prattle of the Shop keeper—or I can sit down with a Gentleman, who will have a little Patience to speak a little more distinctly than common, and to wait a little longer for my Sentences than common, and maintain a Conversation pretty well.

In Travelling the best Way is to dine and sup at the Taverns, with the Company, avec les autres as they express it. You meet here, a vast Variety of Company, which is decent, and after a few Coups du Vin, their Tongues run very fast and you learn more of the Language, the Manners, the Customs, Laws, Politicks, Arts, &c. in this Way, perhaps than in any other. You should preserve your Dignity, talk little, listen much, not be very familiar with any in particular, for their are Sharpers, Gamblers, Quack Doctors, Strolling Comediens, in short People of all Characters, assembled at these Dinners and Suppers, and without Caution, you may be taken into Parties of Pleasure and Diversion that will cost you very dear.

Were I to come to France again, I would wait on the Intendant, Commandant, Mayor &c. of every Place. I would dine, and sup at the Taverns, with the Company. I would go to the Palais, and here the Causes, and to the Comedie and hear the Plays and that as constantly as possible. I would go to Church, whenever I could hear a Sermon. These are the Ways to learn the Language, and if to these are Added, a dilligent study of their Grammars, and a constant Use of their best Dictionaries, and Reading of their best Authors, a Man in one Year may become a greater Master in it. After all, if a Mans Character would admit of it, there is much of the language to be learn'd at the Shops. The female Shop keepers are the most chatty in the World. They are very complaisant—talk a great deal—speak pretty good french, and are very entertaining.

I took a Walk this Morning to the back Part of the little Town of Paimbœuf, and found behind it, a pleasant country Prospect, with one beautifull Country Seat of a Gentleman in sight.

[1] MS: "and."

A violent Wind, and Rain.

The same.

Fair Weather again. My Time has been employed since I have been on board, in writing Answers to my Letters from Paris, Bourdeaux, Passy &c. and in assisting my Son to translate into English which he does in writing Ciceros first Phillippic against Cataline—which we have gone more than half thro. He is also translating into English the french Preface of the Abbey D'olivet, to his Translation of the Phillippics of Demosthenes and the Catalinaires of Cicero.[1] —Are these classical Amusements becoming my Situation? Are not Courts, Camps, Politicks and War, more proper for me?—No, certainly classical Amusements are the best I can obtain on board Ship, and here I can not do any Thing, or contrive any Thing for the public.

A Boat came on board to day with a Custom house Officer to examine and give an Acquit a Caution[2] for a Chest of Tea, which is on board belonging to somebody, I know not whom.

I have been here so long that I find the Cabin to be rather a triste sejour. It is dull to be here alone.

Tullys offices and orations are an agreable Amusement but toujours Tully, is as bad as toujours Perdreaux and infinitely worse than toujours "Sa femme," alluding to the Anecdote of H[enri] 4. which I was told by the Abbey Reynalle.

[1] JA purchased "D'Olivets Phillippics" on 19 April at Nantes for 2 livres, 10 sous (Personal Receipts and Expenditures, printed at the end of 1778, above).
[2] An *acquit à caution* was a customhouse bond.

Spent the Morning in translating with my Son the Carmen Seculare, and the Notes.

There is a Feebleness and a Languor in my Nature. My Mind and Body both partake of this Weakness. By my Physical Constitution, I am but an ordinary Man. The Times alone have destined me to Fame —and even these have not been able to give me, much. When I look in the Glass, my Eye, my Forehead, my Brow, my Cheeks, my Lips, all betray this Relaxation. Yet some great Events, some cutting Expressions, some mean ⟨Scandals⟩ Hypocrisies, have at Times, thrown this Assemblage of Sloth, Sleep, and littleness into Rage a little like a Lion. Yet it is not like the Lion—there is Extravagance and Distraction in it, that still betrays the same Weakness.

1779 AP. 28. WEDNESDAY.[1]

Went up to Nantes from Minden[2] or St. Nazare, before Wind and Tide in 4 Hours. This Morning by C[aptain] Landais who came on board I received a Letter from Dr. F. inclosing one from M. de Sartine, both expressing a Desire, that the Alliance might not sail for some Time, and that I would take my Passage home, with M. Le Chevalier de la Luzerne, the new Ambassador, in one of the Kings Frigates.[3]

This is a cruel Disappointment.—To exchange May for July, and the Alliance for another Frigate, is too much.

Lodged at the Hotel de St. Julien, where I find the Accommodations better than at L'hotel de la Comedie. . . .[4]

Dined at the Hotel, with a Number of Navy Officers, several with the Cross of St. Louis. Drank Tea, at Mrs. Johnsons. Had much Conversation with him about Consuls, Agents. He thinks one Consul enough for the Kingdom with Power of Deputation. This [also,] that a Duty of so much per Ton [should be levied] on all Ships, entering a french Port, for the Relief of unfortunate Americans, Prisoners, Shipwrecked Persons, &c.[5] That no Man should be discharged from a Ship but by the Consul. That six, ten, or twelve Merchants should be appointed to inspect the Consuls accounts, once in 3 Months, &c.

[1] From this point on, through 31 July 1779, the entries are in D/JA/29.

[2] Pointe du Mindin, where the *Alliance* lay at anchor, is across from Saint Nazaire at the mouth of the Loire.

[3] Sartine's letter, dated 20 April 1779, was addressed to Franklin; it requested on behalf of the King that the *Alliance* be ordered to Lorient (Adams Papers). The *Alliance* was soon afterward joined to John Paul Jones' squadron. Franklin's letter, 24 April, enclosing Sartine's, pointed out for JA's consolation that he would be traveling more safely and would have the company of the Chevalier de La Luzerne, "who appears to me a most amiable Man and of very sensible and pleasing Conversation" and "who is to set off in a few Days" (Adams Papers; JA, *Works*, 7:93–94). On the contrary La Luzerne and his party did not arrive at Lorient until 11 June; see entry of 12 June, below. There is a careful study, based mainly on records in the French Ministry of Foreign Affairs, by William E. O'Donnell of *The Chevalier de La Luzerne, French Minister to the United States, 1779–1784*, Bruges and Louvain, 1938.

[4] Suspension points in MS.

[5] The words in brackets have been supplied by the editors to make sense of a defective sentence.

1779. MAY 7TH OR 8TH. FRYDAY.[1]

Mr. Odea of Paimbœuf, Coll. Wibirt[2] and Mr. Ford, dined in the Cabin. O. speaks English perfectly, appears to have read much, is an Admirer of Rousseau and Buffon. W. is silent; has something little in his Face and Air: and makes no great Discovery of Skill or Science.

F. talks as much as ever.[3]

Says, that the Americans at Paris, wished I had remained at Passy, instead of F[ranklin]—that Passy is deserted by the Americans since I came away—that nobody goes there now but B., W. and a young Williams, (which is my Ws. I suppose)[4] who dine there every Sunday. That he has copied Papers for Mr. W[illiam] L[ee] which prove upon F. many Contradictions of himself, &c. That F. told him he did not believe I should go to America—that the Alliance would not be ready for some time—that a Commission would come for me, for some other Court, &c.

That F. did not shew his *Greatness* in the Contract for old Arms, for Soldiers Cloaths at 37 Livres a Suit, or for Virginia Tobacco. Is much puzzled at the Mystery of Jones's Ship, says she is private Property, that therefore L[andais] ought not to be under his Command &c. &c. &c.

I undertook to sound our Engineer this Evening and find he has Knowledge. He says one should begin with the Architecture of Vignol, and draw the five ordres, the Doric, Ionic, Tuscan, Corinthian and composite—Begin with a Pedastal, then the Column, then the Capital, then the ornaments—from civil you may go to military Architecture, and naval if you will. Ces cinque ordres D'Architecture se construissent, par le moyen d'une Echelle divisée en modules, le module en Parties, demi Parties et quart de Partie &c.

He made many Observations to my Son about the Ink, the Instruments, the Pens, the manner of holding the Hand, sitting to the Light of Day or Candle &c. which shew that he knows Something of these Sciences. He is a Designateur. He never had a Master he says.

This Evening arrived Capt. Jones from Baltimore. He sailed 28 March—brings no News Papers nor News. No Dispatches from Congress. No Letters but to Mr. Johnson, and a Packet for Bourdeaux.

[1] Friday fell on 7 May 1779.

[2] Antoine Félix Wuibert (Viebert, Weibert) de Mézières had served as a military engineer in America from June 1776, was captured and exchanged, and later in 1779 accompanied John Paul Jones on the voyage of the *Bonhomme Richard* as an officer of marines (Lasseray, *Les français sous les treize étoiles,* 2:485–487).

[3] Hezekiah Ford was an Anglican clergyman in Virginia before the Revolution (Frederick L. Weis, *The Colonial Churches and the Colonial Clergy of the*

Middle and Southern Colonies, Lancaster, Mass., 1938, p. 116), but there is the utmost variance between his own account and reports widely current in America of how he got to France in the spring of 1778. Ford told the American Commissioners in Paris that he had served as a fighting chaplain of two North Carolina regiments in the service of the United States and that he had been captured and brought to England, whence he "found his Way to Paris" (American Commissioners to Abraham Whipple, 13 June 1778, recommending Ford for the post of chaplain on Whipple's frigate *Providence*; LbC, Adams Papers, copied into JA's Autobiography under its date). (That he actually served in North Carolina is verified by an entry in *The State Records of North Carolina*, 16: 1056.) Whipple needed no chaplain, and Ford started for America on a small cutter, only to be captured (again?) and carried into the island of Jersey, whence he made his way back once more to Paris (Ford to the Commissioners, 25 June, 21 July 1778, PPAmP). Arthur Lee now engaged him as secretary, and he served in that capacity for some months before JA encountered him at Nantes trying again to find passage to Virginia and (as the present and following entries show) displaying very little of the discretion suitable to an impostor, renegade, or spy. In Virginia, however, he was thought by influential persons to be all or at least most of these. When word had reached Virginia that Ford had become a member of Arthur Lee's staff in Paris, Gov. Patrick Henry

wrote the Virginia delegates in Congress, 9 Jan. 1779, that Ford had left the state under British protection, charged with "seditious" activities, and suspected of counterfeiting, and consequently that "Every member of the privy council ... is exceedingly alarmed at the circumstance [of Ford's relationship with Lee], having the most perfect conviction that Mr. Ford is altogether unfit to be near the person[s] of the American commissioners" (Wharton, ed., *Dipl. Corr. Amer. Rev.*, 1:539–540). On 26 Jan. Congress voted to communicate this information to Lee and did so (*JCC*, 13: 116). Lee and Izard refused to believe any part of it, but by the time they heard it Ford was at last on his way home. He arrived early in August and went directly to visit Richard Henry Lee, who advised him to seek a hearing before the Governor and Council of Virginia instead of going to Philadelphia to deliver his dispatches (R. H. Lee, *Letters*, ed., Ballagh, 2:112–113, 119, 122, 145). Soon afterward Ford appeared in Williamsburg and posted a bond of £1,000 for his appearance to answer charges "of certain treasonable practices," but though witnesses were assembled and the hearing put off from time to time, it is not on record that Ford ever appeared to vindicate himself (*Virginia Gazette* [Dixon & Nicolson], 16 Oct. 1779).

⁴ Probably Bancroft, possibly one of the Whartons, and certainly the Jonathan Williams (d. 1780) who had been JA's law clerk. (Franklin's grandnephew Jonathan Williams was at Nantes at this time.)

1779. MAY 9. ⟨*Saturday*⟩ SUNDAY.

The Pilot came on Board this Morning from St. Nazare, and pronounced it unsafe to go out, with this Wind.

F. this Morning, fell to talking.—"Above half the Gentlemen of Paris are Atheists, and the other half Deists. No Body goes to Church but the common People. I wish I could find one honest Man among their Merchants and Tradesmen" &c. &c.

Mr. F., says I, let me be so free as to request of you, when you arrive in America, not to talk in this Style. It will do a great deal of Harm. These Sentiments are not just, they are contracted Prejudices, and Mr. Lee and Mr. Izard too have hurt them selves and the public too by indulging in a similar Language.

F. "Oh! I am no Hypocrite."—Thus this Prater goes on.

Yesterday he wanted me, to get him a Passage on board the french Frigate, that I am to go in. I told him I did not think it would be practicable. And I hope it will not, for I dont wish such a Man to go, in that Ship.

At Dinner, much Conversation about the Electrical Eel which gives a Shock to a ring of Persons like the Touch of a Bottle or Conductor. —What is the Name of this fish?

The Magnet is nothing but Iron Oar, Somebody said at Table, and that the Tendency towards the Pole is in all Iron.—Q[uery].

This afternoon, a Mr. Watkin a Disciple of the great Whitfield as he calls himself, performed divine Service upon the Quarter Deck. He is not learned, but his Prayer was very good for the united States and their Allies, their Army and Gen[eral], their Navy and this Ship and her Commander. His Sermon also was passable.

Our Captain talks much about Batavia, is an Admir[er] of that Duch Settlement in the East Indies.[1]

This Gentleman has been disappointed in Love and in his Ambition—disappointed in the Promotion to which he aspired, and in a Marriage of which he thought himself sure. He has not so much Activity, Dispatch and Decision as [one?] could wish. He seems not to know how to gain or preserve the Affections of his Officers, nor yet how to keep them in Awe. Complaisance, firmness and Steadiness are necessary to the Command of a Ship. Whether it is his imperfect Knowledge of the Language, or his Absence of Mind when poring upon his Disappointments, or any defect in his Temper or Judgment, I know not, but this happy Mixture seems to be wanting. His Lieutenants are smart Men, quick and active—not lettered it is true, but good Seamen, and brave.

[1] Landais had accompanied Bougainville in his voyage of circumnavigation, 1766–1769; see entry of 16 May, below. This officer's fantastically checkered career in the French, American, and French Republican navies has been narrated in Charles O. Paullin, "Admiral Pierre Landais," *Catholic Hist. Rev.*, 17:296–307 (Oct. 1931). Lasseray, *Les français sous les treize étoiles*, 1:255–264, provides a more sympathetic estimate of Landais than can be found in American accounts.

MONDAY MAY. 10.

This Morning the Wind at S.E. The Pilot came on board, the Alliance unmoored and set Sail, for L'orient. A gentle Breeze, fair Weather, and moderately warm.

The 1 Lt. I have made by this War £120 of Prize Money, for which I got six Months Imprisonment, and spent the little that I had. This is all I have got by the War.

The Sand Droguers and Chimney Sweepers in Boston have all turned Merchants and made Fortunes.

Ingraham. Otis says when the Pot boils the Scum rises to the Top.

Eg[o]. The new Cyder, when it ferments sends all the Pummace, Worms, bruised seeds and all sorts of Nastiness to the Top.

People of Fortune have spent their Fortunes, and those who had none, have grown rich.

Ford. I came to France with the highest opinion of Dr. F.—as a Philosopher, a Statesman and as even the Pater Patriae. But I assure you Tempora mutantur.

He has very moderate Abilities, He knows nothing of Philosophy, but his few Experiments in Electricity: He is an Atheist, he dont believe any future State: Yet he is terribly afraid of dying.

This is Fords Opinion. This is his Character of the great Man.

I believe it is too much to say that he is an Atheist, and that he dont believe a future State: tho I am not certain his Hints, and Squibs sometimes go so far as to raise Suspicions:—and he never tells any Body, I fancy that he believes a G[od], a P[urgatory] or f[uture] s[tate].[1] It is too rank to say that he understands nothing of Philosophy, but his own electrical Experiments, altho I dont think him so deeply read in Philosophy, as his Name impute[s].

He has a Passion for Reputation and Fame, as strong as you can imagine, and his Time and Thoughts are chiefly employed to obtain it, and to set Tongues and Pens male and female, to celebrating him. Painters, Statuaries, Sculptors, China Potters, and all are set to work for this End. He has the most affectionate and insinuating Way of charming the Woman or the Man that he fixes on. It is the most silly and ridiculous Way imaginable, in the Sight of an American, but it succeeds, to admiration, fullsome and sickish as it is, in Europe.

When I arrive, I must enquire—concerning Congress, Ennemys Army, R.I., N.Y., G[eorgia], our Army, our Currency, Mass. Bay, Boston &c.

[1] The ambiguous punctuation of this sentence has been retained precisely as found in the MS.

1779. TUESDAY. MAY 11.

Sailing by Belisle, which the English took last War after a Defence of Six Weeks with about 900 Men.

F. still on the Subject. He says that the Contract made by F[ranklin] and D[eane] with the farmers general, was for £40 Pr. Ct.[1] whereas Tobacco was then at 90 and T. Morris made a Contract with them before for £70.[2]

F. and D. to be sure were duped by the Farmers General but F[or]d has nothing accurate in his Head, nothing judicious. He must be mistaken about Tobacco's being at 90. He says farther it was to be du Poieds marquès which makes a difference of 8 Pound in the Hundred against Us.

He says, Deane received from the Banker £1700 st. after he knew he was recalled [and][3] 1100 of it the Morning he went away. And he believes that Deane gave Money to Bancroft that he is now living upon. —It is impossible but he must be mistaken about the sum that D. received, and the Insinuation about Bancroft, is mere Suggestion and Conjecture. There is no End of such Whispers.

Dr. W[indship] told me of Tuckers rough tarry Speech, about me at the Navy Board.—I did not say much to him at first, but damn and buger my Eyes, I found him after a while as sociable as any Marblehead man.—Another of Hinman, that he had been treated with great Politeness by me, and his first Attention must be to see Mrs. Adams, and deliver her Letters.

[1] per hundredweight.

[2] Thomas Morris, half-brother of Robert Morris, had served as agent for both Congress and the Morris interests at Nantes until his death in Jan. 1778. See *Deane Papers*, 2:145–156; Wharton, ed., *Dipl. Corr. Amer. Rev.*, 2:460–463; William Lee, *Letters*, ed. Ford, *passim*. William McCreery informed JA in a letter from Nantes, 29 Sept. 1777: "He

[Thomas Morris] is Drunk at least Twentytwo Hours of every Twentyfour and never without one or two Whores in Company. . . . He neglects all business because he has rendered himself incapable of any. In short, I never saw a man in a more deplorable situation" (Adams Papers).

[3] MS: "at."

WEDNESDAY MAY 12TH.

L[andais] is jealous of every Thing. Jealous of every Body, of all his Officers, all his Passengers. He knows not how to treat his Officers, nor his Passengers nor any Body else.—Silence, Reserve, and a forbidding Air, will never gain the Hearts, neither by Affection nor by Veneration, of our Americans.

There is in this Man an Inactivity and an Indecision that will ruin him. He is bewildered—an Absent bewildered man—an embarrassed Mind.

This Morning he began "You are a great Man but you are deceived. The Officers deceive you! They never do their Duty but when you are on deck. They never obey me, but when you are on deck. The Officers were in a Plott vs. me at Boston, and the Navy Board promised to remove them all from the ship and yet afterwards let them all come on Board."

Conjectures, Jealousies, Suspicions.—I shall grow as jealous as any Body.

I am jealous that my Disappointment is owing to an Intrigue of Jones's. Jones, Chaumont, Franklin concerted the Scheme. Chaumont applied to Mr. De S[artine]. He wrote the Letter.[1] If this Suspicion is well founded, I am to be made the Sport of Jones's Ambition to be made a Commodore. Is it possible that I should bear this? Another Suspicion is that this Device was hit upon by Franklin and Chaumont to prevent me from going home, least I should tell some dangerous Truths. Perhaps, Jones's Commodoreship, and my detention might both concur. Can I bear either? It is hard, very hard, but I must bear every Thing. I may as well make a Virtue of Necessity, for I cannot help my self.

Does the old Conjurer dread my Voice in Congress? He has some Reason for he has often heard it there, a Terror to evil doers.

I may be mistaken in these Conjectures, they may be injurious to J. and to F. and therefore I shall not talk about them, but I am determined to put down my Thoughts and see which turns out.

Mr. Chaumont and his son are here and have been 15 days. But no Chevalier de la Luzerne, nor any french Frigate.

It is decreed that I shall endure all Sorts of Mortifications. There is so much Insolence, and Contempt, in the Appearance of this. Do I see that these People despize me, or do I see that they dread me? Can I bear Contempt—to know that I am despized? It is my duty to bear every Thing—that I cannot help.[2]

As I set in my Quarter Gallery, We are sailing directly into Port Louis, at L'orient, before a fine pleasant Breeze. There is a strong Fortification at the Entrance of this Harbour, at which we were hailed, and asked Whence? Where—Name of Vessell—Captain &c. What an Advantage to Nantes, would such a Port and Harbour as this be?

Went ashore. C. Landais, myself and son, went on Board the poor Richard, saw C. Jones and his officers, Mr. Moylan, Captain Cazneau, Captain Young, &c.

Went to visit Mr. Grondell Commandant des Troupes de Terre, found there Mr. Thevenard, Commandant du Port, Mr. Desaudrèe India Merchant.

Went then to visit Mr. Le Ray de Chaumont, who has been here 15 days with his son.

Went then to visit Mr. Grandville, Commissaire General du Port. Then to the Commissaire des Classes.

Was very politely received, by all these Gentlemen, and Captn. Landais treated with particular respect.

I spoke very freely to Mr. Chaumont, about my situation—told him, I was ill treated—that I had many Jealousies and Suspicions—that I suspected it was an Intrigue.

[1] Sartine's letter to Franklin of 20 April; see entry of 28 April, above. CFA omitted this and the two following paragraphs from his text of JA's Diary.

[2] This paragraph was also omitted by CFA.

THURSDAY. MAY 13TH.

Went on Shore and dined with Captain Jones at the Epèe Royal. Mr. Amiel, Mr. Dick, Dr. Brooke, officers of the Poor Richard, Captain Cazneau, Captain Young, Mr. Ingraham, Mr. Blodget, Mr. Glover, Mr. Conant, Messrs. Moylans, Mr. Maese, Mr. Nesbit, Mr. Cummings, Mr. Tayler, made the Company, with Captain Landais, myself and my Son.

An elegant Dinner we had—and all very agreable.

No very instructive Conversation. But we practiced the old American Custom of drinking to each other, which I confess is always agreable to me.

Some hints about Language, and glances about Women, produced this Observation, that there were two Ways of learning french commonly recommended—take a Mistress and go to the Commedie. Dr. Brookes, in high good Humour—Pray Sir, which in your Opinion is the best? Answer in as good Humour—Perhaps both would teach it soonest, to be sure sooner than either. But, continued I, assuming my Gravity, the Language is no where better spoken than at the Comedie. The Pulpit, the Bar, the Accademie of Sciences, and the faculty of Medicine, none of them speak so accurately as the french Comedie.

After Dinner walked out, with C[aptain]s Jones and Landais to see Jones's Marines—dressed in the English Uniform, red and white. A Number of very active and clever Serjeants and Corporals are employed to teach them the Exercise, and Maneuvres and Marches &c.

After which Jones came on Board our ship.

This is the most ambitious and intriguing Officer in the American Navy. Jones has Art, and Secrecy, and aspires very high. You see the Character of the Man in his uniform, and that of his officers and

Marines, variant from the Uniforms established by Congress. Golden Button holes, for himself—two Epauletts—Marines in red and white instead of Green.

Excentricities, and Irregularities are to be expected from him—they are in his Character, they are visible in his Eyes. His Voice is soft and still and small, his Eye has keenness, and Wildness and Softness in it.

MAY 14. FRYDAY.

On Board all day, ill of a Cold. Many Gentlemen came on board to visit me. A Dr. Brooks, Surgeon to the Poor Richard, drank Tea with me. He seems to be well acquainted with Philosophical Experiments. I led him to talk upon this subject. He had much to say about Phlogiston, fixed Air, Gas &c. About absolute and sensible Heat, Experiments with the Thermometer, to shew the absolute and sensible Heat in Water, Air, Blood &c.

Finding he had Ideas of these Things, I led him to talk of the Ascent of Vapours in the Atmosphere, and I found he had considered this subject.

He mentioned a natural History of N. and S. Carolina, by Catesby in 4 Volumes folio with Stamps of all the Plants and Animals. Price 25 Guineas. He mentioned a Dr. Erving [Irvine] and a Dr. Black of Glasgow, as great Philosophers, whose Hints Priestly had taken.

This Dr. Brooks is a Gentleman of Family, whose father has a great Fortune and good Character in Virginia. Mr. Dick, Captain of Marines, on Board of Jones, is also of good family and handsome fortune in Virginia.

Mr. Gimaet came on board to visit me, Aid de Camp of the Marquis de la Fayette.[1]

[1] Jean Joseph Sourbader de Gimat had accompanied Lafayette to America in the *Victoire* in 1777, returned there again in 1780, and achieved a distinguished military record (Lasseray, *Les français sous les treize étoiles*, 2:418-420).

15 MAY. SATURDAY.

Went on Shore, and dined with Captain Jones at the Mess, at L'Epee Royale. Mr. Hill, Capt. Cazneau, Captn. Young, Mr. Dick, Dr. Brooks &c. Mr. Gourlade, another Aid du Camp of the Marquis[1] &c. Gourlade married a Scotch Lady.—Captain Jones this Morning shewed me a Letter from Lt. Browne, desiring or rather apologizing for leaving the Ship, because of the Word (first) in M. Amiels Commission. I said, I thought Mr. Browne could not serve under M. Amiel. It would be in a manner giving up the Claims of many Lieutenants whose Commissions were dated between his and Mr. Amiels, as well as his own and would expose him to censure. That the Word first was agreed to be inserted by the Commissioners, because We expected that either We or C. Jones would fill up the Commissions to the other Lieutenants of that Ship, and it was intended to give him an Assurance that he should be the first, on board that Ship. It was not so well considered as it ought to have been, to be sure, but could not now be helped. That however the Word first was void; it could not supercede the Date of any former Commission. Mr. Amiel was so urgent to have it in, that it was agreed to, perhaps, too inconsiderately.

After dinner, took a Walk, out of Town, returned and went to view the two Churches, the [least?] of which has some fine Paintings. St. Joseph, St. Joachim, the Virgin, feeling the Babe leap in her Womb, at the sight of Elizabeth, and many others. Some handsome marble Pillars, and two fine Statues in Plaister of Paris.

In the Evening C[aptain] L[andais] chagrined—suspecting Plots among his Officers against him. Had written to Dr. Franklin relating Things to him, &c. &c. Mr. Blodget came in and said, he had one Chest in the Ward Room, which the Officers had ordered him to take away, but as he had but one and they so many, he ventured to wait for the C's orders. That the Officers were now about to treat him better, conscious that they could not treat him worse. Today they invited him to dine in the Ward Room. But he begged Mr. Diggs [Degge] not to invite him. They had d——d him and he could not dine there, yet did not love to refuse, so begged off.

Such is the Danger of Favouritism, in the Government of a Ship as well as of a State. I have had the Pleasure to restore this Ship to Peace and Harmony, and am perswaded, it would have continued. But when I leave here I see plainly all will become unhappy again. There is such a Mixture of Ductility and Obstinacy in the Government of her as will not keep her together. A tender Heart and an obstinate Will sometimes go together. The C. has told M.B.[2] of my Advice that he should not live in the Cabbin. This will raise his Resentment vs. me. And B. will be the Idol still. Yet he will continue to be excluded the Cabin, which will make it worse, for what I know. The Captain is not of an accommodating Humour nor temper. His Resolutions when taken are without Conditions or Exceptions and unalterable, as one would think, yet sometimes too easily and too entirely altered. My Presence has had some degree of Awe upon the Capt. and all the other officers, it has made them endeavour to respect one another. But the Fire is not extinguished, it will break out again.

L. said Honour and Delicacy, are his 2d God.—He shall die poor, and despized,—not by those who know him.—This is an honest Man— But Chagrin and Disappointment are visible in every Thing about him.[3]

He is incapable of all Art. Has no Address or Dexterity at all in managing Men.

P[arson] F[ord] this Morning was upon his Fights and Battles. At such a Time he fought in N.C., such a Time in &c. Once he [fought][4] half an Hour in his shirt tail. Then he got his Rheumatism.— Oh his Groin, his Swelling, his Pains in his Legs, Knees, joints, shoulders, his fever and Ague. If We should have a Battle and he should be sick and killed in his Bed. He had rather be killed ten times upon the Quarter deck, &c.

Coll. Wuibert tells a story. That at Angers a Bishop has been found unconsumed and uncorrupted after being buried many Years. They buried him up again, and is to be dug up again after a certain time, and if found entire, is to be made a saint. His Preservation is to be a Miracle, whereas the Truth is there is salt where he lies. This the Coll. calls Sottise.

[1] In the MS this phrase is interlined without indication where it should be inserted. Lafayette's second aide is not clearly identifiable, but he was not Gourlade, who was a Lorient merchant in partnership with James Moylan (*Cal. Franklin Papers, A.P.S.,* index).

[2] Mr. Blodget. Nathan Blodget was purser of the *Alliance* and a partisan of Landais in the latter's feud with his officers (same; see also Landais' *Memorial, to Justify Peter Landai's Conduct during the Late War,* Boston, 1784, *passim*).

[3] The ambiguous punctuation of this paragraph has been retained as found in the MS.

[4] MS: "found."

MAY 16. SUNDAY.

Went on Shore, and dined with Mr. Moylan. Jones, Landais, Chaumont Pere et Fils, Moylan Frere, Maese, made the Company.

Maese made a sensible Observation, vizt., that he ever found five out of six of the People of England supporting the Measures of Government. That the People of America had been deceived by their Friends in England, by writing that the People were against these Measures.

Letters from England received to day, say, that the last Propositions of Spain for an Accommodation have been rejected by Government, with a Kind of Humour that We have been long used to.

Went after Dinner with Mr. Chaumont, to the House of Mr.

Bouvet, an old Officer of Marine, a Croix de St. Louis, to see the Modell of a Seventy four Gun Ship, that he was Twenty Years in making with his own Hand. Every Sparre, Block, Rope, Iron and Timber in the true Proportions. It is fine comme un Tabatier. In his Shop he has all his Tools, his Chizzells, his Files, &c. and his turning Wheel, Glasses, Mathematical Instruments, &c.

C[olonel] Wuibert told us this Evening of some very ancient and curious Pictures at La Fleche. In one Situation you see H[enri] 4.—in another, at a small distance you see one of his Mistresses, in another a second Mistress. In one Picture viewed from one Point you see a Man, from another Point a Beast.

C.L. told Us of a curious Grate at Nantes, which is ancient and no body knows how it was made. He also entertained Us with an Account of the Indians at Outaheite. The most dextrous Thieves in the World, but the best natured People. Mr. Bougainvilles People sold them, Iron, nails &c. for very great Prices. An Hog for a Deck nail, and a fowl for a Board Nail. He related several Instances of their Ingenuity, in picking Pocketts, and stealing Nails and Bitts of Iron. One of their Priests picked his Pocketts of all the Nails in it, which was all his Money. And a Drol Relation of a Single Combat between the Priest and the Indian that carried him over the River, on his shoulders, for a Nail—which consisted in clinching their Hands together and pushing, untill the Priest fell back, when the other gave him a Fillip upon his Forehead or Nose, which was the Tryumph, and decided the Question about the Property of the Nail.

My Son could not comprehend why they should be so fond of Iron. He was told that Iron made the principal Difference between savage and civilised Nations. That all Arts and Manufactures depended upon Iron &c.

MAY 17. MONDAY.

L. gave Us an Account of St. George at Paris, a Molatto Man, Son of a former Governor of Guadaloupe, by a Negro Woman. He has a sister married to a Farmer General. He is the most accomplished Man in Europe in Riding, Running, Shooting, Fencing, Dancing, Musick. He will hit the Button, any Button on the Coat or Waistcoat of the greatest Masters. He will hit a Crown Piece in the Air with a Pistoll Ball.

Mr. Gimaet came on Board, to go to Port Louis with C[aptain] L[andais]. The Affectation, in the Eyes, features, laugh, Air, gate,

Posture, and every Thing of this Gentleman is so striking, that I cannot but think I see C.J.Q. or C.B. whenever I see him.[1]

Affectation proceeds from Vanity. EASE is the Opposite. Nature is easy, and simple. This Man thinks himself handsome, his Eyes, his Complexion, his Teeth, his Figure, his Step, and Air, have irresistable Charms, no doubt, in his Mind.

L. will never accomplish any great Thing. He has Honour—Delicacy—Integrity—and I doubt not Courage—and Skill, and Experience. But he has not Art.—And I firmly believe there never was, or will be a great Character, without a great deal of Art. I am more and more convinced every day of the Innocence, the Virtue and absolute Necessity of Art and Design.—I have arrived almost at 44 without any. I have less than L. and therefore shall do less Things than even he.

This Evening L. said that Mathematicians were never good Company. That Mathematicks made a Man unhappy. That they never were good writers.

I said no nor the Lawyers—it had been often observed that Lawyers could not write.

L. said that Observation is not just, there are many other Instances of that besides you.—This looks like Art, but was too obvious.

I said, the Roman Lawyers were good Writers. Justinians Institutes were pure as Classicks. Several French Lawyers had been fine Writer[s] as Cochin, &c. and some English Lawyers as Bacon, Clarendon, Couper, Blackstone. But it was a common Observation in England, and I found it as common in Paris, that Lawyers were generally bad Writers.

[1] The first set of initials probably stands for Col. Josiah Quincy, but no satisfactory identification of "C.B." has occurred to the editors.

MAY 18 TUESDAY.

On Board all day, reading Don Quixot.[1]

[1] Surviving among JA's books in the Boston Public Library are a single volume of a six-volume set of *Don Quixote* in French, Paris, 1768, and a four-volume set in Spanish, Madrid, 1777 (*Catalogue of JA's Library*).

MAY 19. WEDNESDAY.

Pleasant. My State is tedious enough, waiting for the Chevalier, and loosing Time and Wind. Expectation is a painful Posture of the Mind, and Suspence, which is a little different, is worse.

This of L'orient is a fine Port and Harbour. Men of War can come up to the Wharf, and they commonly lie not far from it. But there is no such pleasant Prospects of the Country as in Boston Harbour.

1779 MAY 20. THURSDAY.

Went ashore, met a Servant of Mr. Chaumont on the Wharf, who presented me his Masters Compliments and an Invitation to dine which I accepted.

He lodges at Monsieur   who with his Lady and Daughter of Six Years, an Officer of the Navy, Mr. C., my Self and Son made the Company. A rich Dinner for so small a Company. The little Daughter of Six Years, shewed the Effects of early Culture. She sung at Table at my Desire several Songs, with great Ease and Judgment. She behaved as easily, as her mother, her Wit flowed and her Tongue run. Her Countenance was disciplined. Her Eyes and Lips were at her Command. She was very respectful to the Company and very attentive to Decency. Mr. C. went afterwards with me, to see a Magazine of Medicines belonging to the King, a very large Store, in order to get some Jesuits Bark, the best Kind of which I found was Seventeen Livres a Pound.

Found a Courier de l'Europe of the 7th. May. Paliser acquitted, tho reprehended, not unanimously nor honourably. Moultrie's Letter of the 4 Feb. to Lincoln and Putnams to Washington of 2. March.

It is said in this Paper that 121 Privateers and Letters of Marque from 6 to 36 Guns, have been fitted out at N. York, 1,976 Guns, 9,680 Men, and that they have taken 165 Prizes. This must be exagerated.

The 1st of May, the fleet at Portsmouth of more than 400 Sail for N. York, Quebec, Newfoundland and Ireland, put to Sea, convoyed by 6 ships of the Line, besides Frigates and armed Transports.

21. FRYDAY.

Mr. Ingraham and Mr. Merrick dined with me, in the Cabbin.

22 SATURDAY.

Went ashore. Dr. W[indship] revealed to me, a Secret concerning the Parson.—Good God! . . .[1] He is confident. He knows.—The Rheumatism never touches the Glands. It is a confirmed ———. He says, that B[lodget] knows so too.—It must come to an Head. It will break. It will be two months at least. He has purged himself off his Legs. Has exhausted himself by Purges.

(It gets into the Circulations—breaks out in Knots under the Arms—eats away the Roof [of] the Mouth—affects the Nose—if it seises the Lungs, &c.)

A Man of his Cloth. His Character is ruined—&c.

This is the innocent, the virtuous, the religious—&c. This is melancholly, and humiliating indeed! There is English Beauty, at Paris—
English Charmes as well as french. Innocence is not Proof against the
Arts of Paris. Simplicity is a Prey—and Virtue is melted away, by Wine
and Artifice. . . .

Coll. Wuibert drank Tea with me alone this Evening. I had a long,
free and familiar Conversation with him in french and he made me
the Compliment several Times to say that I spoke french very well,
that I understood French perfectly, that I had happily succeeded, tres
heureusement reussi in learning French, that I spoke it fluently, &c.
This flattery was uttered with as much Simplicity as the Duchess
D'Anville. I understood him, perfectly, every Word he said altho he
commonly speaks very indistinctly.

He says that he was several Times with the Solicitor General Wedderburne in London. That Wedderburne speaks and writes french,
very correctly. That he told him, he had spent a dozen Years at Paris
and made many Journeys there besides. That he treated him, with
great Politeness, beaucoup d'honnètete. That he had a List of all the
American Prisoners, with Notes against their Names. That he brought
Letters for W. to some of the family of M. de Noailles, the late Ambassador. That We have many friends in London. That he liked London better than Paris, because the Walking was better, the Streets
were cleaner, and there were Accommodations, on each Side, for
People on foot.

That he has been two hundred Leagues to see his father and family
who live in Champagne, near the frontiers of the Queen of Hungarys
Dominions.

He ran over the Streets in Paris that were commonly the most embarrassed, with Carriages.—C'est un Cahos,[2] &c.—He has promised
to look for me after Vignol's Architecture, &c.

We fell upon the Subject of Religion and Devotion on board the
Men of War. Every french Man of War has a Chaplain who says
Prayers Morning and Evening, regularly. I wished that ours were as
regular.

We fell upon the Subject of Swearing. I asked him, if the french
Sailors swore? He said chaque Instant, every Moment. That H[enri]
4 swore a great deal. Ventre St. Gris—litterally, holy grey belly. I asked
him if this originally alluded to the Vierge. He believed not. I told
him that most of the Oaths had originally Relation to Religion, and
explained to him Zounds—G–ds Zounds—His Wounds—Gods Wounds.

s blood and wounds—His Blood and Wounds—relating to Christ. He said this made him shudder.

Ma foi, Faith, par dieu, &c. It is amazing how Men get the Habit of using these Words, without thinking. I see no Difference between F[rench] and E[nglish] on this Account.

This afternoon, C.L. brought seven or Eight French Gentlemen on board to see the ship, who all admired her. They were genteel, well bred Men.

This Man has a Littleness in his Mien and Air. His face is small and sharp. So that you form a mean Opinion of him from the first Sight. Yet his Eye is good. He maintained a good Character among the American Prisoners, and you find by close Conversation with him that he has a good deal in him of Knowledge.

¹ Suspension points, here and below, in MS.
² Spelling, and therefore the meaning, uncertain; possibly a simple mistake in spelling for "Chaos."

23D. SUNDAY.

Waited in the Morning on Mr. Chaumont, agreed to go tomorrow Morning, on board the Sensible to make my Visit to the Commander.

Went to the Lodging of Mr. Ingraham and Blodget, where about 8 or 10 Americans Breakfast every Morning and drink Punch every Evening.

Took a Walk with Mr. Ingraham about the Town and then went and dined with Mr. Puchelberg. This is a modest and a decent German. He says there is no Protestant Church here. All is Levity, Legèrète. He says this Town is perdu. Amour, Jeu, et Vin, ruin all the Women. The Women drink Brandy like Water.

He says that France is capable of nourishing 48, or 50 Millions of People, but it is not half cultivated. The People are light and lazy.

At Bourdeaux there are 40,000 Protestants—but have no Church. The Workmen, Artisans &c. are Protestants.

This Man has a *Laugh* and a *Grin*, and a *Bow* that are very particular. His Grin is good natured, his Laugh is complaisant, his Bow is aukward to the last degree.

The Peasants in this Country are lazy, and no Wonder, for those who work the whole Year in planting Vines and in making Wine, are obliged to drink Water.

There are many Protestants here, who ne croient pas rien. Ils sont Athèe.

24. MONDAY.

Went with Mr. Chaumont to make my Visit to the Captain of the Sensible,[1] the Frigate in which I am to embark, and was civilly received. Went next on Board the Pallas, where we breakfasted with the Officers, and then viewed the Ship. Went next on board the Poor Richard and took another look at her. Went ashore and dined with C. Jones. The Captain of the Pallas[2] dined there and an Officer of his Marines. Mr. Maese, Mr. Dick, Mr. Hill, Captn. Parks &c.

The Sensible has 28 twelve Pounders upon one deck.

[1] Bidé de Chavagnes, a French officer with whom JA and JQA were to cross the Atlantic twice and who maintained with JA an agreeable correspondence until 1785.

[2] Cottineau de Kerloguin, a French naval officer in American service, commanded the Pallas, a 30-gun frigate, in John Paul Jones' squadron. In the famous action off Flamborough Head, Sept. 1779, the *Pallas* took the *Countess of Scarborough*. According to Lasseray, Cottineau was naturalized as an American citizen in the 1790's, resided in Philadelphia, and died at Savannah in 1808 (*Les français sous les treize étoiles*, 1:167–168).

1779 JUNE 1ST.

Dined on Shore at the Coffee House with Jones, Landais, the two Aids de Camp of the Marquis de la Fayette, Capt. Cotineau.

JUNE 2D. WEDNESDAY.

Dined on Board the Sensible, at the Invitation of the Captn. Mr. Chavan [Chavagnes], with Mr. Thevenard, Mr. Grandville, Mr. Chaumont, &c. &c.

On fait, et defait—mande et contremand. "A Strong Fleet is necessary to defend the Port of Brest."

This Observation, which I had never heard before, struck me. The Dry Docks might be destroyed, the Stores burnt or demolished, the Magazines destroyed, &c. unless the Place could be defended, by the Castle and other Fortifications, with the Land Forces.

1779. JUNE 8. TUESDAY.

Yesterday I sent one Boat with some of my Things, and this Morning another with the Remainder, on Board the Sensible.

Landais has torn open the old Sore, and in my Opinion, has now ruined the Peace of this Ship. He has [an] unhappy Mind. He must ever have something to complain of—something to peave and fret about. He is jealous.

1779 SATURDAY [12 JUNE].

Last night, the Chevalier de La Luzerne arrived, [and] [1] took Lodgings at the Epee Royal, in a Chamber opposite to mine up two Pair of Stairs. He did me the Honour, together with Monsieur Marbois, his Secretary,[2] or rather the Secretary of the Commission, [to visit me] [3] in my Chamber this Morning, and invited me to dine, with him in his Chamber with my Son. The Ambassador, the Secretary, Mr. Chaumont, my Son and myself, made the Company. The Chevalier informs me that he dined with me once, at Count Sarsefields.[4]

I went in the Morning to the Lodging of Monsr. Marbois. He was out, but I found his two Clerks, one of them speaks English very well. They observed to me, that I had been waiting a long time. I said Yes, long enough to have made a sentimental Journey through the Kingdom.—This pleased the English Secretary very much. He said Yoricks Sentimental Journey was a very fine Thing, a charming Piece. I said Yes and that Sterne was the sweetest, kindest, tenderest Creature in the World, and that there was a rich Stream of Benevolence flowing like Milk and Honey, thro all his Works.

M. Marbois shewed me, a Paper from Philadelphia of the 16 Feb. in which is a long Piece, with the Name of Mr. Paine. In it is the Letter, which I remember very well from M.D. proposing P. Ferdinand or M—— B—— to command in Chief.[5] The Name was mentioned of a Marshall, whom I have often heard [Deane] [6] say was one of the greatest Generals in Europe. This is curious—bien extraordinaire, one of the Gentlemen said.

After Dinner, I took a Walk in the Wood.

Beggars, Servants, Garçons, Filles, Decroteurs, Blanchisseuses. Barges, Batteaux, Bargemen. Coffee houses, Taverns. Servants at the Gates of Woods and Walks. Fruit, Cakes. Ice Creams. Spectacles. Tailors for setting a Stitch in Cloaths. Waiters for running with Errands, Cards &c. Cabbin Boys. Coach Hire. Walking Canes. Pamphlets. Ordonances. Carts.

[1] MS: "at."

[2] François Barbé-Marbois, later Marquis de Barbé-Marbois (1745–1837), a French diplomat who was to be repeatedly and significantly concerned with American affairs during his long career; see E. Wilson Lyon, *The Man Who Sold Louisiana . . .*, Norman, Okla., 1942. Marbois wrote his own account of his voyage to America in 1779, but it was addressed to a young lady and is on the whole more playful than informative. An English translation will be found in Eugene P. Chase, ed., *Our Revolutionary Forefathers: The Letters of François, Marquis de Barbé-Marbois during his Residence in the United States as Secretary of the French Legation, 1779–1785*, N.Y., 1929, p. 37–64. See also 20 Nov. 1782, below.

[3] Supplied by the editors for words omitted by the diarist.

⁴ Guy Claude, Comte de Sarsfield (1718–1789), a French military officer of Irish antecedents (*Dict. de la noblesse*, 18:292; Edward MacLysaght, *Irish Families*, Dublin, 1957, p. 261–262; *Ann. Register for 1789*, p. 210). His seat was at Rennes, Brittany, but having gregarious habits he lived much in Paris and later sought out JA's company at The Hague and in London. He had a special fondness for Americans, entertained and corresponded with all those of any prominence who came to Europe, and apparently visited America after the Revolution. In the Adams Papers, besides a long series of letters from Sarsfield, 1778–1789, there is a book-length set of MS essays by him in French on the government and economy of the United Provinces, on Women, Slavery, and other topics, indicating that he had aspirations as a *philosophe*. (These are tentatively dated 1782–1783.) Long extracts from Sarsfield's journal in the Low Countries were copied by JA into his own Diary under date of 10 Oct. 1782, q.v. From London, 6 Sept. 1785, JA wrote Arthur Lee that Sarsfield was there and leading "the Life of a Peripatetic Philosopher.... He ... is the Happyest Man I know.... If a Man was born for himself alone, I would take him for a Model" (Adams Papers; R. H. Lee, *Arthur Lee*, 2:255). And to Sarsfield himself, 21 Jan. 1786, JA wrote: "Among all my acquaintance I know not a greater Rider of Hobby Horses than Count Sarsfield—one of your Hobby Horses is to assemble uncommon Characters. I have dined with you 2 or 3. times at your House in Company with the oddest Collections of Personages that were ever put together. I am thinking if you were here, I would Invite you to a dinner to your taste. I would ask King Paoli, King Brant, Le Chevalier D'Eon, and if you pleased you might have Mr. and Mrs. ——— with whom you dined in America. How much speculation would this whimsical association afford you?" (LbC, Adams Papers).

⁵ This article signed by Thomas Paine appeared in the *Pennsylvania Packet*, 16 Feb. 1779, and incorporates an extract from Silas Deane's letter to the Secret Committee of Foreign Affairs, Paris, 6 Dec. 1776, proposing Prince Ferdinand or Marshal Broglie as suitable persons "to take the lead of your armies" (*Deane Papers*, 1:404–405; 3:361–375).

⁶ Blank in MS.

1779. JUNE 17. THURSDAY.

At 6 O Clock this Morning, Monsieur Chavan, Capitain of the Sensible, sent his Canot, on Shore for me, and mine, and here I am, in full Possession of my Apartment.

Sailed about 3 o Clock, in Company with the Bon Homme Richard Captain Jones, the Alliance Captain Landais, the   Captain Young, the   Captain Cazneau, the Courier de L'Europe Capt.

The Three Friends Capt. Colman, belonging to Mr. Williams of Nantes, which is loaded with a large Quantity of the Chevaliers Baggage, was missing. The Chev[alier] discovered a good deal of sensibility at this. The whole Fleet is obliged to wait for this Captain Colman and loose this fair Wind.

The Chevalier has an Appartment about 8 Feet long and six Wide, upon the Starboard Side of the Quarter Deck. I have another of the same Dimensions, directly opposite to him, on the Larboard. Next behind the Chevalier is the Cabin of the Captain Monsieur Chavan.

Next behind me is the Cabbin of the second in Command of the Frigate. And behind us all at the stern is a larger Room, the Passage Way to which lies between the Chevaliers and the Captains Cabin on one Side, and mine and the Seconds on the other.

In this larger Room, which extends the whole Width of the Quarter Deck, all the Company loll and converse by day. Monsieur Marbois and my little son hang their Cotts there and sleep at night. All the Officers and all the Company, dine, below, in what is called the grand Cabbin.

The Chevalier is a large, and a strong Man, has a singular Look with his Eyes. Shutts his Eye Lids, &c.

M. Marbois the Secretary, is a tall, genteel Man and has a Countenance extreamly pleasant. He has the Appearance of Delicacy, in his Constitution. . . .[1]

Mr. Marbois has two Persons with him, one a French Secretary, the other a Secretaire interprete, who speaks and writes English.

The Maitre D'Hotel has his Wife with him. She seems a well bred Woman. . . .

We are to speak English. This is the Agreement, but there are so few who can speak a Word of English, that 9/10 of the Conversation in spight of our Intentions and Engagements runs into French. We have on board a Dictionary of the Marine, so that We shall soon understand the Names of Things and Actions on Board.

Brown of the Manufactory, is on Board as Pilot for the American Coast. He has received fifty Guineas for it. Such is the Reward for making a Stand, manfully, 10 or 11 Years ago. I told the Story to the Che[valier] who was much pleased with the Narration.[2]

Mr. Hill also, first Lieutenant of the Alliance is on Board but I know not by whose Influence. C. Jones or M. Chau[mont] probably.

[1] Suspension points, here and below, in MS.
[2] This "Story" cannot now be reconstructed.

1779. JUNE 18. FRYDAY.

This Morning, the Monsieur a french Privateer, which sailed out from L'orient as We went into it in the Alliance, came in with four English Prizes, having made Six this Cruise. She and her Prizes saluted the Sensible, and their Salutes were returned.

Received a Card from Mr. Williams 3d., apologising for the 3 friends that the Pilot refused to take charge of her untill the Morning.[1]

I asked a Gentleman how he slept.—Very badly, dans le Sainte

Barbe.—Il faut chercher cet mot la, said I, dans le Dictionaire de Marine.—He ran and brought it and found Le Sainte Barbe to be the Gun Room.—Connoissez vous l'Etymologie Monsieur, said he—Que non, said I.

Sainte Barbe is the Tutelary Sainte of the Cannoniers—Gunners. Each Trade has its Patron. The Shoemakers have Sainte Crispin, &c. and the Gunners Sainte Barbe.

The Sainte Barbe therefore is the Gunroom or the Salle D'Armes, Place of Arms.

There are 9 Persons who sleep in the Sainte Barbe.

The Serruriers have chosen St. Cloud for their Patron, &c.

Mr. Marbois discovered an Inclination to day to slide into Conversation with me, to day. I fell down the Stream with him, as easily as possible. He Thought the Alliance beneficial, to both Countries, and hoped it would last forever. I agreed that the Alliance was usefull to both, and hoped it would last. I could not foresee any Thing that should interrupt the Friendship. Yes, recollecting myself, I could foresee several Things that might interrupt it.—Ay what were they?— I said it was possible, a King of France might arise, who being a wicked Man might make Attempts to corrupt the Americans. A King of France hereafter might have a Mistress, that might mislead him, or a bad Minister. I said I could foresee another Thing that might endanger our Confederation.—What was that?—The Court of France, I said, might, or their Ambassadors or Consuls might, attach themselves to Individuals or Parties, in America, so as to endanger our Union.—He caught at this, with great Avidity, and said it was a great Principle, not to join with any Party. It was the K's Determination and the Chevaliers, not to throw the Weight of the French Court into the Scale of any Individual or Party.

He said, he believed, or was afraid, it had been done: but it was disapproved by the King and would not be done again. . . .[2] He said that the Chevalier and himself would have the favour of the greatest Part, the Generality of the honest People in France, altho there would be Individuals against them.

He said He hoped the United States would not think of becoming Conquerors. I said it was impossible they should for many Ages. It would be Madness in them to think of conquering foreign Countries, while they had an immense Territory, near them uncultivated. That if any one State should have a fancy for going abroad it would be the Interest of all the rest and their Duty to hinder her.—He seemed to be pleased with this.

He said We would explain ourselves wholly, on the Passage. I said, with all my Heart, for I had no Secrets.

All this Conversation was in french, but he understood me, very well, and I him.

He said Mr. Gerard was a Man of Wit, and had an Advantage of them in understanding the Language very well and speaking it easily. I said I believed not much. I had heard it affirmed, by some, that Mr. Gerard spoke English perfectly, but by others, very indifferently. That it was often affirmed that Mr. Franklin spoke French as fluently and elegantly, as a Courtier at Versailles, but every Man that knew and spoke sincerely, agreed that he spoke it very ill. Persons spoke of these Things, according to their Affections.

He said it was Flattery. That he would not flatter, it was very true that both Mr. F. and I spoke french, badly.

A Cutter and a Lugger, hove in Sight, about Noon, and dogged about all the afternoon.

Mr. Marbois began with me, again this Afternoon. Enquired who was Dr. Bancroft?—Who Dr. Berkenhout? &c. &c.[3]

[1] The "Card" has not been found.
[2] Suspension points in MS.
[3] Here follow three and a half blank pages in the MS preceding the second entry dated 18 June. Obviously JA intended to continue his record of the afternoon's conversation with Marbois. In Marbois' epistolary journal of the voyage there is, curiously, only a single bare mention of the Adamses, and that not until 15 July: "I have not told you that Mr. John Adams and his son are passengers with us on the *Sensible*" (Eugene P. Chase, ed., *Our Revolutionary Forefathers*, N.Y., 1929, p. 58).

1779. JUNE 18. FRYDAY.

The orders are to breakfast at 10., dine at 5. and sup at 10.

19. SATURDAY.

The two Privateers, which were in Sight Yesterday, are so still with two others.

Our Captain at length laid too, hoisted his Colours and fired a Gun as a Challenge. One of them hoisted English Colours and fired a Gun, which I suppose was accepting the Challenge. Our Captain gave her two Broad Sides, for the Sake of exercising his Men, and some of his Balls went beyond her, some before and some behind her. I cannot say that any one hit, but there were two which went so well that it is possible they might. It is certain they were frightened, for upon our wearing to give her chase all 4 of them were about in an Instant and run.—But at Evening there were several others in Sight.

20. SUNDAY.

Two Privateers have been in sight all this day. One advanced, and fired several Guns in order to make Us hoist our Colours. But Captain Chavan would not do them that Honour. They are afraid to come near. But this it is.[1] Every day We have a No. in Sight, so that there is no Chance for a Vessell to pass without Convoy.

Our Captain Mr. Chavan has a Cross of St. Louis, and one of his Midshipmen has a Cross of St. Louis. His second has none—he is a youth of 18 or 19, an Enseigne du Vesseau, and very able for his Years. He has a fine Countenance.

The Chevalier de la Luzerne, and M. Marbois are in raptures with my Son. They get him to teach them the Language. I found this Morning the Ambassador, Seating on the Cushing in our State Room, Mr. Marbois in his Cot at his left Hand and my Son streched out in his at his Right—The Ambassador reading out loud, in Blackstones Discourse, at his Entrance on his Professorship of the Common Law at the University, and my Son correcting the Pronunciation of every Word and Syllable and Letter. The Ambassador said he was astonished, at my Sons Knowledge. That he was a Master of his own Language like a Professor. Mr. Marbois said your Son teaches Us more than you. He has Point de Grace—Point d'Eloges. He shews us no Mercy, and makes Us no Compliments. We must have Mr. John.

This Evening had a little Conversation with the Chevalier, upon our American Affairs, and Characters, Mr. Samuel Adams, Mr. Dickinson, Mr. Jay—and upon American Eloquence in Congress and Assemblies as well as in Writing. He admired our Eloquence. I said that our Eloquence was not corrected. It was the Time of Ennius, with Us. That Mr. Dickinson and Mr. Jay had Eloquence, but it was not so chaste, nor pure, nor nervous as that of Mr. Samuel Adams. That this last had written some things, that would be admired more than any Thing that has been written in America in this Dispute.—He enquired after Mr. Dickinson, and the Reason why he disappeared. I explained, as well as I could in French, the Inconsistency of the Farmers Letters and his Perseverance in that Inconsistency in Congress. Mr. Dickensons Opposition to the Declaration of Independancy. I ventured as modestly as I could to let him know that I had the Honour to be the Principal Disputant in Congress against Mr. Dickinson upon that great Question. That Mr. Dickinson had the Eloquence, the Learning and the Ingenuity on his Side of the Question, but that I had the Hearts of the Americans on mine, and therefore my Side of the Question prevailed. That Mr. Dickinson had a good Heart, and an amiable Character. But that his Opposition to Independency, had lost him the Confidence of the People, who suspected him of Timidity and Avarice, and that his Opposition sprung from those Passions: But that he had since turned out with the Militia, against the B[ritish] Troops and I doubted not might in Time regain the Confidence of the People.

I said that Mr. Jay was a Man of Wit, well informed, a good Speaker and an elegant Writer. The Chevalier said perhaps he will not be President when We arrive. He accepted only for a short Time. I said I should not be sorry to hear of his Resignation, because I did not much esteem the Means by which he was advanced to the Chair, it appearing to me that he came in by the Efforts of a Faction at that Moment dominant by Means of an Influence which I was afraid to mention. That I did not care to say what I thought of it.[2]

We fell into a great deal of other Conversation this Evening upon Litterature, and Eloquence ancient and modern, Demosthenes, Cicero, the Poets, Historians, Philosophers. The English, Bacon, Newton &c. Milton &c.

He said Milton was very ancient. I said no, in the Reign of Charles and the Protectorship of Cromwell and the Reign of Charles the Second.—He thought it was much more ancient.

I said there were three Epochas in the English History celebrated for great Men.—The Reign of Elizabeth, the Reign of C[harles] 1. and the Interregnum, and the Reign of Queen Anne.

The C. said Ld. Bolinbroke was a great Man. I said Yes and the greatest Orator that England ever produced.

Mr. Marbois upon this said, it would be easy in France to produce an Orator equal to Bolinbroke. I asked who? John Jac[ques?]—No, Malesherbes. Malesherbes Orations might be placed on a Footing with Demosthenes and Cicero.

[1] Perhaps JA meant to write: "But this is the way it is."
[2] See entry of 12 Feb., above, and note 2 there; also 22 June, below.

MONDAY JUNE 21.

This Morning I found Mr. Marbois recovered of his Sea Sickness. I fell into Conversation with him, about his illness, advised a Dish of Tea, which he readily accepted, told him he must learn to drink Tea in America in order to please the Ladies, who all drank Tea. That the american Ladies shone at the Tea Table. He said, he had heard they were very amiable and of agreable Conversation. I said Yes, but they could not dance, nor sing, nor play Musick, nor dress so well as the European Ladies. But they had Wit and Sense and Virtue.—After a great deal of Chat like this, I asked him—Sir you mentioned last night Malsherbes Orations. Who and What was Malesherbes?—He said Malsherbes was President of the Court of Aids, during the Disputes between the late King and the Parliament of Paris. That he made his orations in the Course of those Disputes. That most of them were not printed, only a few of the latter ones were printed in the Newspapers. That He was banished by the late King with the Parliament, and after the Accession of the present King was recalled and made one of his Ministers, in which Place he continued 18 Months. But finding Things were likely to take a Turn not perfectly agreable to his Mind and that he could not continue in Place with Honour he resigned and lives a private Life in Paris and is happy. He is the Son of a Late Chancellor De lamoignon de Malesherbes, who was a famous Man. He goes by the Name of De la Moignon. He died about five Years ago, and it was thought his Son would take the same Name of Lamoignon, but he choses to go by that of Malesherbes. He is a great Man, an intimate Friend of Mr. De Turgot. Mr. Malesherbes is Uncle to the Chevalier de la Luzerne. I have dined twice, within a few Weeks past, with Mr. Franklin at the House of Mr. Malesherbes, and once with him at Mr. Franklins. The Acquaintance was formed upon Occasion of the Appointment of the C. De la Luzerne to go to America.

I lamented that I had not seen Mr. Malesherbes, said that I had the Pleasure to dine often with Mr. Turgot at his House and at ours. That Mr. Franklin was very intimate with Mr. Turgot, who I thought was a very good Man.—Yes says Mr. Marbois, but a little too systematical and a little too enthusiastical....[1] I said Enthusiasm was sometimes a very good Quality, at least very usefull.—Not for a Minister, says M.M.—Yes for a Minister, in some Cases, and Circumstances.—Ay says he, at sometimes when he can communicate his Enthusiasm to All about him. But at others when his Enthusiasm will be opposed by Millions of People of great Weight, it will not do.

I am very happy to hear of these Connections. I shall discover more of them yet. This Mr. Marbois is one of the best informed, and most reflecting Men I have known in France. I warrant I shall have much Pleasure in his Conversation.

About Three O Clock, the Chevalier and I walking upon Deck, he took me under the Arm, and told me, he had something to communicate to me, which he had bound himself in Honour not to communicate, while he was in France.

Les Espagnols viennent, de se declarer.—Comment, said I?—Aux Anglois said the Chevalier. They have declared that the Court of London having rejected all the Propositions for Peace, which they had made, they were now determined to declare them selves on the side of France, and to assist them with all their Force by Land and Sea, in every Part of the World, and accordingly they have ordered 17 Ships of the Line or 19 to join the Comte D'orvilliere, making up 50 Sail, in the whole. They have a Minister in America, at Congress. And they are to concert with Congress all their military Operations. Without saying any Thing about the Independance of America.[2]—Je ne comprend pas le Politique D'Espagne said I. (This instantly struck me disagreably. I am jealous of some Scheme. The Subtilty, the Invention, the profound Secrecy, the Absolute Silence of these European Courts, will be too much for our hot, rash, fiery Ministers, and for our indolent, inattentive ones, tho as silent as they.) This within Crochets was not said, but is a Reflection of my own. The Chevalier added, The Basis of every Proposition for Peace that Spain has made was, an Acknowledgement of the Independance of Amerique.

He added farther, We i.e. the french have within this Month offered, that if the English would withdraw their Troops from N. York, Rhode Island and Long Island all Things should remain as they were.—Note, this I dont understand. What becomes of Georgia? What was to become of the Sea War? &c.

The Chevalier added, this was rejected by the Court of London....

By this it appears, the Court of Spain have given Mr. Lee the Go by. They may have made a Treaty with Congress by their Ambassador there.

I said the English would make great Depredations upon the Spanish Trade.—How, says the Chev[alier]?—By their little Cutters and Luggers said I.—Oh the Spaniards, said he, dont make an active Commerce like the French. Their Commerce is made in large Vessells, and always well escorted.

This News operates upon my Mind, like the Affair of Sarratoga. It is not good enough and therefore, the Disappointment makes me Mellancholly.

The Chevalier said one other Thing worth Remembrance. He said that The Americans did not know, what their Commerce with France would be. The great and able Merchants had not yet traded to America. Who is it, said He, that has traded to America, but a Parcell of little Rascals, petits Coquins, and Adventurers who have sold the worst Merchandises, for great Prices.—This Conversation was all in french and may not be perfectly translated, but I believe it is.

I have much Satisfaction in reflecting, that in all the Conversations I have yet had with the Chevalier, no unguarded Word has escaped me. I have conversed with that Frankness that makes a Part of my Character, but have said nothing that I did not mean to say.

I find a Gentleman in the Suit of the Chevalier, in the Character of Interpreter and English Master who has written a large Volume upon English Pronunciation and Accent. His Name is Carrè.

[1] Suspension points, here and below, in MS.

[2] Thus punctuated in the MS, but this phrase undoubtedly qualifies the preceding sentence. By the secret Convention of Aranjuez, 12 April 1779, Spain and France agreed that Spain would come into the war against Great Britain if the latter declined the terms of a Spanish proposal of mediation. In May Great Britain did decline, the Spanish and French fleets began to operate together, and on the day JA made the present entry in his Diary Spain declared war on Great Britain. But contrary to the urgent wish of Vergennes, the Spanish government had refused to include in the Convention any guarantee of American independence; Spain became an ally of France but not of the United States; and though she sent "observers" there, there was no officially accredited Spanish minister in the United States until 1784. See Bemis, *Diplomacy of the Amer. Revolution,* ch. 7; Doniol, *Histoire,* vol. 3: ch. 13, especially p. 806–807, 850–851; Frances G. Davenport and Charles O. Paullin, eds., *European Treaties Bearing on the History of the United States and Its Dependencies,* Washington, 1917–1937, 4:145–146.

JUNE 22. TUESDAY.

We have had a fine Wind ever since We came out of L'orient, but it blows fresher today than ever. Yet We go but about 5 Knots, because being obliged to wait for the Three Friends, and the Foudroyant, which sail slow, We cannot carry Sail. With all our Sails We might now go eleven Knots. This is Mercantile Politicks of C[haumont] and W[illiams] in getting the Chevaliers Baggage on Board those Ships.

The Chevalier de la Luzerne, the other day at Mr. De Thevenards Table, gave a terrible Stroke to M. Chaumont. Chaumont said, M. Franklin parle Francais bien.—Oh que non, said the Chevalier, fort mal. Mr. Adams parle mieux que lui.—Yesterday, in a long Conversation with the Chevalier, on the Quarter Deck, he said to me, Vous connoissez les Fondemens de notre Langue tres bien. Vous parlez lentement et avec difficulté, comme un homme qui cherche pour les mots: mais vous ne pechez pas contre la Prononciation. Vous prononcez bien. Vous prononcez, beaucoup mieux que Mr. Franklin. Il est impossible de l'entendre.

Mr. Marbois, with whom I fell into Conversation, this Afternoon very easily upon Deck, said a great many Things that deserve Notice.

He said that Mr. Franklin had a great many Friends among the Gens des Lettres in France, who make a great Impression in France, that he had Beaucoup des Agremens, Beaucoup de Charlatagnerie, that he has Wit: But that he is not a Statesman. That he might be recalled at this Moment, and in that Case, that his Opinion was he would not return to America—But would stay in Paris.

That he heard many of the honest People in France lament that I left France, particularly the Count   and the Marquis de
             That I might possibly return to France or to some other Part of Europe. That the Court of France would have Confidence in any Gentleman, that Congress should ⟨appoint⟩ have Confidence in. That there ought to be a Charge des Affairs or a Secretary, and a successor pointed out, in Case of the Death of Dr. F.

Mr. Marbois said some were of opinion, that as I was not recalled, I ought to have staid untill I was.

I told him that if Congress had directed me to return, I would have returned. If they had directed me to stay untill further orders I should have staid. But as they reduced me to a private Citizen I had no other Duties but those of a private Citizen to fulfill, which were to go home as soon as possible and take Care of my family. Mr. Franklin advised me to take a Journey to Geneva. My own Inclinations would have led me to Holland: But I thought my Honour concerned to return directly home.—He said I was right.

In the Evening I fell into Chat with the Chevalier. He asked me, about Governeur [Gouverneur] Morris. I said it was his Christian Name—that he was not Governor. The Chevalier said He had heard of him as an able Man. I said he was a young Man, chosen into Congress since I left it. That I had sat some Years with his Elder Brother in Congress. That Governeur was a Man of Wit, and made pretty Verses—but of a Character trés legere. That the Cause of America had not been sustained by such Characters as that of Governor Morris or his Colleague Mr. Jay, who also was a young Man about 30 and not quite so solid as his Prediccesor Mr. Laurence [Laurens], upon whose Resignation in the sudden Heat Mr. Jay was chosen. That Mr. Lawrence had a great landed Fortune free from Debt, that he had long Experience in public life and an amiable Character for Honour And Probity. That he is between 50 and 60 Years of Age.

JUNE 23. WEDNESDAY.

This Forenoon, fell strangely, yet very easily into Conversation with M.M.

I went up to him—M.M. said I, how many Persons have you in your

Train and that of the Chevalier who speak the German Language?—
Only my Servant, said he, besides myself and the Chev[alier].—It will
be a great Advantage to you said I in America, especially in Pensilvania,
to be able to speak German. There is a great Body of Germans in P[enn-
sylvania] and M[aryland]. There is a vast Proportion of the City of
Philadelphia, of this Nation who have their Churches in it, two of
which one Lutheran the other Calvinist, are the largest and most
elegant Churches in the City, frequented by the most numerous Con-
gregations, where the Worship is all in the German Language.

Is there not one Catholic, said M.M.?—Not a German Church said
I. There is a Roman catholic Church in Philadelphia, a very decent
Building, frequented by a respectable Congregation, consisting partly
of Germans, partly of French and partly of Irish.—All Religions are
tolerated in America, said M.M., and the Ambassadors have in all
Courts a Right to a Chappell in their own Way. But Mr. Franklin
never had any.—No said I, laughing, because Mr. F. had no—I was
going to say, what I did not say, and will not say here. I stopped short
and laughed.—No, said Mr. M., Mr. F. adores only great Nature, which
has interested a great many People of both Sexes in his favour.—Yes,
said I, laughing, all the Atheists, Deists and Libertines, as well as the
Philosophers and Ladies are in his Train—another Voltaire and Hume.
—Yes said Mr. M., he is celebrated as the great Philosopher and the
great Legislator of America.—He is said I a great Philosopher, but as
a Legislator of America he has done very little. It is universally believed in France, England and all Europe, that his Electric Wand has
accomplished all this Revolution but nothing is more groundless. He
has [done][1] very little. It is believed that he made all the American
Constitutions, and their Confederation. But he made neither. He did
not even make the Constitution of Pensylvania, bad as it is. The Bill
of Rights is taken almost verbatim from that of Virginia, which was
made and published two or three Months before that of Philadelphia
was begun. It was made by Mr. Mason, as that of Pensilvania was by
Timothy Matlack, James Cannon and Thomas Young and Thomas
Paine. Mr. Sherman of Connecticutt[2] and Dr. F. made an Essay towards a Confederation about the same Time. Mr. Shermans was best
liked, but very little was finally adopted from either, and the real
Confederation was not made untill a Year after Mr. F. left America,
and but a few Days before I left Congress.

Who, said the Chevalier, made the Declaration of Independance?—
Mr. Jefferson of Virginia, said I, was the Draughtsman. The Committee consisted of Mr. Jefferson, Mr. Franklin, Mr. Harrison, Mr. R.

and myself,[3] and We appointed [Mr.][4] Jefferson a subcommittee to draw it up.

I said that Mr. Franklin had great Merit as a Philosopher. His Discoveries in Electricity were very grand, and he certainly was a Great Genius, and had great Merit in our American Affairs. But he had no Title to the Legislator of America.

Mr. M. said he had Wit and Irony, but these were not the Faculties of Statesmen. His Essay upon the true Means of bring[ing] a great Empire to be a small one was very pretty.—I said he had wrote many Things, which had great Merit and infinite Wit and Ingenuity. His bonhomme Richard was a very ingenious Thing, which had been so much celebrated in France, gone through so many Editions, and been recommended by Curates and Bishops to so many Parishes and Diocesses.

Mr. M. asked, are natural Children admitted in America to all Priviledges like Children born in Wedlock.—I answered they are not Admitted to the Rights of Inheritance. But their fathers may give them Estates by Testament and they are not excluded from other Advantages.—In France, said M.M., they are not admitted into the Army nor any Office in Government.—I said they were not excluded from Commissions in the Army, Navy, or State, but they were always attended with a Mark of Disgrace.—M.M. said this, No doubt, in Allusion to Mr. Fs. natural Son and natural Son of a natural Son. I let myself thus freely into this Conversation being led on naturally by the Chevalier and Mr. Marbois, on Purpose because I am sure it cannot be my Duty nor the Interest of my Country that I should conceal any of my sentiments of this Man, at the same Time that I due[5] Justice to his Merits. It would be worse than Folly to conceal my Opinion of his great Faults.

[1] MS: "not."

[2] A mistake for Dickinson of Pennsylvania, though Sherman was a member of the committee appointed to draft the Articles, 12 June 1776 (JCC, 5:433). Franklin's rudimentary plan had been submitted to Congress almost a year earlier, July 1775.

[3] A double mistake. The committee appointed on 11 June 1776 to draft a Declaration of Independence consisted of Jefferson, JA, Franklin, Sherman, and Robert R. Livingston, in that order (same, p. 431). But these may have been lapses only of JA's pen and not of his tongue or memory; there is plentiful evidence that he wrote his notes of this conversation when he was sleepy.

[4] MS: "by."

[5] Corrected by CFA to "do," but JA may have meant to write "render due Justice."

JUNE 24. THURSDAY.

Mr. Marbois told a Story of an Ecclesiastic, who pronounced a funeral oration on Marshall Saxe.—He compared him to Alcides, who ballanced long whether he should follow the Path of Virtue or of Sloth, and at last chose the former. But Saxe, after ballancing long, did better by determining to follow both, i.e. Pleasure and Virtue.

This Evening I went into our State Room, where I found Mr. Marbois, alone.—Mr. Marbois, said I, what Books are the best to give a Stranger an Idea of the Laws and Government of France.—I shall surprise you, Sir, said M. Marbois, and I shall make you laugh: But there is no other, but the Almanach Royal.—You say this, said I, laughing, on purpose to make me laugh.—No says he there is no Droit public in France. There are different Customs and Prerogatives in different Provinces. . . .[1] But if you wish I should talk with you, more seriously, there are several Books in which there are some good Notions upon this subject. There are 4 Volumes by Boulainvilliers, of Observations sur l'ancient Gouvernement de France, and 4 Volumes more by the Abby De Fleury on the same Subject.[2]—He ran over a great deal more concerning the Salique Law and the Capitula Regnum francorum &c., which I will be more particular with him about another Time. I mentioned Domat. He said it was excellent on the civil Law: but had little on the Droit public.[3]

How happened it, said I, M.M., that I never saw you at Paris.— You have, said he.—Ay where? said I. I dont remember it.—I dined with you said he at the Count Sarsefields.—I said there was a great deal of Company, but that I had never seen any one of them before. They were all Strangers: but I remember the Count told me, they were all Men of Letters.—There were four Ladies, said M. Marbois, the handsomest of which was the Countess de la Luzerne, the Wife of the Count de la Luzerne. The Count himself was there, who is the Eldest Brother of the Chevalier de la Luzerne. There was another Lady there, who is not handsome and was never married. She is a Sister. —She was the Lady who sat at my left Hand at Table, said I, and was very sociable. I was charmed with her Understanding, altho I thought she was not handsome.

There was a Gentleman there, said I, who asked me if the Mahometan Religion was tolerated in America? I understood he had been in Constantinople, as Ambassador or Secretary to some Embassy. And there was a Bishop there, who came in after Dinner.—Yes said he, he is the Bishop of Langres, another Brother of the Chevalier de la Luzerne.—I fell, said I, unaccountably into a Dispute with that Bishop. He sat down by me, and fell into Conversation about the English and their Conduct, in America. In the Course of the Con- [versation] I said it was the Misfortune of the English that there was no consistent Character among those in Opposition to the Court. No Man who would Adhere to his Principles. The two Hows were in Opposition to the Ministry and the American ⟨War⟩ Measures. But when the Honor and Emoluments of Command were offered them, they accepted to serve under that Ministry and in support of those Measures. Even Keppell, who refused to serve vs. America, was induced to serve vs. France, who were only supporting the Americans.—The Bishop said it was the Will of the K[ing] that must controul public officers.—I said, an officer should beg to be excused, or resign rather than serve against his Conscience.—He said the King's Will must govern.—I said it was a Doctrine I could not understand.—There was a Gentleman present who attended to our Conversation in silence, till this when he said c'est un Doctrine Ecclesiastique, Monseigneur L'Eveque, said he, laughing.

This Bishop, said Mr. Marbois, is no slave, he is a Man of free sentiments. He is Duke et Pair. There are three Bishops, who are Dukes and Peers and Three others who are Counts and Peers, who are always present at the Consecration of our Kings. The Bishop of Langres is one. The Dukes of Normandy, and of Burgundy, used to be present, but as there are not [any?] at present, Monsieur and the Count D'Artois represented them at the Consecration of the present King, about 4 Years ago. The origin of the Custom is not known.

The Chevalier de la Luzerne, said I, is of an high Family.—Yes, said Mr. Marbois, he is of an ancient Family, who have formerly had in it Cardinals and Marechalls of France, but not lately. They were now likely to regain their Splendor for the Three Brothers are all very well at Court.

[1] Suspension points in MS.

[2] A copy of Henri, Comte de Boulainvilliers' work, *Etat de la France . . .* , in 3 folio volumes, London, 1727–1728, is among JA's books in the Boston Public Library; so also is a copy of Claude Fleury's *Droit public de France . . .* , 2 vols., Paris, 1769. The latter is inscribed: "Presented by Monsr. De Tournelle Consul of France at Corunna, on the 19 Decr. 1779 to John Adams"; see entry of 19 Dec., below.

[3] On 30 March 1780, soon after his return to Paris, JA purchased a copy of Jean Domat's great treatise on civil law, *Les loix civiles dans leur ordre naturel . . .* , nouv. édn., 2 vols. in 1, folio, Paris, 1777. It survives among his books in the Boston Public Library.

JUNE 25. FRYDAY.

JUNE 26 SATURDAY.

27 SUNDAY.

JUNE 28 MONDAY.

We have been favoured, in our Voyage hitherto, beyond my utmost Expectations. We have enjoyed a Succession of favourable Winds and Weather, from the Time of our leaving L'orient to this Moment.

The Discipline, on Board this Ship, is a constant Subject of Speculation to me. I have seen no Punishments inflicted, no Blows struck, nor heard scarcely an Angry Word spoken, from the Captain to any of his officers, or from any of the officers to the Men. They live together in greater Intimacy and Familiarity than any Family I ever saw. The Galliard or Quarter Deck, seems to be as open to the foremast Men as the Captain. Captain, all other Officers, the Ambassador, his Train, Common Sailors, and domestic Servants are all walking upon Deck, and sitting round upon Seats on it, upon a footing of perfect Equality that is not seen in one of our Country Town Meetings in America. I never saw so much Equality and Levelling in any Society, whatever. Strange Contrast to a British, or even an American Frigate. Landais is a great Mogul, in Comparison of Chevan.

One of the Officers have favoured me with the following

Etat Major,
De la Fregate du Roy la Sensible.

Messieurs

Bidè de Chavaigne, Capitaine de Vaisseaux Commandant la Fregate.
Le Chevalier de Goabriant [Goësbriand], Enseigne de
   Vaisseaux   Lieutenant de Fregate pour la Campagne.
Le Chevalier D'Arriardant.   idem
Le Chevalier de Pincaire.   idem
   Du Breville.   idem

Garde la Marine

Messieurs

Le Chevalier de Guerivierre.
La Roche de St. Andrè.
   Bergèrac Chirurgien Major.
Le Pere Usem Capucin et Aumonier.[1]

The Diversions on Board the Ship are very curious. The Officers and Men sing and dance in a Ring round the Capstain,[2] on the Quarter deck, in fine Weather. The Men are in Parties at Cards in all Parts of the Ship.

[1] Some of the names in this "Etat Major" are more or less phonetically spelled, according to JA's habit.
[2] Thus in MS. Silently corrected by CFA to "capstan."

1779. JUNE 30. WEDNESDAY.

Mr. Marbois, this Morning, upon my Enquiry, told me, that the Chevalier de la Luzerne is the Grandson of the famous Chancelier de la Moignon by his Mothers Side. That the Marchall Broglie is a Cousin to the Chevalier.

He also told me, that he himself, Mr. Marbois, was born in Metz, where the Comte de Broglie is Commandant. That going lately to Metz to be admitted a Counsellor in Parliament, he journeyed in Company with the Comte.

JULY 2D. FRYDAY.

Walking this afternoon, with Mr. Marbois, upon the Quarter Deck, I said frankly to him, that I had expected that Mr. Garnier would have been sent to America. That I had observed some things in the Conduct of B. and C.[1] which made me conjecture and believe that they were planning to have Mr. G[arnier] succeed Mr. G[érard]. That there was a great Intimacy between B. and Mr. G[arnier].

Between our selves, said Mr. Marbois, I believe that was a Reason, why he did not go.

Mr. G[arnier], said M. Marbois, is a Man of Spirit, and has a great deal of Merit, in England he did us good Service, and he speaks English very well, and understands Affairs very well, but in this Affair of his going out upon this Embassy, I cannot reconcile his Conduct, with a Man of Spirit.

I said, I had the Pleasure of some Acquaintance and a good deal of Conversation with Mr. G[arnier]. That he did me the Honour to visit me, several Times, and I had several long Conversations with him alone; that I was much pleased with his Knowledge of our Affairs from the Beginning, and with his Manners: But I thought him too much connected, and attached to a particular Circle, particularly to B. to whom he seemed to me to have a blind Attachment.

There is Reason to believe, said Mr. Marbois, that Dr. Franklin is not too much pleased with the Appointment of the Chevalier. What is the Reason of the Attachment of Dr. F. to B.?—Because B. is devoted to Mr. D[eane] and because he is the only American at Paris who loves him—all the Americans but him are at present very bitter vs. F....[2] He would probably be very glad to get his G[rand] Son Secretary, but as I fancy he must think him too young to obtain the

Appointment, he will join with Mr. D. in endeavouring to get B.—D. I know from Authentic Information is endeavouring to get B. appointed. That B. was so irregular and excentric a Character, and his Conduct in American Affairs, had been such that I confessed I had an entire Distrust of him.

That at present he and Mr. C. had in a manner the Direction of American Affairs. That C[ongress] might as well appoint Mr. C. their Ambassador. But that he had not the Brains for the Management of such Affairs.

Mr. Marbois said, in Fact, he had the Management but it was altogether improper. That the K[ing] would never suffer any of his Subjects to represent foreign Courts at his, &c.

The Chevalier came up, and said as our Court would take it amiss, if an American Minister should meddle in the Cabals or Intrigues at Versailles, So the United States should resent a french Ministers taking a Part in any Disputes among them. That there was no need of Policy between France and the United States. They need only understand one another. Rien que s'entendre.

I said that in my Youth I had often heard of the Address and Intrigues of the french Court, but I could sincerely say, I had found more Intrigue and finesse among my own Countrymen, at Paris, than among the french.

It is true said the Chev[alier]—our Court at some Periods of our History have mis beaucoup de Ruses dans leur Politique. But, this had never any better Effect than to make Us distrusted by all Mankind.

¹ Here and below in this entry these initials undoubtedly stand for Edward Bancroft and the elder Le Ray de Chaumont.

² Suspension points in MS.

1779 JULY 4TH. SUNDAY.

This Morning, having stepped out of my Cabbin, for a few Minutes, I found upon my Return, that the Compliments of the following Gentlemen, were left chez Moy, on the Anniversary of American Independence,

Le Chevalier de La Luzerne.

Mr. De Marbois.

Mr. Bide de Chavagnes, Capne. des Vaux. du Roy de France, commdnt. la Sensible

Le Chev. de Goisbriand, the Second in Command

Mr. De la Forest.

Mr.   Otto

Mr.   Restif

Mr.   Carrè

I returned Compliments to the Chevr. and the Gentlemen and
Thanks for their kind Congratulations on my Countries Independence,
and sincerely wished, as this was the foundation of the happy Alliance
between France and America, that the latest Posterity of both Countries might have Reason to rejoice in it.

1779. JULY 16. FRYDAY.

Since I have been in this Ship I have read Robertsons History of
America in 4 Volumes, in French,[1] and four Volumes of the Ob-
servateur Anglois, in a series of Letters from my Lord All Eye to my
Lord All Ear.[2]

I am now reading Les Negotiations De Monsieur Le President
Jeannin.[3] He was Ambassador from Henry the fourth, at the Hague,
at the Beginning of the Seventeenth Century, and is reputed one of
the ablest and faithfullest Ambassadors that France ever had. Dossat,
Jeannin and D'Estrades are the 3 first....[4] I am pleased with this
Work, as well because of the Similitude between the Circumstances
of the united Provinces at this Time and those of the united States
at present, as on account of the Wisdom, the Prudence, and Discretion
and Integrity of the Minister.

The Observateur Anglois is extreamly entertaining but it is ruined,
by an Intermixture of Debauchery and licentious Pleasure. It is vastly
instructive to a Stranger, in many curious Particulars of the political
state of France—gives Light upon many Characters. But probably has
much Obloquy.

[1] Among JA's books in the Boston
Public Library are two French editions
of this work, Paris, 1778, and Amsterdam, 1779, each in 4 volumes (*Catalogue of JA's Library*).

[2] An anonymous work by M. F. P.
de Mairobert, first published, with a
pretended London imprint, 4 vols.,
1777–1778, and continued by another
hand or hands; the whole (in 10 vols.,
1777–1786) was given the title *L'espion
anglois; ou, Correspondance secrète entre
Milord All'Eye et Milord All'Ear*, of
which a partial set (vols. 2–5) remains
among JA's books in the Boston Public
Library (LC, *Catalog*, under Mairobert;
BM, *Catalogue*, under "All'Eye, Milord,
pseud."; *Catalogue of JA's Library*, p.
157).

[3] A copy of Jeannin's *Négociations* is

in MQA; see JA's Autobiography under
8 July 1778 and note 9 there. Pierre
Jeannin had negotiated the momentous
twelve-year truce between Spain and
the Low Countries in 1609. C. A. Gérard wrote Vergennes from Philadelphia,
7 May 1779, that he had sounded "plusieurs Délégués [in Congress] des plus
éclairés et des mieux intentionnés" on the
important subject of peace terms. "Je
leur ai fait lire les Lettres du Président
Jeannin que j'avois apportées avec moi
dans l'espérance d'en faire usage. Ils
sont convenus que la même méthode de
terminer leur querelle auroit certains
avantages et pourroit meme devenir indispensable" (Gérard, *Despatches and
Instructions*, p. 626–627).

[4] Suspension points in MS.

1779 JULY 17TH. SATURDAY.

Three Days past We have sounded for the Grand banc but have not found it. By the Reckonings of all the officers, We ought to be now Ten Leagues upon the Banch.

It is surprizing to me, that We have not seen more Fish. A few Whales, a few Porpoises and two Sharks are all We have seen. The two Sharks, We caught, with a Shark Hook and a Bit of Pork for a Bait. We cutt up the first, and threw over board his Head and Entrails, all of which the other, which was playing after the Ship, snatched at with infinite Greediness and swallowed down in an instant. After We had taken him, We opened him, and found the Head and Entrails of his Companion in him.[1]

Mr. Marbois is indefatigable. As soon as he is up, he reads the Correspondance of Mr. Gerard, for some Hours. The Minister it seems has furnished them with a Copy of all Mr. Gerards Letters, which appear to be voluminous. After this He reads aloud, to Mr. Carrè, Mr. Otto, Mr. Restif or Mr. Forrest, one of Congreves or Garricks Plays. Then he writes some Hours.

He is unwilling to let me see Gerards Letters, or what he writes.

[1] Marbois relates this incident, with variant details and some gusto, in his travel journal (Eugene P. Chase, ed., *Our Revolutionary Forefathers*, N.Y., 1929, p. 54–55).

1779. JULY 20. TUESDAY.

I was struck with these Words in a Letter from the President Jeannin to M. Bellegarde of 28 Jany. 1609

Si le Roy "est content de ma Conduite, et de la Diligence et Fidelitè, dont j'use pour executer ponctuellement ce qu'il m'a commandé c'est deja une Espece de recompense qui donne grande Satisfaction à un homme de bien; et quand il ne m'en aviendra rien de mieux, j'en accuserai plutot mon malheur que le defaut de sa bonne volonté. Aussi suis-je si accoustumé à travailler beaucoup, et profiter peu, que j'en ay acquis une habitude qui me rend plus capable de souffrir patiemment la rudesse de cette mauvaise Fortune, sans m'en plaindre, ni murmurer."

It is said that H[enri] 4. altho he honoured Jeannin with his Confidence and Trusts, yet recompensed him very ill, notwithstanding the magnificent Rewards he gave to Sully, whose Modesty, and Delicacy did not hinder him from asking for them.

1779, FRYDAY JULY 30.

We are not yet arrived to the Banc of St. George. Calms, contrary

Winds &c. detain Us. Saw a Whale spouting and blowing and leaping to day in our Wake—a Grampus they say.

1779 JULY 31 SATURDAY.

Found Bottom this Morning on St. Georges Banc. The Weather, the Wind, the Discovery of our Longitude, give Us all, fine Spirits this Morning. The Wind is as good as We could wish it. We are now about to pass the Day and Night of greatest Danger. By the present Appearances, We are highly favoured. But Appearances are often deceitful.

At the Moment I am writing a thick fog comes up, on all Sides, as if directed specially to conceal us from our Ennemies.

I am not so presumptuous as to flatter myself that these happy Circumstances are all ordered for the Preservation of this Frigate, but not to remark them would be Stupidity, not to rejoice in them would be Ingratitude.

If We should be prospered so much as to arrive well, what News shall We find public or private? We may find Dissappointments on Shore.—But our Minds should be prepared for all.[1]

[1] St. George's Bank is about 100 miles east of Cape Cod. On 3 Aug. the *Sensible* entered Boston Harbor. "His Excellency [La Luzerne] and suit landed on General Hancock's wharf, about 5 o'Clock the same afternoon, where they were received by a Committee from the Hon. Council of this State, who were waiting with carriages for their reception; they were conducted to the house late the residence of the Continental General. He was saluted by a discharge of 13 cannon on his landing, from the fortress on Fort-Hill, and every other mark of respect shewn him which circumstances would admit" (Boston *Evening Post and General Advertiser*, 7 Aug. 1779).

From the last entry in JA's accounts printed at the end of 1778, above, it would appear that JA and JQA left the *Sensible* in Nantasket Roads and were rowed to Braintree on 2 August. But in a letter addressed to President John Jay from Braintree on 3 Aug., JA gives *that* day as the date of his arrival—in the letterbook copy as at "Boston Harbour," and in the recipient's copy as at "Nantasket Road" (LbC, Adams Papers; RC, PCC, No. 84, I). The letter to Jay introduces La Luzerne and Marbois in very favorable terms.

1779 NOVEMBER 13TH. SATURDAY.[1]

Took Leave of my Family, and rode to Boston with my Son Charles, nine years of Age last May. At four O Clock went on board the french Frigate the Sensible, Mr. Thaxter,[2] my Son John, twelve Years old last July, and my Servant Joseph Stevens having come on Board in the Morning.—I find the Frigate crouded with Passengers, and Sailors, full 350 Men. They have recruited a great Number here.[3]

[1] First entry in "P[aper] B[ook] No. 30" as labeled and numbered by CFA (our D/JA/30), an unstitched gathering of leaves without cover bearing the

following title in JA's hand on the front leaf: "Journal from 13 Nov. 1779 to 6. January 1780."

On 9 Aug. JA had been elected to represent Braintree in the convention called to frame a new state constitution (*Braintree Town Records*, p. 503). He attended the plenary sessions of that body in the First Church in Cambridge, 1–7 Sept., and presumably again from 28 Oct. to 11 Nov.—that is, throughout its second session, which ended two days before he sailed again for Europe. On 4 Sept. he was named one of a committee of thirty members to draft "a Declaration of Rights, and the Form of a Constitution," to be laid before the Convention at its second session (Mass. Constitutional Convention, 1779–1780, *Jour.*, p. 26). The payroll records of the Massachusetts Council indicate that he was paid £90 for twenty-five days' attendance at committee meetings between the first and second sessions (M-Ar: vol. 170, fol. 413; vol. 171, fol. 20). JA told Edmund Jenings in a letter of 7 June 1780: "I was by the Convention put upon the Committee—by the Committee upon the Subcommittee—and by the Subcommittee appointed a Sub Sub Committee—so that I had the honour to be principal Engineer" (Adams Papers). He was in fact sole draftsman of the earliest form of the instrument which, after some revisions in committee and others in convention, none of them drastic, was adopted by the people in 1780 and is still in force as the organic law of the Commonwealth of Massachusetts, though amended from time to time by later constitutional conventions. With its simple but eloquent preamble on the principle of government by compact, its elevated Declaration of Rights, and its unprecedented clauses requiring state support for education and the encouragement of "literature and the sciences," it is JA's chief monument as a political thinker. In editing his grandfather's writings CFA provided a carefully edited text of the Constitution of 1780, together with commentary and notes showing the modifications of the author's draft (so far as it was then possible to do so) through the point of its adoption by the Convention in its third session, Jan.–March 1780 (*Works*,

4:213–267). Though JA's MS appears to be irretrievably lost, copies of the 1779 printings annotated by members while the Convention was in progress have now come to light, and these will make possible a more complete and accurate presentation of the evolution of the text. See entry of 19 Dec., below, and note 1 there.

Meanwhile, on 27 Sept. 1779, after "a great deal of disagreeable altercation and debate," JA was elected by Congress, on the nomination of Henry Laurens, minister plenipotentiary to negotiate treaties of peace and commerce with Great Britain, and John Jay was elected minister to Spain, leaving Arthur Lee, who was *persona non grata* to the French government, without a post (JCC, 15:1107–1113; John Fell, Diary, in Burnett, ed., *Letters of Members*, 4: 439, 449; see also p. 437–438, 442–450; Lovell to JA, 27, 28 Sept., Adams Papers; Gerry to JA, 29 Sept., same; and Gérard, *Despatches and Instructions*, p. 100–118, 893–898). Thus was settled an issue which had agitated Congress for months and of which perhaps the most lucid account is that by Burnett in his *Continental Congress*, ch. 23. JA's commissions (dated 29 Sept.) and his instructions (see below) were forwarded to him in a letter of 20 Oct. from Samuel Huntington, who had replaced Jay as president of Congress upon the latter's appointment to Spain (Adams Papers; printed in *Works*, 7:119–120). The instructions, though dated 16 Oct., had been adopted by Congress as early as 14 Aug., and the French minister in Philadelphia had had a material part in framing them (JCC, 14:956–966; copied, together with the commissions, from the originals in the Adams Papers, into JA's Autobiography at the beginning of its third and last section, entitled "Peace"). JA accepted his appointment in a letter to Huntington of 4 Nov. (LbC, Adams Papers; also copied into his Autobiography). Gérard and La Luzerne proposed that he take passage in the *Sensible*, which was still in Boston Harbor, and gave orders to Capt. Chavagnes to that effect (La Luzerne to JA, 29 Sept. 1779, Adams Papers; copied into JA's Autobiography along with an undated letter from La Luzerne to Chavagnes).

[2] John Thaxter Jr. (1755–1791), of Hingham, Harvard 1774, first cousin to AA through her aunt, Anna (Quincy) Thaxter. He had studied law in JA's office from 1774 until his admission to the bar in 1777, had at the same time been tutor to the Adams sons, and in 1778 had served as clerk in the office of the Secretary of Congress at York and Philadelphia. He was now going to Europe as JA's private secretary, a post he held until Sept. 1783, when he returned to America bringing the Definitive Treaty with Great Britain. He later settled in Haverhill and practiced law there. This note is largely based on Thaxter's correspondence with various members of the Adams family in the Adams Papers and a small collection of Thaxter family papers in MHi; see also *History of the Town of Hingham, Mass.* [Hingham,] 1893, 3:233; MHS, *Procs.*, 1st ser., 19 (1881–1882):152, 158; JA, *Works*, 3:354–355, 383; Burnett, ed., *Letters of Members*, 7:377.

[3] On the 14th the *Sensible* fell down to King's Roads (now President Roads), and on the 15th it sailed about 10 A.M. (JQA, Diary, 15 Nov. 1779; Francis Dana, Journal, 1779–1780, MHi).

16.

Found a Grammar, entitled, Élémens de la Langue Angloise, ou Méthode pratique, pour apprendre facilement cette Langue. Par M. Siret, A Paris, chez Ruault, Libraire, rue de la Harpe, près de la rue Serpente. 1773. Avec Approbation, et Permission.

24. WEDNESDAY.

On the grand Bank of N[ew] F[ound] L[and].—A few days ago, We spoke an American Privateer, the General Lincoln; Captain Barnes. Wrote Letters by him to my family. Mr. Dana wrote.[1] Mr. Thaxter, Mr. John, and several others.[2]

Heard, since I came on board, several Hints concerning W.; Son of ——.[3] That he has made a great Fortune—by Privateering, by Trade, by buying Sailors Shares, and by gambling. That he has won of C. a great Sum of Money. C., whom nobody pities. That —— has lost Rep[utation] by the Appointment of S., which is probable. That the Son has made Money, by knowing what was wanted for the Navy, and purchasing it, in great Quantities and then selling it, to the Board. That the Agent, B., has made a great fortune. That his Wife is a great Tory. Anecdotes of her Conversation.—That B. would certainly be hanged, if it was not that she was a Tory. Nasty, Poison Paper Money, &c. &c. &c. Not to put that nasty Paper, with our other Money.

Jer[emiah] A[llen] is a very different Man from his Brother J. None of that Wit, Humour, or Fun—none of that volatile Genius appears. There is a Softness, and a Melancholly, in his face, which indicates a Goodness. Not intemperate, or vicious, to Appearance.

¹ Francis Dana (1743–1811), Harvard 1762, lawyer, member of the Massachusetts Council, and delegate to the Continental Congress, 1777–1779, was accompanying JA as "Secretary to my Commission and Chargé D'Affaires" (JA, Autobiography). His later career as diplomat and judge is related in *DAB* and in W. P. Cresson, *Francis Dana . . .* , N.Y. and Toronto, 1930, a work full of careless errors. Dana's papers are in MHi and include a journal kept from Nov. 1779 to Feb. 1780 that has proved useful in annotating JA's Diary for this period.

² JQA's letter to his mother, "At Sea," 20 Nov. 1779, is in Adams Papers.

³ Winslow, son of Gen. James Warren; see JA's Autobiography under this date. James Warren was currently a member of the Eastern Navy Board. His son Winslow sailed for Europe in the following June and wandered from Amsterdam to Lisbon in an unsuccessful search for commercial opportunities and consulships (*Warren-Adams Letters*, vol. 2, *passim*; Winslow Warren's European letters and journals, 1780–1785, MHi: Mercy Warren Papers).

As for the other persons alluded to by initials in this paragraph, plausible guesses as to their identity can be and have been made, but none of these guesses is wholly satisfactory.

25. THURSDAY.

Arose at 4. A fair Wind and good Weather. We have passed the Grand Bank, sounded Yesterday afternoon and found bottom in 30 fathom of Water, on the Eastermost Edge of the Bank.

26. FRYDAY.

Leur Gouvernement, (des Bataviennes) fut un Malange de Monarchie, d'aristocratie, et democratie. On y voioit un chef, qui n'etoit proprement, que le premier des Citoiens, et qui donnoit, moins des ordres, que des Conseils. Les Grands, qui jugeoient les Procés de leur district, et commandoient les Troupes, etoient choisis, comme les rois dans les assemblees generales. Cent Personnes, prises dans la Multitude, servoient de Surveillans a chaque comte, et de chefs aux differens hameaux. La nation entiere étoit en quelque Sorte, une Armée toujours sur pied. Chaque famille y composoit un corps de Milice qui servoit sous le Capitaine qu'elle se donnoit.¹

¹ JA was reading a French work on early Dutch history, but it has not been identified.

1779 DECEMBER [5]. SUNDAY.

We are now supposed to be within 100 Leagues of Ferrol or Corunna, to one of which Places We are bound. The Leak in the Frigate, which keeps two Pomps constantly going, has determined the Captn. to put into Spain.¹

This Resolution is an Embarrassment to me. Whether to travail by Land to Paris, or wait for the Frigate. Whether I can get Carriages,

Horses, Mules &c. What Accommodations I can get upon the Road, how I can convey my Children, what the Expence will be, are all Questions that I cannot answer. How much greater would have been my Perplexity, If the rest of my family had been with me.

The Passage of the Pyrenees is represented as very difficult. It is said there is no regular Post. That we must purchase Carriages and Horses &c. I must enquire.

[1] "29th [Nov.]. The ship is very leaky the passengers are all called to the Pump four times per day 8 oclock A M. 12 oclock 4 oclock P M. and 8 oclock P M." (JQA, Diary). Dana mentions (on the 28th) that Capt. Chavagnes and the other officers were all taking their turns at the pumps (Journal, 1779–1780, MHi). The *Sensible* had encountered heavy weather from the 25th to the 28th, and on the 26th the *Courrier de l'Europe*, a *chasse marée* that had accompanied it to Boston and thus far on the return voyage, was dismasted and probably lost at sea (same).

1779 DECEMBER 7. TUESDAY.

About 11. O Clock discovered Land—two large Mountains, one sharp and steep, another large and broad.—We passed 3 Capes, Finisterre, Tortanes [Toriñaña] and Veillane [Villano].

Yesterday the Chevr. de la Molion gave me some Nuts which he call'd Noix d'Acajou. They are the same which I have often seen, and which were called Cooshoo Nuts. The true name is Acajou Nuts. They are shaped like our large white Beans. The outside Shell has an Oil in it that is corrosive, caustic, or burning. In handling one of these Shells enough to pick out the meat I got a little of this oyl on my fingers, and afterwards inadvertently rubbing my Eyes, especially my Left, I soon found the Lids swelled and inflamed up to my Eyebrow.

8 WEDNESDAY.

Got into Ferrol, where We found the french Ships of the Line, went on Board the General Sade,[1] went ashore, visited the Spanish General Don Joseph St. Vincent, took a Walk about Town, saw a great No. of Spanish and french Officers. Returned on Board the Frigate.[2]

[1] See entry of 13 Dec., below.
[2] JQA's Diary provides a great deal more detail on the entrance to the harbor and the events of this day. This is true occasionally on succeeding days, and Francis Dana's Journal in Spain is also very full. They are cited here, however, only when they clarify or correct JA's Diary.

9. THURSDAY.

Came on Shore with all my family. Took Lodgings. Dined with the Spanish Lieutenant General of the Marine with 24 french and Spanish officers. Don Joseph is an old Officer, but [has] a great deal of Vivacity and Bonhommie.

The Difference between the Faces and Airs of the French and Spanish Officers, is more obvious and striking than that of their Uniforms. Gravity and Silence distinguish the one—Gaiety and Vivacity and Loquacity the others. The Spanish are laced with a broad and even gold Lace, the french with scalloped. The french Wigs and Hair have rows of Locks over the Ears—the Spanish one. The french Bags are small—the Spanish large. The Spaniards have many of them very long Hair queued, reaching down to their Hams almost. They have all a new Cock Aid, which is made up of two a red one and a white in token of the Union of the two Nations.

Went to the Comedy, or Italien opera. Many Officers, few Ladies. Musick and Dancing tolerable. The Language, Italien, not understood. A dull Entertainment to me.

This Evening the French Consul arrived from Corunna,[1] and was introduced to me at my Chamber by the french Vice Consul at this Place. Both made me the politest Offers of Assistance of every Sort.

[1] His name was Detournelle (*Almanach Royal*, 1778, p. 501). The following entries record many kindnesses for which the Adams party were indebted to him.

1779 DECEMBER 10. FRYDAY.

Supped and slept at my Lodgings. Breakfasted on Spanish Chocolate which answers the Fame it has acquired in the World.

Every Body congratulates Us, on our Safe Arrival at this Place. The Leak in the Sensible, increases since she has been at Anchor, and every Body thinks We have been in great danger.

13 MONDAY.

Yesterday, I walked about the Town but there is nothing to be seen, excepting two Churches and the Arsenals, dry docks, Fortifications and Ships of War.

The Inconvenience of this Harbour is, the Entrance is so narrow, that there is no Possibility of going out but when the Wind is one Way, i.e. South East, or thereabouts.

The Three french Ships of the Line here are the Triomphant, the Souverain and the Jason, the first of 80 Guns, the 2d. 74, the 3d. 64.

M. Le Comte de Sade is the Chef D'Escadre or General. Mr. Le Chevalier de Grasse Preville is the Capitaine de Pavillon.[1]

Mr. Le Chevr. de Glandevesse is Capitain of the Souverain.

Mr. de la Marthonie commands the Jason.

[1] The Chevalier de Gras Préville, *capitaine de vaisseau,* 1777 (G. Lacour-Gayet, *La marine française sous la règne de Louis XVI,* Paris, 1905, p. 635). In his Autobiography under this date JA remembered, probably incorrectly, that this officer had been introduced to him as the brother of the famous naval commander Comte de Grasse.

1779 DECR. 14. TUESDAY.

Walked to the Barracks and dry docks, to shew them to Cha[rles]. The Stone of which these Works are made is about as good as Braintree Southcommon Stone. Went into the Church of St. Julien, which is magnificent—Numbers of Devots upon their Knees.

This afternoon We cross the Water to go to Corunna.

We have lodged en la Calle de la Madalena, junto coca, en casa of de Pepala Botoneca.

      Street   near the Head   the House

The Chief Magistrate of this Town is the Corregidor. Last Evening and the Evening before I spent, in Conversation with the Consul, on the Law of Nations and the Writers on that Law, particularly on the Titles in those Authors concerning Ambassadors and Consuls. He mentioned several on the Rights and Duties of Ambassadors and Consuls, and some on the Etiquette and formalities and Ceremonies.

I asked him many Questions. He told me that the Office of Consul was regulated by an Ordinance of the King, but that some Nations had entered into particular Stipulations with the King. That the Consuls of different Nations were differently treated by the same Nation. That as Consul of France he had always claimed the Priviledges of the most favoured Nation. That he enquired what Priviledges were enjoyed by the Consuls of England, Italy, ⟨Holland⟩ Germany &c.

That there is for the Province of Gallice, a Sovereign Court of Justice which has both civil and criminal Jurisdiction. That it is without Appeal in all criminal Cases: but in some civil cases an appeal lies to the Council. That there is not Time for an Application for Pardon for they execute forthwith. That hanging is the capital Punishment. They burn, some times, but it is after death. That there was lately a sentence for Parricide. The Law required that the Criminal should be headed up in an Hogshead, with an Adder, a Toad, a Dog, a Cat, &c. and cast into the Sea. That he looked at it, and found that they had printed those Animals on the Hogshead, and that the dead body was put into the Cask. That the ancient Laws of the Visigoths is still in Use, with the Institutes, Codes, Novelles &c. of Justinian the current law and ordonnances of the King.

That he will procure for me a Passeport from the General, or Governor of the Province, who resides a[t] Corunna, which will secure me all Sorts of facilities as I ride the Country, but whether through the Kingdom or only through the Province of Galicia I dont know.

I have not seen a Charriot, Coach, Phaeton, Chaise, nor Sulky, since I have been in the Place. Very few Horses, and those small, poor and shabby. Mules and Asses are numerous, but small. There is no Hay in this Country. The Horses &c. eat Straw—Wheat Straw.

The Bread, the Cabbages, Colliflowers, Apples, Pears &c. are good. The Beef, Pork, Poultry &c. are good. The Fish are good, excellent Eels, Sardines and other fish and tolerable Oysters, but not like ours.

There has been no frost yet. The Verdure in the Gardens and fields is fresh. The Weather is so warm that the Inhabitants have no fires, nor fire Places but in their Kitchens. They tell us We shall have no colder Weather before May, which is the coldest Month in the Year. Men and Women and Children are seen in the Streets, with bare feet and Legs standing on the cold Stones in the Mud, by the Hour together. The Inhabitants of both Sexes, have black Hair, and dark Complexions with fine black Eyes. Men and Women have long Hair ramilied down to their Waists and even some times to their Knees.

There is little Appearance of Commerce or Industry except about the Kings Docks and Yards and Works. Yet the Town has some Symptoms of growth and Prosperity. Many new Houses are building of Stone, which comes from the rocky Mountains round about of which there are many. There are few goods in the Shops. Little show in their Markett or on their Exchange. There is a pleasant Walk, a little out of Town between the Exchange and the Barracks.

There are but two Taverns in this Town. Captain Chavagne and his Officers are lodged in one, at Six Livres each per day. The other is kept by a Native of America who speaks English and french as well as Spanish and is an obliging Man. Here We could have loged at ⟨Six Livres⟩ a dollar a day each, but We were obliged to give 129 dollars for six days besides the Barber, and a multitude of other little Expences, and besides being kept constantly unhappy by an uneasy Landlady.

Finding that I must reside some Weeks in Spain, either waiting for a Frigate or travelling through the Kingdom, I determined to acquire the Language, to which Purpose, I went to a Bookseller and purchased Sobrino's Dictionary in three Volumes in Quarto, and the Grammatica Castellana which is an excellent Spanish Grammar, in their own Tongue, and also a Latin grammar in Spanish, after which

Monsr. de Grasse made me a Present of a very handsome Grammar of the Spanish Tongue in french by Sobrino.[1] By the help of these Books, the Children and Gentlemen are learning the Language very fast. To a Man who understands Latin it is very easy. I flatter myself that in a Month I should be able to read it very well and to make myself understood as well as understand the Spaniards.[2]

The Consul and Mr. Linde an Irish Gentleman a Master of a Mathematical Academy here, say that the Spanish Nation in general have been of Opinion that the Revolution in America was of a bad Example to the Spanish Colonies and dangerous to the Interests of Spain, as the United States if they should become ambitious and be seised with the Spirit of Conquest might aim at Mexico and Peru.

The Consul mentioned Reynalles Opinion that it was not for the Interest of the Powers of Europe, that America should be independant.

I told the Irish Gentleman, that Americans hated War: that Agriculture and Commerce were their Objects, and it would be their Interest as much as that of the Dutch to keep Peace with all the World, untill their Country should be filled with Population which could not be in many Centuries. That War and the Spirit of Conquest was the most diametrically opposite to their Interests, as they would divert their Attention, Wealth, Industry, Activity &c. from a certain Source of Prosperity, and even Grandeur and Glory, to an uncertain one, nay to one that it is certain they could never make any Advantage of. That the Government of Spain over their Colonies had been such that she never could attempt to introduce such fundamental Innovations as those by which England had provoked and compelled hers to revolt, and the Spanish Constitution was such as could extinguish the first Sparks of discontent, and quel the first risings of the People. That it was amazing to me that a Writer so well informed as Reynale could ever give an Opinion that it was not for the Interest of the Powers of Europe, that America should be independant, when it was so easy to demonstrate that it was for the Interest of every one, except England. That they could loose nothing by it, but certainly would every one gain Something, many a great deal.

It would be a pretty Work to shew, how France, Spain, Holland, Germany, Russia, Sweeden, Denmark would gain. It would be easy to shew it.

[1] The first volume of Francisco Sobrino's *Diccionario nuevo de las lenguas española y francesca*, 6th edn., Brussels, 1760, and the same author's *Grammaire nouvelle espagnolle et françoise ...*, 6th edn., Brussels, 1745, survive among

JA's books in the Boston Public Library (*Catalogue of JA's Library*).

[2] But see JA's second thoughts on learning Spanish, in his Autobiography under this date.

1779 DECEMBER 15. WEDNESDAY.

This Morning We arose at 5 or 6 O Clock, went over in a Boat, and mounted our Mules. Thirteen of them in Number and two Mulateers —one of whom went before for a Guide and the other followed after, to pick up Stragglers. We rode over very bad roads, and very high Mountains, where We had a very extensive Country, appearing to be a rich Soil and well cultivated but very few Plantations of Trees.— Some orange Trees and some Lemmon Trees, many Nut trees, a few Oaks &c. We dined at Hog Bridge, about half Way, upon Provision made by the french Consul, whose Attention and Politeness has been very conspicuous, so has that of the Vice Consul at Ferrol. We arrived at Corunna about seven o Clock and put up at a Tavern kept by Persons who speak french. An Officer who speaks English kept open the Gate for Us to enter, attended Us to our Lodgings, and then insisted on our Visiting the General who is Governor of the Province [1] and a Coll., who commands under him and is Military Governor of the Town. These are both Irish Gentlemen. They made many Professions of Friendship to our Cause and Country. The Governor of the Province, told me he had orders from Court to treat all Americans as their best friends. They are all very inquisitive about Mr. Jays Mission, to know who he is, where he was born, whether ever Member of Congress, whether ever President. When he embarked, in what Frigate, where he was destined, whether to France or Spain, and to what Port of France, Brest, L'orient or Nantes.

The General politely invited me to dine. Said that Spaniards made no Compliments, but were very sincere.

He asked me when this War would finish? I said Pas encore—But when the Kings of France and Spain would take the Resolution to send 20 or 30 more line of Battle Ships to reinforce the Comte d'Estain and enable him to take all the British Forces and Possessions in America.

[1] Don Pedro Martín Cermeño (or Sermeño), who on 18 Dec. issued a passport to JA and his party for their expedition to France. The passport is in the Adams Papers and is reproduced in this volume.

16. THURSDAY.

This Morning the Governor of the Province of Gallice, and the Governor of the Town of Corunna came to my Lodgings at the Hotel du grand Amiral, to return the Visit I made them last Evening. His Excellency invited me to dine with him tomorrow with all my family. He insisted upon seeing my Sons. Said I run a great Risque in taking with me, my Children. Said he had passed not far from my Country, in an Expedition vs. the Portugees. Said that he and every Thing in his Power was at my Service, &c. That he did not speak English, &c.— I told him I was studying Spanish, and hoped that the next Time I should have the Honour to see his Excellency I should be able to speak to him in Spanish. He smiled and bowed. He made some Enquiries about American Affairs and took Leave.

Mr. Dana and I walked about the Town, saw the Fortifications, the Shipping, the Markett, Barracks &c. and returned.

After dinner Mr. Trash and his Mate, of a Schooner belonging to the Traceys of Newbury Port, who have been obliged by bad Weather and contrary Winds to put in here from Bilboa, came to visit me. I gave them Letters to Congress and to my family.[1]

The french Consul came in, and Mr. Dana and I walked with him to the Tour de Fer. This is a very ancient Monument. It is of Stone an hundred foot high. It was intended for a Lighthouse, perhaps as it commands a very wide Prospect of the Sea. It sees all the Vessells coming from the East and from the West. There was formerly a magnificent Stair Case Escalier, winding round it in a Spiral from the Ground to the Top, and it is said that some General once rode to the Top of it, in a Coach, or on horse back. But the Stairs are all taken away and the Stones employed to pave the Streets of Corunna. The Mortar, with which the Stones are cemented is as hard as the Stones themselves, and appears to have a large Mixture of powdered Stone in it.

There are in this Town Three Convents of Monks and two of Nuns. One of the Nunneries, is of Capuchins, very austere. The Girls eat no meat, wear no linnen, sleep on the floor never on a bed, their faces are always covered up with a Veil and they never speak to any Body.

[1] A letter from JA to AA, 16 Dec., is in Adams Papers, and one to Pres. Huntington written the same day in PCC, No. 84, I (copied from LbC, Adams Papers, into JA's Autobiography under this date).

1779 DECEMBER 17. FRYDAY.

The Consul conducted me to the Souvereign Court of Justice. There are three Halls—one of civil Jurisdiction, another of Criminal, and a third of both. The three youngest Judges are the criminal Judges.

The Consul introduced me to the President, and the other Judges and to the Attorney General in their Robes. The Robes, Wigs and bands both of the Judges and Lawyers are nearly like ours at Boston. The President and other Judges and the Procureur du Roi treated me with great Ceremony, conducted me into the Place in the Prison, where the Prisoners are brought out who have any Thing to say to the Judges. Waited on me, into each of the three Halls. Shewed me the Three folio Volumes of the Laws of the Country, which are the Laws of the Goths, Visigoths, Ripuarians &c., incorporated on the Corpus Juris. There are no Seats for any Body in the Halls but for the Judges. Every Body stands. The President told me, that on Monday next there would be an interesting Cause, invited me to come, said he would receive me in Character, and place me by the side of himself on the Bench. Or if I chose to avoid this Parade, he would order an Officer to shew me, a convenient Place to see and hear.

Soon after a Part of an Irish Battalion of Troops was drawn up before the Court House, and made a fine Appearance.

Dined with the Governor, of the Province of Gallicia. Mr. Dana, Mr. Thaxter, Mr. Allen and myself. By the help of two Irish Officers, I had much Conversation with the Governor, who speaks only Spanish.

We sent for our Book of Maps and shewed him, the Position of N.Y. and R. Is., and the Possessions of the English there &c.

Went with the Consul into a Convent of Franciscans. Walked into the Church, and all about the Yards, and Cells.—Here are the Cells of Jealousy, Hatred, Envy, Revenge, Malice, Intrigue &c. said the Consul. There is more Intrigue in a Chapter of Monks for the Choice of a Prior than was employed to bring about the entire Revolution in America. A Monk has no Connections, nor Affections to soften him, but is delivered up to his Ambition, &c.[1] —The Inscriptions over the Cells in Latin Verse were ingenious and good Morals.

Drank Tea with the Consul. The Attorney General was there, and Mr. Logoanere,[2] and the Captain of the french Frigate the [*Belle Poule.*][3]

Inscribed over the Cell of a Monk, at Corunna.

Si tibi pulchra domus, si splendida mensa, quid inde?
Si Species Auri, atque Argenti massa, quid inde?
Si tibi sponsa decens, si sit generosa; quid inde?
Si tibi sint nati; si prædia magna, quid inde?
Si fueris pulcher, fortis, divesve, quid inde?
longus Servorum, si serviat Ordo; quid inde?

Si doceas alios in qualibet Arte; quid inde?
Si rideat mundus; si prospera cuncta; quid inde?
Si prior, aut Abbas, si Rex, si Papa; quid inde?
Si Rota fortunæ te tollat ad astra; quid inde?

Annis si fælix regnes mille; quid inde?
tam cito prætereunt hæc omnia, quæ nihil inde?
Sola manet Virtus, qua glorificabimur inde:
Ergo Deo servi; quia sat tibi provenit inde,[4]
quod fecisse volens in tempore quo morieris
Hoc facias Juvenis, dum corpore sanus haberis.
quod nobis concedas Deus noster. Amen.

[1] In JA's Autobiography under this date the three foregoing sentences are enclosed in quotation marks.

[2] Michel Lagoanere, "a Gentleman who has acted for some time as an American Agent at Corunna" (JA to Huntington, 16 Jan. 1780, LbC, Adams Papers). He gave indispensable aid to the Adams party by arranging for their trip across northern Spain. In addition to long letters of advice on routes and means of travel (17, 26 Dec., Adams Papers), Lagoanere sent JA as a gift a copy of Joseph Mathìas Escrivano's *Itinerario español, o guia de caminos,* *para ir desde Madrid à todas las ciudades* ..., 3d edn., Madrid, 1767, which survives among JA's books in the Boston Public Library and has been useful in verifying contemporary spellings of Spanish place names.

[3] Blank in MS; the name has been supplied from JA's Autobiography.

[4] The sense calls for a full stop here: "Therefore serve God, because it is (will be) to your advantage hereafter. / What you will wish at the time of your death you had done, / Do now while young," &c.

1779 DECR. 18 SATURDAY.

Walked all round the Town, round the Wharves, Slips &c. on the Water and round the Walls vs. the Country.

Afternoon walked, to see the Artillery. 12 Stands of Arms, Cannon, Bombs, Balls, Mortars &c. have been all packed up for Sometime. By the last Post Orders arrived to put up 5000 more in the same Manner, ready to embark, nobody knows where. Saw the Magazines, Arsenals, Shops &c., Carpenters, Wheelwrights, Blacksmiths &c.—shewn Us by the Commandant of Artillery, the Consuls Brother in Law.

The Consuls ⟨Name⟩ Address is De Tournelle Consul de France a la Corogne.

The Governor of the Town is Patricio O Heir.

The Governor of the Province is Don Pedro Martin Sermenio.

Went into the Church of a Convent, found them all upon their Knees, chanting the Prayers to the Virgin, it being the Eve of the Ste. Vierge. The Wax Candles lighted, by their Glimmerings upon the Paint and Gilding made a pretty Appearance and the Music was good.

Dined, with Monsieur De Tournelle the French Consul, in Company, with all my Family, the Regent, or President of the Sovereign Court of the Province of Galicia, the Attorney General, the Administrator of the Kings Revenue of Tobacco, and the Commandant of Artillery, Mr. Lagonaore, &c.

We had every Luxury, but the Wines were Bourdeaux, Champagne, Burgundy, Sherry, Alicante, Navarre, and Vin de Cap. The most delicious in the World.

The Chief Justice and Attorney General expressed a great Curiosity, to know our Forms of Government, and I sent to my Lodgings and presented each of them with a Copy of the Report of the Committee of Convention of Mass. Bay.[1] They said they would have them translated into Spanish, and they should be highly entertained with them.

I have found the Pork of this Country, to day and often before, the most excellent and delicious, as also the Bacon, which occasioned My Enquiry into the manner of raising it. The Chief Justice informed me, that much of it was fatted upon Chesnuts and much more upon Indian Corn, which was much better, but that in some Provinces of Spain they had a peculiar Kind of Acorns, growing upon old Pasture Oaks, which were very sweet and produced better Pork than either Chesnuts or Indian Corn. That there were Parts of Spain, where they fatted Hogs upon Vipers—they cutt off their Heads and gave the Bodies to their Swine, and they produced better Pork than Chesnuts, Indian Corn or Acorns.

These Gentlemen told Us that all Kinds of Grain, would come to a good Markett in this Country even Indian Corn for they never raised more than their Bread and very seldom enough. Pitch, Tar, Turpentine, Timber, Masts &c. would do. Salt Fish, Sperma Cœti Candles, &c. Rice &c. Indigo and Tobacco came from their own Colonies. The Administrator of the Kings Tobacco told me that Ten Million Weight was annually consumed in Spain in Smoking.

We enquired concerning the manner of raising the Kings Revenue. We [were] told that there were now no Farmers General in Spain. That they had been tried, and found prejudicial and abolished. That all was now collected for the King. That he appointed Collectors, for particular Towns or other Districts. That Duties were laid upon Exports and Imports and Taxes upon Lands.

We enquired the manner of raising the Army. Found that some were enlisted for a Number of Years. That others were draughted by Lot, for a Number of Years. And that a Number of Years service entitled to several valuable Priviledges and Exemptions—but the Pay was small.

The Consul gave me two Volumes, Droit public de France: Ouvrage posthume de M. l'Abbé Fleury, compose pour l'education des Princes; Et publié avec des Notes Par J. B. Daragon Prof. en l'Université de Paris.[2]

[1] *The Report of a Constitution or Form of Government for the Commonwealth of Massachusetts: Agreed upon by the Committee . . .* , Boston, 1779, a "committee print" of the earliest text of the Massachusetts Constitution, which was largely JA's own composition; see note 1 on entry of 13 Nov., above.

In his Autobiography under this date JA enlarges on the conversation at this dinner party.

[2] Still among JA's books in the Boston Public Library (*Catalogue of JA's Library*). See also entry of 24 June, above, and note 2 there.

1779 DECR. 20. MONDAY.

Went to the Audiencia, where We saw the four Judges setting in their Robes, the Advocates in theirs a little below and the Attorneys lower down still. We heard a Cause argued. The Advocates argued sitting, used a great deal of Action with their Hands and Arms, and spoke with Eagerness. But the Tone of oratory seemed to be wanting.

1779. DECEMBER 22. WEDNESDAY.

Drank Tea, at Senior Lagoaneres. Saw the Ladies drink Chocolat in the Spanish Fashion.

A Servant brought in a Salver, with a Number of Tumblers, of clean, clear Glass, full of cold Water, and a Plate of Cakes, which were light Pieces of Sugar. Each Lady took a Tumbler of Water and a Piece of Sugar, dipped her Sugar in her Tumbler of Water, eat the one and drank the other. The Servant then brought in another Salver, of Cups of hot Chocolat. Each Lady took a Cup and drank it, and then Cakes and bread and Butter were served. Then each Lady took another cup of cold Water and here ended the Repast.

The Ladies were Seniora Lagoanere, and the Lady of the Commandant of Artillery, the Consuls sister, and another. The Administrator of the Kings Tobacco, the french Consul, and another Gentleman, with Mr. Dana, Mr. Thaxter and myself made the Company.

Three Spanish Ships of the Line, and two french Frigates came into this Harbour this afternoon. A Packet arrived here Yesterday from Havannah.

The Administrator gave me a Map of Gibraltar and the Spanish Ships about it by Sea, and Lines by Land.

December 1779

Orders of Ecclesiasticks

Dominicans, Franciscans, Augustins, only at Corrunna.
Nuns of St. Barbe. Capuchins,[1]

[1] Thus in MS. In his Autobiography under this date JA expands these notes considerably.

1779 DECEMBER 24. FRYDAY.

Dined on Board the Bellepoule, with the Officers of the Galatea and the Bellepoule.

1779 DECEMBER 25. SATURDAY. CHRISTMAS.

Went to the Palace, at 11. o Clock, to take my Leave of his Excellency. Mr. O Heir the Governor of the Town went with me. The general repeated a Thousand obliging Things, which he had said to me, when I first saw him and dined with him.

26. SUNDAY.

At half after two, We mounted our Carriages and Mules, and rode four Leagues to Betanzos, the ancient Capital of the Kingdom of Gallicia, and the Place where the Archives are still kept.[1] We saw the Building, a long Square stone Building without any Roof, opposite the Church. There are in this Place two Churches and two Convents. The last League of the Road was very bad, mountainous and rocky to such a degree as to be very dangerous. Mr. Lagoanere did Us the Honour to bear Us company to this Place. It would appear romantick to describe the House, the Beds, and the People.

[1] The hire of the mules, muleteers, and three carriages (or "calashes") was arranged by the assiduous Lagoanere in an elaborate contract with one Ramon San (or Sanz) of Santiago. The terms, which JA thought piratical, are detailed in Lagoanere's letter to JA of the present date (Adams Papers); see also entry of 4 Jan. 1780 and JA's Autobiography. When departing from La Coruña JA was as yet uncertain whether to proceed to Bilbao and Bayonne by way of Madrid in order to have better roads or to take the shorter but less traveled route directly eastward across northern Spain.

27.

Travelled from Betanzos to Castillano. The Roads still mountainous and rocky. We broke one of our Axletrees, early in the day, which prevented Us from going more than 4 Leagues in the whole.
The House where We lodge is of Stone, two Stories high. We entered into the Kitchen. No floor but the ground, and no Carpet but Straw, trodden into mire, by Men, Hogs, Horses, Mules, &c. In the

Middle of the Kitchen was a mound a little raised with earth and Stone upon which was a Fire, with Pots, Kettles, Skillets &c. of the fashion of the Country about it. There was no Chimney. The Smoke ascended and found no other Passage, than thro two Holes drilled thro the Tiles of the Roof, not perpendicularly over the fire, but at Angles of about 45 deg[rees]. On one Side, was a flew oven, very large, black, smoaky, and sooty. On the opposite Side of the Fire was a Cabbin, filled with Straw, where I suppose the Patron del Casa, i.e. the Master of the House, his Wife and four Children all pigged in together. On the same floor with the Kitchen was the Stable. There was a Door which parted the Kitchen and Stable but this was always open, and the floor of the Stable, was covered with miry Straw like the Kitchen. I went into the Stable and saw it filled on both Sides, with Mules belonging to Us and several other Travellers who were obliged to put up, by the Rain.

The Smoke filled every Part of the Kitchen, Stable, and other Part[s] of the House, as thick as possible so that it was ⟨almost impossible⟩ very difficult to see or breath. There was a flight of Steps of Stone from the Kitchen floor up into a Chamber, covered with Mud and straw. On the left Hand as you ascended the stairs was a stage built up about half Way from the Kitchen floor to the Chamber floor. On this stage was a bed of straw on which lay a fatting Hog. Around the Kitchen Fire, were arranged the Man, Woman, four Children, all the Travellers, Servants, Mulatiers &c. The Chamber had a large Quantity of Indian Corn in Ears, hanging over head upon Sticks and Pieces of slit Work, perhaps an hundred Bushells. In one Corner was a large Bin, full of Rape seed, or Colzal, on the other Side another Bin full of Oats. In another Part of the Chamber lay a Bushell or two of Chesnutts. Two frames for Beds, straw Beds upon them. A Table, in the Middle. The floor had never been washed nor swept for an hundred Years—Smoak, soot, Dirt, every where. Two Windows in the Chamber, i.e. Port holes, without any Glass. Wooden Doors to open and shut before the Windows.

Yet amidst all these Horrors, I slept better than I have done before, since my Arrival in Spain.

1779. DECR. 28. TUESDAY.

Went from Castillan to Baamonde. The first Part of the Road, very bad, the latter Part tolerable.

The whole Country We have passed, is very mountainous and

rocky. There is here and there a Vally, and here and there a Farm that looks beautifully cultivated. But in general the Mountains are covered with Furze, and are not well cultivated. I am astonished to see so few Trees. Scarce an Elm, Oak, or any other Tree to be seen. A very few Walnut Trees, and a very few fruit Trees.

At Baamonde, We stop untill Tomorrow to get a new Axletree to one of our Calashes.

The House where We now are is better, than our last nights Lodgings. We have a Chamber, for seven of Us to lodge in. We shall lay our Beds upon Tables, Seats and Chairs, or the floor as last night. We have no Smoke and less dirt, but the floor was never washed I believe. The Kitchen and Stable are below as usual, but in better order. The Fire in the Middle of the Kitchen, but the Air holes pierced thro the Tiles of the Roof draw up the smoke, so that one may set at the fire without Inconvenience. The Mules, Hogs, fowls, and human Inhabitants live however all together below, and Cleanliness seems never to be tho't of.—Our Calashes and Mules are worth describing. We have three Calashes in Company. In one of them I ride with my two Children John and Charles. In another goes Mr. Dana and Mr. Thaxter. In a third Mr. Allen and Sam. Cooper Johonnot.[1] Our three servants ride on Mules. Sometimes the Gentlemen mount the servants mules— sometimes the Children—sometimes all walk.

The Calashes are like those in Use in Boston fifty Years ago. There is finery about them in Brass nails and Paint, but the Leather is very old and never felt Oil, since it was made. The Tackling is broken and tied with twine and Cords &c. but these merit a more particular Description. The Furniture of the Mules is equally curious. This Country is an hundred Years behind the Massachusetts Bay, in the Repair of Roads and in all Conveniences for travelling.

The natural Description of a Mule may be spared. Their Ears are shorn close to the skin, so are their Necks, Backs, Rumps and Tails at least half Way to the End. They are lean, but very strong and sure footed, and seem to be well shod. The Saddles have large Ears, and large Rims or Ridges round behind. They have a Breast Plate before, and a Breech Band behind. They have large Wooden Stirrips made like Boxes in a semicircular Form, close at one End, open at the other, in which you insert your foot, which is well defended by them against rain and Sloughs. The wooden Boxes are bound round with Iron.

We have magnificent Curb Bridles to two or three. The rest are guided by Halters. And there is an Halter as well as a Curb Bridle to each of the others.

There are Walletts, or Saddle bags, on each made with Canvas, in which We carry Bread and Cheese, Meat, Knives and forks, Spoons, Apples and Nutts.

Mr. Lagoanere told Us, that the Original of the affair of St. Iago, was this. A Shepherd saw a bright Light there in the night. Afterwards it was revealed to an Archbishop, that St. James was buried there. This laid the foundation of a Church, and they have built an Altar, on the Spot, where the Shepherd saw the Light. Some time since, the People made a Vow, that if the Moors should be driven from this Country they would give so much of the Income of their Lands to St. James. The Moors were driven away, and it was reported that St. James was in the Battle on Horse back with a drawn Sword, and the People fulfilled their Vows by Paying the Tribute, but lately a Duke of Alva, a Descendant of the famous Duke, has refused to pay for his Estate, which has occasioned a Law suit, which is carried by Appeal to Rome. The Duke attempted to prove that St. James was never in Spain. The Pope has suspended it. This looks like a Ray of Light. Upon the Supposition that this is the Place of the Sepulture of St. James, there are great Numbers of Pilgrims who visit it every Year from France, Spain, Italy and other Parts of Europe, many of them on foot. St. Iago is called the Capitol of Galicia, because it is the Seat of the Archbishop, and because St. James is its Patron, but Corunna is in fact the Capital as it is the Residence of the Governor, the Audience &c. &c.

[1] Samuel, an eleven-year-old son of Col. Gabriel Johonnot, a merchant of Boston, was being sent to Europe for schooling; see a letter from Sammy's grandfather, Rev. Samuel Cooper, to JA, 14 Nov. 1779 (Adams Papers). JQA's Diary of the voyage and of the journey across Spain naturally contains numerous references to Johonnot, and a boyish but interesting journal of the voyage that was kept by Johonnot himself has also come to rest in the Adams Papers. It bears the title "A Journal by George Beaufort," but internal evidence shows that this is unquestionably a pseudonym, and JQA added a notation, "J. Q. Adams / given him by / S. C. Johonnot" (Adams Papers, Microfilms, Reel No. 330). Placed in school in Passy and later in Geneva, Johonnot became acquainted with young Albert Gallatin, and it was through Johonnot and his grandfather Cooper that Gallatin obtained a post teaching French at Harvard soon after arriving in America (HA, *Gallatin*, p. 15, 38, 39). Johonnot took a bachelor's degree at Harvard in 1783, practiced law in Portland, and in 1791 went to Demerara, British Guiana, "upon a speculation"; he became United States vice-consul and died there in 1806 (JQA, Diary, 3 April 1791; *NEHGR*, 7 [1853]:142).

1779. DECR. 30. THURSDAY.

At Lugo, where We arrived Yesterday. We passed Yesterday the River Minho which originates in the Mountains of Asturies, and flows thro Portugal. We went to see the Cathedral Church at Lugo, which is very rich. A Youth came to me in the street and said he was a Bostonian, a Son of Mr. Thomas Hickling. Went a Privateering in an English Vessell and was taken by the Spaniards.—Unfortunately taken he said.—Unfortunately inlisted I said.—He wanted to make his fortune he said.—Out of your Country, and by fighting against your Country said I.

Two Irish Gentlemen came to pay their Respects to me, Michael Meagher Oreilly and Lewis Obrien. Obrien afterwards sent me a Meat Pie and a minced Pie and two Bottles of Frontenac Wine, which gave Us a fine Supper.

Arrived at Galliego, in very good Season having made Six Leagues and an half from Lugo....[1] Mountainous, but not dangerous as heretofore. About a league back, We passed over a large Bridge over a River called Cara Sedo, which emptyes itself into the Minho, not far from Lugo.

I see nothing but Signs of Poverty and Misery, among the People. A fertile Country, not half cultivated, People ragged and dirty, and the Houses universally nothing but Mire, Smoke, Fleas and Lice. Nothing appears rich but the Churches, nobody fat, but the Clergy. The Roads, the worst without Exception that ever were passed, in a Country where it would be easy to make them very good. No Simptoms of Commerce, or even of internal Trafic, no Appearance of Manufactures or Industry.

We are obliged, in this Journey to carry our own Beds, Blanketts, Sheets, Pillows &c., our own Provisions of Chocolat, Tea, Sugar, Meat, Wine, Spirits, and every Thing that We want. We get nothing at the Taverns, but Fire, Water, and Salt. We carry our own Butter, Cheese, and indeed Salt and Pepper too.

[1] Suspension points in MS.

DECR. 31. FRYDAY.

Rode from Galliego to Sebrero, Seven Leagues. The Journey Yesterday and to day has been very agreable. The Weather, remarkably fair, and dry, and the Roads not so bad as We expected.

There is the grandest Profusion of wild irregular Mountains, that I ever saw—Yet laboured and cultivated every one, to its Summit. The Fields of Grain, are all green. We passed a Rang of Mountains that were white with Snow, and there were here and there banks of Snow on the Mountains We passed over, but no Frost at all in the Ground.

We are now on the highest Ground of all, and within Gun shot of the Line, between Gallice and Leon. The Houses all along are small and of Stone. Some covered with Brick Tile, some with Tile of Stone, but chiefly with Thatch. They interweave a Shrub, of which they make Brooms, among the Straw and bind both together with Wythes. These thatched Roofs are very numerous—But universally dirty, and smoaky. The People wear broad brimmed Hats, or caps made of woolen Cloth like their Coats, Jackets and Breeches which are all of a Colour, made of black sheeps Wool without Dying. The Maragatoes are dressed particularly, in a greasy leathern Jackett &c. But these People will be hereafter more exactly described.[1]

The Mules, the Asses, the Cattle, Sheep, Hogs, &c. of this Country, ought to be more particularly remarked.

[1] This was not done, but see entry of 4 Jan. 1780, below, and CFA's note in JA, *Works*, 3:245.

1780. JANUARY 1ST. SATURDAY.

Arrived at Villa Franca, Seven Leagues. The Road at first was very bad. Steep, sharp Pitches, ragged Rocks, &c. We then came into the Road of Leon, which is made seemingly out of a Rock. It was an excellent Road for a League and an half. We then came to a River, and travelled along the Banks of it for some Leagues. This Way was as bad as the other was good. Miry, rocky, up and down untill We came into a new Road, about two Leagues from Villa franca. Here We found a Road again made entirely by Art, at an immense Expence, but it seems to be made forever. They are going on with the Work. This Work is an Honour to the Nation. It shews that Improvements are coming in, and that Attention is paid to the Ease, Convenience, Utility, Commerce &c. of the People.

The Country We have travelled over to day is the greatest Curiosity I ever beheld—an uninterrupted succession of Mountains of a vast hight. The River Barcarcel flows between two Rows of Mountains, rising on each hand to a vast hight. The most grand, sublime, awful Objects, yet they are cultivated up to their highest summits. There are flourishing fields of Grain, on such steep declivities, near the Summits of Mountains, as I cannot conceive it possible for Horses or Cattle to stand upon them to plough. It must be done with Mules, and I know not even how these or Men either could stand.

The Houses are uniformly the same through the whole Country hitherto—common habitations for Men and Beasts. The same smoaky, filthy holes. Not one decent House have I seen from Corunna.

We passed this Day, the Ruins of an Ancient Castle of the Moors, on the Summit of one of the steepest and one of the highest and one of the most rugged Mountains.

There are in Villa Franca three Parish Churches, one Convent of Men and one of Women. There is an old brick Castle built in feudal Times when Lord was at War with Lord, a defence against Lances, Bows and Arrows and no more—possibly vs. Musquet Balls.

This Evening I bought a Mule, Saddle, Bridle &c. for 62 dollars and an half.

A Description of my Postilion. A little Hat, covered with oyl Cloth, flapped, before. A black, silk Cap of curious Work, with a braided Tail, hanging down his Back in the Spanish fashion. A cotton Handkerchief spotted red and white, around his neck. A double breasted short Jacket and Breeches.

1780. JANUARY 2. SUNDAY.

Rode from Villa franca de el Bierzo Rio P[uen]te. We dined at Ponferrada. We passed through several Villages and over Bridges and Rivers. We passed Campo de Narraya, Cacabelos Rio P[uente] and Ponferrada where We dined. The Country grows smoother.[1]

[1] The cavalcade stopped this night at Bembibre, a village seven leagues beyond Villafranca del Bierzo; both JQA and Dana had difficulty spelling its name in their journals, and JA did not even attempt to in his.

3. M[ONDAY].

Rode to Astorga. We passed through the Town and Country of the Marragattoes. The Town is small—stands on a Brook in a great Plain. We met Coaches, and genteel People as We went into Astorga.

4. T[UESDAY].

Found clean Beds and no fleas for the first Time in Spain. Walked twice, round the Walls of the City, which are very ancient. Saw the Road to Leon and Bayonne, and the Road to Madrid.[1] There is a pleasant Prospect of the Country, from the Walls. Saw the Market of Vegetables, onions and Turnips the largest I ever saw, Cabbages, Carrots &c. Saw the Market of Fuel—Wood, Coal, Turf and brush. Saw Numbers of the Marragato Women, as fine as Squaws and a great deal more nasty.

Crucifixes, Beads and Chains, Earrings and fingerrings in silver, brass, glass &c. about their Necks &c.

Saw the Cathedral Church, which is the most magnificent I have yet seen in Spain. Saw the Parliament House or Casa del Cieudad, where the Corregidor and City Magistrates assemble, to deliberate, and to execute the orders of the King.

This day, was brought me the Gazetta de Madrid of the 24 of December, in which is this Article

Coruña 15 de Diciembre.

Hoy mismo han llegado á esta Plaza el Caballero Juan Adams miembro del Congreso Americano y Su Ministro Plenipotenciario á la Corte de Paris y Mr. Deane[2] Secretario de Embaxada, quienes salieron de Boston el 15 de Noviembre último á bordo de la Fregata Francesa de Guerra la Sensible que entró en el Ferrol el dia 8 del corriente. Trahe la Noticia de que habiendo los Ingleses evacuado a Rhode Island y retirado todas sus Tropas á Nueva Yorck, los Americanos tomaron Possesion de todos los Puestos evacuados.

The Names of the Owner of the Post Chaises,
the Postilions, and the two Lads on foot,
who are with me and my Suite

Senior Raymon San, the Owner of all the Post Chaises and the Mules that draw them, and the Man with whom Mr. Lagoanere made the Contract.
Senior Eusebioo Seberino, the Postilion that drives my Chaise.
Diego Antonio, the Postilion that drives Mr. Allen and S. C. Johonnot.
Joseph Diaz, the Postillion that drives Mr. Dana and Mr. Thaxter.
The Writer, educated at St. Iago.[3]
Juan Blanco.
Bernardo Bria.[4]

This Afternoon a genteel Spaniard came to my Lodgings, to offer me, all sorts of services and good offices, and to enquire if I wanted any kind of Assistance, or if I wanted Cash.—Said he had received a Letter from Mr. Lagoanere at Corunna desiring him, to afford me every Aid in his Power and to furnish me with Money if I wanted.—I thanked him, and desired him to thank Mr. Lagoanere, but to assure him that I wanted nothing, and that I had got so far very well.

[1] At Astorga the party was delayed a day by carriage repairs; and here JA determined to continue eastward through León and Burgos and north to Bilbao instead of turning southeast to Madrid (JQA, Diary, 1, 4 Jan.).

[2] An error (presumably by the newspaper) for "Dana."

[3] "The Writer" was Diaz, but what is meant by this term is uncertain.

[4] JQA made a similar listing in his Diary under 6 Jan. and added the name of the guide and interpreter who completed the staff of the expedition, namely "Senior Miguel Martinus" (i.e. Martinez). See Lagoanere to JA, 26 Dec. 1779 (Adams Papers).

1780. JANY. 5. WEDNESDAY.

Rode from Astorga to Leon, eight Leagues. This is one great Plain. The Road very fine. Great Flocks of Sheep and Cattle. The Sheep of an handsome size, the fleeces of Wool thick, long and extremely fine. The soil rather thin and barren. We passed several smal Villages. The vast rang of Asturias Mountains covered with Snow on our left. The Weather as pleasant as could be, tho cold—some frost and Ice on the Roads. We passed the River and Bridge Orbigo, which in the Spring when swelled with Freshes of melted Snow from the Mountains of Asturias, is a very great River.

Leon, which We entered in the Night, has the Appearance of a large City.

6 THURSDAY.

Went to view the Cathedral Church which is magnificent, but not equal to that at Astorga if to that at Lugo. It was the day of the Feast of the King, and We happened to be at the Celebration of high Mass. We saw the Procession, of the Bishop and of all the Canons, in rich Habits of Silk, Velvet, Silver and Gold. The Bishop, as he turned the Corners of the Church, spread out his Hand to the People, who all prostrated themselves on their Knees as he passed. Our Guide told Us, We must do the same, but I contented myself with a Bow.[1]

Went to see the Council Chamber of the Bishop and Chapter— hung with crimson Damask, the Seats all round crimson Velvet. This Room and a smaller, where the Bishop sometimes took aside some of the Cannons, were very elegant.

Saw the Casa del Ciudad, and the old Castle of King Alphonsus, which is said to be 1936 Years old. It is of Stone, and the Work very neat.

But there is no Appearance of Commerce, Manufactures or Industry. The Houses are low, built of brick and Mud and Pebble stones from the fields. No Market worth notice. Nothing looks either rich or chearfull but the Churches and Churchmen. There is a Statue of Charles 5 in this Church, but very badly done.

There is a School of Saint Mark here as it is called, an Institution for the Education of noble Youths here in Mathematicks and Philosophy.

Dined in Leon, got into our Carriages and upon our Mules about one O Clock, to proceed on our Journey, passed the new Bridge of Leon, which is a beautiful new Piece of Work. It is all of Stone. The

River, which comes down from the Mountains of Asturias, is not now very large, but in the Spring when the Snows melt upon the Mountains it is swelled by the freshes to a very great Size. This River also runs down into the Kingdom of Portugal. Not long after We passed another Bridge and River, which the Peasants told me to call Rio y Puente de Biliarente. This River also comes down from the Asturias and flows down into Portugal. We passed thro several, very little Villages, in every one of which We saw the young People Men and Women dancing, a Dance that they call Fandango. One of the young Women beats a Machine, somewhat like a section of a Drum. It is covered with Parchment. She sings and beats on her drum, and the Company dance, with Each a Pair of Clackers in his and her Hand. The Clackers are two Pieces of Wood, cut handsomely enough, which they have the Art to rattle in their Hands to the Time of the Drum. They had all, Males and Females, wooden shoes, in the Spanish fashion, which is mounted on stilts. We stopped once to look and a Man came out with a Bottle of Wine and a glass to treat Us. We drank his Wine in Complaisance to his Urbanity, tho it was very Sour, and I ordered our Guide to give him somewhat.

We stop to night at a Village called Mansillas, thro which runs another large River from the Asturias, stretching down to Portugal. A great Stone Bridge over it, appears to have been half carried away by the Water in some freshet. This was once a Walled City. The Tours are yet standing all round the Town and the Ruins and Fragments of the Wall and the Appearance of a Foss round it. The Towers were all made of small round Stones, not bigger than two fists, which is the only Kind of Stone to be had here. The Cement is the ancient, which is as hard and as durable as the Stones them selves. I went upon the Top of one of the Towers with Mr. D., Mr. A., and Mr. Charles. The Town appears to be gone to decay, yet there are four or five Churches here still. The People are [*sentence unfinished*]

There are in Leon two Convents of Franciscans, one of Dominicans, one of St. Claudio Benito.

One Convent of Nuns of St. Benito, one of the Conception, one of Descalzas, one of Recoletas.

Canonigos. Cassa de San Isi[dro] one, one Cassa de San Marcus. Nine Parish Churches, including the Cathedral.

The Grandee who is the Proprietor of the Land in and about Leon is the Comte de Luna, a Descendant from the ancient Kings of Leon. He resides in Madrid, and receives about sixty thousand Ducats, or about thirty thousand dollars a Year of Rent, from the Tenants, partly in cash and partly in Grain. He has a Secretary and some other Agents who reside at Leon to collect his Rents. The Grandees of Spain all reside at Madrid. Former Kings, in order to break up the Barons Wars, called all the Nobles to Court, and gave them Employments.

[1] JA enlarges on this incident in his Autobiography under this date. JQA followed the guide's instructions and received a benediction, but remarked in his Diary: "I did not feel the better for it."

[7? JANUARY 1780.] [1]

I have not seen a Chimney in Spain, except one of the french Consul at Corunna. One or two half Imitations of Chimneys in the Kitchens are all that I have seen. The Weather is very cold, the frosts hard, and no fire when We stop, but a few Coals or a flash of Brush in the Kitchen, full of Smoke and dirt, and covered with a dozen Pots and Kettles, and surrounded by 20 People looking like Chimney Sweepers.

[1] First entry in Diary booklet No. 31 as numbered by CFA (our D/JA/31), an unstitched gathering of leaves without cover which contains entries as late as 6 Aug. 1780 but none between 5 Feb. and 27 July. (This is the last of the Diary booklets to which CFA assigned a number.) The present entry, written on the outside front page, is without date but may be reasonably assigned to 7 Jan. in the absence of any entry bearing that date. On the 7th the party traveled six leagues, from Mansilla de las Mulas through the village of El Burgo Ranero, where they dined, to Sahagún, where they visited "the Convent of St. Benedo," which had "nothing singular in it, unless a very large Library shou'd be accounted so," and the Cathedral (Francis Dana, Journal, 1779–1780, MHi).

1780 JANUARY 8. SATURDAY.

Rode from San Juan Segun, to Paredese de Nava. We have passed thro a Village every League. The Villages are all built of Mud and Straw. They have no Timber nor Wood nor Stone. The Villages all appear going to decay. Every Village has Churches and Convents enough in it, to ruin it, and the whole Country round about it, even if they had nothing to pay to the King or the Landlord. But all three together, Church, State and Nobility, exhaust the People to such a degree, I have no Idea of the Possibility of deaper Wretchedness. There are in this little Village, four Parish Churches and two Convents one of Monks and one of Nuns, both of the order of St. Francis.

The Parish Churches, and their Curates are supported here by the Tythes paid by the People. They pay every tenth Pound of Wool, every Tenth Part of Wine, Grain, Honey, in short of every Thing. The good Curates sometimes alieviate the Severity of this by Compositions or Modus's.[1]

425

The Archbishop has Power to do every Thing for the good of the People, that is to make new Parishes or alter old ones at his Pleasure. There are but four Archbishops in Spain. The Archbishop of Saint Iago, has one hundred and Eighty thousand Ducats of Rent a Year.

This War is popular in Spain, the Clergy, the Religious Houses and other Communities have offered to grant large Sums to the King for the Support of it. The English had become terrible to them.

From Astorga to this Place, the face of the Country is altered. It is a plain. But there is little Appearance of Improvement, Industry, or Cultivation. No Trees, of any Kind scarcely. No forrest or Timber or fruit trees. Scarcely any fences except a few mud Walls for Sheep folds.

¹ See OED under Modus, 4: "A money payment in lieu of tithe."

1780. JANUARY. 11TH. TUESDAY.

Arrived at Burgos.¹ We came from Sellada el Camino, 4 Leagues. We had Fog, and Rain and Snow, all the Way, very chilly, and raw. When We arrived at the Tavern, (which is the best in the City, as I am informed, and my Servant went to examine the others,) We found no Chimney. A Pan of Coals in a Chamber without a Chimney was all the Heat We could get. We went to view the Cathedral, which is ancient and very large. The whole Building is supported upon four grant² Pillars, the largest I ever saw. Round the great Altar are represented our Saviour from the Scene of his Agony, on the Mount, when an Angel presents him the Cup, to his Crucifixion, between 2 thieves, his Descent from the Cross and his Ascension into Heaven. The Chapells round the great Altar are the largest I have seen.

Round the Altar, the several Stages are represented. 1. The Agony in the Garden. 2. Carrying the Cross. 3d. Crucifixion between 2 Thieves. 3. Descent. 4. Ascension.

There is no Archbishop, at Burgos. There was one, which made five, but the K[ing] abolished it, and now there are but 4, in the whole Kingdom. There is a Chapell of Saint Iago.

Went into three Booksellers Shops, to search for a Chart or Map of Spain, but could find none, except a very small and erroneous one in a Compendio of History of Spain.

It is five and Twenty Years that I have been, almost constantly, journeying and voyaging, and I have often undergone severe Tryals, great Hardships, cold, wet, heat, fatigue, bad rest, want of sleep, bad nourishment, &c. &c. &c. But I never experienced any Thing like this Journey.—Every Individual Person in Company has a great Cold. We go along ⟨*barking, and*⟩ sneezing and coughing, as if We were fitter for an Hospital than for Travellers, on the Road.

My Servant and all the other Servants in Company, behave worse than ever I knew servants behave. They are dull, inactive, unskillfull. The Children are sick, and in short my Patience was never so near being exhausted as at Present.

Mr. Thaxter is as shiftless as a Child. He understands no Language, neither French nor Spanish, and he dont seem to think himself obliged to do any Thing, but get along, and write his Journal.[3] —In short, I am in a deplorable situation, indeed.—I know not what to do.—I know not where to go.[4]

From this Place We go to Monasterio, which is four Leagues, from thence to Berebiesca [Briviesca], which is four more, from thence to Santa Maria del Courbo, which is two more, from thence to Courbo, which is one, thence to Pancourbo which is two, where the Road parts, to Vitoria and to Bilbao.

Burgos
Monasterio	4.
Berebiesca	4.
S.M. del Courbo	2
Courbo	1
Pancourbo	2

13. Leagues to the Parting of the Roads.

I have taken a Walk about the Town a little. A River runs directly through the Town, and there are several Bridges over it. There is a great Number of Monasteries in it. There is an old ruined Castle on a Hill. But I have not had time to see much. There is a little Appearance of Business, here. Some Trades.

Upon my Inquiry after the Religious Houses in Burgos, our Guide went out and procured me the following Information.

Combentos de Fraires
Franciscos	1.
La Trinidad	1.
Benitos	1.
Augustinos	2
Dominicos	1.
Mercenarios	1.
Carmelitos	1
	8

Combentos de Monjas

Sta. Dorotea Agustinas	1
Sta. Franciscas	2
Carmelitas	1
Agustinas	1
Trinitarias	1
Bernardas	2
Benitas	1
Calatrabas	1
Sn. il de fonso	1

Parroquias 15

Cathedral y St. Iago de la Capilla	2
St. Nicolas	1
Sn. Roman	1
La Blanca	1
Bejarua	1
Sn. Martin	1
Sn. Pedro	1
Sn. Cosmes	1
Sn. Lesmes	1
Sn. Esteban	1
Sn. Gil	1

Total.

De Monjas	10
Frailes	8
Parroquias	15
	33.[5]

We passed through several Villages, this day and rode along a River, and arrived at Bribiesca. The Country a little more hilly than for some time past. But it has a naked and poor Appearance.

[1] From Paredes de Nava the party traveled on 9 Jan. through Palencia to Torquemada, seven leagues; on the 10th from there to a village called by both JA and JQA Sellada el Camino, eight leagues; they reached Burgos just before noon on the 11th (JQA, Diary, 9–11 Jan.; Francis Dana, Journal, 1779–1780, MHi).

[2] Thus in MS. JA may have meant either "granite" or "grand."

[3] No such journal has come to light. Thaxter wrote a number of letters from Spain to his father and to AA that survive but are not very informative.

[4] "... we shall determine at this place whether to go to Bilboa or directly to Bayonne" (JQA, Diary, 11 Jan.).

The decision, as the following itinerary shows, was for Bilbao.

⁵ In his Autobiography under this date JA noted that "the sum total is not conformable to the List," and supposed that some establishments had been omitted by his informant.

1780. JANUARY 12. WEDNESDAY.

Arrived at Bribiesca, where there [are] two Convents, one of Men, the other of Women, both Franciscans, and two Parish Churches.

The Tavern We are in is a large House and there are twelve good Beds in it, for Lodgers. Yet no Chimneys, and the same Indelicacy as in all the others.—Smoke and dirt, yet they give us clean Sheets.

A Spanish Kitchen is one of the greatest Curiosities in the World, and they are all very much alike.

1780 JANUARY 13. THURSDAY.

Rode from Bribiesca to Pancourbo where we dined. We passed thro Courbo, which is a little Village with half a dozen other small Villages in Sight. In every one of them is a Church. Pancourbo is at the Beginning of the Rocks. There is the Appearance of an ancient Carriage Way, up the steepest Part of the Rocks. We passed between two Rows of Mountains consisting wholly of Rocks, the most lofty, and craggy Precipices that I ever saw. These rocky Mountains made the Boundary between the ancient Castile and Biscay. Pancourbo is the last Village in old Castile. At Puente de la Rada, We were stopped by a No. of Officers, and asked if We had a Passeport. I produced my Passport of the Governor of Galicia, they read it, with much Respect and let Us Pass. We came 4 good Leagues this afternoon, and are now at Ezpexo.

We are now at the best public House that I have seen. Yet the Kitchen is a Spanish Kitchen, like all the others, and there is no Chimney in the House.

There is not a Tavern We have been in, but is filled with religious Prints and Images. The Chamber where I now write has two Beds, at the Head of each is a Delph Vessell, for holy Water Agua Santa, or Agua benita. At the Head of each also is a neat Cross about 9 Inches long, with an Image of J.C. in some Metal, Tin, Belmetal, [or] Pewter, upon it. Upon the Wall is a Picture of Vierge de Montcarmel, or Virgo Maria de Monte Carmelo—a great Number of others that I have not Patience to transcribe.

From Ezpexo where We now are, We go to Orduña, which is 4 Leagues, and to Bilbao, which is six.

1780. JANUARY 14. FRYDAY.

Rode from Ezpexo to Orduña, four Leagues. The Road is made all the Way, at a great Expence, but the Descent of the Mountains of Orduña is a great Curiosity. These Mountains are chiefly Rocks, of a vast hight: But a Road has been blown out of the Rocks, from the Hight of the Mountains, quite down into the Valey. After winding round and round a great Way, and observing the Marks of the Drills remaining in the Rocks, the Road at last came to a Steep where the only Method of making a Road for a Carriage up and down is by Serpentining it thus.

There is a fertile Valley, and well cultivated at the feet of these Mountains, in the Center of which is the Village of Orduña. In this narrow Space they have crowded two Convents, one of Frailes the other of Monjas. I saw the lazy Drones of Franciscans at the Windows of their Cells, as We passed. At the Bottom of the Mountains We had a small Toll to pay, for the Support of the Road. The Administrator sent to search our Trunks, but We sent him our Passport which produced a polite Message by his Clerk, that he had seen my Name in the Gazette, that he was very glad I was arrived, wished me Success and Prosperity, and desired to know if I wanted any Thing, or if he could be any Way usefull to me. I returned the Message that I was obliged &c. but wanted nothing.

In the Afternoon, We followed the Road, which pursues the Course of a little River, which originates in the Mountains of Orduña, and rode down between two Rows of Mountains to Lugiando where We put up for the night, four Leagues from Bilbao. It is as dirty and uncomfortable a House as almost any We have seen.

We have met, to day and Yesterday, great Numbers of Mules loaded with Merchandizes from Bilbao. The Mules and their Drivers look very well, in comparison of those We have seen before. Their Burdens are Salted Fish, Sardines, Cod, and a Sort of Fish that We see here very plenty called Besugo. They carry also Horse shoes, ready made in Bilboa, to sell in various Parts of the Kingdom.

The Mountains of Biscay, of Bilboa, of Orduna, and Pancourbo, for by these Names they are called, are the most remarkable that I have seen. Phillip 5. made the first Carriage Road through those of Pancourbo. The present King has done most to those of Orduña.

It was a vexatious Thing to see the beautifull Valley of Orduna, devoured by so many Hives of Drones. It is a beautifull, a fertile and a well cultivated Spot, almost the only one, We have yet seen in Biscay, capable of Cultivation.

1780. JANUARY 15. SATURDAY.

Followed the Road by the Side of the River, between two Rows of Mountains, untill We opened upon Bilboa. We saw the Sugar Loaf some time before. This is a Mountain, in the shape of a Piramid, which is called the Sugar Loaf. The Town is surrounded with Mountains.—The Tavern where We are is tolerable, situated between a Church and a Monastry. We have been entertained with the Musick of the Convent since our Arrival.

Soon after our Arrival Captain Babson and Capt. Lovat made Us a Visit. Lovat is bound for America, the first Wind, and Babson very soon, both in Letters of Mark.

Took a Walk, down the River, which is pleasant enough.

While We were absent our Walk, Mr. Gardoqui and Son came to visit me.[1]

[1] Gardoqui & Son was a mercantile firm at Bilbao with American interests. From Bayonne on 24 Jan. JA wrote to thank the Gardoquis for "the Thousand Civilities and the essential assistance We received at Bilboa" (LbC, Adams Papers). Later correspondence shows that he gave the firm various personal commissions.

JANUARY 16. SUNDAY.

Reposed and wrote.[1]

[1] Among other letters written this day JA addressed a very long one to Pres. Huntington devoted mainly to the geography, commerce, and governmental administration of the maritime provinces of Galicia and Biscay (PCC, No. 84, I; copied from LbC, Adams Papers, into JA's Autobiography under its date).

17. MONDAY.

Dined, with the two Messrs. Gardoquis and a Nephew of theirs. After Dinner the Gentlemen accompanied Us, to the Parish Church over the Way, then to the old Parish Church of St. Iago, which was certainly standing in the Year 1300. The high Altar appears very ancient, wrought in Wooden figures, the Work very neat. The Choir, and the Sacristie &c. as in all others.—We then went to the Chambers of the Board of Trade.

This is a curious Institution. On a certain Day annually in the

Beginning of January all the Merchants of Bilbao meet, write their Names on a Ball or Ballot which is put into a Box, from whence four are drawn by Lott. These four name a certain Number of Councillors or Senators.—But this must be further enquired.

This Board of Trade, first endeavours to make all disputing Merchants agree. If they cant succeed, Application must be made to the Board by Petition in Writing. It is then heard and determined, subject to an Appeal, somewhere.—There is no Consul here from France, England, or Holland—Nor any other Nation. The Board of Trade oppose it.—The Chamber is hung round with Pictures of the present King and Queen, the late King and Queen, &c., with Pictures of the royal Exchange London, the Exchange of Amsterdam, of Atwerp &c.

Captains Babson, Lovatt and Wickes dined with Us. I spoke to Mr. Gardoqui in behalf of fifteen American Prisoners escaped from Portugal, and he consented to furnish them Cloaths to the Amount of six dollars a Man. I told him I had no Authority, and that I could not assure him Repayment, but I believed Congress would do all in their Power to repay him.

There is an Accademy at Bergara, for the Youth of Biscay, Guipuscoa, and Alava.

Yesterday, a Mr. Maroni an Irish Gentleman came to visit me.

The Lands in Biscay are chiefly in the Hands of the People—few Lordships. The Duke of Berwick and the Duke of Medina Cœli have some Estates here, but not considerable. In the Spring Freshes, the Water is deep enough upon Change and in the Streets for Vessells of 100 Tons to float.

1780. JANUARY. 18. TUESDAY.

Spent the Day in Walking about the Town. Walked round the Wharf upon the River, through the Market. Saw a plentiful Markett of Fruit and Vegetables, Cabages, Turnips, Carrots, Beets, Onions &c. Apples, Pairs &c. Raisens, Figs, nuts &c.—Went as far as the Gate, where We entered the Town—then turned up the Mountain by the Stone Stairs, and saw fine Gardens, Verdure and Vegetation. Returned, and viewed a Booksellers Stall. Then walked in succession thro every Street in the Town. Afterwards met Messrs. Gardoquis who went with Us to shew Us a No. of Shops. Glass Shops, China Shops, Trinket Shops, Toy Shops and Cutlary Shops. I did not find any Thing very great. There are several Stores and Shops, however, pretty large and pretty full.

1780. JANUARY 19. ⟨*Tuesday*⟩ WEDNESDAY.

Went down the River, on a Visit to the Rambler a Letter of Mark, of 18 Guns, belonging to Mr. Andrew Cabot of Beverly, Captain Lovatt Commander, and the Phœnix a Brig of 14 Guns belonging to Messrs. Traceys at N[ewbury] Port, Captain Babson Commander.

We were honoured, with two Salutes of 13 Guns each, by Babson and with one by Lovat. We dined at the Tavern on shore and had an agreable day. Went to see a new Packett of the Kings on the Stocks, and his new Rope walks, which are two hundred and ten fathoms long.

1780 JANUARY 31. MONDAY.[1]

On the 20th We left Bilbao, arrived at Bayonne the 23d. Staid one day, there. Sat off for Bourdeaux the 25th. Arrived at Bourdeaux Saturday 29th. Dined Yesterday at the Hotel D'Angleterre at the Invitation of Mr. Bondfield with Sir Robert Finlay and Mr. Le Texier and Mr. Vernon.

Went to the Comedy, saw Amphitrion and Cartouche. Mr. A[rthur] L[ee] at Paris. Mr. I[zard] at Amsterdam. Mr. W[illiam] L[ee] at Brussells.

[1] No space was left in the Diary for the gap of eleven days during which the party traveled on muleback to Bayonne, paid off and dismissed their Spanish retinue of men and mules, bought a post chaise and hired others, and proceeded to Bordeaux. Some details concerning this portion of the journey are provided in JA's Autobiography and in Dana's Journal, 1779–1780 (MHi).

1780. FEB. 1. TUESDAY.

Dined Yesterday, at the Hotel D'Angleterre, with Mr. Maccartey, Mr. Delap, Mr. Vernon, Mr. Bondfield, and my Company, at the Invitation of Sir Robert Finlay. Towards Evening Mr. Cabarras came in with the News of [a] Blow struck by Rodney upon the Spaniards, off Gibraltar.

1780 FEB. 5. SATURDAY.

On Wednesday, the second of Feb. We took Post for Paris, and on Fryday the 4 arrived at Coué, where We lodged, but in the night it rained and froze at the same time untill the Roads were a glare [of] Ice, so that the Postillions informed Us, it was impossible for their Horses which in this Country are never frosted to go.

We passed by Angouleme Yesterday Morning and encircled almost

the whole Town. It stands upon an high Hill and is walled all round—
a fine, Airy, healthy Situation with several Streams of Water below it
and fine Interval Lands. The River Charente runs by it. The Lands are
chiefly cultivated with Wines from Bordeaux to this Place, which afford but a poor Prospect in the Winter. In some Places Wheat is sown
and Vines planted alternately in Ridges.

Great Numbers of the Vineyards are in a Soil that has the greatest
Appearance of Poverty. It is a red Loom, intermixed with so many
Pebbles or small Stones of a reddish Colour, that it looks like an heap
of Stones, or a dry gravell. One would think there was not Earth
enough for the Vines to take root.

Other Vineyards are in a black Sand intermixed with a few small
stones. Others in fine, black, fat, mellow mould.

The numerous Groves, Parks and Forrests in this Country form a
striking Contrast with Spain where the whole Country looks like a
Mans face that is newly shaved, Every Tree, bush and shrub being
pared away.[1]

[1] In the MS a single blank leaf separates the present entry and the next,
which is dated 27 July 1780, the day
on which JA set out from Paris with
JQA and CA for Amsterdam. The Adams
party had arrived in Paris from Bordeaux in the evening of 9 February.
(Dana's Journal, 1779–1780, MHi, fur-
nishes details on the last leg of their long
journey; JQA kept no diary between 31
Jan. and 25 July 1780.) In Paris they
stopped at the Hôtel de Valois in the
Rue de Richelieu, though from entries
recording payments of rent in the personal accounts that follow it appears that
they took a separate house attached to
the hotel. This remained JA's headquarters until he left Paris in July. JQA,
CA, and young Johonnot were placed
in a *pension* academy in Passy conducted by one Pechigny, to whom payments are also recorded in the accounts
that follow. Unsatisfactory as they may
be in lieu of a regularly kept diary, the
accounts tell us a good deal about JA's
daily activities, especially his book buying. But for his attempts to discharge
his public mission and to be otherwise
useful, one must turn to his Autobiography (which does not, however, go
beyond March) and to his correspondence. There one may see with what assiduity he read the news from all quar-

ters of Europe and reported it to Congress. Late in May he told a friend in
Philadelphia: "I have written more to
Congress, since my Arrival in Paris,
than they ever received from Europe put
it all together since the Revolution [be-
gan]" (to Elbridge Gerry, 23 May, CtY).
This may be literally true. He filled one
letterbook after another; for weeks on
end he wrote almost daily dispatches, on
some days addressing two, three, and
even four letters to Samuel Huntington,
filling them with documents copied *in
extenso* from French, British, and Dutch
newspapers. Prevented by Vergennes
from publicly announcing any part of
his mission until the end of March, JA
undertook to improve both his own time
and European opinion of the American cause by concocting paragraphs and
articles for publication in whatever
journals would print them. The elder
Genet had discontinued his *Affaires de
l'Angleterre et de l'Amérique* (see note
on entry of 3 March 1779, above),
but he had ready access to the new
political supplement of the venerable
Mercure de France, which served as a
continuation of the *Affaires*, and for
several months JA happily fed American
propaganda to it. One of his contributions, explaining and defending Congress' recent fiscal measures, had mo-

mentous effects, altering the coolness
with which Vergennes had viewed JA
for some time into anger and hostility,
complicating JA's relations with Franklin, and rendering his position in Paris
highly uncomfortable. The story is too
long to tell here, but it is well summarized by CFA in JA's *Works*, 1:314 ff.,
see also the relevant documents in same,
7:188–203, 211–214; Wharton, ed.,
Dipl. Corr. Amer. Rev., 3:827, 844; 4:
18–19.

[PERSONAL EXPENDITURES, FEBRUARY–JULY 1780.][1]

The Dates of *Receipts*, by whom given and for what Sums.

1780			£	s	d
Feby.	13th.	Joseph Stevens for three Month Wages. 30 Dolls.[2]	150:	0:	0
	15th.	John Thaxter for thirty Louis D'Ors on Account	720:	0:	0
	15th.	Joseph Stevens for Sundries bo't	31:	4:	0
	14th.	C. Hochereau for Books	19:10:		0
	16.	Mr. Morbut for Bread & Butter	10:16:		0
	19.	Auris for Hats	63:	0:	0
	21st.	De Montigny for Courier de L'Europe, & Hague Gazette	84:	0:	0
	21st.	Arnoux for Gazette de France	12:	0:	0
	21st.	Panckoucks, for Mercure de France	30:	0:	0
	26th.	Montagne for Cheese, Prunes &c.	39:	2:	0
March	2	Dinner at Versailles	12:	4:	0
	6	De Montigny for the Gazettes of Leide and Amsterdam	78:	0:	0
		Books	82:10:		0
	8.	Hill for Cloaths	681:15:		0
		Hochereau for Books	17:	6:	0
	9.	Mad[am]e Ruel the Traiteur for Provisions	400:	0:	0
		Mademoiselle Carnu for Handkerfs. Ruffles & Stocks	154:10:		0
		Joseph Stevens for one Month's Wages ending 13th. of March	50:	0:	0
		Miston (Peruquier) for Wigs and dressing	67:	4:	0
		St. Clair (Caffee) for Tea, Milk, Bread and Butter	78:	1:	0
		Joseph Stevens for Sundries bo't	55:10:		0
		Coquelle for Washing, Postage of Letters &c.	27:10:		0

		£	s	d
	Parmentiers for Rent of his House, Wood & Wine	542:	14:	0
	John Thaxter for ten Louis D'Ors on Acct.	240:	0:	0
	Washerwoman	2:	10:	0
	Pacquenot for Wine	26:	0:	0
	John Thaxter for Tea and Sugar	21:	15:	0
	Griffon For Books and Paper	61:	2:	0
	Omitted, paid Mr. Dana for one Dozen of Tea Spoons	95:	6:	8
13th.	Gouyot for Carriage and Horses one month	360:	0:	0
13th.	Gerante for two Pieces of Wine	250:	0:	0
10.	Paid for half a Dozen Stocks, @ 3:10:0	21:	0:	0
	De la vals Rect for Tea, Sugar, Raisins Candles and Flambeau	28:	14:	0
	Backelier Epicier for Dutch Cheese	4:	1:	0
11	Paid Subscription for the Philosophic and politic History of the two Indies[3]	24:	0:	0
12	Paid for M. Moreaus Discourses on the History of France 9. Vol.[4]	41:	0:	0
17.	Paid Mazars for Shoes and Boots	54:	0:	0
	Paid for Sewing Silk 6 Ozs.	18:	0:	0
	Paid for the hire of a Carriage three Days & Coachman	39:	12:	0
19	Hochereau for Books—Theatre D'Education 4 Vol. bound	24:	0:	0
	Dto. for Postage of a Letter	1:	0:	0
	Paid for the American Atlas, Pilot &c. in one Volume[5] 4 1/2 Louis	108:	0:	0
	Paid the Abbè Chalut['s] Servt. for Corks, Shot & bottleing Wine	7:	10:	0
20	Paid for four Quires of Cartridge Paper	10:	0:	0
	Paid Piebot Epicier, for Tea, Sugar &c.	21:	10:	6

Paid Hochereau Bookseller, 30 Louis D'ors, towards the Payment for La Description des Arts et Metiers, in 18 Volumes in Folio, for which I was to

			£	s	d
	give him 750 Liv. and for the Encyclopedia in 39 Volumes in Quarto for which I was to give him 360 Livres [6]		720:	0:	0
21	Paid Pissot for a Grammar of french Verbs, and for Nugents Dictionary [7]		7:10:		0
	Paid for two Pair of black Silk Stockings one Louis D'or.		24:	0:	0
	Paid for a Purse		3:	0:	0
22d.	Paid Pissot for another Grammar of French Verbs		3:	0:	0
	Paid Dto. for The Abbè de Mablys Droits public L'Europe [8]		6:	0:	0
	Paid the Coachman for three day's driving		3:12:		0
23	Paid Daniel, Engraver for two Seals		42:	0:	0
	Paid Mr. Langlois for Carriage three Days		36:	0:	0
24	Paid for 6 yds. Silk 6 Liv. each and 2 oz black sewing Silk,—Fleury		42:	0:	0
29	Paid for the Works of Tacitus with a French Transn. [9]		21:	0:	0
	Paid for the Latin Dicty. of Robert Stephens [10]		48:	0:	0
	Paid for the Eulogium of M: Colbert by Mr. Neckar		1:16:		0
	Paid for the Journal of Paris		24:	0:	0
	Paid for Domats civil Law 26. Liv. and the Voyage Pitoresque de Paris et des Environs 8 [11]		34:	0:	0
April 1.	Paid for two Trunks £40 for a large one and 12 for the Small		52:	0:	0
2	Paid for Duties and Waggonage of a Cask of old red wine of Tonnere. Feuillette de vieux vin rouge de Tonnere.		39:16:		
4	Paid for Chocolat Wine &c.		20:	9:	0
5.	Paid for Tea, Almonds &c.		23:	3:	9
6.	Paid Hochereau for Books. D'Aguesseau, Cochin and Dictionaire D'His-				

		£	s	d
	toire naturell.[12]	647:	0:	0
	Paid Hill the Tayler one Bill	144:	10:	0
	another	223:	0:	0
7.	Paid Chevr. O'Gormon for a Piece of Wine	150:	0:	0
	Paid for Raynals Works and a Voyage thro France [13]	24:	0:	0
7.	Paid for 2 Pieces d'Indien and for Ruffles Necks &c.	153:	0:	0
9	Paid for Dictionaire de l'orthographie [14]	7:	0:	0
10	Paid for Caffees Account for the last Month	18:	13:	0
	Paid Hochereaus Account for Books	188:	0:	0
12.	Paid for the House Rent and furniture, Bottles, Wine &c.	576:	17:	0
	Paid Pacquenot for Wine	10:	0:	0
	Paid Dalley the Baker	15:	0:	0
	Paid Coquelle the Washerwoman	9:	0:	0
	Paid Do. for Postage of Letters	23:	18:	0
	Paid J. Thaxter on Account	240:	0:	0
	Paid Do. for Money lent	26:	8:	0
	Paid Joseph Stevens one Months Wages ending the 13th. of April	52:	10:	0
	Paid Do. for Sundries bo't by him	60:	1:	6
	Paid Ruelle Traiteur	428:	0:	0
13	Paid Hochereau for the Corps diplomatique &c.[15]	940:	0:	0
15	Paid Piebot for Cheese & Tea	56:	13:	6
20	Paid for two Pair of Black Silk Stockings	24:	0:	0
26	Paid for 30 days hire of the Coach, Horses, Coachman &c. 15 Louis	360:	0:	0
	Sent by Captn. C. to Mr. D.[16] in London to pay for Pamphlets &c. 4 Louis	096:	0:	0
	Gave my Son to pay for La Fontaines Fables [17] and for his Brother & S. Cooper at the Comedy	6:	0:	0
	Paid for La Fontaines Fables for Charles	2:	10:	0

			£	s	d
	28	Paid for Singing Birds and Cages	35:10:	0	
May	1	Gave at Biçetre, the bedlam of Paris [18]	9: 0:	0	
	2	Paid for a Pound of black sealing Wax, a Pound of red, and a blank Letter Book	22: 0:	0	
		Paid Subscription for the Journal des Scavans [19]	16: 0:	0	
	5	Paid Dt. for Annales Politiques, Civiles, et literaires [20]	48: 0:	0	
		Paid the Garçon	1: 4:	0	
		Paid for 6 Bottles of white Wine	4:10:	0	
	15	Paid Ruel Traiteur to 10 May	423:15:	0	
		House	432: 0:	0	
		Joseph Stevens	171:12:	0	
		Denis Wages and Dinners	68: 8:	0	
		Bread	15: 0:	0	
		Postage &c.	44: 9:	0	
		Mr. Thaxter	240: 0:	0	
		Stephens's Wages ending 13 May	52:10:	0	
		Marchande de Vin, Garante	180: 0:	0	
		To Caffees Account	2: 9:	0	
		Settled with Mr. Dana so far.			
	17	Paid Mr. Pechini's Account for my Sons John and Charles,[21]	980:10:	0	
	19	Paid Mr. Court de Gebelin,[22] for Subscription for his Greek Dictionary and the Seventh Volume of his Monde primitif and a Thermometer of Raumur	31:10:	0	
	20	Paid the Coach Hire for a Month ending the 17th. 15 Louis and for a pair of additional Horses to go to Versailles on the Day of Pentecote 18 liv.	378: 0:	0	
	27	Paid for the Carriage of a Box of Newspapers and pamphlets from London	9: 6:	0	
		Paid for the Cariage of an hoghead and Case of Bordeaux Wine, and the Duties on the Road	99:10:	0	

439

			£	s	d
	30	Paid the Duties for the Entry into Paris	57:13:	0	
June	1	Paid Cabaret for three Reams of Paper and two Ivory Knives	52: 0:	0	
	9	Paid for Spoons &c.—Mr. Taillepied	823: 0:	0	
	19	Paid for the Waggonage of three Trunks from Brest	72: 0:	0	
	21	Paid for the Coach to the 16 June 15 Louis	360: 0:	0	
	26	Paid for Washing	8:12:	0	
	28	Paid Paule Tailors Account	644: 0:	0	
		Paid Mr. Tyler a Bill of Exchange drawn upon me by Mrs. Adams in favour of Thomas Bumstead & by him inclosed to Mr. John Tyler—100 dollars	535: 0:	0	
July	1	Paid for 12 Ells of Cambrick @ 10 Liv.	120: 0:	0	
	7	Paid Mr. Borzachini for 2 Italian Grammars and 11 Lessons	60: 0:	0	
		Paid for a Piece of Cambrick 12 Ells & 1/2	120: 0:	0	
	8	Paid Molini for Baretti's Italien Dictionary	48: 0:	0	
		Dellitti e Pene	3:		
		Grammatica Del Buomattei [23]	9: 0:	0	
	17	Paid for Linen	67:10:	0	
		Paid for 6 Bottles of Liqueur	27: 0:	0	
		[*In margin*:] Settled with Mr. Dana			
	19	Paid Porters Bill for Postage of Letters &c.	112: 7:	0	
	26	Paid for a months Coach hire	360: 0:	0	
	27	Paid Mr. Pechini one Quarter for my two Sons	650:18:	0	
	28	Paid Taylors Account	170:18:	6	
		Paid Joseph Stevens's Account	100:19:	0	

[1] From Lb/JA/34 (Adams Papers, Microfilms, Reel No. 122), a folio ledger with a trade card inside the front cover reading: "A la Tête Noire, Furgault,

Marchand de Papiers, A l'entrée de la rue de Richelieu, près des Quinze-Vingts, ... à Paris." Following eight pages of accounts, which are at first in Thaxter's hand, including the caption, and afterward in both JA's and Thaxter's hands, the volume contains copies of JA's letters of a much later period, May 1814 – Nov. 1816.

[2] This entry indicates that the exchange rate between the Spanish dollar and the French *livre tournois* was one to five, at least for purposes of common reckoning.

[3] By Abbé Raynal; see Diary entry of 2 Feb. 1779 and note there.

[4] Jacob Nicolas Moreau, *Principes de morale, de politique et de droit public ... ou discours sur l'histoire de France*, Paris, 1777–1779; 9 vols. (*Catalogue of JA's Library*).

[5] *Atlas amériquain septentrional contenant les détails des différentes provinces, de ce vaste continent* ..., Paris, 1778. *Pilote américain* ..., Paris, 1779; 2 vols. in 1. Both of these collections were French reissues of English works and were published by Lerouge, under whose name they are entered in *Catalogue of JA's Library*.

[6] This entry records JA's acquisition of two of the major works of French scholarship of the era. The first was *Descriptions des arts et métiers, faites ou approuvées par Messieurs de l'Académie royale des sciences*, Paris, 1761–1788; 113 cahiers, folio. JA's set, bound in 18 vols., was nearly but not quite complete, only a few parts being published after 1779. He presented it to Harvard College on 5 June 1789, and it is now in the Houghton Library. See Arthur H. Cole and George B. Watts, *The Handicrafts of France as Recorded in the Descriptions des Arts et Métiers 1761–1788*, Boston, 1952, for a history and appraisal of this work and a record of sets in American libraries. The second work was the Diderot-d'Alembert *Encyclopédie, ou dictionnaire raisonné des sciences, des arts et des métiers, par une société de gens de lettres*, 3d edn. Geneva, &c., 1778–1779, of which JA's nearly complete set in 38 vols. survives among his books in the Boston Public Library (*Catalogue of JA's Library*, p.

74); see also *Harvard Library Bull.*, 9:235 (Spring 1955).

[7] The *Catalogue of JA's Library* lists *Les verbes françois ... en forme de dictionnaire*, by Demarville, London, 1773, but only a later edition of Thomas Nugent, *The New Pocket Dictionary of the French and English Languages* ..., London, 1781.

[8] The *Catalogue of JA's Library* lists two sets of Mably, *Le droit public de l'Europe* ..., the first published at Amsterdam in 2 vols., 1748, the second at Geneva in 3 vols., 1776. On Mably see Diary entry of 29 May 1778, above, and note there.

[9] *Traduction complète de Tacite*, Paris, 1777–1779; 7 vols.; Latin and French texts (*Catalogue of JA's Library*).

[10] Robert Estienne, *Thesaurus linguæ latinæ in IV tomos divisus* ..., Basel, 1740–1743; 4 vols., folio (*Catalogue of JA's Library*).

[11] For Domat see Diary entry of 24 June 1779, above, and note 3 there. For the *Voyage pittoresque de Paris* and *Voyage pittoresque des environs de Paris*, frequently cited in notes above, see *Catalogue of JA's Library*, p. 73.

[12] Aguesseau and Cochin were legal writers; see *Catalogue of JA's Library*, p. 8–9, 54. The *Dictionnaire raisonné universel d'histoire naturelle*, Paris, 1775, in 6 vols., was by Valmont de Bomare (same, p. 253).

[13] Probably J. A. Piganiol de La Force, *Nouveau voyage de France; avec un itinéraire, et des cartes* ..., nouv. édn., Paris, 1780 (*Catalogue of JA's Library*).

[14] [Charles Le Roy,] *Traité de l'orthographe françoise, en forme de dictionaire*, nouv. édn., Poitiers, 1775 (*Catalogue of JA's Library*).

[15] Jean Dumont, comp., *Corps universel diplomatique du droit des gens; contenant un recueil des traitez d'alliance, de paix, de trève, de neutralité, de commerce, d'échange* ..., Amsterdam, 1726–1739; 14 vols. in 15, folio (*Catalogue of JA's Library*).

[16] Doubtless Thomas Digges, on whom see Diary entry of 20 April 1778 and note 2, above; also 4 Dec. 1782, note 1, below.

[17] There are copies of La Fontaine's *Fables choisies, mises en vers*, listed in

both the *Catalogue of JA's Library* and in Boston Athenæum, *Catalogue of JQA's Books.* Probably one of these belonged to CA, who, as the next entry in these accounts suggests, wanted a copy of his own.

[18] Described at length in JA to AA, 5 May 1780 (Adams Papers).

[19] JA acquired five volumes of the *Journal des sçavans* (*Catalogue of JA's Library*, p. 132). On this day also, according to a separate and fragmentary record of book purchases elsewhere in the present letterbook, he bought "14 Exemplaires Loix de l'Amerique," paying 35 livres for them. This was a work entitled *Recueil des loix constitutives des colonies angloises, confédérées sous la dénomination d'Etats-Unis de l'Amérique-Septentrionale* ..., Paris, 1778, compiled by one Regnier from the texts of the state constitutions and other American state papers that had appeared in the *Affaires de l'Angleterre et de l'Amérique.* Its curious bibliographical history has been related by Gilbert Chinard in Amer. Philos. Soc., *Year Book 1943,* p. 89–96. Five copies remain among JA's books in the Boston Public Library, one of them bearing MS notes in his hand.

[20] "Dt." probably means "ditto," but JA's copy of the *Annales* has not been found.

[21] Spelled by JQA, probably more correctly, Pechigny. He and his wife conducted the boarding school in Passy in which the Adams boys were placed. JQA wrote engagingly about his school work in a letter to his father without date [ante 17 March 1780] and in another to his cousin, William Cranch, 17 March 1780 (both in Adams Papers).

[22] See entry of 30 Oct. 1778, above, and note.

[23] Copies of Baretti's *Dictionary of the English and Italian Languages* ..., new edn., London, 1771, in 2 vols., and Beccaria's *Dei delitti e delle pene,* Haarlem and Paris, 1780, remain among JA's books in the Boston Public Library (*Catalogue of JA's Library*). The *Grammatica* here mentioned may or may not be Buommattei's *Della lingua toscana ... libre due,* 5th edn., Florence, 1760, which is listed in the *Catalogue.*

1780 JULY 27. THURSDAY. [*]

Setting off on a Journey, with my two Sons to Amsterdam.[1] —Lodged at Compiegne. Fryday night, lodged at Valenciennes. Saturday arrived at Brussells.—This Road is through the finest Country, I have any where seen. The Wheat, Rye, Barley, Oats, Peas, Beans and several other Grains, the Hemp, Flax, Grass, Clover, Lucerne, St. Foin, &c., the Pavements and Roads are good. The Rows of Trees, on each side the Road, and around many Squares of Land.—The Vines, the Cattle, the Sheep, in short every Thing upon this Road is beautiful and plentifull. Such immense fields and heavy Crops of Wheat I never saw any where. The Soil is stronger and richer, than in other Parts.

I lodged in Brussells at L'hotel de L'Imperatrice. The Cathedral Church, the Park, the Ramparts and Canals of this Town, are very well worth seeing.[2]

[1] Having met with absolute resistance at Versailles to discharging any part of his mission to negotiate treaties of peace and commerce with Great Britain, and having offended Vergennes by his importunity on this and unwelcome advice on other matters, JA determined to go to Amsterdam, "to try," as Franklin reported to Congress, "whether something might not be done to render us less dependent on France" (Franklin to Huntington, 9 Aug. 1780,

Writings, ed. Smyth, 8:128). JA went to the Netherlands as a private citizen, not knowing that on 20 June Congress had commissioned him its agent, until Henry Laurens should arrive, to procure a loan there (*JCC,* 17:535–537); his commission, received on 16 Sept., was enclosed in a letter from Lovell and Houston, the Committee on Foreign Affairs (Adams Papers).

[2] Only the first two sentences of the present entry could have been written on 27 July. According to JQA's Diary, which is much more detailed than his father's during this journey, the party arrived in Brussels at 5:30 in the afternoon of the 29th, and JA had a long conversation with Edmund Jenings that evening.

1780. JULY 30. SUNDAY.

Went to the Cathedral Church. A great Feast. An infinite Crowd.[1] The Church more splendidly ornamented than any that I had seen. Hung with Tapestrie. The Church Music here is in the Italian style.

A Picture in Tapestry was hung up, of a No. of Jews stabbing the Wafer, the bon Dieu, and blood gushing in streams, from the B[read?]. This insufferable Piece of pious Villany, shocked me beyond measure. But thousands were before it, on their Knees adoring. I could not help cursing the Knavery of the Priesthood and the brutal Ignorance of the People—yet perhaps, I was rash and unreasonable, and that it is as much Virtue and Wisdom in them to adore, as in me to detest and despise.—Spent the Afternoon, and drank Tea, with Mr. W. Lee, Mr. Jennings, and his Nephew,[2] Mrs. Izard, her two Daughters and Son, and Miss [Steed,][3] Mrs. Lee and her Children &c. An agreable Circle of Americans.

In the Evening Mr. Lee, Mr. Jennings and his Nephew, My two Sons, &c. took a Walk to see the Canals. Vessells of some Burthen come up here, in the Canal which reaches to the Sea. We afterwards walked upon the Ramparts.

In this Town is a great Plenty of stone, which I think is the same with our Braintree North Common stone. It is equally hard, equally fine grain—capable of a fine Polish. I think the Colour is a little darker, than the Braintree stone. There is a new Building here, before which is the Statue of the late Prince Charles, in Front of which are six Pillars, wholly of this stone. Indeed the Steps, and the whole Front is of the same stone.

This Town is the Capital of Brabant, in the Austrian Netherlands. The late Prince Charles was a Brother of the Empress Queen, L'Imperatrice Reine, Unkle of the Emperor and the Queen of France. He was extreamly beloved, by the People, and has left an excellent Character. The Emperor did not like him, it is said. In the late War, the Emperor called upon this Prince for Money. The Prince wrote to dissuade him from it. The Emperor sent again. The Prince wrote back, that he saw They were determined, and they must appoint another Governor of this Province, for he could not execute their orders. Upon this the Imperial Court desisted.

We lodged one night at Antwerp, viewed the Cathedral and the Exchange &c. and went by Moerdyck to Rotterdam, where We arrived, the 4th. August.[4]

[1] MS: "Crown."
[2] "Bordly" (i.e. Bordley), according to JQA's Diary.
[3] Blank in MS; name supplied from JQA's Diary.
[4] According to JQA's Diary the Adamses spent the 31st, 1st, and 2d in sightseeing and in visiting with William Lee and Edmund Jenings in Brussels; on the 3d they traveled in their own carriage to Antwerp; and on the 4th continued in hired carriages to Rotterdam, leaving their carriage in Antwerp.

[LIST OF PERSONS AND FIRMS TO BE CONSULTED
IN THE NETHERLANDS, JULY–AUGUST 1780.][1]

Mr. John de Neufville, et Fils.

Le Chr. de Luxembourg.

Le Chr. de Launay.

Cs. Van der Oudermeulen

M. Grand.

M. Fizeaux.

G. H. Matthes.

Henry du Bois.

Hodshon

Mr. Jean Luzac, Avocat, Leide.

Nicholas and Jacob Van Staphorst.

Mr. Vinman.

Mr. John Gabriel Tegelaer, by the new Market.

Mr. Daniel Crommelin and Sons.[2]

[1] This undated list appears on the last page but one of D/JA/31, separated from the last dated entry (6 Aug. 1780) in that booklet by seventeen blank leaves. It is a fair conjecture that the names, written in JA's most careful, unhurried hand at two different sittings, were put down before JA reached the Netherlands—in Paris, in Brussels, or in both places.

[2] The names are mostly those of Amsterdam merchants or bankers who had American interests that are dealt with in P. J. van Winter's comprehensive study, *Het aandeel van den Amster-* *damschen handel aan den opbouw van het Amerikaansche gemeenebest*, The Hague, 1927–1933, notably Jan de Neufville & Zoon; Fizeaux, Grand & Cie. (which through its partner George Grand was closely associated with Ferdinand Grand, George's brother, the Paris banker for the United States); John Hodshon & Zoon; Nicolaas & Jacob van Staphorst; Jan Gabriël Tegelaar; and Daniël Crommelin & Zoonen. With two of the firms here listed JA was to have very close relations. Jan (or Jean) de Neufville had negotiated with William Lee at Aix-la-Chapelle in 1778 the

unauthorized and abortive "treaty" between the Netherlands and the United States, the text of which, when captured by the British among Henry Laurens' papers in 1780, led to the breach between Great Britain and the Netherlands. The De Neufville firm had refitted John Paul Jones' squadron in 1779 and did its best, after JA's arrival in Amsterdam, to raise a loan for the United States, though the results were extremely disappointing. Besides Van Winter's monograph see his article on De Neufville in *Nieuw Ned. Biog. Woordenboek,* 8:1211–1214. With the Van Staphorst brothers, ardent adherents of the Patriot, or anti-Orangist, party, JA got in touch immediately upon his arrival in Amsterdam (JQA, Diary, 14 Aug. 1780). After American independence

was recognized by the Dutch in 1782, the Van Staphorst firm was one of the syndicate of Amsterdam bankers that floated a succession of loans negotiated by JA. Besides Van Winter's monograph see his article on Nicolaas van Staphorst in *Nieuw Ned. Biog. Woordenboek,* 8: 1285–1286.

Jean Luzac, on the other hand, was a Leyden lawyer, editor of the *Nouvelles extraordinaires de divers endroits* (commonly known as the *Gazette de Leyde*), and professor at the University of Leyden; he became one of JA's most admired and admiring friends and most useful collaborators in the Netherlands (JA–Luzac correspondence, Adams Papers; *Nieuw Ned. Biog. Woordenboek,* 1:1290–1294).

1778 [*i.e.* 1780] AUG. 5.

Lodged at the Mareschall De Turenne. Dined with Mr. Dubblemets.[1] Went to see the Statue of Erasmus, the Exchange, the Churches &c. Mr. Dubblemets sent his Coach in the Evening and one of his Clerks. We rode, round the Environs of the Town, then to his Country Seat, where We supped.—The Meadows are very fine, the Horses and Cattle large. The Intermixture of Houses, Trees, Ships, and Canals throughout this Town is very striking. The Neatness here is remarkable.

[1] The mercantile firm of F. & A. Dubbeldemuts in Rotterdam had some tenuous American connections and was eager to improve them. Probably Franklin, to whom they had addressed various appeals, commended them to JA's attention. They were later vigorous supporters of JA's campaign to obtain Dutch recognition of American independence. See *Cal. Franklin Papers, A.P.S.,* index, and JA–Dubbeldemuts correspondence in Adams Papers.

1778 [*i.e.* 1780] AUG. 6.

Went to the English Presbyterian Church, and heard a sensible sermon, the mode of Worship differs in nothing from ours but in the organ, whose Musick joins in the Singing.

1780 AUG. 28TH. MONDAY.[1]

Heeren Graagt, by de Veisel Straagt. Burgomaster Hooft, D.Z.[2]
Mr. Hartzinck. Scheepen. Heeren Gragt.
M. G. H. Matthes.—burgwal opposite the Lombard.
J. Vandevelde. Agter zyds burgwal.

Mr. Hartzinck is the Son in Law of Madam Chabanel, Mr. Le Roy's Aunt.

Keep us poor. Depress Us. Keep Us weak. Make Us feel our Obligations. Impress our Minds with a Sense of Gratitude. Let Europe see our dependance. Make Europe believe We are in great distress and danger, that other nations may be discouraged from taking our Part. Propagate bad news, to discourage the Merchants and Bankers of Holland from lending Us Money. Is there any Thing in these Jealousies and Insinuations?

Dined with M. Jacob Van staphorst. A dutch minister from St. Eustatia there. A Lawyer, Mr. Calcoon,[3] Mr. Cromellin, Mr. Le Roi, Gillon,[4] Joiner and a Merchant from Hamborough. The Parson is a warm American. The Lawyer made one observation which [I once?] made to Dr. Franklin, that English would be the general Language in the next Century, and that America would make it so. Latin was in the last Century, French has been so in this, and English will be so, the next.

It will be the Honour of Congress to form an Accademy for improving and ascertaining the English Language.[5]

[1] First entry in D/JA/32, a pocket memorandum book with a cover of Dutch decorated paper over boards which have loops for a pencil at the fore-edge. Most of the entries are in pencil, and most of them are undated, but all belong to JA's first months in the Netherlands. Inside the front cover is a notation, probably in the hand of Harriet Welsh, a relative who lived in Boston and who acted occasionally as JA's amanuensis during his old age: "The Dutch book of Mr. John Adams when in Holland in the revolution. June 1823." Among the leaves left blank by JA in the middle of the book are six scattered pages of accounts which are in a hand not even tentatively identified but unquestionably later than 1800. These have been disregarded in the present text. Since this is not a diary in the conventional sense, but a pocket engagement and address book containing occasional diary-like entries, CFA included nothing from it in his edition of JA's Diary. Yet the contents, fragmentary and sometimes cryptic as they are, throw some light on the beginnings of JA's mission to the Netherlands.

From JQA's Diary we learn that the Adamses left Rotterdam on 7 Aug. by canal boat for Delft and went on to The Hague, where JA consulted with the American agent, Charles William Frederic Dumas, and the French ambassador, the Duc de La Vauguyon. They visited Leyden on the 9th, stopping there one night, and proceeded by canal boat via Haarlem to Amsterdam on the 10th, putting up at "l'Hotel des Armes d'Amsterdam." In this city they found numerous Americans, including Alexander Gillon, who enjoyed the title of commodore of the South Carolina navy (Arthur Middleton to JA, 4 July 1778, Adams Papers). Gillon had Dutch relatives and found lodgings for the Adamses next door to his own (JA, *Corr. in the Boston Patriot*, p. 345–346). JA at once set about establishing such commercial, political, and journalistic connections as he could.

[2] That is, Henrik Hooft, Danielszoon, a burgomaster of strongly republican (anti-Orangist) sentiments, who lived on the Heerengracht (Lords' Canal) near Vyzelstraat (Johan E. Elias, *De vroedschap van Amsterdam*, Haarlem, 1903–1905, 2:726).

446

[8] Hendrik Calkoen (1742–1818), later described by JA as "the giant of the law in Amsterdam." See *Nieuw Ned. Biog. Woordenboek*, 3:195–197. Three days later Calkoen addressed a series of questions about the United States and its resources to JA in writing (Adams Papers), to which JA replied in a MS dated 4–27 Oct. 1780 (Adams Papers), afterward printed as *Twenty-Six Letters, upon Interesting Subjects, respecting the Revolution of America* ..., London, 1786; reprinted New York, 1789. JA included them among his letters to the *Boston Patriot*, preceded by an explanation of how they came to be written and the use Calkoen made of them to spread "just sentiments of American affairs" in the Netherlands (JA, *Corr. in the Boston Patriot*, p. 194). CFA also included them, with the explanation, in JA's *Works*, 7:265–312.

[4] Alexander Gillon, of Charleston, S.C., but probably of Dutch origin, had recently acquired a Dutch-built frigate for the use of South Carolina and had named it for that state. He was also attempting to negotiate a loan for his state in Amsterdam and had gone the rounds of the banking and brokerage houses. JA held a respectful opinion of Gillon until after the fiasco of the latter's voyage of 1781, with CA on board. Gillon started from the Texel for America, but after six weeks put in at La Coruña, Spain, where his American passengers made haste to leave the *South Carolina*. See D. E. Huger Smith, "Commodore Alexander Gillon and the Frigate South Carolina," *So. Car. Hist. & Geneal. Mag.*, 9:189–219; John Trumbull, *Autobiography*, ed. Theodore Sizer, New Haven, 1953, p. 75–77.

[5] On 5 Sept. JA developed this idea in a letter to Pres. Huntington proposing the establishment of an "American Accademy, for refining, improving and ascertaining the English Language," to be maintained by Congress in conjunction with "a Library consisting of a compleat Collection of all Writings concerning Languages of every Sort ancient and modern" (LbC, Adams Papers).

29 AUG.[1]

30   Wednesday. Mr. Vanberckle [2]
31   Thursday. Mr. Crommelin opde Keyzers Gragt.

Septr.

1   Fryday. Mrs. Chabanels.
3   Sunday. M. De Neuville, De Neuville
[6]   Wednesday. Bicker [3]
[7]   Thursday.
[10]   Sunday. Cromelin
[12]   Tuesday. Grand
[13]   Wednesday. Chabanell
[14]   Thursday. De Neufville

[1] This list of engagements appears on the last page but one of D/JA/32. The entries may or may not have all been put down on 29 Aug.; space was left for insertions between those that do not fall on successive days.

[2] Engelbert François van Berckel (1726–1796), pensionary of Amsterdam, an early enthusiast in the American cause, and younger brother of Pieter Johan van Berckel, who became the first minister from the Netherlands to the United States, 1783 (*Nieuw Ned. Biog. Woordenboek*, 4:109–111; 2:128–129).

[3] Henrick Bicker (1722–1783), an Amsterdam merchant who in the following month advised JA on his first steps to secure a Dutch loan to the

United States and who proved to JA "a sincere friend and faithful counsellor, from first to last" (Johan E. Elias,

De vroedschap van Amsterdam, Haarlem, 1903–1905, 1:361; JA, *Corr. in the Boston Patriot*, p. 171).

[30 AUGUST.]

School op de Cingel.

30 of August, my Sons went to the Latin School.[1]

Dined at Mr. Vanberkles Pensionary of Amsterdam, with Mr. Bicker and an Officer of the Army.

Mr. Calkoen Keyzers Gragt.

[1] This was the well-known Latin school or academy on the Singel (a canal in the heart of Amsterdam) near the Muntplein (Mint Square). The building is now occupied by the Amsterdam police. There is a contemporary account of the school in *Le guide, ou nouvelle description d'Amsterdam* ..., Amsterdam, 1772, p. 220–222, an anonymous but excellent guidebook, of which JA's copy survives among his books in the Boston Public Library. JQA translated and copied this account into his Diary, 31 Aug., and in later entries tells a little of life at the school. Things did not go well, however, for the precocious JQA under Dutch scholastic discipline. Since he did not know Dutch, he was kept in a lower form, and the Rector, H. Verheyk, found him disobedient and impertinent. As a result, on 10 Nov. JA instructed Verheyk to send both of his sons home (JA–Verheyk correspondence in Adams Papers).

[MISCELLANEOUS MEMORANDA IN AMSTERDAM, AUGUST–SEPTEMBER 1780.][1]

H. Grotius, de Jure Belli ac Pacis.[2]

C. van Bynkershoek

G. Noodt Opera

Apologeticus eorum qui Hollandiæ præfuerunt ab H. Grotio

Considerations sur l'Etude de la Jurisprudence par M. Perrenot.

Janiçon Republik der Vereenigde Nederlanden[3]

Ploos Van Amstel, the first Lawyer of Holland. Mr. Calkoen the next.

Heerens Gragt, pres Vissel Straat. Burgomaester Hooft.

Q. A Society or Academy for the dutch Language, in Germany, Russia, Sweeden, Denmark. The Italian Academy.

2000 Plants and Trees, many Americans.

38,000 florins for the Seat, 216 Acres of Land, between 30 and 40 thousand Vessells pass in a Year in Sight.

Velserhooft.

Muyden. Sluices

Weesop. G in Hogs.[4]

De Geen. [Fine?] Seats

Hofrust. Muyderberg. Mr. Crommelin.

Mr. Crommelin Op de Keyzers Gragt, over de Groenlandse Pakhuyzen. On the Keyzers Gragt opposite the Greenland Warehouses.

M. Van Berckel. Upon the Heerens Gragt, by de Konings Plein.

M. Bicker. Opposite.

M. Hooft—op de Heerens Gragt, by de Vyselstraat.

M. Vanhasselt at M. Wm. Hoofts on the Keysers Gragt, near the Amstel.

M. John Gabriel Tegelaar op de nieuwe Maart.

M. Nicholas Vanstaphorst, op de Cingel, about 50 doors from Jacob.

De La Lande & Fynje—op de Cingel.[5]

Questions. Is it necessary, or expedient to make any Representation, Communication, or Application to the Prince? or States General?

2. Is it prudent to apply to the City of Amsterdam, their Regency or any Persons, concerned in the Government?

3. To what Persons is it best to make the first Communication of my Commission? To Mr. Hooft, Mr. Vanberckel?

4. What House would you advise me to choose? or Houses?

5. Whether it is probable that any Number of Houses would unite in this Plan? and what Houses?

6. Whether any Number of Houses, might be induced, to become responsable for the punctual Payment of the Interest?

7. How much per Cent Interest must be given?

8. How much per Cent Commission to the Banker, or Bankers, House or Houses?

9. Whether it will be necessary to employ Brokers? What Brokers, and what Allowance must they have?

Jan and Dirk van Vollenhoven. Sur le meme Canal avec M. Berckel.

un Courtier. Maakalaar.[6]

Gulian Crommelin; at Mr. John Gasquet on the Rookin opposit the New Chapel.[7]

The Theatre of the War in N. America with the Roads and Tables of the superficial Contents, Distances &c. by an American. Annexed a compendious Account of the British Colonies in North America.

Van Arp. Maakalaar. Next to Mr. Matthes, op de Verweelé Burgwal, over de Lombard

What is the manner of doing Business with the Brokers?
What must be given them?

2100 Guilders, double Rect. to receive for one, 400 Ducats [8]

Monitier & Merckemaer. Brokers in Loans [9]
Mandrillon.
Messrs. Curson & Gouvernieur Cont[inenta]l Agents at St. Eustatia [10]
Monitier & Merckemaer Brokers in Loans.

In het Rondeel op de hoek van de doele Straat [11]
Demter dans le Pijlsteeg [12]

Daniel Jan Bouwens, op de Heeregragt, by de Reguliersgragt. [13]
Reguliers Gragt

⟨Verlam⟩ Printer. Verlem in de graave Straat. Printer of the North holland Gazette.

Daniel Jan Bowens, op de Heeregragt, bij de reguliers Gragt over de hoofd Officier.

	In 1708
La Gueldre	4 1/2
La Hollande	55 1/2
La Zelande	13 1/2
Utrecht	5 3/4
La Frise	11 1/2
L'Overyssell	2 3/4
Groningue & les Ommelandes	6 1/2 [14]

8 feet long.
[9?] Inches diameter of the Mirour.
L'Angle aggrandit 300 fois, the least.

Jacobus van de Wall, over de laaste molen op de Overtoomseweg [15]
Mr. Ploos van Amstel Makelaar
B[...] te Amsterdam

In de Kalverstraat bij Intema & Tiboel boekverkoper. Een Frans en Duits [...], van het werk door Ploos v. Amstel

Agterburgwal by de Hoogstraat [16]
Mr. Wilmart Prince Gragt.
Mr. McCreery lodges, a Pension
Searle [17]

[1] These memoranda are undated and are probably not in chronological order. The "Questions" must have been formulated after JA received, 16 Sept., his temporary commission of 20 June to procure a loan in the Netherlands; see also note 8. A number of the entries, indicated by notes below, were written by persons other than JA, no doubt at his request when he wished to get unfamiliar names, addresses, and other information correctly recorded.

[2] This and the following three entries are in an unidentified hand, perhaps Hendrik Calkoen's. For works by the eminent legal writers Hugo Grotius, Cornelis van Bynkershoek, and Gerard Noodt eventually acquired by JA, see *Catalogue of JA's Library* under their respective names.

[3] JA later acquired an edition in French of Janiçon's *Etat présent de la république des Provinces-Unies* . . . , 4th edn., The Hague, 1755; 2 vols. (*Catalogue of JA's Library*).

[4] Thus in MS. What JA meant by it is unknown to the editors.

[5] The firm of De la Lande and Fynje was the third of the three Amsterdam banking houses (the others being the Van Staphorsts and the Willinks) that joined to raise the first Dutch loan to the United States in 1782.

[6] *Courtier* (French) and *makelaar* (Dutch) are equivalent to the English word broker.

[7] This entry is in an unidentified hand.

[8] This entry can be explained and precisely dated from an isolated entry in Lb/JA/14 reading: "1780 Septr. 21. Recd. of Messrs. Fizeau Grand & Co. Four hundred Ducats or Two Thousand one hundred Guilders, for which I gave a double Rect. to serve as one. This I recd. on Account of M. F. Grand at Paris."

[9–13] These entries are in various unidentified hands.

[14] This table, on a page by itself, doubtless represents the proportions of revenue paid into the common treasury by the seven provinces of the United Netherlands in 1708.

[15] This and the following four entries are in various unidentified hands.

[16] This was JA's own address, written down for him by someone who knew how to spell it, from mid-August 1780 to Feb. 1781. The Agterburgwal was a street on a canal "behind the city wall," and JA lived on it "near High Street." His landlady was "Madame La Veuve du Mr. Henry Schorn" (JA to Francis Dana, 18 Jan. 1781, LbC, Adams Papers). In his letters to the *Boston Patriot* JA remembered that there had been some "remarks" and "whisperings" among the Dutch and among Americans in Amsterdam "that Mr. Adams was in too obscure lodgings," but he considered that these originated with "English spies" (*Corr. in the Boston Patriot*, p. 346). Whatever it may have been then, this section of Amsterdam, near the harbor and railroad station, is anything but respectable now, being on the edge of the area reserved for licensed prostitution. The most prominent landmark nearby is the Oude Kerk.

[17] James Searle of Philadelphia, a member of the Continental Congress, who arrived in Europe in Sept. 1780 to try to obtain a foreign loan for Pennsylvania. See Mildred E. Lombard, "James Searle: Radical Business Man of the Revolution," *PMHB*, 59:284–294 (July 1935).

1781 JANUARY 11. THURSDAY.[1]

Returned from the Hague to Leyden. Was present from 12. to one O Clock, when the Præceptor gave his Lessons in Latin and Greek to my Sons. His Name is Wenshing.[2] He is apparently a great Master of the two Languages, besides which he speaks French and Dutch very well, understands little English, but is desirous of learning it. He obliges his Pupills to be industrious, and they have both made a great Progress for the Time. He is pleased with them and they with him.

John is transcribing a Greek Grammar of his Masters Composition and Charles a Latin one. John is also transcribing a Treatise on Roman Antiquities, of his masters writing. The Master gives his Lessons in French.

This Day Dr. Waterhouse, Mr. Thaxter and my two Sons dined with me at the Cour de Hollande, and after Dinner, went to the Rector Magnificus, to be matriculated into the University. Charles was found to be too young, none under twelve Years of Age being admitted. John was admitted, after making a Declaration that he would do nothing against the Laws of the University, City or Land.

I wish to be informed concerning the Constitution and Regulations of this University. The Number of Professors, their Characters. The Government of the Students both in Morals and Studies. Their Manner of Living—their Priviledges &c. &c.[3]

[1] This and the following scattered entries in Jan.–Feb. 1781 are from Lb/JA/28 (Adams Papers, Microfilms, Reel No. 116), which since it contains copies of a few of JA's letters in 1793–1794 has long been classed as a letterbook though it was begun as a diary. It is a small quarto-sized gathering of leaves stitched into a cover of marbled paper.

It is extremely unfortunate that JA kept no journal during the last months of 1780 when Anglo-Dutch relations came to a crisis that led to war between the two powers, vitally affected JA's status in the Netherlands, and greatly benefited the American cause. However, JA's long and frequent letters to Pres. Huntington and other correspondents constitute a more or less weekly and sometimes daily record of the events leading up to the rupture. Many of these letters were printed first in JA's self-justifying communications to the *Boston Patriot*, 1809–1812 (partly gathered and reprinted in his *Correspondence in the Boston Patriot*); another selection from them was made by CFA in JA's *Works*, vol. 7; and still another (though largely based on earlier printings) by Wharton in his edition of the *Revolutionary Diplomatic Correspondence*, vol. 4. Since relatively little use has been made, especially by European historians, of this mass of information and reflection by a lively observer, JA's correspondence will be printed comprehensively in Series III of the present edition.

The explosion in Anglo-Dutch relations was touched off by the capture at sea of Henry Laurens, when he was at last on his way to his post in the Netherlands, by a British ship in Sept. 1780. In a chest which he threw overboard but which was recovered were found papers which the British government considered evidence of unforgivable conduct on the part of Dutch citizens and especially of E. F. van Berckel, pensionary of Amsterdam and sponsor of the proposed treaty agreed upon at Aix-la-Chapelle, Sept. 1778, by William Lee representing the United States and Jean de Neufville representing the Regency of Amsterdam. (See JA to Huntington, 27 Oct. 1780, LbC, Adams Papers; JA, *Works*, 7:320–321. See also Wharton, ed., *Dipl. Corr. Amer. Rev.*, 2:787–798.) The texts were dispatched at once to the British minister at The Hague, Sir Joseph Yorke, submitted by him to the Stadholder, and a disavowal of the conduct of the Amsterdam Regency demanded. In the Adams Papers, under date of 20 Oct. 1780, are printed texts, in English and Dutch, of the treaty draft and the other offending papers, and also a printed reply (with an English translation in MS) from the Burgomasters of Amsterdam. The latter defended their conduct against the British charges on the grounds, first, that the treaty was contingent on the United States' gaining 'independence, and second, that a commercial treaty with the United States was in the ultimate interest of the whole Dutch trading community. These arguments were not likely to mollify Yorke, who memorialized the States General directly, 10 Nov., demanding that the Amsterdammers be punished for an attempt to violate the sovereignty of the nation and an abrogation of its treaties with England. JA observed that Yorke's action was "outrageous," that Van Berckel had been singled out "for the Fate of Barnevelt, Grotius or De Wit," and that the British were treating a sovereign power as if it were a recalcitrant colony of their own—very much as they had treated America in fact (JA to Huntington, 16, 17 Nov., and to Franklin, 30 Nov.; all letterbook copies, Adams Papers; *Works*, 7:329–330, 331, 338). From this point affairs deteriorated rapidly, but since JA provided a chronology of the climactic events in a letter to Huntington of 5 Jan. 1781 (LbC, Adams Papers; *Works*, 7:352–353), it is unnecessary to say more than that Yorke left The Hague on Christmas or the day before, without taking leave. The question in January, when JA briefly resumed his Diary, was whether the British threats and attacks on their shipping and colonies would bring the Dutch to an abject surrender. Their own

dissensions prevented this, and they drifted into war.

[2] Thaxter spells his name "Wensing" (to JA, 22 Dec. 1780, Adams Papers).

[3] On 13 Dec. Benjamin Waterhouse, who was studying for a medical degree at Leyden, responded to inquiries from JA about schools, tutors, and accommodations for the Adams boys in that city (Adams Papers; see also JA, *Corr. in the Boston Patriot*, p. 572). Encouraged by Waterhouse's reply, JA sent the boys off under Thaxter's care on the 18th (JA to AA, 18 Dec. 1780, Adams Papers). They secured rooms in the house where Waterhouse was living, F. Weller's (or Willer's) on the Langebrug, not far from the Kloksteeg where John Robinson had ministered to his congregation of English Separatists before they sailed to Cape Cod in 1620 (Thaxter to JA, 19 Dec.; JQA to JA, 21 Dec. 1780; both in Adams Papers). As JA notes here, JQA was regularly enrolled as a student in the University early in January; CA was enrolled by special permission on the 29th (Thaxter to JA, 1 Feb. 1781, Adams Papers; Register of Students, MS, Leyden Univ. Libr.). Letters exchanged by JA and JQA in the following months record the older son's progress in his studies, which he found congenial.

12. FRYDAY.

Mr. Mitchel, Mr. Luzac, Dr. Waterhouse, Mr. Thaxter and my two Sons supped with me at the Cour de Holland.

13 SATURDAY.

Returned to Amsterdam, having dined at Haerlem, at the Golden Lion. Went in the Evening to see Ingraham and Sigourney [1] and C[ommodore] Gillon.

Chez la V[euv]e Wynen, dans le premier Wezelstraat, à main gauche. Address of Cerisier.[2]

[1] "There are three Gentlemen, in the Mercantile Way, Mr. Sigourney, Mr. Ingraham and Mr. Bromfield, who are now in this City, and propose to reside here and establish a mercantile House. These Gentlemen are very well known

in the Massachusetts, and therefore it is unnecessary for me to say any Thing about their Characters" (JA to the Massachusetts Board of War, 16 Jan. 1781, LbC, Adams Papers). The three established themselves promptly in business, for in a series of letters in April JA commissioned them to rent and furnish a house in Amsterdam suitable for his residence as minister plenipotentiary; see note on entry of 28 Feb., below.

² Antoine Marie Cerisier (1749–1828), a French publicist and historical writer who had resided for some time in the Netherlands and was active in the Patriot movement (Hoefer, *Nouv. Biog. Générale*). Quite possibly his journalistic activities were subsidized by the French government. JA later said that after reading one of Cerisier's works on Dutch history he traveled to Utrecht to meet the author and found him an agreeable and learned man, at home in French, Dutch, and English, and deeply interested in American affairs. Cerisier moved to Amsterdam, apparently at just this time (early in 1781), "and proposed to publish a periodical paper, with a view to serve our cause. I encouraged this very cordially, and he soon commenced the work, under the title of Le Politique Hollandais, or the Dutch Politician. In this he inserted every thing that he thought would do honor to America, or promote our reputation and interest. His paper was much read, and had a great effect. He was always ready to translate any thing for me into French or Dutch, or out of Dutch into French or English" (JA, *Corr. in the Boston Patriot*, p. 256). In short, Cerisier became one of JA's principal coadjutors in his press campaign to win support for America. In a letter to R. R. Livingston, 16 May 1782, JA commended Cerisier in the warmest terms to the generosity of Congress (LbC, Adams Papers; *Works*, 7:589–590). JA's copies of *Le politique hollandais* survive in the Boston Public Library, and a number of contributions by JA to this journal have been identified. A study of *Le politique hollandais* by W. P. Sautyn Kluit is illuminating on Dutch journalism at this period but not adequate on Cerisier's career (*Handelingen en mededeelingen van de Maatschappij der Nederlandsche Letterkunde te Leiden over het jaar 1882*, p. 3–36). From documents in the Adams Papers it now appears that Cerisier was also the author of the principal statement of the Patriot party's program, a learned and influential work in two volumes entitled *Grondwettige herstelling van Nederlands staatswezen*, Amsterdam, 1784–1786, though his authorship was a secret long and well kept in the Netherlands (Cerisier to JA, 10 Aug. 1786, laid in a presentation copy of the second volume of the *Herstelling* among JA's books in the Boston Public Library; see also JA to John Jay, 3 Oct. 1786, LbC, Adams Papers, printed in *Dipl. Corr.*, 1783–1789, 2:676–677). When the Prussian army invaded the Netherlands in the fall of 1787 and crushed the Patriots' hopes and efforts, Cerisier fled to Paris (letter to JA, 3 Nov. 1787, Adams Papers).

1781. SUNDAY. JAN. 14.

Questions.—How many Ships of War, are determined to be equipped? How much Money have the States General granted for the Navy? Have the States General resolved to issue Letters of Marque? Are the Letters issued? Is there a Disposition to demand them? Will there be many Privateers? How many? Will the Manifesto be published? When? How many Troops are ordered to Zealand? Have the States General taken any Sweedish or Danish Men of War, into their Service? How many? On what Terms?

When will the Decision of the Court of Holland, be made, upon the Conduct of Amsterdam? Will it be this month or next? Who knows what it will be? Why is the decision delayed? What are the

Reasons, Causes, Motives, End and design? Is it not the Influence of the English Party, that still obstructs and retards?

Has Zealand, proposed, or advised, to open a Negotiation, to make up the Quarrel? When. What measures does she propose? [1]

The B. V. Capellen came in. [2] He fears that the Prince and the Proprietors of English Funds will unite, in endeavours to make it up, by a dishonourable Peace.—Mr. V. B. persists that there will be no war. Says it is a Rhodomontade, a Bombino of the English &c. That some Persons have underwritten upon Vessells, on the Faith of Mr. Van berkel, &c.

This Evening call'd upon M. V. Berkel, who was alone, among a Multitude of Papers, obliged to go out at 5 upon Business, made many polite Excuses, and invited me to call the Day after tomorrow, at 4 o clock, being engaged tomorrow. I agreed. I asked him however, whether the States General had resolved to grant Letters of Mark, and he said Yes.—If they were distributed? and he hesitated, as if uncertain. I then excused myself from staying longer, and prayed him to keep his Chamber, but according to the Dutch Fashion he would accompany me to the Door, and make me all the Bows, which the Custom demands, which obliged me to return him, as many.

Q. Is it certain that the Empress of Russia is well inclined towards America? Who has such Information? Has there been any deliberation or Consultation, between the maritime Powers in forming the armed Neutrality, concerning the American Question?

[1] The Province of Zeeland, where the Stadholder's influence was stronger than anywhere else in the country, continued to hold out for pacification instead of war with England; see JA's short treatise on Zeeland in a letter to Congress, 30 Dec. 1780, PCC, No. 84, II, printed in Wharton, ed., *Dipl. Corr. Amer. Rev.*, 4:214–218; also JA to Congress, 15 Jan. 1781, PCC, No. 84, III, printed in same, p. 232.

[2] Joan Derk, Baron van der Capellen tot den Pol (1741–1784), of Zwolle in Overyssel, philosophical leader of the Patriot party in the United Provinces, reformer, and friend of America (*Nieuw Ned. Biog. Woordenboek*, 1:578–581). Van der Capellen had been in correspondence with Gov. Jonathan Trumbull for several years, had in 1779 proposed that an American minister be sent to The Hague, and proved an encouraging friend and faithful adviser to JA throughout his Dutch mission. Virtually all of their correspondence has been published in Van der Capellen's *Brieven*, ed. W. H. de Beaufort, Utrecht, 1879.

1781. MONDAY. JAN. 15.

Visited old Mr. Crommelin and Mr. De Neufville. There is a wonderful Consternation among the Merchants. Many Houses have great difficulty to support their Credit.

1781. FEB 24 [*i.e.* 23?]. FRYDAY.

Went to the Hague, in the Trecht Schuit.[1] At Leyden I have seen
Mr. Vander Kemp,[2] and Mr.   and Mr.
I also visited two large Manufactures, one of Cloth, another of Camblet.

[1] Canal boat or tow-boat. ". . . partly
by the Trech Schuits, that is the Barks
which ply in this Country in the Canals"
(JA to Huntington, 6 April 1781, LbC,
Adams Papers). JA spells the word in a
multitude of ways.

[2] François Adriaan van der Kemp
(1752–1829), Mennonite clergyman,
author, and political radical, was a disciple of J. D. van der Capellen's. He
suffered imprisonment for his anti-Orangist activities and after the collapse of
the Patriot movement fled the Nether-

lands and emigrated to the United
States, 1788. He settled in upper New
York State and lived a scholarly life in
bucolic surroundings for many years.
See *Nieuw Ned. Biog. Woordenboek,*
8:953–958, and Van der Kemp's *Autobiography,* ed. Helen L. Fairchild, N.Y.,
1903, a charming book containing selections from Van der Kemp's extensive correspondence with JA and others,
and much information on the Dutch Patriots, with numerous portraits.

1781 FEB. 28. WEDNESDAY.

At the Arms of Amsterdam.[1]

What can be the Ground of the Malice, of so many, against America?

[1] This implies that JA had given up
his lodgings at Madame Schorn's in the
Agterburgwal. During the early months
of 1781 he was much on the move between Amsterdam, Leyden, and The
Hague, but on 27 April he wrote Edmund Jenings: "I have taken an House
on the Keysers Gragt near the Spiegel
Straat, and am about becoming a Citizen
of Amsterdam—unless their High mightinesses should pronounce me a Rebel,
and expel me their Dominions, which
I believe they will not be inclined to
do" (Adams Papers). The arrangements
were made by the new American firm
in Amsterdam, Sigourney, Ingraham, &
Bromfield, to whom JA wrote a succession of letters from Leyden commissioning them to rent a "large, roomly [*sic*]
and handsome" house "fit for the Hotel
des Etats Unis de L'Amerique," with
detailed directions about furniture, a

carriage, servants, and much else (9,
11, 13 April, all letterbook copies,
Adams Papers; partly printed in JA,
Corr. in the Boston Patriot, p. 426–428).
His new house on the Emperor's Canal
near the Looking-Glass Street was in
keeping with his new status; on 25 Feb.
he had received a letter from Pres. Huntington of 1 Jan. enclosing a commission, with full powers and instructions
voted by Congress on 29 Dec., as "Commissioner . . . to confer, treat, agree and
conclude" with the States General of
the United Provinces "concerning a
treaty of Amity and Commerce" (Adams
Papers). His letter of credence, however,
denominated him "minister plenipotentiary" (enclosure, dated 1 Jan., in Huntington to JA, 9 Jan. 1781, Adams
Papers; see JCC, 18:1204–1217; 19:
17–19). See illustrations of present Keizersgracht No. 529 in this volume.

[ACCOUNTS, JULY 1781.][1]

Expences of a Journey from Amsterdam to Paris. Sat off the 2d of
July from Amsterdam, passed by Utrecht, Gorcum, Breda, Antwerp,

Brussells, Valenciennes &c. and arrived at the Hotel de Valois Rue de Richelieu, Paris the 6th of July, 1781.[2]

£   s   d

July 6. 1781. Expences, on the Road, Fifty four Ducats 1781. July 9. Recd. of Mr. F. Grand at Paris four Thousand Eight hundred Livres, for which I gave him a Rect.   4800: 0: 0

[1] This fragment is the sole entry in an account book (M/JA/2; Adams Papers, Microfilms, Reel No. 181) apparently purchased for use during JA's hurried visit to Paris in the summer of 1781. The volume is a small quarto bound in parchment; the leaves are ruled lengthwise for double-entry accounts, but all except the first two facing pages are blank. On the back cover is a notation in JA's hand: "1781 / Peace."

On 12 March 1781 the States General of the United Provinces at last issued a counter-manifesto to the British denunciation (21 Dec. 1780) of the Anglo-Dutch alliance. JA embodied the counter-manifesto in his letter to Huntington of 18 March (PCC, No. 84, III; Wharton, ed., *Dipl. Corr. Amer. Rev.*, 4:306–313). Now that the long and intense debate over war or submission was finished, JA could consider the timing and method of announcing his powers to treat for an alliance between the United States and the Netherlands —which would require as an antecedent condition Dutch recognition of American sovereignty and would in itself be a necessary antecedent, it was now clear to JA, to raising a substantial loan among the Amsterdam bankers. In consequence he spent the last part of March and the early part of April quietly in Leyden drafting a memorial which emphasized the historical ties between the two nations and the advantages that would flow from close commercial relations between them. This paper, which was to become famous, went through successive drafts and was completed and signed on 19 April, the sixth anniversary of the battles of Lexington and Concord. On this very day JA went to The Hague and began a series of interviews with La Vauguyon, the French ambassador, who, under instructions from Vergennes, did everything in his power to dissuade JA from his purpose but did not succeed. The account of his tussle with La Vauguyon in JA's *Correspondence in the Boston Patriot* (p. 431–434) is, or at least deserves to be, a classic piece of diplomatic narrative; it is reprinted in a long note in JA, *Works*, 7:404–406. In the first days of May, after copies and translations had been prepared, JA first submitted his memorial to Van Bleiswyck, grand pensionary of Holland, which was by far the most powerful of the seven provinces and the one most inclined to be sympathetic to JA's appeal; and next to Baron Lynden van Hemmen, president of the week of the States General. Neither dignitary would receive it officially, but the latter reported his interview with JA to the body over which he presided, and copies of the paper were called for by the deputies to refer to their provincial assemblies. During their interview JA had informed Lynden van Hemmen that he would feel it his duty to have the memorial printed; no objection was raised; and JA's man-of-all-work in The Hague, C. W. F. Dumas, arranged for its publication and distribution in Dutch, French, and English throughout the Netherlands. It was also widely reprinted in Dutch and other newspapers. See JA to Huntington, 3, 7 May 1781, PCC, No. 84, III, printed in Wharton, ed., *Dipl. Corr. Amer. Rev.*, 4:398–399, 401–403; also Dumas to Huntington, 1 May–13 July 1781, same, p. 393–397. Contemporary printings of the memorial in Dutch, French, and English are listed in W. P. C. Knuttel, comp., *Catalogus van de pamflettenverzameling berustende in de Koninklijke Bibliotheek*, The Hague, 1889–1916, Nos. 19506, 19506a, 19507; English texts will be found in JA's *Corr. in the Boston Patriot*, p. 439–448; *Works*, 7:396–404; Wharton, ed., *Dipl. Corr. Amer. Rev.*, 4:370–376.

² In the spring of 1781 the proposals of the Russian and Austrian courts for a mediation between the warring powers took definite shape, and Vergennes, with some reluctance, was obliged to summon JA, the only American representative abroad empowered to discuss peace terms, to Paris for consultation upon them (Bérenger to JA, 5 June 1781, Adams Papers; JA, *Works*, 7:423–424). At Versailles on 11 July Vergennes laid before JA those terms of the proposed mediation which he chose to let him see and which JA, in a series of letters that followed and overwhelmed Vergennes, rejected on the part of the United States. JA later said that these letters "defeated the profound and magnificent project of a Congress at Vienna, for the purpose of chicaning the United States out of their independence" (*Corr. in the Boston Patriot*, p. 133). The essential truth of this assertion has been confirmed by later historians, since it is clear that Vergennes was almost ready at this critical point in the war to compromise France's pledge of independence and throw the United States on the mercy of Great Britain. See CFA in JA's *Works*, 1:334–340; Bemis, *Diplomacy of the Amer. Revolution*, ch. 13, "The Imperial Mediators and France in 1781," especially p. 184, 186–187. The articles of the imperial mediation proposed on 20 May 1781, with the answers of the belligerent powers in Europe, are printed in English in Wharton, ed., *Dipl. Corr. Amer. Rev.*, 4:860–867. JA's record of his part in the abortive negotiation is in Lb/JA/17 (Adams Papers, Microfilms, Reel No. 105), together with rejected and corrected drafts of his own papers and some important sequels. Nearly all of these documents were reprinted in his "second autobiography" (*Corr. in the Boston Patriot*, p. 107–148).

JA left Paris and returned to Amsterdam in the last days of July.